The 1993 BMUG Shareware Disk Catalog

Edited, Produced, Designed, and Scripted by:

Noah Potkin

Hans Hansen

Derrick Schneider

Addison-Wesley Publishing Company
Reading, Massachusetts • Menlo Park, California • New York
Don Mills, Ontario • Wokingham, England • Amsterdam • Bonn
Sydney • Singapore • Tokyo • Madrid • San Juan
Paris • Seoul • Milan • Mexico City • Taipei

To the authors of publicly distributable software, who make the BMUG library possible.

Sponsoring Editor: David Rogelberg
Project Editor: Joanne Clapp Fullagar
Editorial Assistant: Amy Cheng
BMUG Editing Czar: Gray Shaw
Cover Design: Chad Kubo
Set in 8/9.5-point Univers and 14/14-point Futura Bold by Bhagabooks, Berkeley CA

ISBN 0-201-63231-4

1 2 3 4 5 6 7 8 9-MW-9695949392
First Printing, June 1992

Contents

Contents

Welcome

This is *The 1993 BMUG Shareware Disk Catalog.*

This is the fourth such book BMUG has created and is certainly the largest and most comprehensive. In addition to being a catalog of our library, this book is the most complete and up-to-date directory to the vast amount of Shareware and Freeware available in the Macintosh community.

Whether you get your software from BMUG, your local user group, online services, or your friends, this book will tell you what it does, its compatibility, its author, and more.

BMUG is a nonprofit user group dedicated to helping graphical user interface computer users around the world. With over 10,000 members in more than 50 countries, BMUG has claim to being a truly international user group. BMUG has one of the largest and most complete libraries of Publicly Distributable (PD) software in the world.

Welcome

Introduction

How to Read *The 1993 BMUG Shareware Disk Catalog*

The BMUG Disk Catalog contains listings for more than 300 disks and thousands of files. The listings in the catalog are divided into several sections, such as Text, Utilities, HyperCard, and Fonts. Each section begins with a brief description of its contents. Where it is needed, section descriptions include instructions on how to install and use the software listed.

The sections are further divided into categories. For example, Fonts includes Type 1 Fonts, TrueType Fonts, and Bitmapped Fonts. Within the categories are the listings for each individual disk. Within each disk listing, the programs are presented alphabetically. Most descriptions give you basic information about the software, including the name; version number; icon; type of file; method of distribution and requested fee, if Shareware (see "What Is Publicly Distributable Software?"); the author's name and address; a description of what the software does; and the file size in kilobytes. See the illustrated page for a guide to this information.

Gerald and Art organize and maintain the BMUG Disk Library.

Every program in our library comes with some documentation, written either by the author or by the BMUG librarian. This documentation may be in the form of a "Read-Me" file or built into the program. All files in the BMUG PD Library have been checked thoroughly for viruses; we go to great lengths to protect our customers.

BMUG constantly strives to keep the PD Library organized so that you can easily get the programs you want. We have recently restructured the various categories. Disks that have been overhauled use an alphanumeric system (a letter followed by a number). Disks that have not yet been overhauled use a sequential number system (a number only). The letter and number assigned to a disk do not indicate the age of its contents.

The version numbers listed after the name of each file indicate the current version at the time this catalog was printed. To find out whether a program has been updated, call BMUG. If a program has been updated recently, it will be available, usually with some other updated programs, on a special update disk. If the program was updated some time ago, the original disk will contain the update. Either of these disks are available for $4.

Welcome

Anatomy of the Disk Catalog

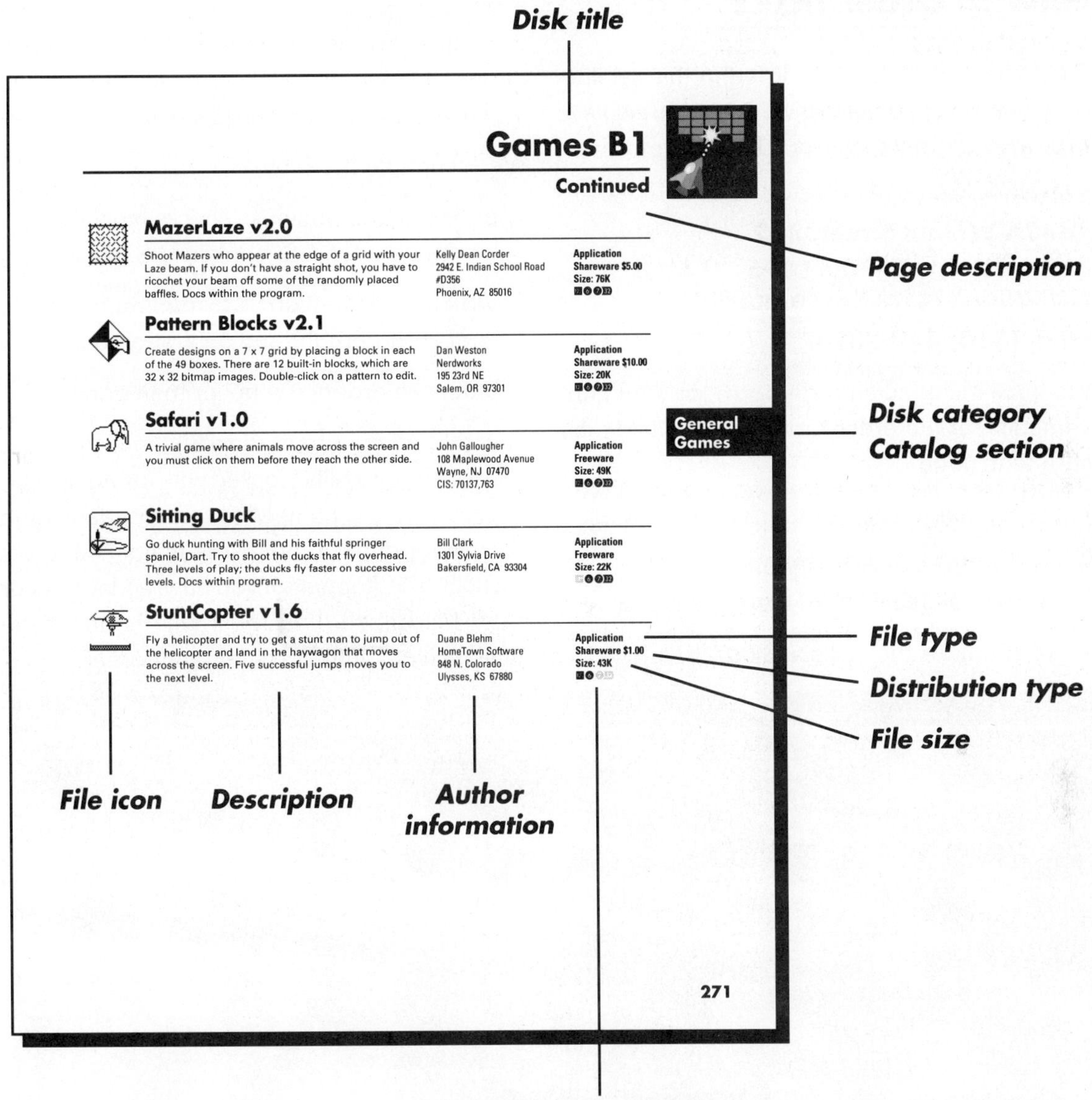

Yes	No	System Compatiblity
12"	12"	Works with Apple's 12 inch color monitor sold with many Macintosh LC systems.
6	6	Works with System 6.
7	7	Works with System 7.
32	32	Works under System 7's 32-bit memory addressing.

Welcome

Introduction

How to Order Disks

To obtain any of the disks listed in this catalog, simply send your order to BMUG. You do not have to be a BMUG member to purchase disks from us.

BMUG
1442A Walnut Street, #62
Berkeley, CA 94709-1496 U.S.Aa
Telephone: (510) 549-2684
Fax: (510) 849-9026

We have included an order form for your convenience. If the order form isn't available, be sure to include

- the full name and number of the disk(s)
- your return address and phone number so that we can reach you if there is any problem
- payment for the disks at $4 each
- shipping charge of $4 for orders of three or more disks. For international orders see the chart on the order form or call our Busiess Office.

We accept payment by

- personal and business checks (checks must be drawn on a U.S. bank in U.S. currency)
- VISA and Mastercard ($15 minimum; include your card number and expiration date)
- purchase orders (by fax or mail only)

Several staff members and a full-time volunteer keep our library fully stocked with preduplicated disks, so there is no need to send us blanks and no wait for duplication! Note that all our disks are 800k 3.5" floppies. If you have a Mac 512k or older Macintosh, you must call us about the availability of 400k disks for your order.

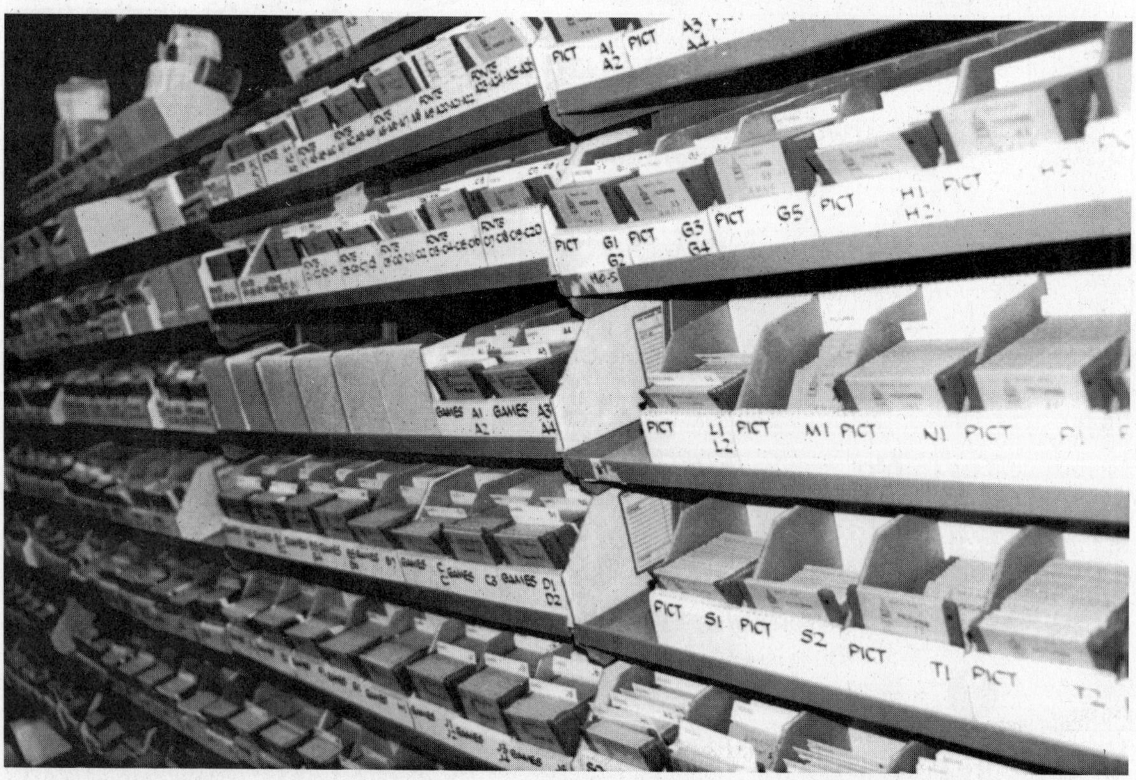

The BMUG PD Library contains hundreds of disks each duplicated and stored in these many shelves.

BMUG Order Form

information

name ______ date ______

company name ______

address ______

city ______ state ______ zip code ______

country ______ day phone ( )

❑ cash ❑ check/money order ❑ credit card ($15 minimum)

VISA/Mastercard number ______

signature ______ expiration date ___/___

Mail to: BMUG, 1442A Walnut Street #62, Berkeley CA 94709-1496
Fax to: (510) 849-9026 **Phone (*Orders Only*):** 1-800-776-2684

*For questions about your order: (510) 549-BMUG [2684]
Please allow 3-4 weeks for delivery. All prices include applicable CA taxes.
Contents, availability, and prices subject to change. (7/92)*

membership

❑ new ❑ renewal ❑ change of address

❑ Individual Membership – 6 months • One Newsletter • One BBS Account • Helpline for 1	$25	$ ______
❑ Individual Membership – 1 year • Two Newsletters • One BBS Account • Helpline for 1	$40	$ ______
❑ Family Membership – 1 year • Two Newsletters • Four BBS Accounts • Helpline for 4	$60	$ ______
❑ Company Membership – 1 year • Four Newsletters (2 of each) • Eight BBS Accounts • Helpline for 25	$100	$ ______

donations

We need your continued support. All donations are tax deductible. BMUG is a 501(c)3 non-profit organization. $ ______

❑ $5 ❑ $15 ❑ $25 ❑ $50 ❑ $100 ❑ Other

software

______ 800k floppy disks $4 each ($3 each for 10 or more) $ ______

List disks by name below, use list on back for reference (or copy and attach):

______

______

______

Item	Member/Non-member	
______ PD-ROM ver. A – Sys. 7 & 32-bit clean	$35/$50	$ ______
______ TV-ROM – includes QuickTime player	$35/$50	$ ______
______ System 6.0.x – 4 800k Disks	$10	$ ______
BMUG Members Only:		
______ System 7.0 – 10 800k Disks & Book	$25	$ ______
______ System 7.0.1 – 6 HD Disks	$15	$ ______

publications

Item	Member/Non-member	
______ Zen and the Art of Resource Editing w/ disk containing ResEdit 2.1.1	$15/$20	$ ______
______ The BMUG Guide to BBSs and Beyond w/ BMUG Disk Telecom A1	$15/$20	$ ______
______ The 1993 Shareware Disk Catalog	$15/$20	$ ______
______ BMUG Newsletter – Back Issues	$7/10	$ ______

❑ Spring '92 ❑ Spring '90 ❑ Fall '90
❑ Fall '89 ❑ Fall '88 ❑ Spring '87

shipping & handling

Rush orders available by phone.

All U.S. orders add $4 *except membership only*

Foreign orders add:

	6 mo. membership, Newsletters, System 7 & Book	1 yr. membership	each Disk Catalog, each BBS Book	other publications	individual disks	PD-ROM, TV-ROM
Canada/Mexico/South America	$6	$12	$15	$3	$1.50	$4
Europe/Asia/Australia	$14	$28	$25	$7	$1	$6

subtotal $ ______

S/H (USA) $ 4.00

S/H (foreign) $ ______

Mail FAX Phone Walk

Please make payment to "**BMUG**" in US negotiable funds, payable through US Banks. Do not send cash.

total $ ______

Welcome

Disk listing for ordering reference

For large disk orders, circle disk numbers below and attach to order form on reverse.

Business

A1 B1 B2 C1 C2 C3 C4 D1 D2 E1

DAs

A1 B1 1 2 3 4 5 6 7 8
9 10 11

Education

A1 A2 A3 A4 A5 A6 1 2 3 4
5 6 7 8 9 10 11 12 14 15
16 17 18 19 20 21 22 23 24 25
26 27 28

Fonts

A1 A2 A3 A4 A5 A6 A7 A8 A9 A10
A11 A12 A13 A14 A15 A16 A17 A18 A19 A20
A21 A22 A23 A24 A25 B1 B2 B3 B4 B5
B6 B7 B8 B9 B10 B11 B12 B13 C1 C2
C3 C4 C5 C6 C7 C8 C9 C10 C11 C12
C13 C14 C15 C16 C17 C18 C19 C20 D1 D2
D3 D4 D5 D6 D7 D8 D9 D10 E1 E2
E3 E4 E5 E6 E7 E8 F1 G1

Games

A1 A2 A3 A4 A5 A6 B1 B2 B3 B4
B5 B6 B7 C1 C2 C3 D1 D2 D3 E1
F1 G1 H1 J1 J2 J3 J4 J5 J6 K1
K2 K3 K4 K5 K6 K7 K8 K9 K10 L1
L2 L3 L4 L5 M1 M2 M3 N1 P1 P2
R1

Graphics

A1 A2 A3 A4 A5 B1 B2 C1 D1 D2
E1 E2 F1

HyperCard Education

A1 A2 A3 A4 A5 B1 B2 B3 B4 C1
D1 D2 D3 D4 E1 E2 F2 G1 H1 J1
K1 K2 L1 L2 L3 L5 L6 L7 L8 M1
M2 N1 N2

HyperCard Games

A1 A2 A3 A4 A5 A6 A7 A8 B1 B2
B3 C1 C2 C3 D1

Paris

A2 A3 A4 B1 B2 C1 C2 C3 C4 C5
D1 D2 D3 D4 D5 E1 E2 E3 E4 F1
G1 H1

Pictures

A1 B1 B2 C1 D1 E1 F1 F2 F3 F4
G1 G2 G3 G4 G5 H1 H2 H3 H4 J1
K1 K2 L1 L2 M1 N1 P1

Programming

A1 B1 C1 E1 F1 G1 H1 J1 K1

Sounds

A1 A2 A3 A4 A5 S1 S2 S3 S4 S5
S6 S7 S8 S9 S11 S12 S13 S14 S15

Telecom

A1 A2 B1 C1 D1 E1 F1 G1

Text

A1 A2 B1 C1 D1 E1

Utilities

A1 B1 B2 C1 C2 D1 D2 E1 F1 F2
G1 G2 G3 G4 G5 H1 J1 K1 L1 M1
N1 N2 P1 R1 R2 S1 T1 T2 V1 W1
X1 X2 X3 Z1

What is Publicly Distributable (PD) Software?

Most people are familiar with the concept of buying software. Like a book, you go to the store and buy it. However, software's digital nature makes duplication and distribution over long distances quite easy. National and international laws make it illegal to copy copyrighted software without the author's permission. Software sold in stores is considered commercial; BMUG does not sell or distribute any commercial software.

Another genre of software is called "Publicly Distributable." Publicly Distributable software is released by the author directly to the user through on-line services, user groups, and many other commercial and noncommercial distribution points. However, authors have some freedom in defining copyrights applicable to the software they write, resulting in a multitude of different copying and usage restrictions on PD software.

When using PD software for the first time, you should look at the *About...* box under the Apple menu or read the "Read-Me" file. This file will give you important information about the version of the software you have, any known incompatibilities, and the conditions under which you may use the software. In addition, it will tell you which type of publicly distributable software it is. We have divided the software in our library into the following categories.

Shareware

Shareware is copyrighted and the author asks for payment if you use it. It is the most common type of software in the realm of PD software. The usual terms are that you may try out the program for a limited amount of time, typically 10 to 30 days, and then decide whether you want to keep it. If you continue to use it, you are requested to send the author a nominal fee, approximately $5 to $40, with an average of $15. Shareware benefits both the user and the author as it allows prices to remain low by avoiding distribution, packaging, and advertising costs. It allows you to try the software and decide whether you like it before spending your money. There is an unstated agreement that the author will update the Shareware when necessary, because he or she is charging money. However, this is not always so and should not be depended upon.

There are many variations on the Shareware theme. For instance, instead of money, some authors simply ask for a postcard stating your appreciation or ask that you donate money to a certain charity. Another variation is software that no longer works after a set time period has passed. This is a not-so-subtle hint to pay your fees.

BMUG strongly believes in the concept of Shareware software and encourages users to support the authors by paying the Shareware fees. When purchasing a disk or CD-ROM through BMUG you are purchasing a collection of PD software. It is your responsibility to honor any fees requested for the software you choose to keep and use. Registering your software by paying these fees makes future releases and updates possible.

Freeware

Many authors like to retain ownership of software by copyrighting it, yet they allow people to copy and use it for free. Many times the author created the program for his or her own purposes, and then realized others might be able to use it. Sometimes these are first at-

tempts by new programmers. Whatever the reason, this is the best software bargain in the world. Probably the most famous piece of freeware is Disinfectant, a highly recommended virus protection program by John Norstad of Northwestern University and his merry band of followers.

Freeware is in many cases the only release of a piece of software and in case of incompatibilities it may become obsolete with no chance of an update.

Public Domain

Public Domain software is not only free, but has no copyright attached to it. You are free to do whatever you want with it. You may rewrite it; fold, spindle, and mutilate it; or even use it in a program you are writing, all with no complaints from the author. The author will generally not provide any kind of follow-up support.

Demoware

Demoware is a special demonstration version of a program and acts as an enticement or teaser to buy the fully functioning piece of software. Demoware is usually identical to the commercial or Shareware version, except that some vital function, such as printing or saving, is disabled. A Demoware version of a Shareware font might have all the vowels missing. Demoware is also sometimes called "crippleware." While not a new concept, Demoware is becoming more more and more prevalent in the PD world. The fewer Shareware fees that are paid, the more often we will see this type or software.

What's an INIT? *or* How to Use the Software

There are many types of files included in the pages of this catalog. So many that their names become a lingo of their own such as "DA," "INIT," "FKEY," and so on. It is important that you know some of this lingo to be able to fully use the programs. The following definitions should help:

DA: DAs or "Desk Accessories" are modeled after calculators, note pads, and various items you keep on your desk while you're doing "real" work. For installation of these files see the introduction to the section on DAs.

FKEY: An FKEY is a file that is installed in the System file itself and can then be accessed from within another application. It allows a certain key configuration to perform an action. For example: Command-Shift-3 is an FKEY that is built into System Software. It creates a picture of your screen in TeachText format and saves it to your hard drive.

INIT: An INIT is a file that loads itself as part of the System when your Mac starts up and modifies some part of the System. INITs are not user configurable. Most of these files show an icon at the bottom of the screen during startup to signify that they are loading. To install these under System 6 simply drop them into the System Folder.

System Extension: This is the System 7 term for an INIT. This includes files that will be accessed in the Chooser. You install these by dropping them in the Extensions Folder. Though dropping them in the System Folder sometimes works, this is not recommended unless you are specifically instructed to do so. Under System 7 you can bypass loading these files by holding down the Shift key upon startup.

cdev: cdev stands for control panel device. Many times these files load some part of themselves into System RAM as would an INIT or System Extension, but unlike INITs, cdevs are configurable by the user. Under System 6 they must be placed in the System Folder and then accessed through the Control Panel under the Apple Menu. Under System 7 some Control Panels are able to be used anywhere, but should usually reside in the Control Panels Folder.

Noah and Hans are looking a little frazzled after a week of 18-hour days working on the Disk Catalog.

What is BMUG?

BMUG is a non-profit organization dedicated to collecting, evaluating, and disseminating information about computers that use graphical interfaces. BMUG is not affiliated with any manufacturer, and represents the interests of over 10,000 users in more than 50 countries around the world. We give users information that will help them use their computers as efficiently and painlessly as possible. All of our meetings, and well as the disks in the software library, PD-ROM, TV-ROM, back issues of the BMUG Newsletter, and other BMUG publications are available to non-members.

BMUG offers local activities in the San Francisco Bay Area. Our Main Meeting is held every Thursday on the UC Berkeley campus in the Physical Sciences Lecture Hall. This weekly meeting is routinely attended by several hundred people. We also offer various Special Interest Groups (SIGs), which focus on particular topics or issues. SIGs meet in the BMUG office unless otherwise specified. All our meetings are open to the public; beginners are always welcome. To find out the schedule, call (510) 849-9114.

Become a BMUG Member

BMUG is financed by membership dues and the sale of our educational products. In order to remain objective in our evaluations of the computer industry, we do not accept advertising in our publications.

Our goal is to provide you with the widest possible array of useful information. Please support us by joining BMUG. Find out why *MicroTimes* listed BMUG as one of the 100 most important influences in the computer industry and said, "BMUG is what every user group dreams of becomming." To become a member, fill out the section on the order form, or call BMUG at (510) 549-2684

Each one-year BMUG Membership includes two issues of the highly acclaimed *BMUG News-*

Welcome

Introduction

letter, at least one account on the BMUG BBS, and free access to our Technical Helpline.

The BMUG Newsletter

Twice a year, BMUG publishes a newsletter full of interesting articles on a variety of subjects. Unlike other user group newsletters, and unlike other Macintosh publications, the *BMUG Newsletter* is over 400 pages long and contains no advertising. Our newsletter is the heart of our activities; it serves as a medium for the exchange of information and contains some of the most honest, insightful commentary in the entire computer industry.

Joining BMUG is the only way to get the current BMUG Newsletter, and we work hard to live up to our members' expectations.

Online Services

The BMUG multi-line electronic Bulletin Board System (BBS) is the crossroads of a larger international network, and an information resource in itself.

It is one of the premier nodes in the EchoMac network on Fidonet and is also part of Usenet and UUCP Mail on the Internet. Each of these non-profit networks is monitored by tens of thousands of computer users in America and abroad.

Most of the latest Publicly Distributable software is available online, and is subjected to the same intense scrutiny for viruses as our disk-based software library. Our multi-line capability gives you fast access 20 hours a day (our BBS processes mail with other systems from 2:30-3:30 pm and 5:30-6:30 am Pacific time), all lines support 300, 1200, or 2400 baud at 510/849-2684; 9600 baud access at 510/849-1795.

The BMUG Helpline

BMUG attempts to supply unlimited technical support for our members over the phone, through online information services, and via fax. BMUG is in constant contact with thousands of computer users who are doing virtually everything imaginable with their machines. We have been doing Macintosh tech support as long as anyone, and we have an incredible knowledge base to draw upon in solving your problems. We can answer virtually any Macintosh question, simple or advanced-just call. We specialize in both beginners' questions and hard-to-find technical tips.

System Software

BMUG is also licensed to sell to its members Macintosh System Software. Many older machines need to use older Systems, and so we carry an entire range, from System 1.1 for the Macintosh 128 to the most current at the time of this writing, System 7.0.1. We also carry many of the System Extensions released by Apple.

BMUG membership packages

One-Year Individual - $40

- Two issues of the BMUG Newsletter per year
- One BBS account
- Unlimited access to the Helpline for 1 person for one year

One-Year Family - $60

- Two issues of the BMUG Newsletter per year
- Four BBS accounts
- Unlimited access to the Helpline for 4 people for one year

One-Year Company - $100

- Four BMUG Newsletters per year—two copies of each issue
- Eight BBS accounts
- Unlimited access to the Helpline for 25 people for one year

Other Products Available from BMUG

The Ever-Growing Library

By their nature, computer programs are transient. What seems the most innovative piece of software ever today, will seem underpowered and wimpy tomorrow. New programs are always becoming available. BMUG attempts to keep pace by releasing new disks with this new software on a constant basis. Thus, many of our most current disks may not be listed in this catalog. For information about our new disks, contact us. You can call BMUG to find out what updates to this catalog will have become available through BMUG.

Update Disks

In an effort to keep the BMUG PD Library as current as possible we periodically create Update Disks. These disks include new releases of software that is already in our library in an older form. This saves the buyer from having to buy the same disk over and over to get the latest release of a particular piece of software. In addition, many times you can get updates to several pieces of software at once since updates to many different programs are included on each update disk. If you want to know if an update version of a program is available, call BMUG.

The BMUG PD-ROM

In addition to the disks in the software library, BMUG has a CD-ROM of Publicly Distributable software. BMUG's PD-ROM has over 400 megs of all System 7 compatible, 32-bit clean software. It is a great source of Shareware and Freeware, including fonts, clip art, utilities, articles, and more. Much of it is unavailable elsewhere.

At about the price of a dozen BMUG disks the PD-ROM represents a very high software per dollar value. BMUG frequently updates the PD-ROM in order to maintain a current offering and has free technical support for registered owners

Zen and the Art of Resource Editing

ResEdit is one of the most fun and useful tools ever designed for the Mac. With this book, ResEdit and the software included you can access the power of ResEdit to personalize your Mac and to make it work for you in the most efficient way possible.

This 240-page book includes System 7 information, tips to ensure the safe use of ResEdit, and comes with a disk containing over 1500k of cool stuff, including the latest version of ResEdit.

The BMUG Guide to Bulletin Boards and Beyond

Starting with a quick guide for beginners, this 550-page book is a practical and thorough introduction to the world of communications, bulletin boards, including BMUG's.

A guide to the Internet, Fidonet, and Rime and a sysop's resource guide, this book is a collection of information never before available in one place, including a list of Macintosh bulletin boards across the country.

Welcome

Introduction

Acknowledgments

Many people deserve credit for what you hold in your hands. No few people can say they *made* this book. BMUG is the product of years of volunteer work, which have made it a place where such a creation as this could happen.

BMUG would like to acknowledge the following for their hard work and dedication in creating this book. We cannot mention them all, but would like to make special mention of those that were more central to its actual production.

Hans Hansen and **Noah Potkin**, Catalog Production Team, more than anyone they can take credit for what you see, from restructuring the design to streamlining the production, these two made it happen.

Derrick Schneider, BMUG Volunteer Extraordinaire, for scripting above and beyond the call of duty. (We hope he graduates anyway.)

Gray Shaw, Assistant BBS Sysop and Volunteer Extraordinaire, for massive amounts of editing and a firm grasp of quality. Gray's amazing editing skills made this book tyypo free.

Dong-Gyom Kim, BMUG Volunteer, for his work on the massive database from which this catalog arose.

Arthur Lau, Disk Librarian, for his unending dedication to the BMUG PD Library. It is truly a work of art.

Gerald Raddatz, Auxilliary Support, for major restructuring efforts and huge amounts of overtime.

Stan Troutner, Disk Duplicator, for his selfless devotion to BMUG and the PD Library. Stan is BMUG's best and only full-time volunteer.

Chad Kubo, artist, for the beautiful cover art on so many of BMUG's books.

Steve Costa, BMUG's Executive Director, for completing the hours and hours of compatibilty checking.

Tim Holmes, BMUG Shortstop, for writing and writing and writing and writing and writing.

Greg Dow, BMUG Board of Directors Chairman, for the creation of the first real BMUG Disk Catalog in 1989 and for programming utilities to make this one.

Tim Bodine, BBS Validation Sysop and Volunteer, who compiled the database for the previous edition.

Lauren Antonoff, BMUG Volunteer, for restructuring the Utilities and Text sections and writing descriptions.

Bernard Aboba, BBS Sysop, for help with the Telecom section.

Karla Aronson, BMUG Project Manager, for her help in making it happen.

The **BMUG Office and Helpline staff** for their usual wonderful assistance: **Alisa**, **Jacqui**, **Michele**, **David**, **Kenny**, **Betsy**, **Mario**, and of course, **Meg**.

In addition to people there were companies and products without which this project could've taken years. For many of our corporate friends, support of user groups is an up-hill battle. Those that have stood by us deserve all the more the thanks we owe them. In alphabetical order they are:

Addison-Wesley: especially **David Rogelberg** for making this edition possible, **Joanne Clapp Fullagar** for her help and support, and **Kathy Traynor** for helping with production issues.

Aldus: for PageMaker 4.2, thanks for the scripting and AppleEvent support.

Canterbury Press: for linoing, especially **Ian Faircloth** for staying up all night.

Claris: for Filemaker Pro, especially **Phil Vahey** and **Brendan McCarthy** for arranging access to a pre-alpha AppleEvent supporting version.

ElseWare: for introducing DataShaper and CheckList to the world.

Fusion Systems: for the use of a TokaMac LC board. (Thanks **Andrew**, **Jennifer**, and **Bob**.)

PLI: for the long term loan of two 600 meg hard drives on which we kept the 450-900 megs of data that make up this catalog. Thanks especially to **Fred Swan**.

Sigma Designs: for a beautiful 19" 24-bit color monitor. Especially **Marshall Goldberg**.

UserLand: For creating Frontier, especially **Tom Petaccia** for the PageMaker Glue Table.

Colophon

The 1993 BMUG Shareware Disk Catalog was designed and produced on Apple Macintosh computers running System 7. The layout of this book was automated by using the AppleEvent scripting capibilities of UserLand Frountier 1.0 in combination with Claris FileMaker Pro 2.0 to store the database and Aldus PageMaker 4.2's layout scripting language. The scripts were run over the course of ten days on two Macintosh IIci's, a Macintosh II fx, a Macintosh LC with a Fusion Data Systems TokaMac LC '040 accelerator, and a PowerBook 170. PostScript illustrations were made using Adobe Illustrator 3.2. Bitmapped graphics were prepared with Adobe Photoshop 2.01.

Proof prints were made on an Apple LaserWriter IIg. Final copy was output to paper on a Linotronic 300 at Canterbury Press in Berkeley.

Type is from the Futura and Univers families from Adobe. Body text is in 8/9.5 point Univers 55. Titles are in 14 point Futura Bold.

The Cover was designed and produced by Chad Kubo in Adobe Illustrator 3.2. Separations were made by Quark Xpress 3.2 output on an Agfa SelectSet 5000 at Hunza Graphics in Berkeley.

Layout and production by Noah Potkin and Hans Hansen. Scripting by Derrick Schneider.

Business

Software to help you make money, organize time, and manipulate data for business and home use.

Business B2

General

General Business

Anesthesia_Fee_Calculator

Template for calculating medical fees associated with receiving anesthesia.

unknown

Excel Worksheets
Public Domain
Size: 26k

AutoExpense

Keeps tracks of expenses associated with an automobile: fuel, service and repair, and insurance. Contains an electronic log book for recording all these expenses that also prints out reports for the three expense categories.

Phil Jurgenson
232 Adams St.
Mankato, MN 56001
GEnie: PJURGENSON

Application
Shareware $10.00
Size: 51k

Bi-Weekly Mortgage

Template for calculating the biweekly payment required for a biweekly mortgage, which is paid back over 21 years.

unknown

Excel Worksheets
Public Domain
Size: 4k

Easy Bills

Excel templates for managing/recording home expenses.

C. Amet
31A Wayne Garden
Collingsood, NJ 08108

Excel Worksheets
Shareware $5.00
Size: 37k

Home Finances aka PacMac

MultiPlan and Excel templates for managing home finances, car and mortgage payments, nutrition analysis, stock portfolios, and more.

Loren Davis
Pacific Associates
238 Merner Drive
Windsor, CA 95492

MultiPlan Document
Shareware $20.00
Size: 6k

Mac a £oan 1.3 v1.3

Calculates regular payments for loans and shows the amount going toward the principal and the interest.

Coconut Info
PO Box 75453
Honolulu, HI 96836
(808) 262-6159

Application
Shareware $6.00
Size: 53k

MacLoan v3.7E

Developed by a CPA to help clients evaluate the different options associated with borrowing money, such as interest rates, monthly payments, and tax consequences.

Robert K. Valentine
10743 Hungerford Pl.
Cerritos, CA 90701

Application
Shareware $15.00
Size: 75k

Medicare MAAC

Calculates the MAAC fee, which physicians can bill patients under the 1987 Medicare law if they are not planning to be a participating member. The laws and fee structures are very complicated for such cases.

Charles S. Ostrov
Minneapolis, MN

Excel Worksheets
Public Domain
Size: 17k

MortCalc v1.8.1

Performs various mortgage calculations: monthly payment tables, loan amortization, sinking fund, time value single payments, and time value annuities.

Phillip E. Leahy III
24 Dogwood Hills Road
Newburgh, NY 12550

Application
Freeware
Size: 75k

Mortgage Amortization v1.0

Package of 3 Excel documents to use as a template for performing mortgage calculations. Determines load payment schedules and amounts.

Linda Custer
BMUG

Excel Template
Freeware
Size: 10k

Retirement Analysis

MultiPlan templates.

unknown

MultiPlan Document
Public Domain
Size: 6k

Business C1

General

General Business

PayMaster

Payroll Excel templates. Highly sophisticated macros for accounting.

Denning Associates
111 Kingussle Court
Cary, NC 27511
(919) 387-1231

Excel Template
Shareware $35.00
Size: 204k

Payroll System

Excel templates for managing the payroll for up to 22 employees. Handles hourly workers, FSLIC, and federal and state taxes. Complete docs in a separate file.

R & D Resources
PO Box 468
Boardman, OR 97818
(503) 481-6878

Excel Worksheets
Freeware
Size: 14k

Small Bus Payroll

Just as the name implies, this is a template for handling the payroll records of a small business.

unknown

Excel Worksheets
Public Domain
Size: 11k

Wagekeeper

Small business bookkeeping templates. Designed to integrate with Bookkeeper (on disk B1).

Connie L. Bass
James R. Barry
1717 Avenue K #221
Lubbock, TX 79401

Excel Templates
Shareware $20.00
Size: 73k

Business C2

General

Calendar v2.2.1

Contructs a calendar for a month. Lets you fill in text for each day of the month (supports multiple fonts within text). Prints using the full paper size.

Jim Studt
LunareWare
342 W. Madison
Kirkwood, MO 63122

Application
Shareware $15.00
Size: 40k

Calendar System

Prints a set of pages that can be put in a notebook and used to keep track of appointments, as well as record time spent working on different consulting jobs. Provides extensive documentation.

Bob Pulgino
1420 N Street NW, #414
Washington, DC 20005
(202) 797-0879

Excel Macrosheet
Shareware $10.00
Size: 15k

CalendarMaker™ v2.2.1

Terrific calendar program. You can specify text and an icon for each day, place a picture on the page with a monthly calendar, print in color, and save calendars as pictures. Great interface, too.

Donald Brown
CE Software
801 - 73rd Street
Des Moines, IA 50312

Application
Shareware $30.00
Size: 72k

Emerge Job Cost

A demo version of a Professional Job Costing & Accounts Payable package. A sophisticated set of spreadsheets, databases, and macros. Some documentation provided.

Robert Snowie
1035 - 75 Street
Edmonton, Alberta
T6K 2S5 CANADA

Excel Worksheets
Demoware
Size: 5k

File Management

FileMaker database for keeping track of paper correspondence stored in a file cabinet. You can create a catalog subdivided by cabinet, drawer, and folder.

Unknown

FileMaker Database
Public Domain
Size: 43k

Mac Mailing v2.2

Maintains mailing lists and prints mailing labels. Sort of a dedicated database for names and addresses. Handles up to 2500 entries with nice data entry, search, and print functions.

IsleSoft
2497 West River Road
Grand Island, NY 14072

Application
Shareware $20.00
Size: 86k

Memo Minder

A talking memo program that speaks a phrase when you start up your Mac. Comes with an application for entering the phrase. MacinTalk is required.

Daniel Gimpelevich
CIS: 76625,3122

System Startup Extension
Freeware
Size: 2k

Reminders v1.01

Displays a short reminder when you boot your Mac if you make it the startup application. Has docs in a separate file.

Bob Patin
Summit Software
112 Hickory Park Lane
Antioch, TN 37013

Application
Shareware $5.00
Size: 26k

Business C2

Continued

Smallview v1.2

Calendar program that you can use as an on-line reference or to print out monthly calendars. For each day, you can specify a very short note and "to do" list of up to 10 items.

Dean Wong
718 Schwerin Street
Daly City, CA 94014

Application
Shareware $12.00
Size: 25k

TheShipper v1.0

Demo version of a complete UPS and Federal Express manifest system. Has on-line help. Demo only works with zip codes 117-118. Full version available for $60.

LPL Industries
70-8 Knickerbocker Avenue
Bohemia, NY 11716
(516) 567-1715

Application
Demoware
Size: 139k

Timecard™ v1.0c

Trivial program for calculating time intervals. Specify the time you start working, length of lunch break, and time you stop working. The program then determines how long you worked.

Michael Barto
B & P Associates
6951 Warner Avenue
Huntington Beach, CA 92647

Application
Public Domain
Size: 16k

TinyCalender

Guess what? This DA displays a tiny calendar of a single month. Starts up with the current month, but you can click arrows to move forward or backward by a month or a year.

unknown

Desk Accessory
Public Domain
Size: 6k

YOAP v0.1a

YOAP stands for Year On A Page. Prints a 12-month calendar on a single page with months arranged in 4 rows and 3 columns. Has no options; just specify the year, and hit a button to print.

Eric D. Boegel
Madison, WI

Application
Public Domain
Size: 9k

Address Book v1.1

Maintains a database of names, addresses, miscellaneous info, and phone numbers. Automatically dials telephone number if you have a modem. Contains a nice index that lets you view 66 names at a time.

Jim Leitch
61 Shaughnessy Blvd.
Willowdale, Ontario
M2J 1H9 CANADA
(416) 849-1532

Application
Shareware $10.00
Size: 48k

Address Book DA v2.5

Maintains address list and allows auto dialing, up to 3 numbers per address. Includes complete on-line help, and logs calls! A neat DA; check it out.

Jim Leitch
61 Shaughnessy Blvd.
Willowdale, Ontario
M2J 1H9 CANADA
(416) 849-1532

Desk Accessory
Shareware $20.00
Size: 97k

Easy Envelopes+ v1.5c

Maintains a list of up to 99 addresses and can print them out directly onto envelopes. Works with any size envelope on both an ImageWriter and a LaserWriter. Has a search function for finding particular addresses. Very nice.

Andrew Welch
Mark 3 Software
29 Grey Rocks Road
Wilton, CT 06897

Desk Accessory
Shareware $15.00
Size: 21k

Kiwi Envelopes!™ v2.03

Quick and simple program for addressing envelopes. Just type in the mailing address and your return address, select the envelope size, and print. You can even adjust the font if you like.

Kiwi Software
6546 Pardall Road
Santa Barbara, CA 93117

Desk Accessory
Freeware
Size: 23k

Business C4

General

Check Book v2.0

FileMaker database for managing a checkbook.

Mark White
459 Liberty Square Road
Boxboro, MA 01719
(508) 263-4322

FileMaker
Database
Freeware
Size: 63k

CheckLedger

Template for recording and categorizing check payments. You can print out summaries for analyzing expenses and business accounting. Not designed for balancing a checkbook.

A. Coblentz

Excel Worksheets
Public Domain
Size: 3k

CK 2.2 v2.2r2

A home checkbook keeper. Logs all your checking activity, including categories for income and expenses. Searches for particular entries and prints reports for budgeting and taxes.

Fernando Salazar
305 Whittier Street NW #202
Washington, DC 20012
CIS: 71550,676

Application
Shareware $15.00
Size: 151k

Exchequer

A payroll program for small businesses. Handles salaried or hourly wages with overtime; calculates Social Security, state, and federal taxes; prints payroll checks, earnings reports, and W-2 forms. Demo version limited to 5 employees.

Philip E. Jurgenson
164 Rita Road
Mankato, MN 56001
(507) 625-2737

Application
Demoware
Size: 163k

Business D1

Stocks and Bonds

Best Answer™ Demo v1.0

An optimization program that determines the best solution to a given business situation by using linear programming techniques. It's an add-on for Microsoft Works or Excel. Demo version only. Retails for $99 through Heizer Software.

Eric Weissmann
Eric Wainwright
Market Engineering Corp.

Application
Demoware
Size: 117k
12" 6 7 32

Real Estate Templates

Excel templates for real estate agents: buyer profiles & qualifications, repayment schedules, sales comparisons, income property comparisons, etc.

unknown

Excel Worksheets
Public Domain
Size: 18k
12" 6 7 32

Schwab v1.0

Calculates the brokerage fees for buying and selling stocks and warrants charged by Charles Schwab & Co., Inc. You have to adjust the template for rate increases since 11/1/86.

Chuck Horton
5209 Camino Sandia NE
Albuquerque, NM 87111

Excel Macrosheet
Shareware $2.00
Size: 9k
12" 6 7 32

Business D2

Stocks and Bonds

Bonds v3.0

Evaluates the yields of municipal, Treasury, and corporate bonds. Considers federal and state taxes and transaction fees when comparing the yields. Interface is sloppy and cumbersome.

H. B. Levine
4666 Cristy Way
Castro Valley, CA 94546

Application
Shareware $3.00
Size: 55k
12" 6 7 32

EE Bonds

Template for determining the value and interest payments of EE Series bonds.

H.L. Killingsworth
R.L. Barrett

Excel Worksheets
Freeware
Size: 63k
12" 6 7 32

Financial Analysis

Large Excel template for a financial analysis of a company: assets, liabilities, capital accounts, profit and loss, cash flow, performance ratios.

unknown

Excel Worksheets
Public Domain
Size: 235k
12" 6 7 32

Financial Calc v1.0

Not a real calculator. Allows you to calculate and compare the time value of money at various levels of interest, period, and payment schedules.

Phil Bush
12385A Naverucj Drive
Maryland Hts, MO 63043

Application
Shareware $10.00
Size: 27k
12" 6 7 32

MacDep v1.0

Macrosheet for calculating depreciation for multi-year investments. User specifies the depreciation factors, so any type of depreciation schedule can be used.

Stuart C. Bowen
CIS: 71226,1373

Excel Macrosheet
Freeware
Size: 10k
12" 6 7 32

MacroStats v1.03

Collection of structured command and function macros for performing statistical calculations: factorial, determination coefficient, correlation coefficient, etc.

Chuck Horton
5209 Camino Sandia NE
Albuquerque, NM 87111
CIS: 72447,2007

Excel Macrosheet
Shareware $5.00
Size: 43k
12" 6 7 32

Airways

A sample spreadsheet showing a capital expenditure analysis for a hypothetical company called Airways Corporation. Shows how to use Excel to forecast costs and expenditures.

Micromentor, Inc.

Excel Worksheets
Freeware
Size: 29k

Commands

Set of simple macros for command tasks and actions. The macros can be executed using keyboard equivalents.

unknown

Excel Macrosheet
Public Domain
Size: 7k

Country Lawyer Kit

Word templates for lawyers and legal clerks. Includes templates for Bill of Sale, Medical Authorization, Promissory Note, Speed Note, Summons (Federal), Waiver, Warranty Deed, Will (Male).

unknown

MS Word Templates
Public Domain
Size: 42k

Engineering Templates

MultiPlan templates.

unknown

MultiPlan Document
Public Domain
Size: 21k

M/10 Key

Macro automatically inserts decimal points in numbers to allow rapid entry of monetary values. For example, 5122 is automatically entered as $51.22. Documentation in a separate file.

R. Steven Dell
9519 Viewside Drive
Dallas, TX 75231
(214) 349-8599

Excel Macrosheet
Public Domain
Size: 3k

M/Generic

Set of macros that implement many keyboard equivalents for Excel commands and operations. Documentation in a separate file.

R. Steven Dell
9519 Viewside Drive
Dallas, TX 75231
(214) 349-8599

Excel Macrosheet
Public Domain
Size: 6k

Pcal v2.11

Personal calendar program that claims to work on the ImageWriter and Apple LaserWriter.

Joseph F. Buchanan
University of Utah

Application
Freeware
Size: 31k

Point-to-Point

Calculates the distance between two locations specified by their longitude and latitude. Also computes the velocity required to travel between the two locations in a specified amount of time.

J. D. Martin
GEnie: Capt.Cumulus

Excel Worksheets
Public Domain
Size: 8k

Business E1

Continued

Misc. Business

Robber! v1.0

Maintains a list of descriptions of items and serial numbers. Use it to keep track of the serial numbers of equipment in case of theft.

Mark H. Eppel
1400 Tuesburg Court
Pontiac, IL 61764

Application
Shareware $1.00
Size: 14k

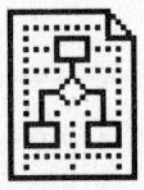

W/M / Currency v0.3

Macros for performing conversions between U.S. dollars and Japanese Yen, and between English and Metric units of weight. For example, converts from $/pound to Yen/kilogram.

Keizo Suzuki
2000 South Eads Street, #934
Arlington, VA 22202

Excel Macrosheet
Shareware $1.00
Size: 5k
12" 6 7 32

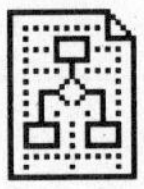

Weights/Measures. v0.4

Macros for converting between English and metric weights and measures, such as from pounds to grams, or feet to meters.

Keizo Suzuki
2000 South Eads Street, #934
Arlington, VA 22202

Excel Macrosheet
Shareware $1.00
Size: 6k
12" 6 7 32

DAs

Desk Accessories are those nifty little programs in your Apple Menu.

To install DAs under System 6:

Use Font/DA Mover 3.8 or later (located on Utilities 2 in your System disk set). 1) Open the Font/DA Mover. 2) Click the Desk Accessory button at the top of the screen. The DAs already installed in your System file appear in the left-hand window. 3) Click on the Open... button on the right. 4) Locate and open the DA suitcase file you wish to install. 5) Select the Desk Accessory you are installing. 6) Click on the Copy button in the middle of the window.

To install DAs under System 7:

1) Simply drag the DA suitcase file onto the System Folder icon. A dialog box saying, "Desk Accessories need to be stored in the Apple Menu Items Folder" will appear. Click OK.

DAs A1

Calculators

Abacus

An abacus with 9 rows of beads. Each row has 2 black beads on the left and 4 white beads on the right.

unknown

Desk Accessory
Public Domain
Size: 2k

Adv Calculator v1.1

This calculator provides advanced scientific and programmer functions, as well as a quick-reference ASCII table.

Desktop CAD, Inc.
607 Rosemont Plaza
Rosemont, PA 19010-1526

Desk Accessory
Shareware $8.00
Size: 10k

Analyst

Some of the financial parts of this demo version of the calculator don't seem to work.

unknown

Desk Accessory
Demoware
Size: 7k

BusAnalyst Calc

Calculator. Same as Analyst on this disk.

unknown

Application
Freeware

Calculator

Simple calculator created using the Dubl-Click Calculator Construction Set. Just the 4 basic functions.

Chuck Fisher

Desk Accessory
Public Domain
Size: 20k

Conversion v1.5.4

Fairly comprehensive general conversion DA. Not as complete as Sci DA, but it does the work for you. Nice interface and all the converting that nonscientific types will ever need. Another best buy!

Rick Johnson
2216 Allen Lane
Waukesha, WI 53186
GEnie: RICK.JOHNSON

Desk Accessory
Shareware $5.00
Size: 43k

Dt Calculator v3.0

A reverse polish notation calculator with scientific functions.

Lars Sundström
Seagull Engineering of Sweden
Box 909
S-220 09 Lund
SWEDEN

Desk Accessory
Freeware
Size: 21k

Financial Calc

Calculator created using the Dubl-Click Calculator Construction Set. A simple financial calculator with the 4 basic functions as well as present and future value computations.

Design Equilibrium

Desk Accessory
Freeware
Size: 23k

FractionCalc v1.1

Feet, inches, and fraction calculator. Convenient for calculating distances in feet and inches, which often involve fractional inches.	Steve Bryan and David Stroval	**Desk Accessory** **Shareware $5.00** **Size: 14k**

Hex Calculator

A simple calculator that does the 4 basic operations and bit shifts in both decimal and hexadecimal modes. Also converts between them.	unknown	**Desk Accessory** **Freeware** **Size: 4k**

IQ 15-C•CALC

A calculator with scientific functions. Emulates HP 15-C calculator.	Rick Billingsley	**Desk Accessory** **Shareware $5.00** **Size: 88k**

MacOhm Calc

This calculator has 3 displays, one each for hex, binary and integer; a simulated paper tape which you can copy to the Clipboard; and a calendar. May not work with recent System versions.	unknown	**Desk Accessory** **Freeware** **Size: 20k**

Mini Sci Calc

Another scientific calculator constructed with the Dubl-Click Calculator Construction Set.	Chris Munger GEnie: CMUNGER	**Desk Accessory** **Freeware** **Size: 26k**

Multi Calc

Calculator created using the Dubl-Click Calculator Construction Set. Conversions for binary, octal, decimal, and hexadecimal formats.	Computer Coach (209) 523-4000	**Desk Accessory** **Freeware** **Size: 19k**

Multi Calc

Calculator created using the Dubl-Click Calculator Construction Set. Conversions for binary, octal, decimal, and hexadecimal formats.	Computer Coach (209) 523-4000	**Desk Accessory** **Freeware** **Size: 19k**

Pocket Calendar v1.2

Displays a small window with a one-month calendar. Comes up initially at the current month/year, but buttons allow you to move back/forward by a month or year.	MacBear ShareWare 92 Maplehurst Road Rochester, NY 14617	**Desk Accessory** **Shareware $3.00** **Size: 5k**

DAs A1

Continued

RPN calc

A reverse polish notation calculator with scientific and financial functions.

Jonathan Hess
7015 E. Aster Drive
Scottsdale, AZ 85254

Desk Accessory
Shareware $10.00
Size: 45k
12" 6 7 32

RPN-C

Reverse polish notation calculator. The memory and the settings are preserved between invocations.

Milton E. Sagen
Department of Physics
Oregon State University
Corvallis, OR 97331
milt@mist.cs.orst.edu

Desk Accessory
Freeware
Size: 34k
12" 6 7 32

SciCon

A list of unit conversion factors.

Don Rittner
CIS: 70057,1325
GEnie: D.Rittner

Desk Accessory
Public Domain
Size: 35k

SmartCal

The calendar DA allows you to save messages, and the INIT reminds you of them when you first start up your Macintosh. You must have System 6.0.x or higher to see reminders.

unknown

Desk Accessory
Freeware

SuperCalc II

Decimal and hexadecimal modes, trigonometric functions, statistics, and metric conversions.

Brad Ferguson

Desk Accessory
Freeware
Size: 25k
12" 6 7 32

Waltham Font(LCD)

A font that looks like the LCD display letters. Included here for use with IQ 15-C•CALC desk accessory.

unknown

Font
Freeware
Size: 29k
12" 6 7 32

Amort

Calculates amortization tables for loans based on the annual percentage rate, number of payments, and amount of the loan or periodic payment.

Roger V. Mitchell
729 Pt. Arguello Road
Oceanside, CA 92054

Desk Accessory
Freeware
Size: 9k

Area Codes

Gives you the locality corresponding to area codes you enter.

unknown

Desk Accessory
Freeware
Size: 3k

AreaCodes/TimeZonesDA v1.0

Telephone area codes for the U.S., Canada, and Mexico circa 1990.

NeoScribe International Inc.
PO Box 469
Middleton, CT 06457
CIS: 71041,15

Desk Accessory
Freeware
Size: 14k

BlackBook

'Little black book' for storing phone numbers or notes. There is a page for each letter of the alphabet and buttons for moving to each page. Has a Find function to search for text.

unknown

Desk Accessory
Public Domain
Size: 4k

Charger DA

A simple time-accounting utility. Enter the cost per minute and leave the DA running. It continuously calculates the total charges.

James Finnigan

Desk Accessory
Public Domain
Size: 6k

Decision

This doesn't seem to work; it crashes.

unknown

Desk Accessory
Public Domain
Size: 14k

Dialer

Dials a number through the serial or sound port that has been saved to the clipboard. Can send commands to a modem. Comes with FKey.

John Hill
Bugless Software Ltd.
PO Box 1097
Mason City, IA 50401

Desk Accessory
Shareware $?
Size: 38k

DiskLock™

Allows you to lock/unlock any local Mac hard disk or floppy. Files on locked disks cannot be modified under normal circumstances.

Jeffrey S. Shulman
PO Box 521
Ridgefield, CT 06877-0521

Desk Accessory
Freeware
Size: 4k

DAs B1

Continued

Business DAs

FastEnvelopeDA 1.0.3 Demo

Good interface. Handles 14+ different stationery sizes, prints bar codes, etc.

Henry Carstens
Vertical Solutions
PO Box 1150
Beaverton, OR 97075

Desk Accessory
Demoware
Size: 121k

Help - Word 3 Commands

A listing of commands and keyboard equivalents for commonly used operations in MS Word 3.01. The list is quite extensive. A handy quick reference.

Jim Moore

Desk Accessory
Public Domain
Size: 13k

Label and Envelope v1.4

Does labels, envelopes, and file cards. You can type the address by hand or copy it from the Clipboard.

Eastgate Systems, Inc.
PO Box 1307
Cambridge, MA 02238

Desk Accessory
Shareware $15.00
Size: 23k

Postal Codes

Displays a scrolling window listing each state and its two-letter postal code abbreviation.

unknown

Desk Accessory
Public Domain
Size: 5k

PT NomoGraph

Displays a pressure/temperature nomograph. For a given observed temperature and pressure, chart shows the temperature corrected to 760 mm Hg.

Roger Simon & Tim Senecal
CU Denver Chemistry Dept.
1200 Larimer Street
Denver, CO 80204

Desk Accessory
Freeware
Size: 11k

Remember? v2.00rm

A utility for remembering appointments and important occasions. Use the DA to enter and browse information. A companion INIT reminds you of impending events when you start up your Mac.

Dave Warker
1330 W. North Street
Egg Harbor, NJ 08215

Desk Accessory
Shareware $?
Size: 77k

Road Atlas

Displays a road map of the continental U.S. with major cities and highways. Clicking on two cities shows the mileage and shortest path between them.

Jim Moore
Vic Hasselblad
Microsparc, Inc.

Desk Accessory
Freeware

Time Logger v2.11

Utility for keeping track of time for the purpose of billing clients. Creates tab-delimited text files. Has docs in a separate file.

Loftus E. Becker, Jr.
41 Whitney Street
Hartford, CT 06105

Desk Accessory
Shareware $15.00
Size: 21k

To Do! DA

Maintains an electronic 'to do' list. For example, store a list of people you need to call with attached notes and phone numbers. Slick interface. Complete docs in a separate file.

Andrew Welch
Mark 3 Software
29 Grey Rocks Road
Wilton, CT 06897

Desk Accessory
Shareware $10.00
Size: 10k

Twelve-C™ Demo

A programmable financial calculator DA. Imitates an HP 12-C calculator. Comes with an installer program to place it in your System file.

Richard F. Reich
Dreams of the Phoenix, Inc.
PO Box 10273
Jacksonville, FL 32247

Application
Demoware
Size: 25k

USDebt v1.4

Displays a random quotation. Then, after about 10 seconds, it displays a running count of the U.S. national debt, which increases by $1 million every two minutes.

Chris Riley
GEnie: CHRISRILEY
riley@cs.ucsd.edu

Desk Accessory
Freeware
Size: 9k

Values

Calculates stock and property values. For a company's common stock, program estimates growth rate and fair market PE ratio. For properties, program estimates cash flow and property value.

James H. Moore, Jr.
4125 Arroyo Trail
Carmel, CA 93923

Desk Accessory
Shareware $5.00
Size: 8k

DAs 1

Desk Accessories

3D Tic Tac Toe

Play a variation of Tic-tac-toe against the computer on a 4 x 4 x 4 grid.

unknown

Desk Accessory
Public Domain
Size: 2k

Afterthought Demo v1.4

Desk accessory text editor designed for programmers. Supports tabs, auto-indenting, and line numbers.

Jimmy Mac Software
P.O. Box 24695
Jacksonville, FL 32241

Desk Accessory
Demoware
Size: 44k

Artisto+ v2.01

Opens and displays MacPaint files and 'PICT' format files. Lets you select a rectangular portion of the image and copy it to the Clipboard.

Tom Taylor
3405 Walton Way
San Jose, CA 95117

Desk Accessory
Shareware $5.00
Size: 14k

Ascii Chart v1.0

Displays a chart of the 128 standard ASCII characters with either decimal, hexadecimal, or octal indexes.

Gertjan Noordman

Desk Accessory
Public Domain
Size: 3k

ASCII-Char v1.0

Presents a chart of the decimal and hexadecimal index for each ASCII character in a specified font. Appears in color on a Mac II. Includes desk accessory version and has docs in a separate file.

Jim Leitch
Toronto, CANADA
(416) 498-0828
CIS: 70416,1532

Application
Freeware
Size: 7k

Basetool v1.32

Converts numbers between binary, decimal, and hexadecimal formats.

Dave Burnard
Fred, Sam, & Dave Software
654 Neilson St.
Berkeley, CA 94707

Desk Accessory
Shareware $5.00
Size: 5k

BCS*Clicker

Continuously displays the coordinates of the mouse. Also computes the distance between two mouse clicks.

Ken Winograd
Boston Computer Society
One Center Plaza
Boston, MA 02108

Desk Accessory
Freeware
Size: 3k

Beacon v2.2

A Finder substitute DA that displays information about files and can launch programs. This is a crippled version of a $15 shareware program.

Lighthouse Systems
RFD 2, Box 189c
Uxbridge, MA 01569

Desk Accessory
Demoware
Size: 23k

BigBen

Puts up a window showing the clock face of Big Ben with the correct time. Properly updates time if the DA is left running.

Ricardo Ettore

Desk Accessory
Public Domain
Size: 10k
12" 6 7 32

Bricks

Simple version of the game Breakout where you control a paddle and must keep a ball in play to knock out bricks.

RainMaker Research Inc.

Desk Accessory
Public Domain
Size: 5k
12" 6 7 32

Calendar v2.1

Draws a monthly calendar above a text notepad. Lets you enter and store text for any day of any year. Provides nice features for navigating to different dates. Has docs within the program. Very nice.

David Oster
Mosaic Codes
2140 Shattuck Ave, Suite 2036
Berkeley, CA 94704

Desk Accessory
Shareware $5.00
Size: 16k
12" 6 7 32

Casio v1.1

Emulates a 4-function digital wristwatch, complete with time and date, stopwatch, alarm clock, mulitple time zones, and more. Contains docs in a separate file.

Ralph Muha
25A Kelly Road
Cambridge, MA 02139

Desk Accessory
Shareware $5.00
Size: 14k
12" 6 7 32

Charger v1.0

A simple time accounting utility. Enter the cost per minute and leave the DA running. It continuously calculates the total charges.

James Finnigan

Desk Accessory
Public Domain
Size: 6k
12" 6 7 32

Checksum (File Checker) v1.0

Displays the file size and checksum for a selected file.

Mike Cohen

Desk Accessory
Freeware
Size: 3k
12" 6 7 32

Compact1

Compacts memory.

unknown

Desk Accessory
Public Domain
Size: 1k
12" 6 7 32

Compact2

Compacts memory.

unknown

Desk Accessory
Public Domain
Size: 1k
12" 6 7 32

DAs 1

Continued

Compress It

A simple file compression program.

Jerry Whitnell
188 Laurel Avenue
Menlo Park, CA 94025
CIS: 76317,2615

Desk Accessory
Shareware $15.00
Size: 21k

ConCode v1.3

Tool for assembly language programmers that demonstrates how various instructions are affected by the status of the condition codes.

John Stogdell Stokess III
Pixel Pathways
P.O. Box 4065
Mt. Penn, PA 19606

Desk Accessory
Shareware $15.00
Size: 7k

Convert

Program for converting between metric and English units.

JAM Software Pty Ltd
27A Nowraine Street
Summer Hill, NSW 2130
AUSTRALIA

Desk Accessory
Shareware $15.00
Size: 25k

DAFile

Displays and modifies the information stored about each file by the Finder, such as its name, type, file creator, and size.

Ken Winograd
2039 Country Club Drive
Manchester, NH 03102
(603) 625-1094

Desk Accessory
Shareware $5.00
Size: 9k

DAFont v3.1

Displays all available fonts in their own font and in all sizes. Also reports statistics about fonts, such as ID number and size. Lets you direct reports to the screen or the printer. Includes docs within program.

Ken Winograd
2039 Country Club Drive
Manchester, NH 03102
(603) 625-1094

Desk Accessory
Shareware $10.00
Size: 29k

DApp v1.1

Install DAs within this application, then run this application to access the DAs. Keeps DAs out of your System file, but probably useful only under MultiFinder.

Steve Bollinger
4297 Sulgrave Drive
Swartz Creek, MI 48473
CIS: 71620,740

Application
Freeware
Size: 4k

dCAD Calculator v2.1

A scientific calculator with additional functions for programmers such as Boolean algebra and bitwise shifts and rotates. There's an application version as well. Thorough docs in a separate file.

Desktop CAD
104 Helecho Court
Thousand Oaks, CA 91362-2712

Desk Accessory
Shareware $8.00
Size: 10k

DeskZap v1.32

Renames, deletes, and copies files. Displays and modifies Finder information. Strips line feeds, control characters, and trailing blanks from text files.

Bruce Tomlin
15801 Chase Hill Blvd. #109
San Antonio, TX 78256

Desk Accessory
Shareware $15.00
Size: 17k

DAs 1

Continued

DiskInfo v1.45

Displays file and volume directories.

David Dunham
Maitreya Design
P.O. Box 1480
Goleta, CA 93116

Desk Accessory
Shareware $10.00
Size: 16k
12" 6 7 32

DiskTop v1.2

Old shareware version of a commercial product. Displays directories and modifies file information.

Gil Beecher
CE Software
801 73rd Street
Des Moines, IA 50312

Desk Accessory
Shareware $39.95
Size: 33k
12" 6 7 32

f(n)key

Creates a menu from which you can run FKEYs (function key programs) instead of having to hit Command-Shift and a number.

Carlos Weber
CIS: 70277,726

Desk Accessory
Public Domain
Size: 2k
12" 6 7 32

File Minder v1.1

File utility that can copy, rename, and delete files.

J M McIntosh
Seanook Software
CIS: 75366,1233

Desk Accessory
Freeware
Size: 11k
12" 6 7 32

FileFixer v1.0b3

Fixes up text files by adding or removing line feeds and filtering out non-printing characters.

Bill Steinberg
CIS: 76703,1027

Desk Accessory
Freeware
Size: 6k
12" 6 7 32

FileMaster v2.3

Displays files and allows you to search for and delete files. Also modifies Finder information and flags.

Alexander Falk
Freistädterstr.150/5/13
A-4040 Linz
AUSTRIA

Desk Accessory
Shareware $25.00
Size: 18k
12" 6 7 32

FileStar v1.0

Displays files and allows you to view and modify file information.

Scott Searle
Searle Software International
P.O. Box 87
Mukilteo, WA 98275

Desk Accessory
Shareware $15.00
Size: 20k
12" 6 7 32

Flow

Makes your Mac screen appear to melt and flow down to the bottom of the screen. Requires that you reboot to quit.

unknown

Desk Accessory
Public Domain
Size: 2k
12" 6 7 32

DAs 1

Continued

FolderMaker v1.0

Creates a new folder. Good for those times when you want to save a file in a new folder from within an application.

Jan Eugenides
P.O. Box 151
Maynard, MA 01754

Desk Accessory
Freeware
Size: 5k

Freemem

Displays the amount of free memory on your Mac.

R. Ettore

Desk Accessory
Public Domain
Size: 2k

Grep / Word Count v1.1

Implementation of the grep and word count functions from UNIX. Search text files for patterns using regular expressions.

Paul DuBois
1220 Capitol Court
Madison, WI 53706

Desk Accessory
Public Domain
Size: 12k

Heap Doctor

Programming tool that displays information about the system and application heaps. Can scramble the heap, which is useful for finding memory management errors.

unknown

Desk Accessory
Public Domain
Size: 3k

HeapInfo

Displays the size of the application heap, number of free bytes and free blocks.

unknown

Desk Accessory
Public Domain
Size: 1k

Icon Maker v2.1

Captures any 32 x 32 pixel region on the screen and turns it into an icon ('ICON' or 'ICN#' resource). Shareware fee is 'what you think it is worth.' Docs in a separate file.

Steve Fine
504 Linden Road
University Park, PA 16802

Desk Accessory
Shareware ?
Size: 11k

Knockout

Simple implementation of the game Breakout. You control a paddle and must keep a ball in play to knock out bricks.

Andy Stadler
Box 603, Occidental College
1600 Campus Road
Los Angeles, CA 90041

Desk Accessory
Freeware
Size: 5k

LabelMaker v1.3

Prints labels on an ImageWriter; it will not print to a LaserWriter. Has space for 6 lines of text.

David Mutter

Desk Accessory
Public Domain
Size: 7k

Mage's DAleks v1.0

Move to avoid the Daleks, insidious creatures from the TV show 'Dr. Who.' Daleks die when they crash into each other. You can randomly teleport, and you can use your sonic screwdriver once per level.

Mage Software
c/o Steve Sheets
P.O. Box 8455
Rolling Meadows, IL 60008

Desk Accessory
Shareware $20.00
Size: 22k

MakePICTfile

Creates a PICT file from a picture you've copied to the clipboard.

unknown

Desk Accessory
Public Domain
Size: 2k

Multi-Scrap

Allows you to create and maintain several Scrapbook files. This version has been updated to support HFS. Original version of the program was written by Bob Luce.

Kevin Mitchell
1321 W. Touhy #2S
Chicago, IL 60626
(312) 274-2418

Desk Accessory
Freeware
Size: 5k

New Scrapbook v2.2

Improved version of the standard Scrapbook DA. Has a selection tool and vertical scroll bars, and it can shrink a picture to fit in the window. Requests a small contribution if you find the program useful.

Tim Waska
4832 - 49 Avenue N.W.
Calgary, Alberta
T3A 0R9 CANADA

Desk Accessory
Shareware ?
Size: 12k

Panic Button

Puts up a window with a panic button. Clicking the button blacks out your screen. Click the mouse to continue. Useful for quickly hiding your screen from prying eyes.

unknown

Desk Accessory
Public Domain
Size: 1k

Show Clipboard

Displays the contents of the clipboard in a scrolling window.

unknown

Desk Accessory
Public Domain
Size: 5k

Stuffclip v1.00

Allows you to copy non-printing ASCII characters to the clipboard.

William Steinberg

Desk Accessory
Freeware
Size: 2k

DAs 2

Desk Accessories

Amortization

Calculates amortization tables for loans based on the annual percentage rate, number of payments, and amount of the loan or periodic payment.

Roger V. Mitchell
729 Pt. Arguello Road
Oceanside, CA 92054

Desk Accessory
Freeware
Size: 9k

Analyse v1.2

Displays a dump of RAM or ROM memory of the Mac starting from a specified address. Can also seach for a specified hex or ASCII string.

Claude Johnson
249 Springhill
Rosemère, Québec
J7A 3G2 CANADA

Desk Accessory
Shareware $10.00
Size: 10k

BigZoomIdle

Screen saver that darkens the screen and displays successive random rectangles that smoothly zoom in and out.

Paul DuBois

Desk Accessory
Public Domain
Size: 3k

Coordinates

Displays the coordinates of the mouse.

E. Wrench

Desk Accessory
Public Domain
Size: 4k

Fade to Black v3.2

Installs a screen saver INIT in your System file that blackens the screen after a specified period of inactivity. Shows the icon of the running application bouncing around the screen on a black background.

Brian L. Matthews
10513 SE 219th Street
Kent, WA 98031

Desk Accessory
Freeware
Size: 36k

FatMouse2

Displays the mouse coordinates and a 16 x 16 pixel FatBits view of the area under the mouse cursor.

Ken Winograd
2039 Country Club Drive
Manchester, NH 03102
(603) 625-1094

Desk Accessory
Shareware $5.00
Size: 3k

Glass

Displays a 16 x 16 pixel FatBits view of the area under the mouse cursor.

unknown

Desk Accessory
Public Domain
Size: 1k

Idle

Screen saver that blackens the screen and displays the icon of the running application bouncing around on a black background.

unknown

Desk Accessory
Public Domain
Size: 2k

immortality v0.94

Automatically calls up a selected desk accessory each time a new application is launched. Useful if you can't run MultiFinder.

Ron Risley
1955 Edgemont Street
San Diego, CA 92102
CIS: 73547,240

System Startup Extension
Freeware
Size: 3k

KeyMouse

Displays a small keyboard so you can 'type' using the mouse. Useful for those who can't use the keyboard.

John B. Halleck
Univ. of Utah Computer Center
3116 Merrill Eng. Building
Salt Lake City, UT 84112

Desk Accessory
Freeware
Size: 6k

LockOUT™ v2.0

Provides password protection for your Mac. Bring up the DA and enter a password. To re-access your Mac, you must re-enter the password. Supplying the wrong password results in having to reboot the Mac.

BEYOND
3865 N. Oracle Road
Tucson, AZ 85705
(602) 323-4547

Desk Accessory
Freeware
Size: 20k

McSink v7.0A

Great DA text editor. Multiple windows and lots of useful utilities for cleaning up text files. Convert space runs into tabs, add and strip linefeeds, include line numbers, and more. By the author of Vantage.

Dave McWherter
Preferred Software, Inc.
5100 Poplar Ave, Suite 706
Memphis, TN 38137

Desk Accessory
Shareware $45.00
Size: 68k

MegaWatcher v85.10.12

Tracks the loading and unloading of resources. Continuously displays the status (in memory, locked, and/or purgeable) of all resources of a specified type. Has docs in a separate file.

unknown

Desk Accessory
Public Domain
Size: 5k

Memory Watch v0.1

Displays a hexadecimal dump of memory from a specified address. Can also modify contents of memory.

Jay Fenton
MacroMind Inc.
1028 W. Wolfram Street
Chicago, IL 60657

Desk Accessory
Shareware $10.00
Size: 5k

MemScan v0.9

Displays a hexadecimal and ASCII dump of memory starting from a specified address.

Michael J. Wise

Desk Accessory
Public Domain
Size: 3k

Message v2.0

Puts up a lightbulb tickertape of a specified text message. Letters are composed of white dots on a black background about 2 inches high. Letters move slowly from right to left across the screen.

Steve Christensen

Desk Accessory
Public Domain
Size: 3k

DAs 2

Continued

miniWRITER™ v1.61

A nice DA text editor. Excellent printing features for either the ImageWriter or LaserWriter. Has option for automatically using smart quotes. Docs in a separate file.

David Dunham
Maitreya Design
P.O. Box 1480
Goleta, CA 93116

Desk Accessory
Shareware $12.00
Size: 36k

MockPackage+

Set of four DAs: MockChart, for graphing a table of numbers; MockTerminal, a terminal emulator; MockPrinter, a text file printer; MockWrite, a text editor.

Don Brown
CE Software
801 - 73rd Street
Des Moines, IA 50312

Desk Accessory
Shareware $35.00
Size: 54k

Moire Idle

Screen saver that displays a moiré line-art pattern moving around on a black background. The shape of the pattern can be adjusted by hitting certain keys on the keyboard.

unknown

Desk Accessory
Public Domain
Size: 5k

Mouseometer

Displays the coordinates of the mouse.

unknown

Desk Accessory
Public Domain
Size: 2k

MW->TEXT

Translates MacWrite documents into text-only files.

unknown

Desk Accessory
Public Domain
Size: 6k

Note Pad II v2.0

Creates a notepad of text indexed by a topic name. Each topic has its own page of text and is listed in a pop-up menu.

Arthur Britto II
1850 Arch Street, #3
Berkeley, CA 94709
(415) 841-7216

Desk Accessory
Freeware

Other... v3.09

Allows you to run desk accessories that aren't installed in the System file. Has docs in a separate file.

Loftus E. Becker, Jr.
41 Whitney Street
Hartford, CT 06105
CIS: 70206,67

Desk Accessory
Shareware $10.00
Size: 12k

Phone Book DA v1.1

Maintains a list of names and associated phone numbers. Searches by either name or number.

Peter Merchant
Engineering Department
U.S. Merchant Marine Academy
Kings Point, NY 11024

Desk Accessory
Public Domain
Size: 7k

Piczle

Displays a scrambled picture of a sketch of a Mac with an apple. Requires you to assemble the pieces in the proper order.

Ricardo Ettore
c/o Dr. C. Krauthammer
4101 Cathedral Avenue
Washington, DC 20016

Desk Accessory
Shareware $5.00
Size: 8k

Poly Idle

Screen saver that displays a line-art polygon moving around on a black background.

unknown

Desk Accessory
Public Domain
Size: 8k

ProCount v1.0

Counts all words in a text file. Can screen for words that are 4 letters or longer.

John Pintar
1709 E. Park Place #35
Milwaukee, WI 53211

Desk Accessory
Shareware $5.00
Size: 5k

Saviour

Can be set up to automatically save documents after a specified number of seconds, number of keystrokes or mouse clicks, or seconds of idle time.

unknown

Desk Accessory
Public Domain
Size: 4k

SetFile v3.3

Displays and modifies file information such as the File Type and Creator. Not compatible with new system software.

Sam M. Roberts
Fred, Dave, & Sam Software
1442A Walnut St., Suite #153
Berkeley, CA 94709

Desk Accessory
Shareware $10.00
Size: 7k

SetSound v1.3

Adjusts the sound-level setting, which is normally set using the Control Panel.

William P. Steinberg

Desk Accessory
Freeware
Size: 1k

Stars v1.8

Screen saver that displays a Star Trek effect of stars whizzing by on the screen.

unknown

Desk Accessory
Public Domain
Size: 6k

Time Logger v2.11

Utility for keeping track of time for the purpose of billing clients. Creates tab-delimited text files. Has docs in a separate file.

Loftus E. Becker, Jr.
41 Whitney Street
Hartford, CT 06105

Desk Accessory
Shareware $15.00
Size: 21k

DAs 2

Continued

Timer v1.2

Displays a running timer that records how long your Mac has been on. Can also display the current time or be used as a stopwatch. Includes docs within program.

John M. Cagle
CIS: 72477,3223

Desk Accessory
Freeware
Size: 6k

Traplist

Displays a list of trap numbers and the corresponding memory address.

unknown

Desk Accessory
Public Domain
Size: 2k

Uriah heap

Displays a graphical representation of the system or application heap showing free space, relocatable and nonrelocatable blocks, purgeable and non-purgeable blocks.

unknown

Desk Accessory
Public Domain
Size: 2k

Utils

Utility for copying, renaming, and deleting files.

unknown

Desk Accessory
Public Domain
Size: 8k

VT52 v1.1

Terminal emulation program that responds to the control sequences of the DEC VT-52 terminal. Does not auto-dial.

DIALECTIX Software Systems
P.O. Box 1998
Cambridge, MA 02138

Desk Accessory
Shareware $10.00
Size: 6k

WeAreTheWord

Hangman game without the hanging man. Guess letters in a computer-selected phrase or type in your own phrase. Suggests a contribution to the USA for AFRICA fund.

unknown

Desk Accessory
Public Domain
Size: 7k

Windows v1.1

Maintains a menu listing all open windows in the current application. Lets you activate a window by selecting its name from the menu.

Marsh Gosnell
35 Godfrey Road
Montclair, NJ 07043

Desk Accessory
Shareware $5.00
Size: 4k

DAs 3

Desk Accessories

DAs

Airports

Lists the 3-letter codes for 240 airports. Clicking on two airport codes shows the distance in nautical miles between the respective airports.

Jim Moore

Desk Accessory
Freeware
Size: 10k
12" 6 7 32

BaseToBase v1.0

RPN calculator that can also handle arithmetic and logical operations on 32-bit numbers in hexadecimal, decimal, octal, or binary format. Docs in a separate file.

A. Remy Malan
1455 SW 211th Avenue
Aloha, OR 97006
(503) 642-0919

Desk Accessory
Freeware
Size: 10k
12" 6 7 32

Bugs Bunny

Displays a clock with Bugs Bunny's face in the middle. Has a sweep second hand and shows the current date.

Jim Moore

Desk Accessory
Public Domain
Size: 6k
12" 6 7 32

BusyorNot v2.0

Dials a phone number and reports whether it is busy or not. If not busy, lets you decide whether to hang up or stay on-line. Includes Pascal source code. A modem is required. No documentation.

Kiron D. Bondale
4195 Beaconsfield Avenue
Montreal, Quebec
H4A 2H4 CANADA

Desk Accessory
Freeware
Size: 15k
12" 6 7 32

DATools

Copies, deletes, and renames files. Also checks the free space left on a disk. Has docs in a separate file.

Kiron D. Bondale
4195 Beaconsfield Avenue
Montreal, Quebec
H4A 2HR CANADA

Desk Accessory
Shareware $5.00
Size: 12k
12" 6 7 32

Draw v2.5

Object-oriented (like MacDraw) drawing program. Standard Mac drawing tools. Also has arrows and hairlines. Docs in a separate file.

Günther Blaschek
Petzoldstr. 31
A - 4020 Linz
AUSTRIA

Desk Accessory
Shareware $30.00
Size: 35k
12" 6 7 32

∑Edit v1.11

An excellent DA text editor designed for programmers and telecommunicators. File length limited only by memory, true tabs, auto-indent, search and replace, cursor-key movement, and more.

Leonard Rosenthol
LazerWare, Inc.
GEnie: MACgician

Desk Accessory
Freeware
Size: 51k
12" 6 7 32

Font Lister

Displays a list of all fonts and corresponding font sizes installed on your Mac. Includes C source code; docs are in a separate file.

Jim Leitch
Toronto, CANADA
(416) 498-0828
CIS: 70416,1352

Desk Accessory
Freeware
Size: 6k
12" 6 7 32

DAs 3

Continued

JoliWrite v2.0

Text editor DA. Instead of installing a menu, text window has a status bar with a pop-up menu. Status bar also shows line and character count and current position. Supports only one window at a time.

Benoît Widemann
68 avenue d'Italie
75013 Paris
FRANCE

Desk Accessory
Shareware $20.00
Size: 62k

MacAlmanac

Gives information about the planets and stars: next time when Venus, Jupiter, and Saturn are in conjunction/opposition, next full moon and equinox, current declination of sun, list of stars at meridian.

unknown

Desk Accessory
Public Domain
Size: 4k

Pager v1.01

Prints a picture of the current screen contents.

unknown

Desk Accessory
Public Domain
Size: 11k

Paint Reader

Views a MacPaint file over the entire screen, using a non-standard interface. Supports zooming, and any selected area may be copied to the Clipboard. Complete version available for $10.

Page Software
P.O. Box C
Bedford, MA 01730

Desk Accessory
Demoware
Size: 6k

ResPeek Demo v2.03

A resource decompiler. Displays list of resources contained in a file. Can decompile resources into RMaker format. Release version, available for $25, allows saving listings to files.

Pierre Omidyar
Dark Designs
P.O. Box 58
Medford, MA 02153

Desk Accessory
Demoware
Size: 21k

Special Calendar

Displays a 6-month calendar, indicating when full moons and holidays occur.

unknown

Desk Accessory
Public Domain
Size: 4k

SueClockCal

Displays a calendar for the current month and an analog clock (has hands). A picture of a woman, presumably named Sue, is in the background.

unknown

Desk Accessory
Public Domain
Size: 11k

Super Ruler v1.1

Places a ruler on the screen either horizontally or vertically. Allows you to adjust scale for different dpi. Very slick. Has docs in a separate file.

Randy Ubillos
COMPUTER:applications, Inc.
12813 Lindley Drive
Raleigh, NC 27609

Desk Accessory
Shareware $10.00
Size: 14k

SuperCalc II

Calculator created with the Dubl-Click Calculator Construction Set. Lots of features: metric conversions, statistics, scientific functions. Docs in a separate file.

Brad Ferguson

Desk Accessory
Freeware
Size: 25k

SysPICTs

Creates a menu listing the pictures (PICT resources) installed in the System and other open files. Lists pictures by resource ID. Displays the picture on the screen when you select an item.

unknown

Desk Accessory
Public Domain
Size: 2k

System Errors Table v3.0

Displays a list of system error numbers and a short description of the error. Explains that little ID number that shows up in the System Bomb dialog box.

Bill Steinberg

Desk Accessory
Freeware
Size: 46k

Transfer v3.0

Creates a menu of all applications on your hard disk or floppy disk. Lets you transfer to an application by selecting the application from the menu.

Clifford Story
Jimmy Mac Software
P.O. Box 24695
Jacksonville, FL 32241

Desk Accessory
Freeware
Size: 12k

Transfer.FKEY v1.00

Function key program that puts up a standard Open File dialog box from which you can select an application to which to transfer. Avoids having to go to the Finder to locate the file.

Peter Bryant
P.O. Box 946
Zephyr Cove, NV 89448

Fkey Resource
Freeware
Size: 2k

Values

Calculates stock and property values. For a company's common stock, program estimates growth rate and fair market PE ratio. For properties, program estimates cash flow and property value.

James H. Moore, Jr.
4125 Arroyo Trail
Carmel, CA 93923

Desk Accessory
Shareware $5.00
Size: 8k

DAs 4

Desk Accessories

DAs

AirBrush v0.1

A painting program with an airbrush tool similar to the one used in ComicWorks and GraphicWorks (commercial programs by MacroMind). Open up an existing painting and touch it up with an airbrush.

unknown

Desk Accessory
Public Domain
Size: 9k

Autolog v3.2

Use in conjuction with a telecommunications program to automate the login process to a mainframe or bulletin board. Handy if your terminal program does not have scripts. Shareware fee is what you think it is worth. Docs provided.

Steve Fine
504 Linden Road
State College, PA 16801

Desk Accessory
Shareware ?
Size: 13k

BlackBook (Little)

A little black book for storing phone numbers or notes. There is a page for each letter of the alphabet and buttons for moving to each page. Has a find function to search for text.

unknown

Desk Accessory
Public Domain
Size: 4k

Clarity

Performs the electronic equivalent of photoreduction by reducing the size of an image to increase resolution. Useful for printing bitmap images on a LaserWriter. Docs in a separate file.

Andrew Welch
Mark 3 Software
29 Grey Rocks Road
Wilton, CT 06897

Desk Accessory
Shareware $10.00
Size: 5k

Command-Shift

Installs a menu listing all available function key programs (FKEYs). Allows you to invoke an FKEY from a menu rather than from the keyboard.

Robert Thomas Curran, Jr.

Desk Accessory
Public Domain
Size: 2k

Craps

A very simple version of craps. No real graphics and you can't adjust your betting. Bet is always $1 on the pass line.

unknown

Desk Accessory
Public Domain
Size: 4k

Decision

This doesn't seem to work; it crashes.

unknown

Desk Accessory
Public Domain
Size: 14k

Default Param

Lists the default settings of the parameter RAM. You usually alter these settings using programs accessed from the Control Panel.

unknown

Desk Accessory
Public Domain
Size: 2k

DiskLock™ v1.0

Allows you to lock/unlock any local Mac hard disk or floppy. Files on locked disks cannot be modified under normal circumstances.

Jeffrey S. Shulman
P.O. Box 521
Ridgefield, CT 06877-0521

Desk Accessory
Freeware
Size: 4k

Help - Word 3 Commands

A listing of commands and keyboard equivalents for commonly used operations in MS Word 3.01. The list is quite extensive. A handy quick reference.

Jim Moore

Desk Accessory
Public Domain
Size: 13k

Jumble DA

A tool for solving 5-letter Jumble puzzles. Type in 5 letters and the program shows you all 120 combinations of those letters. Type in a scrambled word, then scan the list to find the actual word.

Jim Moore

Desk Accessory
Freeware
Size: 4k

MaCube v2.1

Mac version of Rubik's Cube. Uses 6 colors on a Mac II or 6 patterns on a b&w machine.

Kim Gillies
P.O. Box 42344
Tucson, AZ 85733
GEnie: KGILLIES

Desk Accessory
Freeware
Size: 27k

Planets

Displays a diagram of the solar system showing the current locations of the visible planets: Venus, Mars, Jupiter, and Saturn.

unknown

Desk Accessory
Public Domain
Size: 4k

PowerEdit

A text editor DA for programmers. Supports auto-indenting and lets you shift selected text left or right. Has docs in a separate file.

Anson Tsao
3100 Bayview Ave., #6
Willowdale, Ontario
M2N 5L3 CANADA

Desk Accessory
Shareware $20.00
Size: 37k

PT NomoGraph

Displays a pressure/temperature nomograph. For a given observed temperature and pressure, chart shows the temperature corrected to 760 mm Hg.

Roger Simon & Tim Senecal
CU Denver Chemistry Dept.
1200 Larimer Street
Denver, CO 80204

Desk Accessory
Freeware
Size: 11k

QuickB Download v1.15

Use in conjuction with a terminal program to download files from CompuServe using QuickB protocol. Docs in a separate file.

Raymond Lau
100-04 70 Avenue
Forest Hills, NY 11375-5133
CIS: 76174,2617

Desk Accessory
Shareware $15.00
Size: 16k

DAs 4

Continued

DAs

Rhine

The classic test for ESP using the method designed by J.B. Rhine in 1934. A deck of 25 cards with 5 different symbols: star, plus sign, circle, square, and tilde. Try to guess the symbol on the next card.

C. Heilman

Desk Accessory
Freeware
Size: 17k

Road Atlas

Displays a road map of the continental U.S. with major cities and highways. Clicking on two cities shows the mileage and shortest path between them.

Jim Moore
Vic Hasselblad
Microsparc, Inc.

Desk Accessory
Freeware
Size: 22k

Runner v1.0

Utility for running desk accessories under MultiFinder. Install DAs into this application instead of the System file to control the amount of memory allocated for the DA.

Benoît Widemann

Application
Freeware
Size: 13k

Special Key Clip

Allows you to copy the 4 special characters (Command key, check mark, diamond, and apple) to the clipboard. These characters are not available from the keyboard in all fonts.

unknown

Desk Accessory
Public Domain
Size: 2k

StarGazer

Displays the stars in the sky. Lets you adjust the view direction (north or south) and angle (20° to 60°). Shows the name and constellation when you click on a star.

unknown

Desk Accessory
Public Domain
Size: 11k

Terminal DA v1.5

A DA terminal program for logging onto remote computers and bulletin boards. Emulates a VT-52 terminal. Docs in a WriteNow file.

Joachim Lindenberg
Sommerstraße 4, 7500 KA 1
WEST GERMANY

Desk Accessory
Shareware $20.00
Size: 32k

TextDump v1.12

Dumps a text file directly to the modem or printer port. Works only with an ImageWriter.

Darik Datta
#6, 3422 - Parkdale Blvd. NW
Calgary, Alberta
T2N 3T4 CANADA

Desk Accessory
Freeware
Size: 9k

To Do! v1.0

Maintains an electronic "to do" list. For example, store a list of people you need to call with attached notes and phone numbers. Slick interface. Complete docs in a separate file.

Andrew Welch
Mark 3 Software
29 Grey Rocks Road
Wilton, CT 06897

Desk Accessory
Shareware $10.00
Size: 10k

Twelve-C™ Demo v1.1

A programmable financial calculator DA. Imitates an HP-12C calculator. Comes with an installer program to place it in your System file.

Richard F. Reich
Dreams of the Phoenix, Inc.
P.O. Box 10273
Jacksonville, FL 32247

Application
Demoware
Size: 25k

USDebt v1.4

Displays a random quotation. Then, after about 10 seconds, it displays a running count of the U.S. national debt, which increases by $1 million every 2 minutes.

Chris Riley
GEnie: CHRISRILEY
E-mail: riley@cs.ucsd.edu

Desk Accessory
Freeware
Size: 9k

Utilities

A smorgasbord of file, mouse, and keyboard utilities all in one DA. Copy, rename, delete, close, and search for files, display mouse position, show table of ASCII codes, and more. Not fully functional yet.

unknown

Desk Accessory
Public Domain
Size: 37k

DAs 5

Desk Accessories

ASCII$

A special 24-point font in which each character is composed of 3 parts: the character itself, decimal ASCII character code, and hexadecimal ASCII character code. Docs in a separate file.

Dennis Dunkerley
367 Cohasset Drive
Hermitage, PA 16148

Bitmap Font
Shareware $2.00
Size: 27k

AT View v1.0.0

Lists machines connected on an AppleTalk network. Shows node numbers, user names, what's going on, and socket numbers.

Randy Dees
6402 Whitemarsh Vly. Walk
Austin, TX 78746-6155

Desk Accessory
Shareware $5.00
Size: 17k

ClipPrint v1.24

Prints the contents of the Clipboard. Supports bitmaps, PICT files, and text.

Steve Maller
Apple Computer
AppleLink: MALLER1

Desk Accessory
Public Domain
Size: 6k

DAfx v1.30

A complete paint program in a DA. Has most features of the original MacPaint. Pictures cannot be saved or printed in demo version. Extensive docs in a separate file. Supports some esoteric formats.

James K. Miles
Mi Concepts
P.O. Box 8822
Kentwood, MI 49508

Desk Accessory
Demoware
Size: 86k

Fast Calc•SELF

Calculator created using the Dubl-Click Calculator Construction Set. Application installs DA into your System file. Calculator features a calendar and binary/decimal/hexadecimal conversions.

Frank M. Ventura

Application
Public Domain
Size: 29k

InternationalTime

Displays the time and date in 6 different places (Athens, London, Los Angeles, Munich, New York, and Tokyo) based on Eastern Daylight Time.

Ted Sapountzis
Colgate Box K2019
Hamilton, NY 13346

Desk Accessory
Freeware
Size: 11k

Masters Trivia

Displays an alphabetical list of all the winners of the Masters Golf Tournament. Shows the year(s) in which a person won the Masters when you click on their name.

unknown

Desk Accessory
Public Domain
Size: 4k

Memoir DA v1.1

Displays the amount of free memory in bytes. Releases all purgeable blocks and compacts the heap when you click a button. Constantly updates display so you can monitor a program's memory usage.

Andrew Welch
Mark 3 Software
29 Grey Rocks Road
Wilton, CT 06897

Desk Accessory
Freeware
Size: 4k

DAs 5

Continued

MidiHz v1.1

Displays a lists of the frequency (Hz) and note for each index number from 0 to 127 for MIDIs.

Mark Erickson
901 Yorkchester
Houston, TX 77079

Desk Accessory
Freeware
Size: 5k

Positions 24 v1.2d2

A font for chess pieces and chess boards. There is a font character for all 6 chess pieces of both colors and on squares of both colors. Author claims it takes about 20 seconds to type in a chess position. Nice.

Dennis Dunkerley
367 Cohasset Drive
Hermitage, PA 16148

Bitmap Font
Shareware $10.00
Size: 16k

Remember? v2.00rm

A utility for remembering appointments and important occasions. Use the DA to enter and browse information. A companion INIT reminds you of impending events when you start up your Mac.

Dave Warker
1330 W. North Street
Egg Harbor, NJ 08215

Desk Accessory
Shareware $10.00
Size: 22k

Search

Utility for searching for specified text strings in files. Searches single files or all files in a folder. Works with text files as well as documents from several popular word processors.

M&M Assoc.
4947 Grouse Run Drive
Stockton, CA 95207
CIS: 74756,551

Desk Accessory
Freeware
Size: 14k

Sunrise..Sunset

Displays the time of sunset on the current day and the time of sunrise on the next day. Lets you adjust latitude and longitude.

unknown

Desk Accessory
Public Domain
Size: 5k

Text Count

Counts the number of words, sentences, and paragraphs in a text file. Also tabulates the average number of words per sentence and sentences per paragraph. Estimates a grade level for the text.

Stephen Kirkpatrick
CIRCLE Lab
UC Santa Barbara

Desk Accessory
Freeware
Size: 9k

Towers of Hanoi

Plays the classic Towers of Hanoi game with 7 discs. Movement is controlled by buttons rather than by dragging the pieces.

Jim Moore

Desk Accessory
Freeware
Size: 4k

Trax v1.0

We're not quite sure what this does. A dialog box asks you whether you want to print a TrackSheet. Click OK and it looks for a printer.

Mark Erickson
901 Yorkchester
Houston, TX 77079

Desk Accessory
Shareware ?
Size: 6k

DAs 6

Desk Accessories

Advanced Calculator

A scientific calculator with additional functions for programmers such as Boolean algebra and bitwise shifts and rotates. Thorough docs in a separate file.

Desktop CAD, Inc.
607 Rosemont Plaza
Rosemont, PA 19010-1526

Desk Accessory
Shareware $8.00
Size: 10k

MacTalker v1

Speaks text that you type into a dialog box. Requires MacinTalk.

James Joaquin
Viking Technologies, Inc.
P.O. Box 299
Newport, RI 02840

Desk Accessory
Freeware
Size: 20k

Midi Mode DA

Sends MIDI mode messages to a synthesizer from your Mac.

Austin Development
227 Marin Street
San Rafael, CA 94901
(415) 454-9620

Desk Accessory
Freeware

Mini Sci Calc v1.0

Calculator created using the Dubl-Click Calculator Construction Set. A scientific calculator with trigonometric, logarithmic, and statistical functions.

Chris Munger
GEnie: CMUNGER

Desk Accessory
Public Domain
Size: 26k

Peeper v1.0

A viewer for MacPaint-compatible documents. Displays paintings but does not allow editing or modifications.

Matt Holiday
CIS: 73120,2400

Desk Accessory
Freeware
Size: 4k

PrintQueue v5.0

For use with the SuperSpool print spooler. Shows a list of all documents in the queue waiting to be printed.

unknown

Desk Accessory
Freeware
Size: 32k

Scientific Conversion Chart

A list of unit conversion factors.

Don Rittner
CIS: 70057,1325
GEnie: D.Rittner

Desk Accessory
Public Domain
Size: 35k

Scope v1.5

Shows a magnified view (1, 2, 4, or 8 times) of the area under the mouse. Lets you set a timer to take a snapshot of the current magnified view. The view window is resizable.

Tom Lippincott

Desk Accessory
Freeware
Size: 27k

Swiss Watch

Displays a small, approximately 1/2-inch square, clock with hands on the screen.

SuperMac Software
(Nick Gault & Andy Nuss)
485 Potrero Avenue
Sunnyvale, CA 94086
(408) 245-2202

Desk Accessory
Public Domain
Size: 4k

Tide Guide 88

Predicts the tides at 14 different locations on the east and west coasts of the U.S. Displays a graph of the tide level for the current day. Information valid only for 1988.

Zihua
P.O. Box 51601
Pacific Grove, CA 93950

Desk Accessory
Freeware
Size: 30k

Turbo Viewer v1.02

Utility for viewing GIF graphics files. GIF is a graphics file format used mainly on CompuServe. Some features have been disabled in this demo version.

James K. Miles
Mi Concepts
P.O. Box 8822
Kentwood, MI 49508

Desk Accessory
Demoware
Size: 48k

WriteFontSize™ v1.0

Allows you to enter text in any font size (useful for MacWrite users where point size options are limited) and enter special non-printing characters using their ASCII codes. Docs in a separate file.

Jeffrey S. Shulman
P.O. Box 521
Ridgefield, CT 06877-0521

Desk Accessory
Shareware $7.00
Size: 14k

DAs 7

Desk Accessories

Apple Pinouts DA v1.0

Displays tables showing the pinouts for several Mac and Apple II cables/connectors: Super Serial Card (DB-25), ImageWriter I & II, DIN-8, DB-9, SCSI, etc.

Jeff Baudin
MICROMAT
7075 Redwood Blvd., Bay 4
Novato, CA 94947

Desk Accessory
Freeware
Size: 25k

ASCII-DA II

Displays a table showing characters and their ASCII equivalents (in both decimal and hex) for any installed font.

Leonard Rosenthol
LazerWare, Inc.

Desk Accessory
Freeware
Size: 10k

Autolog v3.2

Sends text directly to the serial port. Has docs in a separate file.

Steve Fine
504 Linden Road
State College, PA 16801

Desk Accessory
Shareware $?
Size: 13k

File Tools

Displays and modifies Finder flags and other directory information for a selected file. Also lets you copy, delete, launch, or rename the file.

unknown

Desk Accessory
Public Domain
Size: 8k

GumbyClock

Yet another clock/calendar DA. This one has a picture of a man calling himself Mister Gumby.

unknown

Desk Accessory
Public Domain
Size: 8k

Help - Word 3 Commands

Puts up a scrolling window with a complete listing of commands and keyboard equivalents for commonly used operations in Word version 3.01.

unknown

Desk Accessory
Public Domain
Size: 13k

HexFlags v2.0

Calculates the proper value for the Enable Flags field in a 'MENU' resource. Computes the proper hex value for the enable flags for items you mark as enabled/disabled.

Mark Chally
Chally Micro Solutions
PO Box 4600
West Covina, CA 91791

Desk Accessory
Freeware
Size: 10k

LoMem v1.00

Displays the value of a few low-memory globals, such as CurApName, MemTop, BufPtr, StackBase, HeapEnd, ApplLimit, AppleZone, TheZone, SysZone, MBarHeight, MenuFlash, ScrnBase, etc.

Neal E. Trautman
1701 SW 42nd Street
Fargo, ND 58103

Desk Accessory
Shareware $5.00
Size: 5k

Memory

Displays a small window showing the amount of free memory (RAM) on your Mac.

unknown

Desk Accessory
Public Domain
Size: 3k

MenuShot v1.3

Creates a MacPaint or MacDraw format file of the screen image. Lets you specify a time delay and whether the cursor should be visible. Handy for making screen dumps with a menu down.

John A. Love, III
6413 Wyngate Drive
Springfield, VA 22152

Desk Accessory
Shareware $15.00
Size: 17k

Navigator

Displays the distance and direction from one airport to another. Lists airports by their 3-letter codes.

Jim Moore

Desk Accessory
Public Domain
Size: 16k

NotePad++ v1.0b08

NotePad utility with a lot of features. Multiple notepads with up to 8 pages per notepad, multiple fonts, styles, and colors within a page, rulers, printing, justification. Has an on-line help screen.

Alexander S. Colwell

Desk Accessory
Freeware
Size: 42k

PictDisplay v1.00

Displays up to 9 'PICT' resources that must be pasted into the DA itself using ResEdit or some other resource-copying program.

Neal E. Trautman
1701 S.W. 42nd Street
Fargo, ND 58103

Desk Accessory
Shareware $10.00
Size: 7k

Port Watcher v1.0

Alerts you when information arrives through one of the serial ports on your Mac. Also has a screen saver feature. Useful if you connect to remote computers to perform lengthy operations and want to be notified when something happens.

Steve Fine
504 Linden Road
State College, PA 16801

Desk Accessory
Shareware $?
Size: 10k

Postal Codes

Displays a scrolling window listing each state and its two-letter postal code abbreviation.

unknown

Desk Accessory
Public Domain
Size: 5k

PS Printer

Sends PostScript files to the currently chosen printer.

Scott Gillespie
Reed College

Desk Accessory
Freeware
Size: 7k

DAs 7

Continued

Scrapbooks

Allows you to create and view multiple scrapbook files. Unlike the Scrapbook DA from Apple, this lets you divide data into multiple scrapbooks rather than having just one big scrapbook.

unknown

Desk Accessory
Public Domain
Size: 5k

ShowDA Demo

Demo version of a DA that displays MacPaint format paintings. Has a slideshow feature and commands for easily viewing all paintings in a particular folder. Full version costs $20.

Square Ball, Ink
4011 X Street
Lincoln, NE 68503

Desk Accessory
Demoware
Size: 22k

SilentWriterSelector

Sets the output hopper (one or two) for a NEC SilentWriter Printer.

Timothy S. Smith
1004 West Girard Avenue
Monmouth, IL 61462

Desk Accessory
Shareware $1.00
Size: 11k

Term220 v1.01

A VT-220 terminal emulation program. Docs in a separate file.

Todd Hitt
1447A Cliff Court
Columbus, OH 43204
GEnie: THITT

Desk Accessory
Freeware
Size: 62k

•'TEXT'«»'ttro' v1.0a1

Changes the file type of TeachText files between 'TEXT' and 'ttro'. 'TEXT' files can be edited in TeachText, whereas 'ttro' files are read-only.

Josh & Nick Franco
328 17th Street
Santa Monica, CA 90402

Desk Accessory
Freeware
Size: 4k

TextDump v1.12

Dumps a text file directly to the printer or modem serial port. Allows rapid printing to an ImageWriter. Send the author a postcard if you like the program.

Darik Datta
#6, 3422 Parkdate Blvd. NW
Calgary, Alberta
T2N 3T4 CANADA
CIS: 76146,2573

Desk Accessory
Freeware
Size: 9k

Varityper FontMaster

Great utility for managing your fonts. Can display or print a sample of all your fonts, using a phrase which you specify. Also shows statistics about your fonts, such as ID number, size, etc.

Ken Winograd
Varityper, Inc.
11 Mount Pleasant Avenue
East Hanover, NJ 07936

Desk Accessory
Freeware
Size: 23k

Varityper FontWizard

Terrific utility that tells you everything you want to know about your fonts. Displays statistics, a complete map of all characters, sample text in all sizes and styles. Shows actual names of both screen and printer versions of fonts.

Ken Winograd
Varityper, Inc.
11 Mount Pleasant Avenue
East Hanover, NJ 07936

Desk Accessory
Freeware
Size: 34k

ViewFile v1.00

Displays the contents of any file (resource or data fork) in both hex and ASCII.

Neal E. Trautman
1701 S.W. 42nd Street
Fargo, ND 58103

Desk Accessory
Shareware $10.00
Size: 7k
12" 6 7 32

DAs 8

Desk Accessories

DAs

DA Base v1.4

Allows you to read/modify imported IBM dBASE files with .dbf extensions. Lets you modify only text fields. Works with McMac and Foxbase .dbf files also. Wow!

Vic Rubenfeld
128 14th St., Suite A
Manhattan Beach, CA 90266
CIS: 72416,1215

Desk Accessory
Shareware $14.95
Size: 39k

DAstat...P1.0 v1.0

Calculates P values from Z (binomial distribution), chi-square, t- and F- values, and the degree of freedom. Not a stat calculator. Pleasant interface.

Kaz Matsuki
550 W. Sandhurst Dr. #204
Roseville, MN 55113

Desk Accessory
Shareware $5.00
Size: 21k

Image Window v1.0

Converts MacPaint and TIFF bitmap files to PICT format.

Mike Calbaum
Crossroads Software

Desk Accessory
Freeware
Size: 35k

MaxFiles v1.0

A file management program with a beautiful interface. Not MultiFinder-friendly.

Keisuke Hara
TMUG: Keisuke Hara
MIX: hara
MacEvent: Keisuke Hara

Desk Accessory
Freeware
Size: 141k

melt v1.2

A newer version of the Flow DA. Makes the screen flow. Click to make the screen come back. Author says it's not MultiFinder-friendly.

Gordan A. Arocella
CIS: 73467,01411
GEnie: G. AROCELLA
Delphi & MacNet: GORACO

Desk Accessory
Public Domain
Size: 2k

MISHU™ 2 Demo v2.0

A DA for pasting Chinese characters into documents. $59.00 for students.

Xanatech Inc.
20 Fresh Pond Place
Cambridge, MA 02138
(617) 492-7463

Desk Accessory
Demoware
Size: 21k

Pinyin

Font for the MISHU DA.

Xanatech

Bitmap Font
Demoware
Size: 17k

Quill v1.0

Opens various word processor documents, some with formats intact. Average, but send the guy a postcard!

Sergio Villone
Via Baltimora 122
10100 Torino
ITALY

Desk Accessory
Public Domain
Size: 12k

Suzhou2.0 0-4

Font for the MISHU DA. | Xanatech | **Bitmap Font**
Demoware
Size: 58k

DAs 9

Desk Accessories

DAs

acur Player

DA for looking at the animated cursor resources inside applications.

Jon Wind
CIS: 70167,3444
GEnie: JPWIND
AoL: JWIND

Desk Accessory
Public Domain
Size: 7k

ASCII Chart 3.2 v3.2

The best ASCII DA I've seen! Clicking on a character gives you the ASCII and hex equivalents, along with the key combination. Allows pasting into documents and display of character at 72 points. A best buy!

Jon Wind
CIS: 70167,3444
GEnie: JPWIND
AOL: JWIND

Desk Accessory
Freeware
Size: 10k

Conversion DA v1.5.1

Fairly comprehensive general conversion DA. Not as complete as Sci DA, but it does the work for you. Nice interface and all the converting that nonscientific types will ever need. Another best buy!

Rick Johnson
2216 Allen Lane
Waukesha, WI 51386
GEnie: RICK.JOHNSON

Desk Accessory
Shareware $5.00
Size: 42k

DeskPat v1.2

A DA for modifying the color desktop pattern. An improvement over the editor in the General control panel.

Roy M. Lovejoy III
23636 Algiers Street
Mission Viejo, CA 92691

Desk Accessory
Shareware $10.00
Size: 44k

Gizmo™ DA v1.00

Useful for viewing GIF files. Comes with FKey.

James K. Miles
Mi Concepts
PO Box 8822
Kentwood, MI 49508

Desk Accessory
Demoware
Size: 105k

DAs 10

Desk Accessories

Address Book DA v2.5

Maintains address list and allows auto-dialing, up to 3 numbers per address. Has complete on-line help, and logs calls! A neat DA, check it out.

Jim Leitch
61 Shaughnessy Blvd.
Willowdale, Ontario
CANADA
(416) 849-1532

Desk Accessory
Shareware $20.00
Size: 97k

Dt Calculator v2.1

OK calculator DA with a likable interface.

Seagull Engineering of Sweden
Box 909
S-220 09 Lund
SWEDEN

Desk Accessory
Freeware
Size: 21k

Font Style Info DA/Demo v1.01

Shows installed PostScript fonts corresponding to bitmap font name.

Peter Gutowski
New Century Laser Type
23 Barbara Street
Bloomfield, NJ 07003

Desk Accessory
Demoware
Size: 9k

MW II Command Keys

On-line help for MacWrite II.

John Albert

Desk Accessory
Public Domain
Size: 9k

Time v1.0

Nice alternative to the Alarm Clock DA. You get to pick different faces for an analog watch. Alarm doesn't work when DA is not displayed. Can set pop-up alarm message.

George T. Talbot
24 Judy Ave.
Franklinville, NJ 08322

Desk Accessory
Shareware $10.00
Size: 195k

DAs 11

Desk Accessories

AreaCodes/TimeZonesDA1.0

Telephone area codes for the U.S., Canada, and Mexico circa 1990.

NeoScribe International Inc.
PO Box 469
Middletown, CT 06457
CIS: 71041,15

Desk Accessory
Freeware
Size: 13k

Dialer DA

Dials a number through the serial or sound port that has been saved to the clipboard. Can send commands to a modem. Comes with FKey.

John Hill
Bugless Software Ltd.
PO Box 1097
Mason City, IA 50401

Desk Accessory
Shareware $15.00
Size: 39k

FastEnvelopeDA 1.0.3 Demo

Good interface. Handles 14+ different stationery sizes, prints bar codes, etc.

Henry Carstens
Vertical Solutions
PO Box 1150
Beaverton, OR 97075

Desk Accessory
Demoware
Size: 123k

Education

Educational software for everybody from kids learning the alphabet to scholars analyzing Shakespeare.

Education A1

Shakespeare's Collections

A Midsummer Nights Dream

The Bard's play in 5 Acts.There is a separate document for each Act. Transcribed from the Arthur Bullen's Stratford Town Edition--Victorian Shakespeare.

William Shakespeare
AOL: StephenS18

Microsoft Word document
Public Domain
Size: 120k

Anthony and Cleopatra

The Bard's play in 5 Acts.There is a separate document for each Act. Transcribed from the Arthur Bullen's Stratford Town Edition--Victorian Shakespeare.

William Shakespeare
AOL: StephenS18

Microsoft Word document
Public Domain
Size: 189k

As You Like It

The Bard's play in 5 Acts.There is a separate document for each Act. Transcribed from the Arthur Bullen's Stratford Town Edition--Victorian Shakespeare.

William Shakespeare
AOL: StephenS18

Microsoft Word document
Public Domain
Size: 152k

Comedy of Errors

The Bard's play in 5 Acts.There is a separate document for each Act. Transcribed from the Arthur Bullen's Stratford Town Edition--Victorian Shakespeare.

William Shakespeare
AOL: StephenS18

Microsoft Word document
Public Domain
Size: 112k

Henry V Part 2

The Bard's play in 5 Acts.There is a separate document for each Act. Transcribed from the Arthur Bullen's Stratford Town Edition--Victorian Shakespeare.

William Shakespeare
AOL: StephenS18

Microsoft Word document
Public Domain
Size: 177k

Henry V Part 3

The Bard's play in 5 Acts.There is a separate document for each Act. Transcribed from the Arthur Bullen's Stratford Town Edition--Victorian Shakespeare.

William Shakespeare
AOL: StephenS18

Microsoft Word document
Public Domain
Size: 177k

Twelfth Night

The Bard's play in 5 Acts.There is a separate document for each Act. Transcribed from the Arthur Bullen's Stratford Town Edition--Victorian Shakespeare.

William Shakespeare
AOL: StephenS18

Microsoft Word document
Public Domain
Size: 145k

Cymbeline

The Bard's play in 5 Acts.There is a separate document for each Act. Transcribed from the Arthur Bullen's Stratford Town Edition--Victorian Shakespeare.

William Shakespeare
AOL: StephenS18

Microsoft Word document
Public Domain
Size: 193k

Hamlet

The Bard's play in 5 Acts.There is a separate document for each Act. Transcribed from the Arthur Bullen's Stratford Town Edition--Victorian Shakespeare.

William Shakespeare
AOL: StephenS18

Microsoft Word document
Public Domain
Size: 499k

Henry V Part 1

The Bard's play in 5 Acts.There is a separate document for each Act. Transcribed from the Arthur Bullen's Stratford Town Edition--Victorian Shakespeare.

William Shakespeare
AOL: StephenS18

Microsoft Word document
Public Domain
Size: 184k

Julius Caesar

The Bard's play in 5 Acts.There is a separate document for each Act. Transcribed from the Arthur Bullen's Stratford Town Edition--Victorian Shakespeare.

William Shakespeare
AOL: StephenS18

Microsoft Word document
Public Domain
Size: 383k

King John

The Bard's play in 5 Acts.There is a separate document for each Act. Transcribed from the Arthur Bullen's Stratford Town Edition--Victorian Shakespeare.

William Shakespeare
AOL: StephenS18

Microsoft Word document
Public Domain
Size: 149k

Education A3

Shakespeare's Collections

Loves Labor Lost

The Bard's play in 5 Acts.There is a separate document for each Act. Transcribed from the Arthur Bullen's Stratford Town Edition--Victorian Shakespeare.

William Shakespeare
AOL: StephenS18

Microsoft Word document
Public Domain
Size: 153k

Macbeth

The Bard's play in 5 Acts.There is a separate document for each Act. Transcribed from the Arthur Bullen's Stratford Town Edition--Victorian Shakespeare.

William Shakespeare
AOL: StephenS18

Microsoft Word document
Public Domain
Size: 130k

Much Ado About Nothing

The Bard's play in 5 Acts.There is a separate document for each Act. Transcribed from the Arthur Bullen's Stratford Town Edition--Victorian Shakespeare.

William Shakespeare
AOL: StephenS18

Microsoft Word document
Public Domain
Size: 150k

Othello

The Bard's play in 5 Acts.There is a separate document for each Act. Transcribed from the Arthur Bullen's Stratford Town Edition--Victorian Shakespeare.

William Shakespeare
AOL: StephenS18

Microsoft Word document
Public Domain
Size: 188k

Pericles

The Bard's play in 5 Acts.There is a separate document for each Act. Transcribed from the Arthur Bullen's Stratford Town Edition--Victorian Shakespeare.

William Shakespeare
AOL: StephenS18

Microsoft Word document
Public Domain
Size: 213k

Richard II

The Bard's play in 5 Acts.There is a separate document for each Act. Transcribed from the Arthur Bullen's Stratford Town Edition--Victorian Shakespeare.

William Shakespeare
AOL: StephenS18

Microsoft Word document
Public Domain
Size: 160k

The Merchant of Venice

The Bard's play in 5 Acts.There is a separate document for each Act. Transcribed from the Arthur Bullen's Stratford Town Edition--Victorian Shakespeare.

William Shakespeare
AOL: StephenS18

Microsoft Word document
Public Domain
Size: 149k

Shakespeare's Collections

Measure For Measure

The Bard's play in 5 Acts.There is a separate document for each Act. Transcribed from the Arthur Bullen's Stratford Town Edition--Victorian Shakespeare.

William Shakespeare
AOL: StephenS18

Microsoft Word document
Public Domain
Size: 155k
12" 6 7 32

Richard III

The Bard's play in 5 Acts.There is a separate document for each Act. Transcribed from the Arthur Bullen's Stratford Town Edition--Victorian Shakespeare.

William Shakespeare
AOL: StephenS18

Microsoft Word document
Public Domain
Size: 214k
12" 6 7 32

Romeo And Juliet

The Bard's play in 5 Acts.There is a separate document for each Act. Transcribed from the Arthur Bullen's Stratford Town Edition--Victorian Shakespeare.

William Shakespeare
AOL: StephenS18

Microsoft Word document
Public Domain
Size: 436k
12" 6 7 32

ShakespeareSonnets

The Bard's play in 5 Acts.There is a separate document for each Act. Transcribed from the Arthur Bullen's Stratford Town Edition--Victorian Shakespeare.

William Shakespeare
AOL: StephenS18

Microsoft Word document
Public Domain
Size: 130k
12" 6 7 32

The Taming Of The Shrew

The Bard's play in 5 Acts.There is a separate document for each Act. Transcribed from the Arthur Bullen's Stratford Town Edition--Victorian Shakespeare.

William Shakespeare
AOL: StephenS18

Microsoft Word document
Public Domain
Size: 154k
12" 6 7 32

Education A5

Shakespeare's Collections

A Winters Tale

The Bard's play in 5 Acts.There is a separate document for each Act. Transcribed from the Arthur Bullen's Stratford Town Edition--Victorian Shakespeare.

William Shakespeare
AOL: StephenS18

Microsoft Word document
Public Domain
Size: 174k

The Merry Wives of Windsor

The Bard's play in 5 Acts.There is a separate document for each Act. Transcribed from the Arthur Bullen's Stratford Town Edition--Victorian Shakespeare.

William Shakespeare
AOL: StephenS18

Microsoft Word document
Public Domain
Size: 161k

The Tempest

The Bard's play in 5 Acts.There is a separate document for each Act. Transcribed from the Arthur Bullen's Stratford Town Edition--Victorian Shakespeare.

William Shakespeare
AOL: StephenS18

Microsoft Word document
Public Domain
Size: 222k

Timon Of Athens

The Bard's play in 5 Acts.There is a separate document for each Act. Transcribed from the Arthur Bullen's Stratford Town Edition--Victorian Shakespeare.

William Shakespeare
AOL: StephenS18

Microsoft Word document
Public Domain
Size: 22k

Titus Andronicus

The Bard's play in 5 Acts.There is a separate document for each Act. Transcribed from the Arthur Bullen's Stratford Town Edition--Victorian Shakespeare.

William Shakespeare
AOL: StephenS18

Microsoft Word document
Public Domain
Size: 149k

Troilus And Cressida

The Bard's play in 5 Acts.There is a separate document for each Act. Transcribed from the Arthur Bullen's Stratford Town Edition--Victorian Shakespeare.

William Shakespeare
AOL: StephenS18

Microsoft Word document
Public Domain
Size: 204k

Two Gentlemen of Verona

The Bard's play in 5 Acts.There is a separate document for each Act. Transcribed from the Arthur Bullen's Stratford Town Edition--Victorian Shakespeare.

William Shakespeare
AOL: StephenS18

Microsoft Word document
Public Domain
Size: 135k

King Lear

The Bard's play in 5 Acts.There is a separate document for each Act. Transcribed from the Arthur Bullen's Stratford Town Edition--Victorian Shakespeare.

William Shakespeare
AOL: StephenS18

Microsoft Word document
Public Domain
Size: 189k
12" 6 7 32

Education 1

Education

Digital Logic Simulator v2.5

Nice program for designing and experimenting with digital circuits. Good graphical interface. Docs in a separate file.

Brian Rauchfuss
8915 N 13th Ave.
Phoenix, AZ 85021

Application
Shareware $20.00
Size: 43k

Eliza v1.3

Carries on a simple conversation in English between a psychiatrist (the Mac) and a patient (you). It's based on the classic program by Joseph Weizenbaum discussed in Communications of the ACM, January 1966.

Charles Hayden
438 River Road
Fair Haven, NJ 07701
(201) 747-8560

Application
Public Domain
Size: 21k

Flashcard v1.1

Creates simple flash cards that associate a pair of phrases (a question and an answer). Plays back flash cards in test mode, giving the user a chance to provide the answer to each question.

Bob Ellison
Rice Macintosh Dev. Team

Application
Freeware
Size: 22k

Histogram Maker v1.03

Produces frequency plots from numerical data. Lets you enter data from a text file or the Clipboard. Produces a picture that must be copied into a drawing program for printing.

Bill Engles
Genetics Department
Univ. of Wisconsin
Madison, WI 53706

Application
Shareware $10.00
Size: 51k

Logarithms

Crude program that computes a logarithm given a base and a number. Gives only the integer portion of the log and quits after the computation.

unknown

Application
Public Domain
Size: 6k

MathMaster v2.1

Solves simple, first-year algebra problems. Useful as a teaching tool for students to verify solutions. Extensive docs in a separate file.

Paul Cozza
SoftPlus
PO Box 2442
Gaithersburg, MD 20879
(301) 540-6552

Application
Shareware $17.00
Size: 83k

XYZ Chart v1.0

Three-dimensional charting program. Produces line and scatter plots. Docs in a separate file.

Alan Miller
36 Robert Quigley Dr.
Scottsville, NY 14546
(716) 889-5348

Application
Freeware
Size: 22k

Grade v0.96

Simple gradebook program that records test scores and computes weighted averages. Allows up to 24 grades.

Jerry Keough
Dept. of Mathematics
Boston College
Chestnut Hill, MA 02167

Application
Public Domain
Size: 32k
12" 6 7 32

HandsOn

Graphically constructs and manipulates binary trees. Performs tree traversals, creates binary search trees, and parses expressions with binary operators. Includes docs within the program.

John Glenn
Dartmouth College
Hanover, NH

Application
Freeware
Size: 45k
12" 6 7 32

Mac'N'States v2.1

Displays a map of the U.S. and can zoom in on specific regions. Shows the name, abbreviation, and capital city of each state. Has different modes for learning and testing.

Ed Neu
6761 Deerwood Lane North
Maple Grove, MN 55369
(612) 435-8744

Application
Shareware $15.00
Size: 109k
12" 6 7 32

MEC Demo v1.00

Graphically creates molecular models. Lets you scale molecules in size and view them from different angles.

Rick Wargo
Drexel University
32nd and Chestnut Streets
Philadelphia, PA 19104

Application
Demoware
Size: 105k
12" 6 7 32

Orbital Mixing

Depicts the molecular orbitals derived from two 2p orbitals overlapping in the PI manner.

John R. Meier

Application
Public Domain
Size: 10k
12" 6 7 32

Satellite Locator

Gives the angle at which to point antennas to receive signals from geosynchronous satellites that are available for North America.

Ivan L. Ossander
PO Box 55616
North Pole, Alaska 99705

Application
Public Domain
Size: 86k
12" 6 7 32

Scientist's Helper v2.5

Performs simple graphing and data reduction. Also does multiple regressions, filtering, Fourier transforms, etc. Source code is available from the author.

William Menke
College of Oceanography
Oregon State University
Corvallis, OR 97331

Application
Public Domain
Size: 97k
12" 6 7 32

Tangent

Calculates the tangents at specified points to a sixth-order polynomial function. User specifies the polynomial coefficients. Simple graphics capabilities.

unknown

Application
Public Domain
Size: 17k
12" 6 7 32

Education 2

Continued

Venn v2.0

Graphically displays Venn diagrams for evaluating single-premise arguments and syllogisms.

Richard Wesley
Courseware Dev. Group
Dartmouth College
Hanover, NH

Application
Freeware
Size: 26k

Weinberg v0.52

Equation editor for creating scientific expressions and mathematical equations. Docs within the program.

Allan Bonadio Associates
2000 Center St. #1225
Berkeley, CA 94704

Application
Public Domain
Size: 29k

Algebra Tutor

Demonstrates tutorials for adding terms, multiplying by monomials, raising monomials to powers, etc. Gives hints if you request it. Lets you adust degree of difficulty of examples.

Ken Tilton
CIS: 71460,744 (Mac User Forum)

Application
Shareware $10.00
Size: 104k

FzzPlot v7.2

Analyzes statistical data and creates graphs for showing results. Includes several examples. Has docs in a separate file.

Richard M. Siegel
134 Horseshoe Drive
Williamsburg, VA 23185
(617) 275-4800

Application
Shareware $15.00
Size: 79k

Oyster Demo v2.02

Program creates tutorials. Includes examples for law, ethics, and algebra. Demo version omits the save option.

Hugh Gibbons & Tom Kent
Franklin Pierce Law Center
2 White Street
Concord, NH 03301
(603) 228-1541

Application
Demoware
Size: 75k

SocStat v1.2

Computes statistics on sociological data, and displays results in a window. Also lets you print results.

Dartmouth College
Sociology Laboratory
S. Maker, Project Director
Hanover, NH

Application
Public Domain
Size: 43k

Education 4

Education

Astronomical Events

Lists upcoming dates of astronomical events, i.e. Earth's solstices & equinoxes, and the inferior conjunctions and oppositions of the nearer planets. Crashes occasionally.

unknown

Application
Public Domain
Size: 3k

Binomial Test v1.0

A binomial distribution test program. Computes one- and two-tail tests and provides the randomized probabilities. Docs within the program.

Bill Engels
Genetics Department
University of Wisconsin
Madison, WI 53706

Application
Freeware
Size: 54k

Bright Stars v2.0

Provides north and south views of the night sky in the northern hemisphere. Locates the constellations and principal stars.

Jim Moore
4125 Arroyo Trail
Carmel, CA 93923

Application
Shareware $10.00
Size: 16k

CellPattern v0.9

Generates patterns, such as those used by fabric weavers, by means of cellular automata. When you enter 7 digits, it generates a pattern that fills the screen. Has a few bugs.

Donald B. Siano

Application
Public Domain
Size: 43k

Earthplot v3.0

Provides views of the Earth at any longitude and latitude, and at altitudes of 1,000 to 160,000 miles, but size of Earth remains constant! Results in distortion of contours and meridians, since their spacing varies with altitude.

The Black Swamp Software Co.
MCI: mpeirce
Delphi: mpeirce

Application
Public Domain
Size: 65k

Fish6 v1.001

Author describes it as 'the ultimate (for now) Fisher's Exact Test Program.' This test checks for independence in a 2 x 2 table. Docs within the program.

Bill Engels
Genetics Department
University of Wisconsin
Madison, WI 53706

Application
Freeware
Size: 59k

Geography v0.8

A sort of word game where you and the computer take turns naming geographic locations. Subsequent names must begin with the last letter of the previous name.

William Revelle
Department of Psychology
Northwestern University

Application
Public Domain
Size: 10k

Learning Tool™ Demo v1.0

An electronic notebook for colleges. Use it to store, organize, and search course notes (text and graphics), and to quiz yourself. Instructors can electronically distribute course notes.

John Van Roekel &
Bob Kozma
Arborworks, Inc.
2540 Pittsfield Blvd.
Ann Arbor, MI 48104
(313) 747-7087

Application
Demoware
Size: 105k

MacLinReg

Program performs linear regressions on statistical data. Entry screen provided. MS BASIC source code available for $8.

Jeff Amelse
343 Meadowrue Lane
Batavia, IL 60510
(708) 879-6499

Application
Freeware
Size: 71k

Monte Carlo 2xN v1.01

Uses Monte Carlo techniques to test for independence in a 2 x n contingency table. Includes docs within program.

Bill Engels
Genetics Department
University of Wisconsin
Madison, WI 53706

Application
Freeware
Size: 66k

Monte Carlo RxC v1.0

Uses Monte Carlo techniques to test for independence in an arbitrary-size contingency table. Includes docs within program.

Bill Engels
Genetics Department
University of Wisconsin
Madison, WI 53706

Application
Freeware
Size: 65k

Volume and SA

Calculates the volume or surface area of any sphere, cone, right cylinder, right regular prism, or right regular pyramid.

David Klein
634 Piney Point Rd.
Houston, TX 77024

Application
Shareware $5.00
Size: 8k

Education 5

Education

Convert v1.0

Converts scientific units of measurement from one standard into another, just by entering a value. Complete version is available for $10.

Jim Walker
Flight Engineering
PO Box 661133
Miami Springs, FL 33266

Application
Demoware
Size: 60k

Gravitation Ltd v4.0B

Calculates and displays planetary systems in motion. Lets you enter information for up to 10 planets (mass, distance from sun, and velocity). Comes with many examples. Not bad.

Jeff Rommereide
343 Elma Ave
Laurel Springs, NJ 08021
CIS: 73710,467

Application
Freeware
Size: 37k

MacMORSE v1.0B

Typing a letter on the keyboard produces the sound of the code signal and displays the letter graphically. The send rate is adjustable to 40 w.p.m.

Mark Shapiro
1225 Vienna Drive #199
Sunnyvale, CA 94089

Application
Shareware $5.00
Size: 46k

MiniGuide v2.0

Accesses four modules: History of HyperText, History of Rock & Roll, Automobile Engines, and the Chemical Elements. Uses HyperText to connect the various levels of these informational modules.

Gordon Dougan
Owl International, Inc.
14218 NE 21st Street
Bellevue, WA 98007
(206) 747-3203

Desk Accessory
Shareware $20.00
Size: 60k

OHM v1.0

Calculates ohms, amperes, volts, and watts in an electrical circuit when given the values for any two of these.

Jim Walker
Flight Engineering
PO Box 661133
Miami Springs, FL 33266

Application
Shareware $5.00
Size: 52k

Planets v2.00

A high-precision orbital simulator. Supply information about planets, and the program simulates their orbits.

Joe Hodge

Application
Public Domain
Size: 32k

Sector v1.3

Calculates the area and volume for sectors and segments when given two dimensions of a segment.

Jim Walker
Flight Engineering
PO Box 661133
Miami Springs, FL 33266

Application
Shareware $10.00
Size: 55k

UniCalc v1.3

Calculates many mathematical and trigonometric functions when given one (x) or two (x,y) numbers.

Jim Walker
Flight Engineering
PO Box 661133
Miami Springs, FL 33266

Application
Shareware $10.00
Size: 79k

BrainBusters!

An arithmetic drill for addition. Features musical prompts.

unknown

Application
Freeware
Size: 13k

Math Mountain - ADDITION v2.1

Arithmetic drill for children. Cartoon man climbs farther up the mountain with each correct answer to a math question. Reaching the top results in a spectacular musical cue.

Gary Dauphin
334 Markham Dr.
Slidell, LA 70458

Application
Shareware $10.00
Size: 50k

Monster Chase Math +

Each correct answer to a math question takes you further away from a pursuing monster. With each wrong answer he gains on you...until?!!

Gary Dauphin
334 Markham Dr.
Slidell, LA 70458

Application
Shareware $9.00
Size: 56k

Number Investigator

When you enter any number into the program, it lists many of that number's mathematical characteristics.

Price M. Collins
Trumbull, CT
(203) 261-3764

Application
Freeware
Size: 58k

TimeLines v1.0

Lists several important historical events that occurred on a selected day.

Tommy Manley & Jon Little
ACC - TimeLines
70 Woodland Terrace
Auburn, AL 36830
(205) 821-0470

Application
Shareware $15.00
Size: 7k

Education 7

Education

Cabri v2.5

Tool for teaching and research in graph theory. Definitely not for novices. Support and manual available. Not MultiFinder-compatible.

Laboratoire Structures Discrètes (IMAG)
CNRS USTMG Grenoble, BP 68
38402 St. Martin d' Hères Cedex, FRANCE
laborde@imag.uucp

Application
Freeware
Size: 141k
12" 6 7 32

ChemIntosh Demo

Graphically assembles and draws chemical structures.

Gary Dauphin
334 Markham Drive
Slidell, LA 70458

Desk Accessory
Demoware
Size: 27k
12" 6 7 32

ChemIntosh™ MMCalc

Calculates the molecular weight of a compound when you enter its chemical formula.

SoftShell Co.
PO Box 632
Henrietta, NY 14467
(303) 242-7502

Desk Accessory
Freeware
Size: 17k
12" 6 7 32

Elements v1.2

Provides physical characteristics of the various chemical elements. Uses the Periodic Table.

Flight Engineering
PO Box 661133
Miami Springs, FL 33266

Application
Shareware $20.00
Size: 79k
12" 6 7 32

Education

Ballistic v1.0

Plots trajectories of projectiles given the initial velocity and angle. Air friction and rate of decay are also variables.

Blas Cabrera
Stanford University
Stanford, CA

Application
Freeware
Size: 13k

Einstein v1.0

Simulates mechanics on a rocket moving at velocities near the speed of light.

Blas Cabrera
Stanford University
Stanford, CA

Application
Freeware
Size: 17k

Kepler v1.0

Simulates orbits of planets. Shows how orbits change over a period of years. Only lets you display two planets at once.

Blas Cabrera
Stanford University
Stanford, CA

Application
Freeware
Size: 28k

MacFormula

Calculates the molecular weight of any chemical formula entered into the data entry box.

James E. Deline
Department of Chemistry
University of California
Davis, CA 95616

Application
Shareware $5.00
Size: 14k

MacGraph v5.2

A graphics package constructed for Drexel University. Creates graphs of the various mathematical functions.

Bill Sammons
Instructional Support Group
32nd and Chestnut Streets
Philadelphia, PA 19104

Application
Freeware
Size: 38k

MultiFlow Demo v1.06

Computes information for vapor-liquid fluid flow in a piping system. Demo version cannot save files; uses constant viscosity for liquids and constant molecular weight for vapors.

Kelix Software Systems
(604) 769-6785

Application
Demoware
Size: 100k

MultiReg

Performs multiple linear regression by least-squares analysis. Fits complex mathematical equations to a set of points. Has tests to ensure that assumptions are satisfied.

Bob James
GEnie: BOB.JAMES
CIS: 72325,1615

Application
Public Domain
Size: 140k

Oscillator v1.0

Simulates the motion of a harmonic oscillator (a weight on a spring). Lets you control the extension, time constant, frequency, and phase shift.

Blas Cabrera
Stanford University
Stanford, CA

Application
Freeware
Size: 17k

Education 8

Continued

PadDesign v1.0

Creates designs for impedance-attenuating devices in electronic circuits.

John Knuth
E. 14119 Sunnyside Drive
Veradale, WA 99037
(509) 924-3560

Application
Shareware $5.00
Size: 35k

Potential v1.0

Simulates motion of a ball with both kinetic and potential energy. Lets you specify damping and the shape of the potential well.

Blas Cabrera
Stanford University
Stanford, CA

Application
Freeware
Size: 19k

Regression Analyzer

A program for multiple linear regression.

Steve Brecher
Software Supply

Application
Freeware
Size: 33k

Tiny Tafel v1.0

Has something to do with genealogy, but we seem to have misplaced the documentation file that accompanies this program.

Brian Bechtel

Application
Freeware
Size: 21k

AppleTones v2.0

Lets user compose music using 12 provided building block sounds. Includes docs within the program. Good for learning about repetition, silence, volume and timbre changes in musical composition.

John R. Meier & Jon Appleton
Music Department
Dartmouth College
Hanover, NH 03755

Application
Freeware
Size: 71k

Ax Headroom v1.0

A guitar simulator capable of producing 10 chords.

Harmony Unlimited
PO Box 15101
Newark, DE 19711

Application
Shareware $10.00
Size: 39k

CZ-101/5000 Librarian v0.94

Has a large documentation file that fully explains its many functions. It is, among other things, a tool for modifying MIDI files that makes control of Casio's CZ synthesizers more convenient.

Mike Cohen
2255 Barker Avenue
Bronx, NY 10467
(818) 788-6867

Application
Shareware $25.00
Size: 20k

Ear Trainer v1.2

By means of drills, trains your ability to distinguish the pitch of musical notes and chords.

Lawrence Gallagher
843 Winthrop Ave.
Revere, MA 02151

Application
Shareware $10.00
Size: 28k

Esurientes

Ninth passage from Bach's 'Magnificat.' ConcertWare+ MIDI software and a MIDI sound-generating system are required to play this sound.

J. S. Bach
and an anonymous transcriber

ConcertWare Document
Public Domain
Size: 4k

FB-01 Edit

Editor for the Yamaha Sound Generator FB-01. Enables the user to see and alter the various settings of the voices, instruments, and configurations on the patches for this synthesizer.

Dennis De Mars, #211
2265 Westwood Blvd.
Los Angeles, CA 90064

Application
Shareware $15.00
Size: 107k

MacKeybd

Loads a sound file and then uses the Mac keyboard to play the scale with it. Accompanying it are the sounds of a banjo and various effects.

Terry Bertram
PO Box 772
Claremont, CA 91711

Application
Public Domain
Size: 23k

MIDI Program Selector

Assigns a MIDI channel number to a particular instrumental voice.

Austin Development
227 Marin Street
San Rafael, CA 94901

Desk Accessory
Freeware
Size: 8k

Education 9

Continued

Midi Sequencer v0.1

Records and saves digitized sounds received through the modem port. Can also play these sounds.

Mike Cohen

Application
Freeware
Size: 9k

MIDI Terminal v1.0

Displays the MIDI information coming into your computer from a MIDI device. Translates the hexadecimal MIDI code to ASCII text.

Laurie Spiegel
175 Duane Street
New York, NY 10013

Application
Shareware $15.00
Size: 19k

MIDI>TEXT CONVERT v0.3

Coverts text to MIDI code and vice versa.

David Zacarelli

Application
Freeware
Size: 22k

MIDIdisplay v1.1

Takes the raw data captured by MIDIecho, which accompanies this program, then expands and displays it.

Lee Story
PAN: LSTORY

Application
Public Domain
Size: 16k

MIDIecho v1.1

Filters MIDI data arriving through the modem port and echoes it back out, or to a file. It is accompanied on this disk by MIDIdisplay.

Lee Story
PAN: LSTORY

Application
Freeware
Size: 23k

MIDIScope™ v1.1

Data capture/analysis tool. Features a filter for incoming data; real-time display of key velocities; pressure and control values with peak, average, and histogram; trace buffer triggered by data matcher.

Ralph Muha
Kurzweil Music Systems, Inc.
411 Waverly Oaks Road
Waltham, MA 02154

Application
Freeware
Size: 31k

Education 10

Education

CalcPlot v2.0

A reverse polish notation calculator with graphing capabilities. Generates plots of equations. Has docs in a separate file.

Joseph E. Carroll
4261 Queens Way
Minnetonka, MN 55345

Application
Shareware $10.00
Size: 41k

Evolutions v1.05

Utility program for text files: converts space runs into tabs, removes control characters, and adds and deletes line feeds. Docs within program.

Kevin M. Hoctor
29215 Fox Run Blvd.
Spring, TX 77386
(713) 288-9593

Application
Shareware $10.00
Size: 21k

Fun with Regions II

Illustrates methods of drawing areas and computing areas based on two different algorithms. Based on an article about regions in MacTutor by S. Dubin, T.W. Moore, and S. Kishore.

unknown

Application
Public Domain
Size: 11k

Latin Conjugation Exercises

Tutor for conjugating Latin verbs. Presents user with quizzes and speaks Latin words. Requires MacinTalk.

Joseph Casazza
Jesuit College Prep. School
12345 Inwood Road
Dallas, TX 75244

Application
Freeware
Size: 117k

Latin Declension Exercises

Tutor for declining Latin nouns. Presents user with quizzes and speaks Latin words. Requires MacinTalk.

Joseph Casazza
Jesuit College Prep. School
12345 Inwood Road
Dallas, TX 75244

Application
Freeware
Size: 75k

Magic Square v4.0

Manipulates a magic square, which is a compositional tool for 12-tone composers.

David Rakowski
51 Big Tree Way
Woodside, CA 94062

Application
Freeware
Size: 117k

Numberator

Tool for determining the smallest number of subjects needed to obtain statistically meaningful results. Line-mode interface.

unknown

Application
Public Domain
Size: 20k

Quiz Master v1.1

Interactive learning tool you can use for drill and practice or as a testing medium. Creates multiple choice or true/false quizzes. Docs within program.

Ed Neu, Viking Technologies
The Traver Block
174 Bellevue Avenue
Newport, RI 02840

Application
Freeware
Size: 29k

Education 10

Continued

R-Mapper v1.01

Takes a list of cleavage sites and enzyme symbols and draws a restriction map. Creates a picture that you can copy to the Clipboard. Has docs within program and in a separate file.

Bill Engels
Genetics Department
University of Wisconsin
Madison, WI 53706

Application
Freeware
Size: 85k

Roman Dates v1.0

Converts dates expressed in modern mm/dd/yy (month/day/year) format to the corresponding date in Roman numerals.

Joseph Casazza
Jesuit College Prep. School
12345 Inwood Road
Dallas, TX 75244

Application
Freeware
Size: 43k

Seven Blocks

Simple puzzle game where you must assemble 7 triangular blocks into a specified pattern.

John Kiehl
Jim Boyles
(617) 367-0510

Application
Freeware
Size: 17k

Education

Baby Demo v2.1

Simulates post-op pediatric patients (children) who have had cardiac surgery. Your job is to keep the patient's vital signs within acceptable ranges for 2 hours. Care options are limited in demo version.

TKB International, Inc.
300 North Newport Blvd.
Newport Beach, CA 92663
(714) 631-9020

Application
Demoware
Size: 236k

BLOOD

Shows the shape of the oxygen/hemoglobin dissociation curve for specified conditions of pCO2, pH, and temperature. Line-mode data entry.

Stephen Dubin
BioMed. Eng. & Science Inst.
Drexel University
Philadelphia, PA 19104

Application
Freeware
Size: 15k

Diet Helper v2.0

Tool for determining dietary goals for calories and food intake (carbohydrates, fat, and protein). Checks for consistency in dietary goals. Includes docs within the program.

Stephen Dubin et al.
BioMed Eng. & Science Inst.
Drexel University
Philadelphia, PA 19104

Application
Freeware
Size: 15k

EKTEACH v1.0

Teaches basic aspects of electrocardiogram (EKG) reading. Has docs in a separate file.

Dr. Stephen Dubin
29 Orchard Road
Springfield, PA 19064

Application
Demoware
Size: 27k

macMRI v0.50ß

A simple image-processing system. Comes with several images of the human heart.

Flip Phillips
(415) 499-3600

Application
Freeware
Size: 37k

MEAXIS v0.1

Computes the value of the mean electric axis of electrocardiographic deflections in the frontal plane.

Stephen Dubin
BioMed Eng. & Science Inst.
Drexel University
Philadelphia, PA 19104

Application
Freeware
Size: 31k

Veggies v2.0

Tool for vegetarians to plan diets to maintain a balance of essential amino acids.

Stephen Dubin
BioMed Eng. & Science Inst.
Drexel University
Philadelphia, PA 19104

Application
Freeware
Size: 32k

Education 12

Education

A Turing Machine Simulator v2.0d

A Turing Machine is a device consisting of a control unit that can read/write symbols to a linear tape. This is an important concept in computer science theory. This simulator is quite extensive and has a nice graphical interface.

Jason Castan, et al.
University of Melbourne
AUSTRALIA

Application
Demoware
Size: 155k

Generate Numbers v1.02

Creates a text file containing strings in the following format: a prefix string, a sequence number, and a suffix string. Useful for generating serial numbers for import into a database or spreadsheet.

Brian Bezanson
Manta Software Corporation

Application
Freeware
Size: 57k

NumberCrunch v1.0

A scientific calculator to compute algebraic expressions, define variables and functions, and graph functions. Docs within the program.

Jim Mahoney
PO Box 347
Marlboro, VT 05344

Application
Freeware
Size: 86k

OpenChannel v1.1

Program for civil engineers who work with open channel type hydraulics. Helps design and analyze gravity sewer pipes, storm drains, channels, canals, ditches, and other cross-section hydraulic elements. Docs in a separate file.

Jeff Miles
8853 Lemas Road
Sacramento, CA 95828

Application
Shareware $20.00
Size: 73k

Wind Chill Factor

Calculates the wind chill factor.

unknown

Application
Freeware

Worm Statistics v.05

Calculates and plots statistical information for tables of data. Data entry interface is awkward. No documentation.

George Wolford

Application
Freeware
Size: 42k

XYGraf

Simulates the two-dimensional x-y dynamic model. Seems to be related to quantum mechanics. Includes Pascal source code.

Theordore W. Gray

Application
Public Domain
Size: 23k

Education

Astrology Forecast

A goofy astrology forecast. One paragraph for each of the 12 signs.

Robert Cole
PO Box 884561
San Francisco, CA 94188

MacWrite Document
Public Domain
Size: 8k

MacMath Demo v2.0

Program for teaching children basic math skills (addition, subtraction, multiplication, division). Nice graphical interface. Retail version has a larger variety of problems and extensive use of sound.

Kelix Software Systems
11814 Coursey Blvd. Suite 220
Baton Rouge, LA 70816
(504) 769-6785

Application
Demoware
Size: 252k

MacRoots v5.03

Genealogy program for creating a database of your family history. Also produces charts. Complete manual in a separate file.

Bruce W. Muckala
Itasca Softworks
Route 1, Box 408
Bagley, MN 56621

Application
Shareware $35.00
Size: 287k

Education 15

Education

CLIPS v4.20

Expert sytem shell developed by the Artificial Intelligence Section of NASA at the Johnson Space Center. Documentation provided, but you have to be familiar with expert systems to use this program.

COSMIC
382 E. Broad Street
Athens, GA 30602
(404) 542-3265

Application
Freeware
Size: 211k

DelayCalc v1.5

Calculates delay times in milliseconds for musical notes, given the number of beats per minute.

Don Harriss
dh Productions
910 Celia Way
Palo Alto, CA 94303

Application
Shareware $5.00
Size: 24k

Jupiterium v1.0

Creates a simulation of Jupiter and its Galilean satellites as viewed from Earth through a small telescope. Includes a separate version that uses the 68881 math coprocessor for greater speed. Has docs in a separate file.

Howard L. Ritter, Jr.
29625 2nd Avenue SW
Federal Way, WA 98023
CIS: 71310, 2533

Application
Freeware
Size: 30k

MacAnorous v2.0

Music playing/composition program. Implements a 52-key keyboard and a 4-key drumpad. Pressing a key produces a sound. There are many options for modifying the sounds produced. Sequences can be recorded and played back.

Troy Peery
14 Broad Run Road
Manakin-Sabot, VA 23103

Application
Shareware $10.00
Size: 37k

VocabQuiz v1.4

Multiple-choice tests on both vocabulary and world capitals. Designed for studying for the SAT.

Mike Gleason, Jr.
5705 N. 117th Plaza
Omaha, NE 68164-1432

Application
Shareware $1.00
Size: 52k

Chaos, the application

Fractal-generating program. Supports color. Contains brief docs in a separate file.

Roger Bauchspies
PO Box 5841
Lincoln, NE 68505

Application
Freeware
Size: 61k

IFS Decompression v1.21

Program for decompressing a graphic picture stored in iterated function system (IFS) format. Comes with several sample pictures stored in this format. Includes a separate version that uses the 68881 math coprocessor.

Steve Scandalis
CIS: 70167,2205
GEnie: S.SCANDALIS

Application
Shareware $10.00
Size: 54k

Mactivation v3.2

Interactive simulator for investigating the low-level concepts of associative memory in a parallel distributed processing architecture, more commonly referred to as neural networks. Complete 30+ page manual included.

Mike Kranzdorf
University of Colorado
Optoelectronic Computing Systems Center

Application
Freeware
Size: 66k

Math21 v0.6

Generates 3-D wire-frame plots and 2-D gradient plots of a specified mathematical function. Has hidden-line removal and can show flow lines. Lets you adjust perspective.

Harry Lewis
Jim Matthews
Harvard College

Application
Public Domain
Size: 62k

Education 17

Education

MusicFun v1.0

You identify parts of music and the computer keeps a scorecard. There are several things to work on: note names, key signatures, scales, intervals, triads, sevenths, and inversions. This can also be used with MIDI equipment.

William Ermey
Transcomp
74 Memorial Rd.
Providence, RI 02906
(401) 272-4641

Application
Demoware
Size: 178k

Synchronicity v1.0

Computerized version of the I Ching (Book of Changes). It places you in an Oregon forest and has you concentrate on your question. The actions you use on the keyboard are the basis for the pattern to which the original mathematical principles of the Book of Changes are applied.

Visionary Software
(800) 877-1832 x5
Local: (503) 246-6200

Application
Demoware
Size: 571k

ALG 1/Simplify

Tutor for algebra, part of Homework Tutor Series. Sets up practice problems for you to solve. If you get stuck, it gives you hints.

Ken Tilton
Missing Link Software
P.O. Box 3280
South Amboy, NJ 08879
CIS: 71460,744

Application
Postcardware
Size: 104k

Government Booklet

Information on various booklets published by the government. Gives descriptions of contents, ordering information, and prices. Great for browsing and seeing what's out there.

Joseph Carlis
PO Box 233
North Haven, CT 06473-0233

Application
Shareware $1.00
Size: 21k

Hurricane

Storm-tracking routine for the Southeast U.S. It allows you to track a storm by filling in the blanks. Plug storm info into the program and it tracks it for you. You can customize the location.

Bill Chenault
149 Country Club Rd.
Shalimar, FL 32579

Application
Shareware $10.00
Size: 150k

Math Tutor v1.2

Tutors student in long division. You can choose the size of the divisor and dividend, then work the problem on a grid. The computer checks the accuracy of the work. Program allows for many variables in size and complexity of problems.

J&K Blanchard Enterprises
4611 Bulova St.
Torrance, CA 90503

Application
Shareware $10.00
Size: 22k

Proportions Calendar

Calculates proportions for making FileMaker documents.

D. Heady
MPC
650 S. Park Ave.
Crown Point, IN 46307

Filemaker II
Document
Freeware

Road Atlas

Map of the U.S. Click on city of origin and destination for mileage and major stops along the way.

Vic Hasselblad

Application
Public Domain
Size: 28k

Statsolver v1.0

For use with college-level statistics. Allows you to check various statistics: binomial coefficient, distribution, and histogram; normal distribution of probability and Z-values; nonstandard distribution of probability and Z-values. It also gives you various ways to check hypotheses.

Jack A. Littleton
PO Box 5301
Chico, CA 95927

Application
Shareware
$95927.00
Size: 108k

Education 19

Education

EarTrainer

Test your musical ability. This program drills you on types of musical intervals and chords by playing notes. You select type of chord or interval.

Lawrence P. Gallagher
843 Winthrop Ave.
Revere, MA 02151

Application
Shareware $10.00
Size: 28k

Education

Evolv-o-Matic

Evolution simulation. See critters eat food. See them breed. You can change the parameters for the critters.

Dave Johnson
58 Chenery St.
San Francisco, CA 94131

Application
Freeware
Size: 98k

Morse Code Tutor v1.2

Tutorial for copying Morse code; use it to practice for getting your ham radio license.

Jack Brinde WA 4FIB
2404 Stockton Pl.
Marietta, GA 30666

Application
Shareware $?
Size: 18k

PowerOut v1.02

Program to warn of impending power outages. Shows you amperage and voltage and plots them on an x-y graph.

Josh Pritikin
1404 Greenworth Pl.
Santa Barbara, CA 93108

Application
Freeware
Size: 46k

Education 21

Education

Biorhythm2 v6.1

Shows your biorhythms after you enter your birthday, other information. This program has been around for a long time. Self-disables after 60 days; must set your clock to before 12/31/90 before running!

David A. Bailey
7030 Enright Dr.
Citrus Heights, CA 95621

Application
Demoware
Size: 83k

CalNeva Roads

Map of California and Nevada. Click on origin and destination, and it produces a route map and mileage.

Jim Moore

Application
Freeware
Size: 25k

Jabberwocky v0.1

A remote response system that allows BBS users to read and respond to messages off-line.

Eric Larson
2902 Falls Rd.
Marcellus, NY 13108

Application
Shareware $20.00
Size: 96k

MacFormula 2.0 v2.0

Calculates the molecular weight of a given empirical formula. It can calculate exact mass or average mass. It can also perform elemental analyses and calculate millimoles from milligrams.

James E. Deline
405 Pine Ridge Rd.
San Ramon, CA 94583

Application
Shareware $15.00
Size: 31k

MacMap

Map of Oregon. Pick two cities (names not on map), and it will select best route and print route information. Also gives estimated driving time and mileage. Order other maps from author.

Dick Loucks
Canonical Solutions
6605 SW River Rd.
Hillsboro, OR 97123
(503) 642-7386

Application
Freeware
Size: 102k

MathLock v1.0

Used to lock your computer. Before a child can access games, etc., s/he must solve from 5 to 25 simple math problems. Each correct answer comes with its own sound. A great way to teach kids math.

Mouse Onion Software
PO Box 1252
Hunt Valley, MD 21030-6252

Application
Shareware $10.00
Size: 85k

McHurricane

Hurricane/storm tracking program. Enter your own information and you can track a storm and print maps.

William Chenault
149 Country Club Rd.
Shalimar, FL 62579
(904) 651-2276

Application
Demoware
Size: 147k

NIST Time v1.1

Sets the Mac clock with the atomic clock at the National Institute of Standards and Technology. You need a modem to use this.

Jeffrey Andre

Application
Freeware
Size: 27k

Southwest Roads

Maps of California, Nevada, Arizona, Utah, New Mexico, and Colorado. Click on origin and destination, and it produces a route map and indicates number of miles.

Jim Moore

Application
Freeware
Size: 33k
12" 6 7 32

Education 22

Education

Dr. Circuit v1.0

A design tool for circuit designers. Program creates a circuit from a written description. It solves the math and shows the solution.

Burce Lawton
1813 Cougar Ct.
Virginia Beach, VA 23456

Application
Shareware $20.00
Size: 47k

Projectionist

PICS animation program. Animates a mathematical problem in conjunction with such programs as Mathematica and Theorist. The examples shown are neat.

Allan Bonadio
Prescience Corp.
814 Castro St. #206
San Francisco, CA 94114
(415) 282-5864

Application
Freeware
Size: 68k

UNITize Demo v1.0

A conversion tool for various measurements and formulas.

Rainbow Bridge
4243 Hunt Rd., Ste. 215
Cincinnati, OH 45242

Application
Demoware
Size: 37k

GearCalc

Calculates bicycle gear ratios from wheel size, size of front chain ring, and rear cogs.

Timothy S. Oey

Application
Freeware
Size: 215k

HMO 1.0 v1.0

Performs Huckel molecular orbital calculations. Draw a molecule and specify the number of electrons. Program constructs the secular determinate and complete Eigen vectors and values by Jacobi diagonalization method.

Allan Wissner
Lederle Laboratories
Oncology and Immunology Research
Pearl River, NY 10965
(914) 732-3580

Application
Freeware
Size: 165k

StudioCalc v1.01

Calculates music note values in milliseconds and cue length from beats per minute. Author requests that you send $5 to the American Red Cross Earthquake Relief Fund in lieu of shareware fee.

Don Harrris
dh Productions
910 Celia Way
Palo Alto, CA 94303

Application
Freeware
Size: 35k

Education 24

Education

pop15

A population growth simulator. Comes with docs. Warning: Doesn't support the Apple menu! Author has an article on this program and population growth in our Spring '91 Newsletter.

John K. Dixon
17 Arthur Drive East
Fort Washington, MD

Application
Shareware $5.00
Size: 37k
12" 6 7 32

Education

Education

AmphibianFlash

A set of FileMaker files for making flash cards for common amphibians.

Eric F. Maurer
Dept. of Systematics & Ecology
University of Kansas
Lawrence, KS 66045

FileMaker II
Document
Shareware $?
Size: 47k

Herp Dictionary

A Word dictionary containing the scientific names of the common North American amphibians and reptiles. Registered users are informed of any updates.

Eric F. Maurer
Dept. of Systematics & Ecology
University of Kansas
Lawrence, KS 66045

MS Word
Dictionary
Shareware $3.00
Size: 4k

Kristi's Letters v1.0

A nice program for teaching kids the alphabet. After you type the correct letter, a vocabulary word flashes on the screen. Has sound and color graphics. Comes with MacinTalk 2.0.

Morgan Davis

Application
Freeware
Size: 33k

ReptilianFlash

A set of FileMaker files for making flash cards for common reptiles.

Eric F. Maurer
Dept. of Systematics & Ecology
University of Kansas
Lawrence, KS 66045

Filemaker II
Document
Shareware $?
Size: 82k

Sage v1.01

A program that allows you to start up with quotes from great and not-so-great minds of the human race. Comes with a modifiable text file of quotes.

Irving Software
86 Hiddenwood Drive
Rochester, NY 14616

Application
Freeware
Size: 10k

Education 26

Education

Teacher's RecordKeeper

A large set of Works 2.0 templates that provide examples of using the program for grading and curriculum. Created by two high school teachers.

David & Lorelei Mayer
Beaumont, TX

MS Works
Spreadsheet
Public Domain
Size: 294k

Education

Fonts

The BMUG library contains four types of fonts – Type 1 & Type 3 PostScript, TrueType, and Bitmapped screen fonts.

PostScript fonts come in two parts, screen fonts and printer fonts, and require a PostScript printer or Adobe Type Manager software to print smoothly. TrueType fonts require System 7, or System 6.0.7 or later with the TrueType Extension (contained on all BMUG TrueType disks). Bitmapped screen fonts will not print smoothly on a LaserWriter or other high-resolution printer, but work well for dot matrix printers such as ImageWriters.

To install PostScript fonts:

1) Install the bitmapped font suitcase as instructed for either System 6 or System 7.
2) Drag the PostScript font icons (they ususally look like little laser printers) into the System Folder. If you are using System 7, open the System Folder, then copy the files into the open folder. Don't just drag the PostScript font files onto the System Folder icon, or they may not install properly.

To install bitmapped fonts under System 6:

Use Font/DA Mover 3.8 or later (located on Utilities 2 in your System disk set).
1) Open the Font/DA Mover. 2) Click on the Open... button on the right. 4) Locate and open the font suitcase file you wish to install. 4) Select the fonts to install.
5) Click on the Copy button in the middle of the window.

Font-Type Icons:

 **TrueType**

 **Bitmap**

 **Type 1**

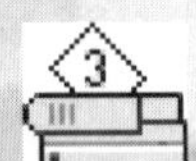 **Type 3**

Fonts A1

Type 1 PostScript

Type 1 Fonts

BlackForest 18, 24

One Style

ABCDEFGHIJKLMNOPQRSTUVWXYZ

abcdefghijklmnopqrstuvwxyz1234567890

How razorback-jumping frogs can level!

Middleton 24

One Style

ABCDEFGHIJKLMNOPQRSTUVWXYZ

abcdefghijklmnopqrstuvwxyz1234567890

How razorback-jumping frogs can level!

PixieFont 12, 18, 24, 36, 48

One Style

ABCDEFGHIJKLMNOPQRSTUVWXYZ

abcdefghijklmnopqrstuvwxyz1234567890

How razorback-jumping frogs can level

Polo-SemiScript 24, 36, 48

One Style

ABCDEFGHIJKLMNOPQRSTUVWXYZ

abcdefghijklmnopqrstuvwxyz1234567890

How razorback-jumping frogs can level!

SlabFace 8, 9, 10, 12, 14, 16, 18, 20, 24, 30, 36, 72, 127

One Style

ABCDEFGHIJKLMNOPQRSTUVWXYZ

ABCDEFGHIJKLMNOPQRSTUVWXYZ1234567890

HOW RAZORBACK-JUMPING FROGS CAN LEVEL!

Albatross 12, 18, 24

One Style

ABCDEFGHIJKLMNOPQRSTUVWXYZ
abcdefghijklmnopqrstuvwxyz1234567890
How razorback–jumping frogs can level!

DavysDingbats 18, 24, 36, 48, 72

One Style

DavysOtherDingbats 24, 36, 48, 72

One Style

Fonts A3

Type 1 PostScript

KonanurKaps 24, 36, 48, 72

One Style

A B C D E F G
H I J K L M N
O P Q R S T U
V W X Y Z

LeftyCasual 24

One Style

ABCDEFGHIJKLMNOPQRSTUVWXYZ

abcdefghijklmnopqrstuvwxyz1234567890

How razorback-jumping frogs can level!

LightsOut 6, 7, 8, 9, 10, 11, 12, 14, 18, 24, 36, 48, 72

One Style

ABCDEFGHIJKLMNOPQRSTUV
abcdefghijklmnopqrstuvw123
How razorback-jumping frogs

LoopDeLoop 24, 48

One Style

ABCDEFGHIJKLMNOPQRSTUVWXYZ

ABCDEFGHIJKLMNOPQRSTUVWXYZ

Luxembourg 12, 24 — One Style

ABCDEFGHIJKLMNOPQRSTUVWXYZ

abcdefghijklmnopqrstuvwxyz1234567890

How razorback-jumping frogs can level!

Math Major 24 — One Style

ABCDEFGHIJKLMNOPQRSTUVWXYZ

abcdefghijklmnopqrstuvwxyz1234567890

]∪ħ⟦→$\tau^{43687}\sigma\rho\vartheta^{2}\varepsilon\upsilon\neq$–ΘωΠπ$\beta^{90}\zeta\cdot\theta,^{1}\lambda\mu\perp$

How razorback-jumping frogs can level!

Fonts A4

Type 1 PostScript

Neuvarese-BoldItalic 10, 12, 24 — One Style

ABCDEFGHIJKLMNOPQRSTUVWXYZ
abcdefghijklmnopqrstuvwxyz12345678
How razorback-jumping frogs can level!

Nordic 12, 24 — One Style

ABCDEFGHIJKLMNOPQRSTUVWXYZ
abcdefghijklmnopqrstuvwxyz1234567890
How razorback-jumping frogs can level!

Ornaments 127 — One Style

ParisMetro 14, 18, 24, 36 — One Style

ABCDEFGHIJKLMNOPQR
STUVWXYZ1234567890

PigNoseTyp 7, 8, 9, 10, 11, 12, 14, 18, 24, 36, 48, 72 — One Style

ABCDEFGHIJKLMNOPQRSTUVWXYZ
abcdefghijklmnopqrstuvwxyz1234567890
How razorback-jumping frogs can level!

Showboat 24, 48, 72

One Style

ABCDEFGHIJK
LMNOPQRSTU

Silicon 12, 24

One Style

ABCDEFGHIJKLMNOPQRSTU
abcdefghijklmnopqrstuv123
How razorback-jumping

StencilCut 24

One Style

ABCDEFGHIJKLMNOPQR
STUVWXYZ1234567890

Time-Italic-Lefty 12, 18, 24

One Style

ABCDEFGHIJKLMNOPQRSTUVWXYZ
abcdefghijklmnopqrstuvwxyz1234567890
How razorback-jumping frogs can level!

Times-Mirror 12, 24

One Style

ABCDEFGHIJKLMNOPQRSTUVWX
abcdefghijklmnopqrstuvwx z1234567890
How razorback-jumping frogs can level!

Fonts A5

Continued

Tribeca 18, 24, 36, 48 — One Style

ABCDEFGHIJKLMNO
PQRSTUVWXYZ
1234567890

UltraBlack 24 — One Style

ABCDEFGHIJKLMNOPQRSTUV
abcdefghijklmnopqrstuv12345
How razorback-jumping frogs!

Andesite 48 — One Style

ABCDEFGHIJKLMN

ANBCEFGHIJKLMNOPQ123

Type 1 Fonts

MesozoicGothic 18, 24 — One Style

ABCDEFGHIJKLMNOPQRSTUVW

XYZ1234567890 RADUE 1990

Patriot 7, 8, 10, 12, 14, 16, C01, 24, 30, 36, 42, 48, 63, 72, 90, 118 — One Style

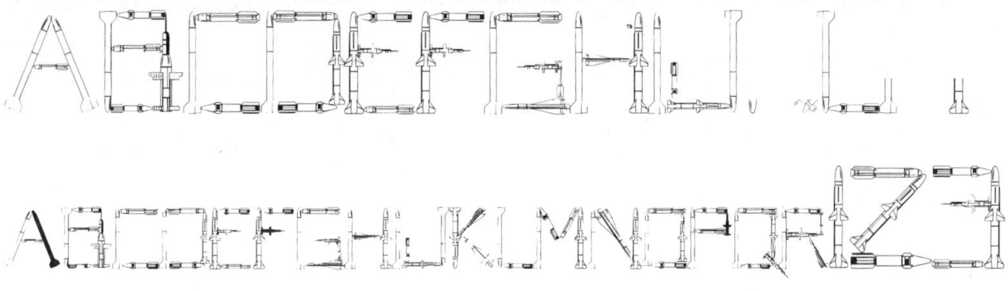

Fonts A7

Type 1 PostScript

CarawayBold 24 — One Style

ABCDEFGHIJKLMNOPQRSTUVW
abcdefghijklmnopqrstuvwx12345
How razorback-jumping frogs!

Crillee 10, 12, 14, 18, 24 — One Style

ABCDEFGHIJKLMNOPQRSTUVWXYZ
abcdefghijklmnopqrstuvwxyz1234567890
How razorback-jumping frogs can level!

GoudyMedieval 10, 12, 24 — One Style

ABCDEFGHIJKLMNOPQRSTUVWX
abcdefghijklmnopqrstuvwxyz1234567890
how razorback-jumping frogs can level!

Premium 48 — One Style

ABCDEFGHIJKLMNOPQRS
abcdefghijklmnopqrstuv12345

Sydney 12, 24 — One Style

ABCDEFGHIJKLMNOPQRSTUVWXYZ
abcdefghijklmnopqrstuv12345

Eire 12, 24 One Style

ABCDEFGHIJKLMNOPQRSTUVW

ABCDEFGHIJKLMNOPQRSTUVWX12345

HOW RAZORBACK-JUMPING FROGS!

InformalOblique 9, 10, 11, 12, 14, 18, 24 One Style

ABCDEFGHIJKLMNOPQRSTUVWXYZ

abcdefghijklmnopqrstuvwxyz1234567890

How razorback-jumping frogs can level!

NewBold 12, 18, 24 One Style

ABCDEFGHIJKLMNOPQRSTUVWXYZ

abcdefghijklmnopqrstuvwxyz1234567890

How razorback-jumping frogs can level!

RansomNote 24 One Style

ABCDEFGHIJKLMNOPQRSTUVW

abcdefghijklmnopqrstuvwxyz123456

How razorback-jumping frogs can!

ReliefDeco 18, 24, 36, 48, 72 One Style

ABCDEFGHIJKLMN

OPQRSTUVWXYZ

1234567890

Fonts A8

Continued

SchwarzWald 24 — One Style

ABCDEFGHIJKLMNOPQRSTUVW

abcdefghijklmnopqrstuvwxyz12345

How razorback-jumping frogs can!

Upsilon 12, 24 — One Style

ABCDEFGHIJKLMNOPQRSTUVWXYZ

abcdefghijklmnopqrstuvwxyz1234567890

How razorback-jumping frogs can level!

Wedgie 18, 24, 36, 48 — One Style

ABCDEFGHIJKL

MNOPQRSTUVW

XYZ123456789

Type 1 Fonts

Type 1 PostScript

DemoRusskijModern 10, 12, 18, 24, 36 — One Style

АБЦДЕФГЧИ
ЙКЛМНОПЯР
СТУВШХЫЗ

RusskijOtkrytyjDemo 10, 12, 18, 24, 36 — One Style

АБЦДЕФГЧИ
ЙКЛМНОПЯР
СТУВШХЫЗ

Shorai 24 — One Style

あつうえおぴろぺぽぷよんのあいうえおなにぬね
もょり゚ぃざどづずぐぜぞぶゅゃべぼがげれば
さとつすくせそふまみむめゆやへほかけしこ
ひてきちはたゎ゚「」 ┐ └ SHŌRAI

Fonts A10

Type 1 PostScript

Type 1 Fonts

BlackChancery 24

One Style

ABCDEFGHIJKLMNOPQR

abcdefghijklmnopqrstuvwxyz123456789

How razorback-jumping frogs can level!

GenoaItalic 24

One Style

ABCDEFGHIJKLMNOPQRSTUVWXYZ

abcdefghijklmnopqrstuvwxyz1 234567

How razorback-jumping frogs can level!

GenoaRoman 24

One Style

ABCDEFGHIJKLMNOPQRSTUVWXYZ

abcdefghijklmnopqrstuvwxyz1 234567

How razorback-jumping frogs can level!

InkaBod 12, 14, 24

One Style

ABCDEFGHIJKLMNOPQRSTUVWXYZ

abcdefghijklmnopqrstuvwxyz1234567890

How razorback-jumping frogs can level!

Medici 10, 12, 18, 24

One Style

ABCDEFGHIJKLMNOPQR

STUVWXYZ1234567890

Type 1 Fonts

Arctic 24 — One Style

ABCDEFGHIJKLMNOPQRSTUVWX
abcdefghijklmnopqrstuvwxyz12345
How razorback-jumping frogs can!

Author 18, 24, 48 — One Style

ABCDEFGHIJKLMNOPQRST
abcdefghijklmnopqrstuvwxyz123456789
How razorback-jumping frogs can level!

BenjaminCaps 24, 48, 72 — One Style

ABCDEFGHIJK
LMNOPQRSTU
VWXYZ

BODIDLYbold 12, 24 — One Style

ABCDEFGHIJKLMNOPQRSTU
abcdefghijklmnopqrstuvw12345
How razorback-jumping frogs!

Fonts A11

Continued

Type 1 Fonts

CarrickCaps 24, 36, 48, 60, 72 — One Style

ABCDEFGHIJKL
MNOPQRSTUVWX

CracklingFire 24, 48, 72 — One Style

ABCDEFGHIJKLMN
OPQRSTUVWXYZ

Flintstone 10, 12, 14, 18, 20, 24 — One Style

ABCDEFGHIJKLMNOPQRSTUVWXYZ
1234567890

Harrington 24 — One Style

ABCDEFGHIJKLMNOPQRSTUVWXYZ
abcdefghijklmnopqrstuvwxyz1234567890
How razorback-jumping frogs can level!

IsadoraCaps 24 — One Style

ABCDEFGHIJKLMNOPQRSTUVWXYZ
1234567890

Fonts A12

Type 1 PostScript

Judas 24 — One Style

ABCDEFGHIJKLMNOPQRSTUVWXYZ1234567890

Kastellar 72 — One Style

ABCDEFG
HIJKLMN

KinigsteinKaps 24, 36, 48, 72 — One Style

ABCDEFGHIJKL
MNOPRSTUVWZ

LeeCaps 18, 24, 36, 48, 60, 72 — One Style

ABCDEFGHIJKLMNOPQR
STUVWXYZ1234567890

Fonts A12

Continued

Type 1 Fonts

LowerEastSide 24, 48, 72

One Style

ABCDEFGHIJKLMNOPQRSTUVWXY

abcdefghijklmnopqrstuvwxyz123456

How razorback-jumping frogs can level!

LowerWestSide 24, 36, 48, 72

One Style

ABCDEFGHIJKLMNOPQRSTUVW

abcdefghijklmnopqrstuvwx1234567

How razorback-jumping frogs can!

Manzanita 24

One Style

ABCDEFGHIJKLMNOPQRSTUVWXYZ

ABCDEFGHIJKLMNOPQRSTUVWXYZ1234567890

HOW RAZORBACK-JUMPING FROGS CAN LEVEL!

Mira 24

One Style

ABCDEFGHIJKLMNOPQRSTUVWXYZ

abcdefghijklmnopqrstuvwxyz1234567890

How razorback-jumping frogs can level!

Fonts A13

Type 1 PostScript

Type 1 Fonts

Playbill 24 — One Style

ABCDEFGHIJKLMNOPQRSTUVWXYZ
abcdefghijklmnopqrstuvwxyz1234567890
How razorback-jumping frogs can level!

Recycle 24, 36, 48 — One Style

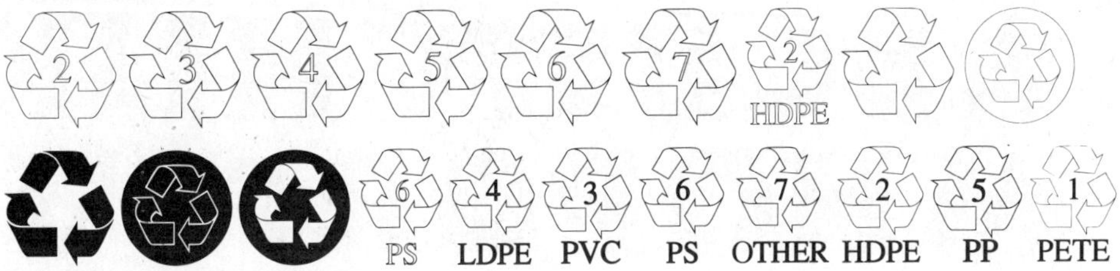

ReynoldsCaps 18, 24, 36 — One Style

ABCDEFGHIJKLMNOPQRSTUVWXYZ

SaintFrancis 18, 24 — One Style

ABCDEFGHIJKLMNOPQRSTUVWXYZ
abcdefghijklmnopqrstuvwxyz1234567890
How razorback-jumping frogs can level!

TempoFont 12, 24 — Plain, Italic

ABCDEFGHIJKLMNOPQRSTUVWXYZ
abcdefghijklmnopqrstuvwxyz1234567890
How razorback-jumping frogs can level!

Fonts A13

Continued

UpperEastSide 12, 14, 18, 24, 36, 48 — One Style

ABCDEFGHIJKLMNOPQRSTUVWXYZ

abcdefghijklmnopqrstuvwxyz1234567890

How razorback-jumping frogs can level!

ZaleskiCaps 24, 36, 48 — One Style

ABCDEFGHIJKL

MNOPQRSTUV

WXYZ12345678

GreenCaps 18, 24, 36, 48

One Style

ABCDEFGHIJKLMNOPQRS

TUVWXYZ1234567890

Muriel 18, 24, 48

One Style

ABCDEFGHIJKLMNOPQRSTUVWXYZ

abcdefghijklmnopqrstuvwxyz1234567890

How razorback-jumping frogs can level!

Rudelsberg 18, 24, 36, 48

One Style

ABCDEFGHIJKLMNOPQRSTUVWXYZ

abcdefghijklmnopqrstuvwxyz1234567890

How razorback-jumping frogs can level!

VarahCaps 24, 48, 72, 96, 120

One Style

ABCDEFGHIJKLM

NOPQRSTUVWXYZ

Ashley 24

One Style

ABCDEFGHIJKLMNOPQRSTUVWXYZ

abcdefghijklmnopqrstuvwxyz1234567890

How razorback-jumping frogs can level!

Fonts A15

Type 1 PostScript

Type 1 Fonts

Dubiel 10, 12, 14, 18, 24, 36 One Style

ABCDEFGHIJKLMNOPQRSTUVWXYZ
abcdefghijklmnopqrstuvwxyz1234567890
How razorback-jumping frogs can level!

DubielItalic 10, 12, 14, 18, 24, 36 One Style

ABCDEFGHIJKLMNOPQRSTUVWXYZ
abcdefghijklmnopqrstuvwxyz1234567890
How razorback-jumping frogs can level!

Lumparsky 24 One Style

ABCDEFGHIJKLMNOPQRSTUVWXYZ
abcdefghijklmnopqrstuvwxyz1234567890
How razorback-jumping frogs can level!

Aarcover 18, 24, 36 — One Style

ABCDEFGHIJKLMNOPQ

RSTUVWXYZ1234567

AdineKirnberg-Script 18, 24, 36, 48 — One Style

ABCDEFGHIJKLMNOPQRSTUVWXYZ

abcdefghijklmnopqrstuvwxyz1234567890

How razorback-jumping frogs can level!

ApplePi 12, 18, 24 — One Style

13457908$_{0123456789}$ P ^{6} e i√1

p ⅛ ¼ ⅓ ⅜ ½ ⅝ ¾ ⅞ ^{2} ⌘

DownWind 24 — One Style

ABCDEFGHIJKLMNOPQRSTUVWXYZ

abcdefghijklmnopqrstuvwxyz1234567890

How razorback-jumping frogs can level!

Jumble 12, 14, 18, 24, 36 — Plain, Italic

DIQBFUYPSELXOZWHRMCVTANGKJ

diqbfuypselxozwhrmcvtangkj6017945283

Pwn mdjwmidql-etohszy umwyc qdz xfafx!

Fonts A16

Continued

Klinzhai 24, 36, 48, 72, 96

One Style

Lemiesz 24, 36, 48

One Style

ABCDEFGHIJKLMN
OPQRSTUVWXYZ
1234567890

MarketBold 24

One Style

ABCDEFGHIJKLMNOPQRSTUVW
abcdefghijklmnopqrstuvwjyz12345
How razorback-jumping frogs can!

Medusa 24

One Style

ABCDEFGHIJKLMNOPQRSTU
abcdefghijklmnopqrstuv12345
How razorback-jumping frogs!

Rothman 24, 36, 48, 72

One Style

ABCDEFGHIJKLMNOPQRSTUVWXYZ
ABCDEFGHIJKLMNOPQRSTUVWXYZ1234567890
HOW RAZORBACK-JUMPING FROGS CAN LEVEL!

Fonts A17

Continued

Type 1 Fonts

Rounders 24 One Style

ABCDEFGHIJKLMNOPQRSTU

ABCDEFGHIJKLMNOPQRSTUVWXYZ123456

How razorback-jumping frogs can level!

Salter 24, 36, 48 One Style

ABCDEFGHIJKLMNOPQR

STUVWXYZ1234567890

SillyconValley 24 One Style

ABCDEFGHIJKLMNOPQRSTUVWXYZ

abcdefghijklmnopqrstuvwxyz1234567890

How razorback-jumping frogs can level!

Starburst 24, 48, 72, 96 One Style

ABCDEFGHIJKLMNOPQR

STUVWXYZ1234567890

Zallman-Caps 24, 48, 72 One Style

ABCDEFGHI

JKLMNOPQR

Brassfield 12, 14, 16, 24

One Style

ABCDEFGHIJKLMNOPQRSTUVWXY

abcdefghijklmnopqrstuvwxyz12345

How razorback-jumping frogs can!

BubbaLove 12, 24, 36

Light, Medium, Bold

ABCDEFGHIJKLMNOPQRSTUVWXYZ

abcdefghijklmnopqrstuvwxyz1234567890

How razorback-jumping frogs can level!

DavysKeyCaps 18, 24, 36

One Style

A B C D E F G H I J K L M N O P Q R

S T U V W X Y Z alt RETURN CAPS LOCK print screen page up ins scroll lock home

↑ ← ↓ → DELETE BACKSPACE option pause SHIFT page down esc TAB end CONTROL

help ⌘ del 1 2 3 4 5 6 7 8 9 0 space

Faktos 14, 18, 24, 36

One Style

ABCDEFGHIJKLMNOPQRSTUVWXYZ

abcdefghijklmnopqrstuvwxyz1234567890

How razorback-jumping frogs can level!

Frankenfont 12, 24, 36

One Style

ABCDEFGHIJKLMNOPQRSTUV

abcdefghijklmnopqrstuvwxyz12345

How razorback-jumping frogs can!

Fonts A19

Type 1 PostScript

Type 1 Fonts

Gallaudet 24, 72

One Style

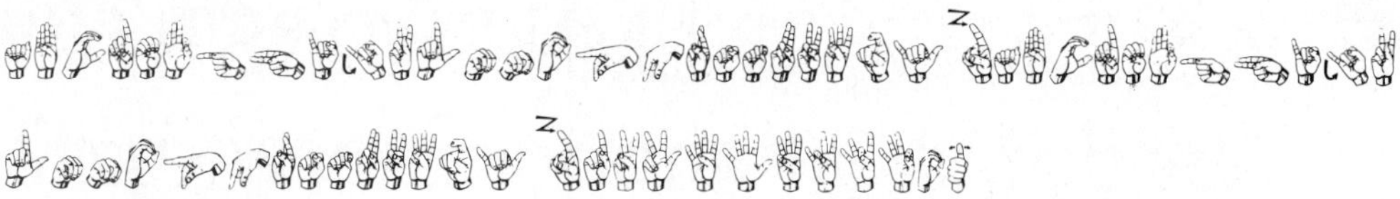

GoodCityModern 24

One Style

ABCDEFGHIJKLMNOPQRSTUVWXYZ
abcdefghijklmnopqrstuvwxyz1234567890
How razorback-jumping frogs can level!

Handwrite-Inkblot 12, 24, 36

One Style

ABCDEFGHIJKLMNOPQRSTUVWXYZ
abcdefghijklmnopqrstuvwxyz1234567890
How razorback jumping frogs can level!

Handwrite-Marker 12, 24, 36

One Style

ABCDEFGHIJKLMNOPQRSTUVWXYZ
abcdefghijklmnopqrstuvwxyz1234567890
How razorback-jumping frogs can level!

Handwrite-Pen 12, 24, 36

One Style

ABCDEFGHIJKLMNOPQRSTUVWXYZ
abcdefghijklmnopqrstuvwxyz1234567890
How razorback-jumping frogs can level!

Fonts A19

Continued

HeFractions 9, 10, 12, 14, 18, 24 — One Style

4/5 2/7 3/4 5/6 6/7 1/6 3/8 7/8 2/5 3/7 4/7 5/7 2/3 3/5 5/8 4/5 2/7 3/4 5/6 6/7

Jeff-Nichols 24, 48, 72 — One Style

ABCDEFGHI
JKLMNOPQR
STUVWXYZ

Jerusalem 14 — One Style

ווצצזש'ג'צ'צש0123456789?

Jumbalaya 12 — One Style

ABCDEFGHIJKLMNOPQRSTUVWXYZ
abcdefghijklmnopqrstuvwxyz1234567890
How razorback-jumping frogs can level

Type 1 Fonts

Fonts A20

Type 1 PostScript

Type 1 Fonts

Kennon 12, 14, 18, 24 — One Style

ABCDEFGHIJKLMNOPQRSTUVWXYZ

abcdefghijklmnopqrstuvwxyz1234567890

How razorback-jumping frogs can level!

Koshgarian-Light 18, 24, 36 — One Style

ABCDEFGHIJKLMNOPQRSTUVWXYZ

abcdefghijklmnopqrstuvwxyz1234567890

How razorback-jumping frogs can level!

Kramer 24, 48, 72 — One Style

ABCDEFGHIJK

LMNOPQRSTUV

WXYZABCDEFGHIJ

KLMNOPQRSTUVWXY

Lassus 24, 48, 72, 120

One Style

OregonWet 24, 36, 48, 60, 72

One Style

ABCDEFGHIJKLMNOPQRSTUVWXYZ

abcdefghijklmnopqrstuvwxyz1234567890

How razorback-jumping frogs can level!

Phonetic-Alphabet 12, 18, 24

One Style

abdefghijklmnoprstuvwxyzæəɣɥ

ɪŋœʃðʊʏʒɑ̃ɑɒɔ̃ʌɚɜθɛ̃ɜɔø¿¡ɛɲ˘ç

Fonts A21

Type 1 PostScript

Type 1 Fonts

LittleGidding 12 One Style

Multiform 24, 36 One Style

ABCDEFGHIJKLMNOPQR
STUVWXYZ1234567890

NeuSansBlack 12, 14, 16, 18, 24 One Style

ABCDEFGHIJKLMNOPQRSTUVWXYZ
abcdefghijklmnopqrstuvwxyz1234567890
How razorback-jumping frogs can level!

NeuSansLight 12, 14, 16, 18, 24 One Style

ABCDEFGHIJKLMNOPQRSTUVWXYZ
abcdefghijklmnopqrstuvwxyz1234567890
How razorback-jumping frogs can level!

NeuSerif 12, 18, 24 One Style

ABCDEFGHIJKLMNOPQRSTUVWXYZ
abcdefghijklmnopqrstuvwxyz1234567890
How razorback-jumping frogs can level!

NewRixFancy 24 One Style

ABCDEFGHIJKLMNOPQRSTUVWXYZ
abcdefghijklmnopqrstuvwxyz1234567890
How razorback-jumping frogs can level!

Orleans 24 One Style

ABCDEFGHIJKLMNOPQRSTU
abcdefghijklmnopqrstuvw12345
How razorback-jumping frogs!

OxNard 24 One Style

ABCDEFGHIJKLMN
OPQRSTUVWXYZ

Sharktooth 10, 12, 14, 18, 20, 24 One Style

ABCDEFGHIJKLMNOPQRSTUVWXYZ
ABCDEFGHIJKLMNOPQRSTUVWXYZ1234567890
How razorback-jumping frogs can level!

Fonts A22

Type 1 PostScript

Type 1 Fonts

Rhyolite 72

One Style

ABCDEFGHIJKLMNOPQRSTUVW

ABCDEFGHIJKLMN1234567890

SansFractions 9, 10, 12, 14, 18, 24

One Style

3/7 7/9 8/9 13/16 11/16 4/7 5/7 2/3 3/5 5/8 4/5 2/7 7/16 3/4 3/16 5/6 1/16 6/7 17/32 17/32

1/32 1/32 — — 15/32 ÷ / 3/32 5/32 9/32 19/32 21/32 23/32 27/32 29/32 31/32 27/32 31/32 25/32 7/32

SchnellerMedium 9, 10, 12, 24

One Style

ABCDEFGHIJKLMNOPQRSTUVWX

abcdefghijklmnopqrstuv1234567890

How razorback-jumping frogs can level!

SeriFractions 9, 10, 12, 14, 18, 24

One Style

3/7 7/9 8/9 13/16 11/16 4/7 5/7 2/3 3/5 5/8 4/5 2/7 7/16 3/4 3/16 5/6 1/16 6/7 1/6 3/8 9/16 1 23/32 29/32

1/32 15/32 15/32 3/32 5/32 9/32 19/32 21/32 23/32 27/32 29/32 31/32 27/32 31/32 25/32 7/32

ShalomOldStyle 24

One Style

טרחבא עהג–כלמנופקרסתשוצזיאוושייוד–ך...

אקושקום

ShalomScript 24

One Style

אקושקום...ב–ויישוא

טרחבא עהג–כלמנופקרסתשוצזי

ShalomStick 24

One Style

אקושקום...ך–ויישוא

טרחבא עהג–כלמנופקרסתשוצז

Fonts A23

Type 1 PostScript

Type 1 Fonts

PostCrypt 12, 24, 48 — One Style

ABCDEFGHIJKLMNOPQRSTUVW

ABCDEFGHIJKLMNOPQRSTUV12345

HOW RAZORBACK-JUMPING FROGS!

Shelldon 24 — One Style

ABCDEFGHIJKLMNOPQRSTUVWXYZ

abcdefghijklmnopqrstuvwxyz1234567

How razorback-jumping frogs can level!

Swifty 24 — One Style

TiFractions 9, 10, 12, 14, 18, 24 — One Style

1/2 1/3 1/4 1/5 1/6 1/7 1/8 1/9 2/3 3/4 2/5 3/5 4/5 5/6 2/7 3/7

4/7 5/7 3/8 5/8 7/8 $\frac{2}{3}$ $\frac{3}{4}$ $\frac{2}{5}$ $\frac{3}{5}$ $\frac{4}{5}$ $\frac{5}{6}$ $\frac{2}{7}$ $\frac{3}{7}$ $\frac{4}{7}$ $\frac{5}{7}$ $\frac{3}{8}$ $\frac{5}{8}$ $\frac{7}{8}$ $\frac{1}{2}$ $\frac{1}{3}$ $\frac{1}{4}$ $\frac{1}{5}$ $\frac{1}{6}$ $\frac{1}{7}$ $\frac{1}{8}$ $\frac{1}{9}$

Uecker 14, 18, 24, 36, 48, 72 — One Style

ABCDEFGHIJKLMNOPQRSTUVWXYZ

ABCDEFGHIJKLMNOPQRSTUVWXYZ 1234567890

HOW RAZORBACK-JUMPING FROGS CAN LEVEL!

Fonts A24

Type 1 PostScript

Andromeda 10, 12, 14, 18, 20, 24 — One Style

ABCDEFGHIJKLMNOPQRSTUVWXYZ

abcdefghijklmnopqrstuvwxyz1234567890

How razorback-jumping frogs can level!

Ann-Stone 24, 48, 72 — One Style

ABCDEFGHI

JKLMNOPQR

STUVWXYZ

Beffle 24, 36, 48 — One Style

ABCDEFGHIJKLMN

OPQRSTUVWXYZ

BellBottom 24 — One Style

ABCDEFGHIJKLMNOPQRSTUVWXYZ

abcdefghijklmnopqrstuvwxyz1234567890

How razorback-jumping frogs can level!

Fonts A24

Continued

Borzoi Reader 9, 10, 11, 12, 24 Plain, Italic, Bold, BoldItalic

ABCDEFGHIJKLMNOPQRSTUVWXYZ
abcdefghijklmnopqrstuvwxyØ123
How razorback-jumping frogs can!

Logger 24, 48, 72 One Style

ABCDEFGHI
JKLMNOP
QRSTUVW
XYZ

BartonLine 9, 10, 12, 14, 18, 24
One Style

DavysBigKeyCaps 18, 24, 36
One Style

A B C D E F G H I J K L M N O P Q R

S T U V W X Y Z ALT RETURN CAPS LOCK PRINT SCREEN ENTER

INS SCROLL LOCK HOME ↑ ← ↓ → DELETE BACKSPACE PAUSE

Handwriting 12, 24, 36, 48
One Style

ABCDEFGHIJKLMNOPQRSTUVWXYZ

abcdefghijklmnopqrstuvwxyz1234567890

How razorback-jumping frogs can level!

Klingo 24
One Style

LED 24
One Style

ABCDEFGHIJKLMNOPQRSTUVWXYZ

abcdefghijklmnopqrstuvwxyz1234567890

How razorback-jumping frogs can level!

LiquidCrystal 10, 12, 24, 72
One Style

AbcdEFGh IJHLMnoP9r

StUuLHY2 1234567890

Fonts A25

Continued

Type 1 Fonts

MachineBlock 24

One Style

ABCDEFGHIJKLMNOPQRSTUVWXYZ12345678

Pepita 24

One Style

ABCDEFGHIJKLMNOPQRSTUVWXY

abcdefghijklmnopqrstuvwxyz1234567890

How razorback-jumping frogs can level!

Rickshaw 14, 18, 20, 24, 36

One Style

ABCDEFGHIJKLMNOPQRSTUVWXYZ

abcdefghijklmnopqrstuvwxyz1234567890

How razorback-jumping frogs can level!

SapirSans 10, 12, 24

Plain, Italic

ABCDEFGHIJKLMNOPQRSTUVWXYZ

abcdefghijklmnopqrstuvwxyz1234567890

How razorback-jumping frogs can level!

TempiFont 18, 24, 36

One Style

A C E G I K M O Q S U W Y

a c e g i k m o q s u w y 1 3 5 7 9

ow a o ack- um i g ogs ca e e !

Continued

Thesisfont 12, 24, 36, 48 — One Style

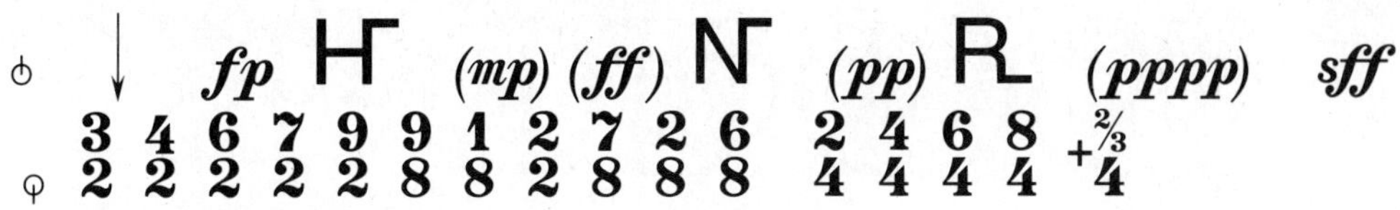

TuxedoVerticle 12, 18, 24, 36, 48 — One Style

ABCDEFGHIJKLMNOPQRSTUVWXYZ

ABCDEFGHIJKLMNOPQRSTUVWXYZ1234567890

HOW RAZORBACK-JUMPING FROGS CAN LEVEL!

Wharmby 24, 48, 72 — One Style

ABCDEFGHIJKLMNOPQ

RSTUVWXYZ2345678

Wiltonian 24 — One Style

ABCDEFGHIJKLMNOPQRSTU

ABCDEFGHIJKLMNOPQRSTUVWXYZ1234567

HOW RAZORBACK-JUMPING FROGS CAN!

Fonts B1

TrueType

TrueType Fonts

Andesite 48

One Style

ABCDEFGHIJKLMN

Architect 10, 12, 48

One Style

ABCDEFGHIJKLMNOPQRSTUVWXYZ
abcdefghijklmnopqrstuvwxyz1234567890
How razorback-jumping frogs can level!

GoudyHundred 10, 12, 14, 16, 18, 24

One Style

ABCDEFGHIJKLMNOPQRSTUVWXYZ
abcdefghijklmnopqrstuvwxyz1234567890
How razorback-jumping frogs can level!

Mazama TrueType 48

One Style

ABCDEFGHIJKLMNOPQ

SaintFrancis 18, 24

One Style

ABCDEFGHIJKLMNOPQRSTUVWXYZ
abcdefghijklmnopqrstuvwxyz1234567890
How razorback-jumping frogs can level!

WinsorDemi (18)

One Style

ABCDEFGHIJKLMNOPQRSTUVWXYZ
abcdefghijklmnopqrstuvwxyz1234567890
How razorback-jumping frogs can level!

DavysDingbatsOption 24
One Style

DavysDingbatsRegular 24
One Style

DavysDingbatsShift 24
One Style

DavysDingbatsShiftOption 24
One Style

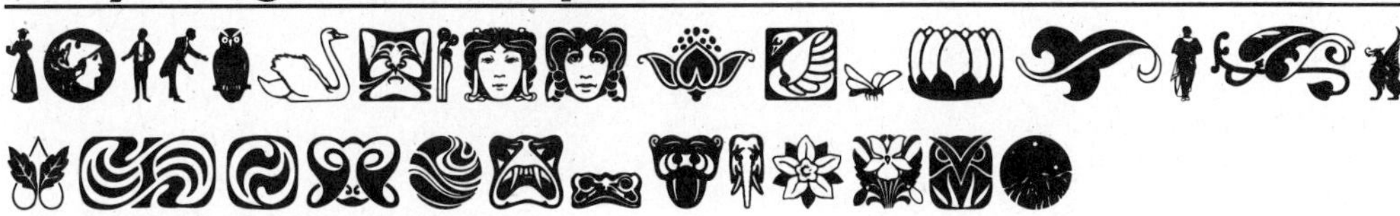

DavysOtherDingbatsOption 24
One Style

Fonts B2

Continued

DavysOtherDingbatsRegular 24 — One Style

DavysOtherDingbatsShift 24 — One Style

TrueType Fonts

Fonts B3

Granite Sans (18)

Plain, Italic, Bold, BoldItalic

ABCDEFGHIJKLMNOPQRSTUVWXYZ
abcdefghijklmnopqrstuvwxyz1234567890
How razorback-jumping frogs can level!

InformalOblique 9, 10, 11, 12, 14, 18, 24

One Style

ABCDEFGHIJKLMNOPQRSTUVWXYZ
abcdefghijklmnopqrstuvwxyz1234567890
How razorback-jumping frogs can level!

Premium TrueType 48

One Style

ABCDEFGHIJKLMNOPQRS

abcdefghijklmnopqrstuvw123

ReliefDeco 18

One Style

ABCDEFGHIJKLMNOPQRSTUVWXYZ
1234567890

Rhyolite TrueType 48

One Style

ABCDEFGHIJKLMNOPQRSTUVWXYZ

ABCDEFGHIJKLMNOPQRSTUVWXYZ123456

Fonts B3

Continued

Wedgie 18

One Style

ABCDEFGHIJKLMNOPQRSTUV
WXYZ1234567890

Albatross 12, 18, 24 One Style

ABCDEFGHIJKLMNOPQRSTUVWXYZ

abcdefghijklmnopqrstuvwxyz1234567890

How razorback–jumping frogs can level!

BODIDLYbold 12, 24 One Style

ABCDEFGHIJKLMNOPQRSTU

abcdefghijklmnopqrstuvw12346

How razorback-jumping frogs?

CartWright 24 One Style

ABCDEFGHIJKLMNOPQRSTUVWXYZ

abcdefghijklmnopqrstuvwxyz1234567890

How razorback-jumping frogs can level!

InkaBod 12, 14, 24 One Style

ABCDEFGHIJKLMNOPQRSTUVWXYZ

abcdefghijklmnopqrstuvwxyz1234567890

How razorback–jumping frogs can level!

Fonts B4

Continued

Judas 24 — One Style

ABCDEFGHIJKLMNOPQRSTUVWXYZ1234567890

LoopDeLoop 24, 48 — One Style

ABCDEFGHIJKLMNOPQRSTUVWX

ABCDEFGHIJKLMNOPQRSTUVWXYZ

OSWALDblack 18, 24 — One Style

ABCDEFGHIJKLMNOPQRSTUVWX

abcdefghijklmnopqrstuvwxyz1234567

How razorback-jumping frogs can level!

BenjaminCaps 24

One Style

ABCDEFGHIJKLMNOPQRST
UVWXYZ

CarrickCaps 24

One Style

ABCDEFGHIJKLM
NOPQRSTUVWXYZ

GreenCaps 18

One Style

ABCDEFGHIJKLMNOPQRSTUVWXYZ1234567890

HorstCaps 18

One Style

ABCDEFGHJKLMNOPQRSTUVWZ

KinigsteinKaps 24

One Style

ABCDEFGHIJKLMNOPR
STUVWZ

KonanurKaps 24

One Style

ABCDEFGHIJKLMN
OPQRSTUVWXYZ

LeeCaps 18

One Style

ABCDEFGHIJKLMNOPQRSTUVWXYZ
1234567890

Fonts B5

Continued

TrueType Fonts

LowerEastSide 24 — One Style

ABCDEFGHIJKLMNOPQRSTUVWXY
abcdefghijklmnopqrstuvwxyz123456
How razorback-jumping frogs can level!

LowerWestSide 24 — One Style

ABCDEFGHIJKLMNOPQRSTUVW
abcdefghijklmnopqrstuvwxyz12345
How razorback-jumping frogs can!

ReynoldsCaps 18 — One Style

ABCDEFGHIJKLMNOPQRSTUVWXYZ

UpperEastSide 24 — One Style

ABCDEFGHIJKLMNOPQRSTUVWXYZ
abcdefghijklmnopqrstuvwxyz1234567890
How razorback-jumping frogs can level!

UpperWestSide 24 — One Style

ABCDEFGHIJKLMNOPQRSTUVWXYZ
ABCDEFGHIJKLMNOPQRSTUVWXYZ1234567890
HOW RAZORBACK~JUMPING FROGS CAN LEVEL!

VarahCaps 24

One Style

ABCDEFGHIJKLM
NOPQRSTUVWXYZ

DownWind 24

One Style

ABCDEFGHIJKLMNOPQRSTUVWXYZ
abcdefghijklmnopqrstuvwxyz1234567890
How razorback-jumping frogs can level!

Fonts B6

TrueType

TrueType Fonts

FrankTimes 24

One Style

ABCDEFGHIJKLMNOPQRSTUVWX
abcdefghijklmnopqrstuvwxyz12345678
How razorback-jumping frogs can level!

IglooLaser 24, 48, 72

One Style

ABCDEFGHIJK
LMNOPQRSTU
VWXYZ12345

PixieFont 12

One Style

ABCDEFGHIJKLMNOPQRSTUVWXYZ
abcdefghijklmnopqrstuvwxyz1234567890
How razorback-jumping frogs can level

Fonts B7

TrueType

Jumble (18) — Plain, Italic

DIQBFUYPSELXOZWHRMCVTANGKJ

diqbfuypselxozwhrmcvtangkj6017945283

Pwn mdjwmidql-etohszy umwyc qdz xfafx!

Kramer (18) — One Style

ABCDEFGHIJKLMNOPQRSTUVWXYZ

ABCDEFGHIJKLMNOPQRSTUVWXYZ

Lemiesz (18) — One Style

ABCDEFGHIJKLMNOPQRSTUVWXYZ

234567890

Logger (18) — One Style

ABCDEFGHIJKLMNOPQRSTUVWXYZ

Medusa 24 — One Style

ABCDEFGHIJKLMNOPQRST

abcdefghijklmnopqrstuv12345

How razorback-jumping frogs!

MiamiNights (18) — One Style

ABCDEFGHIJKLMNOPQRSTUVWXYZ

abcdefghijklmnopqrstuvwxyz1234567890

How razorback-jumping frogs can level!

TrueType Fonts

Fonts B7

Continued

MktBold 24 — One Style

ABCDEFGHIJKLMNOPQRSTUVW
abcdefghijklmnopqrstuvwxyz12345
How razorback-jumping frogs can!

Multiform (18) — One Style

ABCDEFGHIJKLMNOPQRSTUVWXYZ1234567890

Salter (18) — One Style

ABCDEFGHIJKLMNOPQRSTUVWXYZ1234567890

Fonts B8

TrueType

NewBold 12, 18, 24

One Style

ABCDEFGHIJKLMNOPQRSTUVWXYZ
abcdefghijklmnopqrstuvwxyz1234567890
How razorback-jumping frogs can level!

OxNard 24

One Style

ABCDEFGHIJKLMNOPQRS
TUVWXYZ

ParkHaven (24)

One Style

ABCDEFGHIJKLMNOPQRST
abcdefghijklmnopqrstuvwxyz1234567890
How razorback-jumping frogs can level!

RoodCaps (18)

One Style

ABCDEFG
HIJKLMNO
PQRSTUV

Fonts B8

Continued

Rothman (60) — One Style

ABCDEFGHIJKLMNOPQRSTUVWXYZ

ABCDEFGHIJKLMNOPQRSTUVWXYZ 123456789

Rounders 24 — One Style

ABCDEFGHIJKLMNOPQRSTU

abcdefghijklmnopqrstuvwxyz 123456

How razorback-jumping frogs can level!

Rudelsberg (24) — One Style

ABCDEFGHIJKLMNOPQRSTUVWXYZ

abcdefghijklmnopqrstuvwxyz1234567890

How razorback-jumping frogs can level!

SillyconValley (18) — One Style

ABCDEFGHIJKLMNOPQRSTUVWXYZ

abcdefghijklmnopqrstuvwxyz12345678

How razorback-jumping frogs can level!

Sydney (18) One Style

ABCDEFGHIJKLMNOPQRSTUVWXYZ
abcdefghijklmnopqrstuvwxyz1234567
How razorback-jumping frogs can!

Wharmby (48) One Style

ABCDEFGHIJKLMNOPQ
RSTUVWXYZ1234567

ZallmanCaps (60) One Style

ABCDEFGH
IJKLMNOP
QRSTUVWZ

Fonts B9

TrueType

Andromeda (30) — One Style

ABCDEFGHIJKLMNOPQRSTUVWXYZ

abcdefghijklmnopqrstuvwxyz12345678

How razorback-jumping frogs can level!

ArchtextOneType 10, 12, 14, 18, 24 — One Style

ABCDEFGHIJKLMNOPQRSTUVWXYZ

ABCDEFGHIJKLMNOPQRSTUVWXYZ1234

HOW RAZORBACK-JUMPING FROGS CAN!

BikyBold (30) — One Style

ABCDEFGHIJKLMNOPQR

STUVWXYZ1234567890

Borzoi Reader TT 9, 10, 11, 12 — Plain, Italic, Bold, BoldItalic

ABCDEFGHIJKLMNOPQRSTUVWXYZ

abcdefghijklmnopqrstuvwxyz1234567890

How razorback-jumping frogs can level!

Brassfield 12, 14, 16, 24 — One Style

ABCDEFGHIJKLMNOPQRSTUVWXYZ

abcdefghijklmnopqrstuvwxyz123456

How razorback-jumping frogs can!

CarawayBold (18) — One Style

ABCDEFGHIJKLMNOPQRSTUVWXYZ
abcdefghijklmnopqrstuvwxyz1234567890
How razorback-jumping frogs can level!

CracklingFire 24 — One Style

ABCDEFGHIJKLMNOPQRSTUVWXYZ

DavysKeyCaps (18) — One Style

A B C D E F G H I J K L M N O P Q R
S T U V W X Y Z alt RETURN CAPS LOCK print screen page up ins scroll lock home
↑ ← ↓ → DELETE BACKSPACE option pause SHIFT page down esc TAB end CONTROL

FoxTrotMedium (24) — One Style

ABCDEFGHIJKLMNOPQRSTUVWXYZ
ABCDEFGHIJKLMNOPQRSTUVWXYZ123456789
HOW RAZORBACK–JUMPING FROGS CAN LEVEL!

Fonts B10

TrueType

TrueType Fonts

Gallaudet (24)

One Style

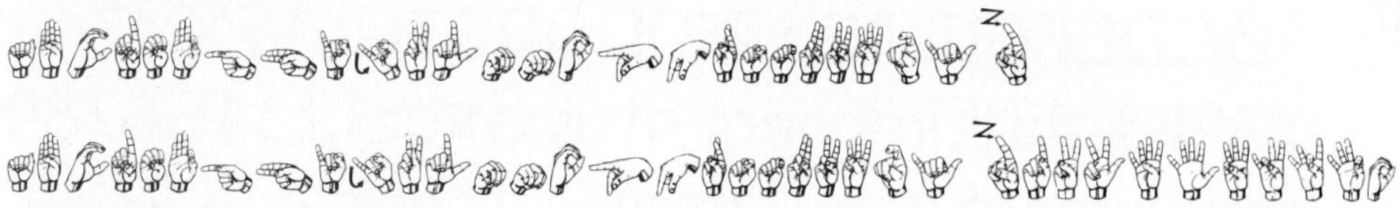

GoodCityModern (24)

One Style

ABCDEFGHIJKLMNOPQRSTUVWXYZ

abcdefghijklmnopqrstuvwxyz1234567890

How razorback-jumping frogs can level!

Groening (36)

One Style

ABCDEFGHIJKLMNOP

QRSTUVWXYZ12345678

HeFractions 9, 10, 12, 14, 18, 24

One Style

3/8 7/8 2/5 3/7 4/7 5/7 2/3 3/5 5/8 4/5 2/7 3/4 5/6 3/8 7/8 2/5 3/7 4/7 5/7 2/3

3/5 5/8 4/5 2/7 3/4 5/6 1/2 1/3 1/4 1/5 1/6 1/7 1/8 1/9

Jumbalaya (24)

One Style

ABCDEFGHIJKLMNOPQRSTUVWXYZ

abcdefghijklmnopqrstuvwxyz1234567890

HOw razorbaCk-jumping frogS Can!

Fonts B10

Continued

Kastellar TrueType 48 — One Style

ABCDEFGHIJKL
MNOPQRSTUV

Kennon 12, 14, 18, 24 — One Style

ABCDEFGHIJKLMNOPQRSTUVWXYZ
abcdefghijklmnopqrstuvwx1234567890
How razorback-jumping frogs can level!

Klinzhai (24) — One Style

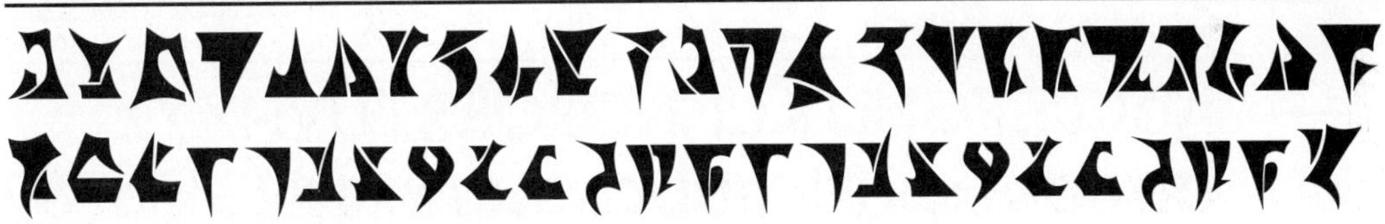

KochRoman (24) — One Style

ABCDEFGHIJKLMNOPQRSTUVWXYZ
abcdefghijklmnopqrstuvwxyz1234567890
How razorback-jumping frogs can level!

Koshgarian-Light (18) — One Style

ABCDEFGHIJKLMNOPQRSTUVWXYZ
abcdefghijklmnopqrstuvwxyz1234567890
How razorback-jumping frogs can level!

Fonts B11

TrueType

TrueType Fonts

Lassus (127) — One Style

LittleGidding (30) — One Style

NeuSansBlack 12, 14, 16, 18, 24 — One Style

ABCDEFGHIJKLMNOPQRSTUVWXYZ
abcdefghijklmnopqrstuvwxyz1234567890
How razorback-jumping frogs can level!

NeuSansLight 12, 14, 16, 18, 24 — One Style

ABCDEFGHIJKLMNOPQRSTUVWXYZ
abcdefghijklmnopqrstuvwxyz1234567890
How razorback-jumping frogs can level!

NeuSerif 12, 14, 16, 18, 24

One Style

ABCDEFGHIJKLMNOPQRSTUVWXYZ
abcdefghijklmnopqrstuvwxyz12345678
How razorback-jumping frogs can!

NewRixFancy (18)

One Style

ABCDEFGHIJKLMNOPQRSTUVWXYZ
abcdefghijklmnopqrstuvwxyz1234567890
How razorback-jumping frogs can level!

Fonts B12

TrueType

TrueType Fonts

ParisMetro 18 — One Style

ABCDEFGHIJKLMNOPQRSTUVWXYZ
1234567890

Phonetic-Alphabet (30) — One Style

abdefghijklmnoprstuvwxyz
æəɣɥɪŋœʃðʊʏʒɔ̃ʌɚɜθɛ̃ɜɔøɛɲ

Polo-SemiScript 24 — One Style

ABCDEFGHIJKLMNOPQRSTUVWXY
abcdefghijklmnopqrstuvwxyz12345678
How razorback-jumping frogs can level!

SansFractions 9, 10, 12, 14, 18, 24 — One Style

3/8 9/16 5/16 7/8 2/5 2/9 4/9 5/9 3/7 7/9 8/9 13/16 11/16 4/7 5/7 2/3 3/5 5/8 4/5 2/7 7/16 3/4 3/16 5/6 1/16 3/8 9/16
5/16 7/8 2/5 2/9 4/9 5/9 3/7 7/9 8/9 13/16 11/16 4/7 5/7 2/3 3/5
5/8 4/5 2/7 7/16 3/4 3/16 5/6 1/16 1/2 1/3 1/4 1/5 1/6 1/7 1/8 1/9

SchnellerMedium — One Style

ABCDEFGHIJKLMNOPQRSTUVWX
abcdefghijklmnopqrstuvwxyz123456
How razorback-jumping frogs can!

Sharktooth (24) — One Style

ABCDEFGHIJKLMNOPQRSTUVWX

ABCDEFGHIJKLMNOPQRSTUVWXYZ123456789

HOW RAZORBACK–JUMPING FROGS CAN LEVEL!

Stone Runes 96 — One Style

Wiltonian 24 — One Style

ABCDEFGHIJKLMNOPQRSTU

ABCDEFGHIJKLMNOPQRSTUVWXYZ12345678

HOW RAZORBACK-JUMPING FROGS CAN!

ZaleskiCaps 24 — One Style

ABCDEFGHIJKLMNOPQ

RSTUVWXYZ12345678

Fonts B13

TrueType

SeriFractions 9, 10, 12, 14, 18, 24 — One Style

$\frac{3}{8}$ $\frac{9}{16}$ $\frac{5}{16}$ $\frac{7}{8}$ $\frac{2}{5}$ $\frac{2}{9}$ $\frac{4}{9}$ $\frac{5}{9}$ $\frac{3}{7}$ $\frac{7}{9}$ $\frac{8}{9}$ $\frac{13}{16}$ $\frac{11}{16}$ $\frac{4}{7}$ $\frac{5}{7}$ $\frac{2}{3}$ $\frac{3}{5}$ $\frac{5}{8}$ $\frac{4}{5}$ $\frac{2}{7}$ $\frac{7}{16}$ $\frac{3}{4}$ $\frac{3}{16}$ $\frac{5}{6}$ $\frac{1}{16}$ 3/8 9/16

7/8 2/5 2/9 4/9 5/9 3/7 7/9 8/9 13/16 11/16 4/7 5/7 2/3 3/5 5/8

4/5 2/7 7/16 3/4 3/16 5/6 1/16 1/2 1/3 1/4 1/5 1/6 1/7 1/8 1/9

Showboat 24 — One Style

ABCDEFGHIJKLMNOPQRSTUV
WXYZ

Starburst 24 — One Style

ABCDEFGHIJKLMNOPQR
STUVWXYZ1234567890

TiFractions 9, 10, 12, 14, 18, 24 — One Style

$\frac{3}{8}$ $\frac{7}{8}$ $\frac{2}{5}$ $\frac{4}{7}$ $\frac{5}{7}$ $\frac{2}{3}$ $\frac{3}{5}$ $\frac{5}{8}$ $\frac{4}{5}$ $\frac{2}{7}$ $\frac{3}{4}$ $\frac{5}{6}$ 3/8 7/8 2/5 3/7 4/7 5/7 2/3

3/5 5/8 4/5 2/7 3/4 5/6 1/2 1/3 1/4 1/5 1/6 1/7 1/8 1/9

ToneAndDebs — One Style

ABCDEFGHIJKLMNOP

QRSTUVWXYZ12345

Tribeca 18

One Style

ABCDEFGHIJKLMNOPQRSTUVWXYZ
234567890

Zallman-Caps (72)

One Style

ABCDEF
GHIJKL
MNOPQR
STUVWZ

Fonts C1

Adobe Screen Fonts

Courier 10, 12, 14, 18, 24 — Plain, Italic, Bold, BoldItalic

ABCDEFGHIJKLMNOPQRSTUVWXYZ
abcdefghijklmnopqrstuvwxyz1234567890
How razorback-jumping frogs can!

Helvetica 10, 12, 14, 18, 24 — Plain, Italic, Bold, BoldItalic

ABCDEFGHIJKLMNOPQRSTUVWXYZ
abcdefghijklmnopqrstuvwxyz1234567890
How razorback-jumping frogs can level!

Helvetica Narrow 10, 12, 14, 18, 24 — Plain, Italic, Bold, BoldItalic

ABCDEFGHIJKLMNOPQRSTUVWXYZ
abcdefghijklmnopqrstuvwxyz1234567890
How razorback-jumping frogs can level!

Symbol 10, 12, 14, 18, 24 — One Style

ΑΒΧΔΕΦΓΗΙϑΚΛΜΝΟΠΘΡΣΤΥςΩΞΨΖ
αβχδεφγηιφκλμνοπθρστυϖωξψζ1234567890
Ηοω ραζορβαχκ−φυμπινγ φρογσ χαν λεϖελ!

Times 10, 12, 14, 18, 24 — Plain, Italic, Bold, BoldItalic

ABCDEFGHIJKLMNOPQRSTUVWXYZ
abcdefghijklmnopqrstuvwxyz1234567890
How razorback-jumping frogs can level!

Avant Garde 10, 12, 14, 18, 24

Plain, Italic, Bold, BoldItalic

ABCDEFGHIJKLMNOPQRSTUVWXYZ
abcdefghijklmnopqrstuvwxyz1234567890
How razorback-jumping frogs can level!

Bookman 10, 12, 14, 18, 24

Plain, Italic, Bold, BoldItalic

ABCDEFGHIJKLMNOPQRSTUVWXYZ
abcdefghijklmnopqrstuvwxyz1234567890
How razorback-jumping frogs can level!

New Century Schoolbook 10, 12, 14, 18, 24

Plain, Italic, Bold, BoldItalic

ABCDEFGHIJKLMNOPQRSTUVWXYZ
abcdefghijklmnopqrstuvwxyz1234567890
How razorback-jumping frogs can level!

Optima 10, 12, 14, 18, 24

Plain, Italic, Bold, BoldItalic

ABCDEFGHIJKLMNOPQRSTUVWXYZ
abcdefghijklmnopqrstuvwxyz1234567890
How razorback-jumping frogs can level!

Palatino 10, 12, 14, 18, 24

Plain, Italic, Bold, BoldItalic

ABCDEFGHIJKLMNOPQRSTUVWXYZ
abcdefghijklmnopqrstuvwxyz1234567890
How razorback-jumping frogs can level

Fonts C2

Continued

Souvenir 10, 12, 14, 18, 24 — Four Weights

ABCDEFGHIJKLMNOPQRSTUVWXYZ
abcdefghijklmnopqrstuvwxyz1234567890
How razorback-jumping frogs can level!

Zapf Chancery 10, 12, 14, 18, 24 — One Style

ABCDEFGHIJKLMNOPQRSTUVWXYZ
abcdefghijklmnopqrstuvwxyz1234567890
How razorback-jumping frogs can level!

Zapf Dingbats 10, 12, 14, 18, 24 — One Style

Adobe Screen Fonts

American Typewriter 10, 12, 14, 18, 24

Plain, Bold

ABCDEFGHIJKLMNOPQRSTUVWXYZ
abcdefghijklmnopqrstuvwxyz1234567890
How razorback-jumping frogs can level!

Benguiat 10, 12, 14, 18, 24

Plain, Bold

ABCDEFGHIJKLMNOPQRSTUVWXYZ
abcdefghijklmnopqrstuvwxyz1234567890
How razorback-jumping frogs can level!

Friz Quadrata 10, 12, 14, 18, 24

Plain, Bold

ABCDEFGHIJKLMNOPQRSTUVWXYZ
abcdefghijklmnopqrstuvwxyz1234567890
How razorback-jumping frogs can level!

Garamond 10, 12, 14, 18, 24

Plain, Italic, Bold, BoldItalic

ABCDEFGHIJKLMNOPQRSTUVWXYZ
abcdefghijklmnopqrstuvwxyz1234567890
How razorback-jumping frogs can level!

Glypha 10, 12, 14, 18, 24

Plain, Italic, Bold, BoldItalic

ABCDEFGHIJKLMNOPQRSTUVWXYZ
abcdefghijklmnopqrstuvwxyz1234567890
How razorback-jumping frogs can level!

Fonts C3

Continued

Helvetica Light 10, 12, 14, 18, 24

Plain, Italic

ABCDEFGHIJKLMNOPQRSTUVWXYZ
abcdefghijklmnopqrstuvwxyz1234567890
How razorback-jumping frogs can level!

Lubalin Graph 10, 12, 14, 18, 24

Plain, Italic, Bold, BoldItalic

ABCDEFGHIJKLMNOPQRSTUVWXYZ
abcdefghijklmnopqrstuvwxyz1234567890
How razorback-jumping frogs can level!

Machine 10, 12, 14, 18, 24

One Style

ABCDEFGHIJKLMNOPQRSTUVWXYZ1234567890

Adobe Screen Fonts

Galliard 10, 12, 14, 18, 24

Plain, Italic, Bold, BoldItalic

ABCDEFGHIJKLMNOPQRSTUVWXYZ
abcdefghijklmnopqrstuvwxyz1234567890
How razorback-jumping frogs can level!

Helvetica Condensed 10, 12, 14, 18, 24

Four Weights

ABCDEFGHIJKLMNOPQRSTUVWXYZ
abcdefghijklmnopqrstuvwxyz1234567890
How razorback-jumping frogs can level!

Korinna 10, 12, 14, 18, 24

Plain, Italic, Bold, BoldItalic

ABCDEFGHIJKLMNOPQRSTUVWXYZ
abcdefghijklmnopqrstuvwxyz1234567890
How razorback-jumping frogs can level!

Melior 10, 12, 14, 18, 24

Plain, Italic, Bold, BoldItalic

ABCDEFGHIJKLMNOPQRSTUVWXYZ
abcdefghijklmnopqrstuvwxyz1234567890
How razorback-jumping frogs can level!

New Baskerville 10, 12, 14, 18, 24

Plain, Italic, Bold, BoldItalic

ABCDEFGHIJKLMNOPQRSTUVWXYZ
abcdefghijklmnopqrstuvwxyz1234567890
How razorback-jumping frogs can level!

Fonts C4

Continued

Trump Mediaeval 10, 12, 14, 18, 24 — Plain, Italic, Bold, BoldItalic

ABCDEFGHIJKLMNOPQRSTUVWXYZ
abcdefghijklmnopqrstuvwxyz 1234567890
How razorback-jumping frogs can level!

Adobe Screen Fonts

Fonts C5

Adobe Screen Fonts

Bodoni 10, 12, 14, 18, 24 — Plain, Italic, Bold, BoldItalic

ABCDEFGHIJKLMNOPQRSTUVWXYZ
abcdefghijklmnopqrstuvwxyz1234567890
How razorback-jumping frogs can level!

Century Old Style 10, 12, 14, 18, 24 — Plain, Italic, Bold

ABCDEFGHIJKLMNOPQRSTUVWXYZ
abcdefghijklmnopqrstuvwxyz1234567890
How razorback-jumping frogs can level!

Cheltenham 10, 12, 14, 18, 24 — Plain, Italic, Bold, BoldItalic

ABCDEFGHIJKLMNOPQRSTUVWXYZ
abcdefghijklmnopqrstuvwxyz1234567890
How razorback-jumping frogs can level!

Franklin Gothic 10, 12, 14, 18, 24 — Three Weights

ABCDEFGHIJKLMNOPQRSTUVWXYZ
abcdefghijklmnopqrstuvwxyz1234567890
How razorback-jumping frogs can level!

Goudy 10, 12, 14, 18, 24 — Plain, Italic, Bold, BoldItalic

ABCDEFGHIJKLMNOPQRSTUVWXYZ
abcdefghijklmnopqrstuvwxyz1234567890
How razorback-jumping frogs can level!

Fonts C5

Continued

Park Avenue 10, 12, 14, 18, 24 — One Style

ABCDEFGHIJKLMNOPQRSTUVWXYZ

abcdefghijklmnopqrstuvwxyz1234567890

How razorback-jumping frogs can level!

Sonata 10, 12, 14, 18, 24 — One Style

Adobe Screen Fonts

Fonts C6

Adobe Screen Fonts

Aachen Bold 10, 12, 14, 18, 24
One Style

ABCDEFGHIJKLMNOPQRSTUVWXYZ
abcdefghijklmnopqrstuvwxyz1234567
How razorback-jumping frogs can!

Brush Script 10, 12, 14, 18, 24
One Style

ABCDEFGHIJKLMNOPQRSTUVWXYZ
abcdefghijklmnopqrstuvwxyz1234567890
How razorback-jumping frogs can level!

Freestyle Script 10, 12, 14, 18, 24
One Style

ABCDEFGHIJKLMNOPQRSTUVWXYZ
abcdefghijklmnopqrstuvwxyz1234567890
How razorback-jumping frogs can level!

Hobo 10, 12, 14, 18, 24
One Style

ABCDEFGHIJKLMNOPQRSTUVWXYZ
abcdefghijklmnopqrstuvwxyz 1234567890
How razorback-jumping frogs can level!

Fonts C6

Continued

Letter Gothic 10, 12, 14, 18, 24 Plain, Italic, Bold, BoldItalic

ABCDEFGHIJKLMNOPQRSTUVWXYZ
abcdefghijklmnopqrstuvwxyz1234567890
How razorback-jumping frogs can!

News Gothic 10, 12, 14, 18, 24 Plain, Italic, Bold, BoldItalic

ABCDEFGHIJKLMNOPQRSTUVWXYZ
abcdefghijklmnopqrstuvwxyz1234567890
How razorback-jumping frogs can level!

Orator 10, 12, 14, 18, 24 Plain, Italic

ABCDEFGHIJKLMNOPQRSTUVWXYZ
ABCDEFGHIJKLMNOPQRSTUVWXYZ1234567890
HOW RAZORBACK-JUMPING FROGS CAN!

Prestige Elite 10, 12, 14, 18, 24 Plain, Italic, Bold, BoldItalic

ABCDEFGHIJKLMNOPQRSTUVWXYZ
abcdefghijklmnopqrstuvwxyz1234567890
How razorback-jumping frogs can!

Revue 10, 12, 14, 18, 24 — One Style

ABCDEFGHIJKLMNOPQRSTUVWXYZ
abcdefghijklmnopqrstuvwxyz1234567890
How razorback-jumping frogs can level!

Stencil 10, 12, 14, 18, 24 — One Style

ABCDEFGHIJKLMNOPQRSTUVWXYZ
1234567890

Tiffany 10, 12, 14, 18, 24 — Three Weights

ABCDEFGHIJKLMNOPQRSTUVWXYZ
abcdefghijklmnopqrstuvwxyz1234567890
How razorback-jumping frogs can level!

University Roman 10, 12, 14, 18, 24 — One Style

ABCDEFGHIJKLMNOPQRSTUVWXYZ
abcdefghi klmnopqrstuvwxyz1234567890
How razorback- umping frogs can level

Fonts C7

Adobe Screen Fonts

Adobe Screen Fonts

Carta 10, 12, 14, 18, 24 — One Style

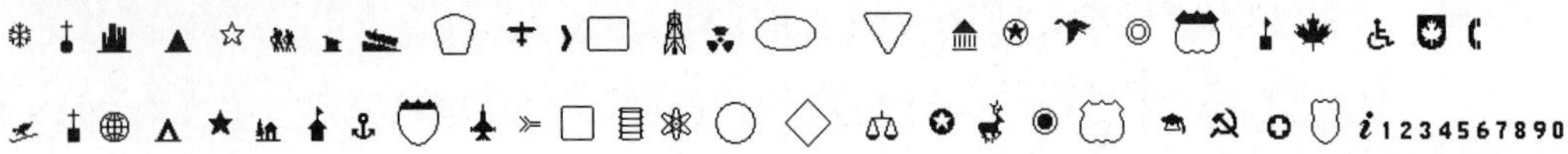

Futura Book 10, 12, 14, 18, 24 — Three Weights

ABCDEFGHIJKLMNOPQRSTUVWXYZ
abcdefghijklmnopqrstuvwxyz1234567890
How razorback-jumping frogs can level!

Lucida 10, 12, 14, 18, 24 — Plain, Italic, Bold, BoldItalic

ABCDEFGHIJKLMNOPQRSTUVWXYZ
abcdefghijklmnopqrstuvwxyz1234567890
How razorback-jumping frogs can level!

Univers 55 10, 12, 14, 18, 24 — Four Weights

ABCDEFGHIJKLMNOPQRSTUVWXYZ
abcdefghijklmnopqrstuvwxyz1234567890
How razorback-jumping frogs can level!

Univers Condensed 10, 12, 14, 18, 24 — Three Weights

ABCDEFGHIJKLMNOPQRSTUVWXYZ
abcdefghijklmnopqrstuvwxyz1234567890
How razorback-jumping frogs can level!

Stone Informal 10, 12, 14, 18, 24 Three Weights

ABCDEFGHIJKLMNOPQRSTUVWXYZ
abcdefghijklmnopqrstuvwxyz1234567890
How razorback-jumping frogs can level!

Stone Sans 10, 12, 14, 18, 24 Three Weights

ABCDEFGHIJKLMNOPQRSTUVWXYZ
abcdefghijklmnopqrstuvwxyz1234567890
How razorback-jumping frogs can level!

Stone Serif 10, 12, 14, 18, 24 Three Weights

ABCDEFGHIJKLMNOPQRSTUVWXYZ
abcdefghijklmnopqrstuvwxyz1234567890
How razorback-jumping frogs can level!

Fonts C9

Adobe Screen Fonts

Adobe Screen Fonts

Corona 10, 12, 14, 18, 24

Plain, Italic, Bold

ABCDEFGHIJKLMNOPQRSTUVWXYZ
abcdefghijklmnopqrstuvwxyz1234567890
How razorback-jumping frogs can level!

Eurostile 10, 12, 14, 18, 24

Three Weights

ABCDEFGHIJKLMNOPQRSTUVWXYZ
abcdefghijklmnopqrstuvwxyz1234567890
How razorback-jumping frogs can level!

Excelsior 10, 12, 14, 18, 24

Plain, Italic, Bold

ABCDEFGHIJKLMNOPQRSTUVWXYZ
abcdefghijklmnopqrstuvwxyz1234567890
How razorback-jumping frogs can level!

Futura 10, 12, 14, 18, 24

Three Weights

ABCDEFGHIJKLMNOPQRSTUVWXYZ
abcdefghijklmnopqrstuvwxyz1234567890
How razorback-jumping frogs can level!

Futura Condensed 10, 12, 14, 18, 24

Four Weights

ABCDEFGHIJKLMNOPQRSTUVWXYZ
abcdefghijklmnopqrstuvwxyz1234567890
How razorback-jumping frogs can level!

Belwe Light 10, 12, 14, 18, 24

Three Weights

ABCDEFGHIJKLMNOPQRSTUVWXYZ
abcdefghijklmnopqrstuvwxyz1234567890
How razorback-jumping frogs can level!

Caslon 3 Roman 10, 12, 14, 18, 24

Plain, Italic

ABCDEFGHIJKLMNOPQRSTUVWXYZ
abcdefghijklmnopqrstuvwxyz1234567890
How razorback-jumping frogs can level!

Caslon 540 Roman 10, 12, 14, 18, 24

Plain, Italic

ABCDEFGHIJKLMNOPQRSTUVWXYZ
abcdefghijklmnopqrstuvwxyz1234567890
How razorback-jumping frogs can level!

Goudy Extra Bold 10, 12, 14, 18, 24

One Style

ABCDEFGHIJKLMNOPQRSTUVWXYZ
abcdefghijklmnopqrstuvwxyz1234567890
How razorback-jumping frogs can level!

Goudy Heavyface 10, 12, 14, 18, 24

Plain, Italic

ABCDEFGHIJKLMNOPQRSTUVWXYZ
abcdefghijklmnopqrstuvwxyz1234567
How razorback-jumping frogs can!

Fonts C10

Continued

Helvetica Compressed 10, 12, 14, 18, 24 — One Style

ABCDEFGHIJKLMNOPQRSTUVWXYZ
abcdefghijklmnopqrstuvwxyz1234567890
How razorback-jumping frogs can level!

Helvetica Extra Compressed 10, 12, 14, 18, 24 — One Style

ABCDEFGHIJKLMNOPQRSTUVWXYZ
abcdefghijklmnopqrstuvwxyz1234567890
How razorback-jumping frogs can level!

Italia Book 10, 12, 14, 18, 24 — Three Weights

ABCDEFGHIJKLMNOPQRSTUVWXYZ
abcdefghijklmnopqrstuvwxyz1234567890
How razorback-jumping frogs can level!

Lucida Sans Roman 10, 12, 14, 18, 24 — Plain, Italic, Bold, BoldItalic

ABCDEFGHIJKLMNOPQRSTUVWXYZ
abcdefghijklmnopqrstuvwxyz123456789
How razorback-jumping frogs can level!

Memphis Medium 10, 12, 14, 18, 24

Four Weights

ABCDEFGHIJKLMNOPQRSTUVWXYZ
abcdefghijklmnopqrstuvwxyz1234567890
How razorback-jumping frogs can level!

Fonts C11

Adobe Screen Fonts

Eras Book 10, 12, 14, 18, 24 Six Weights

ABCDEFGHIJKLMNOPQRSTUVWXYZ
abcdefghijklmnopqrstuvwxyz1234567890
How razorback-jumping frogs can level!

Helvetica 25 Ultra Light 10, 12, 14, 18, 24 Plain, Italic

ABCDEFGH JKLMNOPQRSTUVWXYZ
abcdefgh kmnopqrstuvwxyz1234567890
How razorback- ump ng frogs can eve !

Helvetica 35 Thin 10, 12, 14, 18, 24 Plain, Italic

ABCDEFGHIJKLMNOPQRSTUVWXYZ
abcdefghijklmnopqrstuvwxyz1234567890
How razorback-jumping frogs can level!

Helvetica 55 Roman 10, 12, 14, 18, 24 Plain, Italic

ABCDEFGHIJKLMNOPQRSTUVWXYZ
abcdefghijklmnopqrstuvwxyz1234567890
How razorback-jumping frogs can level!

Helvetica 75 Bold 10, 12, 14, 18, 24 Plain, Italic

ABCDEFGHIJKLMNOPQRSTUVWXYZ
abcdefghijklmnopqrstuvwxyz1234567890
How razorback-jumping frogs can level!

ITC Kabel Medium 10, 12, 14, 18, 24 Five Weights

ABCDEFGHIJKLMNOPQRSTUVWXYZ
abcdefghijklmnopqrstuvwxyz1234567890
How razorback-jumping frogs can level!

Janson Text 10, 12, 14, 18, 24 Plain, Italic, Bold, BoldItalic

ABCDEFGHIJKLMNOPQRSTUVWXYZ
abcdefghijklmnopqrstuvwxyz1234567890
How razorback-jumping frogs can level!

MICR 10, 12, 14, 18, 24 One Style

1234567890

OCR A 10, 12, 14, 18, 24 One Style

ABCDEFGHIJKLMNOPQRSTUVWXYZ
abcdefghijklmnopqrstuvwxyz123
How razorback-jumping frogs!

Fonts C11

Continued

OCR B 10, 12, 14, 18, 24

One Style

ABCDEFGHIJKLMNOPQRSTUVWXYZ
abcdefghijklmnopqrstuvwxyz123
How razorback-jumping frogs!

Adobe Screen Fonts

Fonts C12

Adobe Screen Fonts

Clarendon 10, 12, 14, 18, 24 — Three Weights

ABCDEFGHIJKLMNOPQRSTUVWXYZ
abcdefghijklmnopqrstuvwxyz123456789
How razorback-jumping frogs can level!

Helvetica 45 Light 10, 12, 14, 18, 24 — Plain, Italic

ABCDEFGHIJKLMNOPQRSTUVWXYZ
abcdefghijklmnopqrstuvwxyz1234567890
How razorback-jumping frogs can level!

Helvetica 65 Medium 10, 12, 14, 18, 24 — Plain, Italic

ABCDEFGHIJKLMNOPQRSTUVWXYZ
abcdefghijklmnopqrstuvwxyz1234567890
How razorback-jumping frogs can level!

Helvetica 85 Heavy 10, 12, 14, 18, 24 — Plain, Italic

ABCDEFGHIJKLMNOPQRSTUVWXYZ
abcdefghijklmnopqrstuvwxyz123456789
How razorback-jumping frogs can level!

Kaufmann 10, 12, 14, 18, 24 — Plain, Bold

ABCDEFGHIJKLMNOPQRSTUVWXYZ
abcdefghijklmnopqrstuvwxyz1234567890
How razorback-jumping frogs can level!

Fonts C12

Continued

Adobe Screen Fonts

New Caledonia 10, 12, 14, 18, 24 — Four Weights

ABCDEFGHIJKLMNOPQRSTUVWXYZ
abcdefghijklmnopqrstuvwxyz1234567890
How razorback-jumping frogs can level!

Peignot Demi 10, 12, 14, 18, 24 — Three Weights

ABCDEFGHIJKLMNOPQRSTUVWXYZ
abcdefghijklmnopqrstuvwxyz1234567890
How razorback-jumping frogs can level!

Times Ten Roman 10, 12, 14, 18, 24 — Plain, Italic, Bold, BoldItalic

ABCDEFGHIJKLMNOPQRSTUVWXYZ
abcdefghijklmnopqrstuvwxyz1234567890
How razorback-jumping frogs can level!

Fonts C13

Adobe Screen Fonts

Americana 10, 12, 14, 18, 24 Three Weights

ABCDEFGHIJKLMNOPQRSTUVWXYZ
abcdefghijklmnopqrstuvwxyz12345678
How razorback-jumping frogs can level!

Clearface Regular 10, 12, 14, 18, 24 Four Weights

ABCDEFGHIJKLMNOPQRSTUVWXYZ
abcdefghijklmnopqrstuvwxyz1234567890
How razorback-jumping frogs can level!

Serif Gothic 10, 12, 14, 18, 24 Six Weights

ABCDEFGHIJKLMNOPQRSTUVWXYZ
abcdefghijklmnopqrstuvwxyz1234567890
How razorback-jumping frogs can level!

Fonts C14

Adobe Screen Fonts

Adobe Screen Fonts

Caslon Open Face 10, 12, 14, 18, 24

One Style

ABCDEFGHIJKLMNOPQRSTUVWXYZ
abcdefghijklmnopqrstuvwxyz1234567890
How razorback-jumping frogs can level!

Centennial 10, 12, 14, 18, 24

Four Weights

ABCDEFGHIJKLMNOPQRSTUVWXYZ
abcdefghijklmnopqrstuvwxyz1234567890
How razorback-jumping frogs can level!

Century Expanded 10, 12, 14, 18, 24

Plain, Italic

ABCDEFGHIJKLMNOPQRSTUVWXYZ
abcdefghijklmnopqrstuvwxyz1234567890
How razorback-jumping frogs can level!

Frutiger Roman 10, 12, 14, 18, 24

Five Weights

ABCDEFGHIJKLMNOPQRSTUVWXYZ
abcdefghijklmnopqrstuvwxyz1234567890
How razorback-jumping frogs can level!

Serifa Roman 10, 12, 14, 18, 24

Four Weights

ABCDEFGHIJKLMNOPQRSTUVWXYZ
abcdefghijklmnopqrstuvwxyz1234567890
How razorback-jumping frogs can level!

Avenir 10, 12, 14, 18, 24 — Six Weights

ABCDEFGHIJKLMNOPQRSTUVWXYZ
abcdefghijklmnopqrstuvwxyz1234567890
How razorback-jumping frogs can level!

Garamond 3 10, 12, 14, 18, 24 — Plain, Italic, Bold, BoldItalic

ABCDEFGHIJKLMNOPQRSTUVWXYZ
abcdefghijklmnopqrstuvwxyz1234567890
How razorback-jumping frogs can level!

Stempel Garamond 10, 12, 14, 18, 24 — Plain, Italic, Bold, BoldItalic

ABCDEFGHIJKLMNOPQRSTUVWXYZ
abcdefghijklmnopqrstuvwxyz1234567890
How razorback-jumping frogs can level!

Universal Greek+Math Pi 10, 12, 14, 18, 24 — One Style

ΑΒΨΔΕΦΓΗΙΞΚΛΜΝΟΠΘΡΣΤΘΩϬΧΥΖ
αβψδεφγηιξκλμνοπϑρστθωφχυζ+−×÷=±∓
Ηοφ ραζορβαψκ‴ξθμπινγ φρογσ ψαν λεωελ)

Universal News+Commercial Pi 10, 12, 14, 18, 24 — One Style

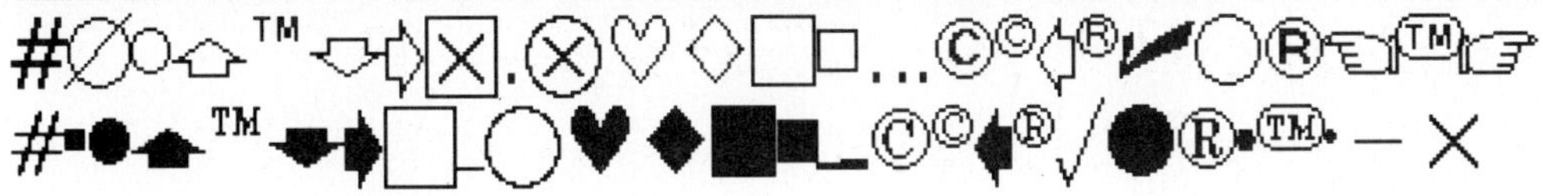

Fonts C15

Continued

Weiss 10, 12, 14, 18, 24

Three Weights

ABCDEFGHIJKLMNOPQRSTUVWXYZ
abcdefghijklmnopqrstuvwxyz1234567890
How razorback-jumping frogs can level!

Antique Olive Roman 10, 12, 14, 18, 24 Four Weights

ABCDEFGHIJKLMNOPQRSTUVWXYZ
abcdefghijklmnopqrstuvwxyz123456789
How razorback-jumping frogs can level!

Concorde Roman 10, 12, 14, 18, 24 Plain, Italic, Bold, BoldItalic

ABCDEFGHIJKLMNOPQRSTUVWXYZ
abcdefghijklmnopqrstuvwxyz1234567890
How razorback-jumping frogs can level!

Gothic 13 10, 12, 14, 18, 24 One Style

ABCDEFGHIJKLMNOPQRSTUVWXYZ
abcdefghijklmnopqrstuvwxyz1234567890
How razorback-jumping frogs can level!

Life Roman 10, 12, 14, 18, 24 Plain, Italic, Bold

ABCDEFGHIJKLMNOPQRSTUVWXYZ
abcdefghijklmnopqrstuvwxyz1234567890
How razorback-jumping frogs can level!

Tempo Heavy Condensed 10, 12, 14, 18, 24 Plain, Italic

ABCDEFGHIJKLMNOPQRSTUVWXYZ
abcdefghijklmnopqrstuvwxyz1234567890
How razorback-jumping frogs can level!

Fonts C16

Continued

Walbaum Roman 10, 12, 14, 18, 24 Plain, Italic, Bold, BoldItalic

ABCDEFGHIJKLMNOPQRSTUVWXYZ
abcdefghijklmnopqrstuvwxyz1234567890
How razorback-jumping frogs can level!

Bauhaus Medium 10, 12, 14, 18, 24 Five weights

ABCDEFGHIJKLMNOPQRSTUVWXYZ
abcdefghijklmnopqrstuvwxyz1234567890
How razorback-jumping frogs can level!

Cochin 10, 12, 14, 18, 24 Plain, Italic, Bold, BoldItalic

ABCDEFGHIJKLMNOPQRSTUVWXYZ
abcdefghijklmnopqrstuvwxyz1234567890
How razorback-jumping frogs can level!

Hiroshige Medium 10, 12, 14, 18, 24 Four Weights

ABCDEFGHIJKLMNOPQRSTUVWXYZ
abcdefghijklmnopqrstuvwxyz1234567890
How razorback-jumping frogs can level!

Sabon 10, 12, 14, 18, 24 Plain, Italic, Bold, BoldItalic

ABCDEFGHIJKLMNOPQRSTUVWXYZ
abcdefghijklmnopqrstuvwxyz1234567890
How razorback-jumping frogs can level!

Fonts C18

Adobe Screen Fonts

Arnold Boecklin 10, 12, 14, 18, 24 — One Style

ABCDEFGHIJKLMNOPQRSTUVWXYZ
abcdefghijklmnopqrstuvwxyz1234567890
How razorback-jumping frogs can level!

Dom Casual 10, 12, 14, 18, 24 — Plain, Bold

ABCDEFGHIJKLMNOPQRSTUVWXYZ
abcdefghijklmnopqrstuvwxyz1234567890
How razorback-jumping frogs can level!

Fette Fraktur 10, 12, 14, 18, 24 — One Style

ABCDEFGHIJKLMNOPQRSTUVWXYZ
abcdefghijklmnopqrstuvwxyz1234567890
How razorback-jumping frogs can level!

Folio Bold Condensed 10, 12, 14, 18, 24 — One Style

ABCDEFGHIJKLMNOPQRSTUVWXYZ
abcdefghijklmnopqrstuvwxyz 1234567890
How razorback-jumping frogs can level!

Folio Medium 10, 12, 14, 18, 24 — Four Weights

ABCDEFGHIJKLMNOPQRSTUVWXYZ
abcdefghijklmnopqrstuvwxyz1234567890
How razorback-jumping frogs can level!

Helvetica Inserat Roman 10, 12, 14, 18, 24 — One Style

ABCDEFGHIJKLMNOPQRSTUVWXYZ
abcdefghijklmnopqrstuvwxyz1234567890
How razorback-jumping frogs can level!

Linoscript 10, 12, 14, 18, 24 — One Style

ABCDEFGHIJKLMNOPQRSTUVWXYZ
abcdefghijklmnopqrstuvwxyz1234567890
How razorback-jumping frogs can level!

Linotext 10, 12, 14, 18, 24 — One Style

ABCDEFGHIJKLMNOPQRSTUVWXYZ
abcdefghijklmnopqrstuvwxyz1234567890
How razorback-jumping frogs can level!

Post Antiqua Roman 10, 12, 14, 18, 24 — Plain, Bold

ABCDEFGHIJKLMNOPQRSTUVWXYZ
abcdefghijklmnopqrstuvwxyz1234567890
How razorback-jumping frogs can level!

Present Script 10, 12, 14, 18, 24 — One Style

ABCDEFGHIJKLMNOPQRSTUVWXYZ
abcdefghijklmnopqrstuvwxyz1234567890
How razorback-jumping frogs can level!

Fonts C19

Adobe Screen Fonts

Adobe Screen Fonts

Akzidenz Grotesk 10, 12, 14, 18, 24

Four Weights

ABCDEFGHIJKLMNOPQRSTUVWXYZ
abcdefghijklmnopqrstuvwxyz1234567890
How razorback-jumping frogs can level!

Bauer Bodoni 10, 12, 14, 18, 24

Plain, Italic, Bold, BoldItalic

ABCDEFGHIJKLMNOPQRSTUVWXYZ
abcdefghijklmnopqrstuvwxyz1234567890
How razorback-jumping frogs can level!

Impressum 10, 12, 14, 18, 24

Plain, Italic, Bold

ABCDEFGHIJKLMNOPQRSTUVWXYZ
abcdefghijklmnopqrstuvwxyz123456789
How razorback-jumping frogs can level!

New Aster 10, 12, 14, 18, 24

Four Weights

ABCDEFGHIJKLMNOPQRSTUVWXYZ
abcdefghijklmnopqrstuvwxyz1234567890
How razorback-jumping frogs can level!

VAG Rounded Thin 10, 12, 14, 18, 24

Four Weights

ABCDEFGHIJKLMNOPQRSTUVWXYZ
abcdefghijklmnopqrstuvwxyz1234567890
How razorback-jumping frogs can level!

Adobe Screen Fonts

AGaramond 10, 12, 14, 18, 24

Lots of Styles

ABCDEFGHIJKLMNOPQRSTUVWXYZ
abcdefghijklmnopqrstuvwxyz1234567890
How razorback-jumping frogs can level!

Candida 10, 12, 14, 18, 24

Plain, Italic, Bold

ABCDEFGHIJKLMNOPQRSTUVWXYZ
abcdefghijklmnopqrstuvwxyz1234567890
How razorback-jumping frogs can level!

Franklin Gothic #2 10, 12, 14, 18, 24

Lots of Styles

ABCDEFGHIJKLMNOPQRSTUVWXYZ
abcdefghijklmnopqrstuvwxyz12345678
How razorback-jumping frogs can level!

Fonts D1

Type 3

AppleFont 9, 10, 12 — One Style

ABCDEFGHIJKLMNOPQRSTUVWXYZ
abcdefghijklmnopqrstuvwxyz1234567890
How razorback-jumping frogs can level!

ArchiSample 12 — One Style

ABCDEFGHIJKLMN PQRSTUVWXYZ
abcd fghijklmnopqr tuvwxyz12345 7890
How razorback-jumping frog can l v l!

Armadillo 12, 14, 18, 24, 36, 72 — One Style

BMUGAsianFont 18, 24 — One Style

北上下あいうさしすなにぬまみむりるきようか
ら夏、と分?あいうえおかきくけこさし封寺春
秋季涼冷李甲邦考孝らゑあいうくけあいよ

DraftsmanDemo 12

One Style

ABCDEFGHIJK MNOPQRSTUVWXYZ
abcdefgh jklmn pqrstuvwxyz1234567890
H w raz rback-jump nq fr qs can level!

FatAppleFont 12

One Style

ABCDEFGHIJKLMNOPQRSTUVWXYZ
abcdefghijklmnopqrstuvwxyz1234567890
How razorback-jumping frogs can level!

KabelBold 14

One Style

ABCDEFGHIJKLMNOPQRSTUVWXYZ
abcdefghijklmnopqrstuvwxyz1234567890
How razorback-jumping frogs can level!

KabelPlain 14, 18

One Style

ABCDEFGHIJKLMNOPQRSTUVWXYZ
abcdefghijklmnopqrstuvwxyz1234567890
How razorback-jumping frogs can level!

Slant Informal 12

One Style

ABCDEFGHIJKLMNOPQRSTUVWXYZ
abcdefghijklmnopqrstuvwxyz1234567890
How razorback-jumping frogs can level!

ThinAppleFont 12

One Style

ABCDEFGHIJKLMNOPQRSTUVWXYZ
abcdefghijklmnopqrstuvwxyz1234567890
How razorback-jumping frogs can level!

Fonts D2

Type 3

Type 3 Fonts

ArchiMedium 9, 10, 12 — One Style

ABCDEFGHIJKLMNOPQRSTUVWXYZ
ABCDEFGHIJKLMNOPQRSTUVWXYZ1234567890
HOW RAZORBACK-JUMPING FROGS CAN LEVEL!

Chester 9, 10, 12 — One Style

ABCDEFGHIJKLMNOPQRSTUVWXYZ
abcdefghijklmnopqrstuvwxyz1234567890
How razorback-jumping frogs can level!

ClassicaHeavy 14 — One Style

ABCDEFGHIJKLMNOPQRSTUVWXYZ
abcdefghijklmnopqrstuvwxyz1234567890
How razorback-jumping frogs can level!

ClassicaItalic 18 — One Style

ABCDEFGHIJKLMNOPQRSTUVWXYZ
abcdefghijklmnopqrstuvwxyz1234567890
How razorback-jumping frogs can level!

ClassicaRoman 18 — One Style

ABCDEFGHIJKLMNOPQRSTUVWXYZ
abcdefghijklmnopqrstuvwxyz1234567890
How razorback-jumping frogs can level!

Faustus 12 — One Style

ABCDEFGHIJKLMNOPQRSTUVWXYZ
abcdefghijklmnopqrstuvwxyz1234567890
How razorback-jumping frogs can level!

GeneralElectric 12, 14, 18, 20, 24, 30, 36, 48

One Style

GENERAL ELECTRIC

Gordon 24

One Style

ABCDEFGHIJKLMNOPQRSTUVWXYZ

abcdefghijklmnopqrstuvwxyz1234567890

How razorback-jumping frogs can level!

IBMKlone 12, 24

One Style

ABCDEFGHIJKLMNOPQRSTUVWXYZ

abcdefghijklmnopqrstuvwx123

How razorback-jumping frogs!

MiamiNights 18

One Style

ABCDEFGHIJKLMNOPQRSTUVWXYZ

abcdefghijklmnopqrstuvwxyz1234567890

How razorback-jumping frogs can level!

ParkHaven 14

One Style

ABCDEFGHIJKLMNOPQRSTUVWXYZ

abcdefghijklmnopqrstuvwxyz1234567890

How razorback-jumping frogs can level!

Type 3 Fonts

Fonts D2

Continued

RichardMurray 14

One Style

ABCDEFGHIJKLMNOPQRSTUVWXYZ
abcdefghijklmnopqrstuvwxyz1234567890
How razorback-jumping frogs can level!

Scrapart 48

One Style

SketchDemo 24

One Style

ABCDEGHIJKLMNOPQRSTUVWXYZ
abcdfghijklmnopqstuvwxyz123456

Style 14

One Style

ABCDEFGHIJKLMNOPQRSTUVWXYZ
abcdefghijklmnopqrstuvwxyz1234567890
How razorback—jumping frogs can level!

ToulouseLautrec 12

One Style

ABCDEFGHIJKLMNOPQRSTUVWXYZ
abcdefghijklmnopqrstuvwxyz1234567890
How razorbackumping frogs can level!

Cuneifont 12, 14, 18, 24

One Style

ABCDEFGHIJKLMNOPQRSTUVWXYZ
abcdefghijklmnopqrstuvwxyz1234567890
How razorback-jumping frogs can level!

Flintstone 12, 24, 48, 72

One Style

ABCDEFGHIJKLMN
OPQRSTUVWXYZ
1234567890

Kathlita 12

One Style

ABCDEFGHIJKLMNOPQRSTUVWXYZ
abcdefghijklmnopqrstuvwxyz1234567890
How razorback-jumping frogs can level!

Fonts D3

Continued

ModernPrintBold 14, 18, 24 — One Style

$25 gets the rest BCDEFGHIJKLMNOPQRS $25 gets the rest UVWXYZ

abcd $25 gets the rest fghijklmnopqr $25 gets the rest tuvwxyz1234567890

How razorback-jumping fog $25 gets the rest can l $25 gets the rest v $25 gets the rest l!

SansSerif 18 — One Style

ABCDEFGHIJKLMNOPQRSTUVWXYZ

abcdefghijklmnopqrstuvwxyz1234567890

How razorback-jumping frogs can level!

UtilSamp 36 — One Style

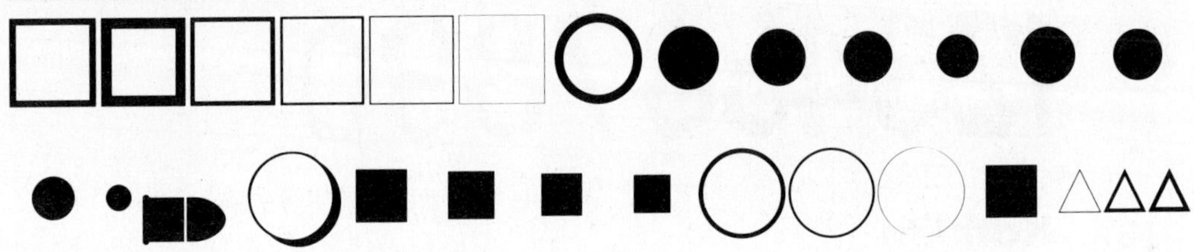

Fonts D4

Type 3

Canaith 14, 24 — One Style

ABCDEFGHIJKLMNOPQRSTUVWXYZ
abcdefghijklmnopqrstuvwxyz123456
How razorback-jumping frogs can level!

ChiTown 12 — One Style

ABCDEFGHIJKLMNOPQRSTUVWXYZ
abcdefghijklmnopqrstuvwxyz1234567890
How razorback-jumping frogs can level!

HelveticaFractions 12, 24, 48 — One Style

$\frac{1}{1}$ $\frac{1}{2}$ $\frac{1}{3}$ $\frac{1}{4}$ $\frac{1}{5}$ $\frac{1}{6}$ $\frac{1}{7}$ $\frac{1}{8}$ $\frac{1}{9}$ $\frac{0}{0}$ $\frac{2}{2}$ $\frac{2}{3}$ $\frac{3}{4}$ $\frac{2}{5}$ $\frac{5}{6}$

$\frac{2}{7}$ $\frac{3}{8}$ $\frac{2}{9}$ $\frac{0}{1}$ $\frac{4}{7}$ $\frac{7}{8}$ $\frac{5}{9}$ $\frac{0}{3}$ $\frac{7}{9}$ $\frac{5}{7}$ $\frac{8}{9}$ $\frac{6}{7}$

Type 3 Fonts

Fonts D4

Continued

ModernPrintBold 14, 18, 24

One Style

$25 gets the rest BCDEFGHIJKLMNOPQRS $25 gets the rest UVWXYZ

abcd $25 gets the rest fghijklmnopqr $25 gets the rest tuvwxyz1234567890

How razorback-jumping fog $25 gets the rest can l $25 gets the rest v $25 gets the rest l!

Type 3 Fonts

*OCR 12

One Style

ABCDEFGHIJKLMNOPQRSTUVWXYZ1234567890

HOW RAZORBACK-JUMPING FROGS CAN LEVEL

Patriot 36

One Style

ABCDEFGHIJKLMN

AB C DEFG H I J K L M NOP Q R

1234567890

Rodchenko 10,12, 14, 18, 24, 36

One Style

ABCDEFGHIJKLMNOPQRSTUVWXYZ

abcdefghijklmnopqrstuvwxyz1234567890

How razorback-jumping frogs can level!

Thomas 9, 10, 12, 14, 28, 36

One Style

ABCDEFGHIJKLMNOPQRSTU
abcdefghijklmnopqrstuvwxyz123
How razorback-jumping frogs can!

TiffanyHG 14, 18, 24

One Style

ABCDEFGHIJKLMNOPQRSTUVWXYZ
abcdefghijklmnopqrstuvwxyz1234567890
How razorback-jumping frogs can level!

Trondheim 9, 12, 18, 24

One Style

Fonts D5

Type 3

Type 3 Fonts

Alison 9, 12, 14, 18, 20, 24, 36, 48 — One Style

ABCDEFGHIJKLMNOPQRSTU

abcdefghijklmnopqrstuvwxyz1234567890

How razorback-jumping frogs can level!

ElGarrett 10, 12, 18, 24, 36, 42, 48, 60 — One Style

ABCDEFGHIJKLMNOPQRSTUV

abcdefghijklmnopqrstuvwxyz1234567890

How razorback-jumping frogs can level!

FutaruBoldCond 12, 18, 24, 36, 48 — One Style

ABCDEFGHIJKLMNOPQRSTUVWXYZ

abcdefghijklmnopqrstuvwxyz1234567890

How razorback-jumping frogs can level!

JacksonvilleOldStyle 12, 24

One Style

ABCDEFGHIJKLMNOPQRSTUVWXYZ
abcdefghijklmnopqrstuvwxyz 1234567
How razorback-jumping frogs can level!

Fonts D6

Type 3

Type 3 Fonts

Author 18, 24, 48

One Style

ABCDEFGHIJKLMNOPQRST

abcdefghijklmnopqrstuvwxyz123456789

How razorback-jumping frogs can level!

BlackForest 18, 24

One Style

ABCDEFGHIJKLMNOPQRSTUVW

abcdefghijklmnopqrstuvwxyz1234567890

How razorback-jumping frogs can level!

ElzevierCaps 48, 72, 96

One Style

ABCDEFGHIJ

KLMNOPQRS

TUVWXYZ

EncycloFont 10, 12, 14, 18, 24 One Style

GreekAntiParticles 9, 10, 12, 18, 20, 24 One Style

ΑΒΧΔΕΦΓΗΙϑΚΛΜΝΟΠΘΡΣΤΥςΩΞ
ΨΖαβχδεφγηιφκλμνοπθρστυϖωξψζ

IglooLaser 24, 48, 96 One Style

ABCDEFGHIJKLMNOPQRSTUVWXYZ
1234567890

Middleton 24 One Style

ABCDEFGHIJKLMNOPQRSTUVWXYZ
abcdefghijklmnopqrstuvwxyz1234567890
How razorback-jumping frogs can level!

Princeton 10, 12, 20, 24 One Style

ABCDEFGHIJKLMNOPQRSTUVWXYZ
abcdefghijklmnopqrstuvwxyz123456
How razorback-jumping frogs can!!

Fonts D7

Type 3

Cornwall 24 — One Style

ABCDEFGHIJKLMNOPQRSTUVWXYZ

abcdefghijklmnopqrstuvwxyz1234567890

How razorback-jumping frogs can level!

Heidelberg 12, 14, 18, 24, 28, 36 — One Style

ABCDEFGHIJKLMNOPQRSTUVWXY

abcdefghijklmnopqrstuvwxyz1234567890

How razorback-jumping frogs can level!

ModernPrintBold 14, 18, 24 — One Style

$25 gets the rest BCDEFGHIJKLMNOPQRS $25 gets the rest UVWXYZ

abcd $25 gets the rest fghijklmnopqr $25 gets the rest tuvwxyz1234567890

How razorback-jumping frog $25 gets the rest can l $25 gets the rest v $25 gets the rest l!

PostCrypt 24, 48, 72, 96 — One Style

ABCDEFGHIJKL

MNOPQRSTUVW

XYZ123456789

Fonts D8

Type 3

Type 3 Fonts

MunchnerCapsAtoM 72, 96, 120

One Style

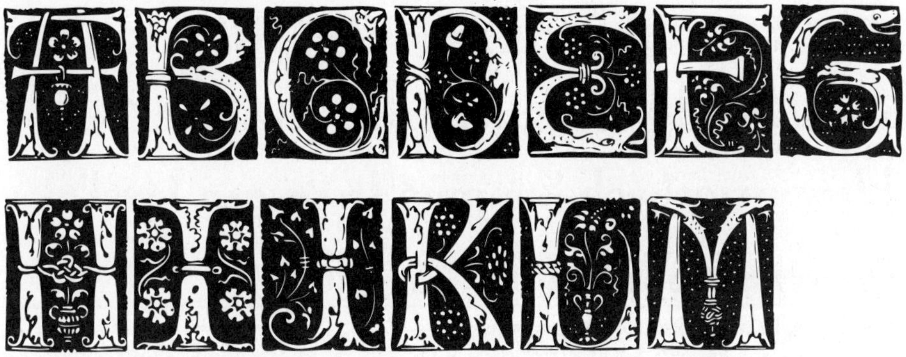

MunchnerCapsNtoZ 72, 96, 120

One Style

WoodcutDropCaps 48, 72, 96

One Style

WoodcutDropCapsTwo 48, 72, 96

One Style

Fonts D9

Type 3

Type 3 Fonts

GraphicLight 12, 13, 14, 18, 24, 48 — One Style

ABCDEFGHIJKLMNOPQRSTUVWXYZ
abcdefghijklmnopqrstuvwxyz1234567890
How razorback-jumping frogs can level!

LarcombeCapsAtoI 72, 96, 120 — One Style

LarcombeCapsJtoR 72, 96, 120 — One Style

LarcombeCapsStoZ 72, 96, 120 — One Style

Chasline 24

One Style

ABCDEFGHIJKLMNOPQRSTUVWXYZ

abcdefghijklmnopqrstuvwxyz1234567890

How razorback-jumping frogs can level!

StymieLight 12, 24

One Style

ABCDEFGHIJKLMNOPQRSTUVWXYZ

abcdefghijklmnopqrstuvwxyz1234567

How razorback-jumping frogs can level!

Fonts E1

Bitmap

Aldous 12, 18, 24, 36
One Style

ABCDEFGHIJKLMNOPQRSTUVWXYZ
1234567890

Alice 12
One Style

ABCDEFGHIJKLMNOPQRSTUVWXYZ
abcdefghijklmnopqrstuvwxyz1234567890
How razorback-jumping frogs can level!

Art Deco 9, 12, 18, 24, 36
One Style

ABCDEFGHIJKLMNOPQRSTUVWXY
abcdefghijklmnopqrstuvwxyz1234
How razorback–jumping frogs can!

Basel 48
One Style

ABCDEFGHIJK
abcdefghijkml23

Beverly Hills 9, 10, 12, 14, 18, 20, 24, 28, 36, 48
One Style

ABCDEFGHIJKLMNOPQRSTUVWXYZ
abcdefghijklmnopqrstuvwxyz123456789
How razorback-jumping frogs can level!

Bitmap Fonts

Beverly Hills Large 36, 72 — One Style

ABCDEFGHIJKLMNOP
abcdefghijklmnopqr123

Black Shadow 48 — One Style

ABCDEFGHIJKLMNOPQRSTUV
abcdefghijklmnopqrstuv123

Bubbles 14, 24 — One Style

ABCDEFGHIJKLMNOPQRSTUVWXYZ
abcdefghijklmnopqrstuvwxyz1234567890
How razorback-jumping frogs can level!

Camelot 12, 24 — One Style

ABCDEFGHIJKLMNOPQRST
abcdefghijklmnopqrstuvwxyz123456
How razorback-jumping frogs can level!

Candy 24 — One Style

ABCDEFGHIJKLMNOPQRSTU
abcdefghijklmnopqrs123
How razorback-jumping!

Fonts E1

Continued

Cartoon 12

One Style

ABCDEFGHIJKLMNOPQRSTUVWXYZ
abcdefghijklmnopqrstuvwxyz1234567890
How razorback-jumping frogs can level!

Cavanaugh 18, 36

One Style

ABCDEFGHIJKLMNOPQRST
abcdefghijklmnopqrstuvwxyz1234567890
How razorback-jumping frogs can level!

Centura 9, 12, 18, 24, 36

One Style

ABCDEFGHIJKLMNOPQRSTUVWX
abcdefghijklmnopqrstuvwxyz123
How razorback-jumping frogs!

Circus 12, 18, 24, 36

One Style

ABCDEFGHIJKLMNOPQRSTUVWXYZ
abcdefghijklmnopqrstuvwxyz1234567890
How razorback-jumping frogs can level!

Fonts E1

Continued

Bitmap Fonts

Clinton 24 — One Style

Coptic 10, 20 — One Style

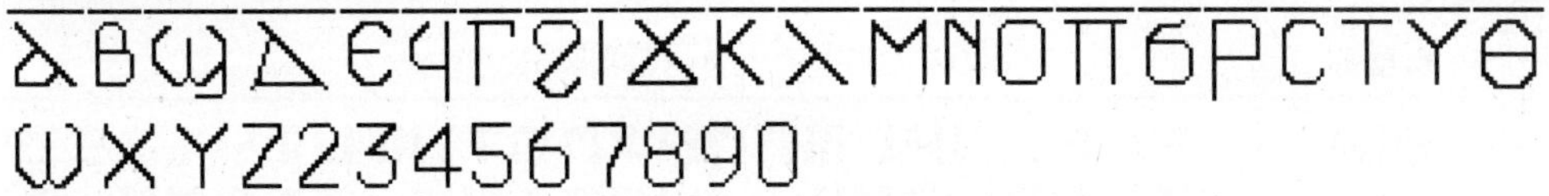

Cream 10, 12 — One Style

ABCDEFGHIJKLMNOPQRSTUVWXYZ
abcdefghijklmnopqrstuvwxyz1234567890
How razorback-jumping frogs can level!

Cursive 12 — One Style

ABCDEFGHIJKLMNOPQRSTUVWXYZ
abcdefghijklmnopqrstuvwxyz1234567890
How razorback-jumping frogs can level!

Dali 24 — One Style

ABCDEFGHIJKLMNOPQRSTUVWXY
abcdefghijklmnopqrstuvwxyz1234567
How razorback-jumping frogs can level!

Fonts E1

Continued

Demotic 20 — One Style

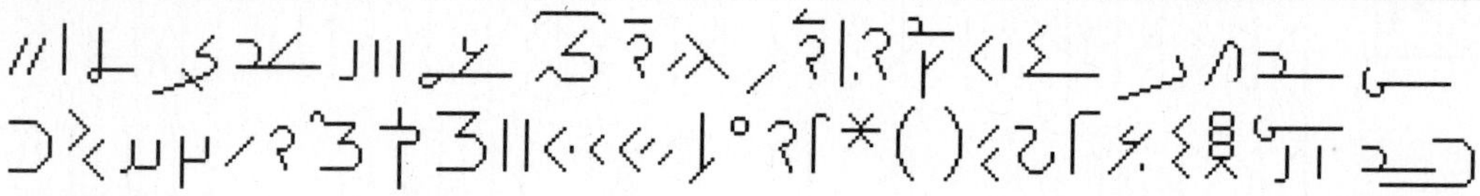

Elvish 12 — One Style

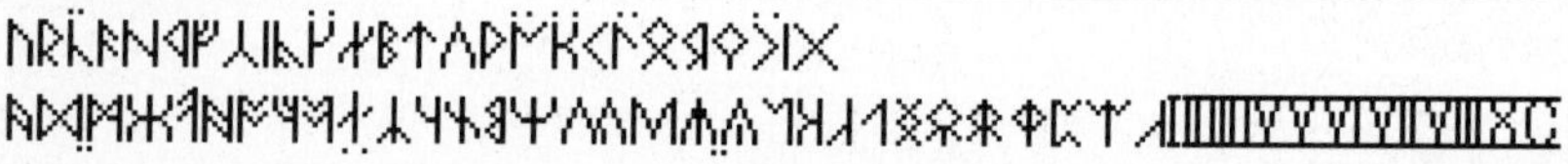

Eon 12 — One Style

abcdefghijklmnopqrstuvwxyz123456
HOW razorback-jumping frogs can!

Epsilon 12, 18, 24 — One Style

ABCDEFGHIJKLMNOPQRSTUVW
abcdefghijklmnopqrstuvwx123
How razorback-jumping frogs!

Fancy caps 72 — One Style

ABCDE
FGHIJK
1234567

Bitmap Fonts

Fargo 48

One Style

ABCDEFGHIJKLMNOPQRSTUV

abcdefghijklmnopqrstuv123

Finney 12, 24

One Style

ABCDEFGHIJKLMNOPQRSTUV

ABCDEFGHIJKLMNOPQRST123

Fletcher 12, 18, 24

One Style

ABCDEFGHIJKLMNOPQRSTUVW

abcdefghijklmnopqrstuv123

How razorback-jumping frogs!

Godfrey 12, 24

One Style

ABCDEFGHIJKLMNOPQRSTUVWXY

abcdefghijklmnopqrstuvwx123

How razorback-jumping frogs!

Fonts E1

Continued

Hollywood Thin 24

One Style

ABCDEFGHIJKLM
NOPQRSTUVWXYZ

Houston 36

One Style

ABCDEFGHIJKLMNOPQR
abcdefghijklmnopqrst123
How razorback-jumping!

Infocom 36

One Style

acehkmnruvwz
ABCDEFGHIJKLM123

Isengard 18

One Style

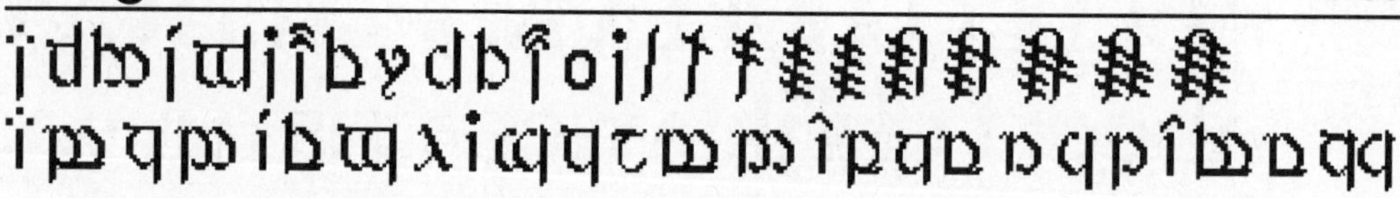

Memphis 24

One Style

ABCDEFGHIJKLMNOPQRSTUVWXYZ
abcdefghijklmnopqrstuvwxyz1234567890
How razorback–jumping frogs can level!

Obliqe 12, 18
One Style

ABCDEFGHIJKLMNOPQRSTUVWXYZ
abcdefghijklmnopqrstuvwxyz1234567890
How razorback-jumping frogs can level!

Padova 12, 24
One Style

ABCDEFGHIJKLMNOPQRS
abcdefghijklmnopqrstu123
How razorback-jumping!

Palo Alto 36
One Style

ABCDEFGHIJKLMNOPQ
abcdefghijklmnopq123

Premiere 24
One Style

ABCDEFGHIJKLMNOPQRSTUVW
abcdefghijklmnopqrstuvwx123
How razorback-jumping frogs!

Ravenna 12, 24
One Style

ABCDEFGHIJKLMNOPQRSTUVW
abcdefghijklmnopqrstuvwxy123
How razorback-jumping frogs!

Fonts E1

Continued

Bitmap Fonts

Rivendell 14

One Style

Spokane 18

One Style

ABCDEFGHIJKLMNOPQRSTUVWXYZ
abcdefghijklmnopqrstuvwxyz1234
How razorback-jumping frogs can!

Thomas 10, 12, 14, 24

One Style

ABCDEFGHIJKLMNOPQRSTUVWXYZ
abcdefghijklmnopqrstuvwxyz1234567890
How razorback-jumping frogs can level!

Tile 18, 24

One Style

ABCDEFGHIJKLMNOPQRSTUVW
abcdefghijklmnopqrstuvwxy123
How razorback-jumping frogs!

Tombstone 24

One Style

ABCDEFGHIJKLMNOPQR
STUVWXYZ1234567890

Ultra 24

One Style

ABCDEFGHIJKLMNOPQRSTUV
abcdefghijklmnopqrstuvwx123
How razorback-jumping frogs!

Venice 14, 24, 28

One Style

ABCDEFGHIJKLMNOPQRSTUVW
abcdefghijklmnopqrstuvwxy123
How razorback-jumping frogs!

White Shadow 48

One Style

ABCDEFGHIJKLMNOPQRSTU
abcdefghijklmnopqrstu123

Fonts E2

Bitmap

Alexis 24 — One Style

ABCDEFGHIJKLMNOPQRSTUVWXY
abcdefghijklmnopqrstuvwxyz1234567
How razorback-jumping frogs can level!

Armonk 12, 24 — One Style

ABCDEFGHIJKLMNOPQRSTUVWXY
abcdefghijklmnopqrstuvwy123
How razorback-jumping!

Bauhaus 10, 20 — One Style

ABCDEFGHIJKLMNOPQRSTUVWXYZ
abcdefghijklmnopqrstuvwxyz12345
How razorback-jumping frogs can!

Boxie 10 — One Style

ABCDEFGHIJKLMNOPQRSTUVWXYZ
abcdefghijklmnopqrstuvwxyz1234567890
How razorback-jumping frogs can level!

Brennero 12, 24 — One Style

ABCDEFGHIJKLMNOPQRST
abcdefghijklmnopqrst123
How razorback-jumping!

Broadway 24 — One Style

ABCDEFGHIJKLMNOPQRSTU
abcdefghijklmnopqrs123
How razorback-jumping!

Bubbles 14, 24 — One Style

ABCDEFGHIJKLMNO
abcdefghijklmnopqrstuv123
How razorback-jumping!

Cavanaugh 18, 36 — One Style

ABCDEFGHIJKLMNOPQRSTUVWXYZ
abcdefghijklmnopqrstuvwxyz1234567
How razorback-jumping frogs can!

Century 18, 24 — One Style

ABCDEFGHIJKLMNOPQRSTUVWX
abcdefghijklmnopqrstuvwxyz123
How razorback-jumping frogs!

Chancery 24 — One Style

ABCDEFGHIJKLMNOPQRS
abcdefghijklmnopqrstuvwxyz123456
How razorback-jumping frogs can!

Fonts E2

Continued

Bitmap Fonts

Cologne 10, 20 — One Style

ABCDEFGHIJKLMNOPQRSTUVWXYZ
abcdefghijklmnopqrstuvwxyz123456
How razorback-jumping frogs can!

Detroit 24 — One Style

ABCDEFGHIJKLMN
OPQRSTUVWXYZ

Dots 24 — One Style

abcdefghijklmnopqrstuvw
xyz1234567890
how razorback-jumping!

Frazier 9, 12, 18, 24 — One Style

ABCDEFGHIJKLMNOPQRSTUVW
abcdefghijklmnopqrstuv123
How razorback-jumping!

Fonts E2

Continued

Bitmap Fonts

Hollywood 18 — One Style

ABCDEFGHIJKLMNOPQRSTUVWX
abcdefghijklmnopqrstuvwxyz123
How razorback-jumping frogs!

Hood River 12 — One Style

ABCDEFGHIJKLMNOPQRSTUVWXYZ
abcdefghijklmnopqrstuvwxyz1234567890
How razorback-jumping frogs can level!

International 12, 24 — One Style

Jones 18 — One Style

ABCDEFGHIJKLMNOPQRSTUVWXYZ
abcdefghijklmnopqrstuvwxyz1234567
How razorback-jumping frogs can!

Fonts E2

Continued

Kalona 9 — One Style

ABCDEFGHIJKLMNOPQRSTUVWXYZ
ABCDEFGHIJKLMNOPQRSTUVWXYZ1234567890
HOW RAZORBACK-JUMPING FROGS CAN LEVEL!

Köln 10, 20 — One Style

ABCDEFGHIJKLMNOPQRSTUVWXYZ
abcdefghijklmnopqrstuvwxyz1234567
How razorback-jumping frogs can!

kroY weN 12 — One Style

ABCDEFGHIJKLMNOPQRSTUV WXYZ
abcdefghijklmnopqrstuvwxyz 1234567890
How razorback+jumping frogs can level!

L.A. 12, 24 — One Style

ABCDEFGHIJKLMNOPQRSTUV
abcdefghijklmnopqrstuv123
How razorback-jumping!

Lambda 18, 24 — One Style

ABCDEFGHIJKLMN
abcdefghijklmnopq123
How razorback-jumping!

Bitmap Fonts

Continued

LED 24

One Style

A B C D E F G H I J K L M N O P Q

R S T U V W X Y Z 1 2 3 4 5 6 7

Lilliput 9, 18

One Style

ABCDEFGHIJKLMNOPQRSTUVWXYZ

abcdefghijklmnopqrstuvwxyz 1234567890

How razorback-jumping frogs can level!

Long Island 12, 18

One Style

A B C D E F G H I J K L M N O P Q R S T U V W X

a b c d e f g h i j k l m n o p q r s t u v w x Y 1 2 3

How razorback-jumping frogs!

Madrid 18, 24

One Style

ABCDEFGHIJKLMNOPQRSTUVWXYZ

abcdefghijklmnopqrstuvwxyz1234567

How razorback-jumping frogs can!

Fonts E2

Continued

Manhattan 12, 24 — One Style

ABCDEFGHIJKLMNOPQRSTUVWXY
abcdefghijklmnopqrstuvwxyz12345
How razorback-jumping frogs can!

Marie 12 — One Style

ABCDEFGHIJKLMNOPQRSTUVWXYZ
abcdefghijklmnopqrstuvwxyz1234567890
How razorback-jumping frogs can level!

McCloud 36 — One Style

ABCDEFGHIJKLMN
abcdefghijklmnop123
How razorbacks jump!

Microsoft 10 — One Style

ABCDEFGHIJKLMNOPQRSTUVWXYZ
abcdefghijklmnopqrstuvwxyz1234567890
How razorback-jumping frogs can level!

Milano 12, 24 — One Style

ABCDEFGHIJKLMNOPQRST
abcdefghijklmnopqrst123
How razorback-jumping!

NY Nights 12, 24

One Style

ABCDEFGHIJKLMNOPQRSTUVWX
abcdefghijklmnopqrstuvwxy123
How razorback-jumping frogs!

Omega 24

One Style

ABCDEFGHIJKLMNO
abcdefghijklmnopqrs
How razorbacks jump!

Rangers 18

One Style

ABCDEFGHIJKLMNOPQRSTUVWX
ABCDEFGHIJKLMNOPQRSTUVWX123
HOW RAZORBACK-JUMPING FROGS!

Ravenna 12, 24

One Style

ABCDEFGHIJKLMNOPQRSTUVW
abcdefghijklmnopqrstuvwx123
How razorback-jumping frogs!

Fonts E2

Continued

Bitmap Fonts

Rome 18, 36

One Style

ABCDEFGHI JKLMNOPQRSTUVWXYZ
abcdefghi jklmnopqrstuvwxyz1234567890
How razorback-jumping frogs can level!

San Quentin 24

One Style

ABCDEFGHIJKLMNOPQRSTUVWXY
abcdefghijklmnopqrstuvwxyz1234
How razorback-jumping frogs!

Scan 48

One Style

ABCDEFGHIJK
abcdefghijkl23

Script 12, 18

One Style

ABCDEFGHIJKLMNOPQRSTUVWXYZ
abcdefghijklmnopqrstuvwxyz1234567890
How razorback-jumping frogs can level!

Seattle 9, 10, 20

One Style

ABCDEFGHIJKLMNOPQRSTUVWXYZ
abcdefghijklmnopqrstuvwxyz123
How razorback-jumping frogs can!

Shoppe 24

One Style

ABCDEFGHIJKLMNOPQRSTUVW
abcdefghijklmnopqrstuvwx123
How razorback-jumping frogs!

Silicon Val 12

One Style

ABCDEFGHIJKLMNOPQRSTUVWXYZ
abcdefghijklmnopqrstuvwxyz1234567890
How razorback-jumping frogs can level!

Small 9, 10, 18, 20

One Style

ABCDEFGHIJKLMNOPQRSTUVWXYZ
abcdefghijklmnopqrstuvwxyz1234567890
How razorback-jumping frogs can level!

Stencil 12, 24

One Style

ABCDEFGHIJKLMNOPQRSTUVWXYZ

Stiletto 14, 28

One Style

ABCDEFGHIJKLMNOPQRSTUVWXY
abcdefghijklmnopqrstuvwxy123
How razorback-jumping frogs!

Fonts E2

Continued

Tiffany 12, 24 — One Style

ABCDEFGHIJKLMNOPQ
abcdefghijklmnopqrs123
How razorback-jumping!

Tinytown 9 — One Style

ABCDEFGHIJKLMNOPQRSTUVWXYZ
abcdefghijklmnopqrstuvwxyz1234567890
How razorback-jumping frogs can level!

Ultra 12, 14, 24 — One Style

ABCDEFGHIJKLMNOPQRSTUV
abcdefghijklmnopqrstuvw123
How razorback-jumping frogs!

Uncial 18 — One Style

ABCDEFGHIJKLMNOPQRSTUVWXYZ
abcdefghijklmnopqrstuvwxyz1234567890
How razorback-jumping frogs can level!

Vancouver 9, 10, 12, 14, 18, 20, 24 — One Style

ABCDEFGHIJKLMNOPQRSTUV
abcdefghijklmnopqrstuv123
How razorback-jumping!

Wall Street 9, 10, 12, 14, 18, 20, 24, 28, 36 One Style

ABCDEFGHIJKLMNOPQRSTUVWX

abcdefghijklmnopqrstuvwxy123

How razorback-jumping frogs!

Zurich 10, One Style

ABCDEFGHIJKLMNOPQRSTUVWXYZ

abcdefghijklmnopqrstuvwxyz123456

How razorback-jumping frogs can!

Fonts E3

Bitmap

Bitmap Fonts

APL 12, 24 — One Style

α ⊥ ∩ ⌊ ε ⍲ ∇ ∆ ⍳ ∘ ⍞ ⎕ ⍂ ⊤ ○ ⍱ ⍭ ρ ⌈ ⍕ ↓ ∪ ω ⊃ ↑ ⊂

ABCDEFGHIJKLMNOPQRSTUVWX↑123

Austin Econ 9, 10, 12, 18, 20, 24 — One Style

ABCDEFGHIJKLMNOPQRSTUVWX

abcdefghijklmnopqrstuvwx123

αβχδεφγηνVκλμNøπθρστυUω

Babylon 9, 18 — One Style

ABCDEFGHIJKLMNOPQRSTUVWXYZ

ABCDEFGHIJKLMNOPQRSTUVWXYZ1234567890

HOW RAZORBACK-JUMPING FROGS CAN LEVEL!

Camelot2 12, 24 — One Style

ABCDEFGHIJKLMNOPQRST

abcdefghijklmnopqrstuvwxyz123456

How razorback-jumping frogs can level!

ChicMath 9, 12, 18, 24
One Style

ABCDEFGHIJKLMNOPQRSTUVWXYZ
abcdefghijklmnopqrstuvwxyz1234567890
α β ψ δ ■ φ γ θ Π ℓ κ λ μ ℳ ε π χ ρ σ τ ▲ ⇔ ω

Copenhägen 9, 12, 18, 24
One Style

ABCDEFGHIJKLMNOPQRSTUVWXY
abcdefghijklmnopqrstuvwx123
How razorback-jumping frogs!

Dover 8, 10, 12
One Style

ABCDEFGHIJKLMNOPQRSTUVWXYZ
abcdefghijklmnopqrstuvwxyz1234567890
How razorback-jumping frogs can level!

Dover PS 12
One Style

ABCDEFGHIJKLMNOPQRSTUVWXYZ
abcdefghijklmnopqrstuvwxyz1234567890
How razorback-jumping frogs can level!

Eire 12, 24
One Style

ABCDEFGHIJKLMNOP
ABCDEFGHIJKLMNOPQ123
HOW RAZORBACKS JUMP!

Fonts E3

Continued

Elite 12 — One Style

ABCDEFGHIJKLMNOPQRSTUVWXYZ
abcdefghijklmnopqrstuvwxyz1234567890
How razorback-jumping frogs can level!

Fractions 9, 10, 12, 14, 18, 20, 24 — One Style

1/4 1/5 1/6 1/7 1/8 1/9 2/2 Ā Ē Ī Ō Ū Ȳ 5/6 ā b̄ c̄ ē ī ŋ
7/8 5/8 3/7 š ǒ 3/5 ý 4/9 0/2 ǣ ȯ œ̄ 4/5 4/7 5/9 0/3 ě ỳ ǔ ī

Monaco 8, 12 — One Style

ABCDEFGHIJKLMNOPQRSTUVWXYZ
abcdefghijklmnopqrstuvwxyz1234567890
How razorback-jumping frogs can level!

Nordic 12

One Style

ABCDEFGHIJKLMNOPQRSTUVWXYZ
abcdefghijklmnopqrstuvwxyz1234567890

How razorback-jumping frogs can level!

Nordic-f 9, 12, 18

One Style

ABCDEFGHIJKLMNOPQRSTUVWXYZ
abcdefghijklmnopqrstuvwxyz1234567890
How razorback-jumping frogs can level!

Palo Alto 12, 24

One Style

ABCDEFGHIJKLMNOPQRSTUVWXY
abcdefghijklmnopqrstuvwxyz1234
How razorback-jumping frogs can!

Pica 10, 20

One Style

ABCDEFGHIJKLMNOPQRSTUVWXYZ
abcdefghijklmnopqrstuvw123
How razorback-jumping!

Pica2 10

One Style

ABCDEFGHIJKLMNOPQRSTUVWXYZ
abcdefghijklmnopqrstuvwxyz1234567890
How razorback-jumping frogs can level!

Fonts E3

Continued

Script Math 12 — One Style

ABCDEFΓHIJKLMNOPQRΣTUVWXYZ

𝒜ℬ𝒞𝒟ℰℱ𝒢ℋℐ𝒥𝒦ℒℳ𝒩𝒪𝒫𝒬ℛ𝒮𝒯𝒰𝒱𝒲𝒳𝒴𝒵⊂⊃∧◁▷×⊕⊗∩⌐

αβψδεφγ□□Δ□λμ□ωπχρστΘφΛξθζ∃∄∨∀∞∇±∓<>≅≡ιν⇓∴⊎⌐

Troyes 10, 12, 20, 24 — One Style

זטס׳הולדרפסמלךלחןיעכקג3נש

1234567890

Washington DC 9, 12, 18, 24 — One Style

ABCDEFGHIJKLMNOPQRSTUVWX

abcdefghijklmnopqrstu123

How razorback-jumping!

Apple I 18

One Style

ABCDEFGHIJKLMNOPQRSTUVWXYZ
abcdefghijklmnopqrstuvwxyz1234567890
How razorback-jumping frogs can level!

Athens 18

One Style

ABCDEFGHIJKLMNOPQRSTUVWXYZ
abcdefghijklmnopqrstuvwxyz1234567890
How razorback-jumping frogs can level!

Atlantic City 36

One Style

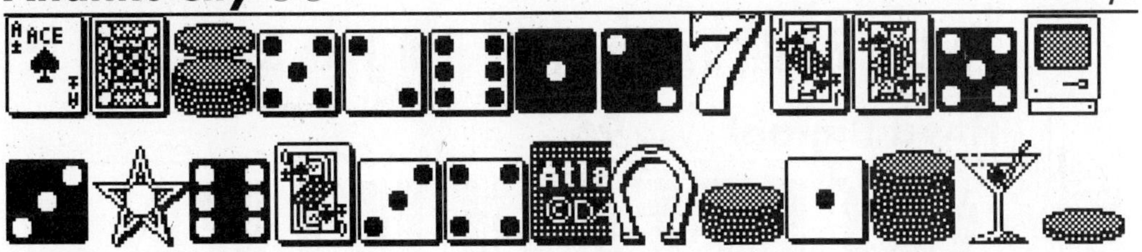

Bolzano 12, 24

One Style

ABCDEFGHIJKLMNOPQRST
abcdefghijklmnopqrst123
How razorback-jumping!

BostonII 9, 10, 12, 14, 18, 20, 24

One Style

ABCDEFGHIJKLMNOPQRSTUVW
abcdefghijklmnopqrstuvw123
How razorback-jumping!

Fonts E4

Continued

BostonII–W 7, 8, 9, 10, 11, 12, 14, 16, 18, 20, 24 — One Style

ABCDEFGHIJKLMNOPQRSTUVWXY
abcdefghijklmnopqrstuvwxyz123
How razorback-jumping frogs!

Bugatti 9, 12, 18, 24 — One Style

ABCDEFGHIJKLMNOPQRSTUVWXYZ
abcdefghijklmnopqrstuvwxyz1234567890
How razorback-jumping frogs can level!

Hlwd Bigfoot 48, 96 — One Style

ABCDEFGHIJKLMN
OPQRSTUVWXYZ

Lake Geneva 9, 10, 12, 14, 18, 20, 24 — One Style

1/4 1/5 1/6 1/7 1/8 1/9 2/2 Ā Ē Ī Ō Ū Ȳ 5/6 ā b̄ c̄ ē ī ŋ̄ 7/8
5/8 3/7 Š Ǒ 3/5 4/9 ý 0/2 ǣ o œ̄ 4/5 4/7 5/9 0/3 ě ỳ ǔ ǐ

Linear B 12, 24

One Style

MicroBoston 12, 24

One Style

ABCDEFGHIJKLMNOPQRSTUVWXYZ

ABCDEFGHIJKLMNOPQRSTUVWXYZ1234567890

HOW RAZORBACK-JUMPING FROGS CAN LEVEL!

MiniBoston 12, 24

One Style

ABCDEFGHIJKLMNOPQRSTUVWXYZ

abcdefghijklmnopqrstuvwxyz1234567890

How razorback-jumping frogs can!

Minneapolis 18

One Style

ABCDEFGHIJKLMNOPQRSTUVWXYZ

abcdefghijklmnopqrstuvwxyz1234567890

How razorback-jumping frogs can level!

Old Church Slavonic 12

One Style

АБЧДЄФГЭИЖКЛМНОПЯРСТУВШХЩЗ

абчдєфгэіжклмнопѩрстоу вшх щз1234567890

Зоw разорбаук-жоумпінг фрогс уан левел!

Fonts E4

Continued

Phoenix 12, 14 — One Style

ABCDEFGHIJKLMNOPQRSTUVWXYZ
abcdefghijklmnopqrstuvwxyz1234567890
How razorback-jumping frogs can level!

Playbill 62, 124 — One Style

ABCDEFGHIJKLMNOPQRS
abcdefghijklmnopqrstu123

Pompeii 12, 24, 48 — One Style

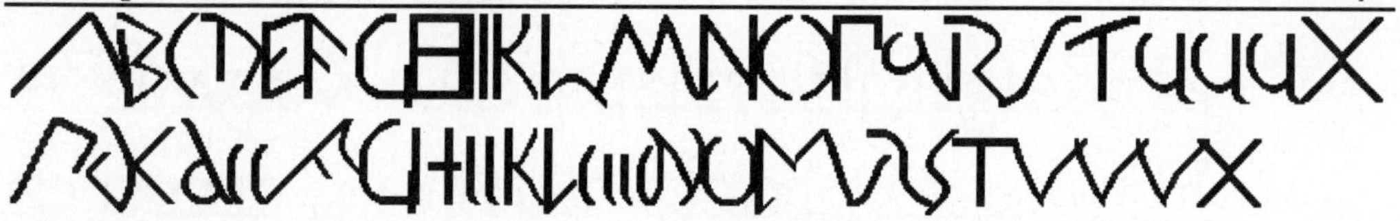

Sierra 12, 24 — One Style

ABCDEFGHIJKLMNOPQRSTUVW
abcdefghijklmnopqrstuv123
How razorback-jumping!

Torino 12, 24 — One Style

ABCDEFGHIJKLMNOPQRST
abcdefghijklmnopqrst123
How razorback-jumping!

Toronto 9 — One Style

ABCDEFGHIJKLMNOPQRSTUVWXYZ
abcdefghijklmnopqrstuvwxyz1234567890
How razorback-jumping frogs can level!

TorontoFix 9 — One Style

ABCDEFGHIJKLMNOPQRSTUVWXYZ
abcdefghijklmnopqrstuvwxyz1234567890

How razorback-jumping frogs can level!

Tucson 10 — One Style

ABCDEFGHIJKLMNOPQRSTUVWXYZ
abcdefghijklmnopqrstuvwxyz1234567890
How razorback-jumping frogs can level!

Versal 18, 36, 72 — One Style

ABCDEFGHIJKLMNOPQR
RSTUVWXYZ

Fonts E4

Continued

Vienna 18 One Style

ABCDEFGHIJKLMNOPQRSTUVWXYZ
abcdefghijklmnopqrstuvwxyz1234567890
How razorback-jumping frogs can level!

Wartburg 18, 36 One Style

ABCDEFGHIJKLMNOPQRSTUVWXYZ
abcdefghijklmnopqrstuvwxyz1234567890
How razorback-jumping frogs can level!

Neshota **8, 9, 10, 12, 14, 16, 18, 20, 24, 27, 28, 30, 32, 36, 40, 42, 48, 54, 56, 60, 64, 72**

One Style

ABCDEFGHIJKLMNOPQRSTUVWXYZ
abcdefghijklmnopqrstuvwxyz1234
How razorback-jumping frogs can!

Fonts E6

Bitmap

Bitmap Fonts

Clairvaux 9, 10, 12, 14, 18, 20, 24, 28, 36, 40, 48, 72 One Style

ABCDEFGHIJKLMNOPQRSTUVWXYZ
abcdefghijklmnopqrstuvwxyz1234567890
How razorback-jumping frogs can level!

Clairvaux Caps 18, 20, 24, 36, 40, 48, 72 One Style

ABCDEFGHIJKLMNOPQ
RSTUVWXYZ1234567890

York 9, 10, 12, 14, 18, 20, 24, 28, 36, 40, 48, 72 One Style

ABCDEFGHIJKLMNOPQRSTUVWXYZ
abcdefghijklmnopqrstuvwxyz1234567890
How razorback-jumping frogs can level!

York Caps 18, 20, 24, 36, 40, 48, 72 One Style

ABCDEFGHIJKLMNOPQRS
TUVWXYZ1234567890

5th Ave-Bold 72

One Style

BCbcl

Band Wagon 72

One Style

BCDFl

School Marm 126

One Style

BCbcl

Wanted 106

One Style

BCDFGH!

Fonts E8

Bitmap

Bitmap Fonts

Amdahl 18, 36 — One Style

abcdefghijklmnop
qrstuvwxyz1234

APPLE ICONS 14 — One Style

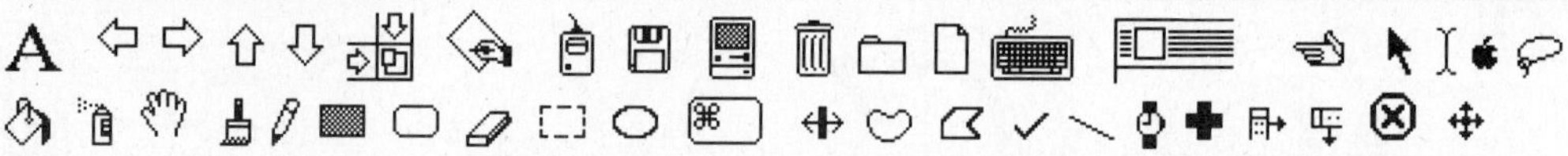

Beneventan 9, 12, 18, 24 — One Style

ABCDEFGHIJLMNOPQRSTUVWX
abcdefghiklmnopqrstuvwxyz

Clairvaux 27, 30, 36 — One Style

ABCDEFGHIJKLMNOPQRSTU
abcdefghijklmnopqrstuvwx123
How razorback-jumping frogs!

Dragon 24 — One Style

ABCDEFGHIJKLMNOPQRSTUVWX
abcdefghijklmnopqrstuvwx123
How razorback-jumping frogs!

Fonts E8

Continued

Lamoni 9, 18, 24, 36, 48, 54, 60, 72, 108 — One Style

ABCDEFGHIJKLMNOPQR

STUVWXYZ1234567890

Meranda 12, 14, 18, 24, 28, 36 — One Style

ABCDEFGHIJKLMNOPQRSTUVWXYZ
abcdefghijklmnopqrstuvwxyz123
How razorback-jumping frogs!

Muscatine 9 — One Style

ABCDEFGHIJKLMNOPQRSTUVWXYZ
abcdefghijklmnopqrstuvwxyz1234567890
How razorback-jumping frogs can level!

NASA 24, 48 — One Style

ABCDEFGHIJKLMNOPQ
ABCDEFGHIJKLMNOPQRSTUVWXYZ123
HOW RAZORBACK–JUMPING FROGS!

Newton 9 — One Style

ABCDEFGHIJKLMNOPQRSTUVWXYZ
abcdefghijklmnopqrstuvwxyz1234567890
How razorback-jumping frogs can level!

Fonts E8

Continued

Oregon 10, 12, 14 — One Style

ABCDEFGHIJKLMNOPQRSTUVWXYZ
abcdefghijklmnopqrstuvwxyz1234567890
How razorback-jumping frogs can level!

Oregonclose 9, 10, 12, 18, 24 — One Style

ABCDEFGHIJKLMNOPQRSTUVWXYZ
abcdefghijklmnopqrstuvwxyz1234567890
How razorback-jumping frogs can level!

Orygun 9, 12, 18, 24 — One Style

ABCDEFGHIJKLMNOPQRSTUVW
abcdefghijklmnopqrstuvw123
How razorback-jumping frogs!

Ouragon 12, 18, 24 — One Style

ABCDEFGHIJKLMNOPQRSTUVWXYZ
abcdefghijklmnopqrstuvwxyz1234567890
How razorback-jumping frogs can level!

Strike Easy 12, 24 — One Style

~~ABCDEFGHIJKLMNOPQRSTUV~~
~~abcdefghijklmnopqrst123~~
~~How razorback-jumping!~~

York 27, 30, 36 — One Style

ABCDEFGHIJKLMNOPQRSTUV
abcdefghijklmnopqrstuV123
How razorback-jumping!

Fonts F1

Symbols

Atlantic City 36 — One Style

BillsDingbats 30 — One Style

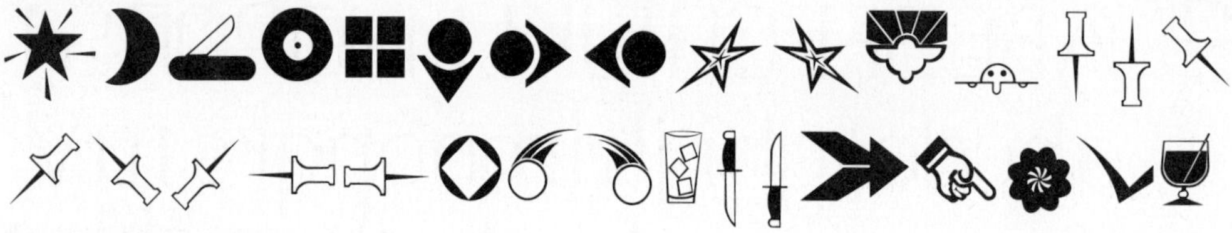

Braille.eng 24 — One Style

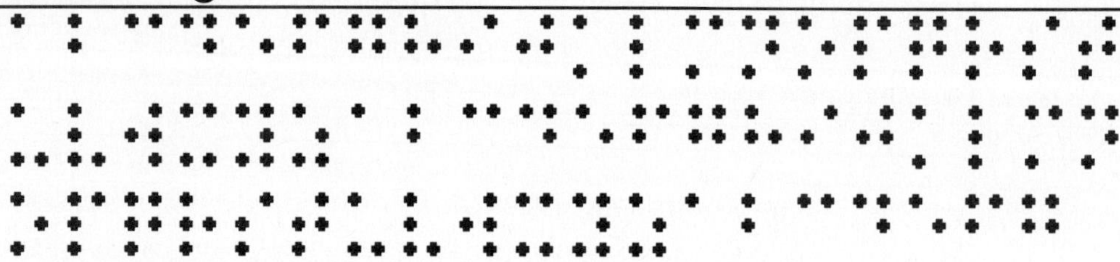

Doodiddles 12, 14, 24 — One Style

Gibson 24 — One Style

Icon 12

One Style

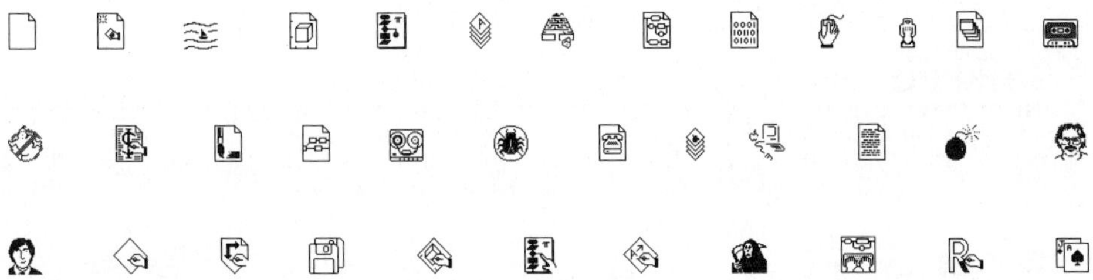

International 36

One Style

Las Vegas 36

One Style

Miscpix 24

One Style

Mobile 18

One Style

Fonts F1

Continued

Poker 20 — One Style

A♣◇♡JKQ♠103456789

Taliesin 18 — One Style

Symbols Fonts

Toyland1 36 — One Style

Toyland2 36 — One Style

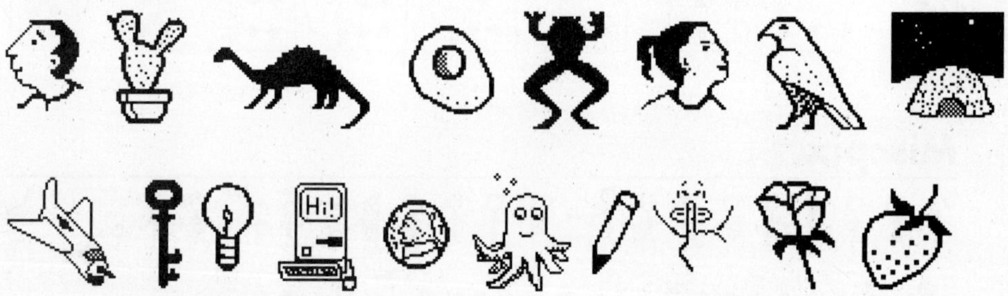

VBraille.eng 24 — One Style

ABCDEFGHIJKLMNOPQRST

abcdefghijklmnopqr123

How razorbacks jump!

Abu Dhabi 24

One Style

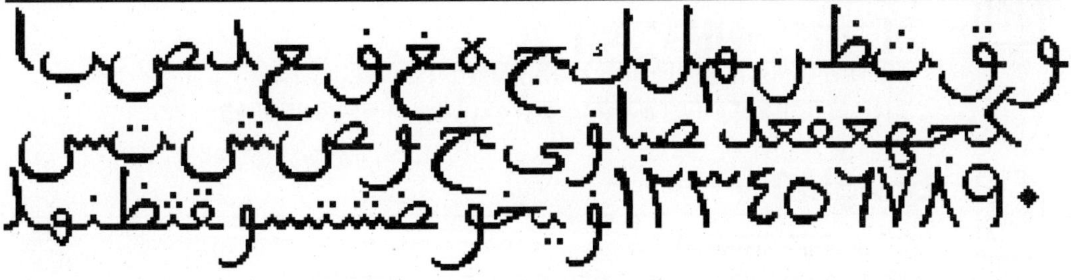

Arabic 12

One Style

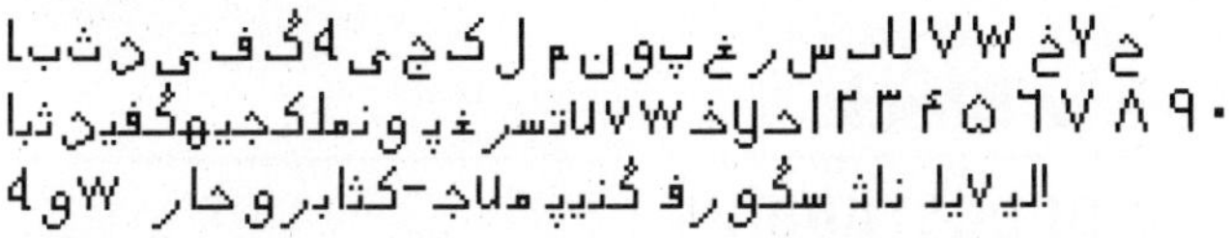

Bangkok 12, 24

One Style

ฤฉฏฎโฌ๎ฌ ษ๋ศ์ฯญฑฆธ๊อ

ฟแกำด้เร่าสทีนยๆพหะือไปัผภฤุคตจ

๎นไ พฟผนพิฟแาขี่ทยรีเ คพนเห แฟี สำอำส

bangla 12

One Style

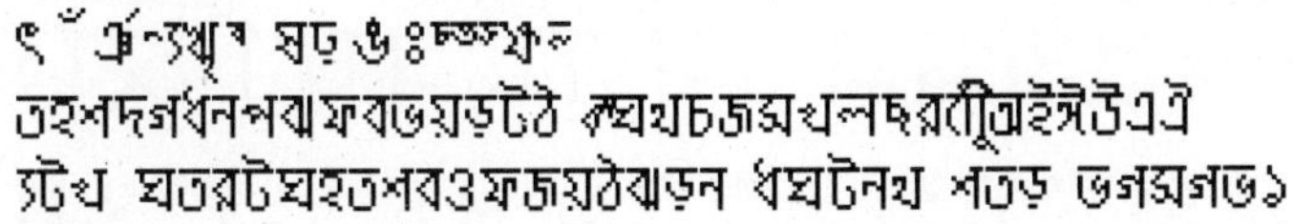

BANGLA V1.1 12

One Style

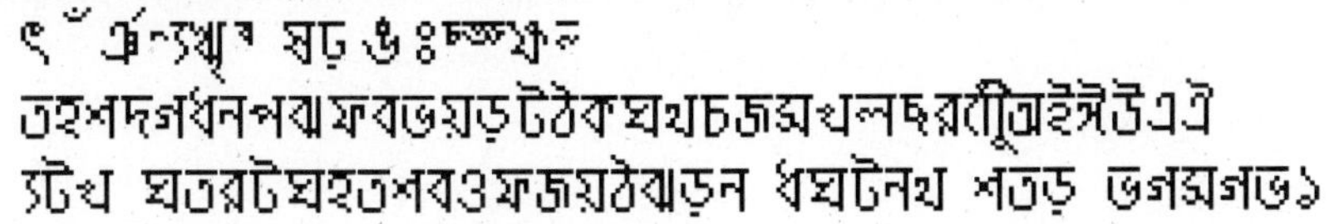

Fonts G1

Continued

bangla2 12
One Style

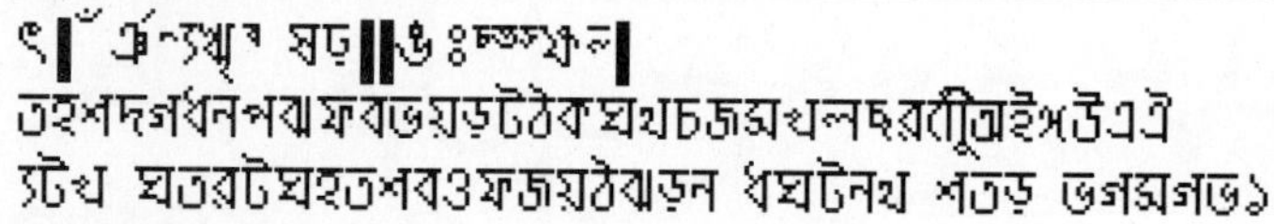

bangla3 12
One Style

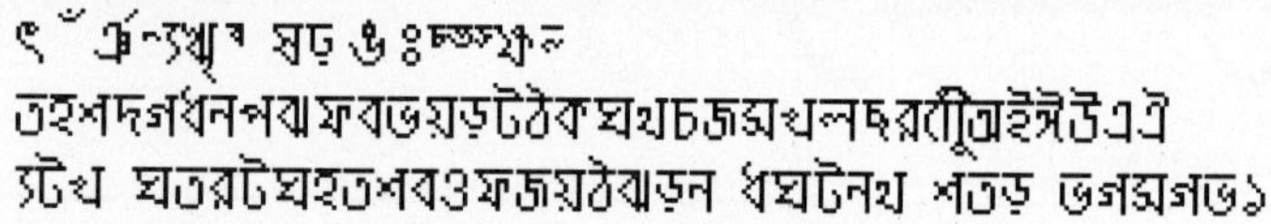

Chicago w Hebrew Block 12
One Style

ABCDEFGHIJKLMNOPQRSTUVWXYZ
abcdefghijklmnopqrstuvwxyz1234567890
How razorback-jumping frogs can level!

Cyril 12
One Style

А Б Ц Д Е Ф Г Ч И Ж К Л М Н О П Ё Р С Т У В Ш Х Ю З
а б ц д е ф г ч и ж к л м н о п ё р с т у в ш х ю з 1 2 3 4 5 6 7 8 9 0
Ч о ш р а з о р б а ц к - ж у м п и н г ф р о г с ц а н л е в е л !

Devanagari 24
One Style

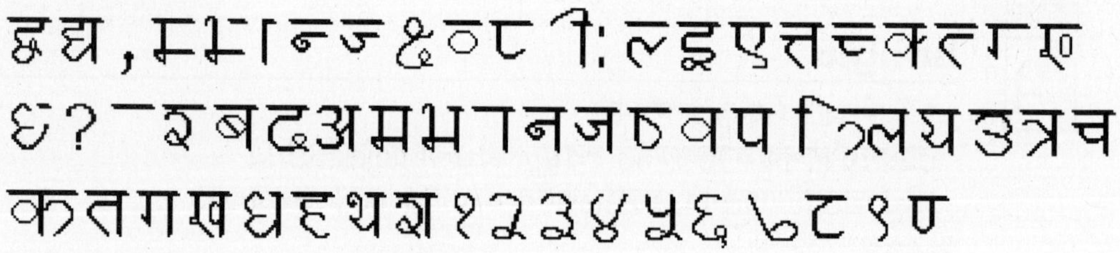

Foreign Fonts

Foreign Fonts

Gdansk 9, 12, 14, 18, 24 — One Style

ABCDEFGHIJKLMNOPQRSTUVWXYZ
abcdefghijklmnopqrstuvwxyz123
How razorback-jumping frogs can

Geneva w Hebrew Stick 9, 12, 18, 24 — One Style

ABCDEFGHIJKLMNOPQRSTUVWXYZ
abcdefghijklmnopqrstuvwxyz1234567890
How razorback-jumping frogs can level!

Greek 10, 20 — One Style

ABCΔEFΓHIΘKΛMNOΠΦPΣTΨXΩΞΥZ
αβcδefγηιθκλμνoπφρστψχωξυς 123456
Hoω ραζoρβαcκ-θψμπινγ fρoγσ cαν!

Greek.A 12, 18 — One Style

ABΨΔEΦΓHIΞKΛMNOΠ PΣTΥΩ XΘZ
αβψδεφγηιξκλμνoπ£ρστυωςχθζ1234567890
Hos ραζoρβαψκ-ξυμπινγ φρoγσ ψαν!

Greek.D 10, 20 — One Style

ABCΔEFΓHIΘKΛMNOΠΦPΣTΨXΩΞΥZ
αβcδefγηιθκλμνoπφρστψχωξυς 123456
Hoω ραζoρβαcκ-θψμπινγ fρoγσ cαν!

Fonts G1

Continued

Foreign Fonts

Greek Doriza 10, 12, 18, 20, 24 — One Style

ΑΒΞΔΕΦΓΗΙΘΚΛΜΝΟΠ□ΡΣΤΥ□ΩΧΨ
αβξδεφγηιθκλμνοπρστυ□ωχψζ1235
Ηοω ραζορβαξκ-θυμπινγ φρογσ!

Greek Sparta 18, 20, 24 — One Style

ΑΒΞΔΕΦΓΗΙΘΚΛΜΝΟΠ□ΡΣΤΥ□ΩΧ
αβξδεφγηιθκλμνοπρστυ□ωχψζ1234
Ηοω ραζορβαξκ-θυμπινγ φρογσ!

Hebrew Cursive 24 — One Style

ABCDEFGHIJKLMNOPQRSTUVWX
abcdefghijklmnopqrstuvwx123
How razorback-jumping frogs!

Hiragana 24 — One Style

がぞずぐよげごやづゆよわびばでどやわぎ
んぢぜゆじだざかそすくうけこなつにぬね
ひはてとあえきおちせいしたさ1234567890

Japanese 12, 24 — One Style

ナモム スネノハツヒフヘリラ
テトサセニソ メシミタマなも

Fonts G1

Continued

Kana 12, 18 — One Style

サトツスクセソマフミムメンヲヘホカケシコヒテキチ
ハタさとつすくせそまふみむめんをへほかけしこひて
きちはたあいうえおなにぬねの

Krakow 9, 10, 12, 14, 18, 20, 24, 36 — One Style

ABCDEFGHIJKLMNOPQRSTUVWXYZ
abcdefghijklmnopqrstuvwxyz1234567890
How razorback-jumping frogs can level§

Leningrad 24 — One Style

АБЦДЕФГХИЖКЛМНОПЧРСТУВ
абцдефгхижклмнопчрстузшй123
Хощ разорбацкэжумпинг фрогс!

Monaco w Hebrew Typewriter 9 — One Style

ABCDEFGHIJKLMNOPQRSTUVWXYZ
abcdefghijklmnopqrstuvwxyz1234567890
How razorback-jumping frogs can level!

Fonts G1

Continued

Foreign Fonts

Moscow 12, 24 — One Style

ФИСВУАПРШОЛДЬТЩЗЙКЫЕГМ

фисвуапршолдьтщзйкыегмцч

New York w Hebrew Block 9, 12, 18, 24 — One Style

ABCDEFGHIJKLMNOPQRSTUVWXYZ

abcdefghijklmnopqrstuvwxyz1234567890

How razorback-jumping frogs can level!

Rehovot 10, 12, 20, 24 — One Style

שנבגקכעיןחלךצמםפ[illegible]ר

דאוה'סטז1234567890

Saigon 12 — One Style

A B C D E Đ G H I J K L M N O P Q R S T U V Ẩ X Y Â

a b c d e đ g h i j k l m n o p q r s t u v ẩ x y â ấ à ẩ ã ạ ô ó ò ổ õ

Hoẩ raẩorbackọjumping đrogs can levelÁ

Salamis 10, 18, 20 — One Style

ΑΒΨΔΕΦΓΗΙΞΚΛΜΝΟΠ[illegible]ΡΣΤΥΩϜΧΘΖ

αβψδεφγηιξκλμνοπϙρστυωςχθζ1234567890

Ηος ραζορβαψκ-ξυμπινγ φρογσ ψα!

Siloam 10 — One Style

□□□□□□□□□□□□□□□□□□□□□□□□□□□

□□□□□□□□□□□□□□□□□□□□□□□□□□□□□1234567890

□□□ □□□□□□□□□□-□□□□□□□ □□□□□ □□□ □□□□□

Smolensk 12 — One Style

АБЧДЕФГЬИЙКЛМНОПЪРСТУВЩХЫЗ
абчдефгьийклмнопърстувщхыз1234567890
Ьощ разорбачк-йумпинг фрогс чан левел!

Sparta 10, 20 — One Style

ΑΒΨΔΕΦΓΗΙΞΚΛΜΝΟΠϞΡΣΤΥΩϜΧΘΖ
αβψδεφγηιξκλμνοπϙρστυωςχθζ1234
Ηος ραζορβαψκ-ξυμπινγ φρογσ ψαν!

Troyes 10, 12, 20, 24 — One Style

דר[אין]פסמלךלחןיעכקגזנב
זטם´הול1234567890

Foreign Fonts

Games

Take a break from your productive life and have some fun.

Games A1

Color Games

Assault v2.0

A minor tactical-level war game. Move your tanks and men across a battlefield, destroy pillboxes for points. Good warlike sounds.

Brad Sanders
PO Box 1205
Lawrence, KS 66044-1205

Application
Shareware $5.00
Size: 262K
12" 6 7 32

Battle Cruiser1 v1.0

A variation on Battleship. Has good sounds and graphics, but not very engaging.

Ray White
3804 Seventh Street
Sachse, TX 75048

Application
Shareware $2.00
Size: 73K

Star 'Roids v5.4.1

A pretty good Mac version of the arcade game Asteroids. Good graphics and sound effects.

Jason Ferrara
1032 Harvard Drive
Yardley, PA 19067

Application
Shareware $10.00
Size: 98K
12" 6 7 32

Strike Force! v1.1

A variation of Stratego with extra features and options. Demo version is good for 30 days.

Keith Lambert
Red Line Software
PO Box 900931
San Diego, CA 92190

Application
Demoware
Size: 163K

Solarian II v1.04

★ 1.04

Star Wars-type arcade game, requires a kill-or-be-killed attitude. Great graphics and sound. Destroy all the things on a level to move up to the next one. Comes with documentation.

Stick Software
Ben Haller
32 Deer Haven Drive
Ithaca, NY 14850

Application
Shareware $25.00
Size: 743K
12" 6 7 32

Games A3

Color Games

Color Kaleidoscope v1.0

Draws constantly changing color patterns. Prone to crashing.

John Connolly
Beaverton Digital Systems
PO Box 1626
Beaverton, OR 97075

Application
Freeware
Size: 27K

Color Save The Farm v3.2

Protect your cornfield and henhouse from the crows and foxes. Your hunter aims his gun and shoots the unfortunate beasts.

Bill Clark
2308 Gambel Oak Way
Bakersfield, CA 93311

Application
Shareware $3.00
Size: 141K
12" 6 7 32

Dropper v1.1

Arrange matching bricks in a horizontal, vertical, or diagonal pattern to eliminate them from the playing area. Similar to Columns, Tetris, and Brickwell.

C.K. Haun
Ravenware Software
22045 McClellan Rd.
Cupertino, CA 95014

Application
Shareware $5.00
Size: 110K
12" 6 7 32

Stained Glass

A great game. You remove colored panes in order until only one is left. The fewer moves the better.

Nick Schlott
1016 E. El Camino Real #227
Sunnyvale, CA 94087

Application
Shareware $25.00
Size: 348K
12" 6 7 32

Bonk v1.0

Cross out the annoying bald faces to get to higher levels. Think C source code is available for $25.

Mike Darweesh
68 Kensington Court
Rochester, NY 14612
eslo@andrew.cmu.edu

Application
Shareware $10.00
Size: 222K

Diamonds v1.5

A nice color variation on Brick-Out. Funky music plays in the background while you play. Color only.

Oliver Dreer
Im Egg 35
CH-4147 tesch
SWITZERLAND
ordreer@iiic.ethz.ch

Application
Shareware $20.00
Size: 390K

Level Mover v1.0

Allows you to change the order of levels in Diamonds v1.5.

Oliver Dreer
Im Egg 35
CH-4147 tesch
SWITZERLAND
ordreer@iiic.ethz.ch

Application
Freeware
Size: 14K

Games A5

Color Games

Glypha II v1.0

In an Egyptian temple, you must battle Sphinxes with only your lance and winged steed. This is a nice color arcade-type game; b&w version also available.

John Calhoun
PO Box 442258
Lawrence, KS 66044

Application
Shareware $10.00
Size: 349K

Iraq Attack v1.02

Shoot up Iraqi aircraft and shipping in the Gulf with your assault helicopter; take out some oil wells for extra points. Makes ominous sounds. Is this politically correct?

Mark Adams
11215 Research Blvd. #2036
Austin, TX 78759

Application
Shareware $10.00
Size: 458K

Games A6

Color Games

Fun in Space! v2.0

Simple game where you navigate a space ship, pick up communications buoys, and avoid crashing into a planet.

Eric Snider

Application
Freeware
Size: 18K

MacCribbage v1.0

A color cribbage game. Play against the computer. Shareware fee is whatever you think it's worth.

Tim Wasko
4832 49th Ave. NW
Calgary, Alberta
T3A 0R9 CANADA

Application
Shareware ?
Size: 251K
12" 6 7 32

Worms! v1.0

Displays a window of squiggling, colorful worms. It's based on the December 1987 Scientific American 'Computer Recreations' article.

T.M. Herbst

Application
Public Domain
Size: 17K

Games B1

General Games

Bird Race

Bet on bird races. There are six birds (too bad they all look the same) with different odds. Place a bet, then let them race. Computer keeps track of your winnings, and speaks if MacinTalk is installed.

unknown

Application
Public Domain
Size: 45K

BlobMgr Demo

A collection of 16 different games: puzzles, word games, strategy games, and more. Each game is in a separate window, and all 16 windows can be displayed at the same time.

Paul DuBois

Application
Public Domain
Size: 72K

Dragon™

Command your 8 knights to slay a dragon who is lurking in the forest, which is a 10 x 15 grid. In a single turn, you can move or pivot one of your knights. Kill the dragon before it kills you.

Mark Nutter
PO Box 5252
Laurel, MD 20707

Application
Shareware $5.00
Size: 71K

Enigma v1.0

A puzzle game along the lines of Rubik's Cube. Two interlocked circles composed of various patterns must be rotated to obtain a specified configuration.

Joe Sensendorf
1224 Eva Avenue
Los Altos, CA 94022

Application
Shareware $5.00
Size: 21K

HangMan Plus v1.0

The classic game of Hangman. Enter your own words or let the Mac pick them from a one of 12 categories. A landscape scene shows an increasingly morbid gallows with each miss. In color on a Mac II.

Ken Winograd
2039 Country Club Drive
Manchester, NH 03102
(603) 625-1049

Application
Shareware $10.00
Size: 45K

Hedges v1.1

Move a ball from the lower left-hand corner of the playing window to the upper right-hand corner; maneuver around walls and hedges.

Michael D. Speir
PO Box 6835
Tampa, FL 33608-6835

Desk Accessory
Shareware $3.00
Size: 18K

Hot Air Balloon v2.1

Fly a hot-air balloon and avoid trees, utility poles, and a stork. The scenery moves past as you control the height of the balloon. Gain points for flying in free air, lose points for running into things.

Bill Clark
1301 Sylvia Drive
Bakersfield, CA 93304
GEnie: DERRELLCLARK

Application
Freeware
Size: 30K

MadMaze

Make your way through a maze while time runs out. There are 4 locked doors that each require a key.

Michael D. Speir
PO Box 6835
Tampa, FL 33608-6835

Desk Accessory
Shareware $3.00
Size: 19K

MazerLaze v2.0

Shoot Mazers who appear at the edge of a grid with your Laze beam. If you don't have a straight shot, you have to ricochet your beam off some of the randomly placed baffles. Docs within the program.

Kelly Dean Corder
2942 E. Indian School Road
#D356
Phoenix, AZ 85016

Application
Shareware $5.00
Size: 76K

Pattern Blocks v2.1

Create designs on a 7 x 7 grid by placing a block in each of the 49 boxes. There are 12 built-in blocks, which are 32 x 32 bitmap images. Double-click on a pattern to edit.

Dan Weston
Nerdworks
195 23rd NE
Salem, OR 97301

Application
Shareware $10.00
Size: 20K

Safari v1.0

A trivial game where animals move across the screen and you must click on them before they reach the other side.

John Gallougher
108 Maplewood Avenue
Wayne, NJ 07470
CIS: 70137,763

Application
Freeware
Size: 49K

Sitting Duck

Go duck hunting with Bill and his faithful springer spaniel, Dart. Try to shoot the ducks that fly overhead. Three levels of play; the ducks fly faster on successive levels. Docs within program.

Bill Clark
1301 Sylvia Drive
Bakersfield, CA 93304

Application
Freeware
Size: 22K

StuntCopter v1.6

Fly a helicopter and try to get a stunt man to jump out of the helicopter and land in the haywagon that moves across the screen. Five successful jumps moves you to the next level.

Duane Blehm
HomeTown Software
848 N. Colorado
Ulysses, KS 67880

Application
Shareware $1.00
Size: 43K

Games B2

General Games

Brickwell v1.0

Catch falling bricks on a paddle. Purpose is to arrange matching bricks in a horizontal, vertical, or diagonal pattern after dropping them off the paddle. A variation on Columns and Tetris.

David W. Lee
Internet/USENET:
dwl@garnet.Berkeley.EDU...
...!ucbvax!garnet!dwl

Application
Freeware
Size: 114K
12" 6 7 32

GunShy v1.2.1

Addictive game where you try to match pairs of tiles with the same icon. Tiles on the edges must be removed before tiles on the inside can be accessed. Rules within the program.

E.C. Horvath
c/o UnitMac, Inc.
PO Box 237
Holmdel, NJ 07733

Application
Freeware
Size: 46K
12" 6 7 32

MacNinja v3.0

Neat arcade-style karate game. Pretty good.

Ron Minor
2304 Canosa Ave.
Las Vegas, NV 89104

Application
Shareware $10.00
Size: 170K
12" 6 7 32

MaCube v2.1

Mac version of Rubik's Cube. Uses 6 colors on a Mac II or 6 patterns on a b&w machine. Rotate sides by clicking on them with the mouse. Excellent.

Kim Gillies
P.O. Box 42344
Tucson, AZ 85733
GEnie: KGILLIES

Desk Accessory
Freeware
Size: 27K
12" 6 7 32

Rubik's Wrap

A fun game if you liked Rubik's Cube. It's also in color if you have a color Mac.

Dennis Johnson
19 Taurus Ave
Oakland, CA 94611

Application
Shareware $5.00
Size: 28K

Shanghai Demo v1.0D

Game is played with 144 mah-jongg tiles arranged in a dragon-shaped pyramid. Try to remove all tiles, two at a time, according to a few simple rules. Demo version is limited to one arrangement.

Brodie Lockard
Activision, Inc.

Application
Demoware
Size: 50K
12" 6 7 32

ADD

A talking addition program. Very simple; intended for children working on addition at the 1st and 2nd grade level.

Mike Kazmierczak
X Systems
32-F Stratford Hills
Chapel Hill, NC 27514-3239

Application
Shareware $5.00
Size: 42K

Apples

Puzzle of 3 x 3 array of squares. Each square is actually just one face of one of 9 cubes with a different symbol on each. Rotate the cubes until the faces with the apples are showing.

Michael D. Speir
PO Box 6835
Tampa, FL 33608-6835

Desk Accessory
Freeware
Size: 20K

Daleks v0.3

Move around and avoid the Daleks, insidious creatures from the TV show 'Dr. Who.' A new version of this program by a different author is also on this disk.

Johan Strandberg

Application
Public Domain
Size: 17K

DAleks

Move to avoid the Daleks, insidious creatures from the TV show 'Dr. Who.' Daleks die when they crash into each other. You can randomly teleport, and you can use your sonic screwdriver once per level.

Mage Software
c/o Steve Sheets
PO Box 8455
Rolling Meadows, IL 60008

Desk Accessory
Shareware $20.00
Size: 22K

Follower

Computer shows you a sequence of different boxes and you have to reproduce the sequence. Author requests donations for People For the American Way.

C. K. Haun
RavenWare Software/
Mac Div.
4009 Pacific Coast Highway
Torrance, CA 90505

Application
Charityware
Size: 14K

Haul It v2.1

Haul cargoes from city to city for pay. The trucker with the most money at the end of the game wins.

Don Collum
7105 Halstead Lane
Raleigh, NC 27613

Application
Shareware $10.00
Size: 125K

HeloMath

Cute game for teaching basic math. An answer to a math problem is displayed and you must fly a helicopter and shoot the tank displaying the equation that evaluates to that answer.

Mark Day
4265 Midland Road
Saginaw, MI 48603

Application
Shareware $5.00
Size: 42K

HexPuzzle v3.0

A puzzle game that the author describes as a 'combination lock.' You must flip and move tiles in the correct sequence, trying to remove them from the board. Instructions are unclear.

Kenneth J. Brody
24 Berkley Lane
Scarsdale, NY 10583
CIS: 71455,225

Application
Shareware $5.00
Size: 11K

Games B3

Continued

MacSimon v1.0

A b&w computer version of the electronic kids' game Simon.

Michael Abramowicz
19 Locust Ave.
Larchmont, NY 10538

Application
Shareware $5.00
Size: 36K

New Daleks v2.0

Move around and avoid the Daleks, insidious creatures from the TV show 'Dr. Who.' Daleks are destroyed when they run into each other. Teleport or use your sonic screwdriver if you get into trouble.

Bob Arning
CIS: 70347,705

Application
Public Domain
Size: 24K

Plato's Cave v2.4.1

The object is to determine the contents of a cave with only a flashlight and your ability to reason. The cave is square and divided into rooms. It contains both mirrors and absorbers that influence what you can see with your flashlight.

Michael Wiplich

Application
Freeware
Size: 82K

ThinkFast Demo v1.0

Tests reaction time to complete simple tasks, such as discerning if two objects or groups of letters are the same; remembering a sequence of letters; and matching patterns.

unknown

Application
Public Domain
Size: 43K

Fool's DEMO

Fool's Errand demo. Solve logic and word puzzles. Some of the puzzles are really good, although the commercial version has many more of them.

Cliff Johnson
Miles Computing, Inc.

Application
Demoware
Size: 141K

Lawn Zapper v1.0

Mow a lawn, go to jail! Seriously, the object of this game is to mow a lawn without hitting the obstacles.

Imperial Software
1208 White Ave.
Baltimore, MD 21237

Application
Shareware $10.00
Size: 366K
6 7 32

Games B5

General Games

Break the Bricks

A variation of the arcade game BreakOut. Move a paddle back and forth to keep a ball in play and knock out bricks. Graphics and sound are not very good.

Richard J. Kalagher
1841 Nigel Court
Vienna, VA 22180

Application
Freeware
Size: 8K

Brickles v7.0

A somewhat interesting version of the arcade game BreakOut. Has options for adjusting the ball speed and number of paddles. Sound and graphics are adequate but nothing spectacular.

Ken Winograd
2039 Country Club Drive
Manchester, NH 03102
(603) 625-1094

Application
Shareware $5.00
Size: 23K

CairoShoot v1.2

A shooting gallery game with a twist. You must shoot a specific number of only certain targets within a time limit to advance to the next round. Fee of $3 for a key to access all program features.

Duane Blehm
HomeTown Software
848 N. Colorado
Ulysses, KS 67888

Application
Demoware
Size: 65K

Faulty Towers Of Hanoi v2.0

Object of the game is to move a stack of disks from one pile to another; you place larger disks on top of smaller.

Forest Lake Senior High
School Math Dept.,
Attn: Kevin D. Lee
6101 Scandia Trail N.
Forest Lake, MN 55025

Application
Shareware $6.00
Size: 61K

Gobbler v1.0

A version of Snake, a classic computer game.

Les Blatt
21 Suffolk Avenue
Maplewood, NJ 07040

Application
Shareware $10.00
Size: 58K

Mac_Pong II v1.0

Mac version of the video game Pong. Two players each control a paddle and must keep a ball in play. Miss and you lose the point.

David L. O'Connor
3663 Woodhaven Circle
Hamburg, NY 14075

Application
Shareware $5.00
Size: 13K

MacChase v1.45+

Mac version of the arcade game PacMan. You can create your own levels or use any of the 25 levels supplied by the author. Requests $10 if you like the game and can afford it.

Kevin L. Gong
1302 Navellier Street
El Cerrito, CA 94530-2449

Application
Freeware
Size: 61K

UnBreakout v1.0

Defend the bricks from being hit by a ball. A necessary twist on BreakOut, the classic arcade game.

M. C. Sumner

Application
Freeware
Size: 38K

Card Magic v1.06

A card trick program.

Roscoe Associates
Attn: CM-1
322 Mall Blvd. #315
Monroeville, PA 15146

Application
Shareware $3.00
Size: 67K

Dot-to-Dot Construction Set v1.0

An educational game to help children (ages 4 to 8) learn numbers, letters, and words. Construct dot-to-dot pictures of Mickey Mouse, a fish, and a spider. As the dots are connected, music plays and the image is revealed to encourage finishing. Docs in a separate file.

Paul Cozza
SoftPlus
PO Box 2442
Gaithersburg, MD 20879

Application
Shareware $17.00
Size: 71K

MacPuzzle v1.0

Program contains 25 different puzzles where you try to fit together several irregular pieces to form a specific shape. Look at the icon for a small sample. Docs within the program.

Bill McQuitty
4206 16th Avenue
Moline, IL 61265

Application
Public Domain
Size: 72K

PUZZ'L v1.0

Jigsaw puzzle solving game. Comes with two puzzles and you can build your own. Pieces can have irregular shapes.

Duane Blehm
HomeTown Software
848 N. Colorado
Ulysses, KS 67880

Application
Shareware $3.00
Size: 76K

Something's Hidden Here!

Trivial gimmick to amuse young children. Hit a button and a picture is drawn that is quickly hidden by black paint. Use the mouse as an eraser to remove the paint and reveal the picture.

Domino Arts
907 Norwood Drive
Norwalk, IA 50211

Application
Public Domain
Size: 211K

Tic-Tac-Toe-Too™

Players alternate turns selecting squares in a grid that can have anywhere from 3 to 15 squares per side. Object is to get more 3-in-a-row sequences than your opponent. Two players required.

unknown

Application
Public Domain
Size: 7K

TicTacToeTooa v1.0

Tic-tac-toe against the computer. Grid size is configurable.

Rico Vaccaro

Application
Demoware
Size: 26K

TTT.1.1 v1.1

Basic tic-tac-toe game. The o's are eyes that wink at you.

Anthony Carlisle
Huntingdon College
1500 E. Fairview Ave.
Montgomery, AL 36194-6201

Application
Shareware $3.00
Size: 19K

Games B7

General Games

Amps v3.0(B2)

Game of chase. You have to avoid the attacking Amps and the walls. Instructions included.

Paul A. Perkins
104-0 Stephanis Drive
Cary, NC 27511
GEnie: AM-WEB

Application
Freeware
Size: 14K

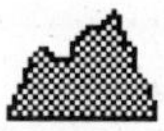

Donkey Doo™

A version of the arcade game Donkey Kong.

Gary Dauphin

Application
Freeware
Size: 65K

Glider+3.0 v3.0

Navigate a paper glider through different rooms. Watch out for air vents!

John Calhoun
1201 Oread #4
Lawrence, KS 66044

Application
Shareware $15.00
Size: 127K

Glypha v2.0

In an Egyptian temple, you must battle sphinxes with only your lance and winged steed. Arcade-style game.

John Calhoun
1201 Oread #4
Lawrence, KS 66044

Application
Shareware $8.00
Size: 137K

Iggy Iggopolis v2.0

Capture territory by moving around the screen and laying down fences while avoiding Zuuls (which look like crabs) and Zamfir (who looks like PacMan). Keys are used for movement.

Dave Bayard
2133 Williamstowne Drive
Richmond, VA 23235
(804) 276-9590

Application
Freeware
Size: 41K

MacConcentration

Take turns revealing pairs of tiles from a grid. If you match a pair, your turn continues. If not, the tiles are re-hidden and the next player chooses. From 1 to 4 players can compete.

Daryl L. Scott
CIS: 75046,704

Application
Freeware
Size: 35K

MacMatch v1.0

Play the game Concentration just as in the TV show, matching two tiles at a time to reveal pieces of a rebus (picture puzzle). The rebus and the tiles are in a MacPaint file you can edit. Nice.

Eagle I. Berns
735 La Para Avenue
Palo Alto, CA 94306

Application
Shareware $20.00
Size: 21K

ProMatch v1.2

A version of Concentration (pairs win points). You can play against another person or the computer.

Barry Jay Bruns
PO Box 602
Niagara Falls, NY 14302-0602

Application
Shareware $10.00
Size: 53K

Runaround

Two-player game where each player controls a line that continuously grows. Players can change the direction in which their line grows. First one to run into a line or hit the screen edge loses.

Allen Hartgraves
38 Glenmore Road
Pueblo, CO 81001

Application
Shareware $5.00
Size: 16K

Social Climber v1.00

Try to climb up a building by weaving back and forth across each floor. You must avoid the elevators that move up and down at various speeds. Game has truly annoying sound effects.

CSI Design Group
PO Box 50510
St. Louis, MO 63105

Application
Shareware ?
Size: 32K

Games C1

Arcade Games

Arcade Games

Columns v1.1

Columns is a game in which you manipulate patterned tiles to form sequences of 3 boxes of the same pattern arranged horizontally, vertically, or diagonally. In other words, any 3 patterns win points. Great game.

Chris Christensen
6901 Chiala Lane
San Jose, CA 95129

Application
Shareware $5.00
Size: 77K

Crab Attack II v1.0

The great arcade game with great sounds. Stay alive on the beach while being attacked by many different creatures. Incompatible with MultiFinder.

Scott and Andrew Lindsey

Application
Freeware
Size: 364K

MacTris v1.0

Hmm, looks like Tetris to me.

TVark Productions
Kevin Vigor
129 South 700 East #4
Salt Lake City, UT 84102

Application
Shareware $10.00
Size: 21K

Tetrix v1.1

Similar to the commercial game Tetris. You manipulate the falling groups of tiles to form a straight line across the playing area. Each filled-in line is then eliminated. The object is to get rid of as many tiles as possible.

Mac version: Steve Johnson
Code: Quentin Neill

Application
Freeware
Size: 51K

Toxic Ravine v1.1

Save the environment by eliminating trash in the toxic ravine from your blimp. You can also rescue garbage robots uncovered while bombing the trash. Very entertaining. Story in documentation could have come from 'Strange Stories.'

Glenn R. Wichman
1128 Briarcroft Rd.
Claremont, CA 91711

Application
Shareware $5.00
Size: 231K

Continuum v1.0

A very impressive arcade game where you control a spaceship and must destroy enemy bases on the surface of a planet. Comes with an editor that can modify the terrain of the planet's surface. Shareware fee is whatever you think it's worth.

Randy Wilson
82D Escondido Village
Stanford, CA 94305

Application
Shareware ?
Size: 132K
12" 6 7 32

Leprechaun™ Demo v2.6

Demo version of a commercial game where you control a Leprechaun and try to push a pot of gold onto a rainbow. Each level has different obstacles. Demo has 20 levels. Retail version has over 100 levels and a level editor. Color graphics and sound.

Shodan
PO Box 4456
Berkeley, CA 94704
(415) 849-9475

Application
Demoware
Size: 585K
12" 6 7 32

Games C3

Arcade Games

Express Lane! v1.1

Practice your checkout counter skills. Simple game that can waste 5 minutes of your time before you know it! Has some screen redraw problems.

Bob Grubb
6612 Thorman Road
Port Charlotte, FL 33981

Application
Shareware $15.00
Size: 80K

Hextris v1.0

A variant of Tetris that uses shapes based on hexagonal blocks. A nice twist on Tetris. Source code is available in Think C, X Windows, and ATK for $25.

Dave Markley
410 Bonshire Road
Akron, OH 44319

Application
Shareware $10.00
Size: 56K

Pararena v1.3

Remember the movie starring James Caan called Rollerball? Steal your opponent's ball and skateboard to the basket for a slam-dunk. Try it, you'll like it! Has a touch of color.

John Calhoun
PO Box 442258
Lawrence, KS 66044

Application
Shareware $8.00
Size: 297K

Tron v2.1

A network version of Tron Cycles. Try to cut your opponent off by drawing a line in front of him/her.

Andrea Viscovich &
Andrea Pellizzon
tina@alessia.dei.unipd.it
turner@alessia.dei.unipd.it

Application
Shareware $5.00
Size: 113K

Wacky Wheel! v1.0

'Wheel of Fortune' without Vanna. You can modify the phrases and the prizes if you want.

Andrew Welch
29 Grey Rock Road
Wilton, CT 06897

Application
Shareware $10.00
Size: 193K

Darts v1.0

Mac version of Darts. Lets you play the following games: 301, 501, 1001, Round the Clock, and Cricket. Instructions included. Shareware fee is whatever you think it's worth.

Robert Boylan
54 Howe Rd.
Coram, NY 11727

Application
Shareware ?
Size: 72K

Dragon v2.10

Play the board game Go on either a 9 x 9 or a 20 x 20 board. Estimated strength is about 17 kyu. Very little documentation on how to use the features of the program.

Liu Don-Yeuh
Dept. of Comp. Sci. & Info. Eng.
National Taiwan Univ.
Taipei, Taiwan
REPUBLIC OF CHINA

Application
Freeware
Size: 69K

Flip It v1.0

Othello for the computer. When you place your tile at the ends of a line of opponents' tiles, they 'flip' over and change to yours. 8 x 8 playing area.

Kevin Clark
8049 Janes #E
Woodridge, IL 60517

Application
Freeware
Size: 24K

Go v1.0B2

Play the game of Go on a 20 x 20 board. Play against the computer or another person. Option for two players to compete on separate Macs using the modem port.

James Logan
BYU 403 CB
Provo, UT 84602
(801) 378-3617

Application
Freeware
Size: 99K

Hex v1.0

Two-player strategy game played on a board composed of hexagonal cells. One player tries to construct a continuous path vertically, the other player horizontally. Play against another human or the Mac. Board size is adjustable.

Andrew McDaniel
Michail H. Dickman
12923 Point Pleasant Drive
Fairfax, VA 22033

Application
Shareware $5.00
Size: 39K

Influence v2.1

A dungeon exploration game with a unique interface. Rooms are hexagonal cells. May be played with one person or with two people playing cooperatively. Docs in a separate file.

Eagle I. Berns
735 La Para Avenue
Palo Alto, CA 94306

Application
Shareware $20.00
Size: 113K

MacLuff v7.0

Play the game of Five-in-a-row, where you and the Mac alternately place markers on a grid. The first one to get 5 in a row either across, up and down, or diagonally wins.

Ronald Karlson
Dept. of Telecom. & Comp. Sys.
Royal Institute of Technology
S-100 44 Stockholm
SWEDEN

Application
Public Domain
Size: 31K

MacPente v2.0

Play the board game Pente, where you and the Mac take turns placing stones on a Go board. Object is to get 5 in a row or make 5 jumps (by flanking adjacent pairs of opponent's pieces).

Fred Moulden, Jr.
11109 Riaza Square #9
St. Louis, MO 63138

Application
Shareware $10.00
Size: 61K

Mystery Box v1.00

Opponent hides balls in a 8 x 8 grid, and you try to find them by firing rays into the grid. Rays are absorbed if they hit a ball and deflected if they pass next to a ball. Play against the Mac or another human.

Keith Lambert
3433 Marathon Drive
San Diego, CA 92123
CIS: 75076,34

Application
Shareware $5.00
Size: 41K

Reversi v2

Play the game Othello on an 8 x 8 board. Players take turns placing pieces on the board, trying to convert the opponents pieces to their own color. You play against the computer. Fee is a donation to the Donald Beaulieu Vision Fund.

Robert Woodhead

Application
Charityware
Size: 17K

This Ain't Othello v0.01

Play the board game Othello. The Mac talks to you if MacinTalk is installed, and you can choose either 'Nice' or 'Downright Obnoxious' comments. The Mac is not a particularly good player.

Gary Thompson
5916E S. Jellison Street
Littleton, CO 80123
CIS: 72447,2455

Application
Freeware
Size: 24K

Backgammon v1.0

A decent Mac version of the board game Backgammon with adequate graphics. Play against the Mac or another opponent. Doubling cube is implemented. Assumes you know how to play backgammon.

Stephen D. Young
Debra Willrett
1516 Cormorant Court
Sunnyvale, CA 94087

Application
Freeware
Size: 31K
12" 6 7 32

Betwixt v3.51

Two-player strategy game played on a 12 x 12 board. One player tries to construct a vertical path and the other a horizontal path across the grid using pegs and bridges. Docs within the program.

Christopher Amet
'Dr. C' Software
31A Wayne Gardens
Collingswood, NJ 08108

Application
Shareware $10.00
Size: 36K
12" 6 7 32

Closure

Three-dimensional board game with 4 levels. You play against the Mac and alternate placing tiles on a 4 x 4 x 4 matrix. It's a little bit like Othello. Has a demonstration play mode for learning how to play.

Christopher Gross
Viking Technologies, Inc.

Application
Freeware
Size: 45K
12" 6 7 32

Consternation v1.0

Game where two players try to move 4 marbles around a board from the base row to the home row. Moves are determined by rolling a single die. Play against the Mac. Docs within the program.

M. D. Brownsworth
Human Factors Software
2409 Gilham Road
Eugene, OR 97401

Application
Demoware
Size: 66K
12" 6 7 32

Knight's Tour v4.00

Mac program for trying to solve the classic Knight's Tour mathematical puzzle. The puzzle is to move a chess knight to every square on the chess board, visiting each square only once. A solution is provided in a separate file.

Gavriel State
Nepean, Ontario
CANADA

Application
Public Domain
Size: 21K

MacYahtzee

Plays the dice game Yahtzee. Roll five dice and try to form specified poker hands. Supports up to 4 players. The Mac rolls the dice and keeps track of the scoring.

Ed Vrcich
Emerald City Software
2104 SW 306 Place
Federal Way, WA 98023

Application
Freeware
Size: 11K
12" 6 7 32

OutFlank v1.0

Game similar to Go with an 8 x 8 playing board. Provides human vs. human, human vs. computer, and computer against itself playing modes.

Steven L. Gilbert

Application
Public Domain
Size: 23K
12" 6 7 32

Stratego v0.95

Plays the board game Stratego. One player competes against the Mac, which is a pretty poor player. However, game has a nice interface, and complete rules are provided within the program.

Ken McLeod
Blue Cloud Software Ventures
550 W. Exeter Avenue
La Habra, CA 90631

Application
Freeware
Size: 122K
12" 6 7 32

Games D2

Continued

Triple Yahtzee v1.0

Plays the dice game Yahtzee where you try to assemble poker hands using dice. It's Triple because you must make each possible hand 3 times. Supports up to 4, all human, players.

John Sullivan
GEnie: j.w.sullivan

Application
Freeware
Size: 36K
12" 6 7 32

3D Checkers v2.0

Plays a game of checkers on a 3-D projection of a standard checkerboard. Play against another person or against the computer. Full-feature version is sold for $10.

Fred Moulden, Jr.
1109 Riaza Square #9
St. Louis, MO 63138

Application
Demoware
Size: 50K

GNU Chess v3.0.2

The Free Software Foundation helped develop this excellent chess game. This is not an official release by them.

Airy André
airy@cernvax.cern.ch
CalvaCom: AA10

Application
Freeware
Size: 73K

KnightEdit v1.4

A chess game that allows you to import text files of chess games (in long algebraic format). Also has some really alternative chess pieces.

Jesse Carpenter
PO Box 80743
Albuquerque, NM 87198-0743
CIS: 73617,1743

Application
Shareware $5.00
Size: 126K

NetChess v1.5b1

Play chess over an AppleTalk network. This version works under AppleShare 2.0.1; other compatibilities unknown. Players can save a game between sessions.

Donald Way
109 - 4th Street
Hoboken, NJ 07030

System Startup Extension
Shareware $5.00
Size: 23K

NetChess DA v1.5b1

DA version of NetChess. Play chess over an AppleTalk network. This version works under AppleShare 2.0.1; other compatibilities unknown. Players can save a game between sessions.

Donald Way
109 - 4th Street
Hoboken, NJ 07030

Desk Accessory
Shareware $5.00
Size: 60K

Games E1

Solitaire Games

Baker's Dozen v2.0

A solitaire game. Cards are dealt out and you have to stack up an entire suite, in order, from the aces.

Eric Snider
4941 Woodcliff Hill Rd.
West Bloomfield, MI 48033

Application
Shareware $10.00
Size: 67K

Canfield v1.0

Plays the solitaire card game Canfield. Graphics are poor, and there's no sound during play. Rules are included within the program.

Michael A. Casteel
Computing Capabilities Corp.
465-A Fairchild Drive
Mountain View, CA

Application
Freeware
Size: 33K

Chinese Puzzle v1.0

A solitaire card game played with two decks of cards. Game requires skill, luck, and a lot of concentration. Docs within program and in a separate file.

Andrew Kirby
CIS: 72560,373
GEnie: A.Kirby1

Application
Freeware
Size: 32K

Fifteens v1.0

A solitaire card game that requires luck and skill, as well as quickness. High scores are ranked according to how quickly you can complete the game. Instructions included within the program.

Phil Bush
12385A Maverick Dr.
Maryland Heights, MO 63043

Application
Shareware $8.00
Size: 43K

Forty Thieves v2.0

Two deck solitaire game. Forty cards are dealt in 10 columns of 4 cards each. Build a suit from ace to kings.

Eric Snider
4941 Woodcliff Hill Rd.
West Bloomfield, MI 48033

Application
Shareware $10.00
Size: 74K

Golf (Card Game) v1.0

Plays the solitaire card game Golf. Reasonable graphics. Rules included within the program.

Michael A. Casteel
788 Edale Drive
Sunnyvale, CA 94087
CIS: 76174,2461

Application
Shareware $10.00
Size: 48K

King Albert

A solitaire card game. Although no rules are provided, the method of play is similar to other solitaire games: build up foundation from ace to king, place red 8 on black 9, etc.

M. Conrad

Application
Public Domain
Size: 16K

Klondike v3.6

Plays the solitaire card game Klondike. Maintains scores based on how many cards have been played to the foundation for up to 4 players. Includes docs within the program.

Michael A. Casteel
Unison Software, Inc.
415 Clyde Avenue
Mountain View, CA 94043

Application
Shareware $10.00
Size: 52K

Pyramid !!! v1.01

Plays the solitaire card game Pyramid. Graphics are OK, but there's no sound. Rules provided within the program.

Phil Bush
12385A Maverick Drive
Mayland Heights, MO 63043

Application
Shareware $5.00
Size: 42K

Solitaire v1.0

Plays the solitaire card game Klondike. Build up the foundation from ace to king, with the usual 'black 9 on the red 10' for cards on the tableau. Poor graphics and a clumsy interface.

Ron Aldrich

Application
Public Domain
Size: 9K
12" 6 7 32

Solitaire 1.1 v1.1

Various solitaire card games: East Haven, Klondike, Spiderette, Westcliff, Will o' the Wisp, and Yukon. For the solitaire aficionado.

Steve Boyd
Universal Imaging Corp.
502 Brandywine Parkway
West Chester, PA 19380

Application
Shareware $5.00
Size: 147K
12" 6 7 32

Spider

A solitaire card game. Color version on the same disk; b&w version is $10 shareware fee.

Steven R. Weiss
1753 Ivywood Drive
Ann Arbor, MI 48103

Application
Shareware $20.00
Size: 141K
12" 6 7 32

Games F1

Card Games

Card Games

Cribbage

Mac version of the two-player card game Cribbage. You play against the computer. Complete rules and instructions provided within the program.

Chris Christen
Elegant Solutions
6901 Chiala Lane
San Jose, CA 95129

Application
Freeware
Size: 75K

Euchre v2.5

Card game played with a deck of 24 cards, 9 through ace in each suit, by two teams of two people. Computer can supply from 0 to 3 of the other players. Play is similar to Bridge. Complete rules and instructions within program.

Christopher Jones
24335 Hampton Hill
Novi, MI 48050

Application
Shareware $10.00
Size: 45K

Hearts v1.6

A fair to middling implementation of the Hearts card game. Play against 3 computer-controlled opponents who, unfortunately, are much too easy to beat.

Loki Engineering, Inc.

Application
Freeware
Size: 41K

MacSeven

Opponents alternate playing a card that must match either the suit or rank of the last card played. Queens are wild. Must draw a card if you can't play one. Win by getting rid of all your cards.

unknown

Application
Public Domain
Size: 11K

Pai Gow v0.9

Plays the gambling game Pai Gow, which uses both dice and dominoes. Object is arrange 4 dominoes into two pairs with a higher ranking than that of the banker. Docs within the program.

David Millers
5451 Lemon Hill Avenue
Sacramento, CA 95824

Application
Shareware $5.00
Size: 31K

Pokeno

Form 10 poker hands on 5 x 5 grid by placing cards one at a time. Each row and column is a separate hand. The better the hands, the more points you get.

Arno Clabaugh
PO Box 4416
Simi Valley, CA 93063

Application
Shareware $15.00
Size: 66K

Precision Cribbage

Excellent Mac version of the two-player card game Cribbage. Play against the computer, which has variable skill levels. Good graphics and animation.

Doug Brent
1299 Oak Knoll Drive
San Jose, CA 95129

Application
Freeware
Size: 189K

Bill's Casino

Plays the card game Blackjack and simulates a slot machine. Not very sophisticated, but the graphics are pleasant and it's easy to play. Docs within the program.

Derrell Clark
GEnie: DERRELLCLARK

Application
Public Domain
Size: 88K

Black Jack Trainer v3.0

Improve your Blackjack game.

Gilbert W. Rogers
PO Box 1171, Postal Station M
Calgary, Alberta
T2P 2K9 CANADA

Application
Shareware $10.00
Size: 137K

BlackJack v1.0

A simple version of the Blackjack card game. Does not support betting, and the only options are hit and hold. Computer deals the cards but does not add them up for you.

Michael Schirpke
CIS: 70167,505

Application
Freeware
Size: 42K

Blackjack v3.1

Blackjack game for the serious player. Options for adjusting the rules and displaying card-counting information. Computer deals and tracks betting. Room for 7 hands at the table.

Dave Dickel
817-A Jennifer Lane
Costa Mesa, CA 92626
CIS: 72356,510

Application
Freeware
Size: 54K

Macjack v2.1

A nice 21 game that is in color on a Mac II.

Lance Gharat
2581 California Park Drive
#206
Chico, CA 95928

Application
Shareware

Size: 74K

Games H1

Casino Games

MacBandit v1.2

Slot machine simulator with nice graphics. Not MultiFinder-compatible.

Dan Jacoby
2014 Timbers Hill Road, Apt. F
Richmond, VA 23235

Application
Shareware $10.00
Size: 61K

MacCasino v1.00

Plays the casino games Roulette and Chuck-A-Luck as well as a slot machine simulation. Tracks your winnings (or losses). Includes graphics that are adequate but nothing spectacular.

Neil Jacobson
9 Linvale Lane
Bridgwater, NJ 08807

Application
Shareware $10.00
Size: 169K

Mouse Craps v1.0

A nice simulation of the dice game Craps. Supports Pass, Come, Field, Hard Way, and One-Roll bets. You can also take up double odds on your point. Drag your chips onto the Craps layout.

William E. Seyler
8 Cassidy
Las Vegas, NV 89115

Application
Shareware $15.00
Size: 38K

Royal Trick-Track

A dice game supposedly played in pubs throughout England. Throw two dice and try to cover 9 markers. Sum of the dice must equal the sum of the markers covered. Docs within the program.

Mark Mains
Custom Graphics
2509 - 47th Street
Des Moines, IA 50310

Application
Shareware $6.00
Size: 80K

The High Roller™ v2.0

A dice-rolling program suitable for use in fantasy role-playing games. Handles multiple dice with any number of faces. Has useful summing functions such as adding the two highest of 6 dice rolled.

John F. Windeknecht
Tweble Computing
815 Dartmouth Drive
Rochester, MI 48063

Application
Shareware $15.00
Size: 33K

Video Poker for Fun

Five-card draw, just as you'd play at a casino.

John Maggiora
9565 Brentford Dr.
Highlands Ranch, CO 80126

Application
Shareware $5.00
Size: 261K

VideoPoker v2.0

Plays video poker (5 card draw) and Hi-Lo just as at a casino. Lets you place a bet before a hand is dealt; payoff is based on your final hand. Has options for playing at Las Vegas, Reno, or Atlantic City odds.

Eric Zimmrman
8433-B Summerdale Road
San Diego, CA 92126

Application
Shareware $15.00
Size: 69K

Bus'd Out v0.25

Multi-player maze game designed for Macs connected on a AppleTalk network, but you can play solo against the computer. The object is to kill the other players. Good 3-D graphics. You can even send nasty messages to the other players.

Gene Tyacke
Lance Saleme
Greg Seitz
Apple Computer, Inc.
Cupertino, CA 95015

Application
Freeware
Size: 40K

Call of Cthula Char. Gentr. v1.0.1

Character generator for the Call of Cthulu, a fantasy role-playing game. It allows exporting of text documents (character sheets). You can pick your skills and profession.

Paul M. Lemieux
905 Union Street
Cary, NC 27511

Application
Freeware
Size: 57K
12" 6 7 32

Cap'n Magneto

Interactive animation adventure game where you must recover the Crown of Control. Movement and actions are controlled by on-screen buttons. Docs within the program.

Al Evans
PowerTools
1206 Karen Avenue
Austin, TX 78757

Application
Shareware $20.00
Size: 109K

CavernQuest! v1.0

Adventure game with graphics and sound. You must explore a cavern, gather potions and magical items, fight monsters, solve puzzles, and fulfill your secret quest.

Brain Booker
ADC Games
PO Box 32360
Columbus, OH 43232

Application
Demoware
Size: 201K

Scarab of RA v1.2

You are an archeologist exploring the Great Pyramid of Ra. You must navigate through the maze-like passages and find 3 sacred talismans. Pick up useful objects along the way. Great game.

Rick Holzgrafe
Semi-Colon Software
PO Box 371
Cupertino, CA 95015-0371

Application
Shareware $10.00
Size: 188K
12" 6 7 32

Games J2

Adventure Games

NetHack v2.3e1

Mac version of the popular UNIX adventure game Hack. Explore a dungeon with your faithful dog Rayner. Collect gold and magical items, avoid or kill monsters. Retains the UNIX interface.

Byron Han
Apple Computer, Inc.
Cupertino, CA

Application
Freeware
Size: 317K

NetTrek v2.0

Star Trek game where you pilot a Terran, Romulan, or Klingon ship. Up to 5 people can play against each other on a network, or play solo against the Mac. Seek out and destroy your opponents. Great game.

Randy Carr
10340 Glenview Avenue
Cupertino, CA 95014

Application
Shareware $25.00
Size: 141K

Delphi Chronicles™ Demo

Demo of the Delphi Chronicles adventure game. As captain of the U.S.S. Pegasus, you are to solve the disappearance of the scientists at Alpha Sirius I on Mars. Instructions included.

Dennis Stamiris & Mark Day
Den Mark Software
4265 Midland Road
Saginaw, MI 48403

Application
Demoware
Size: 90K

Lost in Las Vegas

Demo version of the commercial game Deja Vu II: Lost in Las Vegas, a text and graphics adventure game with excellent digitized sound. This version only lets you play the opening portion of the game.

ICOM Simulations, Inc.
(312) 520-4440

Application
Demoware
Size: 61K

Adventure Games

AdventureMaker v1.0

Creates text adventure game for use with the Adventure! DA also on this disk. Lets you write text descriptions for your own adventure, then run it using the DA.

Patricia B. Smith
Epiboly Software
325 E. 79th St., Apt. 13d
New York, NY 10021

Application
Freeware
Size: 74K

Adventures Plus

Plays text and graphics adventure games. Has an editor for creating such games where you incorporate MacPaint images with descriptions of objects and locations and specify commands.

T & T Software
109 Tee Circle
Salem, VA 24153

Application
Shareware $5.00
Size: 156K

Colossal Cave Adventure

Mac version original text adventure game, usually just called Adventure. A real piece of computer game history. Explore the colossal cave and bring back the treasures.

David R. Malmberg et al.
Softworks
43064 Via Moraga
Mission San Jose, CA 94539

Application
Freeware
Size: 124K

Moria v4.874

Dungeon simulation game. Game time can extend for months. Has many different character types to choose from.

Robert Alan Koeneke

Application
Freeware
Size: 376K

Crystal Quest Sample

Demo version of the commercial game Crystal Quest. It's a fast-moving action game where you must gather up crystals while shooting and avoiding all sorts of nasties. Limited to 5 levels.

Patrick Buckland
Greene Inc.
15 Via Chualar
Monterey, CA 93940

Application
Demoware
Size: 105K
12" 6 7 32

Dungeon of Doom v5.4

Great graphics adventure game where you explore levels of a dungeon, which is laid out as an irregular grid of squares. Formerly shareware, it is now a demo version of The Dungeon Revealed.

John Raymonds
CIS: 76174,205

Application
Demoware
Size: 175K
12" 6 7 32

Investigator No. 1

You are a private investigator and must solve a murder case: check out locations, inspect evidence, interview suspects and witnesses. Get different responses depending on your approach. Register program for $9 to get info needed to solve case.

James R. Chiles
PO Box 38078
Dallas, TX 75238

Application
Demoware
Size: 216K
12" 6 7 32

MasterMaze

Text and graphics adventure game where you must rescue Princess Heather from the Wizard's Lair.

R. B. Hatton
2636 Oxbow
Great Bend, KS 67530

Application
Shareware $7.50
Size: 257K
12" 6 7 32

Games J6

Adventure Games

C & W Adventure

Text game in which you search a 'colossal' cave for a fortune.

Adventure/James Associates
7329 Meadow Court
Boulder, CO 80301

Application
Shareware $10.00
Size: 146K

Castle of Sordoth v1.1

Text adventure game where you must enter Sordoth's Castle, find his legendary sword and armor, and defeat the Platinum Dragon that has been terrorizing the local residents of Kryaack.

Timothy A. Dorcas, Jr.
511 Hope Street
Providence, RI 02906
CIS: 73627,1247

Application
Shareware $5.00
Size: 42K

Hunting the Eland

Text adventure game with a line-mode interface. Descriptions are printed on a teletype-like window and you type in your commands.

Dave Dubin
269 Orchard Road
Springfield, PA 19064

Application
Freeware
Size: 22K

Portal v1.03

Science fiction adventure game. Based on the classic mainframe game.

Michael Detlefsen

Application
Shareware $10.00
Size: 124K

Strange Hotel v5.0

Text adventure game where you explore a strange hotel. Has a line-mode interface where text descriptions are printed and you must type in your commands. Shareware fee is whatever you think it's worth.

Aaron Andrade
6009 Highland Drive
Salt Lake City, UT 84121

Application
Shareware ?
Size: 73K

The Journey

All-text adventure game. You are on a ship and must figure out what is going on. Type commands in a line-mode interface.

Gary Dauphin
334 Markham Drive
Slidell, LA 70458

Application
Shareware $5.00
Size: 76K

Haunted House v1.5

World Builder adventure game where you are sent into a haunted house to retrieve 6 different artifacts. You must also sleep overnight in the house.

John Wedoff
700 S. Lombard
Oak Park, IL 60304

Application
Shareware $2.00
Size: 177K
12" 6 7 32

Radical Castle v2.0

World Builder adventure game where you are a squire who has irked the king by having an affair with his daughter. To avoid a death sentence, you must recover a stolen oracle.

Christopher Kent Wigginton
462 Dewane Drive
El Cajon, CA 92020

Application
Shareware $5.00
Size: 358K
12" 6 7 32

Games K2

World Builder Games

Find the Heart

World Builder adventure game where you must find your stolen heart. Game scenario was created by an 8-year-old boy.

Joshua Chapman
c/o Jerry Chapman
PO Box 21366
Indianapolis, IN 46221

Application
Freeware
Size: 106K

INTRUDER v1.1

World Builder adventure game where you are a mercenary/bounty hunter in the year 4592 and are about to take on a new job. Nice digitized sounds.

Dave Kellum
35949 Avenue 13 1/4
Madera, CA 93638

Application
Shareware $?
Size: 1K

The puzzle piece search

World Builder adventure game where you must find 4 pieces of a puzzle, which is a picture of two animals. Game scenario was created by an 8-year-old boy.

Joshua Chapman
c/o Jerry Chapman
PO Box 21366
Indianapolis, IN 46221

Application
Shareware $5.00
Size: 247K

The Village v1.04

World Builder adventure game where you are a weary traveler trying to get back home. Game has over 150 locations. You don't get the sound library until you pay the shareware fee.

Bill Cameron
c/o Beyond Adventure
PO Box 186
Oxford, OH 45056

Application
Shareware $15.00
Size: 321K

Sands of Time v1.09

World Builder adventure game where you are secret agent Elroy Centron and have been enlisted for a super-secret project designed to halt the erosion of the world's intelligence.

Jeff Wheeler
Seminole Valley Software
6607 Kiowa Trace NE
Cedar Rapids, IA 52401

Application
Shareware $10.00
Size: 125K

Spear of Destiny

World Builder adventure game where you are a priest who must retrieve the Spear of Destiny from the catacombs under the Black Mountains. Nice graphics and sound.

Lloyd Bernhardt
Jason Rennie
Randy McCallum

Application
Freeware
Size: 613K

Games K4

World Builder Games

Enchanted Pencils (PG) v.99

World Builder adventure game where you go on a bizarre journey to find three enchanted pencils. If you send $10 and are old enough, you will receive an adult version of this adventure.

Andy Backer
1267 Willow Avenue
Louisville, KY 40204
(502) 451-2105

Application
Freeware
Size: 405K

Terrorist

World Builder adventure game that satirizes the television show 'Mister Rogers' Neighborhood.' Explore Mr. Rogers' house and neighborhood. Defeat adversaries by flashing a smile or throwing a shoe.

Michail E. Hoffmann
Matthew R. Montgomery
1602 Rochester Street
Caldwell, ID 83605

Application
Shareware $5.00
Size: 517K

P-W Adventure

World Builder adventure game that is the official adventure of Pewamo-Westphalia High School. You must find the treasure inside the school building and escape.

Brad Pohl
Larry Schafer
Jamie Rademacher

Application
Public Domain
Size: 218K

The Phoenix

World Builder adventure game based on the movies 2001 and 2010. It's the year 2066, and you find the Starship Discovery (from 2010) drifting in space. Your job is to get the ship back to Earth.

Lance Havoc

Application
Freeware
Size: 425K

Games K6

World Builder Games

Schmoozer v3.0

World Builder adventure game where you are a musician in the late 1980s. Your quest is to get gigs and make it to the big time.

Michael J. Bruno
5911 Buena Vista Avenue
Oakland, CA 94618

Application
Freeware
Size: 223K

Maze for the Questing Beast

World Builder adventure game where you must explore a maze, solve puzzles, and defeat the Questing Beast.

Andrew Duthie
Aftermath Software
5921 Long Meadow Rd.
Nashville, TN 37205

Application
Shareware $5.00
Size: 134K

Mike's House v1.0

World Builder adventure game where you must find all the objects you need to take a shower and get to the bathtub. You must defeat evil critters and avoid hidden traps in the house.

Mike Rippe
SomeWare
PO Box 83
Hanover, NH 03755

Application
Freeware
Size: 89K

The Hotel Caper v1.0

World Builder adventure game where Detective Sally Sunday must rescue Daring Drake and disarm a bomb planted underneath the bank. Separate file with documentation.

Bruce & Aeron Muckala
Rt. 1, Box 408
Bagley, MN 56621

Application
Shareware $5.00
Size: 231K

Zoony™

World Builder adventure game where you are the court jester, Bingo, and must retrieve the King's ring, which was stolen by the Royal Zookeeper.

Brad Pettit
E. 4212 10th Street
Spokane, WA 99202

Application
Shareware $5.00
Size: 157K

World Builder Games

Odyssey Demo v1.0

World Builder adventure game where you wake up on the spaceship Discovery II, with a vague memory of a black object and a mission your father never completed. Sounds a bit like 2001, doesn't it? Full-featured version available for $10.

George Bolger
151 Old Farm Lane
Lake Marian, IL 60110

Application
Demoware
Size: 256K

Quester-The Forbidden Lands

World Builder adventure game where you must explore a mysterious land, finding weapons and magical objects along the way. You must pay shareware fee to receive the password needed to complete the game.

Andy Schafer
50 Fairfax Drive
Chagrin Falls, OH 44022

Application
Shareware $10.00
Size: 255K

Space Adventure

World Builder adventure game where you awaken out of suspended animation on a crippled spaceship about to self-destruct. Your challenge is to escape unharmed. Instructions included.

Richard Reuss
RJR Publishing Co.
230 Hilton Ave., Suite 103
Hempstead, NY 11550

Application
Shareware $5.00
Size: 155K

Wizard's Warehouse

World Builder adventure game where the Wizard asks you to collect a few things from the Wizard's Warehouse. Your task is to safely return with all the items. Instructions included.

Andrew W. Duthie
ODD Enterprises
5921 Long Meadow Road
Nashville, TN 37205

Application
Shareware $2.00
Size: 160K

Karth II v1.0

World Builder adventure game that is a sequel to Karth of the Jungle. The jungle creatures are tougher and more numerous. You must have completed the original version before you can play this sequel.

Erik R. Batzloff
3001 Lake East Drive,
Apt. 1032
Las Vegas, NV 89117

Application
Shareware $10.00
Size: 200K

Karth of the Jungle

World Builder adventure game where you must explore a jungle and avenge the death of your mentor. Comes with a nice 7-page story explaining the plot of the adventure.

E. R. Batzloff
3001 Lake East Drive, #1032
Las Vegas, NV 89117

Application
Shareware $10.00
Size: 97K

Sword of Siegfried v1.0

World Builder adventure game that introduces you to the world of Teutonic mythology as used by Richard Wagner in his Ring cycle of operas. Object is to gather items and explore everything.

Bob Skinner
Dennis Bowers
CIS: 72157,1570

Application
Freeware
Size: 233K

World Builder Games

Swamp Witch

World Builder adventure game where you try to rescue your parents from the malevolent Swamp Witch. Very well done with excellent sound and graphics. Goes far beyond the typical World Builder interface with greater use of interactive graphics.

Jim Thomas
PO Box 103
Coosada, AL 36020

Application
Shareware $5.00
Size: 735K
12" 6 7 32

Bumper Ships v1.1

Multi-player space wars game. You need to hook two or more Macs together either on a network, with direct cables, or through modems.

Jeffrey S. Shulman
PO Box 1123
Piscataway, NJ 08854-1123

Application
Shareware $10.00
Size: 38K

Destroyer v1.0

Variation of the board game Battleship. Two players position 5 ships on a 10 x 10 grid and take turns shooting at each other's ships. Rules included within the program.

Frank A. Marafino, Jr.

Application
Freeware
Size: 30K

Empire Builder Demo v1.0

War game based on the classic Empire game found on many VAX mainframes. Try to conquer the world by wiping out the computer's military forces. You need to capture cities, amass armies, build transportation, and explore new territory.

Christopher Eliot
PO Box 371
Leeds, MA 01053

Application
Demoware
Size: 133K

Fire Zone v1.0v

Control a tank that moves and shoots using the keyboard. Destroy mines and other enemies. However, you must be in constant motion because your tank has no brakes.

Kelly T. Kirk

Application
Freeware
Size: 74K

Mines v1.01

Try to traverse a 16 x 16 grid filled with a specified number of mines. Moving to a safe square tells you how many mines are on the 8 adjacent squares. You die if you hit a mine. Docs within the program.

Daniel Griscom
The Computer Museum
300 Congress Street
Boston, MA 02210

Application
Freeware
Size: 28K

SubWar!!!

Submarine war game. Poor graphics and no sound. Difficult to figure out how to play. Some on-line instructions provided.

Kelly D. Corder
2942 E. Indian School Rd
#D356
Phoenix, AZ 85016

Application
Shareware $10.00
Size: 83K

Torpedos

Simple shooting game where you fire torpedoes from the bottom of the screen and try to hit one of the many ships that speed horizontally across the screen.

Bill Sammons

Application
Public Domain
Size: 15K

Games L2

War Games

Artillery v2.0.1

Try to shoot an immobile opponent on the other side of a hill. You and your opponent cannot change positions. Players take turns shooting at one another.

Kirk Crawford
1214 - 19th Street
Hermosa Beach, CA 90254

Application
Shareware $10.00
Size: 160K

Ashes

A morbid little nuclear war fantasy with similarities to the arcade game Missile Command. Poor graphics, not very interesting.

Stanley A. Crane et al.
Stoneware
50 Belvedere Street
San Rafael, CA 94901

Application
Freeware
Size: 20K

Ballistics v2

Two-player game where each person has a missile turret located in mountainous terrain. Each specifies an angle and velocity and fires simultaneously. Hit the other guy's turret to win.

Eric Vaughen

Application
Public Domain
Size: 15K

Missile v3.0

Defend your cities from missile attack. A version of the classic arcade game Missile Command.

Robert M. Munafro

Application
Freeware
Size: 10K

O.G.R.E.

Some sort of military battle simulation game. You place infantry and armaments on a battlefield and try to defend against an attack by an ogre. No instructions provided.

Paulo Felcher

Application
Public Domain
Size: 51K

Tank Commander

Two-player tank game where each player controls two tanks. Kill the opponent by shooting and laying mines. Compete against the Mac or another player. Above-average graphics.

Brian Sutter
Viking Technology, Inc.

Application
Freeware
Size: 60K

TankWar v1.0

Two-player tank game. Tanks fight it out on a maze-like battlefield. You must maneuver to get a shot at your opponent. Shots ricochet a few times before they disappear.

Kelly D. Corder
2942 E. Indian School Rd.
#D356
Phoenix, AZ 85016

Application
Shareware $5.00
Size: 21K

Desert Storm Demo v1.0

Complete a mission to destroy a nuclear facility in Iraq. Arcade-style game.

Bungie Software
PO Box 7877
Chicago, IL 60680-7877
(312) 493-2849

Application
Demoware
Size: 254K

Games L4

War Games

Strike Jets Demo v2.05

Jet-to-jet combat in the Middle East. Has neat interface and is interesting if you're into air combat. Comes with two working scenarios.

Blue Cow Software
11 North Avenue #7
Providence, RI 02906
CIS: 71020,3022

Application
Demoware
Size: 460K
12" 6 7 32

War Games

'bot Arena v1.0.1

Have robots battle it out for supremacy of the arena. Icons represent robots. Similar to RoboWar.

John Davis
FUGE Software
10 Thoreau Road
Lexington, MA 02173

Application
Shareware $15.00
Size: 122K
12" 6 7 32

'bot Developer v1.0.1

A robot editor for the game 'bot Arena.

John Davis
FUGE Software
10 Thoreau Road
Lexington, MA 02173

Application
Shareware $15.00
Size: 119K
12" 6 7 32

RoboWar v2.1.2

Pick groups of robots and watch them battle one another. Graphics are slim, but they do the job; not for all tastes. Robot editor is built in. Similar to 'bot Arena.

David Harris
E.C. Box 36
3 Ames Street
Cambridge, MA 02139

Application
Shareware $10.00
Size: 237K
12" 6 7 32

Games M1

Star Trek Games

Star Trek

World Builder adventure game where you are Captain Kirk commanding the Enterprise. You must survive attacks from robots, Klingons, etc. Excellent sound and graphics. Must boot from game disk.	William C. Appleton	**Application** **Freeware** **Size: 49K** 12" 6 7 32

Star Trek trivia quiz

Asks 26 multiple-choice trivia questions about the television series 'Star Trek.' Anyone who has seen all the episodes a few times should be able to correctly answer almost all the questions.	Tom Phillips Phillips Software 1633 Commonwealth Avenue West Newton, MA 02165	**Application** **Freeware** **Size: 17K** 12" 6 7 32

MacTrek v1.1

Implementation of the classic Star Trek game with a Mac interface. Navigate through an 8 x 8 grid of star systems to destroy the Klingons. Shareware fee is whatever you think it's worth.

Travis Butler
8008 Hauser Drive
Lenexa, KS 66215
GEnie: T.BUTLER

Application
Shareware ?
Size: 63K
12" 6 7 32

ST game

Crashes under System 6.0.2.

unknown

Application
Public Domain
Size: 47K
12" 6 7 32

Star Fleet Battles v4.1

Utility for use with Star Fleet Battles game by Task Force games and ADB. No documentation. Shareware fee is whatever you think it's worth.

Douglas Hicks
6089 Rowland Street,
Apt. 1E
Balston Spa, NY 12020
CIS: 71355,264

Application
Shareware ?
Size: 40K
12" 6 7 32

Games M3

Star Trek Games

Star Trek Episodes DA v1.3

List of all Star Trek episodes, including the original series, animated series, motion pictures, and Next Generation series through the end of season 4.

Daniel A. Segel
daniels@xstor.com
AOL: Dan Segel
GEnie: D.SEGEL

Desk Accessory
Freeware
Size: 26K

Star-Trek.guide

Synopsis of the original Star Trek episodes with ratings.

Saul Jaffe
sf-lovers-request@rutgers.edu

Text Document
Freeware
Size: 26K

Star-Trek-Animated.guide

Sysnopsis of Star Trek animated series episodes.

Saul Jaffe
sf-lovers-request@rutgers.edu

Text Document
Freeware
Size: 13K

Star-Trek-STTNG.guide

Synopsis of Star Trek: The Next Generation episodes.

Saul Jaffe
sf-lovers-request@rutgers.edu

Text Document
Freeware
Size: 57K

StarShipMac! v1.5

Move StarShipMac! through the galaxy seeking and destroying Klingon vessels.

Bob Grubb
6612 Thorman Road
Port Charlotte, FL 33981

Application
Freeware
Size: 162K

The Trivia Mac v1.02

Trivia question program. You can add your own categories, questions and answers, and sounds.

Skip Burrell
1313 No. 111th Plaza #1320
Omaha, NE 68154

Application
Shareware $10.00
Size: 47K

Trek v1.2

Your mission is to patrol a portion of the Federation space and to remove hostile ships from all your patrol quadrants.

Robert A. Koch
attn: Registration W190
1416 N. 112th Plaza #2802
Omaha, NE 68154

Application
Shareware $12.00
Size: 144K

Asteroids

Play a version of the arcade game Asteroids. Goal is to break up asteroids by firing a ray. Helps to play if you are depressed. A great way to get over floundering love affairs.

unknown

Application
Public Domain
Size: 23K

Shuttle 88

Pilot the space shuttle to the space station and try to capture and repair U.S. satellites on the way. Watch out for meteors and Russian satellites! Nice graphics. Docs in a separate file.

Ron Minor
Route 2 Box 65
Lula, GA 30554

Application
Shareware $9.95
Size: 171K

Spacestation Pheta v1.0.1

Move a spaceman across platforms and up and down ladders to get to the other side of the screen. Demo version is limited to 10 levels. For a $9.95 fee, get 80 levels and an editor to create your own screens.

Tad Woods
T&T Software
109 Tee Circle
Salem , VA 24153

Application
Demoware
Size: 98K

Stellar Imperium v1.01

Destroy enough of the Klystrons ships in the alotted time and you can advance to the next level. Try to make Admiral!

Daniel Delamatta
275 South St. Ext.
Coventry, CT 06238

Application
Shareware $10.00
Size: 104K

The Pleiades Incident v1.0

You command a military space vessel and must defend yourself against an enemy attack. Decide how to allocate energy between shields, weapons, and engines. Limited graphics and sound.

Allan Goff
Zero Sum, Inc.
PO Box 121
Citrus Heights, CA 95611

Application
Demoware
Size: 51K

Utaan Attack ////

Shoot space ships before they reach the ground. Move the target site and shoot with the mouse.

Gary Dauphin
334 Markham Drive
Slidell, LA 70458

Application
Shareware $4.00
Size: 83K

Space Games

Games P1

Word Games

Ars Magna™ v1.0

An anagram generator. Enter a phrase and the program displays or prints a list of phrases composed of English words that use all the same letters. Has a line-mode interface.

Michael Morton
Boston Computer Society
One Center Plaza
Boston, MA 02108

Application
Shareware $10.00
Size: 28K

Lembracs v1.1

Unscramble jumbled 3- to 8-letter words.

Michael D. Speir
PO Box 6835
Tampa, FL 33608-6835

Application
Shareware $10.00
Size: 40K

MacWord Hunt v2.0

Find as many words as you can in a grid of letters within a specified time. Options for a 4 x 4 or a 5 x 5 grid. You must write down your words on paper. Full-featured version is sold for $10.

Fred Moulden, Jr.
1109 Riaza Square #9
St. Louis, MO 63138

Application
Demoware
Size: 71K

PhrazeCrazePlus v1.01

Mac version of the popular game show 'Wheel of Fortune.' Spin the wheel, buy a vowel, solve the puzzle. Complete with music and a game show host and model. Very well done.

Bradley R. Pettit
E. 4212 10th Street
Spokane, WA 99202

Application
Shareware $10.00
Size: 135K

WordFind 1.3ß v1.3ß

Creates word search puzzles, which are grids of letters in which words are hidden. Specify a list of words and a grid size; the program does the rest. Pascal source code provided.

Matthew Weinstein
2128 Hayes Street
San Francisco, CA 94117

Application
Freeware
Size: 25K

WordSmith

A 5 x 5 array of random letters appears on the playing board. The letters of a word can go in any direction; each letter must be adjacent to the next.

Michael D. Speir
PO Box 6835
Tampa, FL 33608-6835

Application
Shareware $10.00
Size: 46K

CrossMaster v0.2

Crossword puzzle processor. Has an editor where you can enter your own puzzle. Once it is entered, you can click on spaces and the clue is highlighted in an adjacent window. A great program.

Patrick J. Stevenson
26 Roberts Street #223
Fargo, ND 58102

Application
Freeware
Size: 57K

CrossWise v1.4

A solitaire crossword puzzle game. Make up words and place them in a crossword puzzle grid until you can't add any more.

Michael D. Speir
PO Box 6835
Tampa, FL 33608-6835

Application
Shareware $10.00
Size: 89K

CrossWiseDA v2.1

A solitaire crossword puzzle game in a DA. Make up words and place them in a crossword puzzle grid until you can't add any more.

Michael D. Speir
PO Box 6835
Tampa, FL 33608-6835

Desk Accessory
Shareware $7.00
Size: 23K

Jumble

Tool for solving Jumble word puzzles that shows all 120 combinations of 5 letters. Type in a scrambled word, then scan the list to find the actual word.

James H. Moore, Jr.
4100 Rustic Avenue
Paducah, KY 42001

Application
Freeware
Size: 4K

Snigs

Diplays a made-up word and its definition, such as 'BIZOOS n. The millions of tiny individual bumps that make up a basketball.' These are called 'Snigs'. You get a new Snig each time you hit a button.

Gary Dauphin

Application
Freeware
Size: 60K

Webster's Revenge Demo

Find as many words as you can in a 4 x 4 array of letters within a specified time limit. Point out your words with the mouse. Play against the computer. Demo version limits the number of configurations.

Jeffrey Morris & David Jordan
Loki Engineering
55 Wheeler Street
Cambridge, MA 02138

Application
Demoware
Size: 71K

Wheel v1.0

Another version of 'Wheel of Fortune.' Graphics aren't very good, and there's no sound. Has a few bugs also. Shareware fee is whatever you think it's worth.

Bob Boylan
391 Birchwood Road
Medford, NY 11763

Application
Shareware ?
Size: 22K

Will of Fortune

Demo version of a 'Wheel of Fortune' game. Three players compete. Hold down the spin button to spin. Guess letters, buy vowels, or solve the puzzle. Speaks if MacinTalk is installed.

William Rhodes
704 Harris Point Drive
Virginia Beach, VA 23455

Application
Demoware
Size: 57K

Word Search Game

RBD2

Allows you to create word search puzzles by entering a list of words (maximum 40 characters) that the program hides in a user-specified matrix of characters. Instructions included within the program.

Bobby Diggins
RBD2
7036 Madelynne Way
Anchorage, AK 99504

Application
Public Domain
Size: 26K
12" 6 7 32

Ax Headroom v1.0

A guitar simulator capable of producing 10 chords. Fretting is controlled by the keyboard; plucking or strumming is performed by passing the cursor over the 6 strings. Good sound quality.

Harmony Unlimited
PO Box 15101
Newark, DE 19711

Application
Shareware $10.00
Size: 39K

Face the Music v1.0763

Asks 24 mulitple-choice music trivia questions.

Rick Frank
SoftBrains, Ltd.

Application
Public Domain
Size: 13K

Fortune v1.01

Displays random bits of 'wisdom' similar to those found in fortune cookies. Click to keep displaying fortunes. Automatically quits to the Finder if you leave it idle for a few seconds.

David Fry
Dept. of Math., Harvard Univ.
1 Oxford Street
Cambridge, MA 02138

Application
Freeware
Size: 4K

Golf Mac Way

Mac version of Golf. You choose the clubs and play to avoid the obstacles. Graphics are pretty good, but you don't see yourself strike the ball or get to watch the flight of the ball. Also, you have no control over direction and strength of your swing.

Gary Dauphin
334 Markham Drive
Slidell, LA 70458

Application
Shareware $10.00
Size: 62K

LOTTO 54 v1

A program for picking 6 numbers for each dollar category in the New York Lotto 54 lottery.

Tracker!

Application
Freeware
Size: 82K

Lotto Chooser

A spreadsheet and macro that allow you to calculate the odds of winning a lottery. Also picks numbers for you.

David McGregor
AOL: David517
GEnie: D.McGregor1

Excel Spreadsheet
Public Domain
Size: 4K

Lotto wheeler v2.0

For California's Lotto 6/49. Chooses numbers for you.

Michael Powell
PO Box 5246
Napa, CA 94581-0246

Application
Freeware
Size: 94K

LottoBalls II

Picks 3 to 6 numbers for a 49-number lotto game.

Allen Chapman

Application
Freeware
Size: 15K

LottoMania v1.02

Configurable lotto program. Interface is bare-bones, but it does the job.

unknown

Application
Public Domain
Size: 78K

MacLucky v1.0d

Pick your lotto number with MacLucky.

Keep It Simple Software
PO Box 285
Fairfax City, VA 22030-0285

Application
Demoware
Size: 52K

Occult Pick•It

Program has 3 modules: answers yes/no questions using Tarot cards; characterizes people based on their names using numerology; makes recommendations using I Ching.

Larry B. Hunter
1212 S. 7th Street
Philadelphia, PA 19147

Application
Shareware $10.00
Size: 137K

Graphics

Graphics programs of all sorts.

Graphics A1

General Graphics

AddLPrep v1.2

Adds the PostScript code from the Laser Prep file to the beginning of a PostScript text file. Modifies Apple's LaserWriter files to get a PostScript disk file from non-Apple laser printers.

Software101
15151 Old Ranch Road
Los Gatos, CA 95030

Application
Shareware $20.00
Size: 7k

Apple Font

PostScript program defining a font from Century's LaserFonts collection.

Michael Mace
Century Software, Inc.
2483 Hearst #175
Berkeley, CA 94709

Text File
Freeware
Size: 37k

Artisto+ v2.01

Views MacPaint and PICT files. Lets you select any portion of the image and copy it into the clipboard.

Tom Taylor
MegaMot
3405 Walton Way
San Jose, CA 95117

Desk Accessory
Shareware $10.00
Size: 14k

Banner v1.0

Type text in a dialog box; program prints out the text in large letters on an ImageWriter.

John Gregory
PowerTools Software
5059 San Aquario Drive
San Diego, CA 92109

Application
Freeware
Size: 16k

Banner Maker v1.2.3

New twist to the old Banner program. Make small to medium size banners. Use ATM with it for better results.

Jeffrey Backes
1201 Main Street
Higgins, MO 64037
CIS: 72227,1130

Application
Shareware $15.00
Size: 39k

Clarity v1.0

Rescales bitmap images from the clipboard so that they take full advantage of the currently selected printer. Includes docs within the program.

Andrew Welch
Mark 3 Software
29 Grey Rocks Road
Wilton, CT 06897

Application
Shareware $8.00
Size: 33k

Convert][To Mac v0.9

Translates Apple II high-resolution graphics into MacPaint format. Contains documentation in a separate file. Comes with another application to convert Mac graphics to Apple II format also. Not compatible with later Mac systems.

James E. Hopper and
John B. Matthews
7135 Springboro Pike
Dayton, OH 45449

Application
Public Domain
Size: 5k

Direct ACL v1.0

This is the direct-connect file that establishes a connection to an HP LaserJet with a Pacific Data PS cartridge hooked to the serial port. Works with SuperSpool and other spoolers.

Scott Anderson

PS script document
Public Domain
Size: 2k

EPS->PICT v1.1

Converts Encapsulated PostScript (EPS) files into standard Mac PICT files, which can then be copied to the clipboard for importing into other programs.

Altsys Corporation

Desk Accessory
Freeware
Size: 7k

Font List

PostScript program for printing a list of the fonts installed in a LaserWriter.

Michael Mace

Text File
Freeware
Size: 1k

Good LaserWriter Tech Notes

Two transcripts of several messages posted to CompuServe discussing problems and techniques for printing to a LaserWriter.

unknown

Text File
Public Domain
Size: 10k

JoyPaint v1.2

Displays MacPaint drawings and can scroll them in any direction by using a simulated JoyStick. Lets you flip drawings horizontally and/or vertically and invert them. Contains documentation in a separate file.

John Stogdell Stokes III
Pixel Pathways
PO Box 4065
Mt. Penn, PA 19606

Application
Freeware
Size: 10k

LaserFix v2.0

Allows the output of PostScript printing to disk. This version lets you name the output file and decide whether to use LaserPrep. Author requests you send money to American Cancer Society if you use.

David P. Sumner
1009 Walters Lane
Columbia, SC 29208
(803) 786-2980

System StartUp Extension
Charityware
Size: 4k

LaserLAB v1.0

Fiddles with bitmap images such as those created with MacPaint or other painting programs. Can adjust such images so they look better on a LaserWriter and create high-resolution effects.

Wayne Moore & Dave Ewing
In Focus Technologies
PO Box 185
Niwot, CO 80544

Application
Freeware
Size: 46k

LaserWriter Update v1.0b1

Updates LaserWriter driver for System 6.x so that it can output PostScript to a file on disk instead of sending it to the printer. Turn it on and off from the Chooser. Handy!

Ron Breger
AOL: RonBreger

Application
Freeware
Size: 5k

LPDownloader v1.15

Downloads LaserPerfect fonts and text files containing PostScript programs to Apple LaserWriters.

unknown

Application
Public Domain
Size: 11k

Graphics A1

Continued

General Graphics

MakePaint v1.1

Converts PICT files or pictures on the clipboard into MacPaint files.

Alan Dahlbom

Application
Public Domain
Size: 8k

PAINT Ranger

Changes the creator of all paint files on a selected disk. For example, it changes all FullPaint files into MacPaint files, and vice versa.

Neil Swartz
Chicago, IL

Application
Public Domain
Size: 11k

Paint to RMaker v1.0

Converts MacPaint images into RMaker text format; a tool for programmers who want to include pictures with applications.

Carlos A. Rimola

Application
Freeware
Size: 21k

PaintFlipper v1.0

Loads up to 10 MacPaint images into memory. Lets you flip between them with keys 0 through 9.

Jeff Miller

Application
Freeware
Size: 6k

PaintMover v0.03

Open a file, choose the options, select a region, and drag it to the output window. Options include scale, rotate, smooth, thin, and inverse. Documentation in a separate file.

Bill Atkinson
Apple Computer, Inc.

Application
Freeware
Size: 13k

PaintShow

Reads list of MacPaint files and shows them in slide show fashion. Includes documentation in a separate file.

Michael Green & Robin Casady

Application
Public Domain
Size: 25k

Rotate Paint v1.0

Rotates and flips (horizontally or vertically) MacPaint drawings.

Bernard Gille
4409 Avonshire
Plano, TX 75024

Application
Shareware $5.00
Size: 6k

SelectPicture v1.0

Individually selects and displays a MacPaint drawing to fill the screen.

Mark S. Wall

Application
Public Domain
Size: 8k

Start-up off

PostScript program for turning off the startup page that is printed when a LaserWriter is turned on. Use a PostScript downloading program (available on other BMUG disks) to send this file to your printer.

Michael Mace
Century Software, Inc.
2306 Cotner
Los Angeles, CA 90064

PostScript File
Freeware
Size: 1k

Start-up on

PostScript program for turning on the startup page that is printed when a LaserWriter is turned on. Use a PostScript downloading program (available on other BMUG disks) to send this file to your printer.

Michael Mace
Century Software, Inc.
2306 Cotner
Los Angeles, CA 90064

PostScript File
Freeware
Size: 1k

SuperConvert v1.0

Utility program for converting images between different file formats. Converts between TIFF, ThunderScan, and LaserBits formats. Can also convert any of those 3 formats to EPS.

Dana Gregory
Eric Zocher
Silicon Beach Software, Inc.
(619) 695-6956

Application
Freeware
Size: 60k

ViewPaint v1.5

Manipulates MacPaint and StartupScreen documents. Can open, scroll, convert, and print either type of file. Works with large screens, too.

Steve Dagley - SSA Designs
PO Box 360096
Melbourne, FL 32936-0096
CIS: 76174, 2661

Application
Shareware $5.00
Size: 24k

YAPS

Stands for Yet Another Paint Scroller. Views paintings. Supports multiple windows and can display paintings at normal size or zoomed out to see the entire page.

John P. MacVeigh
CIS: 72467, 2141

Application
Freeware
Size: 9k

Graphics A2

General Graphics

3D-Edit v1.5

Drawing program for creating 3-D images. Create spheres, cubes, cylinders, and pyramids. Window displays 4 views of the drawing. You can adjust the perspective and remove hidden lines.

Colin Olson
Route 1, Box 287k
Van Alstyne, TX 75095

Application
Shareware $15.00
Size: 49k

AniRama v1.00

Simple program for creating an animation from 15 paintings. Import paintings into this program, set the time delays, and let 'er rip.

Dennis L. King

Application
Freeware
Size: 9k

Bezier DA

Paint program that draws Bézier curves. Has a pencil, straight line, and selection tool, also. All images are bitmaps, however, so the Bézier curves will not be smooth if printed on a LaserWriter.

Chris Heilman
CIS: 70566,1474

Desk Accessory
Freeware
Size: 16k

Dynamo v1.0 c

Animation program that creates, edits, and displays smoothly moving line drawings. Docs within the program. A more advanced version of this program is available for $35.

Michael Everest
Event One
222 Del Norte Avenue, Dept. I
Sunnyvale, CA 94086

Application
Shareware $10.00
Size: 67k

Graphix v0.5

Simple 3-D animation, variable views of a rotating moving pyramid. Formal name is No Blue Screen Required.

Michael E. Gaines
37 East Gibbons Street
Linden, NJ 07036
GEnie: M.GAINES

Application
Freeware
Size: 37k

Henon Map (area)

Plots the Henon Map, an area preserving iterstive processes. Primitive version of a program developed to teach the mathematics of chaos and fractal geometry.

Bernt Wahl
Wahl Street Software
PO Box 7534
Santa Cruz, CA 95061

Application
Freeware
Size: 27k

PicSynch v1.0

Plays a sound file and displays a painting at the same time. Contains docs within the program.

Tom Stark
551 Lakeside Drive
Sedro Woolley, WA 98284
CIS: 73775,1262

Application
Shareware $10.00
Size: 19k

PS Printer

Sends text files containing PostScript programs to a LaserWriter.

Scott Gillespie
Reed College

Desk Accessory
Freeware
Size: 7k

WriteFontSize™ v1.0

Allows you to enter text in any font size (useful for MacWrite users where point size options are limited) and enter special non-printing characters using their ASCII codes. Contains docs in a separate file.

Jeffrey S. Shulman
PO Box 521
Ridgefield, CT 06877-0521

Desk Accessory
Shareware $7.00
Size: 14k

Graphics A3

General Graphics

Aquarium v2.0

Displays fish on your screen. Includes Pascal source code.

unknown

Application
Public Domain
Size: 27k

Diatom v1.0

Drawing program based on the Fourier transform. Creates line-art patterns based on user-supplied parameters. Docs describe the mathematical basis of the drawings.

Chris Capener
PO Box 994
Cupertino, CA 95015-0994

Application
Freeware
Size: 33k

Escher Draw v1.0b

Working with Escher is a lot like FatBits in MacPaint. Each time you put a bit down, it gets transformed into the symmetry you select.

R. Moravec
WAM 124
University Ave. #201
Palo Alto, CA 94301

Application
Freeware
Size: 95k

Globe v1.2

Displays a spinning globe, which is a little less than 2 inches in diameter. Intended to run as a background task under MultiFinder. Looks nice on a color machine.

Paul Mercer

Application
Freeware
Size: 12k

LAZlife v2.0c

Play the 'game' of Life, a form of cellular automata that roughly simulates the growth and decline of populations. Cells rapidly appear (are born) and disappear (die), creating animated pattern. Shareware fee is whatever you think it's worth.

Larry (LAZ) Hutchinson
6950 SW Juniper Terrace
Beaverton, OR 97005

Application
Shareware ?
Size: 20k

Lines

Displays b&w line-art graphics.

George A. Nelson
201 Main Street
Medway, MA 02053

Application
Freeware
Size: 9k

MacEyes v1.1

Displays a pair of eyes that follow the movements of the mouse. It's cute when running in the background under MultiFinder.

Duncan Sinclair
40 Switchback Road
Bearsden G61 1AD
UNITED KINGDOM

Application
Freeware
Size: 10k

QuickDraw Fun

Displays b&w line-art graphics.

unknown

Application
Public Domain
Size: 5k

Rays v1.0

Description	Author	Type
Displays line-art graphics in b&w. Even draws over the scroll bars.	Michael Mounier	**Application** **Public Domain** **Size: 2k**

Ripple 1

Description	Author	Type
Draws a checkerboard sheet undulating in a breeze. Warning: There doesn't seem to be any way to quit the program except by rebooting!	unknown	**Application** **Public Domain** **Size: 3k**

Ripple 2

Description	Author	Type
Draws a series of hexagonal posts that rise and fall in waves. Warning: There doesn't seem to be any way to quit this program except by rebooting!	unknown	**Application** **Public Domain** **Size: 4k**

Tree v1.0

Description	Author	Type
Displays line-art graphics in b&w. Source code available for $5.	Dana Gregory Ventana Software 3721A Balboa Terrace San Diego, CA 92117	**Application** **Freeware** **Size: 9k**

Graphics A4

General Graphics

FastPaintPrint

Opens and prints MacPaint format paintings (PNTG).

unknown

Application
Public Domain
Size: 6k

FlipTIFF v1.0

Converts a TIFF file between Motorola and Intel formats.

Ed McCreight
Richard Chon
Brian Bezanson
Pot O' Gold Software

Application
Freeware
Size: 85k

Fonds

Set of 3 resource files containing replacement 'FOND' resources for HyperCard, MacDraw, and MacPaint. You need to use ResEdit to install them. Helps avoid conflicts with the internal fonts in these programs.

John Friedman
CIS: 71350,2360

Resource Files
Public Domain
Size: 3k

MultiRuler v1

Displays a vertical ruler with increments in picas, inches, or points. Designed for use under MultiFinder with word processors that only have a horizontal ruler.

Martin Simoneau
200 De Beaujeu
Ste-Hyacinthe, Quebec
J2S 7P6 CANADA

Application
Freeware
Size: 10k

Notebook v2.0

A little program for creating notebook pages with both graphics and text. Sort of a simple paint program where each document can be composed of multiple pages that you can flip through.

Kevin Parichan

Application
Freeware
Size: 66k

PCXtc v0.8

A viewer for files created in the PCX graphics format used on MS-DOS machines. Docs in a separate file. This version does not support DAs. Version 1.0 of this program is available for $5.

John Papiewski
PO Box 7444
Elgin, IL 60121-7444

Application
Freeware
Size: 45k

PICT Loader

Displays pictures stored as PICT resources in files. Loads pictures into memory, then stores them in other files. For example, you could extract pictures from your favorite game.

Jim Moore
4125 Arroyo Trail
Carmel, CA 93923

Application
Freeware
Size: 6k

Preview v1.4

A screen printer driver that allows printed output to be viewed on the screen. Pages are displayed one at a time in miniature; clicking on the miniature shows the page at actual size.

Randy Ubillos
COMPUTER:applications, Inc.
12813 Lindley Drive
Raleigh, NC 26714

Chooser Extension
Shareware $10.00
Size: 10k

R-Mapper v1.5

A program for molecular biologists. Takes a list of cleavage sites and enzyme symbols and draws a restriction map. Creates a picture that can be copied to the Clipboard. Includes docs within program and in a separate file.

Bill Engels
Genetics Department
University of Wisconsin
Madison, WI 53706

Application
Freeware
Size: 80k

Snap v1.0

You can select any rectangular area of the screen and copy the image to a window. The image can then be inverted, copied to the Clipboard, saved as a PICT file, or printed. Useful under MultiFinder only.

Mac Whackers
Craig, John, and Mike

Application
Freeware
Size: 23k

SnapShot™ Installer v1.0

Installs a function key (FKEY) program that takes snapshots of the screen. Works with color and large-screen monitors and with menus pulled down. Demo version; limited to 12 uses.

Mike Whittingham
Mark 3 Software
215 Thayer Pond Road
Wilton, CT 06897

Application
Shareware $15.00
Size: 118k

Super Ruler v1.1

Places a ruler on the screen horizontally or vertically. You can adjust the scale for different dpi. Very slick. Includes docs in a separate file.

Randy Ubillos
COMPUTER:applications, Inc.
12813 Lindley Drive
Raleigh, NC 27609

Desk Accessory
Shareware $10.00
Size: 14k

Graphics A5

General Graphics

Bomber v1.0

Puts a System bomb Alert box on the screen with a Restart button and a grayed-out Resume button. The Restart button moves if you try to position the mouse over it. Click the grayed-out button to quit.

unknown

Application
Public Domain
Size: 4k

Cursor demo v1.0beta

A demonstration of animated cursors: an hourglass, a one-handed clock, and a two-handed clock.

Mike Morton

Application
Freeware
Size: 6k

Curves v1.0

Draws 3 types of curves defined by a recursive pattern. Lets you draw each curve at 4 different resolutions.

John S. Rhoades

Application
Public Domain
Size: 5k

Fractal Magic

Fractal-generating program. Has problems running under MultiFinder.

Scott Ettinger
1373 NW Cocoanut Point Lane
Stuart, FL 34994

Application
Shareware $10.00
Size: 15k

Galaxy

Fills the screen with slowly moving stars on a black background. Screen looks very much like the program's icon.

unknown

Application
Public Domain
Size: 2k

Geographics II Demo v2.00b

Interesting program for creating and viewing maps, floor plans, perspective views, etc. Maintains an index of all the constitutive elements that compose a drawing.

David M. George
332 Palermo Drive
St. Louis, MO 63011

Application
Demoware
Size: 90k

Googly Scrooge

Draws a picture of Scrooge McDuck with google eyes that wiggle back and forth.

Neil Shapiro

Application
Freeware
Size: 49k

Graphics

Draws 3 different spirograph-like patterns on the screen.

Terry Gintz

Application
Public Domain
Size: 22k

Insane v1.0

Draws a spiral pattern on the screen. Looking at it for a long time could possibly drive you insane.

unknown

Application
Public Domain
Size: 7k

Julia

Fractal-drawing program that illustrates the Fatou-Julia construction when P(z) is quadratic.

Richard Koch

Application
Public Domain
Size: 10k

MadMenus

Bizarre program that displays what the author calls a 'video telegram.' Text flashes across the screen as if quickly scanning a bunch of menus. Must use ResEdit to change the text of the message.

Howard Katz

Application
Public Domain
Size: 4k

Maze 3D

Displays a 3-D perspective drawing of a maze.

unknown

Application
Public Domain
Size: 4k

More Chaos v1.0

Draws chaotic patterns using from 3 to 6 base points. From a starting point, pixels are plotted halfway between the current point and a randomly selected base point.

Henry Seurer
109 Kansas City Street
Rapid City, SD 57701

Application
Freeware
Size: 14k

Pattern* v1.2

Nice string-art, moiré pattern generator. Lets you set the parameters that control the drawing process. The ultimate in meditative aids.

M. Murray
PO Box 9992
Atlanta, GA 30319

Application
Shareware $20.00
Size: 7k

Pattern Blocks v2.1

Create designs on a 7 x 7 grid by placing a block in each of the 49 boxes. There are 12 built-in blocks, which are 32 x 32 bitmap images. Double-click on a pattern to edit it. Nice interface.

Dan Weston
Nerdworks
195 - 23rd NE
Salem, OR 97301

Application
Shareware $10.00
Size: 20k

Pattern Librarian v1.0

Tool for creating libraries of patterns, which are 8 x 8 bitmaps. Has a scrolling window with a grid of cells. Double-clicking on a cell brings up a FatBits editor for modifying its pattern.

Eagle I. Berns
Holly Thomason
735 La Para Avenue
Palo Alto, CA 94306

Application
Shareware $20.00
Size: 38k

Graphics A5

Continued

Pattern Maker v2.0

Displays windows with a variety of animated patterns. Has options for 5 basic types of patterns: bouncing shapes, rapidly flashing shapes, Life, flashing patterns, and random arcs. Nicely done.

Ron Ullmann
Moose Software Products
PO Box 9442
Stanford, CA 94305

Application
Shareware $10.00
Size: 47k

rae

Little balls with happy faces (just like the program's icon) drop from the top of the screen, bounce a few times, and come to rest. Let it run for a few minutes and watch the balls pile up.

unknown

Application
Public Domain
Size: 5k

RobotArm

Cute program where you control a robot arm with the mouse. Blocks can be created by pressing keys and then manipulated using the robot arm. Arm can also fire a laser beam to destroy blocks.

Brian Westley

Application
Freeware
Size: 16k

Spline Demo v2

Program for experimenting with properties of B-splines and Catmull splines. Click the mouse to position the control points, then let the program draw the spline curve.

Steve Splonskowski
PO Box 11349
Eugene, OR 97440

Application
Freeware
Size: 14k

Trix

Draws a rapidly moving string-art pattern on the screen.

unknown

Application
Public Domain
Size: 2k

Wide Flight

Small white stars on a black background whiz by you on the screen.

unknown

Application
Public Domain
Size: 2k

ZoomShapes v1.0

Draws moving string-art moiré patterns on the screen. Has options for setting the shape and speed and playing beep sounds. You can use it as a screen saver by hiding the menu bar.

Eric Knight
Crystal Creations
809 Timber Lane
Nashville, TN 37215

Application
Freeware
Size: 16k

Metalware v1.1

Display and edit a data file that defines the shape of a part. You can mail the file on a floppy disk to a service bureau, which can quote a price for the part and machine it for you.

Thorson & Co.
PO Box 360850
Miliptas, CA 95035-0850

Application
Freeware
Size: 36k

Minicad v2.4

Two mid-level CAD (Computer-Aided Design) programs for 2-D and 3-D drawing. Demo version doesn't cut, copy, paste, print, or save. Docs in a separate file.

Richard Diehl
Diehl GraphSoft
3246-K Normandy Woods Drive
Ellicott City, MD 21043

Application
Demoware
Size: 328k

SITZ CAD

A 2-D CAD program. Demo version limits the number of objects that can be stored. Full version available for $40. Extensive docs in a separate file.

Mike Sitz
10438 Jellison Way
Broomfield, CO 80020

Application
Demoware
Size: 311k

Graphics B2

CAD Software

CADD Level 1 Demo v1.1.3

A demo of a full-featured CAD program. It will not save or print, though. One meg of memory may be a little low for this demo.

Generic Software
(800) 228-3601

Application
Demoware
Size: 338k

Objex Demo v1.0

A new kind of drawing program: links objects by Cartesian equations.

Softstream International Inc.
19 White Chapel Dr.
Mt. Laurel, NJ 08054
(800) 262-6610

Application
Demoware
Size: 120k

Area Properties v1.0

Finds the area, centroid, and moment of inertia of any shape that has been saved as a picture (PICT) or painting (PNTG). Requests a donation to help the homeless if you use the program.

William Weiss
2500 Ptarmigan Drive #1
Walnut Creek, CA 94595
(415) 937-3091

Application
Shareware $?
Size: 50k

Design Demo v0.093

Demo version of a program that assists in graphical thinking. Operates similar to a drawing program where you create nodes (graphic objects) and connections (lines). Saving and printing are disabled. Docs in a separate file.

Meta Software Corporation
55 Wheeler Street
Cambridge, MA 02138
(617) 576-6920

Application
Demoware
Size: 197k

DesignScope Demo v1.00

Simulation program for designing component circuitry. Place electronic system blocks on a worksheet and construct a block diagram. Then assign parameter values and run the simulator to view the waveforms. Saving and printing disabled.

Bob Diamond
BrainPower, Inc.
24009 Ventura Boulevard
Calabasas, CA 91302

Application
Demoware
Size: 215k

Graphics D1

Drawing, Painting, and Graphing

CompuGraph v1.0v19

This one is hard to pin down. It can be used as a relational idea processor. It can handle animation and full text.

Klex Software, Inc.
25633 Branchaster
Farmington Hills, MI 48018
(313) 477-6800

Application
Shareware $40.00
Size: 108k
12" 6 7 32

DesignerDraw Demo

Draws diagrams such as structure charts, flow charts, dataflow diagrams, and organization charts. Diagrams are composed of boxes, connecting lines, and text. Some docs within the program.

Paul M. Hyman
417 Associate Road
Suite A-197
Brea, CA 92621

Application
Demoware
Size: 80k
12" 6 7 32

XVT-Draw v1.0B2

A simple object-oriented drawing program, much like MacDraw or the draw layer of SuperPaint. Creates PICT files.

Marc J. Rochkind
Advanced Programming Ltd.
Box 17665
Boulder, CO 80308

Application
Shareware $25.00
Size: 107k
12" 6 7 32

Crystal Paint™ Demo v1.02

Demo version of a unique program for painting crystal-like images and patterns characterized by some form of symmetry. Comes with several sample images.

Great Wave Software
5353 Scotts Valley Drive
Scotts Valley, CA 95066
(408) 438-1990

Application
Demoware
Size: 113k

Grapher DEMO v1.0

Has many nice graphing features. Get working version from the author.

Steve Scarborough
17030 Los Alimos Street
Granada Hills, CA 91433
(818) 831-7647

Application
Demoware
Size: 113k

GraphToolz v1.19c

Graphs and solves functions of a single variable. Functions can include polynomial, trig, and logarithmic terms. Numerically solves for roots, max and min, and integrals.

Tom Saxton
15500 NE 11th #D308
Bellevue, WA 98007

Application
Shareware $15.00
Size: 53k

Kid Pix v1.0

A easy-to-use painting program. Lots of tools and can save in PICT and MacPaint format. This is the original version; it's now commercial.

Craig Hickman
615 East 39th Ave
Eugene, OR 97405
(503) 683-5562

Application
Freeware
Size: 102k

PaintTools v1.0.0

Turbo Pascal unit for supporting the basic Mac paint tools. Source code and an example application are included.

Kevin Parichan

Application
Freeware
Size: 16k

Graphics E1

LaserWriter and PageMaker Software

PageMaker Templates II

Set of 9 templates for PageMaker 2.0. Samples of resumes, newsletters, business cards, envelopes, letterheads, and invitations are included.

unknown

PageMaker 2.0
Documents
Public Domain
Size: 734k
12" 6 7 32

LaserWriter and PageMaker Software

Generic Business Reply Template

A MacDraw template for printing business reply postcards, those little postage-paid cards you get from companies for ordering merchandise or requesting more information.

Dan Wood

MacDraw Document
Public Domain
Size: 6k

Laser ConTemplates Demo v3.1a

PostScript templates for creating impressive visual effects. This demo package includes a clipped button, name cards, spiral text, and a letterhead. Just fill in text from a dialog box. Retail version with 30 templates available for $74.

Greg Kruckewitt
Lupin Software
PO Box 4009
Davis, CA 95617-4009

Application
Demoware
Size: 43k
12" 6 7 32

Laser Disk Labels

Template for printing floppy disk labels on a LaserWriter. Comes with step-by-step instructions on how to create labels using nice paper and double-sided tape.

Bill Santos
3999 N. Chestnut, Suite 327
Fresno, CA 93726
CIS: 76625,3513

MacDraw Document
Shareware $10.00
Size: 8k
12" 6 7 32

PageMaker Templates I v.99

Set of PageMaker templates useful for business. They help lay out business cards, letterheads, envelopes, signs, labels, diplomas, and postcards. Separate PageMaker documentation file.

Robert Elliott Purser
P.O. Box 466
El Dorado, CA 95623

PageMaker 1.0 & 2.0 Files
Public Domain
Size: 377k
12" 6 7 32

Template For Business Cards

A MacDraw template for laying out standard business cards. Page is set up for 10 cards.

Dan Wood

MacDraw Document
Public Domain
Size: 2k

Graphics F1

Graphics Utilities

Halftone v1.0

Displays and prints grayscale images. Uses halftone patterns for display. Communicates with LaserWriter directly in PostScript; LaserWriter uses its own halftone patterns for printing.

Chris Capener
PO Box 994
Cupertino, CA 95015-0994

Application
Freeware
Size: 22k

PostScript template

Library of PostScript shapes and fill patterns for use with Aldus FreeHand, a commercial drawing program.

unknown

Aldus FreeHand Document
Freeware
Size: 2k

PseudoPS

An interpreter that handles a small subset of PostScript commands. Reads PostScript programs from text files and displays the graphics on the screen. C source code is included.

Craig E. Rasmussen
Center for Atmospheric & Space Science
Utah State University
Logan, Utah 84322-4405

Application
Freeware
Size: 36k

Retouch v1.2

Manipulates b&w and 8-bit gray-cale images. Works with TIFF, MacPaint, and PICT file formats. Touches up scanned images and produces special effects. Includes docs in a separate file.

Allen Akin
784 Palo Alto Avenue
Palo Alto, CA 94301
CIS: 72247,2635

Application
Shareware $20.00
Size: 94k

TeX Preview v0.1.0

Views documents written using the TeX text formatting language.

SARA
PO Box 4613
1009 AP Amsterdam
THE NETHERLANDS

Application
Freeware
Size: 59k

TeXSetScrap v0.0.1

Converts a picture on the Clipboard to a file with TeX commands so you can typeset pictures with TeX.

Rick Jansen
SARA
THE NETHERLANDS

Application
Freeware
Size: 8k

Vision Lab v0.65

Graphics conversion utility that handles GIF, PICT, MacPaint, PixelPaint, and ThunderScan file formats. Worth trying just to see the About box. Some C source code is included.

John Raymonds
CIS: 76174,205
GEnie: RAYMONDS

Application
Freeware
Size: 140k

HyperCard

Fun and educational HyperCard stacks for the whole family!

Note: Many HyperCard stacks are multi-disk packs.

HyperCard

HyperCard Education

Laura's Letters

HyperCard Education A1

Teaches alphabet and spelling of simple words.

unknown

Freeware
Size: 228k

Libby's Letters

HyperCard Education A1

Teaches alphabet and simple spelling through a kind of matching game.

Rick Montgomery
The Center of the Universe
25 Muirfield Green Lane
Midlothian, VA 23112

Public Domain
Size: 98k

Sight•Words v2.0

HyperCard Education A1

Find the correct word when MacinTalk speaks to you.

Lloyd Fruchtman
2778 Hearthstone Circle
Marietta, GA 30062

Freeware
Size: 71k

A,B,Cs

HyperCard Education A2

Click on the background to hear a letter and see a picture that begins with that letter. If you guess the real name of the picture right, it plays a little tune. And more!

Curt Morrison (SysOp)
Newton Corner
Newton, MA
(617) 964-6088

Freeware
Size: 327k

Drew's ABCs v1.1

HyperCard Education A2

Teaches the alphabet by associating a picture of an object whose name begins with the given character. Also teaches counting from one to ten.

Marty Harnish
7316 Old Mill Run
Fort Worth, TX 76133

Shareware $5.00
Size: 115k

Ed's Talking Speller

HyperCard Education A2

Click on letters to make words and hear the computer spell and read the word!

Ed Hensley
Eddie's Diner
160 W. Pine Street
Stockton, CA 95204

Shareware $5.00
Size: 239k

Education HyperCard

Flash Cards

HyperCard Education A2

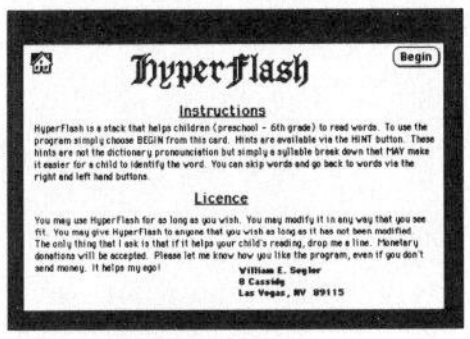

A stack that helps children read. Match words to pictures.

William E. Seyler
8 Cassidy
Las Vegas, NV 89115

Freeware
Size: 40k

Spelling

HyperCard Education A3

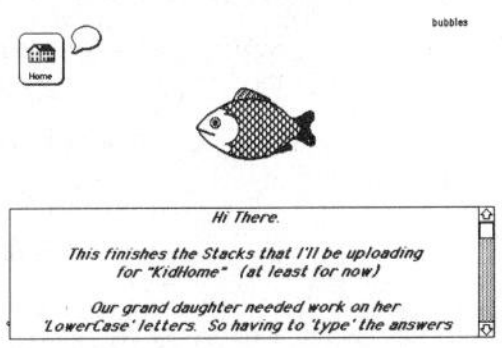

Spelling test. User level must be set higher than Typing.

unknown

Size: 34k

Spelln B Fun

HyperCard Education A3

Practice spelling. MacinTalk speaks back with advice.

R. J. Kelly
13130 W. Hampton Avenue
Butler, WI 53007

Shareware $5.00
Size: 166k

Education HyperCard

Talking Spelling Stack

HyperCard Education A3

Stack tests spelling. Requires MacinTalk.

Paul Wilson
POBox 2163
Largo, FL 34649

Freeware
Size: 183k

Addition

HyperCard Education A4

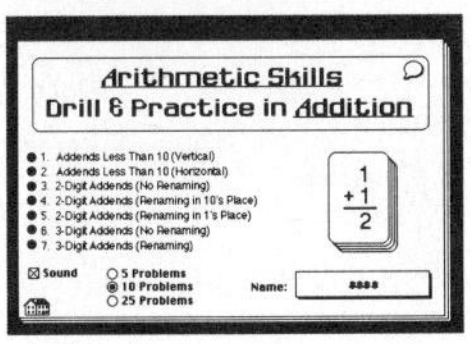

Test skills in adding 1-3 digit numbers.

Lawrence O. Hill
804 Temple Street
San Diego, CA 92106

Shareware $5.00
Size: 96k

Caroline's Counting

HyperCard Education A4

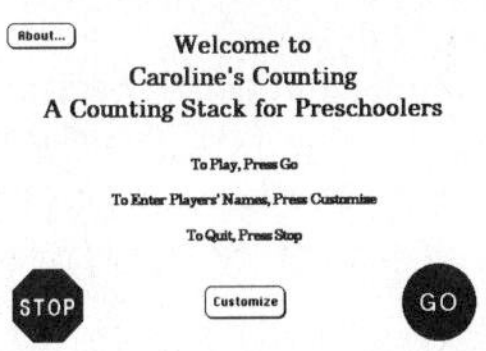

Count the objects appearing on the screen, and the computer will tell you if you're right.

Paul Dobbs

Freeware
Size: 102k

HyperCard

HyperCard Education

Let's do MATH

HyperCard Education A4

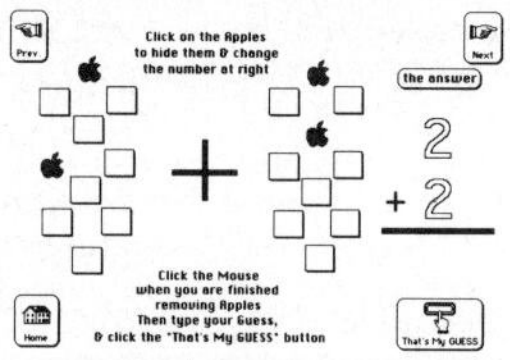

Test your addition and subtraction skills.

unknown

Size: 26k

Mad Math Minute v2.0

HyperCard Education A4

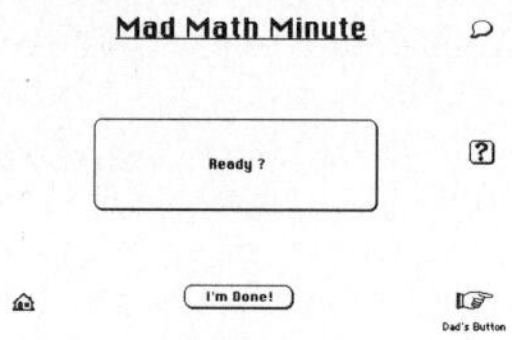

Speed test of addition skills. You can adjust the goal as you progress.

Hans Kruse
775 Rodney Drive
Nashville, TN 37215

Freeware
Size: 16k

Mr. Moo's Math

HyperCard Education A4

Test addition, subtraction, multiplication, and division skills. Levels range from very easy to very hard.

Mike Gleason, Jr.
5705 N. 117th Plaza
Omaha, NE 68164-1432

Shareware $1.00
Size: 426k

Subtraction

HyperCard Education A4

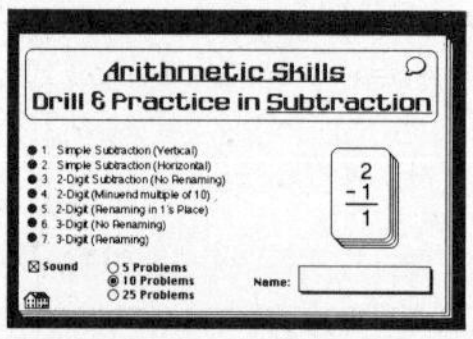

Test skills in subtracting 1-3 digit numbers. Companion to the Addition stack.

Lawrence O. Hill
804 Temple Street
San Diego, CA 92106

Shareware $5.00
Size: 86k

ASL Spelling v2.2

HyperCard Education A5

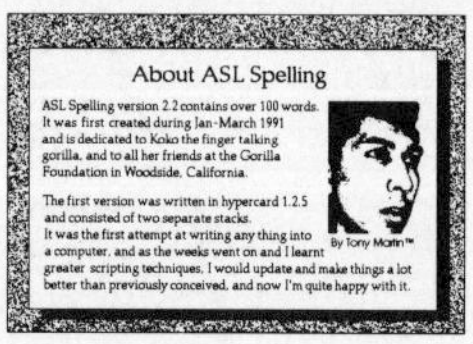

American Sign Language finger spelling practice stack. It shows how to spell words in ASL and also tests your reading skill. Author requests a $10 donation to Gorilla Foundation, PO Box 620–640, Woodside, CA 94062.

Tony Martin

Freeware
Size: 790k

Finger Helper

HyperCard Education A5

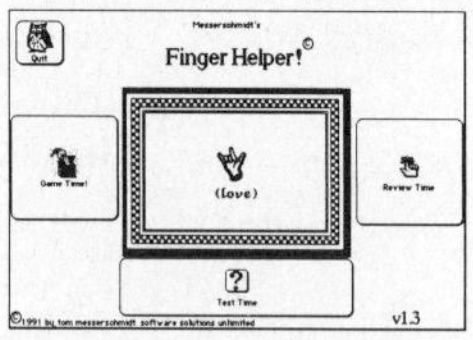

ASL finger spelling practice stack. Comes with two supplementary stacks: Game Time and Hand Shapes.

Tom Messerschmidt
Software Solutions Unlimited
165 Blossom Hill Road #276
San Jose, CA 95123

Freeware
Size: 83k

Education HyperCard

Game Time

HyperCard Education A5

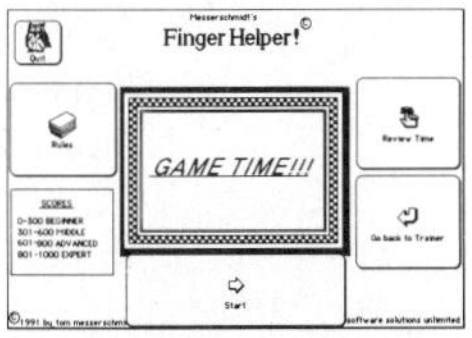

Lets you practice ASL finger spelling. For use with Finger Helper stack.

Tom Messerschmidt
Software Solutions
165 Blossom Hill Rd. #276
San Jose, CA 95123

Freeware
Size: 42k

Hand Shapes

HyperCard Education A5

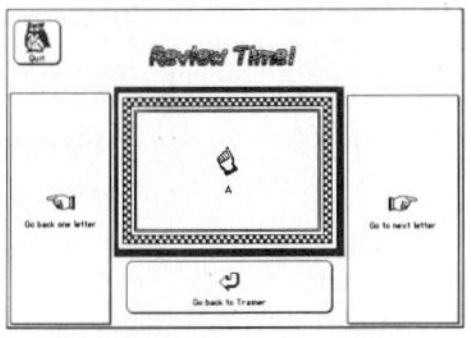

Shows hand shapes for ASL alphabet. For use with Finger Helper stack.

Tom Messerschmidt
Software Solutions
165 Blossom Hill Rd. #276
San Jose, CA 95123

Freeware
Size: 18k

Exegesis Tools v3.2

HyperCard Education B1

It doesn't do anything, but 'it's simply a place to store all those bits of information an exegete collects as she/he digs into the Scripture.' Included in the 4-disk set (HyperCard Education B1-1, -2, -3, and -4).

Mark Spaulding
Foundation Software
354 Canner Street #607
New Haven, CT 06511

Shareware $2.00
Size: 176k

Holy BibleStack© v1.9

HyperCard Education B1

Complete Holy Bible (King James Version). 'In addition to its function as a powerful, exhaustive concordance, [its] search feature...allows it to function both as a cross-reference and topical Bible.' This is a 4-disk set (HyperCard Education B1-1, -2, -3, and -4).

Shane Kiser
Holy Mountain Softw.
2775 Fountain Circle
Sarasota, FL 34235

Shareware $25.00
Size: 5106k

666

HyperCard Education B2

Calculates numbers from given words or phrases, based on Theomatics. More fun than spinning records backwards to detect Satanic references, and just as strange!

Mike Pfeiffer

Shareware $9.95
Size: 45k

HolyHyper!

HyperCard Education B2

A tool to keep track of one's favorite verses and notes about them. Also good for Bible study information.

Joel W. Gerdeen
Gospel/Ware
6240 Alden Way
Fridley, MN 55432

Freeware
Size: 47k

HyperCard

HyperCard Education

Romans Study — HyperCard Education B2

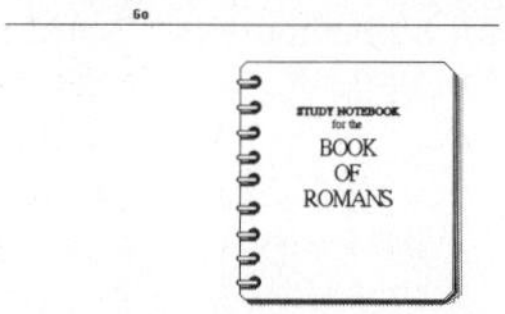

Bible study help. Explains terms in Romans.

Tom Gabrielli

Freeware
Size: 192k

St. John Holy BibleStack© — HyperCard Education B2

The book of St. John in a HyperCard Stack. The complete Holy BibleStack is shareware $25.

Holy Mountain Software

Freeware
Size: 184k

macBible Sampler — HyperCard Education B3

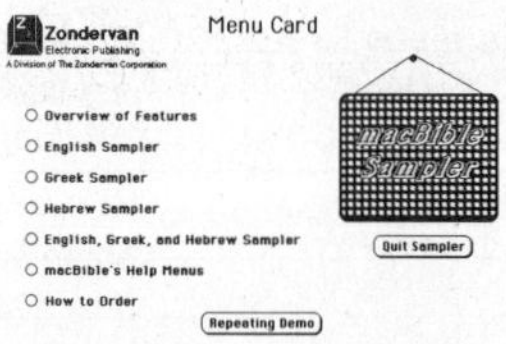

Demo of macBible program.

Zondervan Electronic Publishing

Demoware
Size: ?k

If Monks Had Macs... v2.5.7 — HyperCard Education B4

Quotes from the manual: 'IF MONKS HAD MACS... is about a time before capitalism, and a freedom beyond free enterprise.' 'Stacks crisscross the world of an idea rather than a catalogue of facts and images.' Amazing multistack game. Three-disk set.

Brian Thomas
riverTEXT
PO Box 2517
Portland, OR 97208

Freeware
Size: 2863k

Gradebook v2.02L — HyperCard Education C1

Stack for maintaining classroom gradebook. Mostly for college-level teachers. The long version.

Bangs L. Tapscott
4608 Lanark Road
Salt Lake City, UT
84124

Shareware $18.75
Size: 296k

Gradebook v2.02S — HyperCard Education C1

Stack for maintaining classroom gradebook. Mostly for college-level teachers. The short version.

Bangs L. Tapscott
4608 Lanark Road
Salt Lake City, UT
84124

Shareware $18.75
Size: 288k

BrainStack

HyperCard Education D1

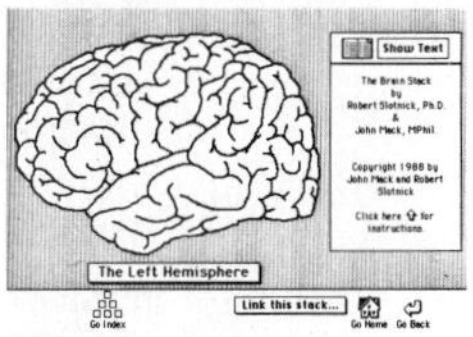

Explains the functions of various parts of the human brain.

John Mack and Robert Slotnick

Freeware
Size: 148k

Ear

HyperCard Education D1

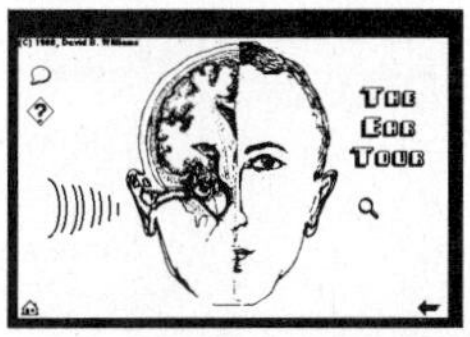

Designed for a psychomusicology course, this stack illustrates the anatomy of the human ear.

David B. Williams
Professor of Music
Illinois State University
Normal, IL 61761

Freeware
Size: 103k

Flash Anatomy Demo

HyperCard Education D1

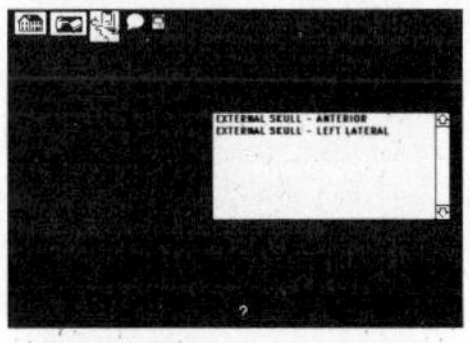

Demo version of a series of flashcard-type stacks for learning anatomical terms. This stack shows two views of the human skull.

Peter Lyte
2115 NW Aspen
Portland, OR 97210

Demoware
Size: 60k

Neurotour

HyperCard Education D1

This stack illustrates the human nerve system, with views of ever-increasing magnification.

Jim Ludtke

Freeware
Size: 311k

AIDS v7.02

HyperCard Education D2

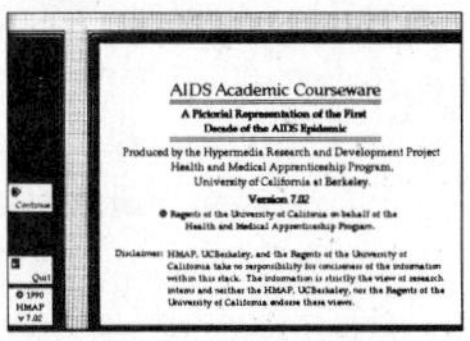

A review of the first decade of the AIDS epidemic.

Hypermedia Research and Development Project
Health and Medical Apprenticeship Program
University of California

Freeware
Size: 618k

AIDS Clock

HyperCard Education D2

Clock showing the toll of the AIDS epidemic.

Michael Tidmus

Freeware
Size: 40k

HyperCard

HyperCard Education

Abortion v3.01

HyperCard Education D3

A review of the abortion issue in various aspects.

Hypermedia Research and Development
Health and Medical Apprenticeship Program
University of California

Freeware
Size: 500k

Adult CPR Stack

HyperCard Education D4

Illustration of how to perform CPR on adults. Does not substitute for an accredited course.

Sylvan Rogers
465 Waller Street
San Francisco, CA
94117

Shareware $5.00
Size: 392k

Baby CPR

HyperCard Education D4

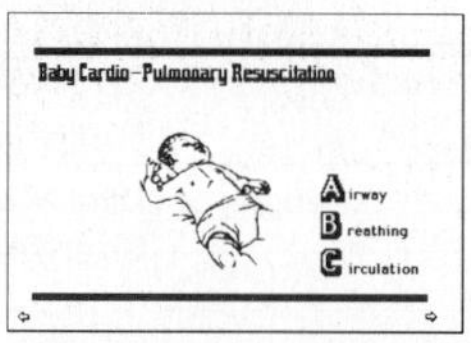

Illustration of how to perform CPR on infants. Does not substitute for an accredited course.

Sylvan Rogers
465 Waller Street
San Francisco, CA
94117

Shareware $5.00
Size: 160k

Chemistry HTB v1.0

HyperCard Education E1

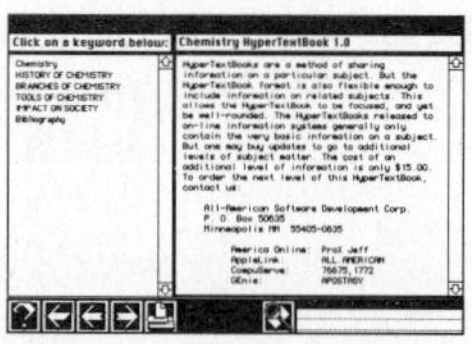

The first of the HyperTextBook series on chemistry. Sort of a demoware. An additional level of the subject matter may be ordered for $15.

All-American Software Development Corp.
PO Box 50635
Minneapolis, MN
55405-0635

Freeware
Size: 85k

Hyperchem

HyperCard Education E1

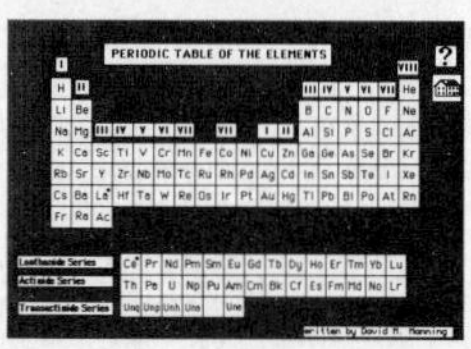

When you click on a chemical element in the periodic table, it shows brief specifics on the element.

David M. Manning
GEnie: D.Manning12

Freeware
Size: 40k

Periodic Table

HyperCard Education E1

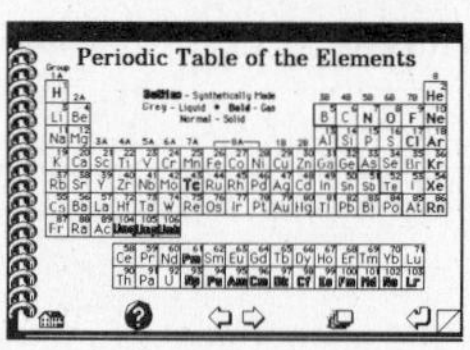

Periodic table with information on each chemical element.

Pisces Publishing
616 Rancheria Suite C
Chico, CA 95926
CIS: 72307,2100
GEnie: B.MENELL

Freeware
Size: 74k

Periodic Table

HyperCard Education E1

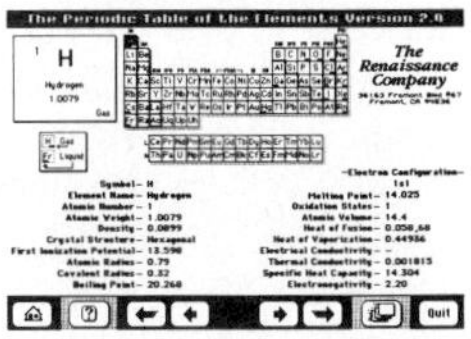

Another periodic table stack with lists of properties of chemical elements. The name of the file on the disk is 'Periodic Table 2' to distinguish it from other stacks of the same name.

The Renaissance Company
36163 Fremont Blvd. #67
Fremont, CA 94536

Freeware
Size: 104k

Periodic Table v1.0

HyperCard Education E1

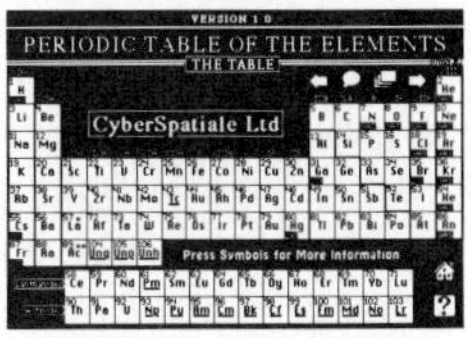

Yet another periodic table stack with information on individual element's chemical properties. Also lists isotopes. The name of the file on the disk has a period in it to distinguish it from other stacks of the same name.

Jeffrey Kirk Johnson
2542 Chilton Way
Berkeley, CA 94704

Freeware
Size: 89k

Conservation ?'s v1.21p

HyperCard Education E2

Collection of over 200 questions concerning conservation biology; intended to stimulate discussions. This stack originates from a seminar at San Francisco State University.

Jeremy John Ahouse
c/o Waves Consulting and Development
5957 Shattuck Avenue
Oakland, CA 94609

Freeware
Size: ?k

Bird Calls

HyperCard Education F2

A variation of Bird Stack that includes bird call sounds. Demo version.

Richard J. Wald
1 Dogberry Lane
Ridgefield, CT 06877

Demoware
Size: 125k

Bird Stack II

HyperCard Education F2

Gives information on various bird species with illustration. Useful for birdwatching.

Richard J. Wald
1 Dogberry Lane
Ridgefield, CT 06877

Shareware $10.00
Size: 315k

First Fleet v2.0US

HyperCard Education G1

The stack describes the First Fleet, under Captain Arthur Phillip, from Portmouth, England, to Port Jackson, Australia, 1787–1788. Australian History. Comes with a database stack, a help stack, and sound files. Two-disk set.

Peter Lynden
11 Toohey Avenue
Westmead, NSW 2145
AUSTRALIA

Shareware $15.00
Size: 1957k

HyperCard

HyperCard Education

Kids Can Save the Earth v1.1 — HyperCard Education H1

This series of stacks teach kids about the environmental problems we face and how to solve them. Good audio-visual effects. This is a 6-disk set.

Kids of the Earth (Assembled by Karen Rall and Amanda Goodenough)

Freeware
Size: 4148k

Family Tree v1.0 — HyperCard Education J1

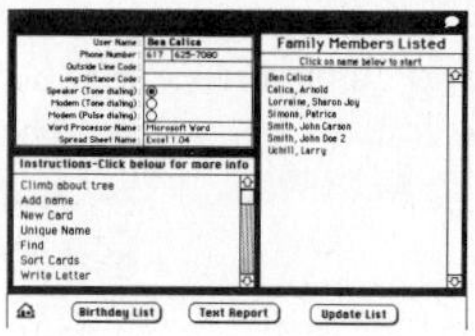

Keep in touch with family members with this genealogy program. It will dial their telephone number or even start your favorite word processor and fill out the heading for you so that you can write a letter.

Jim Palms
PO Box 70218
Bellevue, WA 98007

Shareware $5.00
Size: 73k

Genealogy — HyperCard Education J1

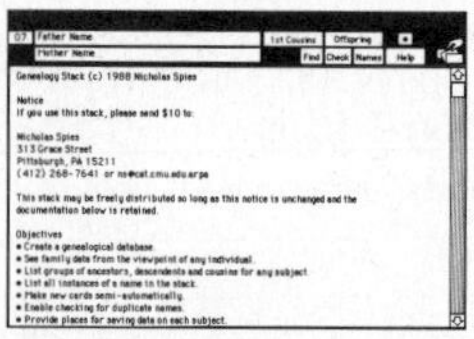

Keeps family tree data.

Nicholas Spies
313 Grace Street
Pittsburgh, PA 15211

Shareware $10.00
Size: 78k

Genealogy Data Base — HyperCard Education J1

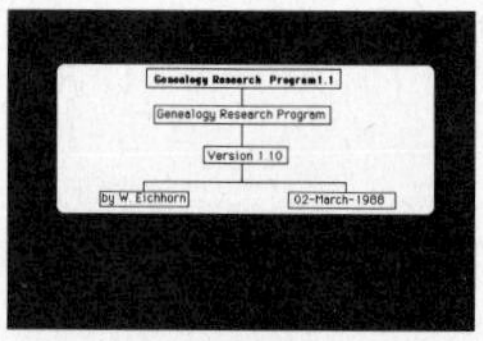

Stack to keep a genealogy database.

Kevin Mennitt
208 Baker Avenue
Westfield, NJ 07090

Shareware $5.00
Size: 67k

Horoscope v1.1 — HyperCard Education K1

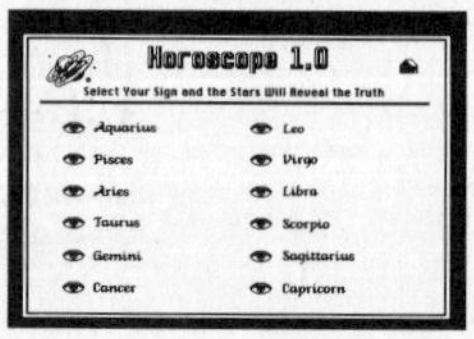

A simple stack that tells your fortune. Be prepared to be insulted, though. You probably want to (and can) write in your own fortune. The name of the file on disk is 'Astrology.'

unknown

Freeware
Size: 42k

Tarot Engine — HyperCard Education K1

Four-card Tarot reading that quickly tells your fortune. (An accompanying stack may be missing.)

Walter Kafton Minkel
3425 NE 18th Avenue
Portland, OR 97212

Freeware
Size: 209k

Education HyperCard

Tarot Major Arcana

HyperCard Education K1

The Major Arcana, which consists of 22 cards from the Tarot deck, is explained.

Susan Lewis
PO Box 10529
Calder Square
State College, PA 16805

Freeware
Size: 439k

Book of Changes v1.1

HyperCard Education K2

Stack generates a hexagram for your question and interprets the result.

Kevin T. Boyd
PO Box 488
Orange, CA 92666

Shareware $10.00
Size: 311k

I-Ching v1.0

HyperCard Education K2

This stack explains trigrams, hexagrams, Yin and Yang and gives your hexagram reading.

Mutant Machinations

Freeware
Size: 259k

Tao Te Ching

HyperCard Education K2

Annotation of the first chapter of Dao De Jing (Tao Te Ching).

unknown

Freeware
Size: 183k

AOL French

HyperCard Education L1

Flashcard stack for learning French vocabulary (or any other language). It can import vocabulary from a text file you prepare.

Richard Tuckerman

Freeware
Size: 12k

French Lessons

HyperCard Education L1

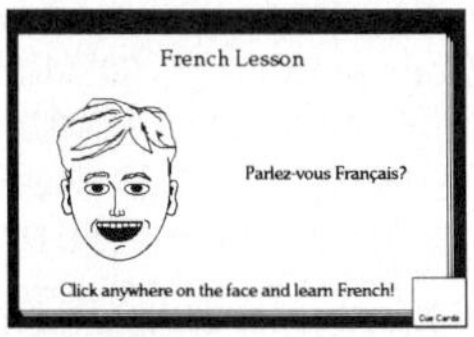

Click on any part of the picture of a face and you will hear the French word. Consists of just one card. Missing a supplementary stack.

unknown

Freeware
Size: 54k

HyperCard

HyperCard Education

Pig Latin v2.0

HyperCard Education L1

Converts any word you type into Pig Latin.

Aaron Caine
64 South Bow Road
Hooksett, NH 03106

Shareware $5.00
Size: 97k

Thai Tutor I

HyperCard Education L1

Teaches you how to pronounce numbers and other simple words in Thai.

Dave Short, Brian Hughes, and Dukita Short
50 Maverick Drive
Dayton, OH 45431

Shareware $25.00
Size: 727k

Learn to Read Russian 1.1

HyperCard Education L2

First in the Teach Yourself Russian stackbook (a three-disk set). Learn Cyrillic alphabet and basic Russian pronunciation. Includes extensive digitized sounds.

Prof. Martin P. Rice
701 McClung Tower
University of Tennessee
Knoxville, Tennessee
37919

Freeware
Size: 276k

Learn to Read Russian 4

HyperCard Education L2

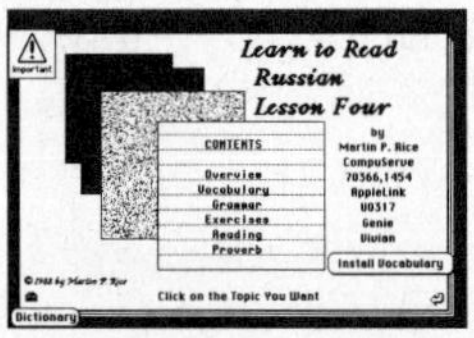

Learn to Read Russian Lesson 4. Sixth in the Teach Yourself Russian stackbook (a three-disk set).

Martin P. Rice
CIS: 70366,1454
AppleLink: U0317
GEnie: Vivian

Freeware
Size: 306k

Learn to Read Russian 5

HyperCard Education L2

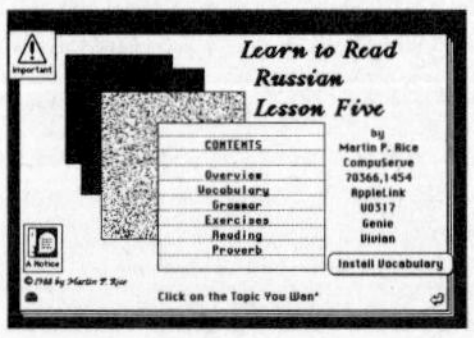

Learn to Read Russian Lesson 5. Seventh in the Teach Yourself Russian stackbook (a three-disk set).

Martin P. Rice
CIS: 70366,1454
AppleLink: U0317
GEnie: Vivian

Freeware
Size: 374k

Read More Russian

HyperCard Education L2

Second in the Teach Yourself Russian stackbook (a three-disk set). More practice reading and pronouncing Russian before the actual study of the language. Assumes familiarity with the material in Learn to Read Russian 1.1 stack.

Prof. Martin P. Rice
701 McClung Tower
University of Tennessee
Knoxville, Tennessee
37919

Freeware
Size: 273k

RUSS3

HyperCard Education L2

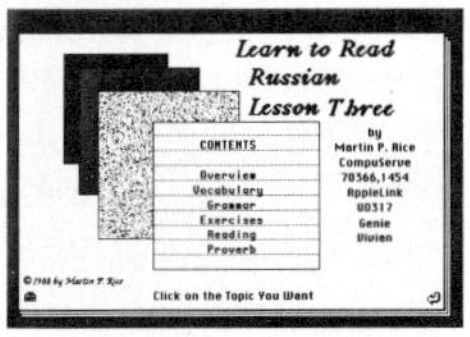

Learn to Read Russian Lesson 3 (a three-disk set). Fifth in the Teach Yourself Russian stackbook.

Martin P. Rice
CIS: 70366,1454
AppleLink: U0317
GEnie: Vivian

Freeware
Size: 339k

Russian 1

HyperCard Education L2

Learn to Read Russian Lesson 1 (a three-disk set). This is the third in the Teach Yourself Russian stackbook. Assumes the familiarity with the material in Learn to Read Russian 1.1 and Read More Russian stacks, which are the first two in the series.

Martin P. Rice
CIS: 70366,1454
AppleLink: U0317
GEnie: Vivian

Freeware
Size: 277k

Russian 2

HyperCard Education L2

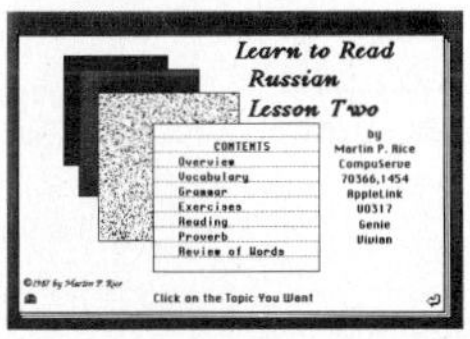

Learn to Read Russian Lesson 2 (a three-disk set). Fourth in the Teach Yourself Russian stackbook.

Martin P. Rice
CIS: 70366,1454
AppleLink: U0317
GEnie: Vivian

Freeware
Size: 385k

Russian Noun Tutor

HyperCard Education L2

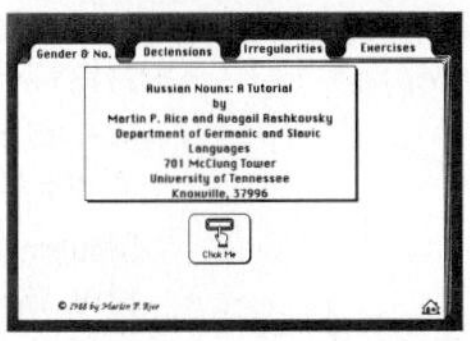

A combined tutorial and drill for the study of Russian nouns. Covers gender, declensions, and irregularities. Includes exercises. Note that this stack is part of a three-disk set.

Martin P. Rice & Avagail Rashkovsky
701 McClung Tower
University of Tennessee
Knoxville, 37996

Freeware
Size: 235k

Russian Vocabulary

HyperCard Education L2

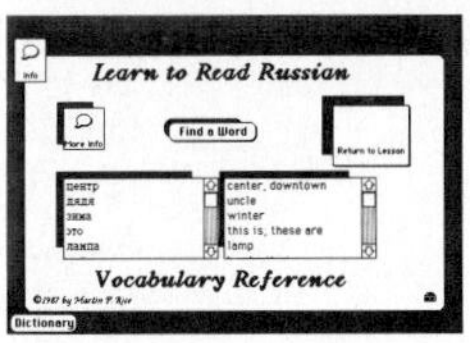

Dictionary stack to accompany the Learn to Read Russian stack series. Note that this stack is part of a three-disk set.

Martin P. Rice

Freeware
Size: 15k

Russian Stack

HyperCard Education L3

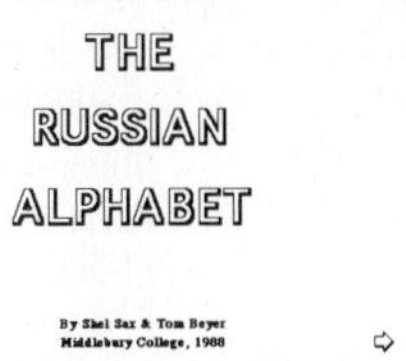

Learn Russian alphabet and simple words. Digitized sounds are included for pronunciation practice.

Shel Sax & Tom Beyer
Middlebury College

Freeware
Size: 767k

HyperCard

HyperCard Education

a/e Japan (kana)

HyperCard Education L5

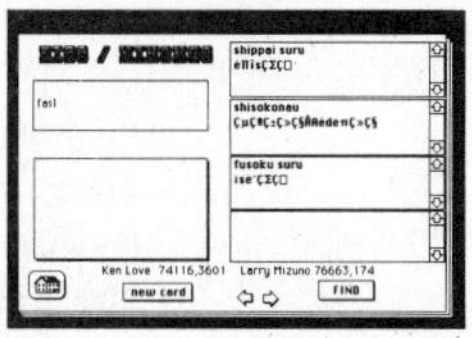

An English-Japanese wordbook. Contains many words starting with the characters a-f, and is extendable. Looks useful for keeping personalized wordbook. It seems to use a Japanese font which is not provided with the stack. No docs.

Ken Love & Larry Mizuno

Freeware
Size: 273k

Japan A to E

HyperCard Education L5

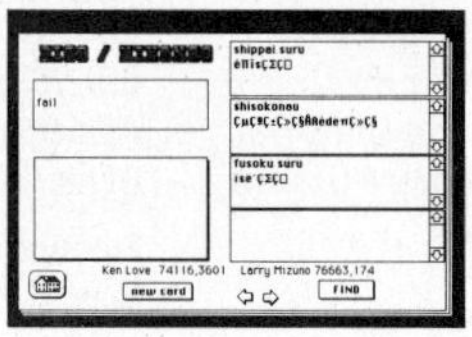

In the same format as the stack a/e Japan (kana), it contains some 2600 entries of English words and their Japanese equivalents. No docs.

Unknown

Freeware
Size: 401k

Japanese Drills

HyperCard Education L6

This stack contains a lesson on writing a Japanese word in Kanji characters. It's not really a language instruction stack; rather, it's a demo of how sound can be utilized for such a stack.

Unknown

Demoware
Size: 366k

Learn Kana

HyperCard Education L6

Flash cards for learning the two systems of Japanese characters: Hiragana and Katakana. Contact the author for the shareware fee.

Sid Webb
1113 Fincastle Rd.
Lexington, KY 40502
GEnie: S.WEBB

Shareware $?
Size: 136k

Learn Japanese

HyperCard Education L6

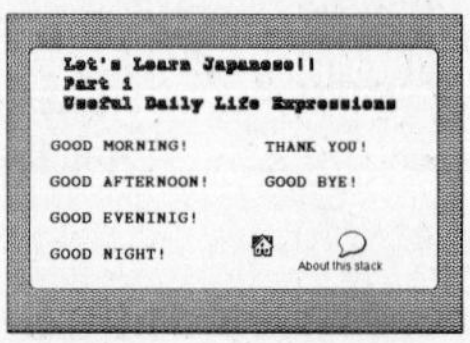

Learn six useful Japanese phrases. Contains sounds for pronunciation.

Makoto & Kyoko Ozaki
304-6 Katamachi,
Shinjuku
tokyo 160, Japan

Freeware
Size: 348k

Lexical Engineer- Kanji Demo

HyperCard Education L6

A demo of an electronic English-Japanese dictionary with sound for Japanese pronunciation. Contains five word pairs.

Bio-grammatical Engineering

Demoware
Size: 153k

Education HyperCard

HyperCard Education

Italian Survival Guide — HyperCard Education L7

A combination phrasebook and English- Italian dictionary. Phrases are arranged according to topics.

Maria Lima
5110 Frich Drive
Pittsburgh, PA 15227

Shareware $20.00
Size: 171k

Ted's Traveler's Spanish v1.0 beta — HyperCard Education L7

Spanish phrasebook for travelers. Sounds by a MacinTalk-like synthetic voice.

Theodore Micceri
527 Lantern Circle
Temple Terrace, FL
33167

Shareware $5.00
Size: 62k

Esperanto — HyperCard Education L8

A brief but complete introduction to the grammar (and some vocabulary) of the international language Esperanto. Requires MacinTalk for sound. If you like it, you are expected to send somthing to the author.

Michael Urban
P.O. Box 24560
Los Angeles, CA
90024

Freeware
Size: 486k

Guitar Chording v1.0d — HyperCard Education M1

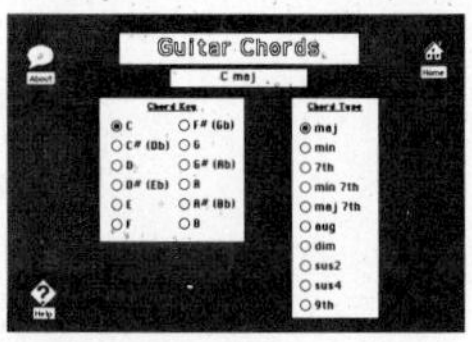

Shows the guitar fret positions for various chords and plays them. Some nonelementary chords are missing from this version.

Paul Lemieux
904 Jason Court
Cary, NC 27511

Shareware $5.00
Size: 103k

Guitar Font — HyperCard Education M1

Guitar Font I & II. Font for guitar fret position notation. You won't find a separate font file on this disk; rather it's installed in the Guitar Chording stack and carries a separate shareware fee.

Paul Lemieux
904 Jason Court
Cary, NC 27511

Shareware $5.00
Size: 8k

The Guitar Tutor — HyperCard Education M1

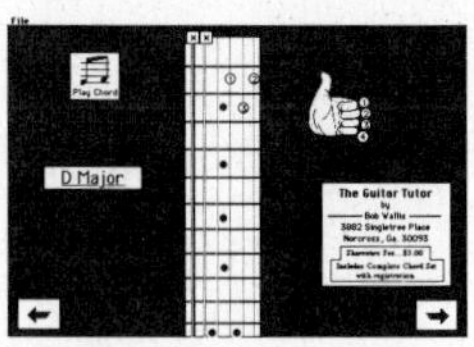

Illustrates how to play C, D, E, F, and G chords on a guitar.

Bob Wallis
3882 Singletree Place
Norcross, GA 30093

Shareware $3.00
Size: 347k

HyperCard

HyperCard Education

Tunes v1.0 — HyperCard Education M1

Plays the tune you type in either by using alphabetical note names or by clicking the keys on an organ keyboard picture.

Ike Nassi and Friends

Freeware
Size: 100k

Heather's Notes — HyperCard Education M2

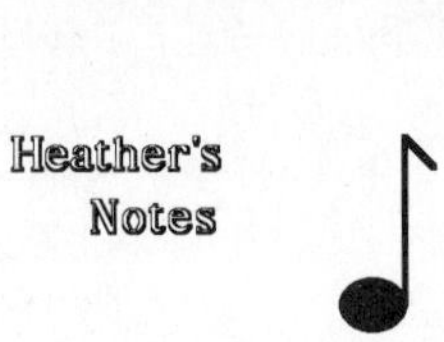

Drill for reading the C and the F clefs.

Larry Veinott
Route 2, Box 378
Lisbon, NY 13658

Shareware $5.00
Size: 64k

Keyboard #2 v1.0 — HyperCard Education M2

Lets you hear some tunes and the note you choose in different sounds.

Ed Kietlinski
Micro Maniaxs
PO Box 1597
Rutherford, NJ 07070

Freeware
Size: 153k

Music HTB v1.0 — HyperCard Education M2

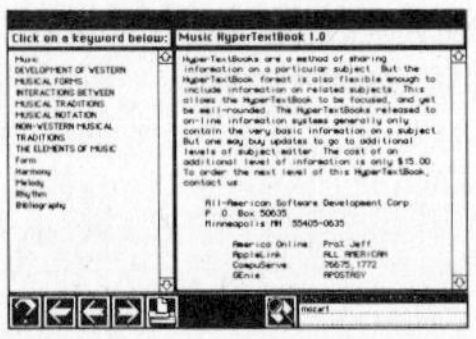

The first of the HyperTextBook series on music. Sort of a demoware. An additional level of the subject matter may be ordered for $15.

All-American Software
Development Corp.
PO Box 50635
Minneapolis, MN
55405-0635

Shareware $15.00
Size: 91k

Astro Almanac — HyperCard Education N1

Describes major astronomical events for 1988.

John Deecken

Freeware
Size: 24k

Astronomy & Astrophysics HTB — HyperCard Education N1

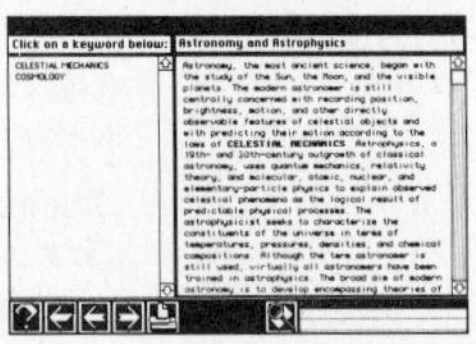

One of the HyperTextBook series. Covers astronomy and astrophysics. Sort of a demoware. An additional level of the subject matter may be ordered for $15.

All-American
Software
Development Corp.
PO Box 50635
Minneapolis, MN
55405-0635

Shareware $15.00
Size: 58k

Astronomy History HTB

HyperCard Education N1

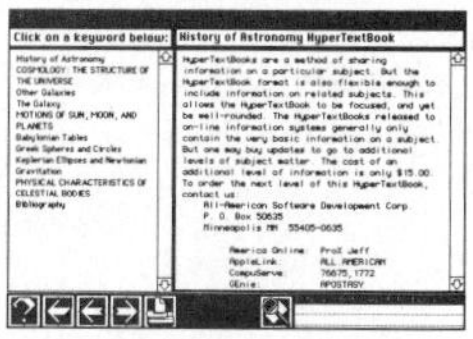

One of the HyperTextBook series. Covers history of astronomy. Sort of a demoware. An additional level of the subject matter may be ordered for $15.

All-American Software Development Corp.
PO Box 50635
Minneapolis, MN
55405-0635

Shareware $15.00
Size: 64k

Q&A v1.01

HyperCard Education N1

Astronomy question and answer stack. It comes with 4 stacks that contain the actual questions and answers (Cosmology, Stars, Galaxies, and History). These stacks are customizable with your own sets of questions and answers.

Douglas O. S. Wood
Deptartment of Astronomy
University of Wisconsin
475 N. Charter Street
Madison, Wisconsin 53706

Shareware $5.00
Size: 179k

Solar System HTB v1.0

HyperCard Education N1

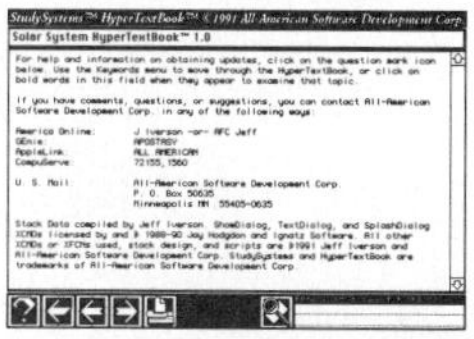

One of the HyperTextBook series. Covers the astronomy of the Solar System. Sort of a demoware. An additional level of the subject matter may be ordered for $15.

All-American Software Development Corp.
PO Box 50635
Minneapolis, MN
55405-0635

Shareware $15.00
Size: 91k

Oct '87 Manifest

HyperCard Education N2

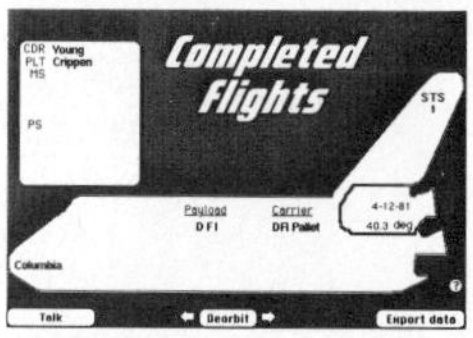

Describes the completed, assigned, or requested flights of Space Shuttles. A postcard is requested if you use this stack.

Dr. Mike Kobrick
MS 300-233
Jet Propulsion Lab.
4800 Oak Grove Drive
Pasadena, CA 91101

Freeware
Size: 164k

Shuttle Info v1.0

HyperCard Education N2

Describes various parts of the Space Shuttles, and their flights and schedules. Postcardware: Send the author a postcard if you use this stack.

Rick Stickle
13006 Golden Oak Drive
Laurel, MD 20708

Freeware
Size: 303k

Shuttle Information '89

HyperCard Education N2

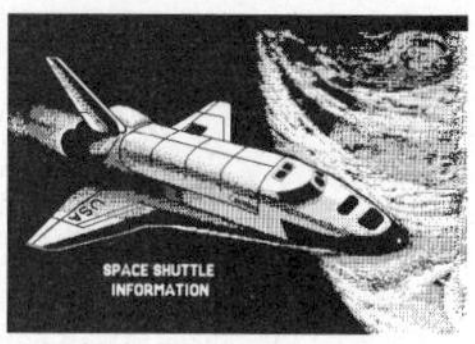

Describes various parts of the Space Shuttles, and their flights and schedules. This is the 1989 version of the earlier Shuttle Info stack. Postcardware: Send the author a postcard if you use this stack.

Rick Stickle
13006 Golden Oak Drive
Laurel, MD 20708

Freeware
Size: 325k

Space • Software

HyperCard Education N2

This stack contains information about various programs written for the Macintosh that involve NASA, the aerospace business, or space exploration.

Shawn Harrison
NASA Area Macintosh Users (NAMU)
403 NASA Road 1, #384
Webster, TX 77598

Freeware
Size: 66k

Inigo Gets Out

HyperCard Games

The story of the adventures of Inigo the cat, who wanted to go outside. You get different stories by clicking on different parts of the cards. A Good storybook for small children. One of the AmandaStories series.

Amanda Goodenough
The Voyager Company
2139 Manning Avenue
Los Angeles, CA 90025

Freeware
Size: 155k

Inigo Takes a Bath

HyperCard Games A1

Inigo the cat takes a bath all by himself! A little story for small children. One of the AmandaStories series.

Amanda Goodenough
1025 Martin Road
Santa Cruz, CA
95060-0721

Shareware $9.95
Size: 180k

Your Faithful Camel

HyperCard Games A1

Adventures of the Faithful Camel. Another stack from the AmandaStories.

Amanda Goodenough
1025 Martin Road
Santa Cruz, CA
95060-0721

Shareware $9.95
Size: 409k

Monster Hunt v1.1

HyperCard Games A2

Venture into an ancient cave to kill a monster and return with the trophy.

Kendall J. Redburn
Prophecy Software
3650 Silverside Road #3
Wilmington, DE 19810

Shareware $10.00
Size: 773k

Mr. Potatohead v1.4

HyperCard Games A2

Complete the picture of Mr. Potatohead from the parts you get by rolling a die.

Bill Robertson
microPRINT
214 Third Avenue
Waltham, MA 02154

Freeware
Size: 58k

Code for Kids

HyperCard Games A3

Encode simple stories using Cairo font. Students are given the keys for the alphabetic correspondence and are supposed to decode the story.

Rob Weinberg
356 San Pablo Terrace
Pacifica, CA 94044

Freeware
Size: 43k

HyperCard

HyperCard Games

Dot to Dot 1 — HyperCard Games A3

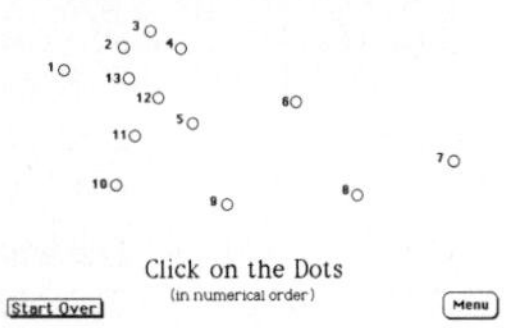

Connect the dots to see the hidden picture.

Ron LeMay

Freeware
Size: 72k

HyperZoo — HyperCard Games A3

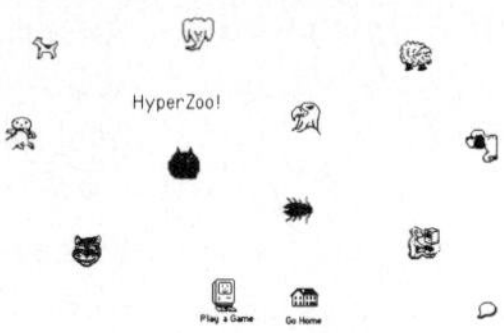

Do you know the names of these animals?

Ron Pejril
GEnie: R.Pejril

Freeware
Size: 141k

Knight Adventure — HyperCard Games A3

Sir Knight rescues the Princess. An adventure game written by a 10-year-old.

Marshall Ward
1924 Coral Gardens Dr.
Wilton Manors, FL
33306

Freeware
Size: 224k

Time for Heather — HyperCard Games A3

For kids learning how to read the clock.

Larry Veinott
Route 2, Box 378
Lisbon, NY 13658

Shareware $5.00
Size: 74k

Where Is My Triangular Hat? — HyperCard Games A3

Where should I go to find my triangular hat?

Kazutoshi Otani

Freeware
Size: 94k

Sir Knight — HyperCard Games A4

The High Wizard Spindus must be destroyed to save the kingdom. Consists of 9 stacks. The authors don't specify the shareware fee.

Juri Hobbs and Kathy Hobbs
PO Box 212
Wauna, WA 98395

Shareware $?
Size: 21k

Blah! v1.1

HyperCard Games A5

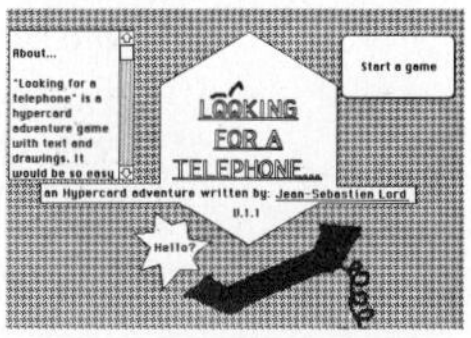

You just had an auto accident and are looking for a phone. An adventure in a strange house.

Jean Sebastien Lord
311 Notre-Dame
St-Lambert P.Q.
J4P 2K2 CANADA

Shareware $15.00
Size: 480k

DragonSword

HyperCard Games A6

Kill the dragon and meet the damsel.

Nat Ingalls

Freeware
Size: 305k

Solo Adventure

HyperCard Games A6

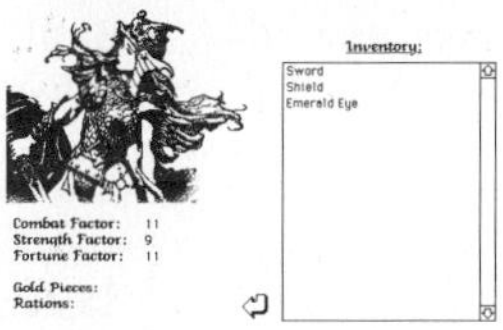

A customizable adventure game.

Dan Horn

Freeware
Size: 146k

SpaceEscape

HyperCard Games A6

Escape from the cell you were thrown into after being captured by the enemy Drools.

Steve Merel
400 Ardmore Avenue
Manhattan Beach, CA
90266

Shareware $15.00
Size: 305k

Criminals

HyperCard Games A7

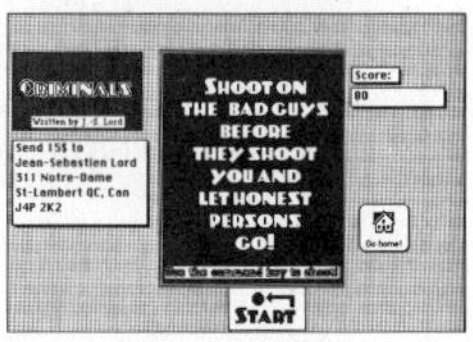

Shoot the criminal before you get killed!

Jean-Sebastien Lord
311 Notre-Dame
St-Lambert Q.C.
J4P 2K2 CANADA

Shareware $15.00
Size: 325k

Spot's Adventure

HyperCard Games A7

Bring Spot the dog, who changes into a mouse, back to the lab and turn him back into himself.

Brian Risk
Professional Macintosh Services
PO Box 522
Chapel Hill, NC 27514

Shareware $5.00
Size: 495k

Concentration v1.1

HyperCard Games A8

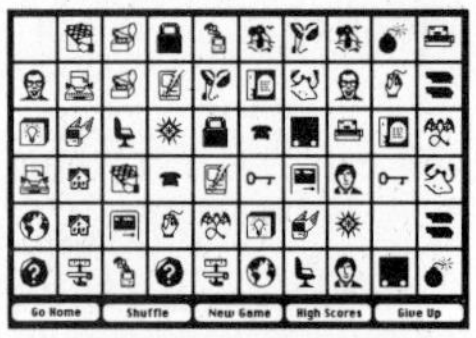

Match icons by memory.

Richard Davis

Freeware
Size: 56k

Concentration v3.0

HyperCard Games A8

Match cards by memory. Can be played by one or two players.

Sioux Lacey

Public Domain
Size: 80k

Gopher Tag

HyperCard Games A8

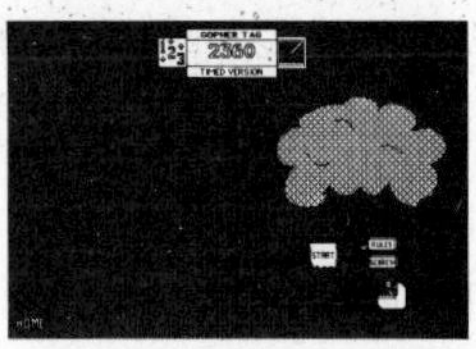

Tag the gophers that pop up on the screen. Has two modes: timed or scored.

Greg Tjosvold
1237 Nestor Street
Coquitlam, British Columbia
V3E 1H4 CANADA

Shareware $7.00
Size: 35k

Just for Fun1

HyperCard Games A8

Contains a number game card and several cards illustrating illusions.

Steve Stanley
10637 Direct River Drive NW
Coon Rapids, MN 55433

Freeware
Size: 122k

Memory Match

HyperCard Games A8

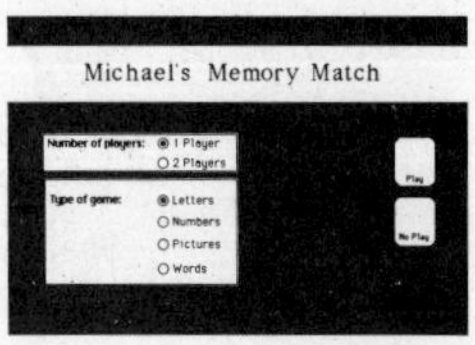

Another memory/matching game.

unknown

Freeware
Size: 49k

Tower of Hanoi

HyperCard Games A8

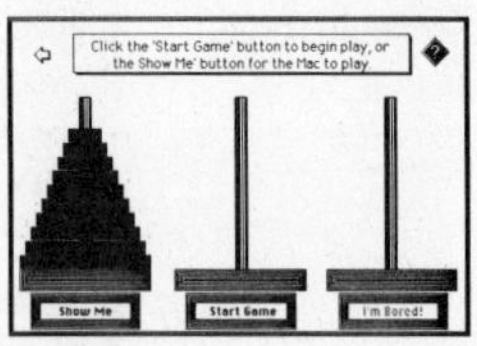

The classic game of Tower of Hanoi. Move disks from one pole to another without disturbing the order. Up to 10 disks.

Richard Lee Floyd
5326 Silva Avenue
El Cerrito, CA 94530

Freeware
Size: 59k

Games
HyperCard

TrainSet v1.2C

HyperCard Games A8

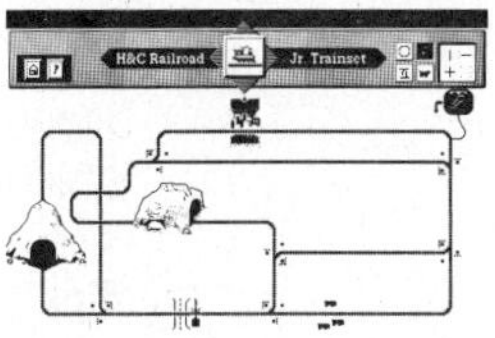

A digital train set. Requires HyperCard 1.2.

VIA, Inc.

Freeware
Size: 68k

Yahtzee v4.0

HyperCard Games A8

A poker dice game. You can play against the Mac or another player, or just watch the Mac play against itself.

Ian Summerfield
60 Tenby Drive
Luton, Bedfordshire
LU4 9BL ENGLAND

Shareware $20.00
Size: 42k

Hoodwinked

HyperCard Games B1

A Star Trek role-playing adventure game.

Christopher A. Faria
3909 Swiss Avenue
Box 452
Dallas, TX 75204

Shareware $20.00
Size: 769k

Lunar Lander

HyperCard Games B1

You are in charge of landing a spacecraft on the moon without crashing it.

Chris Calabrese

Freeware
Size: 112k

Interplanetary Struggle v1.0

HyperCard Games B2

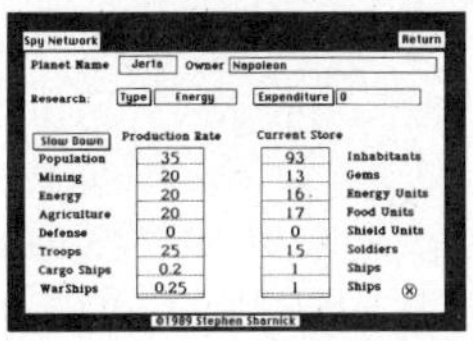

You are the ruler of a planet, and you are to control the resources and the population.

Stephen Sharnick
PO Box 3494
Danbury, CT 06810

Shareware $5.00
Size: 65k

Moon Base Alpha v1.1

HyperCard Games B2

Information stack for the 'Space: 1999' TV series. Lots of trivia with sounds, maps, and pictures.

CSUC Dr. Who Fan Club

Freeware
Size: 747k

Games
HyperCard

HyperCard

HyperCard Games

4X4 — HyperCard Games B3

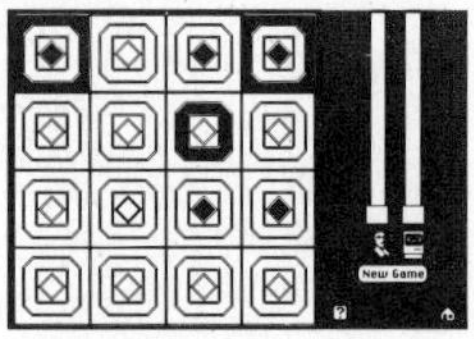

A Tic-tac-toe-like game with a 4X4 board.

Bruce Wilson and
Michael Niemack
1239 E. Palm Street
Altadena, CA 91001

Shareware $7.00
Size: 95k

Adventure Construction Kit — HyperCard Games B3

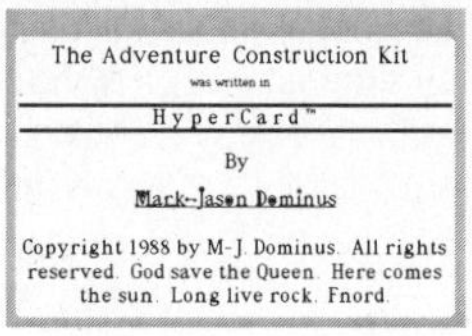

Tools for creating adventure game stacks.

Mark-Jason Dominus
250 W. 94th Street
New York, NY 10025

Freeware
Size: 68k

Battle of Britain — HyperCard Games B3

Set in the year of 1940, you are charged with the air defense of all southern England against German invasion.

René Vidmer

Freeware
Size: 289k

Tilt v1.2 — HyperCard Games B3

A game of medieval jousting.

Neil Shapiro and Mike
Gilbert

Shareware $10.00
Size: 168k

Code Buster v2.0 — HyperCard Games C1

Guess which color is in which slot. You have 10 tries.

Steven Fuchs
SWF Software
PO Box 129
Coram, NY 11727

Freeware
Size: 71k

Horror Trivia v1.0 — HyperCard Games C1

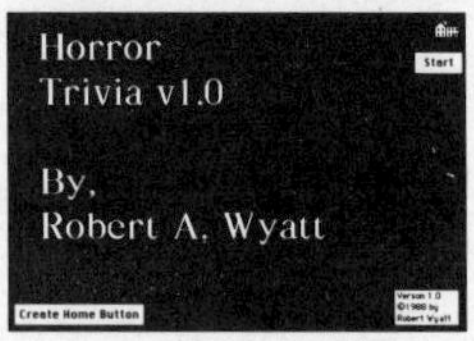

Horror film trivia questions.

Robert A. Wyatt
PO Box 388
Berryville, VA 22611

Freeware
Size: 488k

Mastermind

HyperCard Games C1

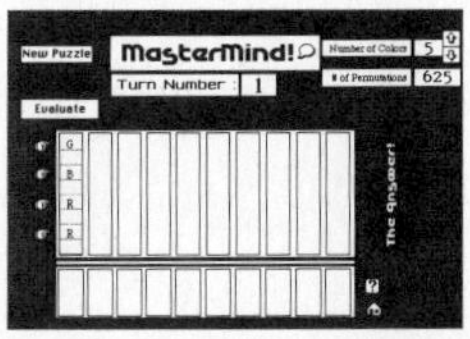

Guess which color is in which slot. You have ten tries. The same game as the Code Buster stack, with slightly different layout.

Steven Fuchs
SWF Software
PO Box 129
Coram, NY 11727

Freeware
Size: 29k

By Love Insured v0.98

HyperCard Games C2

A fictional soap opera, a nonlinear HyperBack Novel, AmandaStories for grownups. Click on buttons and construct the story yourself.

Ellen Chait
Virtual Communications
2323 Carleton Street
Berkeley, CA 94704

Shareware $10.00
Size: 695k

BUDDY-O-MATIC

HyperCard Games C3

Create your own buddy-movie plot by answering 58 multiple-choice questions.

Chuck Price
95 Higgins Court
Baton Rouge, LA
70808

Freeware
Size: 448k

SolitaireStack

HyperCard Games C3

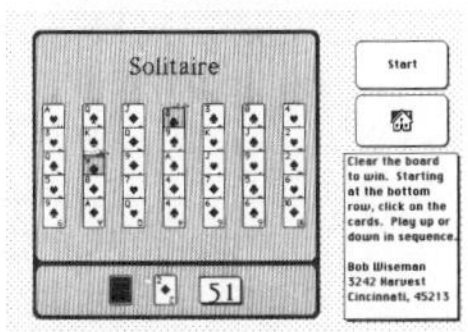

Solitaire card game.

Bob Wiseman
3242 Harvest
Cincinnati, OH 45213

Freeware
Size: 116k

Tangram

HyperCard Games C3

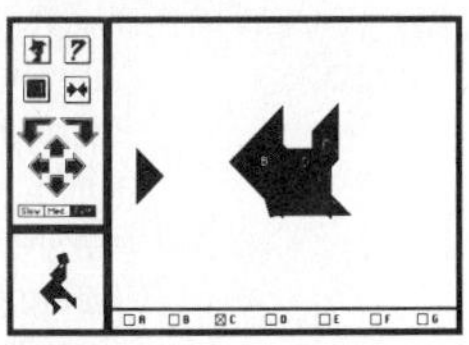

Seven pieces that make up a square are to be rearranged without overlap so that they will form the shape of a chosen silhouette.

Martin Lewis
9801 Fair Tide Circle
Huntington Beach, CA
92646

Shareware $5.00
Size: 129k

Tic Tac Toe

HyperCard Games C3

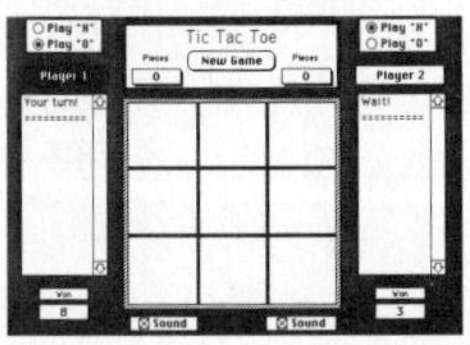

Tic-tac-toe game.

unknown

Freeware
Size: 295k

Games HyperCard

HyperCard

HyperCard Games

CALotto 2.0

HyperCard Games D1

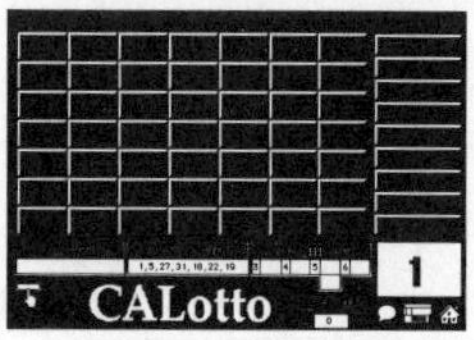

California Lotto simulation game.

Andrew Burns
843-1/2 S. Curson Avenue
Los Angeles, CA 90036

Shareware $10.00
Size: 42k

D&D Dice v1.1

HyperCard Games D1

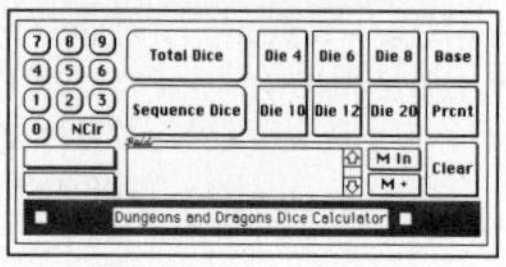

Dungeons and Dragons dice calculator. A calculator designed especially for making calculations that involve a series of random numbers.

Reid Raymond

Freeware
Size: 16k

Day at Racetrack v.9

HyperCard Games D1

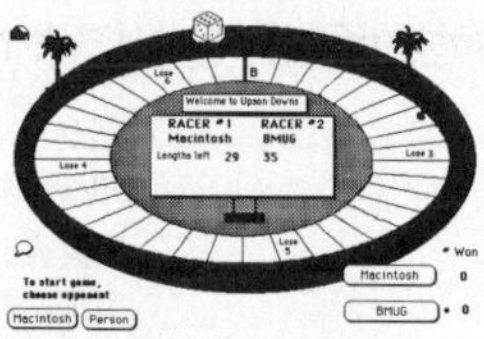

A racing game.

Dan Kittay
CIS: 73277,3034

Freeware
Size: 89k

Dicey v2.0

HyperCard Games D1

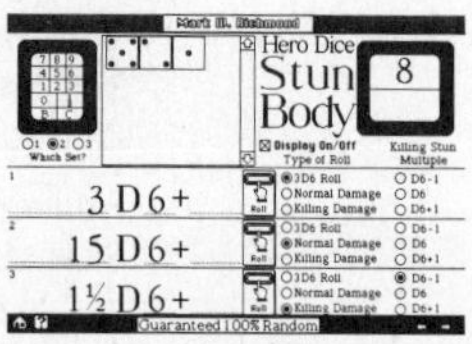

A utility stack for throwing dice.

Mark W. Richmond
12008 Wycliff Lane
Austin, TX 78727

Freeware
Size: 133k

DieRoller Demo

HyperCard Games D1

This stack demonstrates how to roll dice in HyperCard using either HyperTalk or an XCMD.

Dave Newman
CIS: 74107,2401
GEnie: DAVE-NEWMAN
ARPA:
Newman.pasa@Xerox.com

Freeware
Size: 25k

Guess the Number

HyperCard Games D1

Guess a number between 2 and 19.

Rod Riggenbach

Freeware
Size: 215k

HyperCraps v1.02

HyperCard Games D1

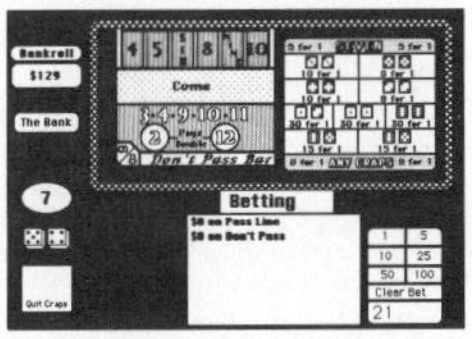

A limited version of the craps game.

Robert S. Fuller, et al.
Infostat
PO Box 243
Neenah, WI 54957

Shareware $12.50
Size: 32k

HyperSlots

HyperCard Games D1

A digital slot machine.

Bill Ritzdorf
Starving Programmers Software
25815 111th Avenue SE
Kent, WA 98031

Shareware $20.00
Size: 64k

Lotto-Six

HyperCard Games D1

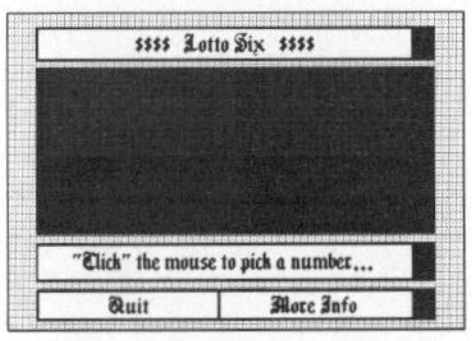

Helps you pick 6 numbers in the range of 1–49, which are used in lotteries.

Al Handley
3720 Collins Avenue
#701
Miami Beach, FL
33140

Shareware $3.00
Size: 45k

LottoBlaster

HyperCard Games D1

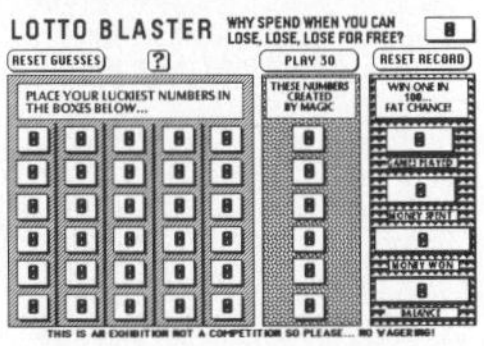

Quoting the author, 'Why spend when you can lose, lose, lose for free?' Another Lotto game.

David Vallone
32 W. Anapamu #277
Santa Barbara, CA
93101
CIS: 71071,400

Freeware
Size: 46k

LottoMaster

HyperCard Games D1

Generates 6 random numbers for use with Florida Lotto. If you win, send 1% in to the author.

Martin Rubinstein
MRU Software
9214 NW 48th Street
Sunrise, FL 33351

Shareware $?
Size: 32k

Pick Six

HyperCard Games D1

Another 6-number picker for lottery. Winners should send in 10% to the author.

John R. Roberts
3 Rio Grande Drive
Chelmsford, MA
01824

Shareware $?
Size: 24k

HyperCard

HyperCard Games

Random Sentence Generator

HyperCard Games D1

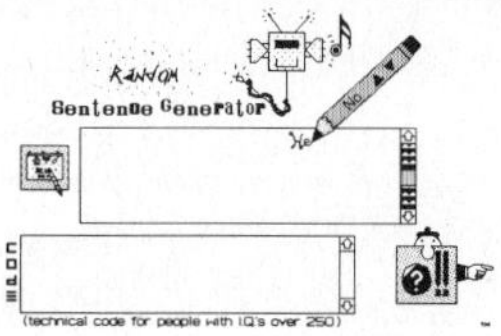

Generates random sentences based on editable word database.

unknown

Freeware

Size: 118k

Games
HyperCard

Paris

Paris

Paris was Apple's code name for the Mac II, so this section contains all sorts of Mac II-specific software including applications, color pictures, color icons, sounds, DAs, and FKEYs.

Paris Picture-Type Icons

 Flex

 Flex Slide

 GIF

 Pict

 Pixel Paint

 Startup Screen

Paris A2

GIF Pictures

Cartoon Gauls

Cubola2

Egmont

Caveman

Fry Guy

Geoscape

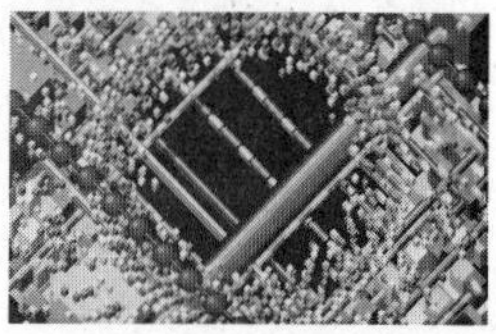

Rock Band

London-GIF

MC68020.GIF

Meek

Moons

Phobos.GIF

Paris A2

Continued

Puffin-GIF

Sun and Moon-GIF

Torot

White Horse

XC68030.GIF

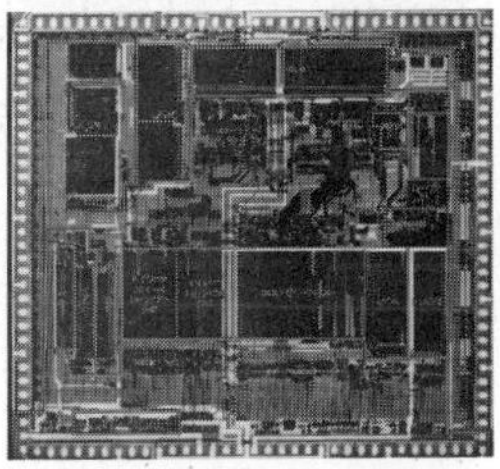

Paris A3

GIF Pictures

A2000

Aquarium

Blue Porsche

Car2

Cartoon

Death Star

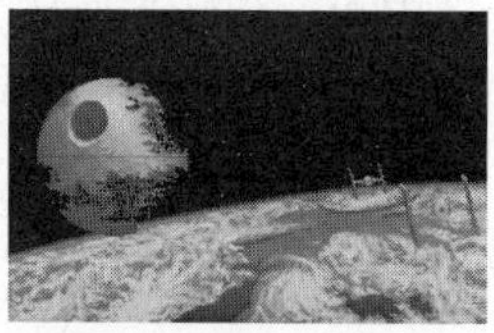

Eiffel Tower

Emerald City

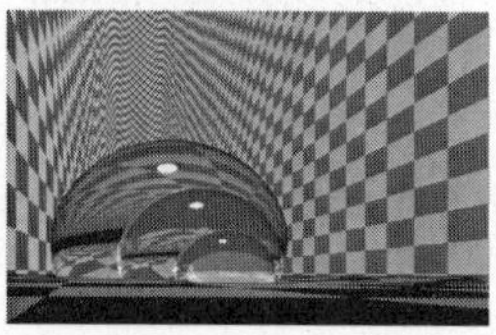

Floor Plan

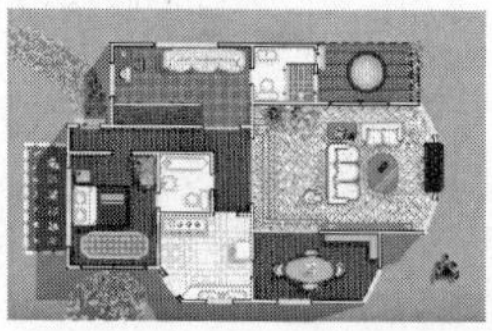

Floral Wonder

Fox Puppy

Cartoon Cat

Paris A3

Continued

Gold Porsche

Green Porsche

Guru

ImLate

Jigger

Jimmy

Laser Weapons

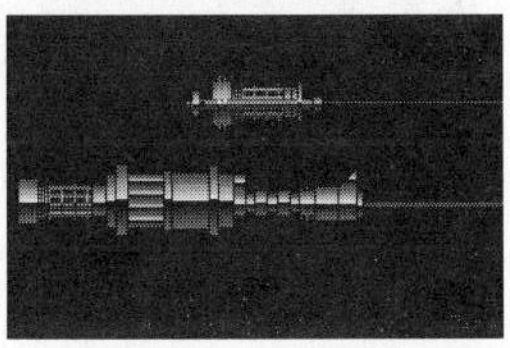

Legends

Mac Meltdown

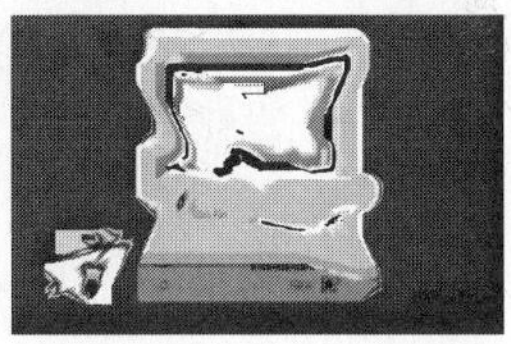

Mazda Rx7

Morris

Ninja 900

Paris A3

Continued

Noid

Panther

Pegasus

Red Porsche

RoboHand

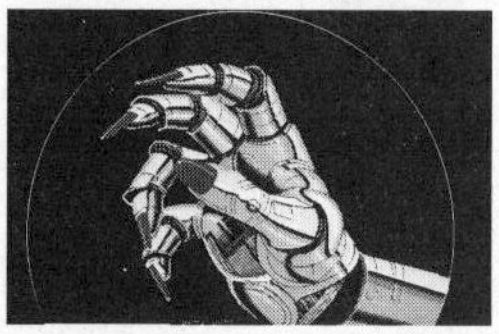

Robot

Ruger Pistol

Sachs Castle 1990

Sachs Self Portrait

Saucer Attack

Spy vs Spy

Star Destroyer

Paris A3

Continued

Time Crystal

Uncle Jack

Vampire

XWing

YWing

Paris A4

GIF Pictures

Apollo

Buzz Aldrin

Challenger

Earth

Grand Canyon

Kitty

Lunar Rover

Monument Valley

Red Rock

Paris B1

Fractals

Mandelbrot v4.81

Draws the Mandelbrot and Julia fractals. Works in color and allows palette animation. Supports different resolutions; zooms in on selected area. Includes docs in a separate file. Has problems under MultiFinder.

Jesse Jones
1821 E. Thomas, Apt. 103
Seattle, WA 98112

Application
Shareware $25.00
Size: 70k
12" 6 7 32

MandelZot v2.0

One of the best fractal-generating programs around. Explore the Mandelbrot set in full color and zoom selected areas by up to a factor of one trillion! Excellent docs clearly explain all the numerous features. Runs in the background under MultiFinder.

Dave Platt
Coherent Thought Inc.
(415) 493-8805
dplatt@coherent.com

Application
Freeware
Size: 80k
12" 6 7 32

Paris B2

Fractals

Ani-Mandel v1.2

Plots both the Mandelbrot and Julia sets. Animates colors, zooms in and out, shows info about the complex plane. Docs in a separate file.

Mark Lankton
1275A Bear Mountain Drive
Boulder, CO 80303

Application
Freeware
Size: 27k

Animated Fractal Generator

Fractals in color using Mandelbrot and Julia sets. Requires FPU and Color QuickDraw.

Jerry Goldstein
1051 - 12th Street #4
Santa Monica, CA 90403

Application
Demoware
Size: 151k

Bugglings v1.5

This program simulates life in a test tube, with tiny bugs swimming around, feeding on food particles.

Chuck Shotton
c/o BIAP Systems
PO Box 580622
Houston, TX 77258-0622

Application
Shareware $5.00
Size: 34k

Cellular Automatons v0.1

Calculates and displays the evolution of an array of cellular automatons. Presents statistics about the simulation and generates interesting color patterns. Includes docs in a separate file.

Douglas Wood
Center for Astrophysics,
MS 42
60 Garden Street
Cambridge, MA 02138

Application
Freeware
Size: 88k

JuliaSet v5.1b0

Draws the Julia set fractal pattern in color. Lets you specify the horizontal and vertical speed. Includes MPW assembly language source code.

Ray Sanders
Green Grass Software, Inc.
P.O. Box 570
Dunedin, FL 34697-0570

Application
Shareware $5.00
Size: 4k

Mac II Fractals

Draws fractal pattern on screen in garish colors. Slow; does nothing else.

Unknown

Application
Public Domain
Size: 3k

Paris C1

Color PixelPaint Pictures

PixelPaint Viewer v0.5

Displays color pictures created by the commercial program PixelPaint. Views full-size and half-size documents.

Keith McGreggor
Pixel Resources, Inc.

Application
Freeware
Size: 17k

Abdominal Aorta

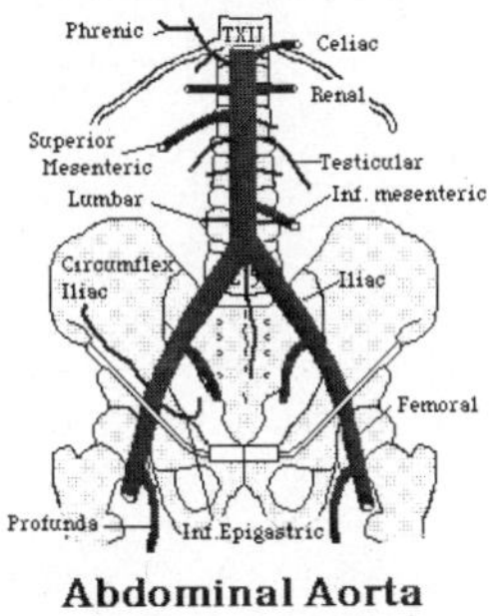

blue Marble

Circle

Pictures
Paris

Flightless Fawl

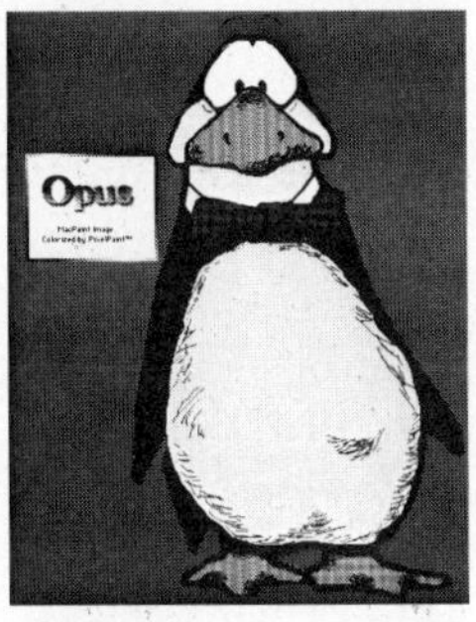

Egyptian Queen

Ferrari Mondial

Final Froggy

Heart 2

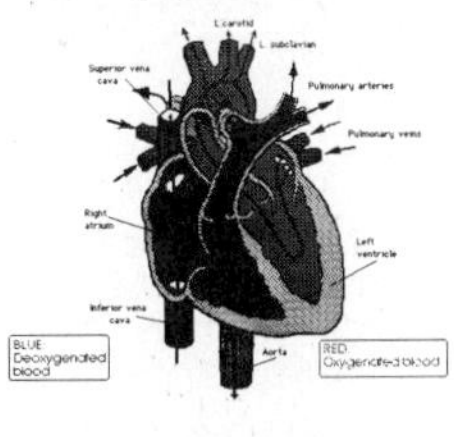

Keith's Trip #1

Paris C1

Continued

Model

Outside BMUG

Paris C2

Color Pictures

Caution

Egyption Office

Red Giant

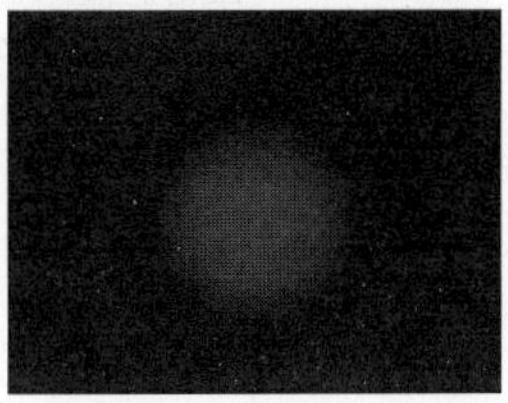

Street

Town Brawl

Unicorn

Pictures
Paris

White Dragon

Paris C3

Color Pictures

GrayView v1.9.8a4

Designed primarily to convert ThunderScan SCAN documents to gray-scale images. Has limited paint capabilities for manipulating and viewing images.

David S. Fry
81 Irving Street
Cambridge, MA 02138

Application
Freeware
Size: 99k

Ai Tran Landscape

Ball Startup

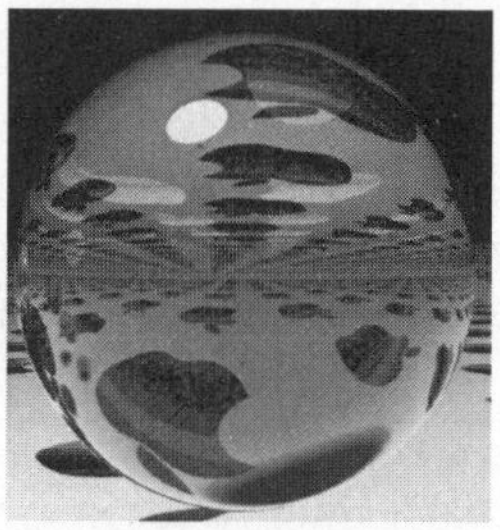

Bill Startup

Geisha Startup

Creation2.pict

Cube

Juggler

Lizards.pict

Marat.pict

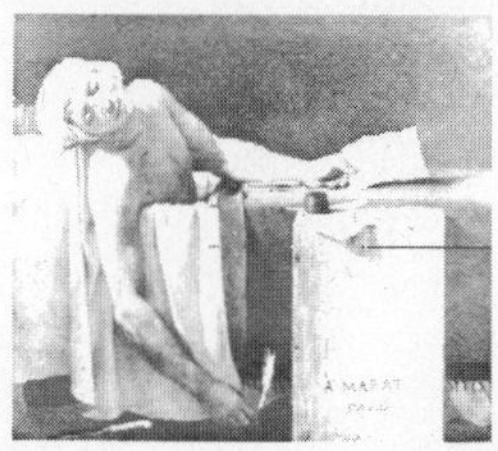

Einstein

Paris C4

Color Pictures

FlexReader II v1.10

Reads pictures in Flex format. Comes with lots of color pictures.

Steve Blackstock
Random Dot Software
40 Bartlett Ave.
Lexington, MA 02173

Application
Freeware
Size: 50k

Bikini.flx

Bobcat

Bouganvilla

Bozo

Doe

EarthRise

Moth

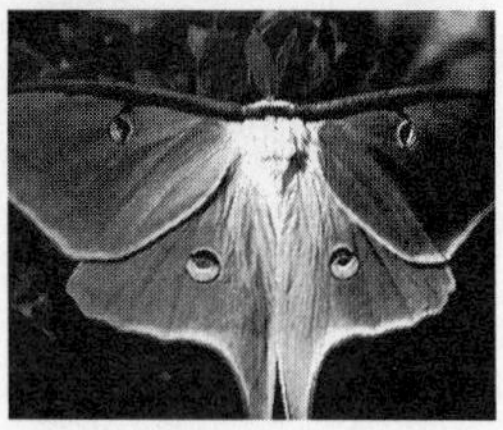

Mum

Parrot

Color Pictures

SFBay

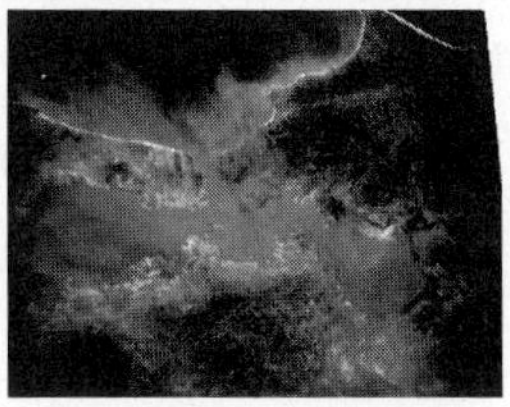

SFBay.flx

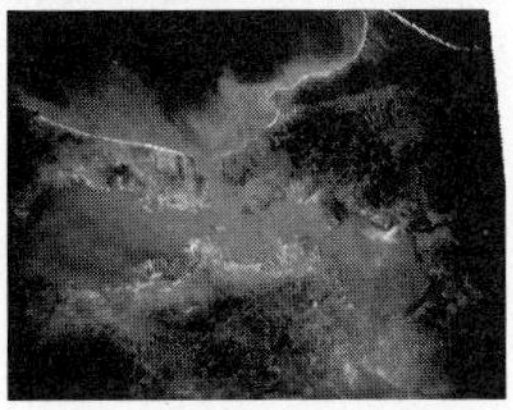

Susanna

Tetcha

Paris C5

Color Pictures

GIF Converter v2.2d1

Converts PICT and GIF files to many other formats.

Kevin A. Mitchell
PO Box 803066
Chicago, IL 60680-3066

Application
Shareware $40.00
Size: 284k

Jedi

Laser

Mirror spheres

Toys

Two Mirrors

Accuracy v1.7

Checks the accuracy of mathematical calculations (round-off errors) on your Mac. Checks +, -, *, /, trig, exponential, and square root functions. Has a few bugs. Includes Pascal source code.

Jim Roberts
PC Tech Journal
Ziff Communications Co.

Application
Freeware
Size: 13k

ColorBits v1.0

Color Bits is an editor for bitmapped resources.

Ben Haller
Stick Software
32 Deer Haven Drive
Ithaca, NY 14050

Application
Shareware $10.00
Size: 70k

ColorBoxes_by_Neal_Trautman

Rapidly draws colored rectangles in a window.

Neal Trautman

Application
Public Domain
Size: 12k

Colorize v2.00

Colorizes window frames, controls, and menus of existing applications.

Neal Trautman
1701 SW 42
Fargo, ND 58103

Application
Shareware $5.00
Size: 12k

Dawn v2.0.2

Dawn allows you to specify a PICT format startup screen and accompanying sound.

Frank Price
612 Doheny Rd.
Beverly Hills, CA 90210

Control Panel
Extension
Shareware $20.00
Size: 47k

ExtraColor v1.2

This cdev allows you to color your cursor to any color in the color picker.

Giuseppe Carnevale
via Ugo Niuttia 36
80128 Napoli
ITALY

Control Panel
Extension
Shareware $10.00
Size: 17k

PictDisplay v1.0

Displays PICT resources with ID=0 (used for startup screens); displays PICT data files (created by drawing programs); converts PICT data files into PICT resources for use as startup screens.

Jan Eugenides
PO Box 151
Maynard, MA 01754

Application
Public Domain
Size: 7k

Player INIT v1.0

Plays the sound of the transporter from Star Trek when you turn on your Mac.

Apple Computer, Inc.

System Startup
Extension
Freeware
Size: 116k

Paris D1

Continued

Rainbow

Displays constantly changing color patterns on the screen. Very impressive in 256-color mode.

Keith McGreggor
Pixel Resources, Inc.

Application
Public Domain
Size: 7k

Random Art v0.5

Draws random color objects on the screen: lines, rectangles, ovals, and arcs in various colors and fill patterns.

Ted Lowery
4631 Twisted Oaks Drive
Apt. 2004
Raleigh, NC 27612

Application
Public Domain
Size: 6k

SANE Mark v1.0

Runs benchmark tests to determine how fast your Mac runs. Has 6 tests for measuring math and graphics performance. Lets you compare computing speeds of different Macs or determine how INITs affect your system performance.

Bartley H. Calder, Jr.
106 Hooper Hill Road
New Boston, NH 03070
GEnie: B.CALDER

Application
Freeware
Size: 31k

Screen-Dump][v1.0

Installer program for 3 function key programs: two perform a b&w screen dump whether you are in color or not, one dumps a 256-color picture of the screen. Docs within the program.

Mike Whittingham
Mark 3
215 Thayer Pond Road
Wilton, CT 06897

Application
Shareware $12.00
Size: 134k

SD->AlertSound v1.0

Converts Sound Designer files to 'snd' resources which you can use as alert sounds (beeps).

John Connolly
Beaverton Digital Systems
PO Box 1626
Beaverton, OR 97075

Application
Public Domain
Size: 28k

Sound->Beep

Converts SoundCap files into 'snd ' resources.

Frederick Computer &
Electronics Corporation
11301 Tree View Lane
Monrovia, MD 21770

Application
Shareware $10.00
Size: 7k

Sound->Snd

Converts sounds into 'snd' resources.

unknown

Application
Public Domain
Size: 8k

Soundoff][

Plays sounds when the system starts up.

Frederick Computer &
Electronics Corporation
11301 Tree View Lane
Monrovia, MD 21770

System Startup Extension
Shareware $15.00
Size: 2k

Spectra

Displays 6 different color pictures/effects. Cycles colors once a picture is drawn, creating an interesting color animation.	Jim Stout CIS: 73240,2052 GEnie: JSTOUT	**Application** **Public Domain** **Size: 10k** 12" 6 7 32

Spirograph Mac II

Draws color line-art images on the screen.	unknown	**Application** **Public Domain** **Size: 2k** 12" 6 7 32

Paris D2

General

ApplicationMenu

Provides a menu of currently running applications under MultiFinder so that you can switch between them.

Larry Rosenstein
102 Muir Ave
Santa Clara, CA 95051

System Startup
Extension
Freeware
Size: 2k

AutoIdle v1.0a10

A screen saver that blanks the screen after 5 minutes of inactivity. Docs in a separate file.

Larry Rosenstein
Apple Computer, Inc.
20525 Mariani M/S 32-E
Cupertino, CA 95014

System Startup
Extension
Freeware
Size: 4k

Color Fonts

Color fonts! Wow!

Interactive Software
57 Post Street #811
San Francisco, CA 94104
(415) 956-2660

Fonts
Public Domain
Size: 133k

Flash

Allows you to select up to 100 GrayView documents (files of type 'gray' with PICT resources of ID=0 in them) and rapidly flashes them on the screen. Contains docs in a separate text file.

David Fry
81 Irving Street
Cambridge, MA 02138

Application
Freeware
Size: 6k

Picture Colorizer v1.0

Adds color to existing MacPaint bitmap images. Lets you assign colors to rectangular regions in the image. Includes docs in a separate file.

Scott Neufeld
6 Lake Road
Peekskill, NY 10566

Application
Shareware $10.00
Size: 54k

Retouch v1.3

Manipulates b&w and 8-bit gray-scale images. Works with TIFF, MacPaint, and PICT file formats. Lets you touch up scanned images and produce special effects. Contains thorough docs in a separate file.

Allen Akin
784 Palo Alto Avenue
Palo Alto, CA 94301
CIS: 72247, 2635

Application
Shareware $20.00
Size: 94k

aShowPict/zHidePict

Pair of INITs for displaying a color picture at startup using the picture's own color table instead of the System's color table. Pictures look funny if a color table other than their own is used.

Bill Band

System Startup Extension
Freeware
Size: 1k

Color Cursor

Colorizes your arrow cursor in the same manner as the Apple menu icon. A rainbow cursor with green, yellow, orange, red, and blue colors.

Matthias Urlichs
CIS: 72437,1357

System Startup Extension
Public Domain
Size: 3k

Diagnostic Sound Sampler

A little program that plays several of the diagnostic failure sounds for the Mac II.

Mark Lentczner
Apple Computer, Inc.

System Startup Extension
Public Domain
Size: 3k

Fish! v2.0

A truly unique and wonderful program that turns your desktop into a aquarium. Fish (or any other color icons) swim across your desktop in the background. Must see to appreciate.

Ed Fries
Bogus Software
15600 NE 8th Street #A3334
Bellevue, WA 98008

Control Panel Extension
Shareware $22.95
Size: 85k

Flock

Author calls it an experiment in particle systems. A collection of about 10 small, white squares move about the screen somewhat like a flock of birds.

Keith McGreggor
Pixel Resources, Inc.

Application
Public Domain
Size: 8k

Imagine v1.0

Imagine is an advanced image-processing program.

Bill Connor
2425 North Park Blvd #1
Cleveland Hts., OH 44106

Application
Freeware
Size: 413k

Kaleidoscope

Draws color line-art patterns on the screen.

MacMaster Systems

Application
Freeware
Size: 5k

Menu Color v1.1.1b0

A control panel device that allows you to change the colors of menus.

Mike Pinkerton
2136 Owls Cove Lane
Reston, VA 22091

Control Panel Extension
Freeware
Size: 10k

Paris D3

Continued

Møire v3.22

A very nice screen saver. After a specified period of inactivity, screen darkens and a moving moiré pattern is displayed. In color on a Mac II. Docs in a separate file.

John Lim
18 Nottingwood Street
Doncaster East 3109
Victoria
AUSTRALIA

Control Panel
Extension
Shareware $10.00
Size: 13k

PalEdit v1.1b0

Tool for editing color palettes. Has many advanced features, including support for CMY, RGB, and two other color standards. Saves palettes in raw or HDF formats. Edits the entire palette graphically.

NCSA Research
University of Illinois
605 E. Springfield Ave.
Champaign, IL 61820

Application
Freeware
Size: 113k

¶RestoreCLUT

Part of the ScreenMaster package. RestoreCLUT prevents the screen from looking awful when ScreenMaster is set to the SMScreen option. ScreenMaster is also on this disk.

unknown

System Startup
Extension
Shareware $?
Size: 3k

ScreenMaster v2.6

Controls the screen size of any 13-inch monitor. Did not work on a 5-meg Mac II with an Apple 13-inch color monitor running System 6.0.2 (claimed the Control Panel could not get enough memory).

Frank Proce
AOC Software
612 Doheny Road
Beverly Hills, CA 90210

Control Panel
Extension
Shareware $5.00
Size: 17k

WindCntl Color v1.1b0

A control panel that allows you to alter the colors of the dialog boxes, windows, text, highlighting, etc. of your Mac's system.

Mike Pinkerton
2136 Owls Cove Lane
Reston, VA 22091

Control Panel
Extension
Freeware
Size: 12k

Bouncer

Shows the Apple logo bouncing around a black background. You can increase the number of Apple logos; also supports variable speeds.

Jim Stout
CIS: 73240,2052
GEnie: J.G.Stout

Application
Freeware
Size: 13k

ColorFun

Draws color circles on the screen. Lets you specify the number of circles, circle radius, and hollow or filled circles.

Scott Neufeld
6 Lake Road
Peekskill, NY 10566

Application
Freeware
Size: 51k

Contour81 v1.0

Creates contour maps, 3-D surface plots, and pictures from lists of 3-D data, up to 1000 points. Includes good docs in a separate file.

Technical Software Systems
PO Box 56
Millburn, NJ 07041-1008

Application
Shareware $10.00
Size: 58k

Easy Color Paint v0.4

A basic color paint program designed for children under 12 years of age. Program has pattern, FatBits, and cut & paste features.

Bruce Ballard
55 Clinton Ave.
New Providence, NJ 07974

Application
Freeware
Size: 33k

Just Print

Comes with GIFConverter. Prints out any Glue format documents.

Kevin A. Mitchell
PO Box 803066
Chicago, IL 60680-3066

Application
Freeware
Size: 4k

Lines and Circles

Draws animated color patterns on the screen. Lets you choose between animating colors, drawing lines, or drawing circles. Allows you to modify drawing parameters from a dialog box.

Jerry Goldstein

Application
Public Domain
Size: 13k

Petals v00-100

Displays a colorful and moving set of flower petals. Works in the background under MultiFinder.

Kent A. Behrends
CIS: 72447, 2533

Application
Freeware
Size: 12k

StarMac II

Star plotter (color).

William H. Klein
879 S. Mary Ave.
Sunnyvale, CA 94087

Application
Shareware $5.00
Size: 105k

Paris D4

Continued

Tears v1.0

Puts up a window with falling teardrops. Operates in the background under MultiFinder.

Steve Morein
44 Kinnan Way
Basking Ridge, NJ 07920

Application
Public Domain
Size: 8k

Tears(MAC II) v1.0

Puts up a window with falling teardrops. Operates in the background under MultiFinder. Lets you change the color of the background screen and the teardrops. Buggy; bombs frequently.

Steve Morein
44 Kinnan Way
Basking Ridge, NJ 07920

Application
Public Domain
Size: 9k

Worms ! v1.0

Displays a window of squiggling, colorful worms. Based on the December 1987 Scientific American 'Computer Recreations' article.

T. M. Herbst

Application
Public Domain
Size: 17k

Image v2.27

Program for analyzing, editing, and color-coding gray-scale and color images. May be cool.

Wayne Rasband
NIH/RSB
Bldg 36, Room 2A-03
Bethesda, MD 20892

Application
Public Domain
Size: 84k

Paris E1

Color Icons

Color Icon FKEY

An FKEY of unknown function.

unknown

FKEY Resource
Document
Public Domain
Size: 5k

Icon Colorizer v1.6

Allows you to use 8-bit color icons in System 6.x.

Robert P. Munafo
239 Clinton Road
Brookline, MA 02146
(617) 738-0650

System Startup
Extension
Freeware
Size: 25k

Icon Lab v1.1b

Icon Editor is a paint-like editor to create icl8 color icon resources. The palette used to build an icl8 is the 8-bit system default.

Tom Wasko
4832 49th Avenue NW
Calgary, Alberta
T3A 0R9 CANADA

Application
Shareware ?
Size: 43k

iContraption v1.0.1

iContraption is an icon family organizer. The concept is similar to font family organizers. Icon nuts of the world, UNITE!

Tom Poston
Immedium Design
2114 Lockhart Drive
Charlotte, NC 28203-6040

Application
Shareware $20.00
Size: 164k

SunDesk v1.1

Allows color icons in System 6.0.x. Nice if you haven't gone to System 7 and you want color icons.

Frédéric Miserey
nOne Corp.
13, Boulevard Pasteur
51100 Reims
FRANCE

System Startup
Extension
Freeware
Size: 11k

SunDesk Strip v1.2.2

This program creates a SunDesk icon file that contains only icons that match those in your Desktop file; this could speed up SunDesk significantly.

Morgan Davis Group
10079 Nuerto Lane
Rancho San Diego, CA 92078-1736

Application
Freeware
Size: 28k

351 Color Icons in 31 files

(samples below)

Adobe Stuff Icon Vault -4047 | Adobe Stuff Icon Vault -4064 | Adobe Stuff Icon Vault -4046 | Adobe Stuff Icon Vault 256 | Adobe Stuff Icon Vault 15500 | America Online Icon Vault 136 | America Online Icon Vault 135 | America Online Icon Vault 134

America Online Icon Vault 132 | America Online Icon Vault 131 | America Online Icon Vault 130 | America Online Icon Vault 129 | America Online Icon Vault 128 | America Online Icon Vault -16455 | Compact Pro Icon Vault 128 | Compact Pro Icon Vault 129

Color Icons
Paris

1,867 Color Icons in 245 files

(samples below)

BarTender Animated Icons 128	BarTender Animated Icons 127	BarTender Animated Icons 126	BarTender Animated Icons 125	BarTender Animated Icons 124	BarTender Animated Icons 123	BarTender Animated Icons 122	BarTender Animated Icons 121
CalendarMaker/ IconMover Icons -25523	CalendarMaker/ IconMover Icons -25526	CalendarMaker/ IconMover Icons -25522	CalendarMaker/ IconMover Icons -25524	CalendarMaker/ IconMover Icons -25525	Colorizer Icons -25582	Colorizer Icons -25581	Colorizer Icons -25583
Colorizer Icons -25584	DOCMaker Icons -30969	DOCMaker Icons -30968	DOCMaker Icons -30967	MacProof Icons -25535	MacProof Icons -25530	MacProof Icons -25531	MacProof Icons -25532
MacProof Icons -25534	MasterJuggler Icons 30090	MasterJuggler Icons 30099	MasterJuggler Icons 30100	MasterJuggler Icons 30096	MasterJuggler Icons 30095	MasterJuggler Icons 30097	MasterJuggler Icons 30091
MasterJuggler Icons 30093	MasterJuggler Icons 30098	MasterJuggler Icons 30092	MenuFonts Icons 12347	MenuFonts Icons 12346	MenuFonts Icons 12345	SAM Icons 5151	SAM Icons 5150
Serius89 Programmer Icons -31172	Serius89 Programmer Icons -31173	Serius89 Programmer Icons -31171	Serius89 Programmer Icons -31170	After Dark Icons 16053	After Dark Icons 16052	Banner Maker Icons 30081	Banner Maker Icons 30080
myDiskLabeler Icons 30066	QuicKeys Icons 30088	QuicKeys Icons 30087	QuicKeys Icons 30089	QuicKeys Icons 30086	QuicKeys Icons 30085	QuicKeys Icons 30084	QuicKeys Icons 30083
QuicKeys Icons 30081	QuicKeys Icons 30080	READ-IT! O.C.R. Icons 30060	READ-IT! O.C.R. Icons 30061	READ-IT! O.C.R. Icons 30062	READ-IT! O.C.R. Icons 30063	READ-IT! O.C.R. Icons 30064	Ready,Set,Go! Icons 30058
Ready,Set,Go! Icons 30056	Ready,Set,Go! Icons 30055	Ready,Set,Go! Icons 30054	Ready,Set,Go! Icons 30053	Ready,Set,Go! Icons 30052	Ready,Set,Go! Icons 30051	Ready,Set,Go! Icons 30050	Switch-A-Roo Icon 30068

Paris E3

Color Icons

1,874 Color Icons in 327 files

(samples below)

101 icon families sample 128	101 icon families sample 129	101 icon families sample 130	101 icon families sample 131	101 icon families sample 132	101 icon families sample 133	101 icon families sample 134	101 icon families sample 135
101 icon families sample 137	101 icon families sample 138	101 icon families sample 139	Adobe Separator Icl8s 2468	AfterDark 2.0 icl8s -4064	AfterDark 2.0 icl8s -4063	AfterDark 2.0 icl8s -4062	Boomerang Icl8 10031
ColorDesk icl8s 132	Disinfectant Icl8s 6429	Disinfectant Icl8s 6430	Disinfectant Icl8s 6431	Disinfectant Icl8s 6432	Finder Icl8's 129	Finder Icl8's 130	Finder Icl8's 131
Finder Icl8's 133	Finder Icl8's 134	Finder Icl8's 135	Finder Icl8's 136	Finder Icl8's 137	Fortune Icl8s 7386	INIT Scope Icl8 14551	MacsBug Icl8 11432
MandleColor Icl8 18260	Mathematica Icl8s 587	Mathematica Icl8s 3130	Mathematica Icl8s 7546	Mathematica Icl8s 17058	MS Mail 2.0 Icl8 31636	Partition Icl8s 3089	Partition Icl8s 12800
Partition Icl8s 25411	Partition Icl8s 28155	Partition Icl8s 300	PhotoShop Appl Icl8 25411	Programmer Key Icl8 11012	SCSI Probe Icl8 14466	StrataFlight icl8s 130	StrataFlight icl8s 133
Switch-a-roo Icl8 8686	Timbuktu Icl8 7216	TurboCache Icl8 18420	Virtual 2.0 Icl8s 134	Virtual 2.0 Icl8s 135	Escapade icon family -4064	Escapade icon family -4064	Escapade icon family -4048
A Few icl8s 7040	A Few icl8s 7041	A Few icl8s 2051	A Few icl8s 135	A Few icl8s 145	A Few icl8s 170	A Few icl8s 240	A Few icl8s 243
A Few icl8s 370	A Few icl8s 400	A Few icl8s 515	A Few icl8s 516	A Few icl8s 725	Bricicns 6016	Bricicns 6019	Bricicns 6020

CIcon Edit v1.1

An application for making cicn resource icons. Supports only 16 colors.

AppleSauce Designs
c/o Ben Haller
32 Deer Haven Drive
Ithaca, NY 14850

Application
Freeware
Size: 17k

System CICNs

Contains colorized versions of the icons used in Alert boxes (stop, information, and caution). Lets you cut and paste these icons into your System using a resource copier or editor.

Scott Anguish
Mark Steinberg
Graphic Applications
(919) 852-1608

Application
Freeware
Size: 7k

778 Color Icons in 32 files

(samples below)

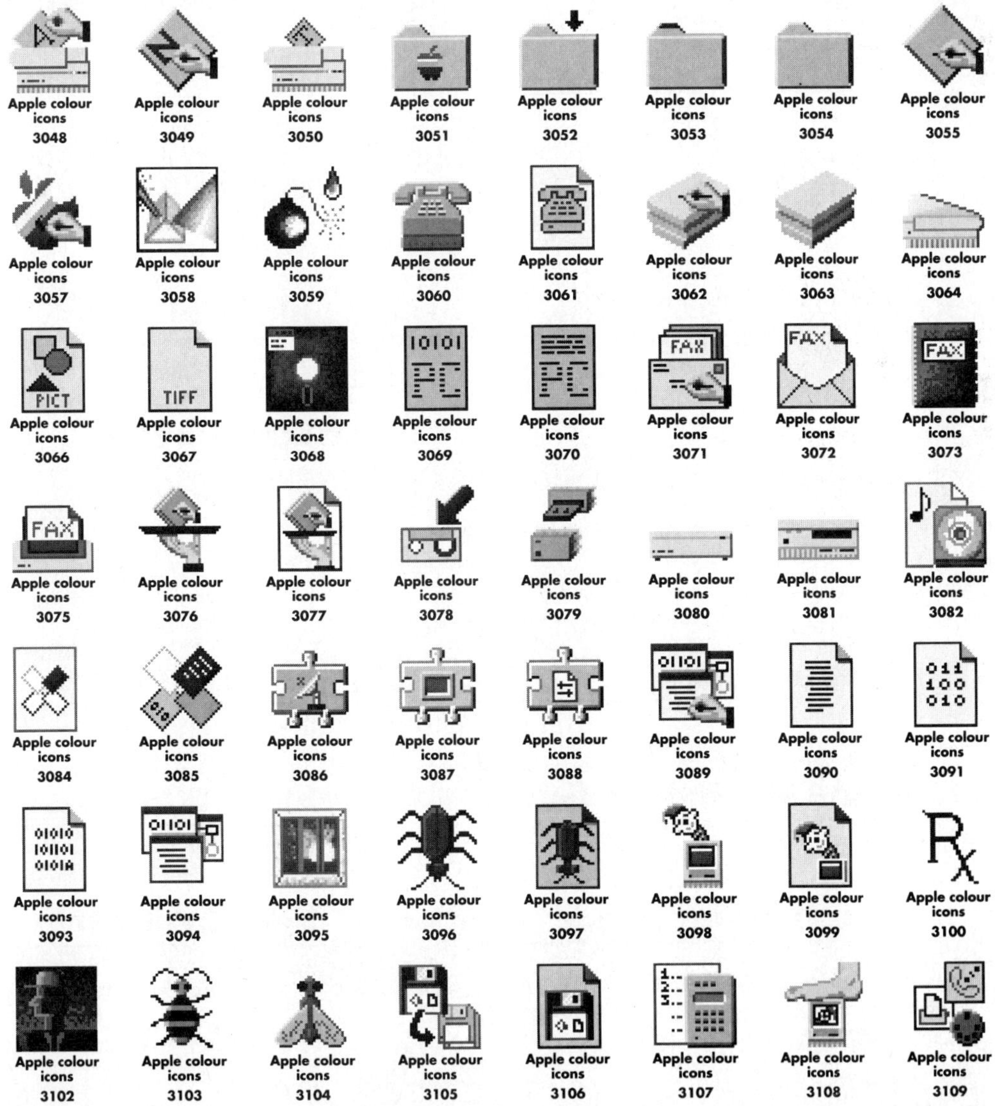

Paris F1

Sounds

Baby Lamb Beep
Size: 12k

Bridge Noise
Size: 52k

Dave's Window
Size: 35k

Elephant
Size: 22k

Frog
Size: 31k

Fung Riff
Size: 15k

Hi
Size: 16k

Kirk Here
Size: 29k

Meep Meep
Size: 11k

Piano
Size: 12k

Shall We Play a Game
Size: 46k

Spam Beep
Size: 16k

Warp
Size: 38k

Bottled Bach
Size: 12k

Dave Beep
Size: 13k

Dragnet
Size: 169k

Fred Flintstone
Size: 33k

FTroop2
Size: 21k

Guitar Beep
Size: 38k

Illogical
Size: 12k

Lamb Beep
Size: 13k

Ni
Size: 7k

Sea Lion Beep
Size: 5k

Slide Whistle
Size: 7k

Spin Cylinder
Size: 24k

You Can't do That
Size: 19k

Blender v1.0

For calculating the number of steps required to make smooth blend transitions between two colors in programs such as Illustrator or Aldus FreeHand.

Rick Johnson/Graffix
2216 Allen Lane
Waukesha, WI 53186
GEnie: RICK.JOHNSON

Desk Accessory
Shareware $1.00
Size: 24k

ColorFinder

ColorFinder is an INIT that allows your applications, documents, folders, volumes, and other icons to be displayed in full color.

Chris Derossi
Apple Computer
20525 Mariani Ave., MS27-AJ
Cupertino, CA 95041

System Startup Extension
Freeware
Size: 157k

Façade v1.0.1

Allows you to assign special icons to your disks.

Greg Marriot
Apple Computer
20525 Mariani Ave. MS-46z
Cupertino, CA 95014

System Startup Extension
Freeware
Size: 3k

Finder Color Icons v1.0b1

Displays color icons on your desktop. Does not work with System 7 (and it never will).

Robert P. Munafo
239 Clinton Road
Brookline, MA 02146
(617) 738-0650

System Startup Extension
Freeware
Size: 140k

HodgePodge v2.0

Cellular automaton extension of the game of Life, where each cell can exist in a state from 0 to n.

Fred Condo
GEnie: F.Condo
BBS: (818) 339-4704

Application
Freeware
Size: 122k

Kolor v1.0

Lets you customize your Mac desktop by colorizing controls (buttons, scroll bars, etc.), windows, menus, and text highlighting.

Russ Wetmore
Apple Computer, Inc.
101 Los Gatos Blvd. #5
Los Gatos, CA 95032

Control Panel Extension
Freeware
Size: 18k

loads of icons

Forty or so icons. Part of the Façade software package. You can use ResEdit to edit and place these icons into your favorite programs or the System.

John Singer

Façade Resource Document
Freeware
Size: 14k

ResCicn v1.0b3

Color icon editor for older versions of ResEdit (prior to v2.0). Install by copying resources into a copy of ResEdit. We recommend that you get ResEdit 2.x+ instead.

Frédéric Miserey

Old ResEdit Template
Freeware
Size: 39k

Colorizing Paris

Paris H1

Mac II DAs and FKEYs

Cache Control v1.1

Lets you turn off/on the instruction cache on a 68020 machine (Mac II), and both the instruction and data cache on a 68030 machine (SE/30, IIcx). Some older programs have problems if these caches are on.

Jim Hamilton
2914 Aftonshire Way, #13102
Austin, TX 78748

Control Panel Extension
Shareware $10.00
Size: 5k

Cache Control FKey

Function key that toggles on/off the Mac II instruction cache.

Kiyomasa Ono
Advanced Products Design
Shinjuku 6-28-10 1002
Tokyo 160
JAPAN

Function Key
Public Domain
Size: 2k

cachectrl v1.0

Turns the Mac II instruction cache on or off. Some programs run on a Mac II only when the instruction cache is off.

John Foderaro
GEnie: jkf
ARPA: jkf@berkeley.edu
uucp: ucbvax!franz!jkf

Application
Public Domain
Size: 3k

Clutter v1.0

Displays the current color table(s) for the screen(s) that the Clutter DA window spans. Shows all available colors (up to 256) in a small grid and lets you edit colors by double-clicking on them.

Don Leeper
CIS: 70157,1670
AppleLink: D0428

Desk Accessory
Freeware
Size: 6k

Color Puzzle

A color version of the Puzzle DA that comes with the System (on the Utilities Disk). Has15 numbered pieces on a 4 x 4 grid with one open space. Shift the pieces to get them in numerical order.

unknown

Desk Accessory
Public Domain
Size: 11k

Color SnapShot™ v1.0

Installs a function key program for taking color snapshots (screen dumps) of the screen. Saves to size different file formats. Has option for including pull-down menus in the snapshot. Program includes docs.

Mike Whittingham
Mark 3 Software
215 Thayer Pond Road
Wilton, CT 06897

Application
Shareware $12.00
Size: 112k

ColorDreams

Rapidly draws random color rectangles on the screen. Provides no apparent way to get back to the Finder from this program.

unknown

Desk Accessory
Public Domain
Size: 1k

ColorKey v1.3b0

Change your screen depth through an FKEY instead of by a control panel.

Mike Pinkerton
2136 Owls Cove Lane
Reston, VA 22091

FKEY
Freeware
Size: 7k

ColorSave

Performs a screen dump in glorious color. Saves the file in PICT format as 'Screen x,' where x increments from 0 to 9. Works the same as the built-in screen dump FKEY, except that this one works in color.

unknown

Function Key
Public Domain
Size: 2k

DeskPat v1.2

A DA for modifying the color desktop pattern. An improvement over the editor in the General control panel.

Roy M. Lovejoy III
23636 Algiers Street
Mission Viejo, CA 92691

Desk Accessory
Shareware $10.00
Size: 44k

FKey Manager v3.0

Organizes function-key commands (FKEYs) into sets with an interface similar to that of the Font/DA Mover.

Carlos Weber

Application
Freeware
Size: 50k

Klutz v1.0

Allows you to modify color lookup tables (CLUTs). Handy for viewing them…if you're interested.

Bill Steinberg
CIS: 76703,1027
GEnie, Delphi & MacNet: BillS

Desk Accessory
Freeware
Size: 10k

MaCube v2.1

Mac version of Rubik's Cube. Use the mouse and buttons to rotate faces of the cube. In color.

Kim Gillies
PO Box 42344
Tucson, AZ 85733
GEnie: KGILLIES

Desk Accessory
Freeware
Size: 27k

Simpsons Color Clock

A Simpsons color clock. The whole family is in stylish clothing!

unknown

Desk Accessory
Public Domain
Size: 18k

Switch-A-Roo v1.4

Switches Mac II monitors between two user-specifed display modes, such as 256-color and b&w. A must for HyperCard users.

Bill Steinberg
CIS: 76703,1027
AppleLink: X0542
MacNet: BillS

Function Key
Freeware
Size: 15k

Toggle Cache

Turns the Mac II instruction cache on or off.

Jan Eugenides

Control Panel Extension
Public Domain
Size: 3k

Paris

Pictures

Black & white and grayscale pictures of all sorts.

Picture-Type Icons

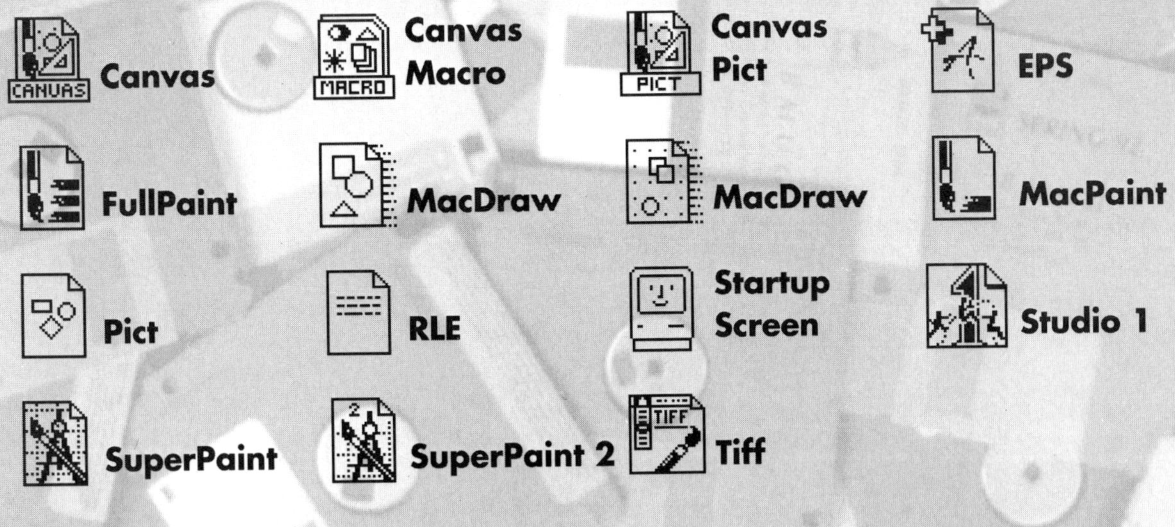

Pictures A1

Startup Screens

A Apple

Andromeda

Another Galaxy

ArmadilloStart

B Apple

BearStart

Startup Pictures

Bird

BombStart

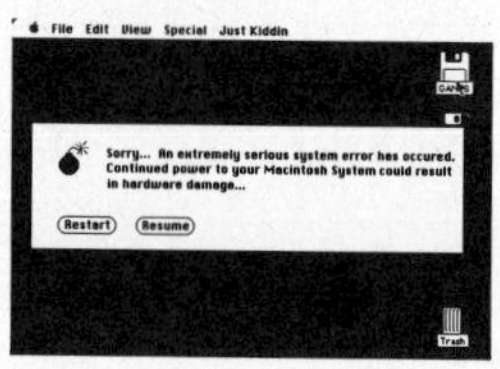

ButterfliesStart

C Apple

Cheshire Cat

Clint Start

CopyIIStart

Crashex

Dragon

Earth

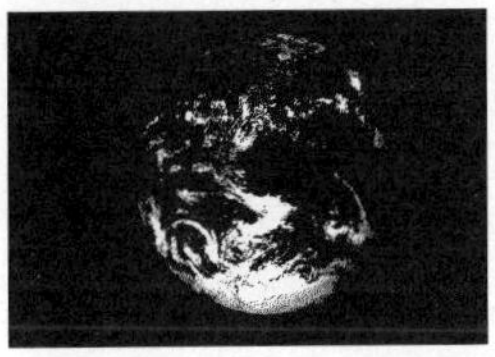

Engine Start

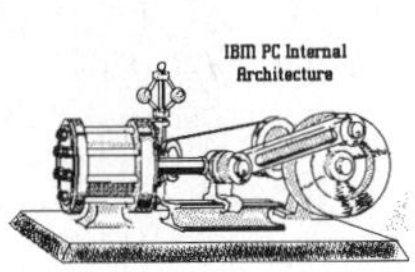

FunkArtistStart

StartupScreen OPUS

Pictures B1

Personalities

Bert & Ernie

Bogart

Clint Eastwood

Ed Sullivan

Geraldo

Golf Cartoons

Personality Pictures

Jack Webb

Jet Car

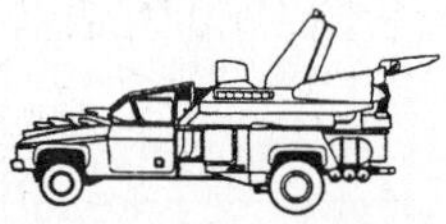

Jetthruster

Louis Armstrong

New York New York

Overthruster

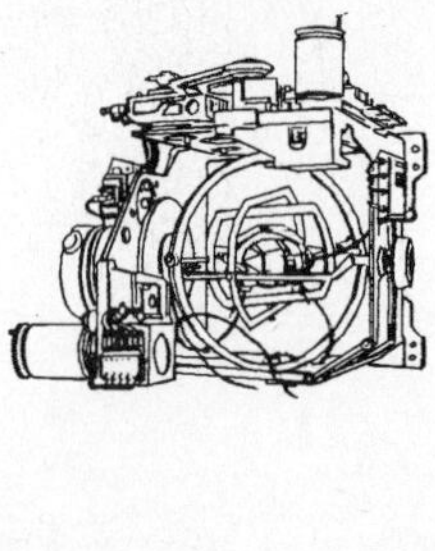

Pecos?

President Reagan

Rock-N-Roll

Ronnie Reagan

SCREEN Maker 11

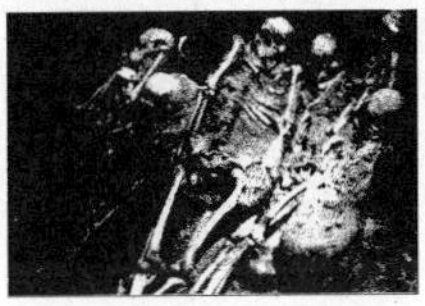

The Mac Group

SCREEN Maker 12

The Mac Group

SCREEN Maker 13

SCREEN Maker 16

The Mac Group

SCREEN Maker 18

SCREEN Maker 19

The Mac Group

SCREEN Maker 21

The Mac Group

Pictures B2

Personalities

Albert

Ben Franklin

Crying Girl

Duke Kahanamoku

Executive

Geisha TS

Interesting#2

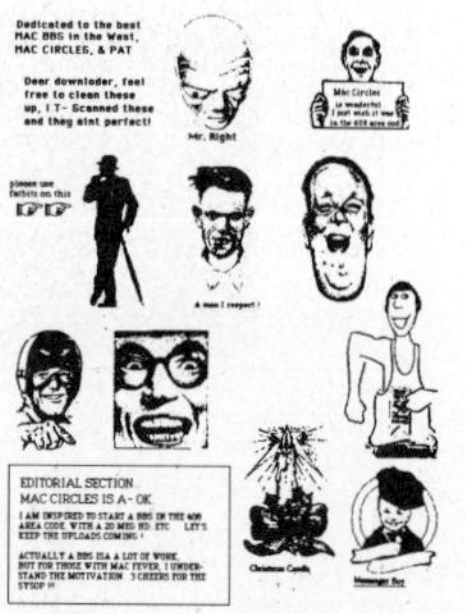

Koala

Occupations

Rogue's Gallery

Skull Lady

Thinker

Washington

Pictures C1

Anatomy

Anatomy

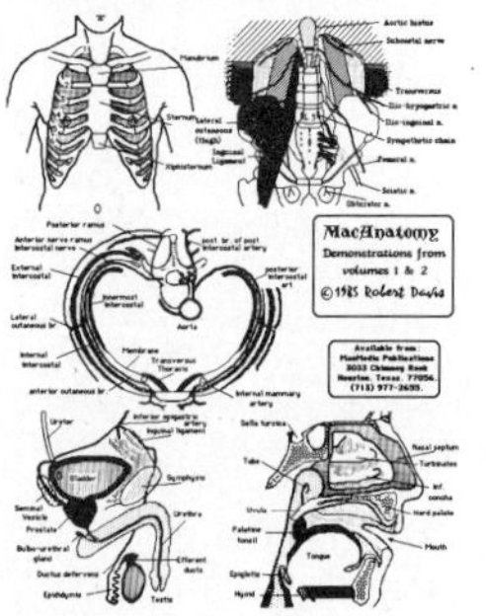

Body Building

Eye

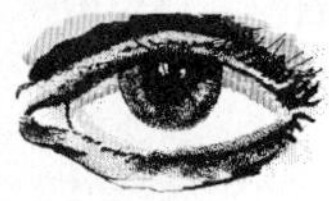

Eyes

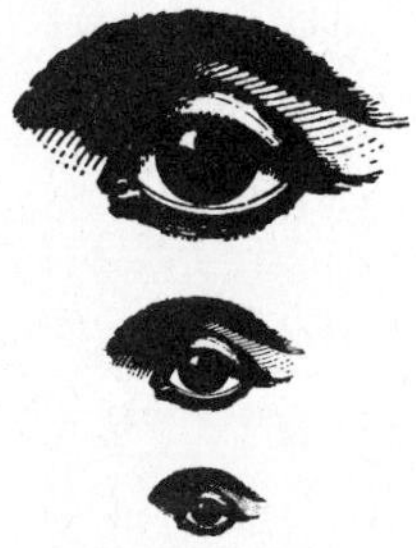

Eyes1

Eyes2

FemHead 01

FemHead 02

FemHead 03

FemHead 04

FemHead 05

FemHead 06

Pictures C1

Continued

FemHead 07

FemHead 08

FemHead 09

FemHead 10

FemHead 11

FemHead 12

FemHead 13

FemHead 14

FemHead 15

Hands

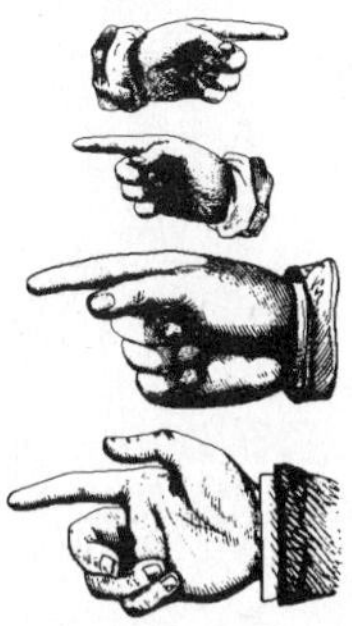

Hands 1

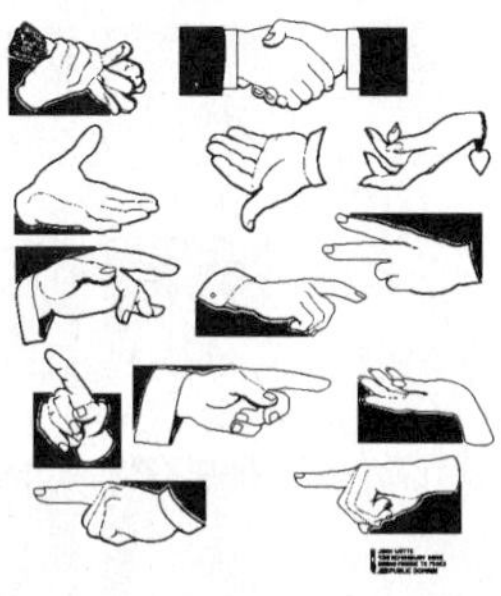

Hands 2

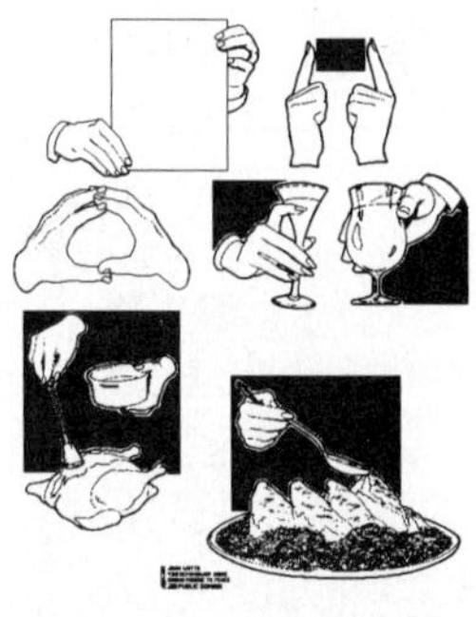

Pictures C1

Continued

Hands 3

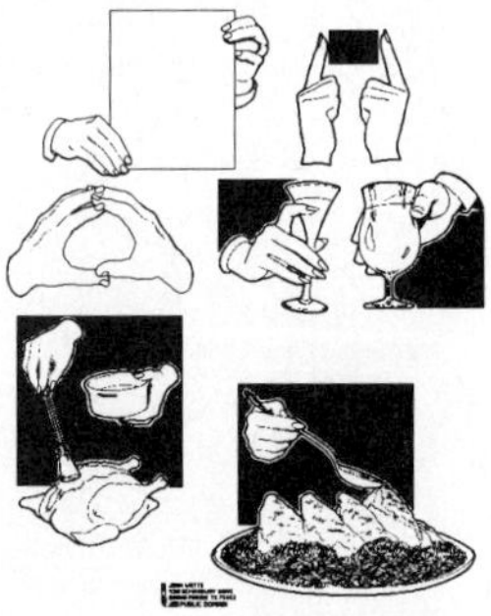

Hands 4

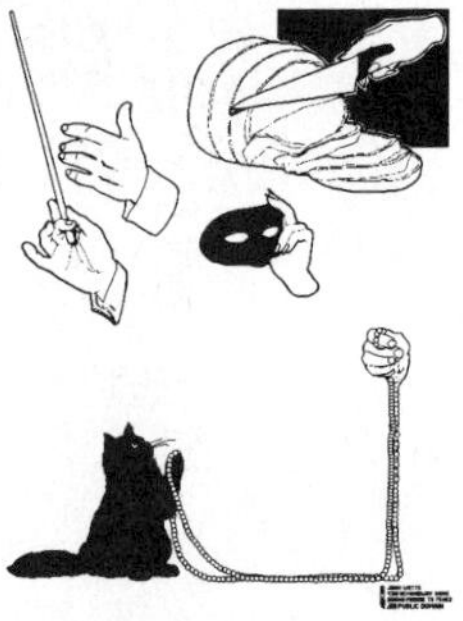

Mens Head 1

Mens Head 10

Mens Head 11

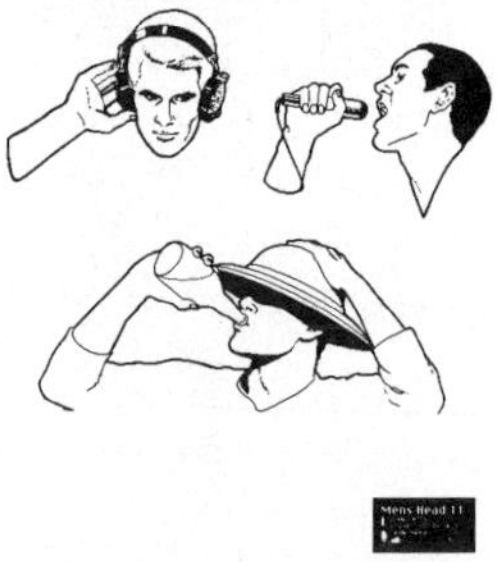

Mens Head 2

Mens Head 3

Mens Head 4

Mens Head 5

Mens Head 6

Mens Head 7

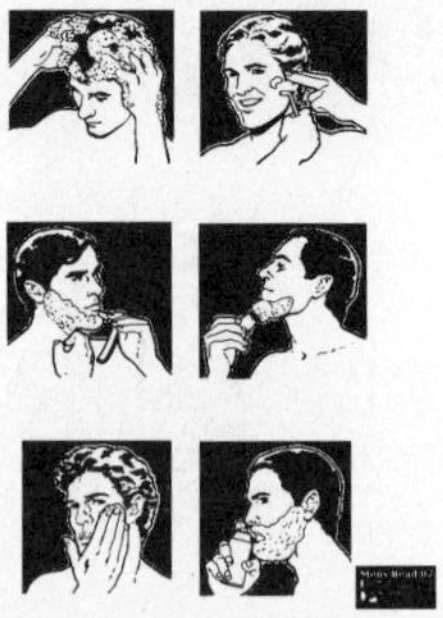

Mens Head 8

Pictures C1

Continued

Mens Head 9

More Muscle

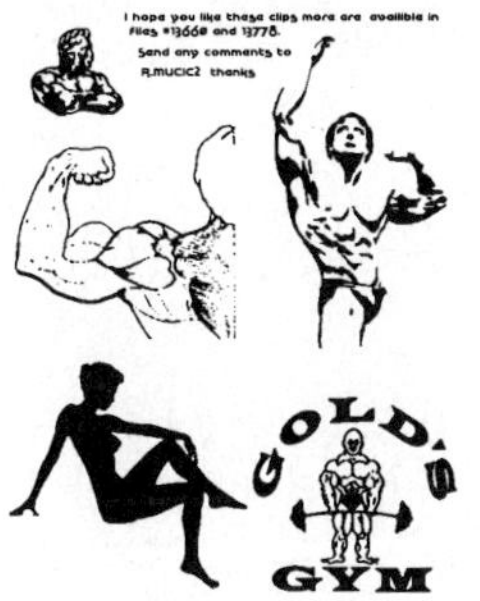

Sad Eyes

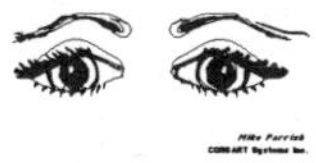

Anatomy Pictures

Pictures D1

Science

100% Natural

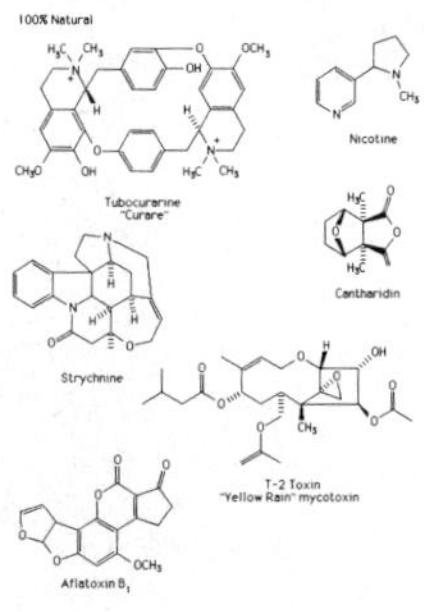

Anti-viral Drugs

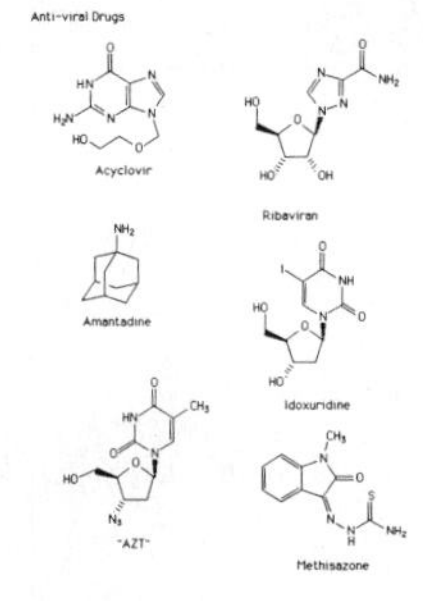

Antibiotics

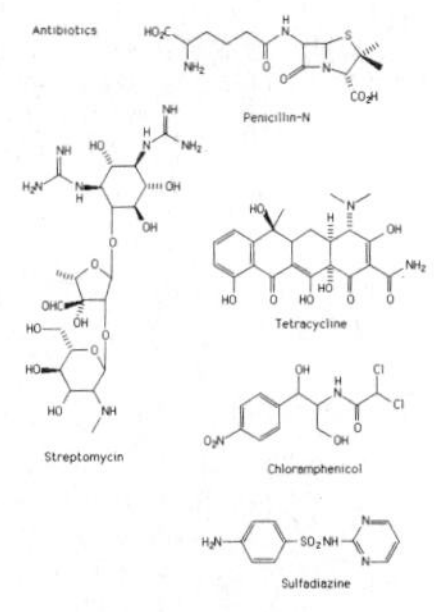

Better Living ?

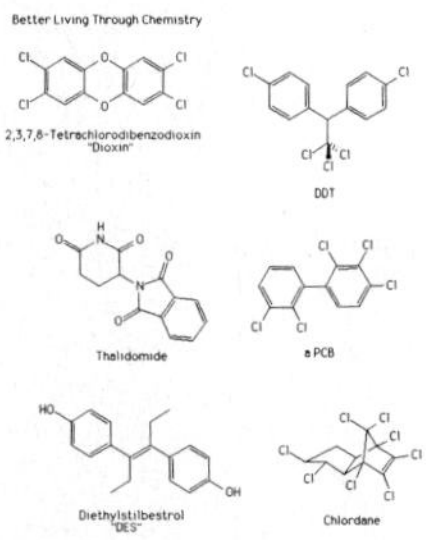

Central America

Changes in State

CW Agents

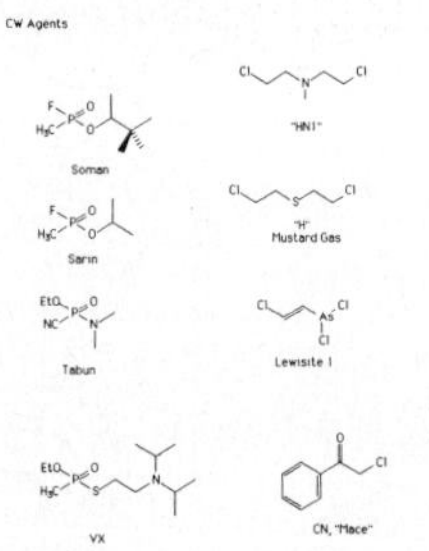

Designer Drugs

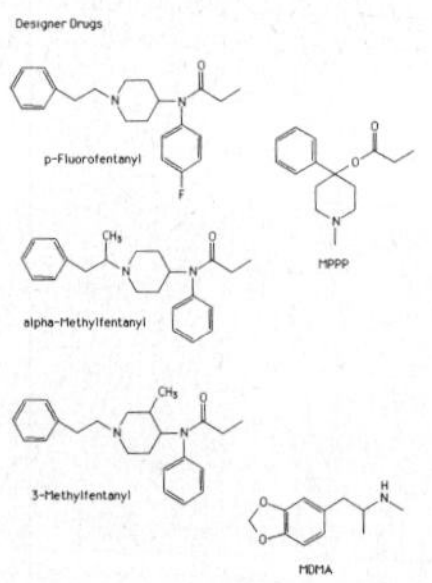

Earth's Interior

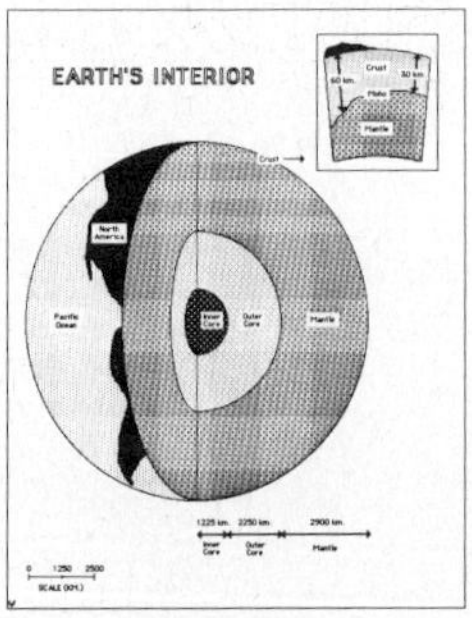

Energy Sources

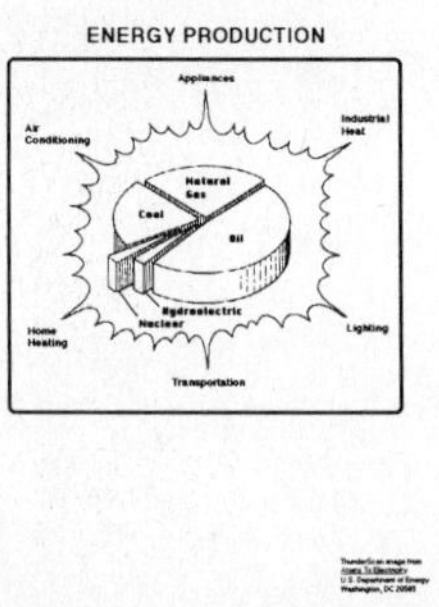

Folding & Faulting

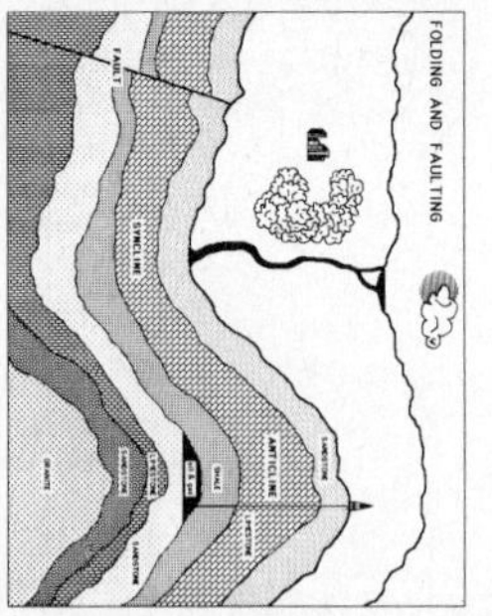

Geologic Puzzles

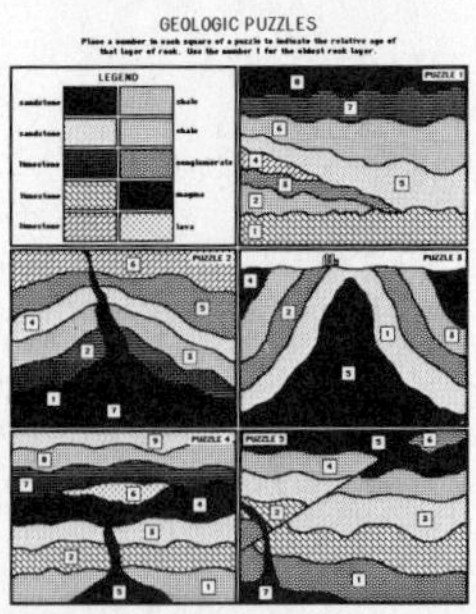

Introduction

Just Say No

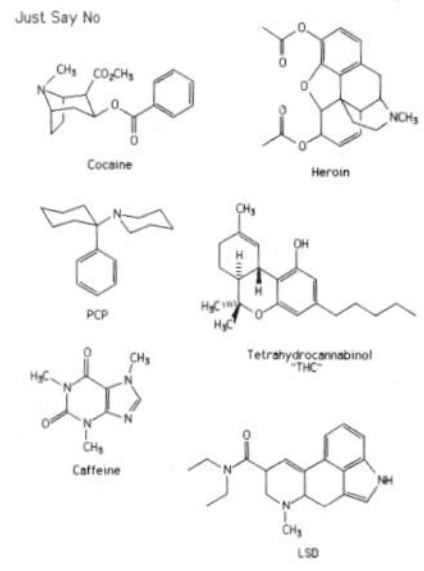

Landscapes

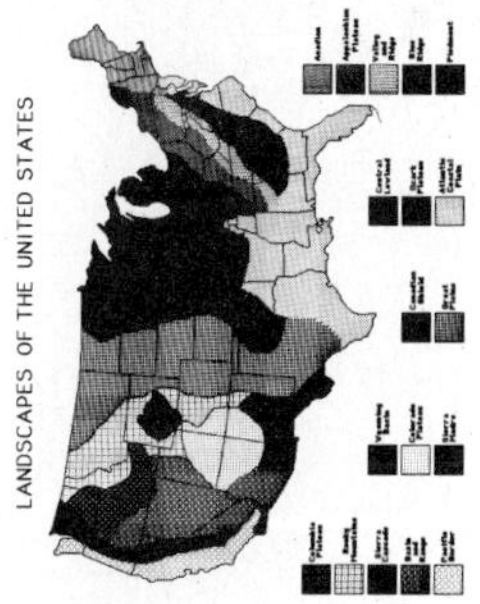

Maya 1

Maya 2

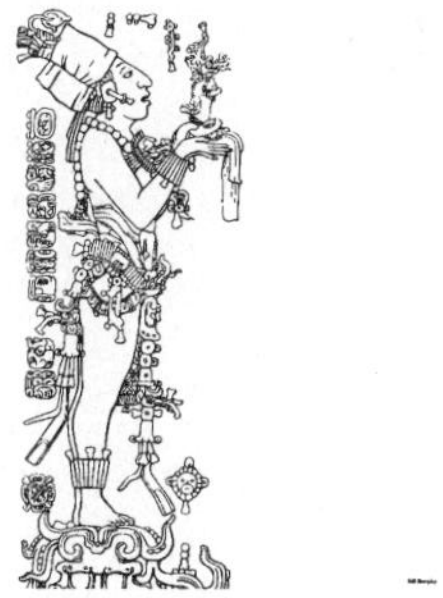

Maya 3

Ocean Currents #1

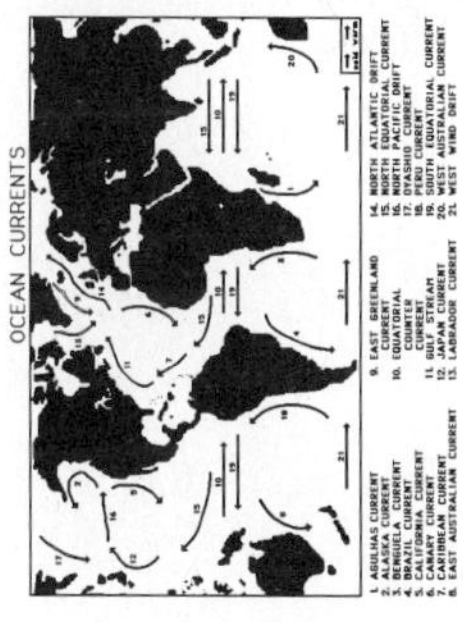

Ocean Currents #2

OTC

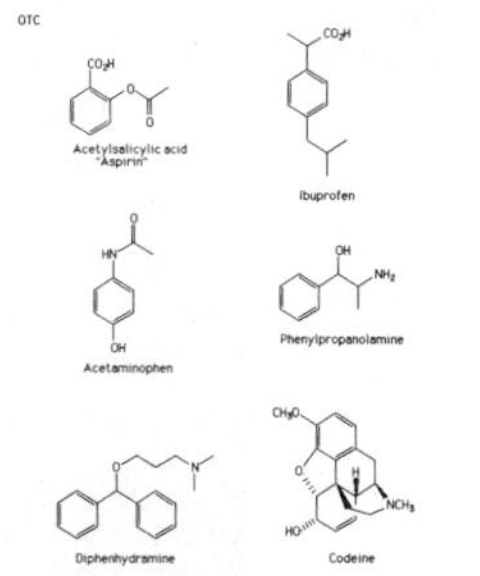

Powers of Ten

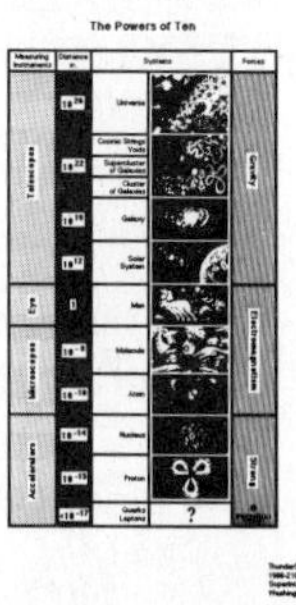

Rivers of the U.S.

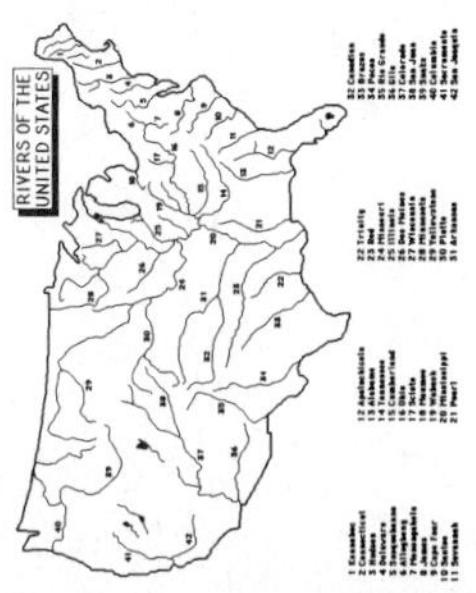

Sharks

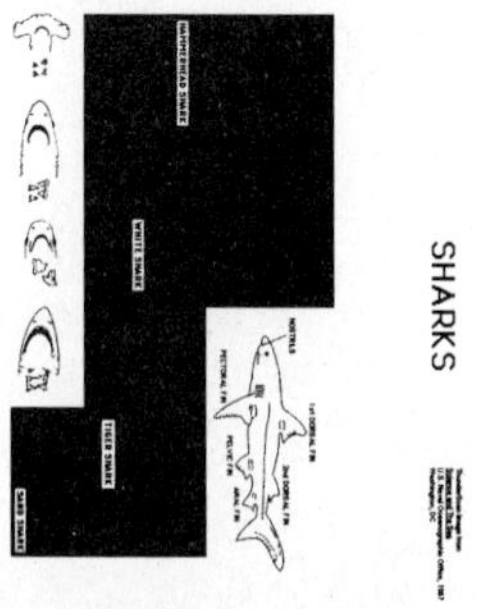

Pictures D1

Continued

Tools of Earth Science

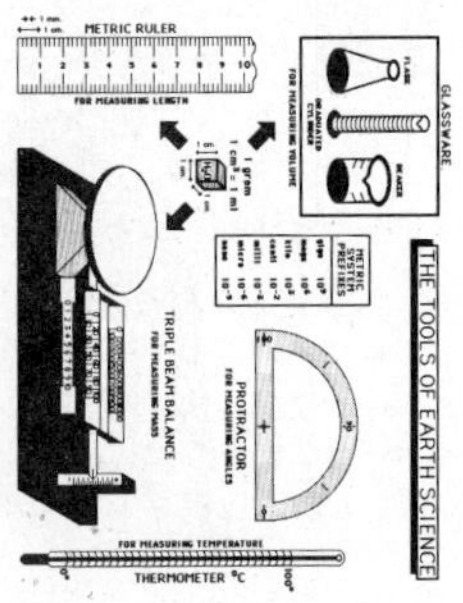

Tsunami

Types of Faults

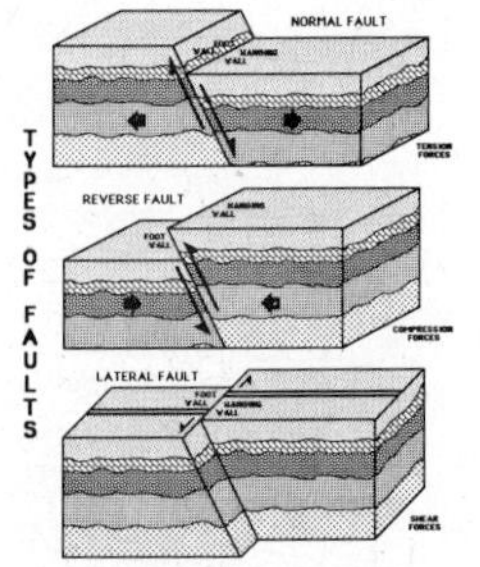

Types of Volcanoes

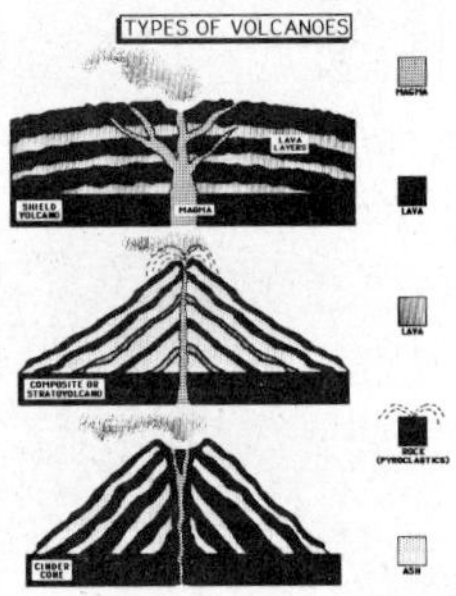

Vitamin B12

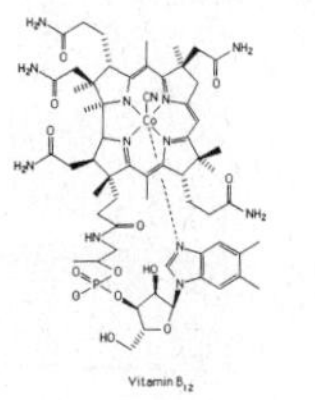

Vitamins

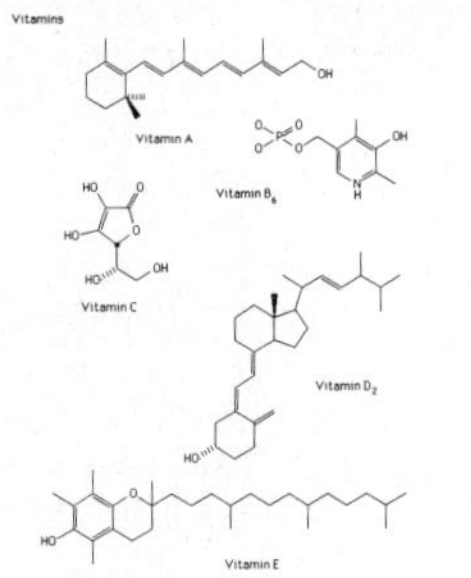

Volcanic Structures

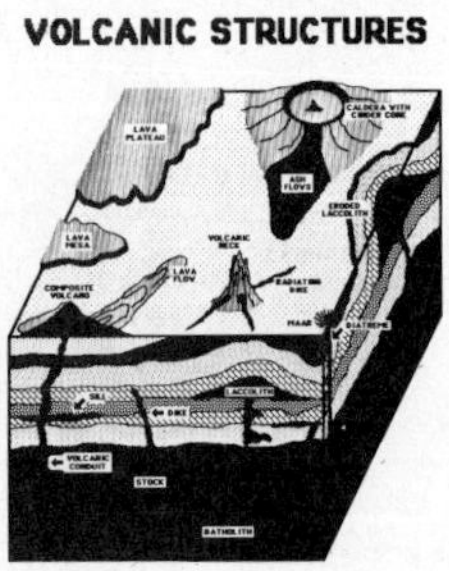

Water Cycle

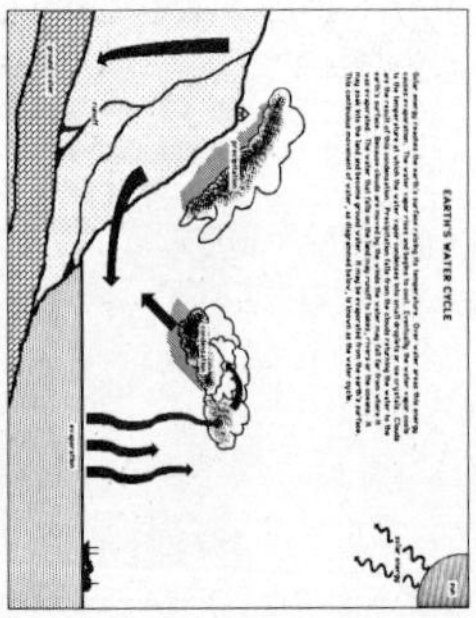

Watersheds of the U.S.

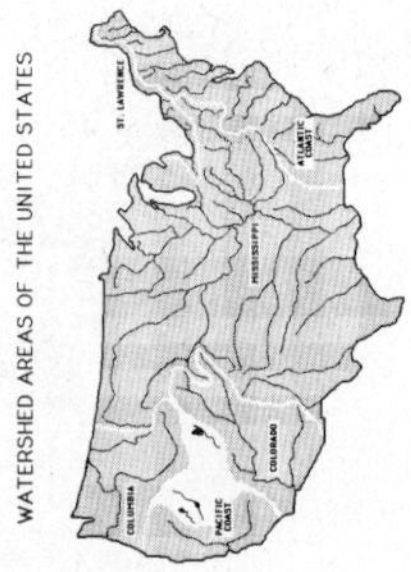

Science Pictures

TIFF Format Pictures

3 Nuns

$1.00 Shareware (one time fee!)
"3 Nuns.TIFF"
Page One Publications, PO Box 33097
Austin, TX 78764 (512)444-4593
GEnie: R.WEST4
CompuServe: 72047,1136

Anchor & Mermaid

$ 1.00 Shareware
Page One Publications
PO Box 33097
Austin, TX 78764

Watch this BBS for more quality shareware graphics from Page One Publications!

Baby in Womb

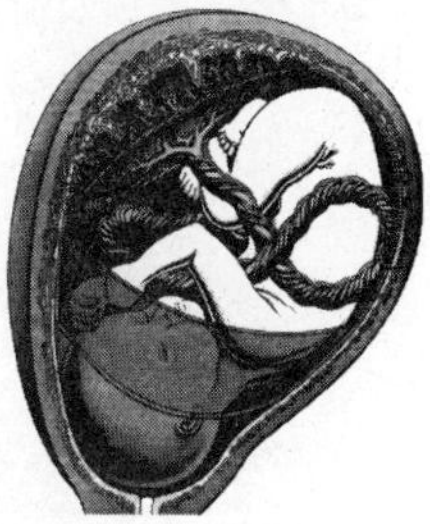

$4.00 Shareware Fee--Page One Publications, PO Box 33097, Austin, TX 78764
(512) 444-4593 / CompuServe 72047,1136 / GEnie Ron West

BackPacker

$1.00 Shareware (one time fee) "BackPacker.TIFF"
Page One Publications, PO Box 33097, Austin, TX 78764

CandleLady

$1.00 SharewareFee
(One Time Fee)
"CandleLady.TIFF"
Page One Publications
PO Box 33097, Austin, TX 78764
GEnie: R.WEST4

Carnation

$1.00 SAREWARE FEE
(ONE TIME FEE!)
"CARNATION.TIFF"
PAGE ONE PUBLICATIONS
PO BOX 33097, AUSTIN, TX 78764
(512) 444-4593
GENIE: R.WEST4
COMPUSERVE: 72047,1136

Clown

Faces

$1.00 SharewareFee (One time fee!)
"Faces.TIFF"
Page One Publications, PO Box 33097,
Austin, TX 78764 (512) 444-4593
GEnie: R.WEST4
CompuServe: 72047,1136

Flower Corner 1

$ 1.00 Shareware fee "Flower Corner 1"
Page One Publications, PO Box 33097, Austin, TX 78764
(512)444-4593 / CompuServe: 72047,1136 / GEnie: R.West4

FlowerGirl

FlowerHatLady

$1.00 SharewareFee (One Time Fee) "FlowerHatLady.TIFF"
Page One Publications, POBox 33097, Austin, TX 78764
(512)444-4593 GEnie R.WEST4 CompuServe 72047,1136

Kayaking

$1.00 Shareware (one time fee) "Kayaking.TIFF"
Page One Publications, PO Box 33097, Austin, TX 78764

Pictures E1

Continued

LadyDreamer

Neptune

NoSmoking

On The Beach

PalmTree

Pirate & Treasure Chest

Small Frame

Snow Shoeing

The Mooring

Young Lady

TIFF Format Pictures

Ball and Chain

Grasshopper.TIFF

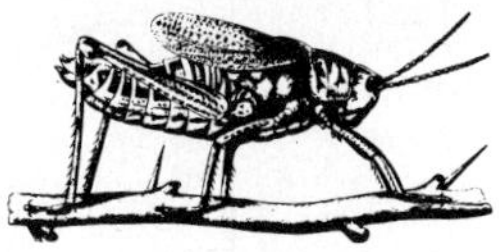

Naked Dwarf.TIFF

Trojan Horse.TIFF

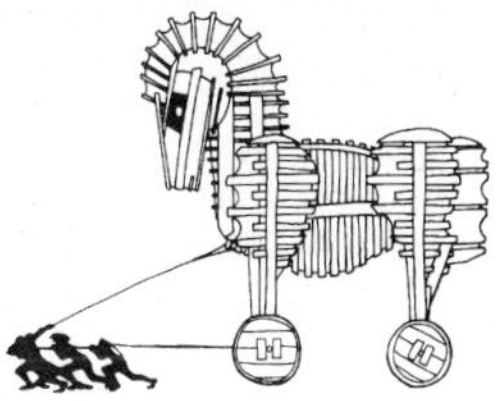

Pictures F1

EPS Format Pictures

California

CalState

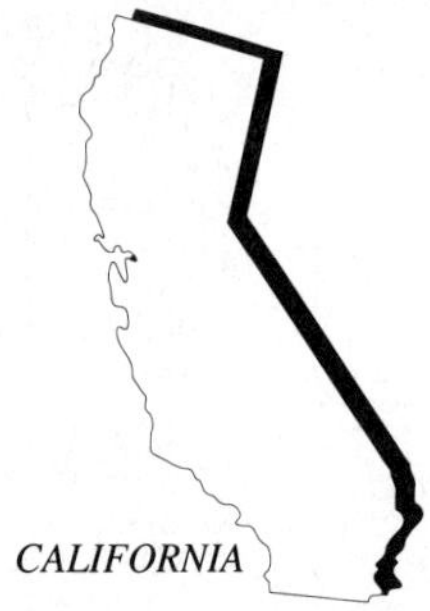

SolarSystem

Stars & stripes

Texas

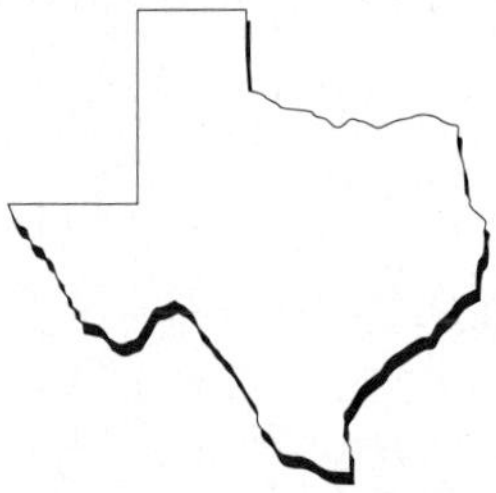

USA

World Map

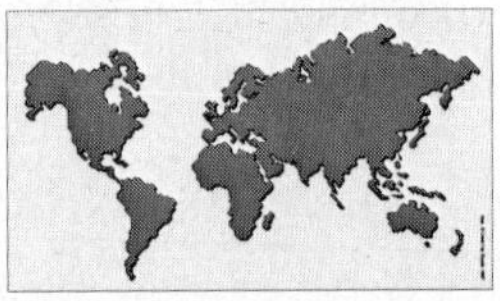

EPS Format Pictures

Angel

Beethoven

Bird of Paradise

CamelsatOasis

Cap'n Gloval

Cargo Van

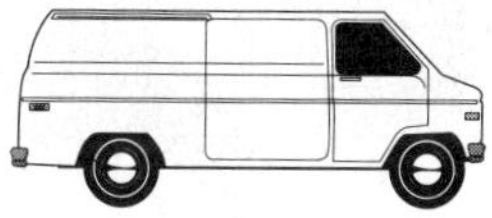

Female 1

Female 2

Female 3

Female 4

Female Operator

GirlStaring

Pictures F2

EPS Format Pictures

Holmes silhouette

InvisbleMan

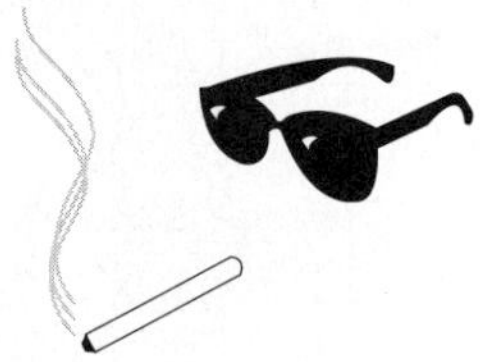

Joggers3

John Anderson

Left fist

Lion

Magic rabbit

Male 1

Male 2

Male 3

Male Silhouette

Male Waiter

EPS Format Pictures

Man with Tuxedo

Mona Lisa

Adobe Illustrator™ artwork by
Dave Hollen (GEnie = D.HOLLEN)

Opus

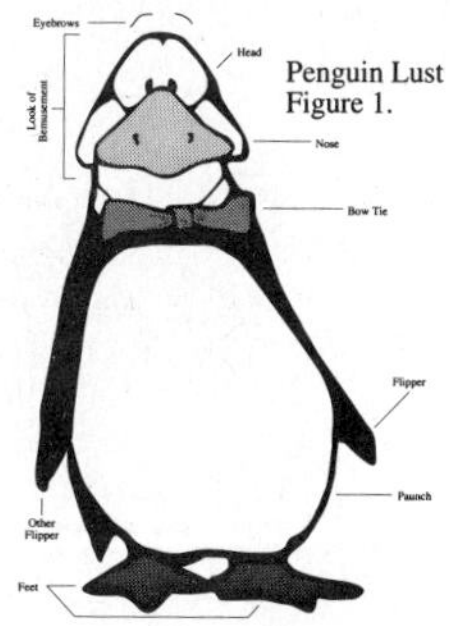

Panda

Patriarch

Pointing Finger

Sad mask

SeaLife

Tigers

Turkey Eating

Women

Zebra

Pictures F3

EPS Format Pictures

A OK Hand 1

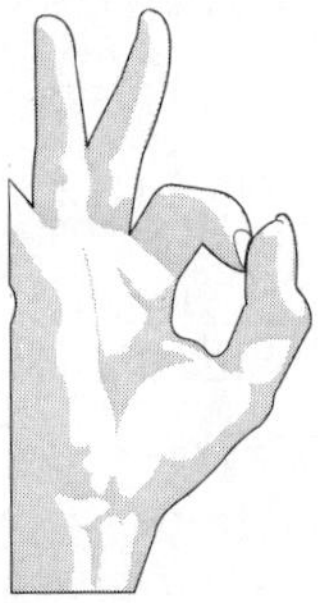

A OK Hand 2

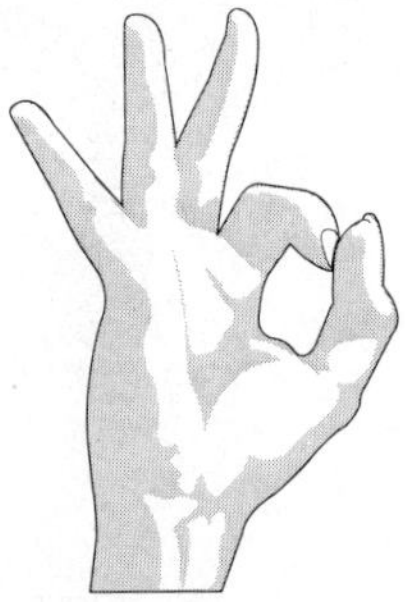

An example of a typical

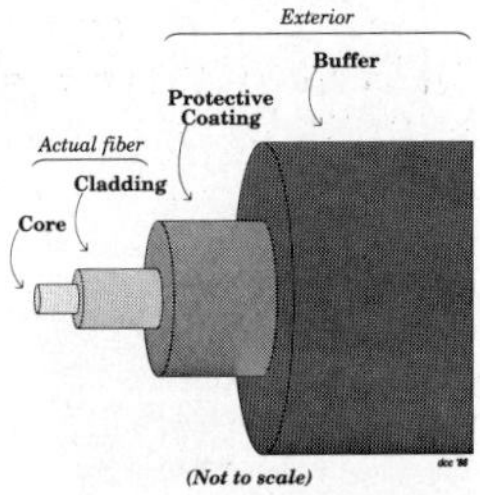

AW Rating

Axe Beak

Blackboard

Brush

Burst 1

Burst 2

Burst 3

Business Phone

CD

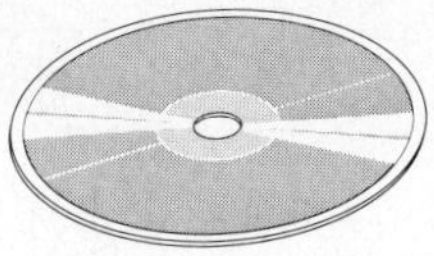

Closed padlock

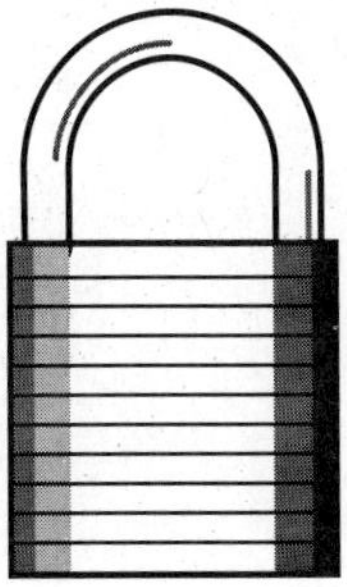

CreditCards

Diskette

Dividers

Drafting

DynaMac

Fat pencil

Keys

No magnets

Open padlock tilt

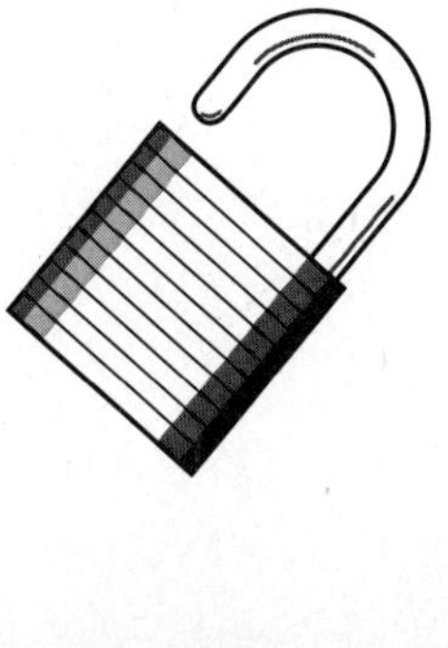

Pushpin

Scissors

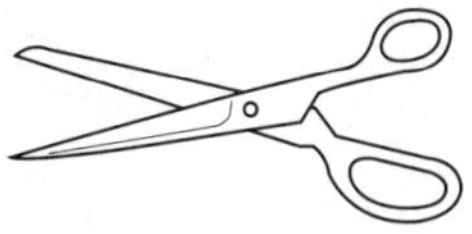

Pictures F3

Continued

Scroll

Snowflake

Snowflake 1

Snowflake 2

Snowflake 3

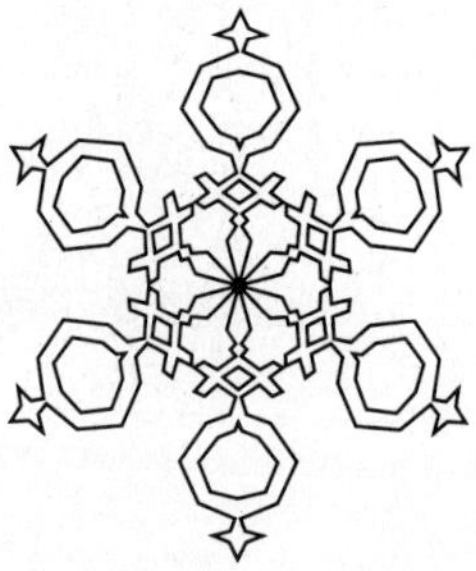

Snowflake 4

SpotlightLeft

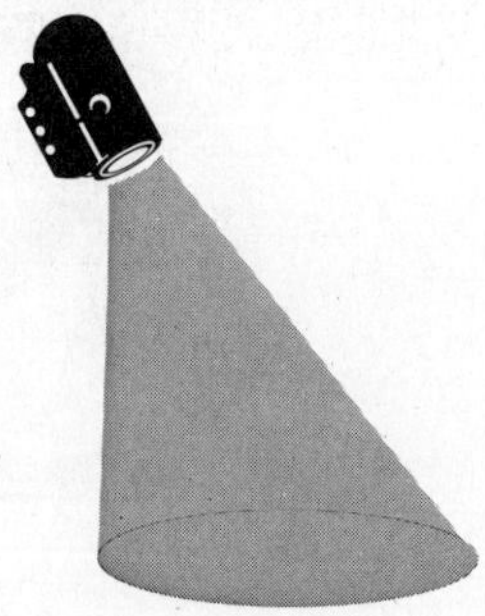

Spring/Fall clocks

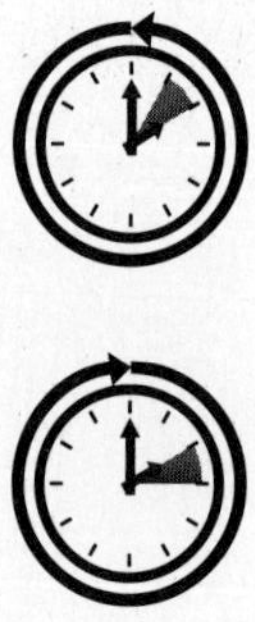

StarburstSample

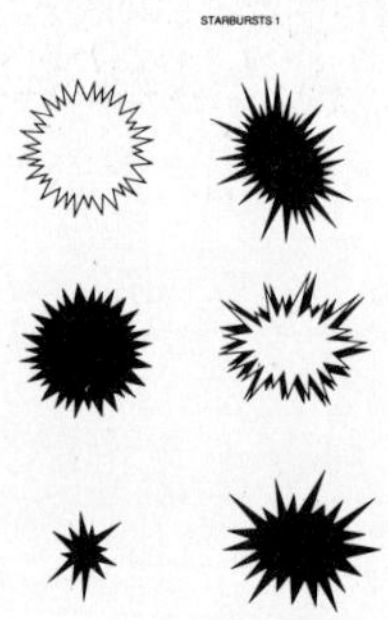

Treasure Chest

35mm Camera

announcing

Automobile 1

Automobile 2

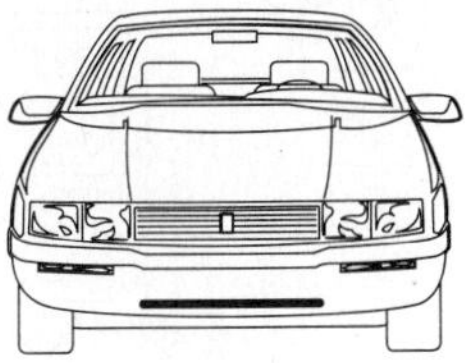

Balloons

Battle Axe

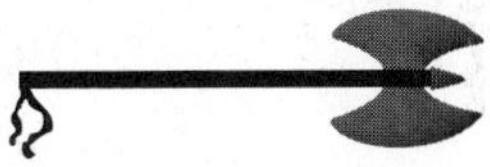

Pictures F4

Continued

Ink Well

Letter in a Slot

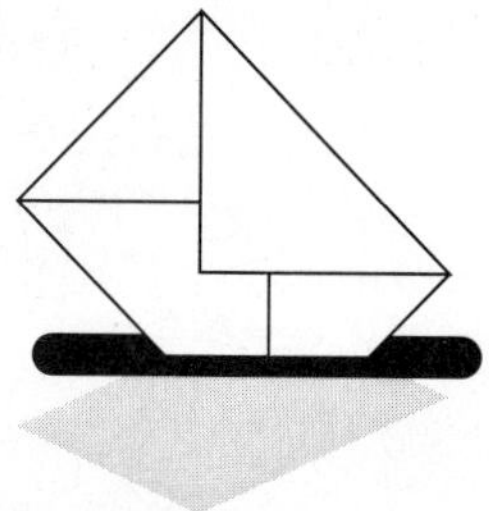

Light Bulb

Lock & Key

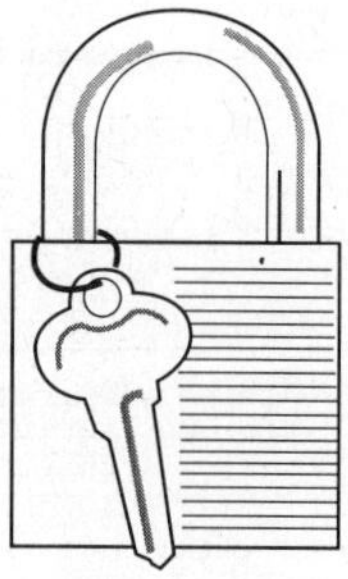

Mac

Mac Se

Microscope

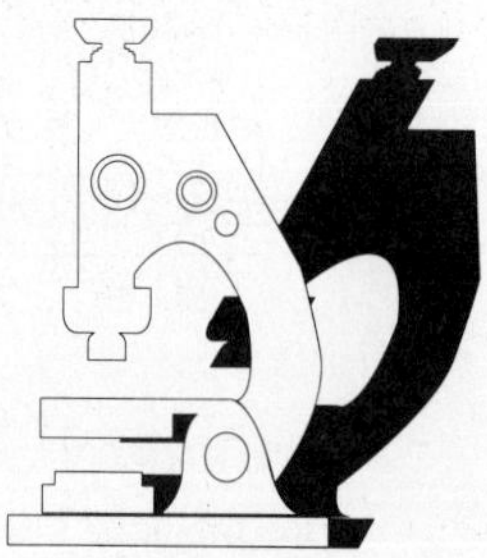

Paperclip

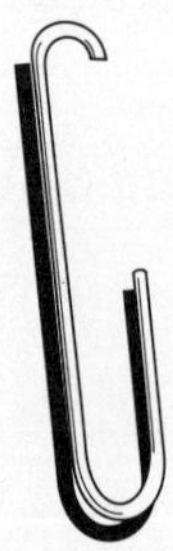

Pen Border

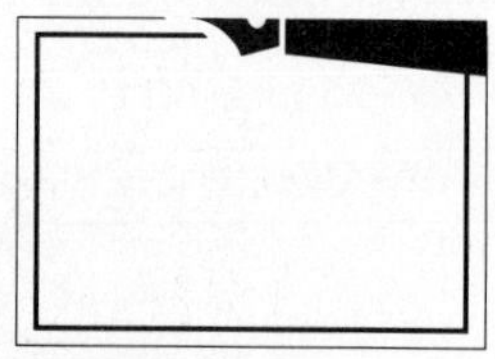

Pen H

Pen V

Phone Handset

Pictures F4

Continued

Pocket Watch 1

Pocket Watch 2

Santa #1

Santa 2

Satellite Dish

Ship

Sitting Pretty

Spitfire

Stereo&Speakers

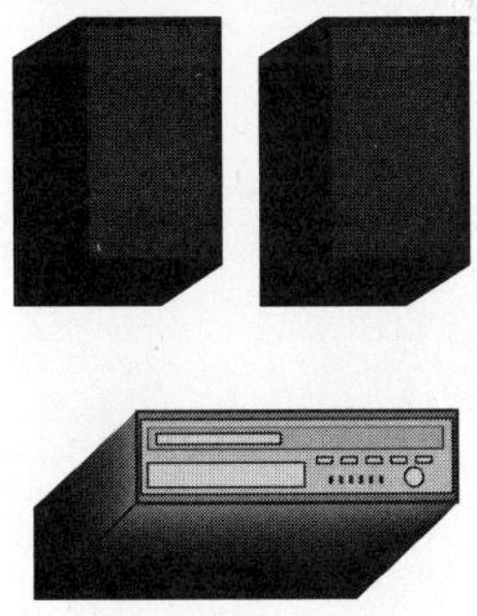

Swiss knife

Sword

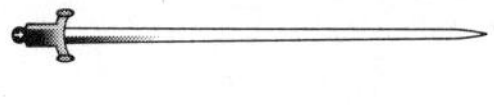

Sword 1

Pictures F4

Continued

Telephone

Trident

Umbrella

Xmas tree

EPS Format Pictures

Pictures FA1

EPS Pictures of the United States

Alabama.eps

Alaska.eps

Arizona.eps

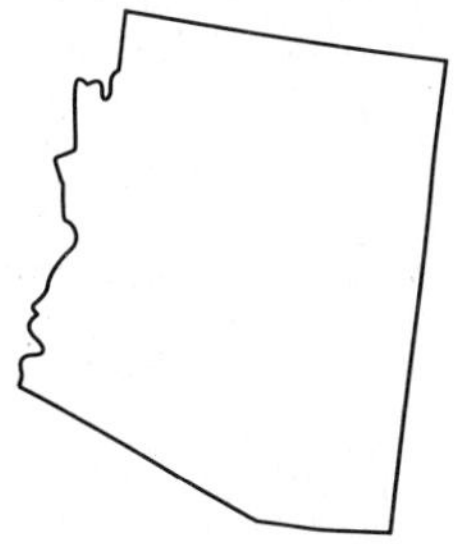

Arkansas.eps

California.eps

Colorado.eps

Connecticut.eps

Delaware.eps

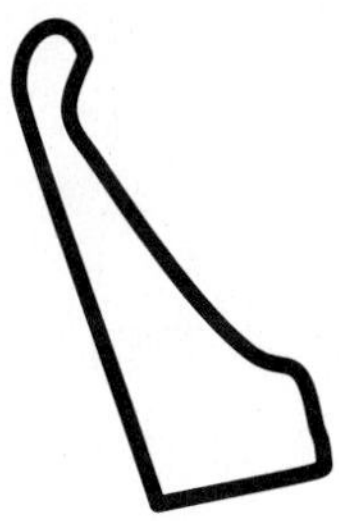

Florida.eps

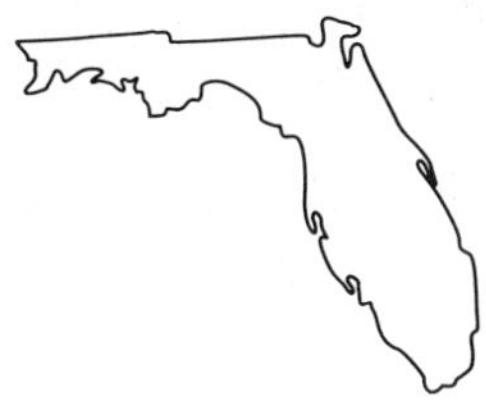

Georgia.eps

Hawaii.eps

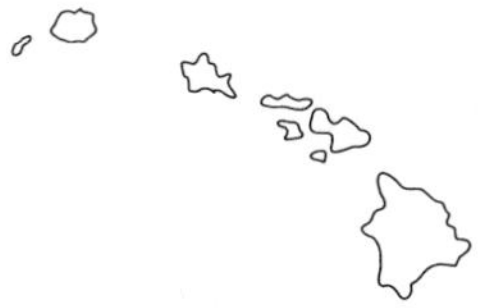

Idaho.eps

Pictures FA1

Continued

Illinois.eps

Indiana.eps

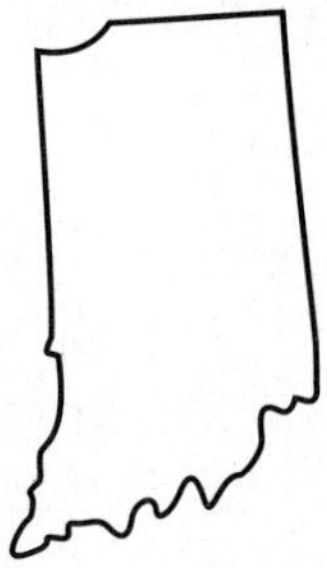

Iowa.eps

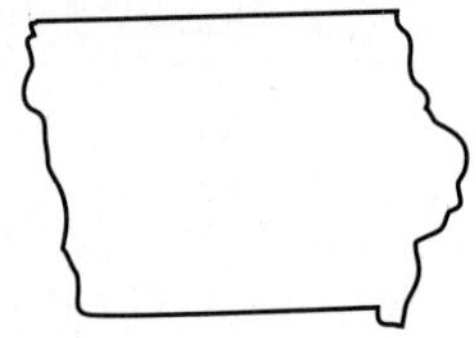

Kansas.eps

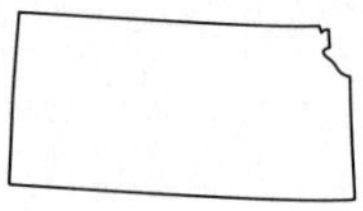

Kentucky.eps

Louisiana.eps

Maine.eps

Maryland.eps

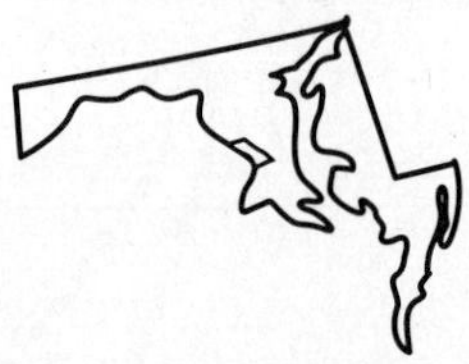

Massachusetts.eps

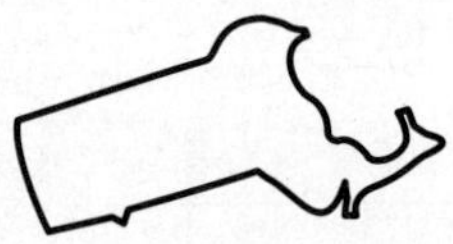

Michigan.eps

Minnesota.eps

Pictures FA2

EPS Pictures of the United States

Mississippi.eps

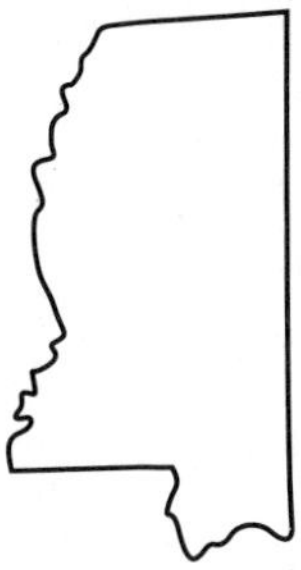

Missouri.eps

Montana.eps

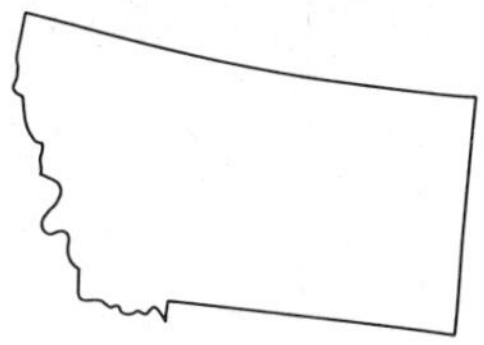

Nebraska.eps

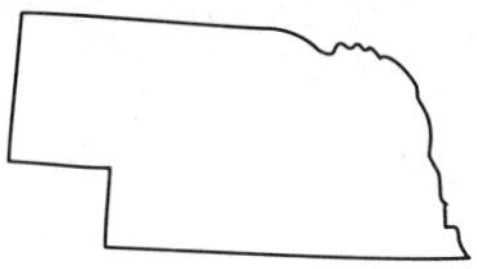

Nevada.eps

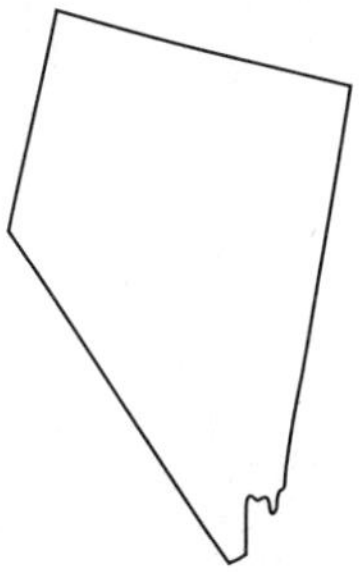

New Hampshire

New Jersey.eps

New Mexico.eps

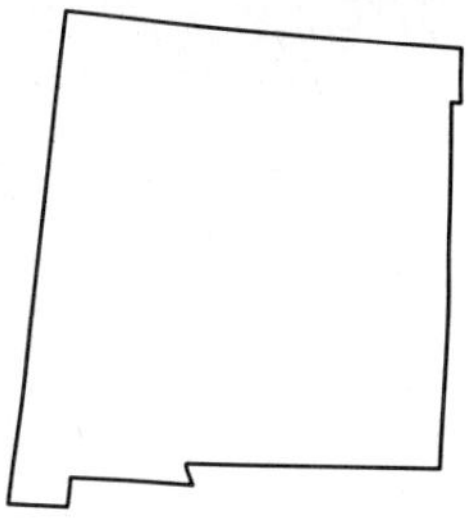

New York.eps

North Carolina

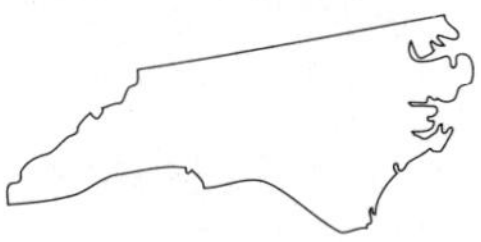

North Dakota.eps

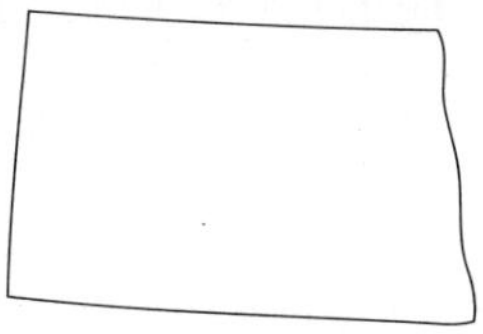

Ohio.eps

Pictures FA2

Continued

Oklahoma.eps

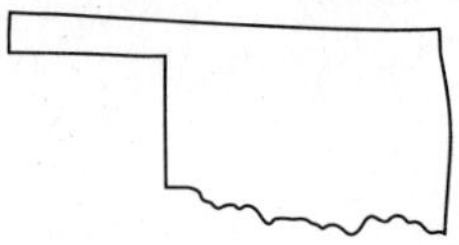

Oregon.eps

Pennsylvania.eps

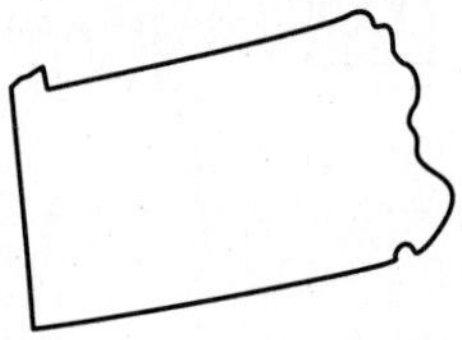

Rhode Island.eps

South Carolina

South Dakota.eps

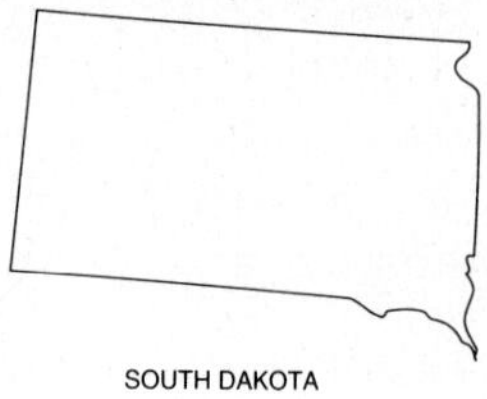

Tennessee.eps

Texas.eps

Utah.eps

Vermont.eps

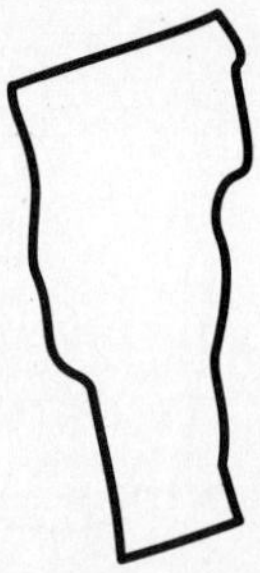

Virginia.eps

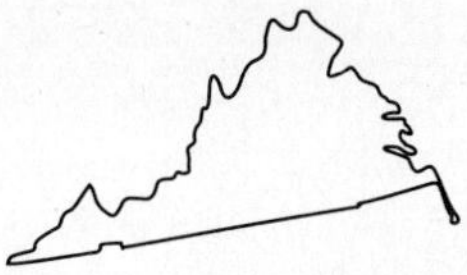

Washington.eps

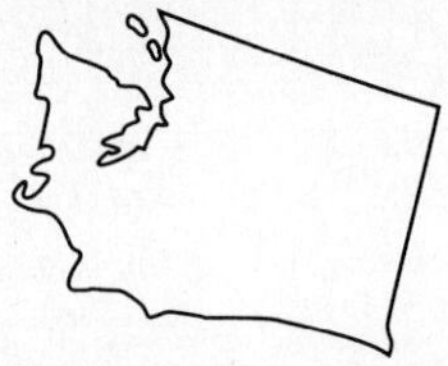

West Virginia.eps

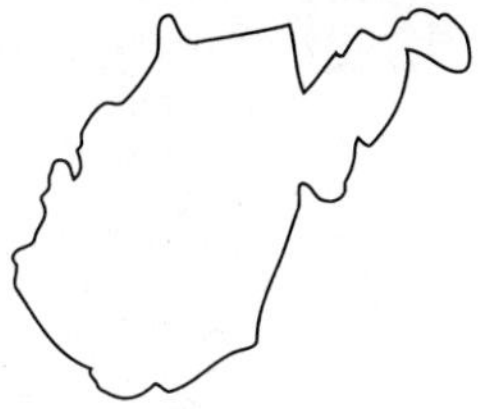

WEST VIRGINIA

Pictures FA3

EPS Pictures of the United States

Alabama.EPS

Alaska.EPS

Arizona.EPS

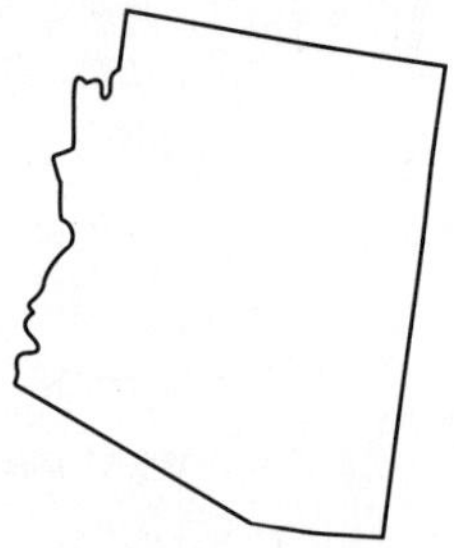

Arkansas.EPS

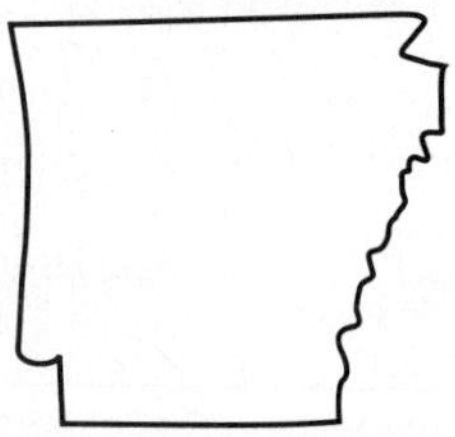

California.EPS

California.EPS.

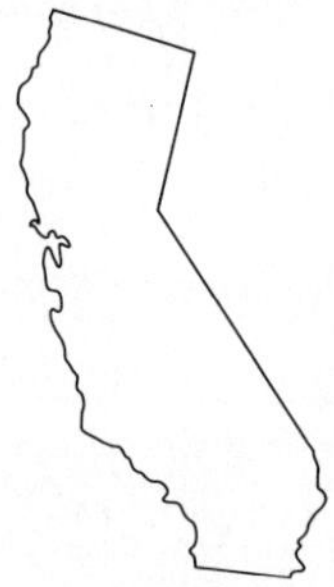

CalSateEPS

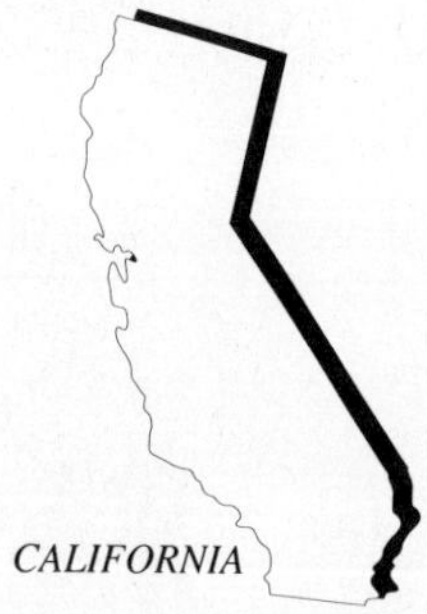

Colorado.EPS

Connecticut.EPS

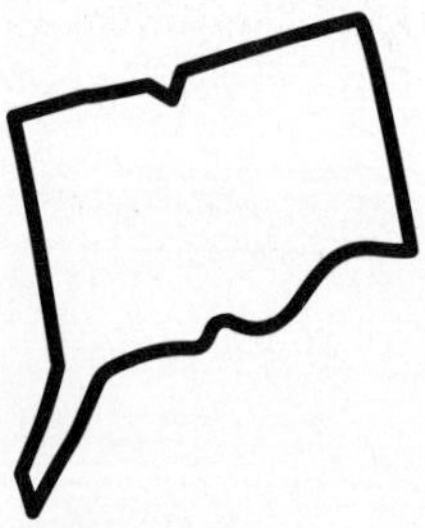

Delaware.EPS

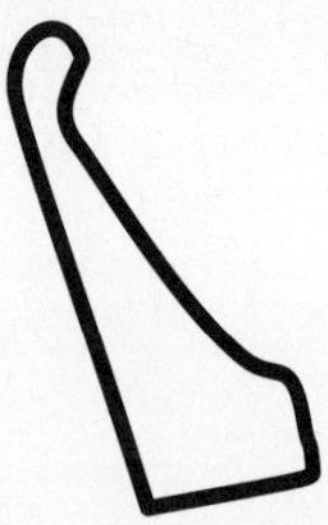

Florida.EPS

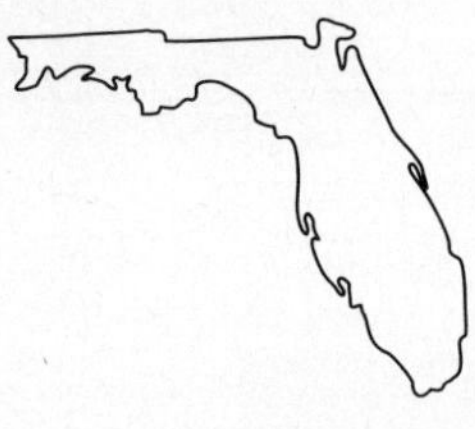

Georgia.EPS

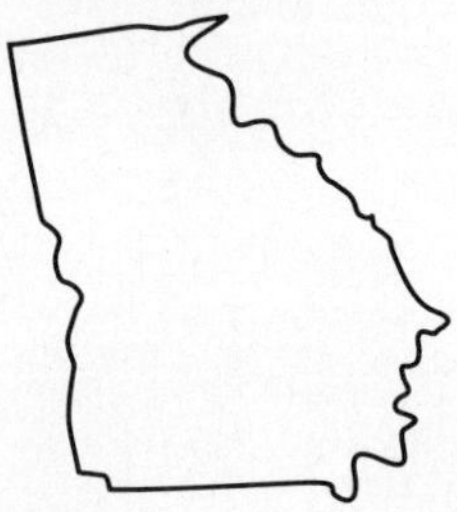

Pictures FA3

Continued

Hawaii.EPS

Idaho.EPS

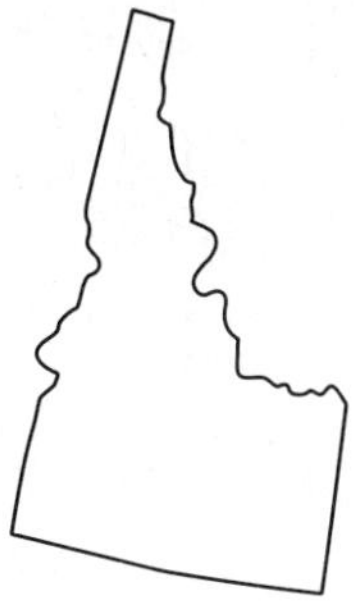

Illinois.EPS

Indiana.EPS

Iowa.EPS

Kansas.EPS

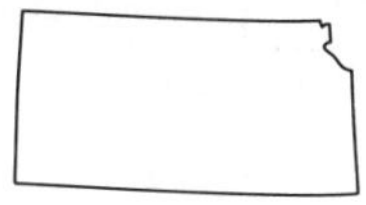

Kentucky.EPS

Louisiana.EPS

Maine.EPS

Maryland.EPS

Massachusetts.EPS

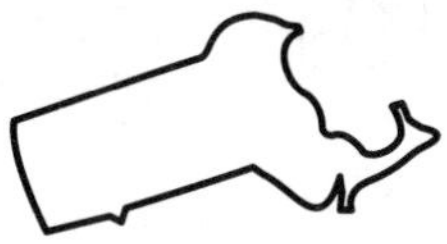

Michigan.EPS

Pictures FA3

Continued

Minnesota.EPS

Mississippi.EPS

Missouri.EPS

Montana.EPS

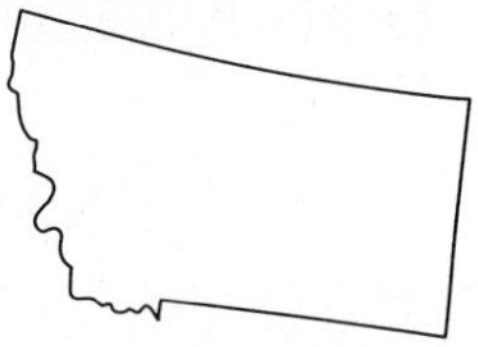

N. Carolina.EPS

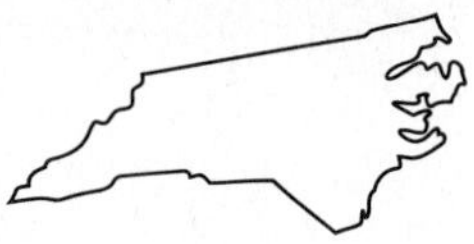

N. Dakota.EPS

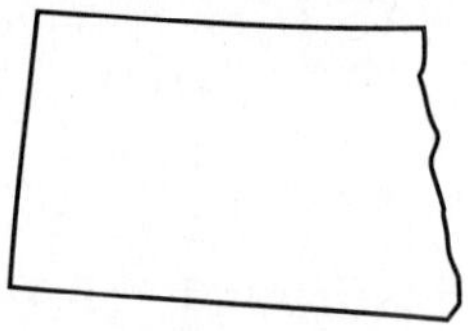

Nebraska.EPS

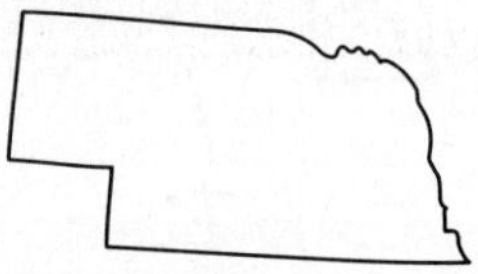

Nevada.EPS

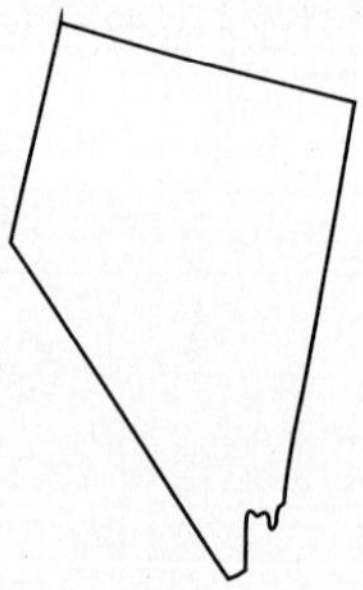

New Hampshire

New Jersey.EPS

New Mexico.EPS

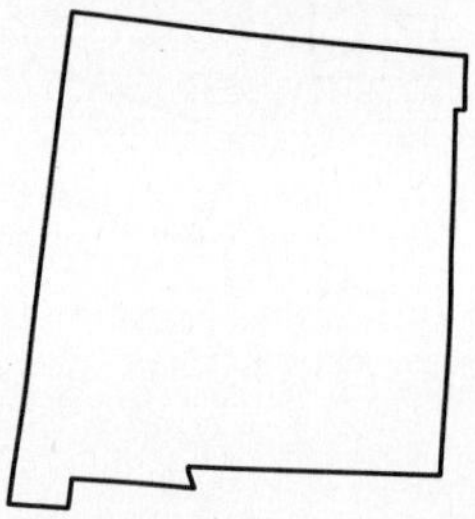

New York.EPS

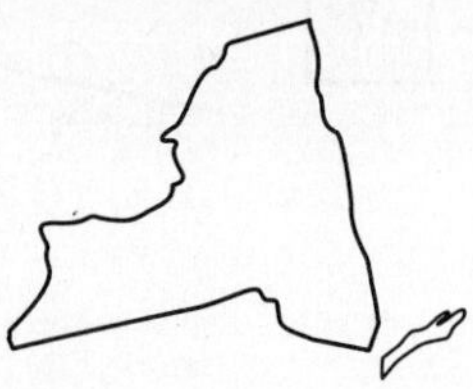

Ohio.EPS

Oklahoma.EPS

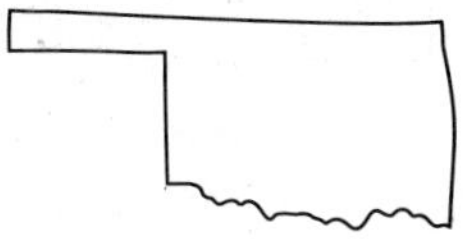

Oregon.EPS

Pennsylvania.EPS

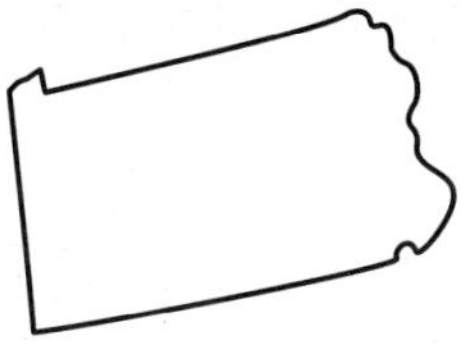

Rhode Island.EPS

S. Carolina.EPS

S. Dakota.EPS

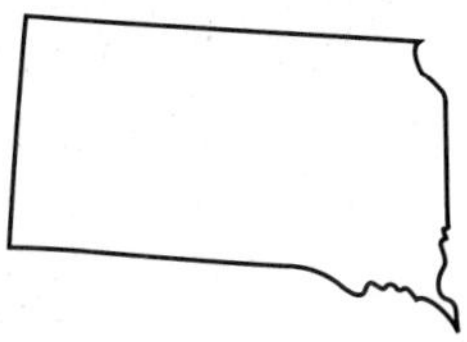

Tennesee.EPS

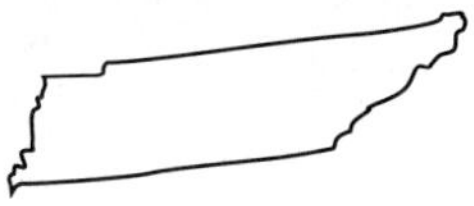

Texas.EPS

US map.EPS

USA EPS.

USMap.epsf

Pictures FA3

Continued

Utah.EPS

Vermont.EPS

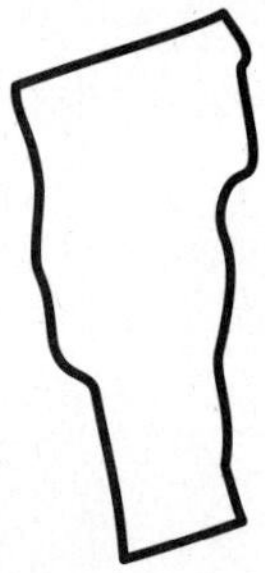

Virginia.EPS

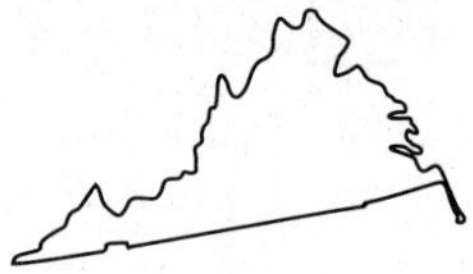

W. Virginia.EPS

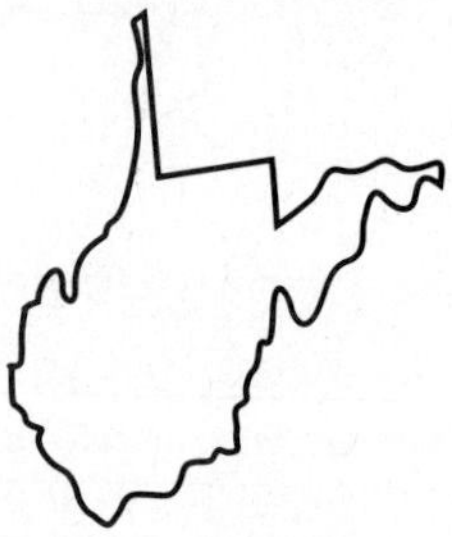

Washington.EPS

Wisconsin.EPS

Wisconson.eps

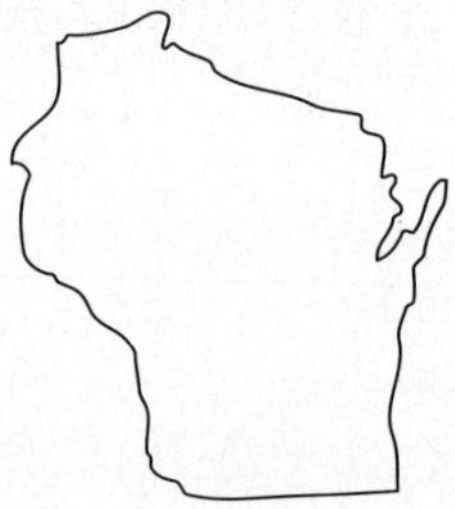

WISCONSON

Wyoming.EPS

MacPaint & MacDraw Pictures of the United States

Alabama.

Alaska.

Arizona.

Arkansas.

California.

Colorado.

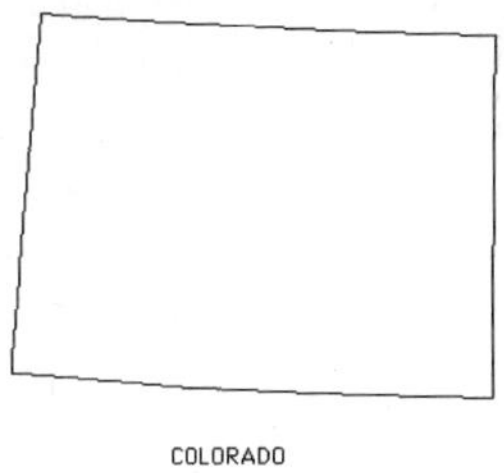

Connecticut

Connecticut.

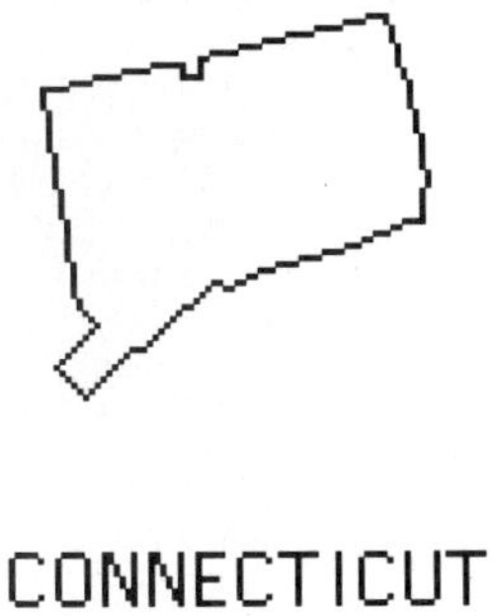

Delaware.

Florida.

Georgia.

Hawaii.

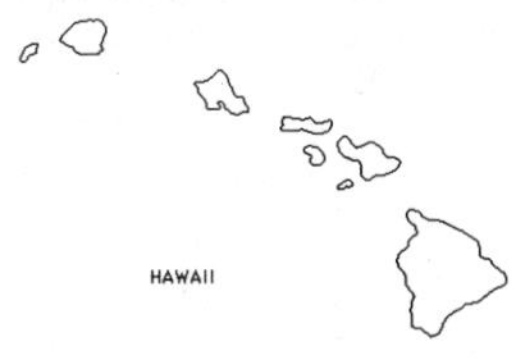

Pictures FA4

Continued

Idaho.

Illinois

Illinois.

Indiana.

Iowa.

Kansas.

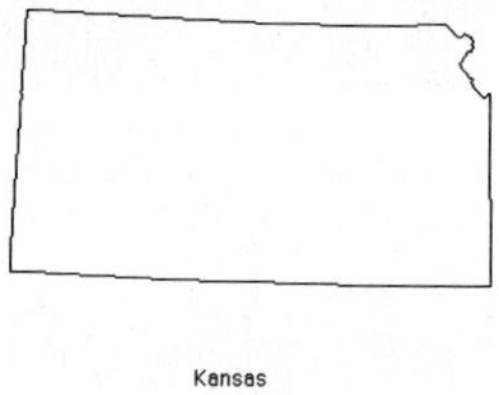

Kentucky.

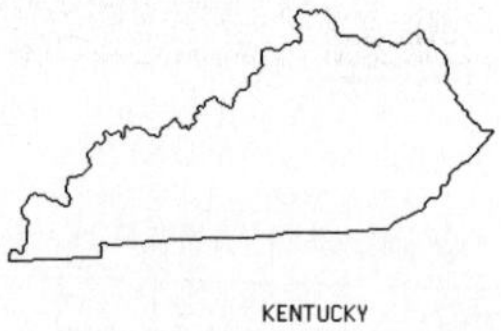

Louisiana

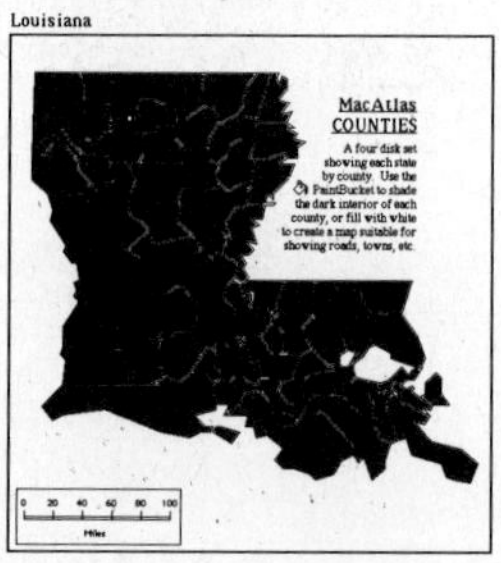

Louisiana.

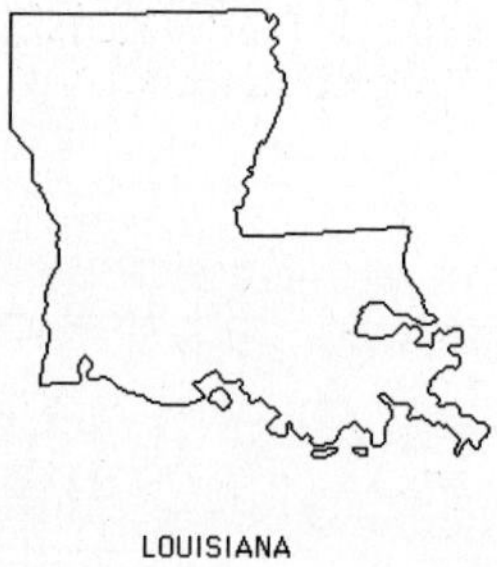

Louisiana.draw

Louisiana Map

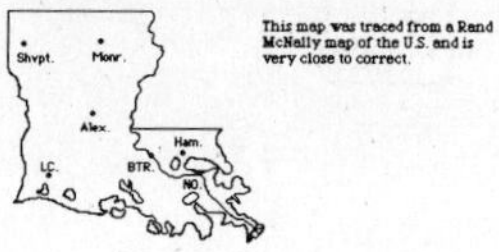

Maine.

Maryland.

Massachusetts

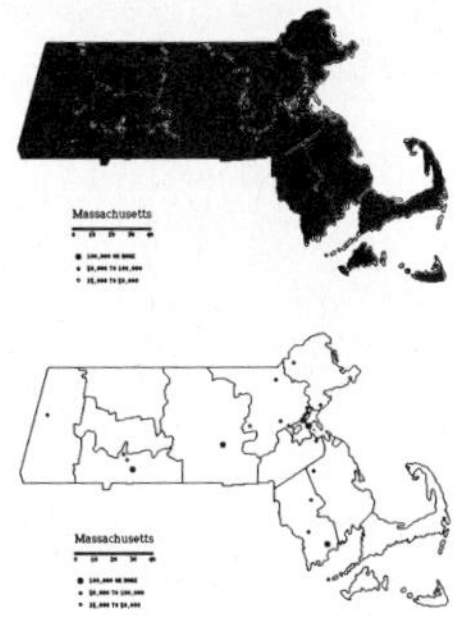

Massachusetts.

Michigan

Michigan][

Michigan.

Minnesota.

Mississippi.

Missouri.

Montana.

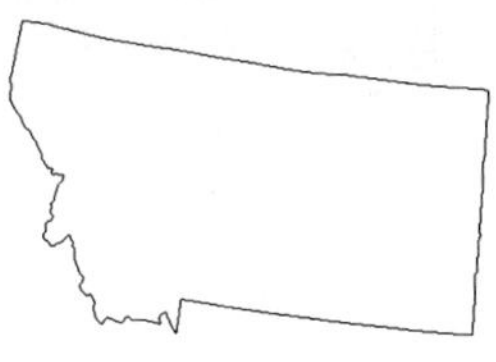

Nebraska.

Nevada.

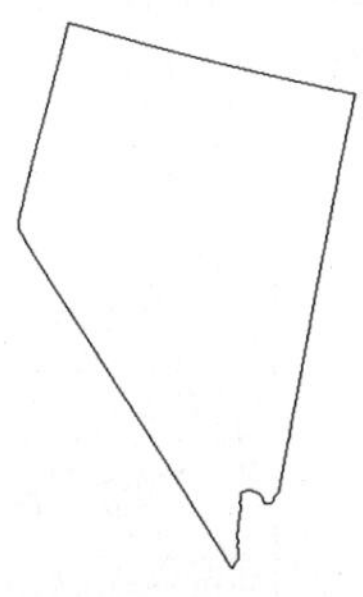

Pictures FA4

Continued

New Hampshire

New Hampshire.

New Jersey.

New Mexico.

New U.S. (Texas View)

New York.

New York State

North Carolina.

North Dakota.

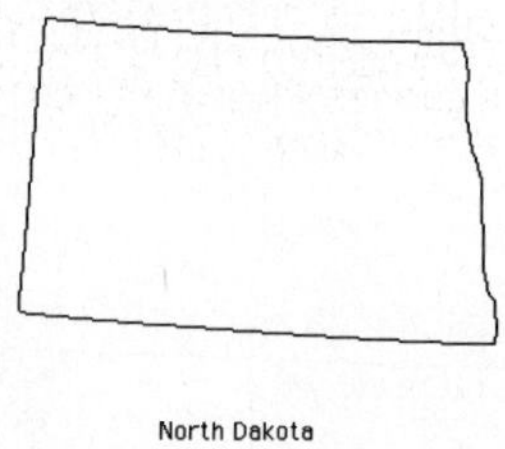

Ohio.

Oklahoma.

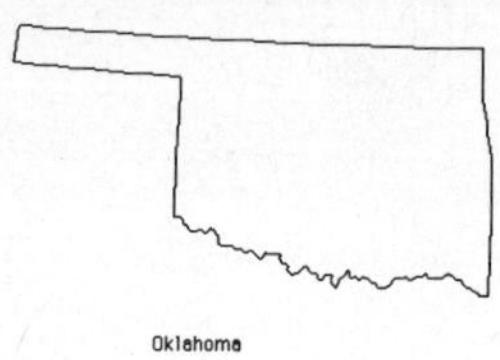

Oregon.

Pennsylvania.

Rhode Island.

South Carolina.

South Dakota.

Tennessee.

Texas

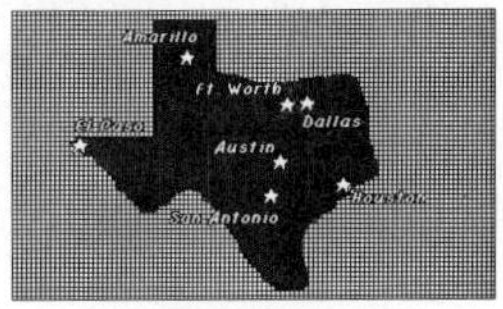

Texas.

Texas2

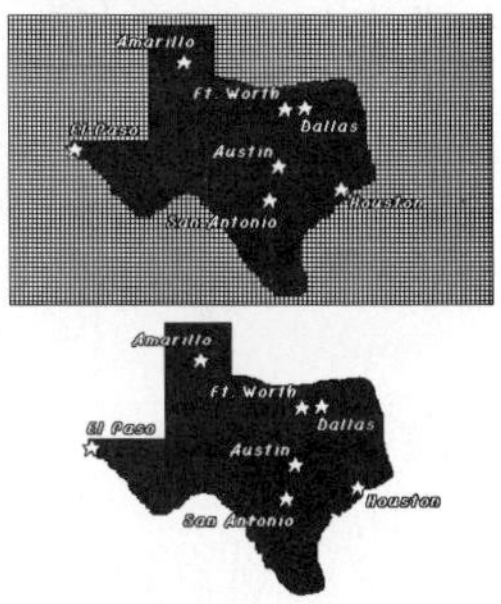

.U.S. Map

U. S. Map

U.S. MAP

.U.S. Map-2.

Pictures FA4

Continued

.U.S. Map-3

USA Draw Sample

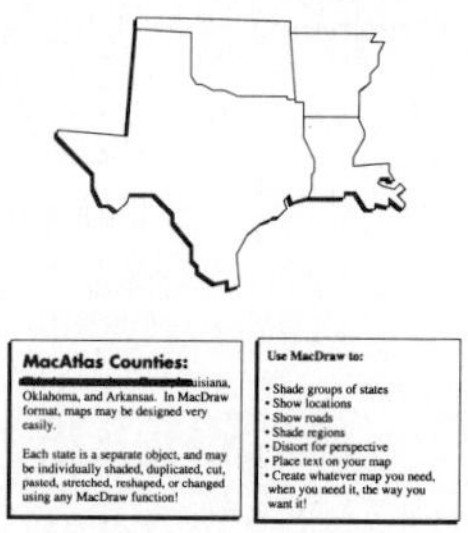

USA info

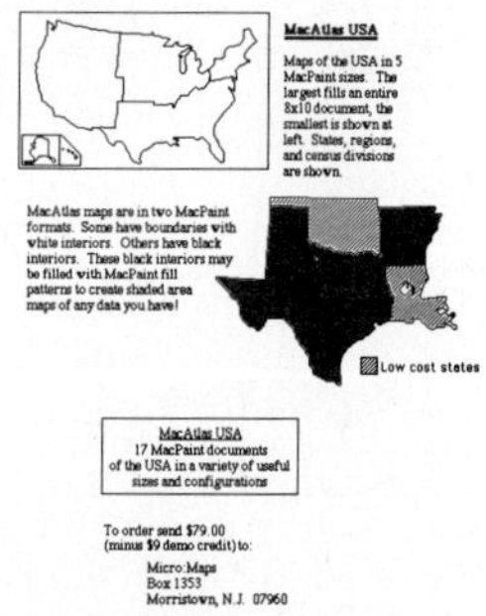

USA Paint Sample

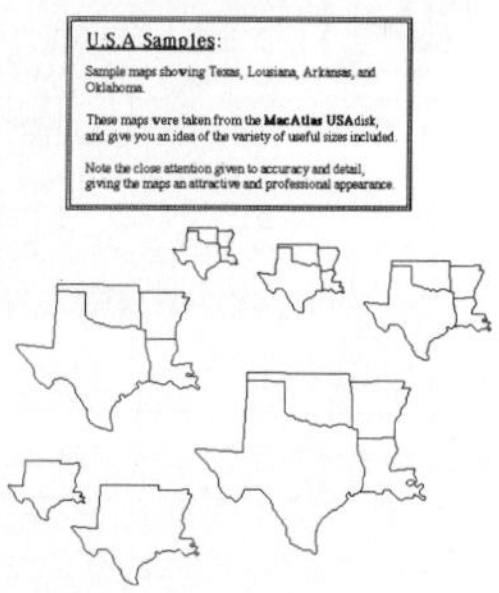

.USA/Micro.

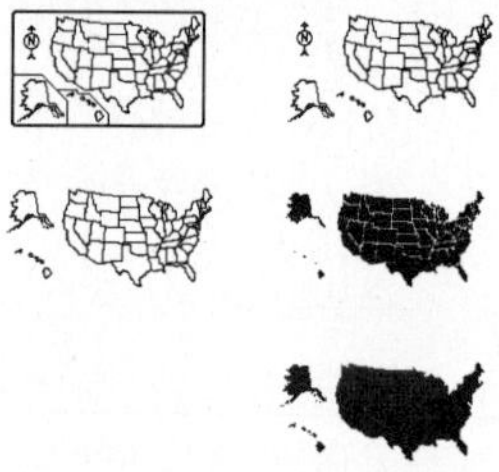

USMapSample

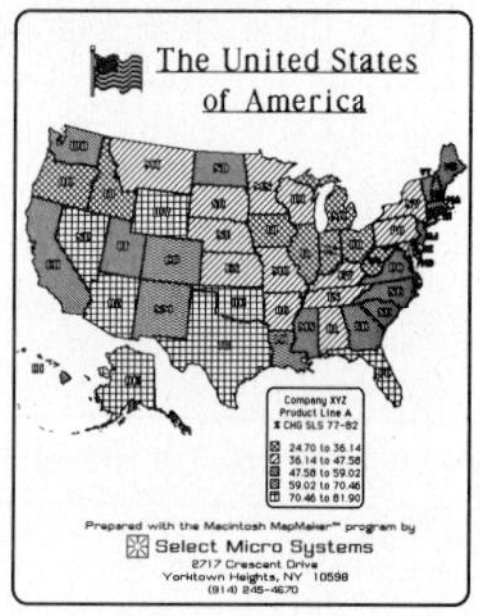

Utah.

UTAH

Vermont.

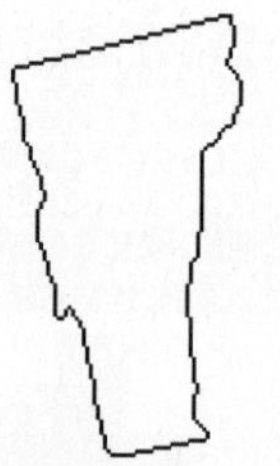

VERMONT

Virginia.

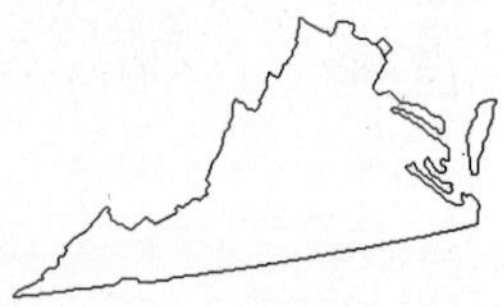

VIRGINIA

Washington.

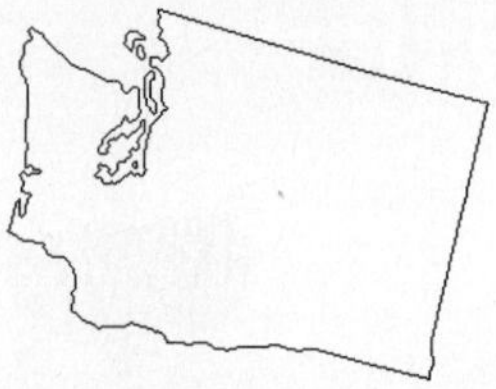

WASHINGTON

West Virginia.

WEST VIRGINIA

Wisconsin.

WISCONSIN

Wyoming.

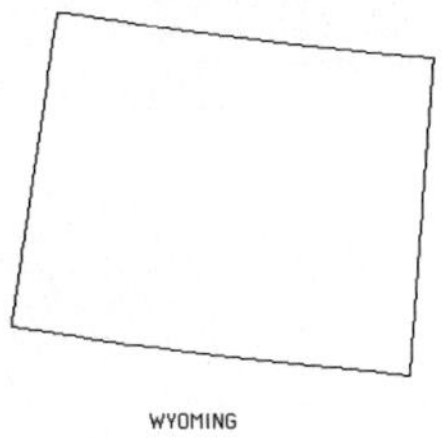

Pictures G1

PICT Format Pictures

1-Point Perspective

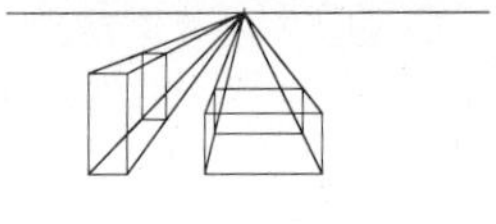

2-point perspective

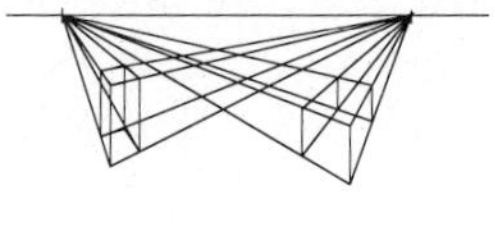

3-D Drawing

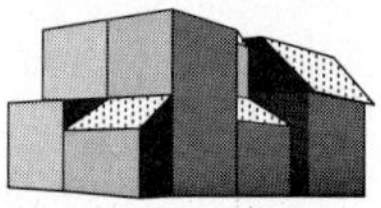

Abc Medical

About MAC PasteUp

About MAC PasteUps

PasteUps FONTS

Apple Logo @10% screen

Assorted Macros

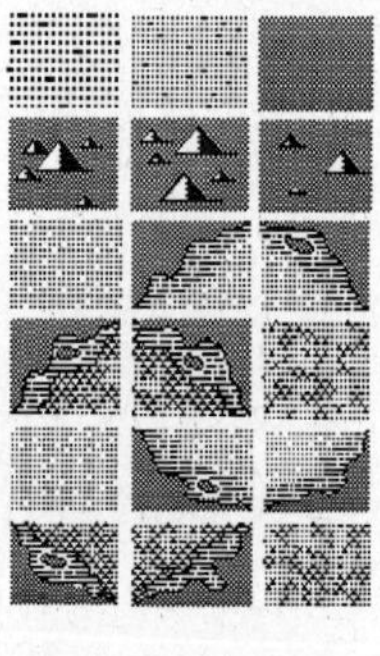

Beckett org

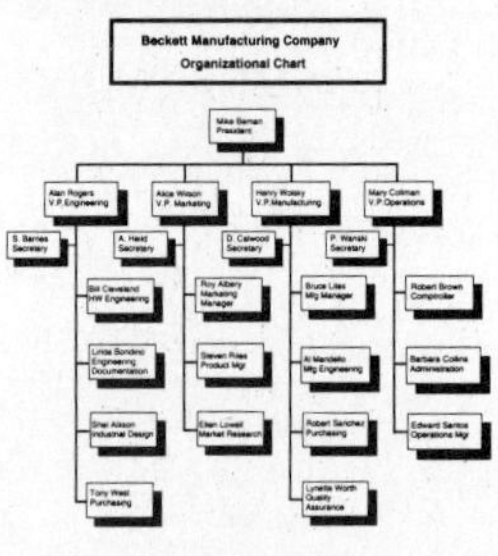

border

Pictures G1

Continued

Candle & Bowl

Cassette

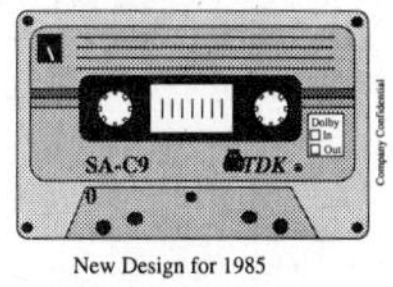

Cassette Label Template

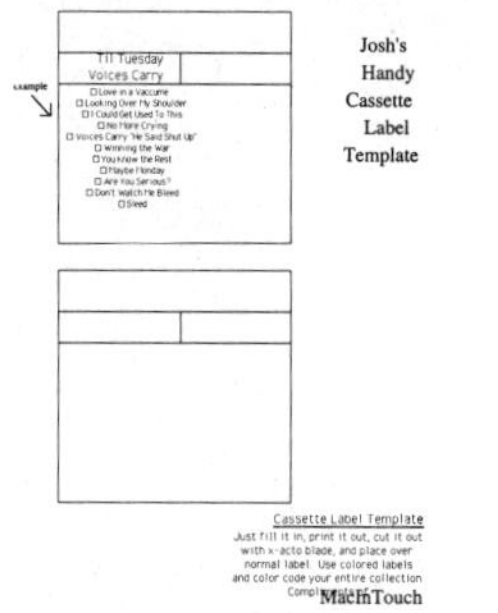

Column

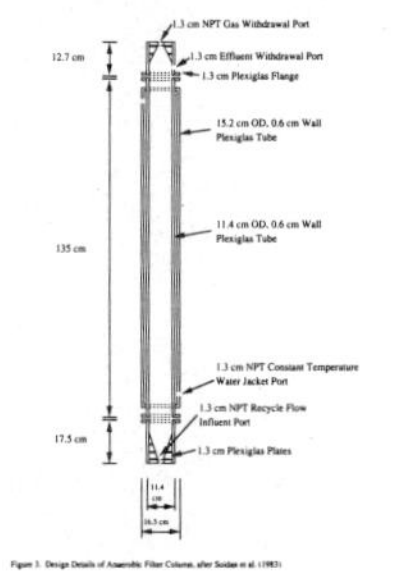

Corners Macros

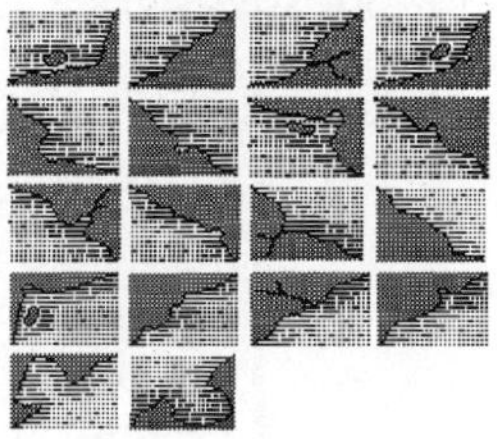

DeckerComm.

Effectiveness

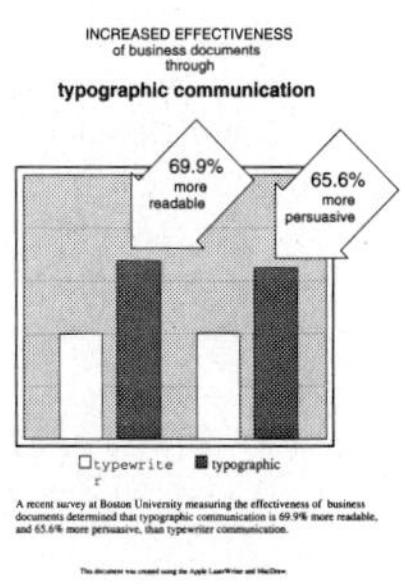

EnlargedPrintArea.PLP

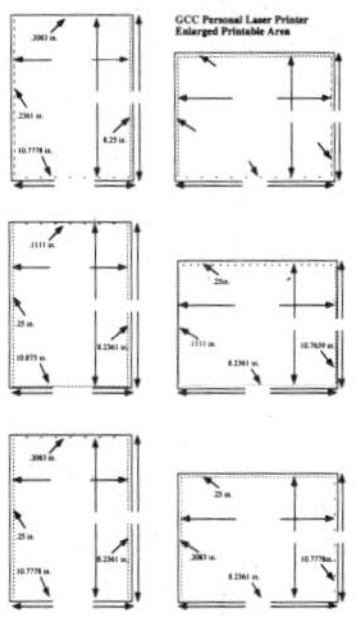

Names Macros

NomalPrintArea.PLP/LW

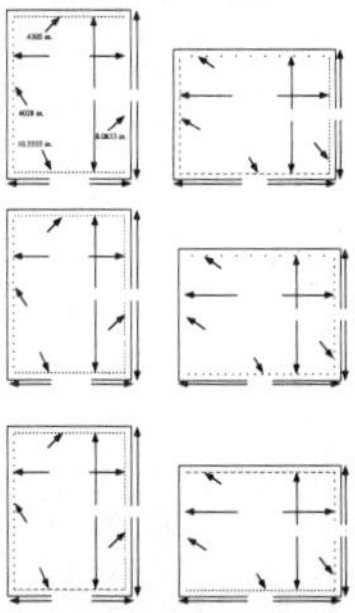

Scenario Construction Kit

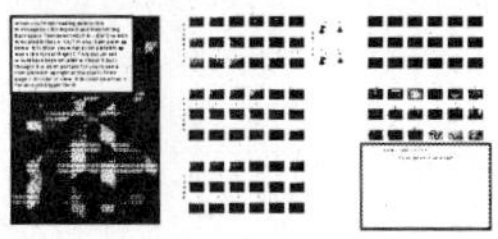

Ships Macros

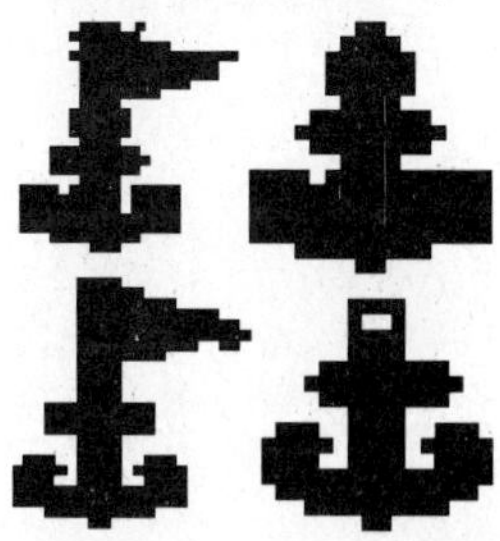

PICT Pictures

Pictures G1

Continued

Shore Macros

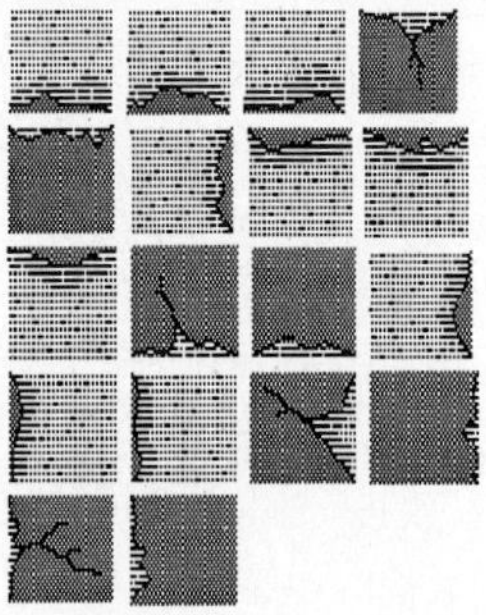

Storybook.pict

Symbols Macros

TypiCorp Inc.

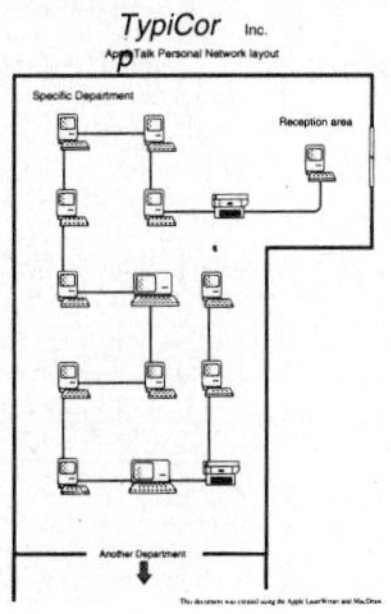

Waterfalling2

WM Wine Form

PICT Pictures

Pictures G2

PICT Format Pictures

Bits and Pieces 4

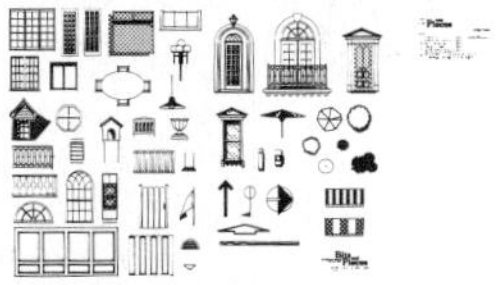

Cat & Mouse 1

Cat & Mouse 2

Cat & Mouse 3

Cat & Mouse 4

Cat & Mouse 5

Cat & Mouse 6

DrawArt One

DrawArt Two

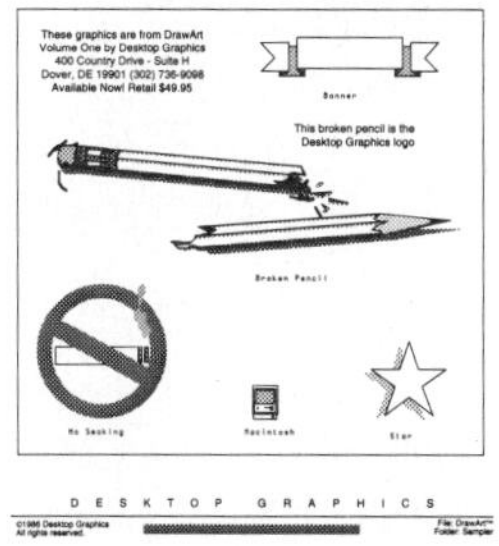

Enterprise

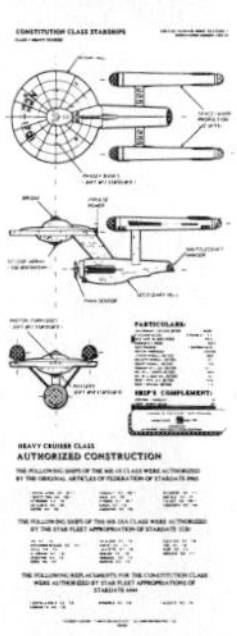

Exploded Disk

F-14 side view

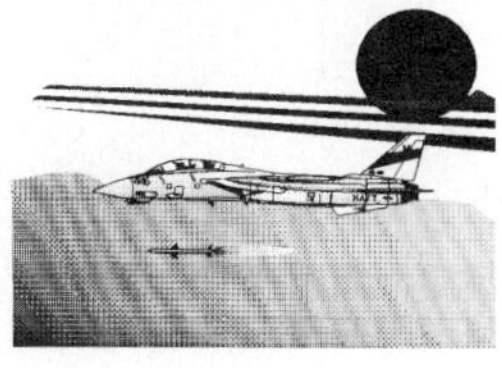

PICT Pictures

Pictures G2

Continued

Guided Tour

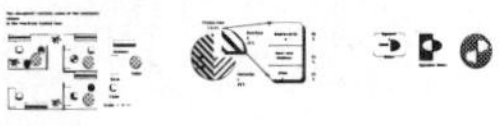

Hurricane grid2

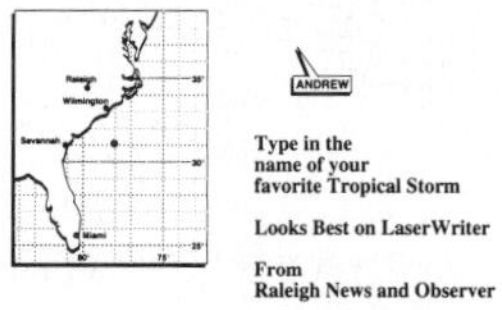

Icons

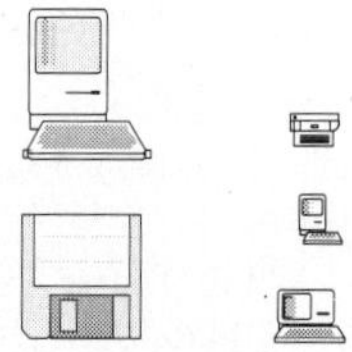

Isometric Drawing

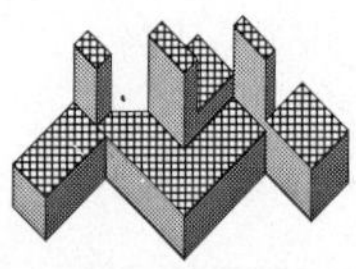

Long Way Baby

Mac Hardware

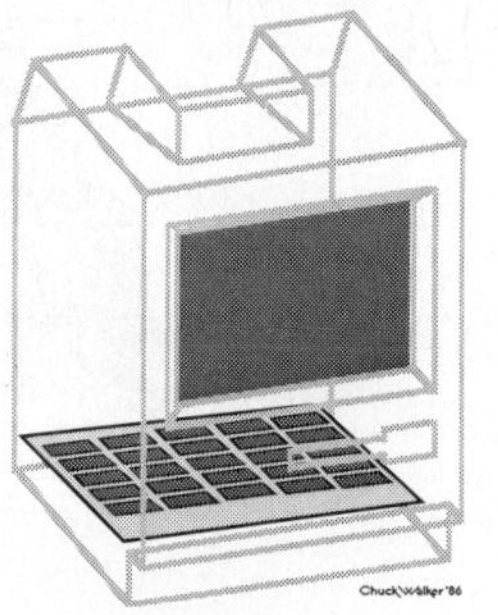

Mac SE.PICT

McPic!s 1 & 2

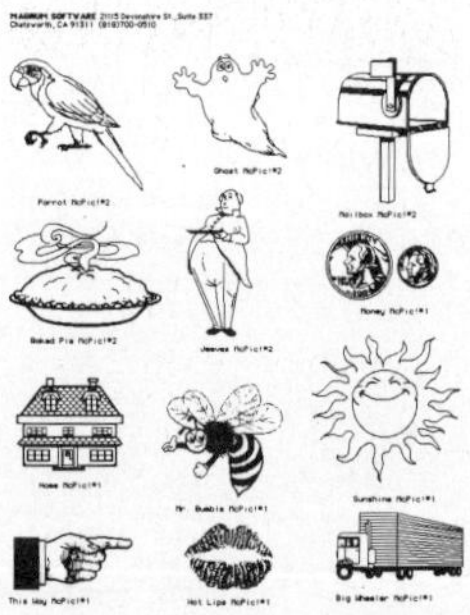

order form/misc

Q-ART

Shrubs 1.samples

Shrubs 2.samples

Business cards

Connecticut

digi seal

Illinois

Louisiana

MacChimney 2

Manual Example

May Calendar

Name Tags

NCC-1701A.draw

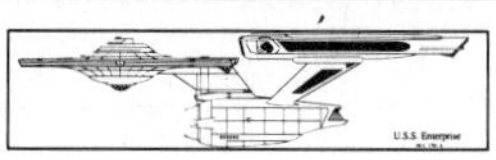

Net Title

New York State

Pictures G3

Continued

Orbiter Views

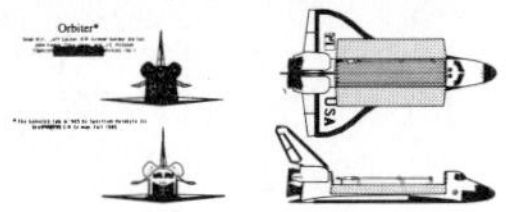

Piper Cub

Ribbon rev1.1

Scan

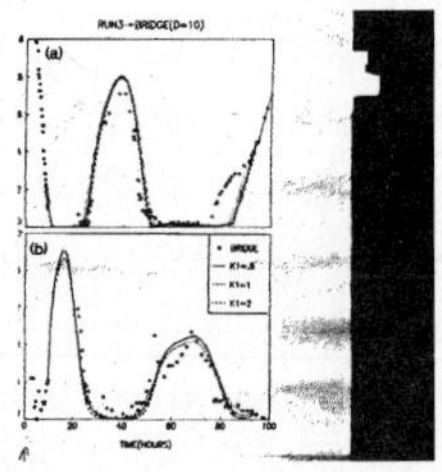

Scan+Chart=Draw

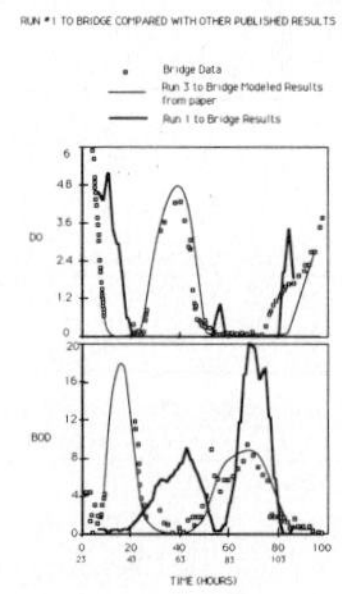

Seal rev1.4

smallNY

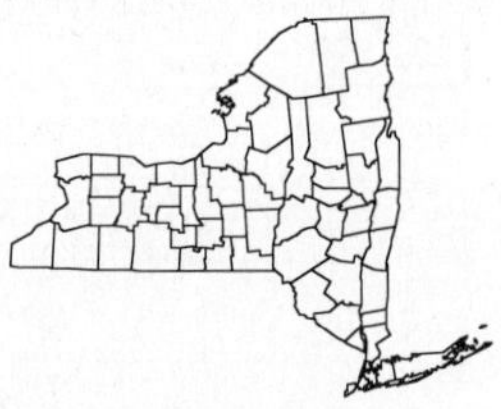

South America

Star rev1.4 (PICT)

Still

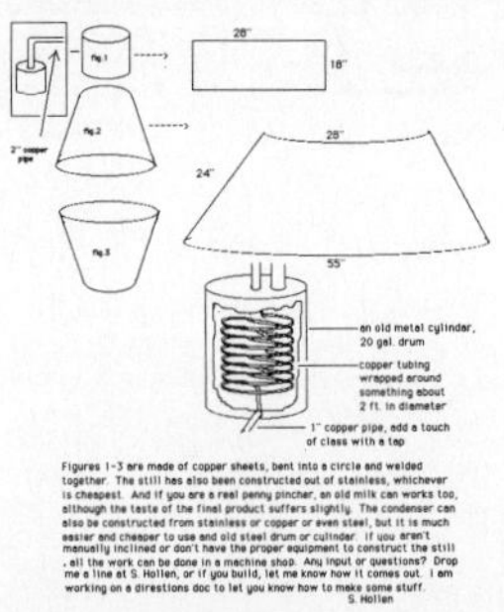

U. S. Area Codes

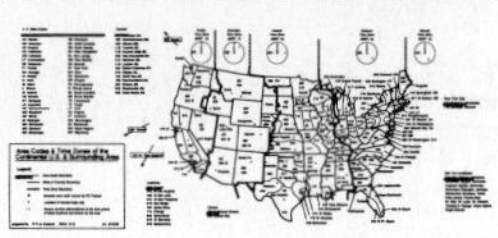

U. S. Map

PICT Pictures

USA Draw Sample

Pictures G4

PICT Format Pictures

$3 press

Baby Buggy

Bicycle

Birds

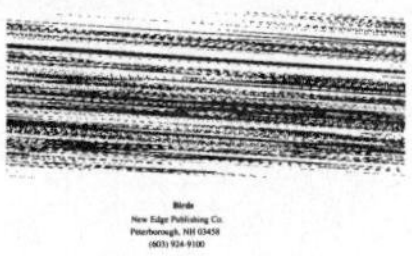

Canoe

Couple (man)

Couple (woman)

Fine gent

Flower 1

Flower 2

Flower border

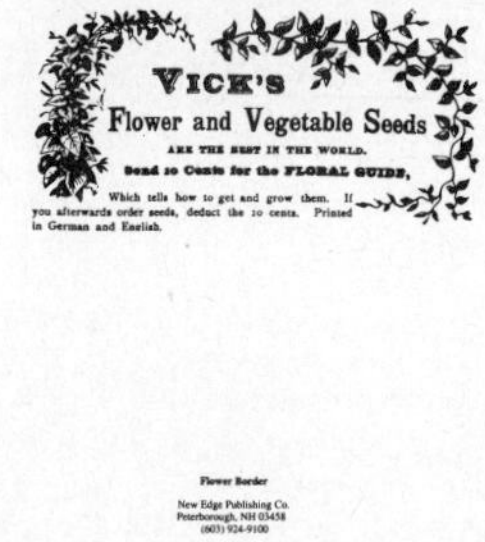

Gent

Pictures G4

Continued

Horse/Trolly

Lady 1

Lil Bo Peep

Lustro

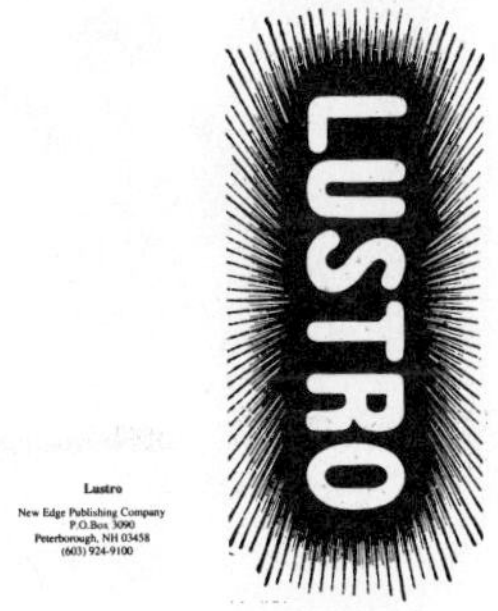

Old gent

Poor Fellow

Young gent

Pictures G5

PICT Format Pictures

Press 2

Press 2
New Edge Publishing Company
P.O.Box 3090
Peterborough, NH 03458
(603) 924-9100

Press 3

Press 3
New Edge Publishing Co.
Peterborough, NH 03458
(603) 924-9100

Projector

Projector
New Edge Publishing Company
P.O.Box 3090
Peterborough, NH 03458
(603) 924-9100

Reserved

Reserved
New Edge Publishing Company
P.O.Box 3090
Peterborough, NH 03458
(603) 924-9100

Santa

Santa
New Edge Publishing Company
P.O.Box 3090
Peterborough, NH 03458
(603) 924-9100

School Boy

SCHOOL BOY
New Edge Publishing Company
P.O.Box 3090
Peterborough, NH 03458
(603) 924-9100

PICT Pictures

Spool

Spool
New Edge Publishing Company
P.O.Box 3090
Peterborough, NH 03458
(603) 924-9100

Spoon

Spoon
New Edge Publishing Company
P.O.Box 3090
Peterborough, NH 03458
(603) 924-9100

Tennis

Tennis
New Edge Publishing Company
P.O.Box 3090
Peterborough, NH 03458
(603) 924-9100

Tomato

Tomato
New Edge Publishing Company
P.O.Box 3090
Peterborough, NH 03458
(603) 924-9100

Violin

Violin
New Edge Publishing Company
P.O.Box 3090
Peterborough, NH 03458
(603) 924-9100

4th of July

Apple - Halloween

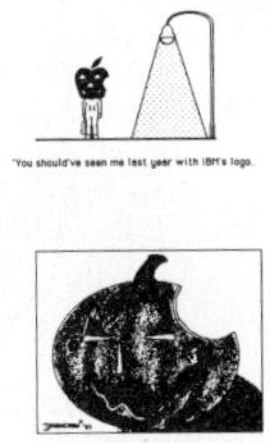

Be My Valentine 1

Big Valentine

Bunny Card

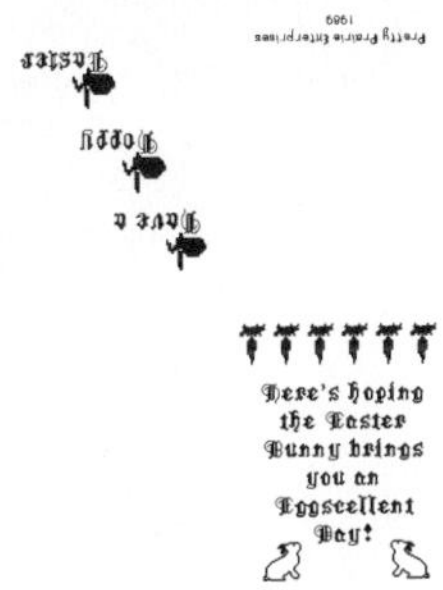

Ceremonial

Cornucopia.eps

Easter Bunny

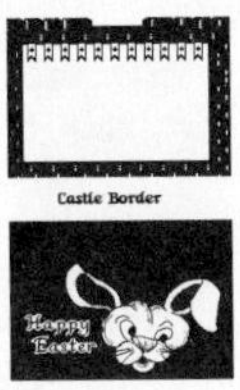

Golden gate

Halloween 1

Halloween Images

Happy Birthday

Pictures H1

Continued

Hearts 2

Leprechaun

Miss Liberty

Mother'sDay

New Years Clip Art

Pumpkin carve

Holiday Pictures

Rose/Valentine

Summer Fun

Thanksgiving 1

Thanksgiving 2

Thanksgiving 3

Thanksgiving 4

TinkerToys

Valentine Art

Valentine's

Veterans Day

Pictures H2

Holidays

Holiday Pictures

A Christmas Story

Christmas

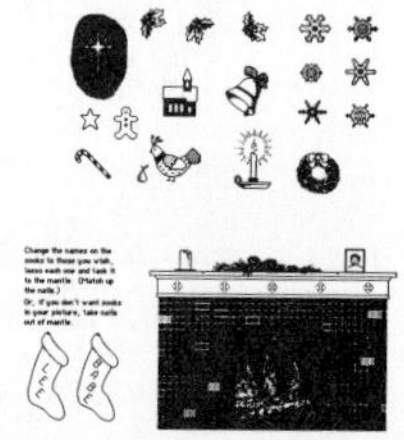

Christmas 3

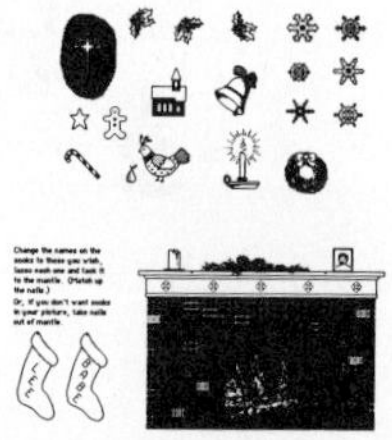

Christmas Tree

Club Mac Santa Cover

Club Mac Santa Cover

CowboySanta.MAC

DadWreath

Decorative Corners 1

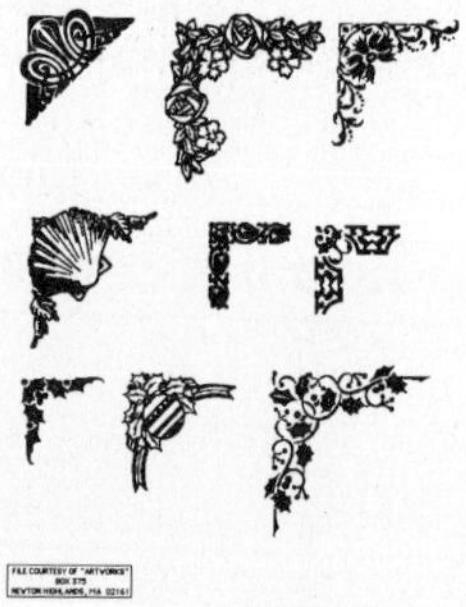

Decorative Corners 2

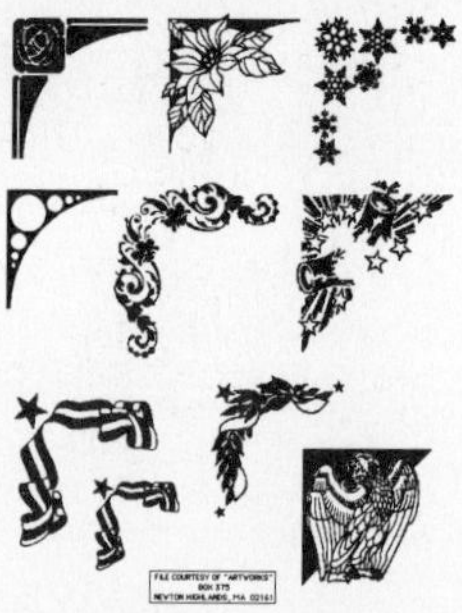

Disk w Bow

Durer-Nativity Scene

GraphicTree

Holiday Mail

Holiday Tags

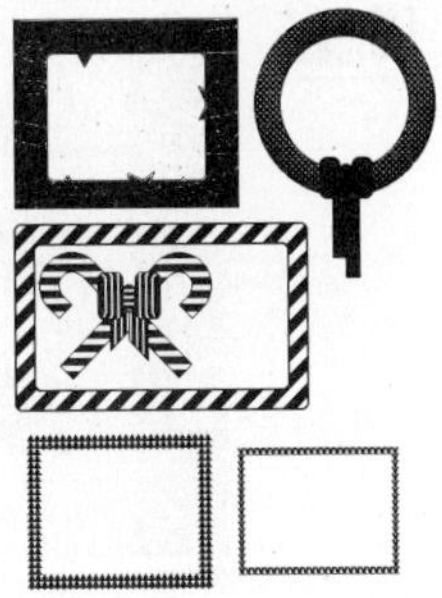

HolidaySamples

Mac Ornament

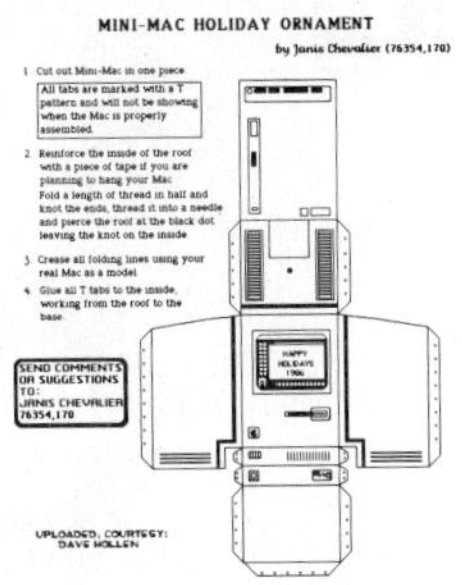

MacTidings

New Year

Ornament 1

Ornament 10

Ornament 11

Ornament 12

Ornament 18

Pictures H2

Continued

Ornament 19

Ornament 2

Ornament 4

Ornament 5

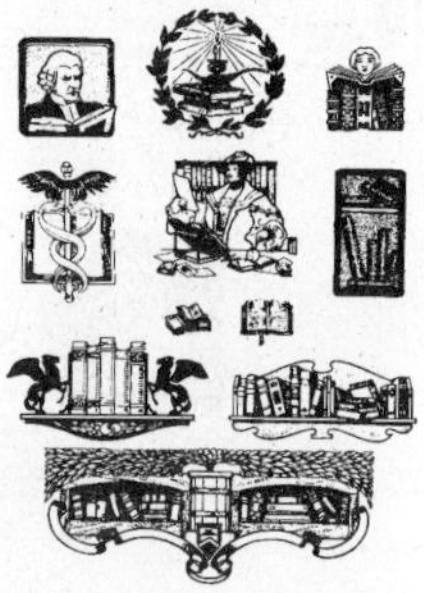

Ornament 7

Ornament 8

Ornament 9

Ornaments

Rudolf

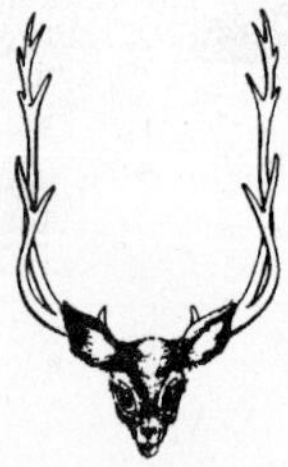

Santa

Santa 1

Santa 3

Santa 4

Santa 5

Santa 6

Santa & Elves

Santa & Reindeer

Santa's Mac

SantaBalloon

SantaCartoon

SantaCowboy

Santas(TNA)

Pictures H3

Continued

Sleigh Ride

Snowman

Stockings

ThreeWiseMen

ThreeWiseMen.MAC

TRoU Dec. Cover

Winter 2

Wreath light

X-mas Card Template

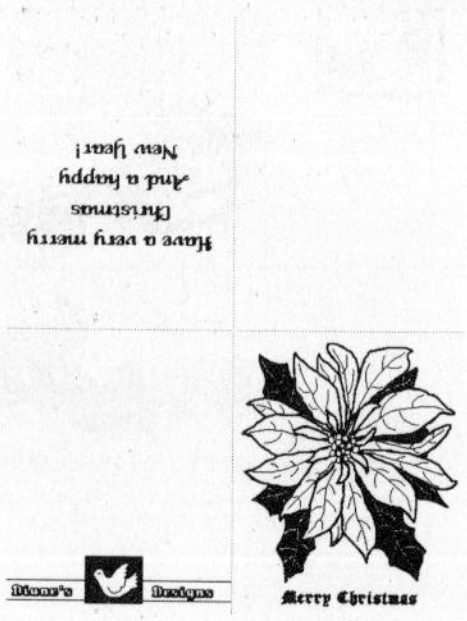

Xmas 1

Xmas 2

Xmas 3

Pictures H3

Continued

Xmas 4

Xmas baby

Xmas Card 0

Xmas Card 1

Xmas Card 2

Xmas Card 3

Xmas Toys

Xmas tree

Pictures H4

Holidays

Bells.eps

Christmas Bells

Christmas tree

Decorative Frame

Decorative Frame 2

Decorative Frame 3

Gift EPS

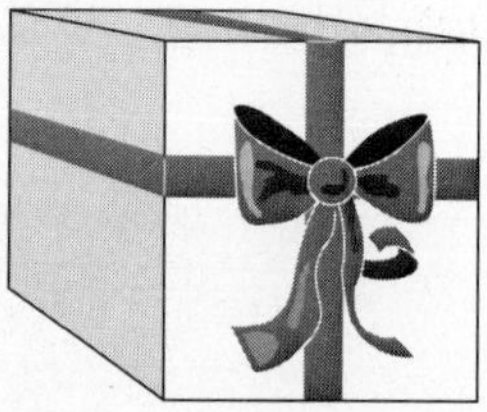

Holly.eps

Holly & Wreath

Ornament 1.EPS

Ornament 2.eps

Ornament 3.eps

Pictures H4

Continued

Ornament 4.eps

Ornament 5.eps

Ornament 6.eps

Ornament 7.eps

Santa 1.eps

Santa 2.eps

Santa 3.eps

Santa 4.eps

Tree.eps

Pictures H5

Holidays

holly.tif

mryxmas.tif

ornament.tif

pinecone.tif

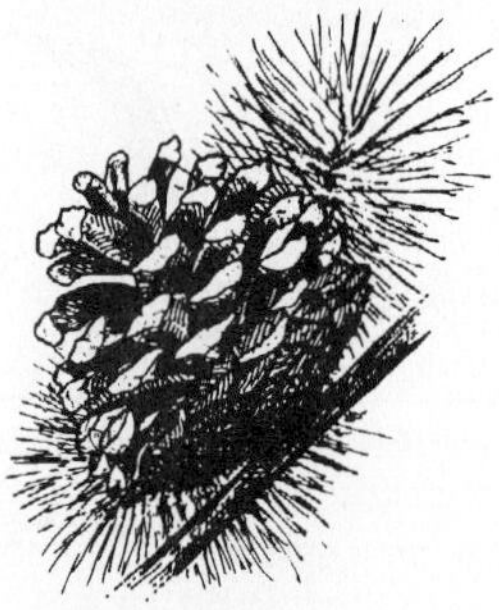

snowflak.tif

snowman.tif

stockngs.tif

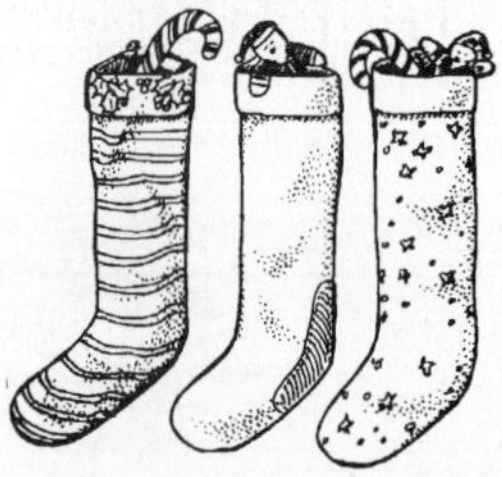

xmastree.tif

xmaswrth.tif

yulelog.tif

Pictures H6

Holidays

angel.tif

elf.tif

nativity.tif

santa.tif

santafac.tif

wisemen.tif

Holiday Pictures

Pictures J1

Cartoons

Banana

Banana Jr.

Banana jr 9000

Basselope

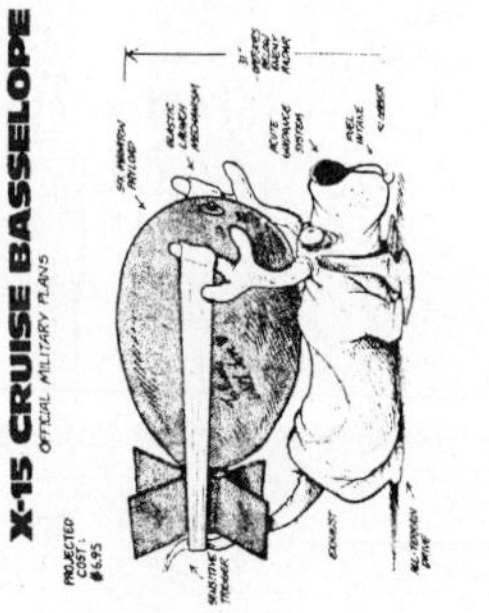

Bear/Raccoon

Betty Boop

Bill

Bill Speaks

Bill the Cat 1

Bill the Cat 2

Bill the Cat 3

Bill The Cat 4

BloomCountyDisks

Cartoon Pictures

Pictures J1

Continued

Bugs

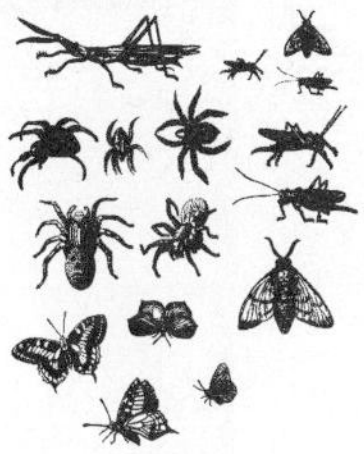

Bulldog

Bully

Cutter

Cutter 2

DiskArt

Garfield

Goat/Donkey

Hemorrhoidogram

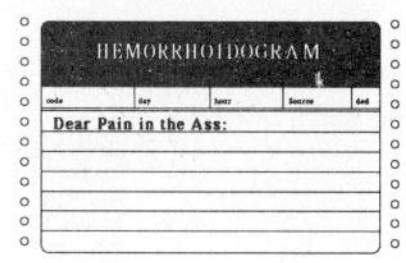

Horse/Cow

Iron Man

JOKER

Cartoon Pictures

Pictures J1

Continued

Kitty

Lion

MacComix/Verbum

Milo

Opi

Opus 2

Opus' amazement

Opus Qual Time

Out of Order

Penguin Lust

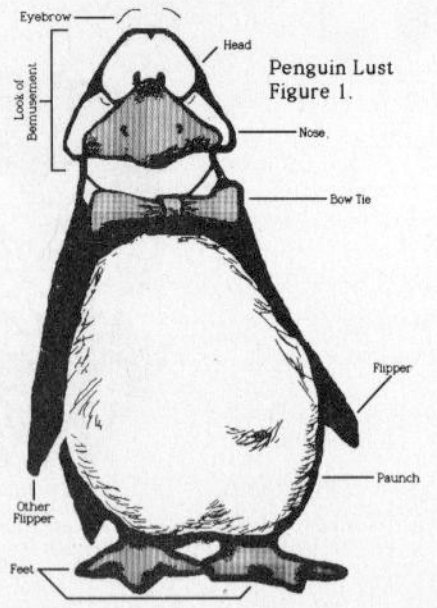

Pigs

Retired

Pictures J1

Continued

Simple Beasts 1.1

Squirrels

Xmas Opus

Pictures K1

Animals

Arabesq

Bears

Bird Scroll

Birds

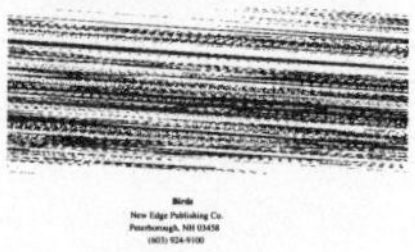

Birds 1

Birds 2

Animal Pictures

Black Beauty

Camel/Elephant

Cat

Cheeta

ClipArt

Dinosaurs Pg 1

Dinosaurs Pg. 2

Dinosaurs Pg. 3

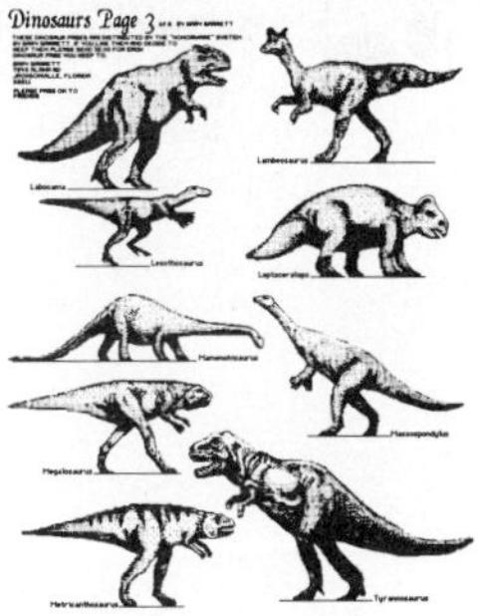

Dinosaurs Pg.4

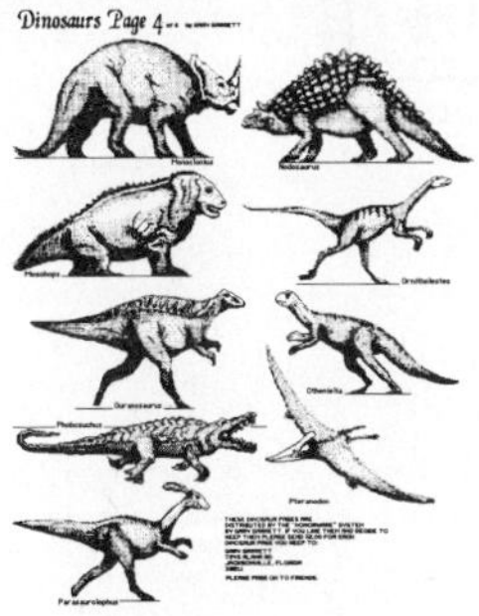

Dinosaurs pg.5

Dinosaurs Pg.6

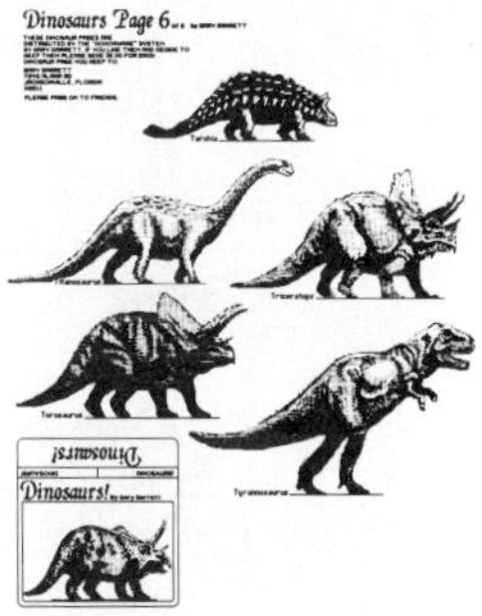

DivingBird

Eagle

Eagle Screen

Elephant line

Elephants

Fish

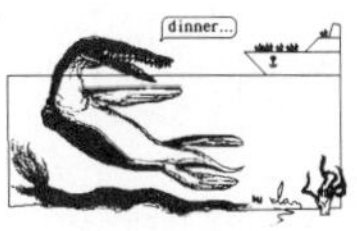

Fleur De Lis

Pictures K1

Continued

Frog on Pad

Goose

Gulls

Horse

Horses 1

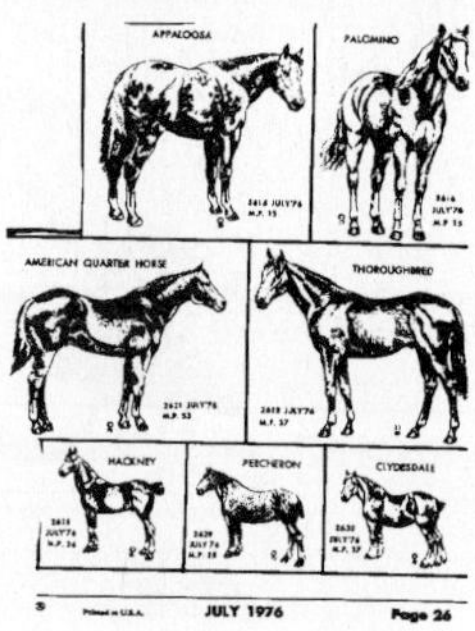

Horses 2

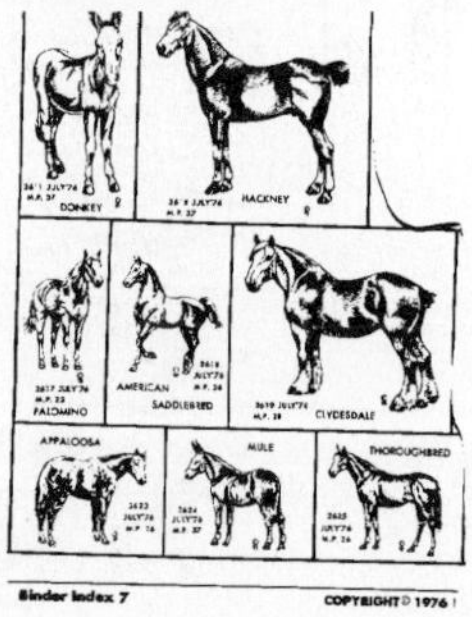

Horses 3

HyperAnimals

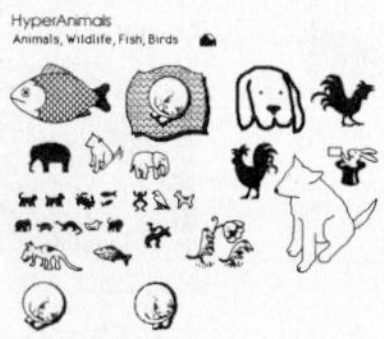

Oriental

Animal Pictures

Pictures K2

Animals

3 D stars

Borders 18 (Thick)

Borders 20

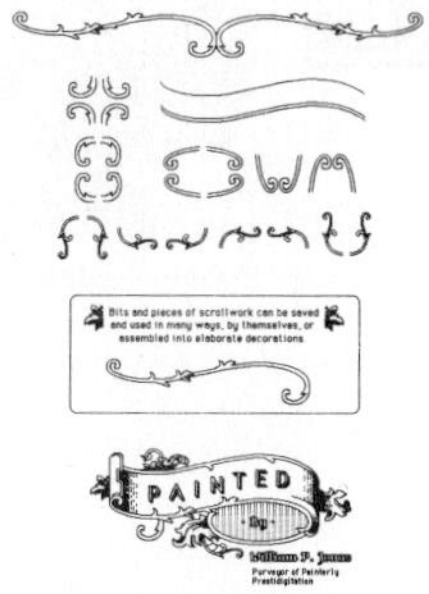

Geometric

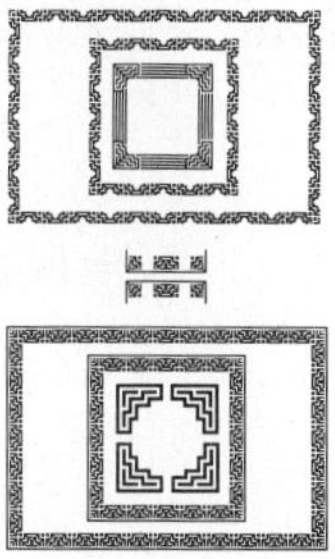

Ichthyocentaurus

Loon

Meander

Monkeys

Owl

Panda

Persian Flowers 2

Rodeo

Animal Pictures

Pictures K2

Continued

Seahorse

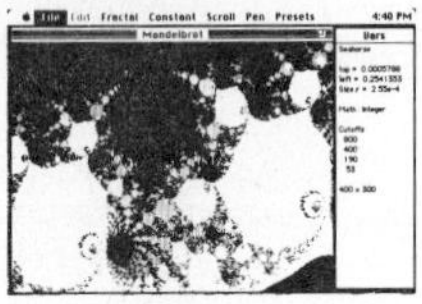

Speedy Turtles

Squirrel MAC

Star shell

Stars Rows

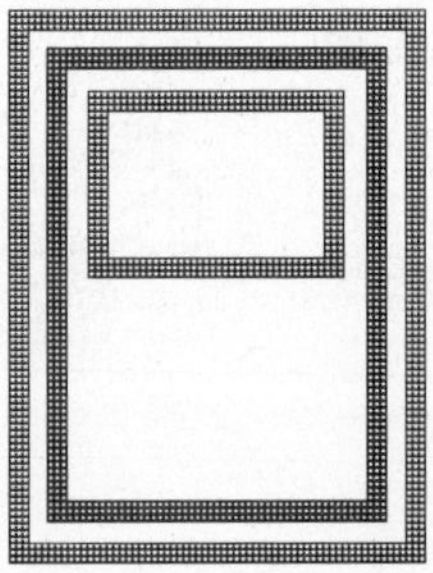

Swans

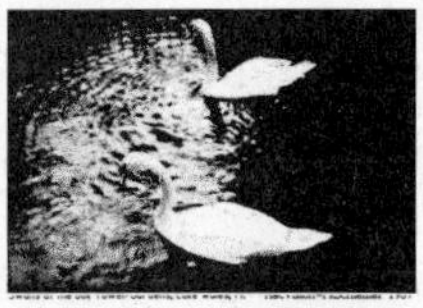

Tiger

White Arab

White Horse

Winged Horse

Yellow Iris

Yellow Iris--line drawing

Pictures K3

Animals

Archaeopteryx

Brontosaurus.TIFF

Dinosaur1EPS

Dinosaur2EPS

Dinosaurs Pg 1

Dinosaurs Pg. 2

Dinosaurs Pg. 3

Dinosaurs Pg.4

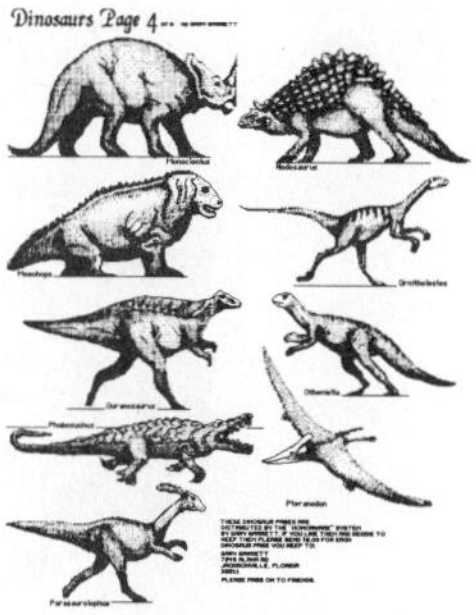

Dinosaurs pg.5

Dinosaurs Pg.6

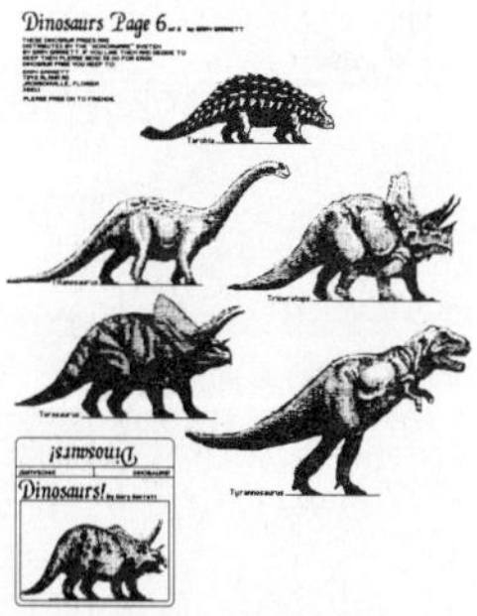

Struthers

Triceratops.TIFF.

Pictures L1

Small Picture Collections

4th of July

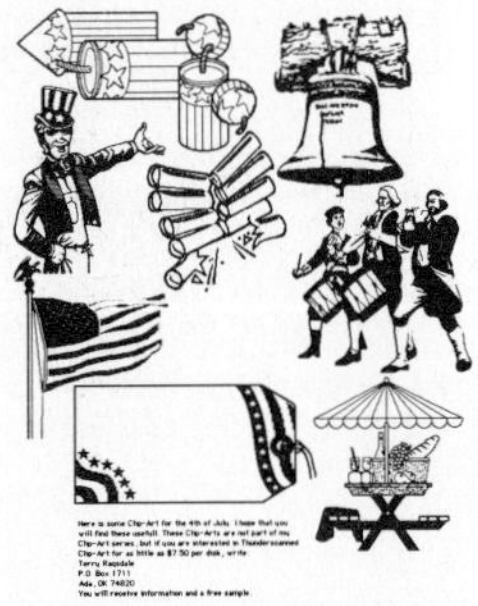

Babygrnd.pnt

BANANAJR.RLE

CATHY'S MARK

Clip #1

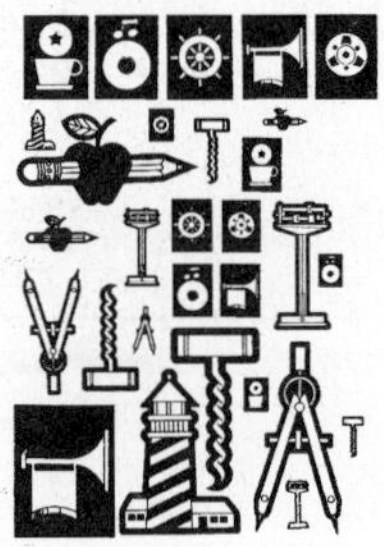

Clip #2

Clip #3

Clip #4

Clip #5

Clip #6

Clip #7

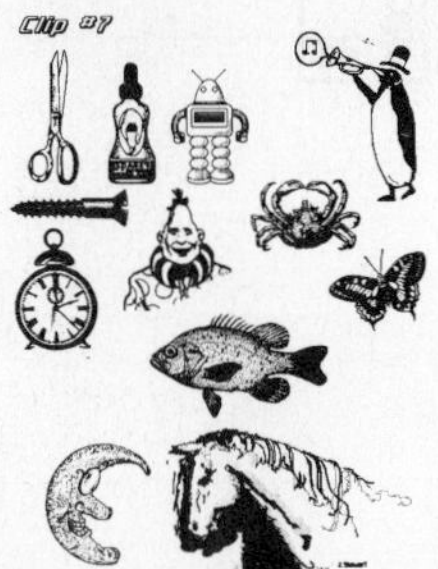

Clip #8

Clip #9

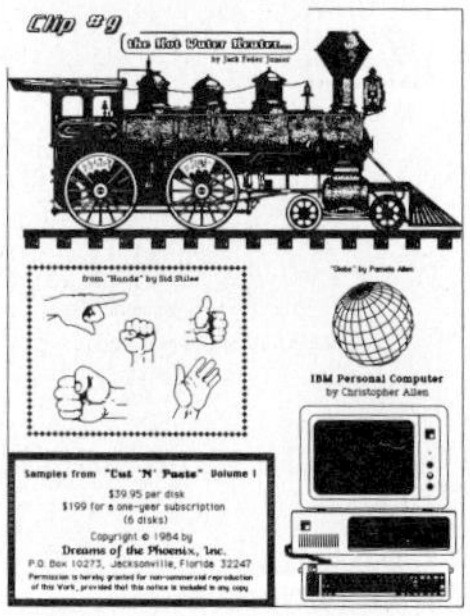

Cut 'N Paste

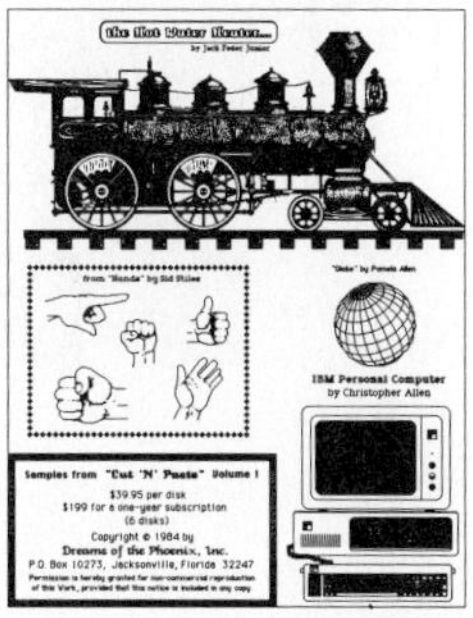

Document Decorations

Duet.pnt

FLASHER.RLE

Full-Page Message

Welcome to Sampler S-2

in the SunShine Graphics Library for the Macintosh™

This disk is being distributed as shareware
If you want to keep these pictures, please send $12 to

SunShine
Box 4351
Austin, Texas 78765

You can also write for a free description of the dozens of disks of artwork available for just $12 apiece, or $10 each if you buy three or more. Good computer artwork doesn't have to be expensive!

As you can see from this sampler, the pictures in the SunShine Graphics Library are large and of high quality. The range of topics is equally large, and new disks will continue to appear in the future.

The images in the SunShine Graphics Library stand on their own as beautiful pictures, but you can add text to use them for cards, ads, signs, T-shirt transfers, report covers, etc. Because the pictures are large and detailed, they work well when blown up to poster size with programs like MacBillboard™, PosterMaker™, and Full Paint™.

Each design included on these disks can give rise to many others. The INVERT command produces a negative image that is often as pleasing as the original. Repeated use of the TRACE EDGES command can produce attractive new designs, too. In conjunction with that command you can also use the PAINT BUCKET to fill in some of the new regions thus created.

GARFIELD.RLE

Header Directory

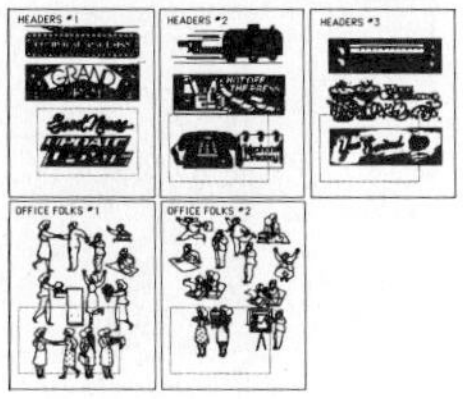

Headers #1

Small Pictures

Headers #2

Headers #3

JGIRL.RLE

Pictures L1

Continued

LetsDuet.pnt

MEGABD.RLE

Office Folks #1

Office Folks #2

PIX 4 ASST

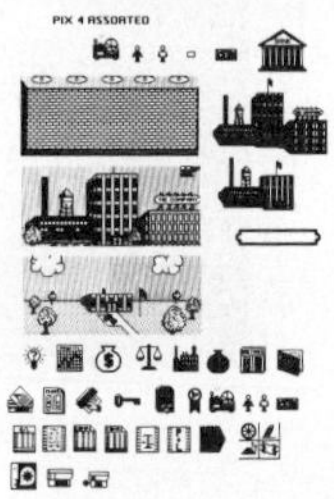

Rests.pnt

Ripper Art

TIGER.RLE

UTAMARO Art-1

UTAMARO Art-2

UTAMARO Art-4

UTAMARO Art-5

Wild Tulip

From Disk # 19: Full-Page Floral Wallpaper Patterns, Volume 2
SunShine Box 4351 Austin Texas 78765

Pictures L2

Small Picture Collections

Application Icons

Birdz

Birdz 2

Bump.3D

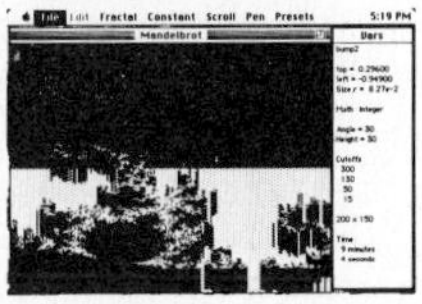

ChipWits icons

Corners

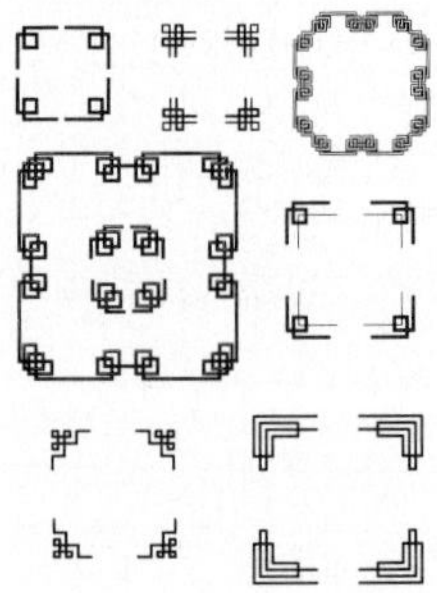

Corners 1

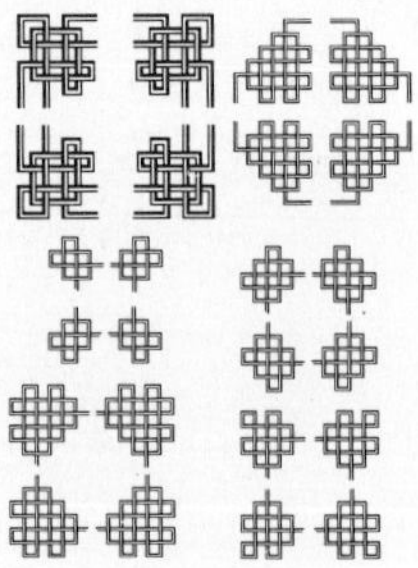

Disk Label Maker

Disk Labels#1

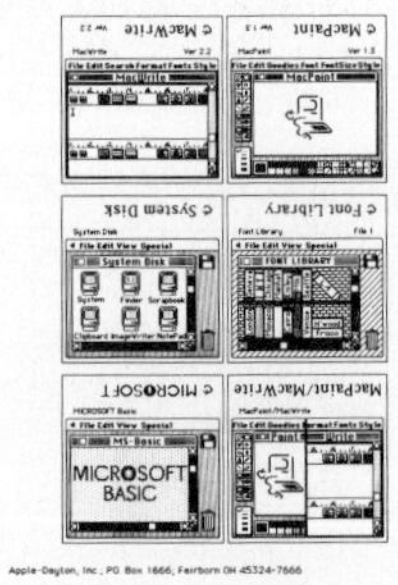

Disk Labels#2

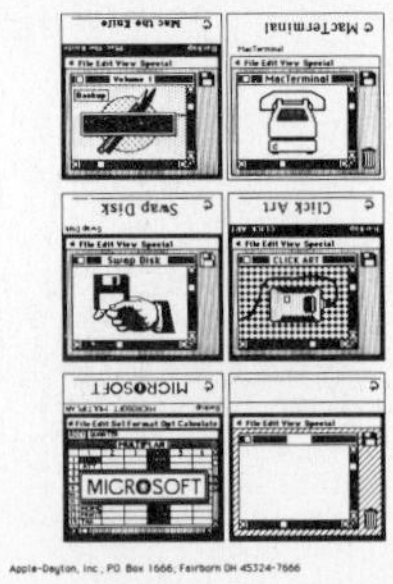

Disk Labels#3

Disk Labels#4

Document Icons

Fancy Minature.o

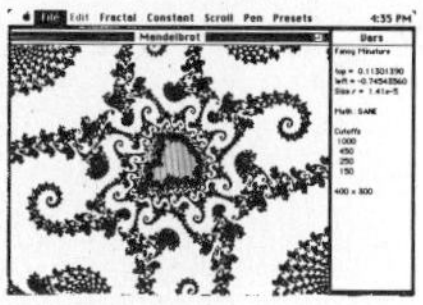

Hook.o

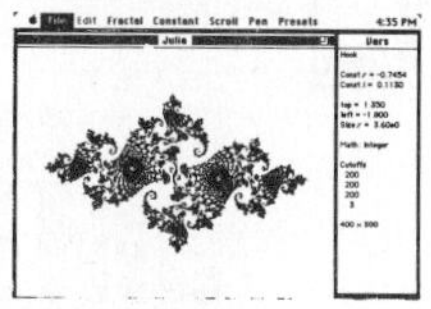

Hyper-Homes

HyperIcons

MacJacket

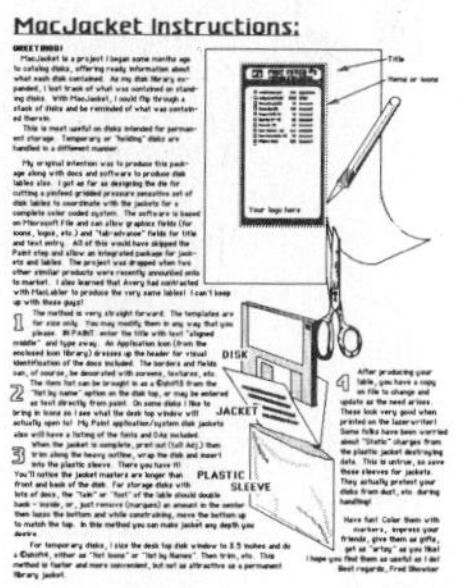

Master Jacket Outlines

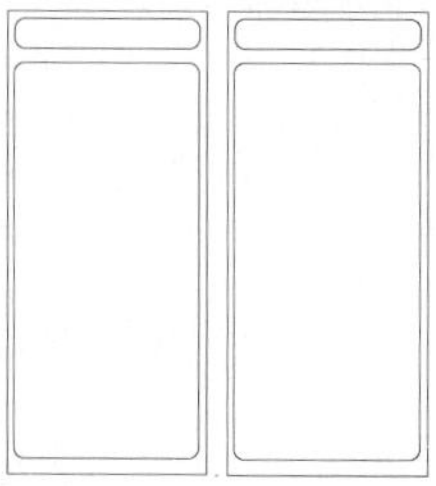

Minature3

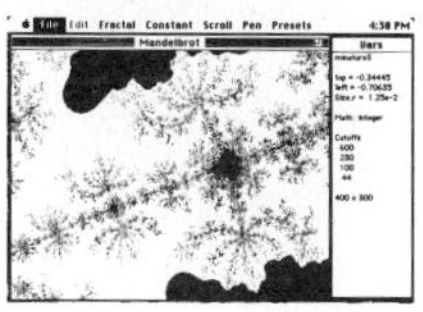

One Man's Icons

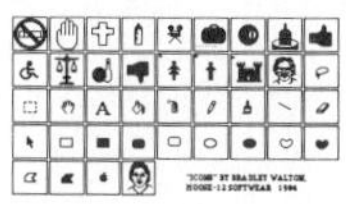

Patriotic

Patterns 1

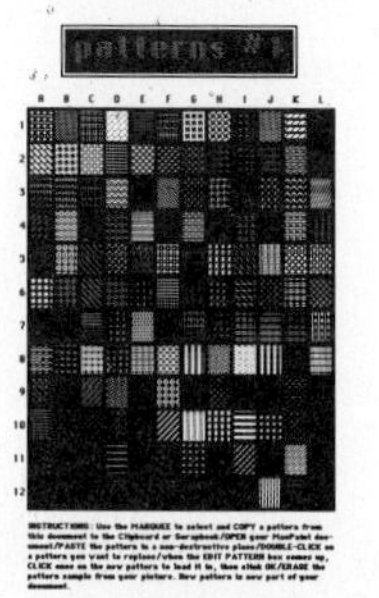

Patterns 2

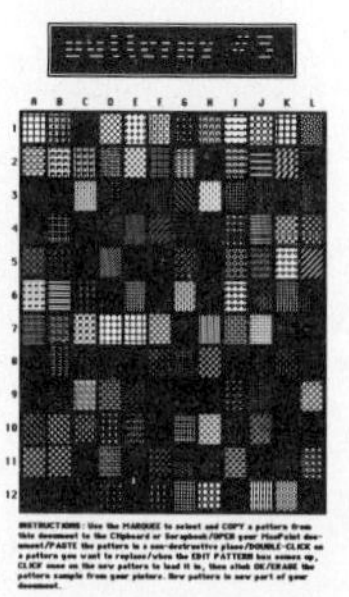

Pictures L2

Continued

Patterns 3

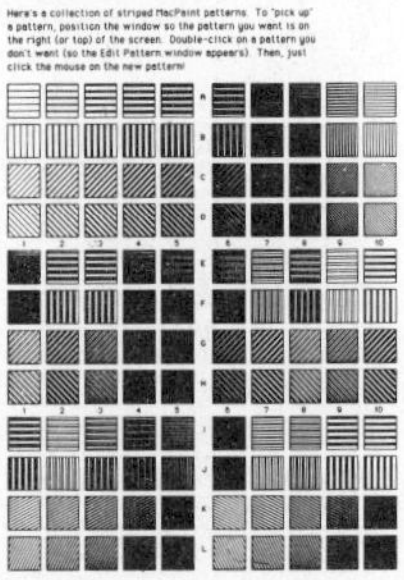

Patterns 5

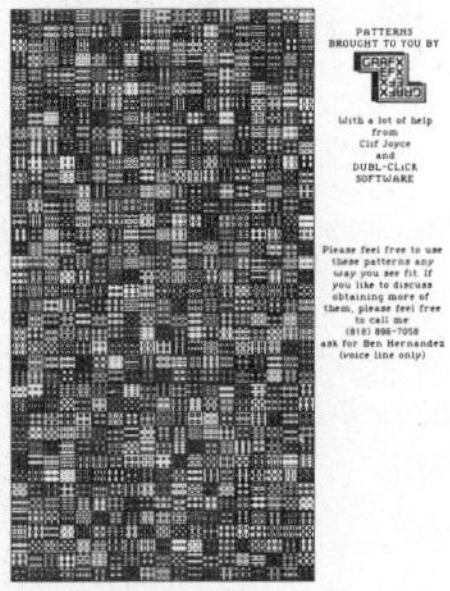

Spike.3D

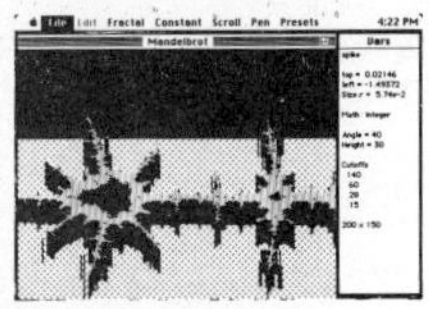

Still More Icons

System Icons

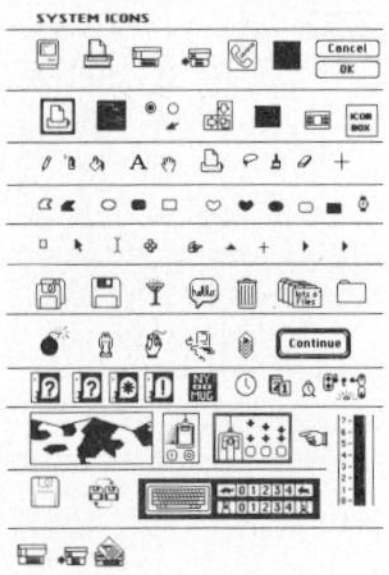

Whorls.o

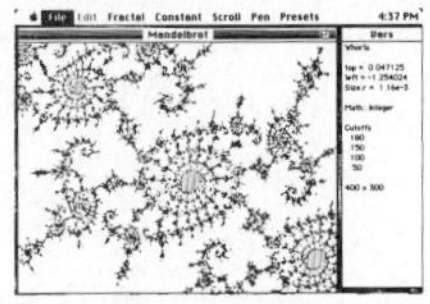

Small Pictures

Cognitive

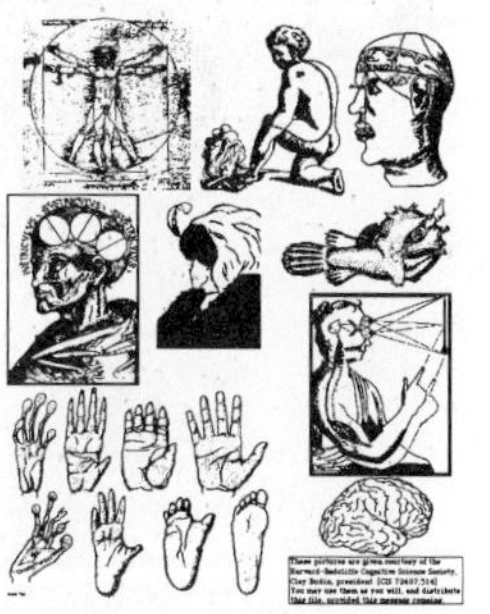

Cool Dudes

D.C. Things

Fall Activities

Greeters 1

Greeters 2

Kids 1

Kids 2

Kids 3

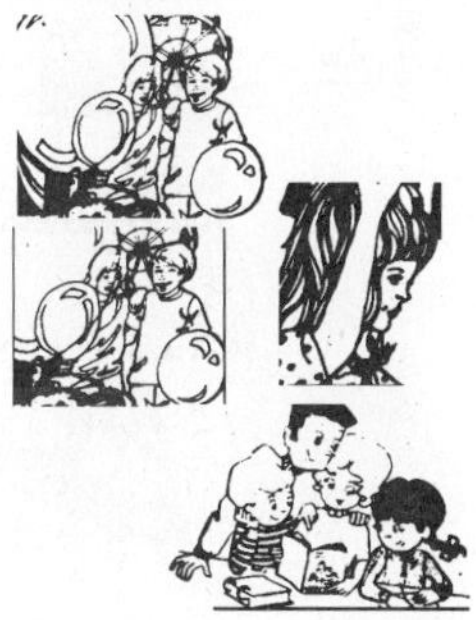

Kids 4

Kids 5

Kids 6

Pictures M1

Continued

Kids 7

Kids at Desks

Letters

More Bibles

OlympicLogos#1

OlympicLogos#2

School 1

School 2

School 3

School 4

Speed of Light Graph

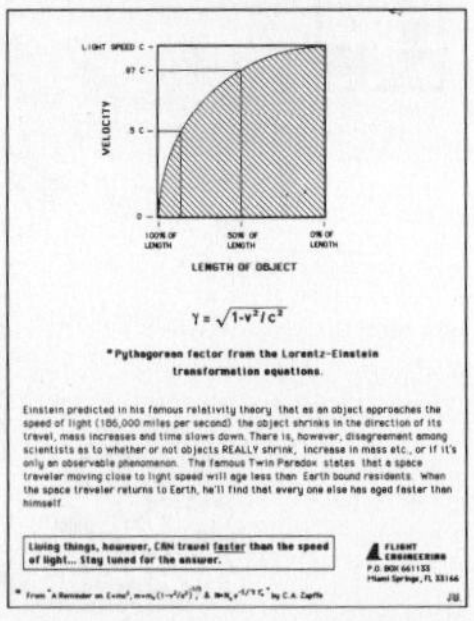

Summer+grad+eat+movie

Education Pictures

Pictures M1

Continued

The Great Seal

TinkerToys

Youth service people

Zodiac

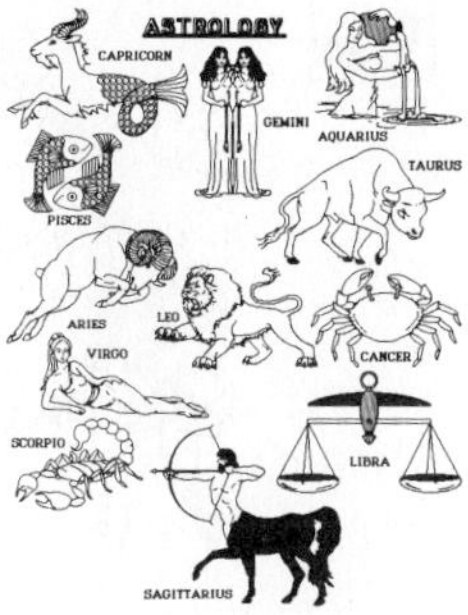

Pictures N1

Fantasy

2Swords

Adventure Warrior

Barbarian

Bruce

Castle

Cherubs

Clean Hacker

Cowboy.pnt

Devil

Dragon

Dragon 1

Dragon 2

Fantasy Pictures

Pictures N1

Continued

Dragon 3

Dragon 4

Dragon3

DUNE

Franky

Friends of Rocky

Heavey Metal

Helmet

Hydra

Killer

LVL7-10 Wiz

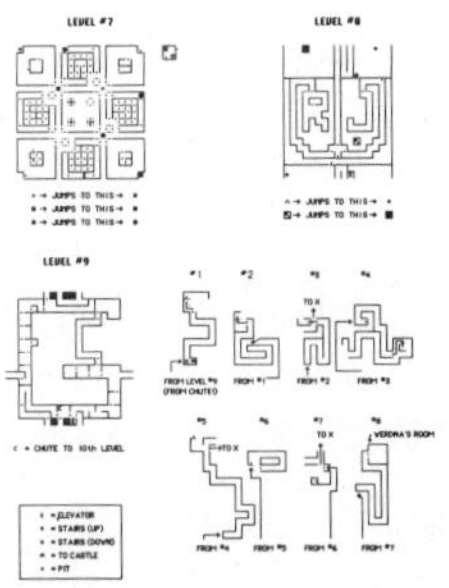

Machen/Black Seal

Pictures N1

Continued

Mandala

Merlin

Prometheus

Romance

Skeleton

Warrior

Fantasy Pictures

Warrior 2

Warrior TS

Warriors

Zork

adversary

Angel

angry

Anti Christ 1

Awana poster

Bad Outfit

Bash

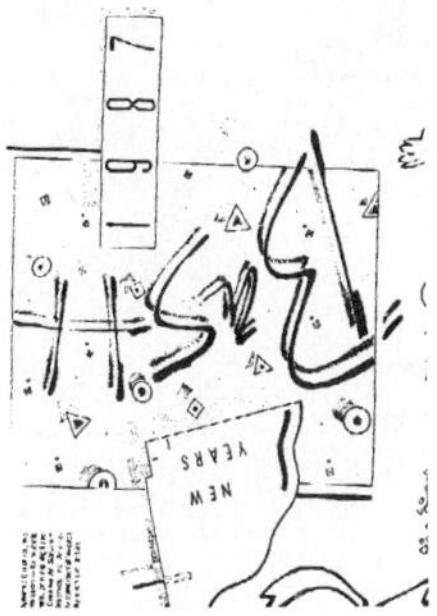

BookMan

Bookplate 1

Bookplate 2

Bookplate 3

Bully

Pictures P1

Continued

Burn Out

Card Death

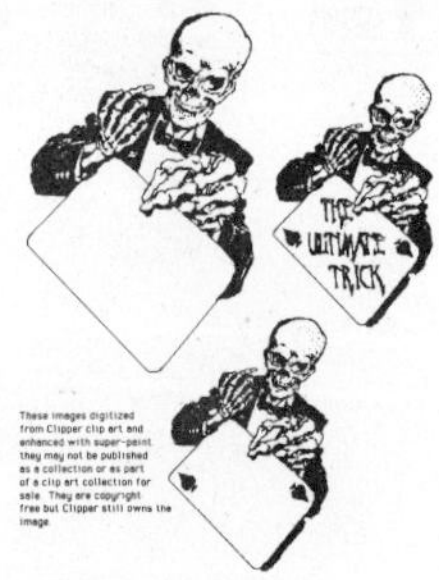

Christ's love

Colonialist

Dallas Lady

Dallas Man 1

Dark Horse

Date

Digging deeper

Doll kit

Earth normal

Easter Jesus

Eastern confed

Gossip Monster

Guys 1

guys 2

Guys 3

Hairy Bloke

Halloween 1

Halloween 2

Hands 1

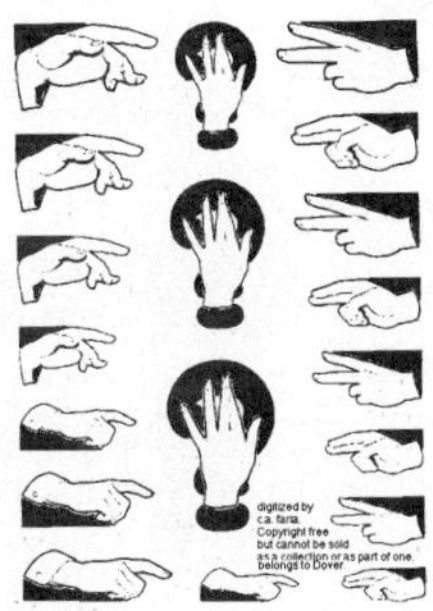

Hands 2

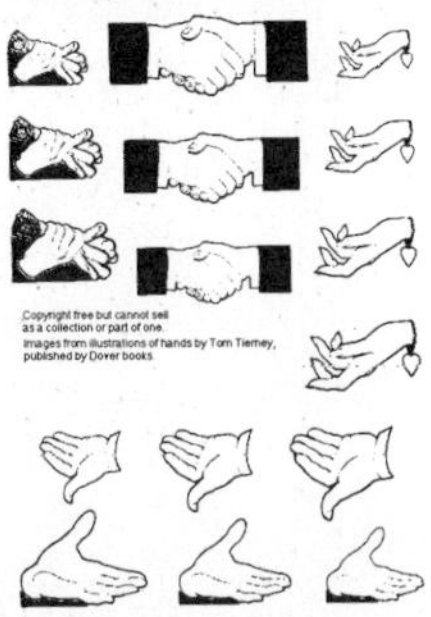

Hands 3

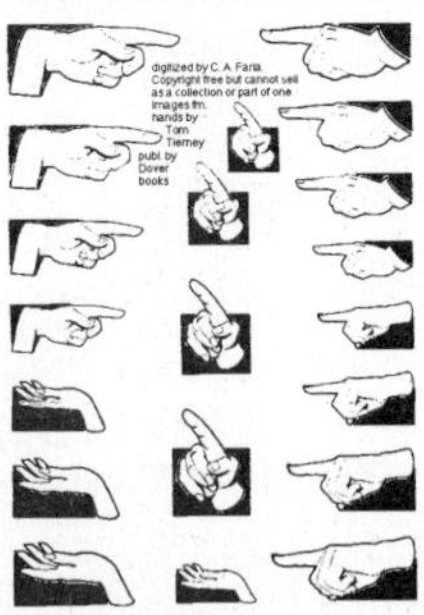

Hands 4

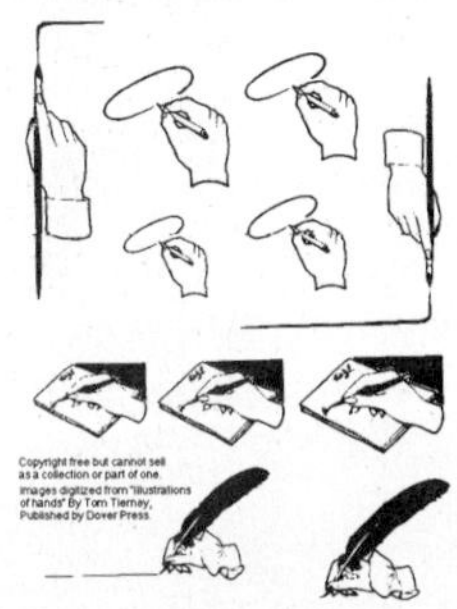

Pictures P1

Continued

Hands 5

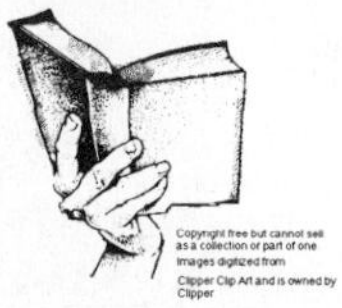

Jewish 1

Jewish 2

Jewish 3

Jewish scriptures

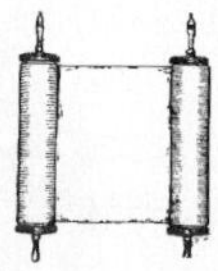

Kool Kids

Kool Kids 2

Man on Ladder

More Bibles

Lady 1

lady & bum

Lady Magician

Little Girl 1

Little Girl 2

Maranatha Backgr

Maranatha Jesus

MoneyEater Monster

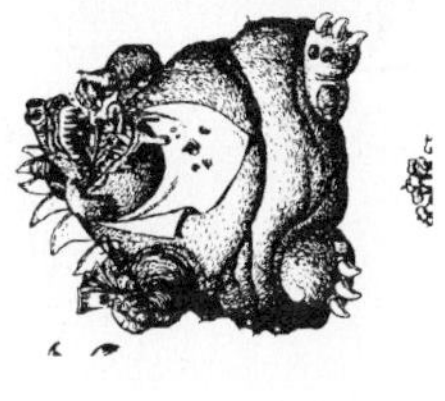

New Year

No Lady

Not Pass

Office Stuff 1

Pictures P2

Continued

Old english

Old lady

Pale Horse

Parchement open

Party kids

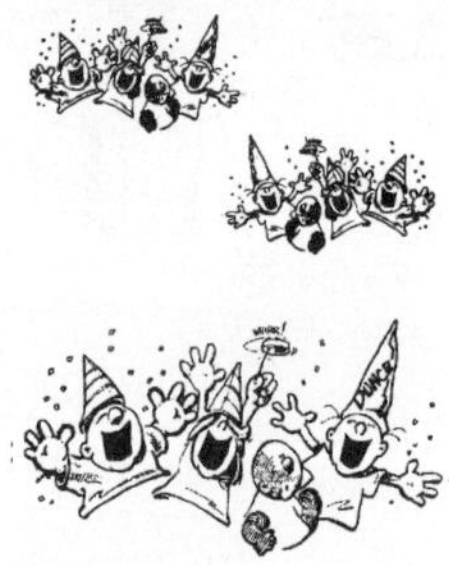

Persecution

General Pictures

Pile of Books

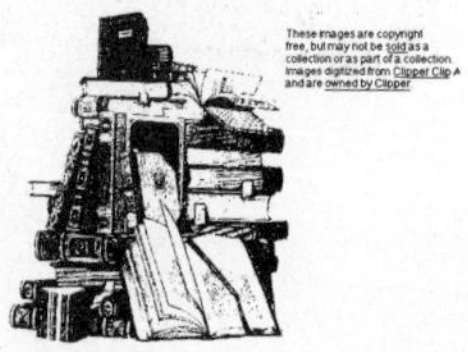

Piper

PosterMan

Prayer

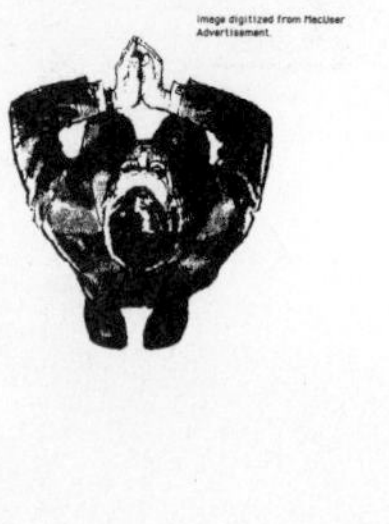

Pretty Face 2

Roman empire

Roman empire fill

ropes

Runner

Runner 4

Running Log

Samurai (PCS)

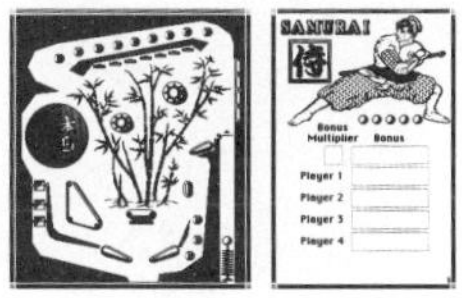

Sign man 1

Sign men

Sign men 2

Sign men 3

Sin Monster

Sneaker

Pictures P2

Continued

Soldiers and Tanks

South.confed.map

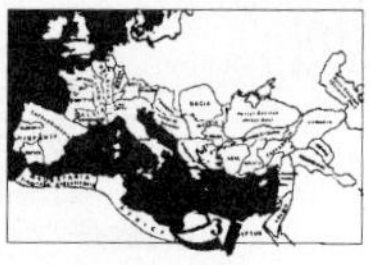

Supermac

Surf's up

Surf's up 1

Temple

Ten crowns

The Coup

TimeEater Monster

We B Jammin'

Who is

Witch

General Pictures

Pictures R1

Assorted Pictures

Airman

AppleBus

Be My Valentine

Beaver/Playin' Mac

Bite

CloneClown

DeskTop Pict

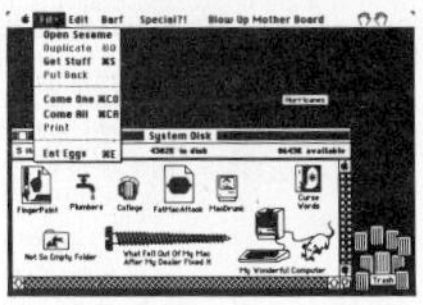

Dino

Dragon Wins

Exchange.pnt

Expose

Fiesta and Trees

Pictures R1

Continued

Flowchart

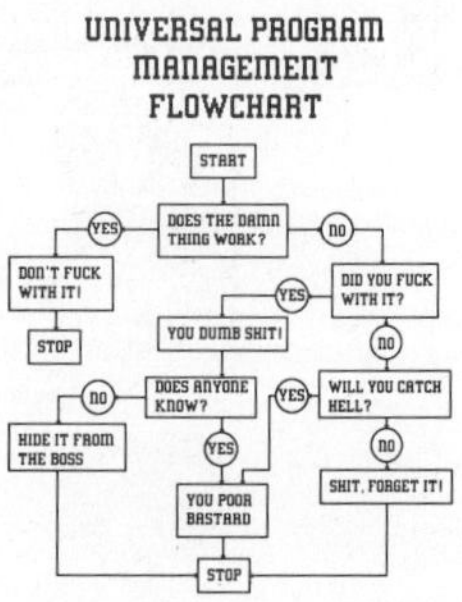

Garfield

Hacker Comic

Hacker Humor

Holiday Lane

Holidays

InsideMacPaint

Kamikaze Bees

Liar's Club Certificate

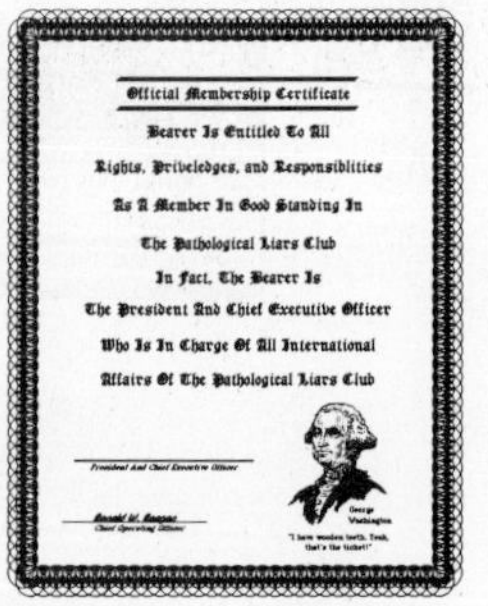

Listen Up!

Macs & Axes

Meadow Guard

MoveTheWorld

Nanny

NASA

Nerd Comic II

Nerd Comix

New U.S. (Texas View)

Assorted
Pictures

Pictures R2

Assorted Pictures

Nanny

Nerd Comic II

Nerd Comix

"No" Stuff

Notice

Ø Oon Board

OKIE

Pencil

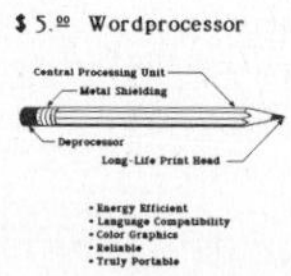

Portland Oregon

Post Office

Power User

Randy's BMW

Recipe.pnt

Rest of Us Chip

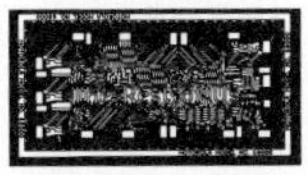

Roman Army-pt

Salesman

Santa's Mac

Sects

SoftSell.pnt

SputnickFish

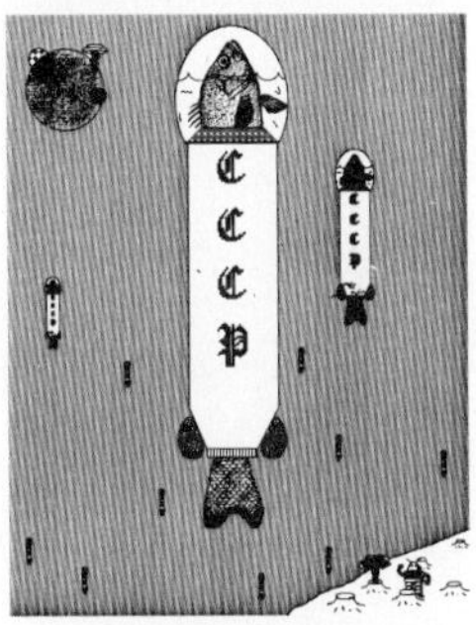

Stooges

Weird People

Windows.pnt

Wing

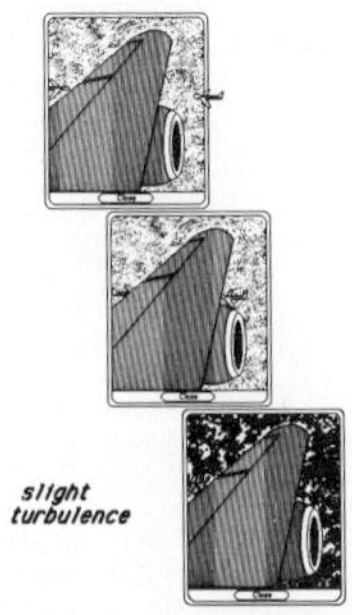

Assorted Pictures

Pictures R2

Continued

Winnebiko

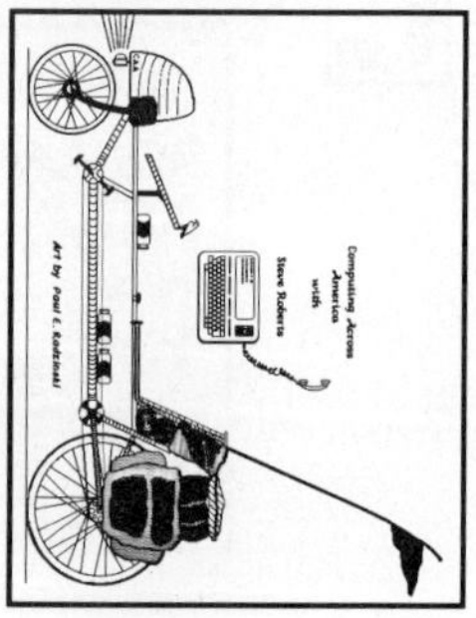

Zog

"Hey! Look what Zog do!"

Background

BIG Hand

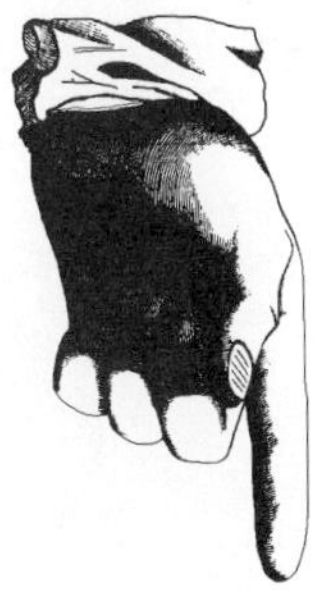

BizClips

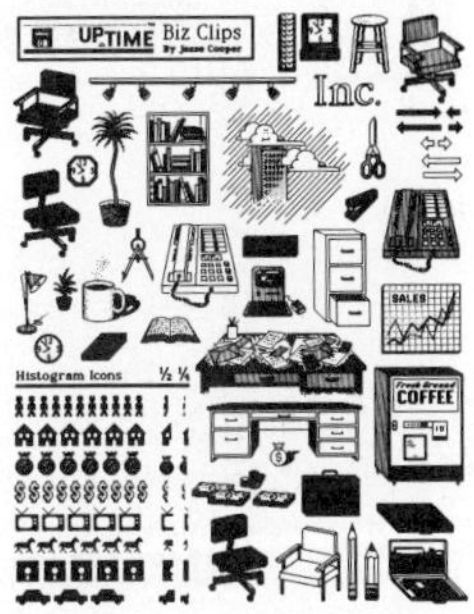

BLTWich

Bridgewalk

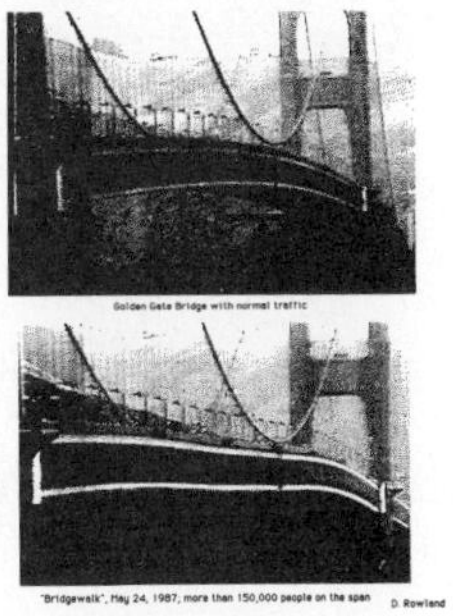

Clip Art

Clips 2

Congrats

Copyright

Court

Crown Floral

Cute/House

Pictures S1

Continued

Deco

Definitivo

Delicate

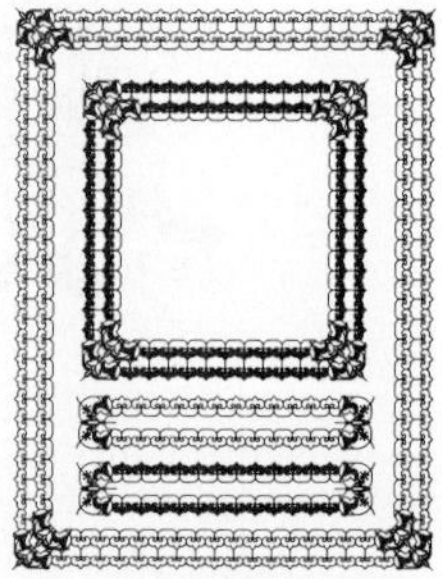

Dewdrop

Diamonds

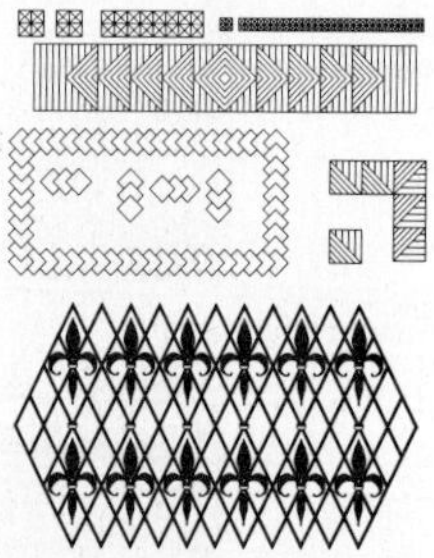

Don't Panic

Dune.3

Eyeglasses

Fair Days

Fatbit 2

Fatbit 3

Fatbits

FatBits ABC Patterns

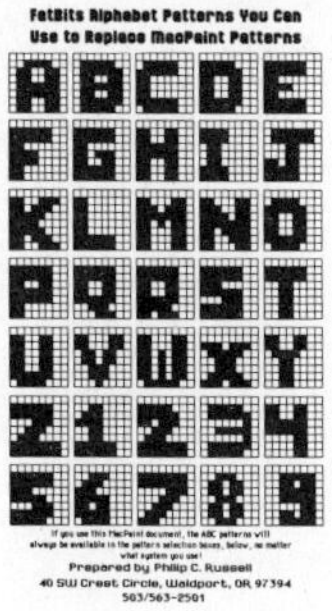

Fist

Garage Sale

Glove

HandPlant

House

Howdy Do

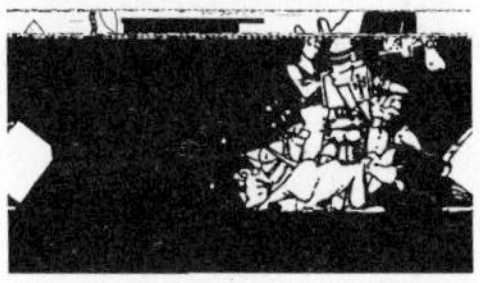

Kei

More Pictures

Pictures S2

More Pictures

Golden gate

Lrg. Scroll

MacLectic Clip Art

Martini

Misc 1

Nouveau

Office

Open Door

Orns2

Photo Equipment

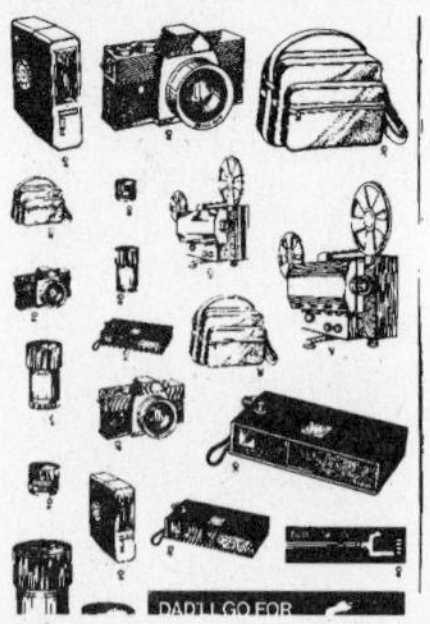

Play Card

Publications

Pictures S2

Continued

Quality

Ribbons

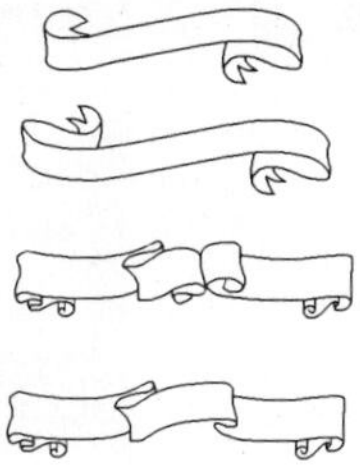

Sacrifice

Scrap 1

Scrap 2

Scrap 3

Set Design

Shinsui

SignBoard

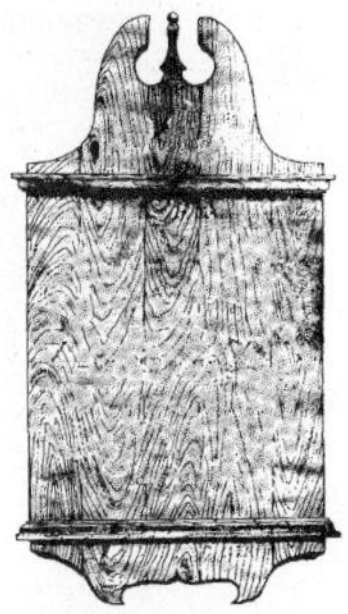

Small Frames

Square

Supervisors

Pictures S2

Continued

Tarot

Three Frames

Thumbs up

Tiles

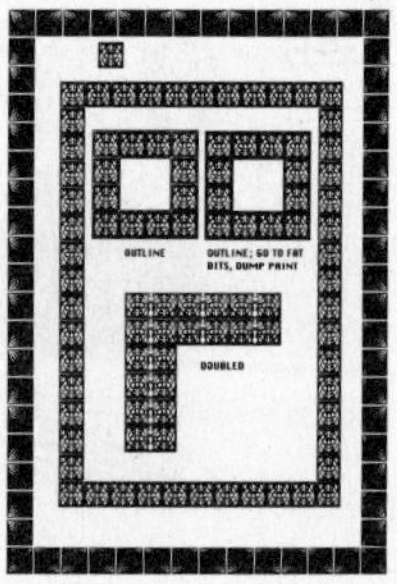

Twilight

Wanted

Watch

4Planes

AIR CONVOY

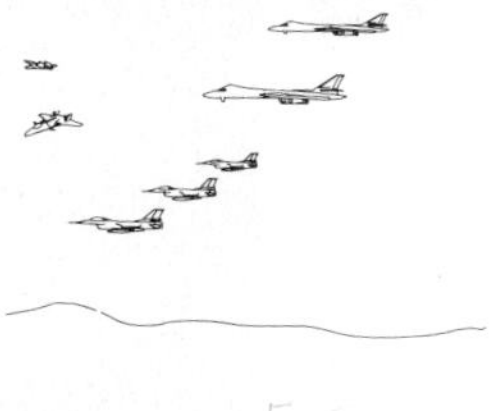

Aircraft 1

Aircraft 2

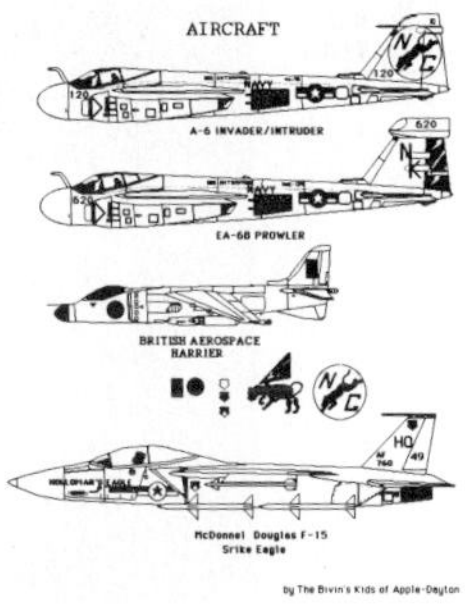

B-1B

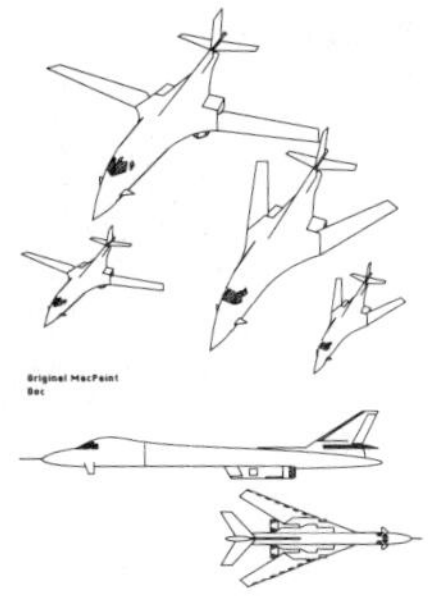

B-52/helicopters

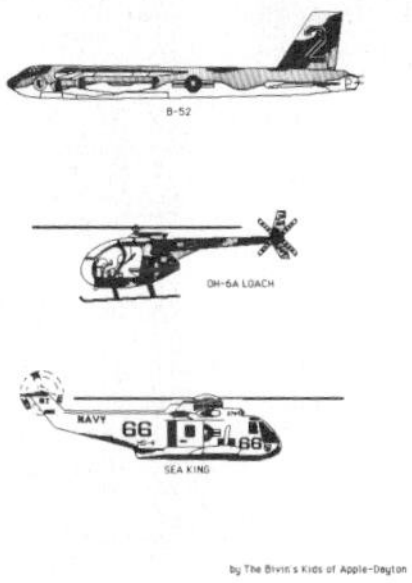

Black/F-15 Side

BMP-1

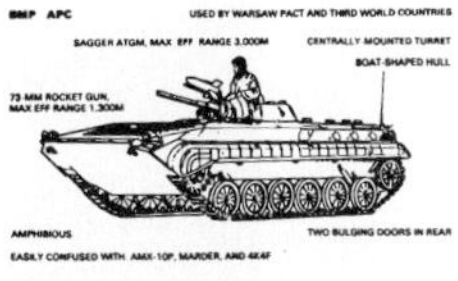

BMP-1a

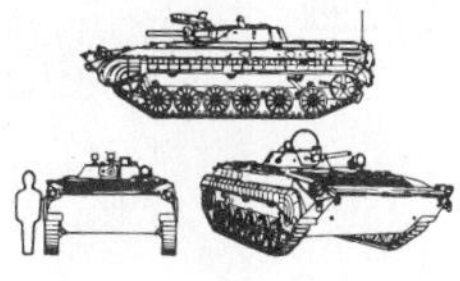

BMP-2

BMP-2a

BTR-70

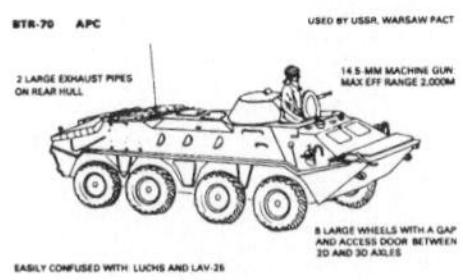

Pictures T1

Continued

BTR-70a

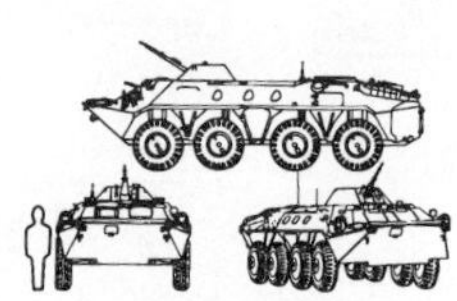

Chicago

Copter

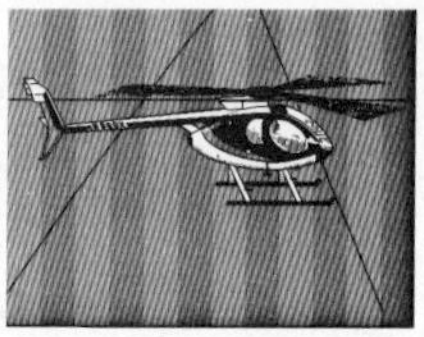

Current US Aircraft

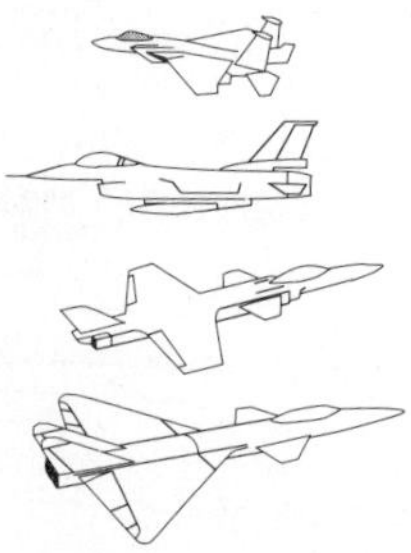

DC9

dsrv 2

dsrv1

dsrv3

F-14

F-16

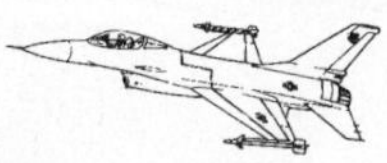

F-19

Fokker Triplane

Foxbat?

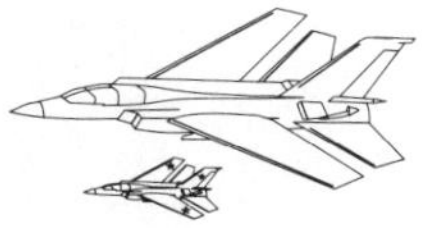

GeeBee

Helicopters

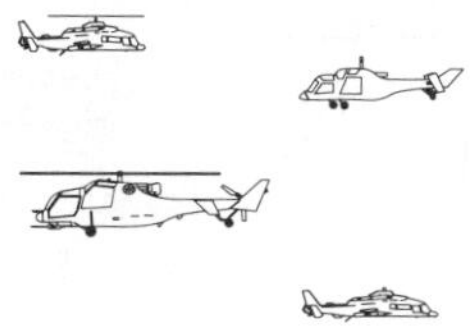

HUD F-4.1

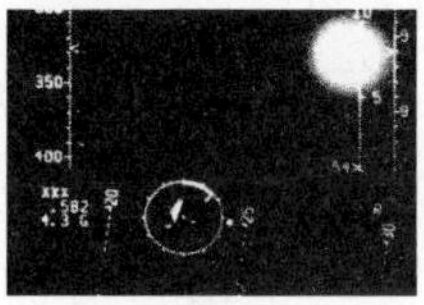

Lockheed U-2

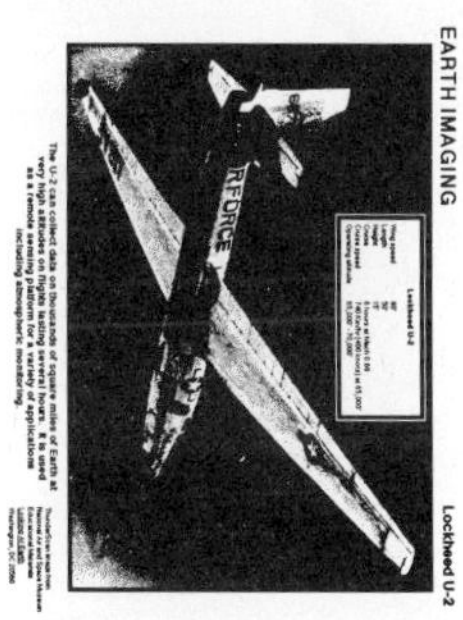

M113-APC-ACAL

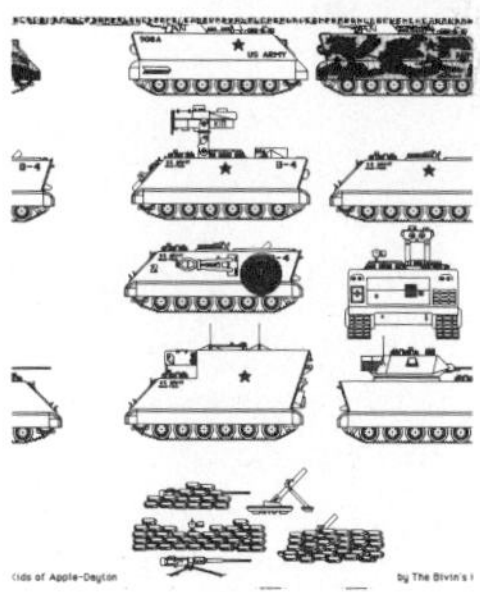

Misc Ships

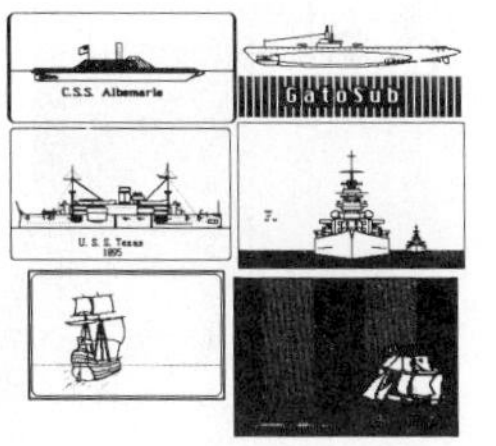

NATO Aeroplanes

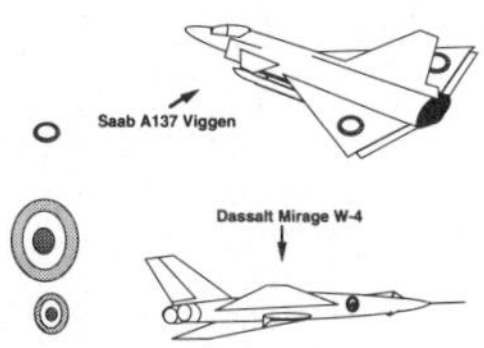

Naval

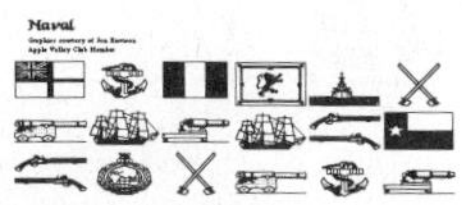

plane

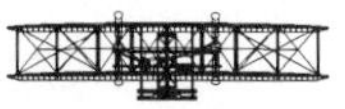

Russian MiG

SU-122

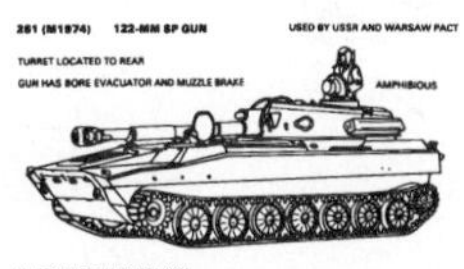

Pictures T1

Continued

SU-122a

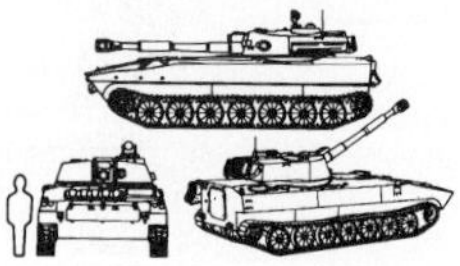

Submarine

T-64

T-64a

T-72

T-72a

TR-1

Tu-26

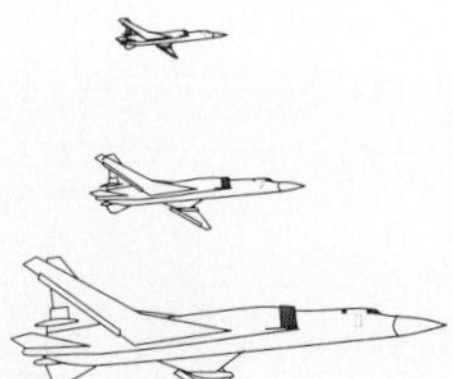

Wings

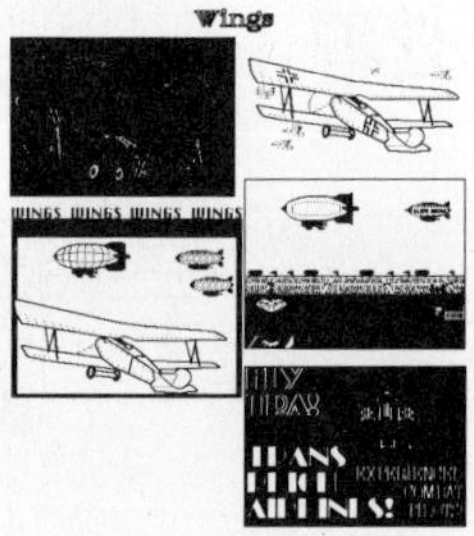

Wright Flyer

ZSU 23-4

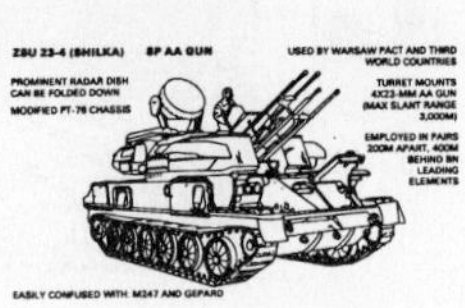

ZSU 23-4a

7 Seas

Bike

Bikes and Camper

Bimota Cycle

Car Logos

F1 Racers

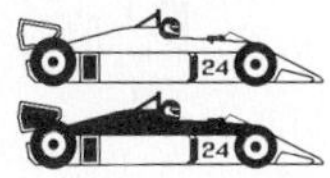

Ferrari

Hi Speed Proc

Jalopy

Lamborghini

Learjet

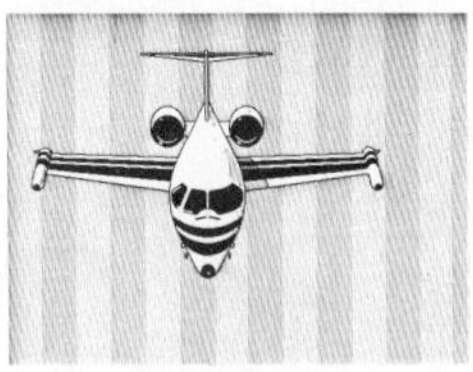

Old Cars

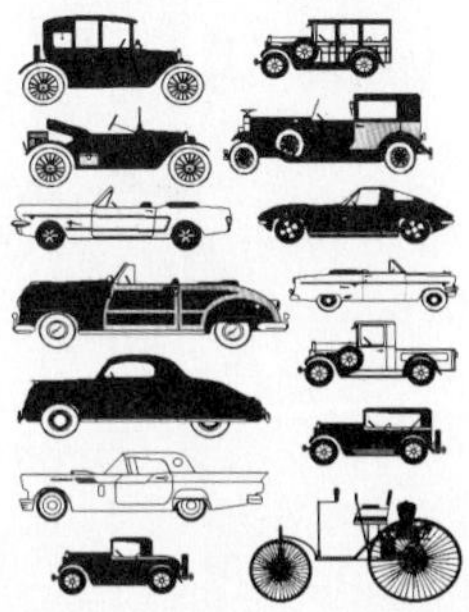

Pictures T2

Continued

Porsche 928

Porsche959

Racing 1

Racing 2

Racing 3

Racing 4

Racing a

Rail Logos

Ship of the Line

Signals1

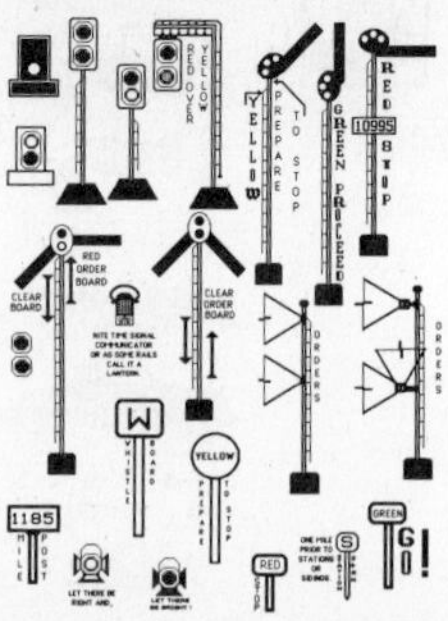

Signals2

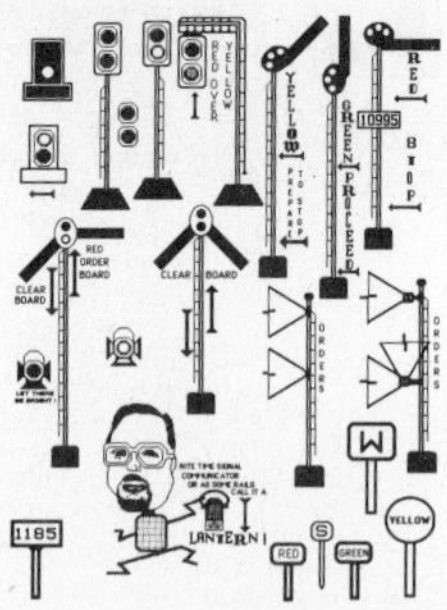

Sky/Skin/Jet

Pictures T2

Continued

Testerossa

Trainset

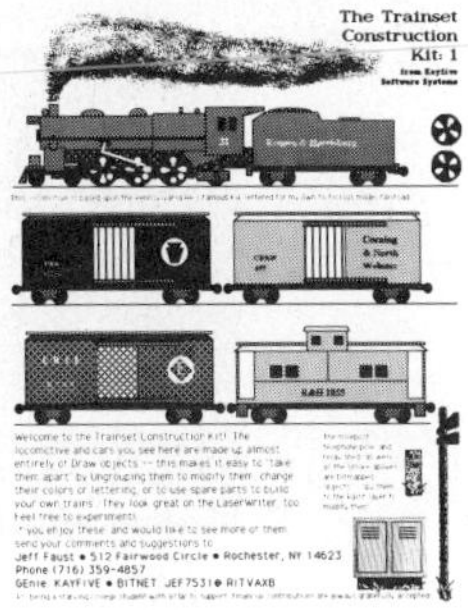

Trans 1

Trans 2

Trans 3

Trans 4

Trans 5

Trans 6

Transport Pictures

Pictures T3

Transportation

Balloon Photo

Chal Over Earth AD

Enterprise

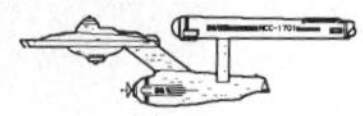

Enterprise1

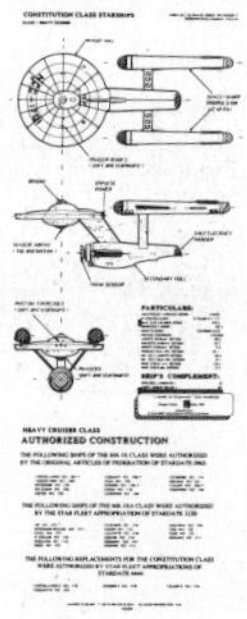

FederationSeal

Klingon Battlecruiser

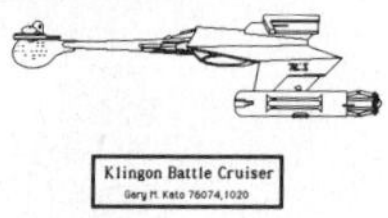

Transport Pictures

Klingon Cruiser

Launch II AD

Lost in Space

Moon

R2D2

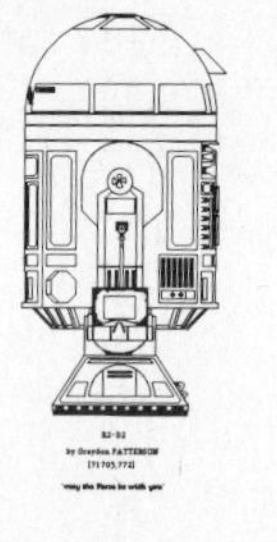

Robot

Saturn

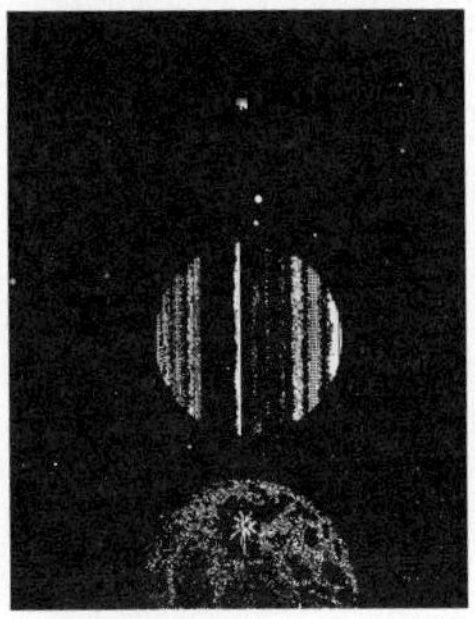

Scout

SDF-1

SF World

Shuttle & Moon Walk

Space Station

SpaceShip

Spiral Galaxy 1

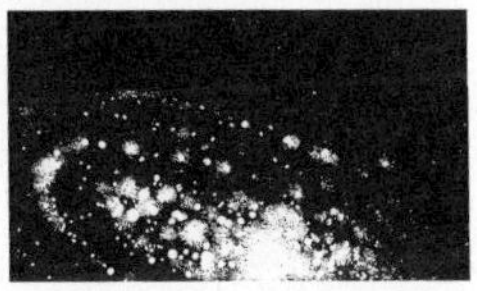

Star shell

Stars

Stars Rows

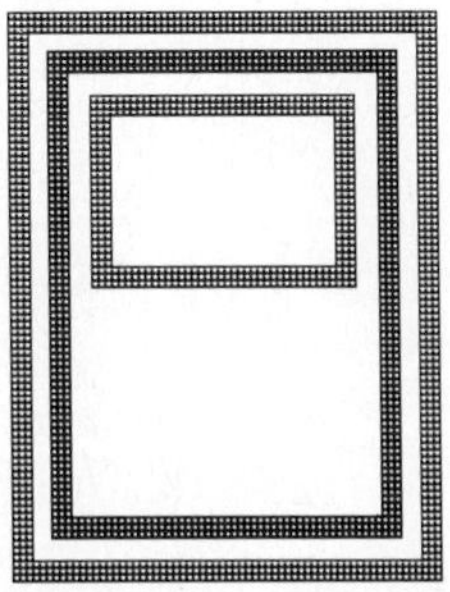

Starships

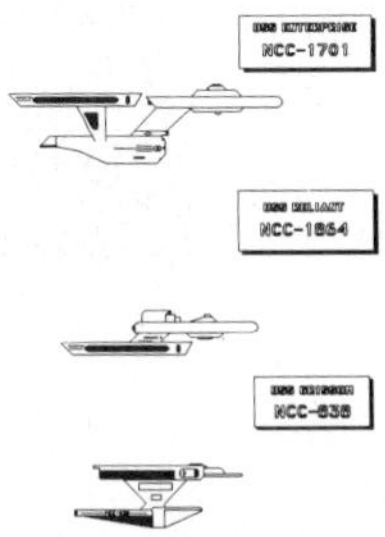

Transport Pictures

Pictures T3

Continued

U.S.S. Enterprise

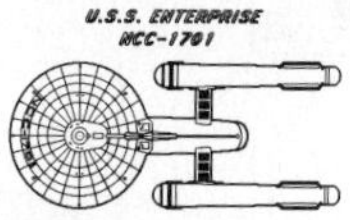

Voyager

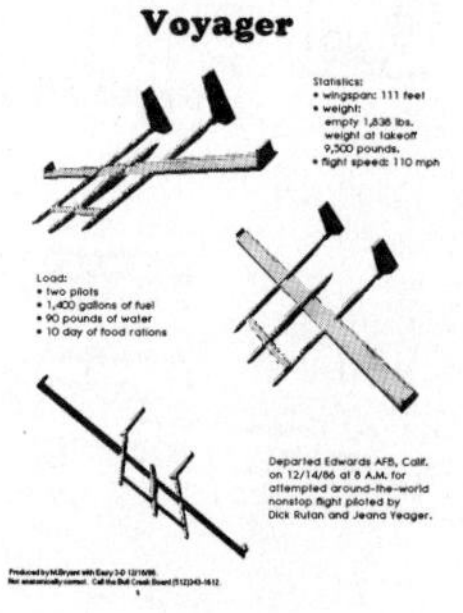

Transportation

Pictures U1

Geography

Map Pictures

Africa

Asia

Canada

Central America

CntyMapSample

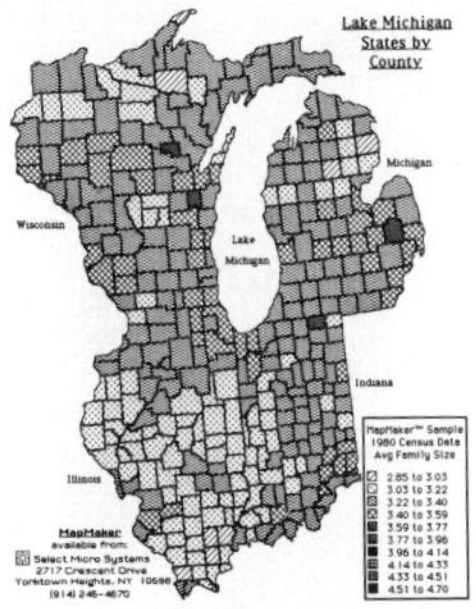

Europe

Globes

Hurricane Map

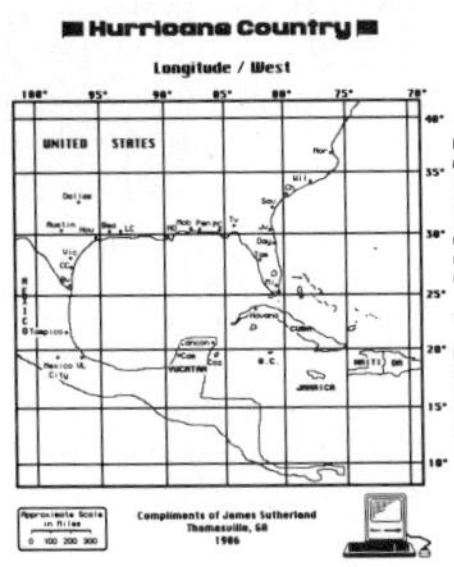

Kenya

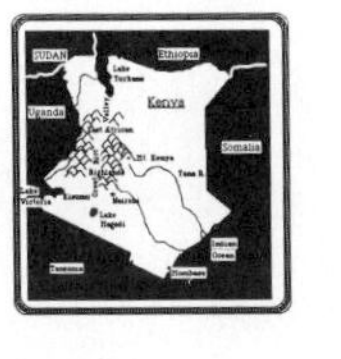

Louisiana

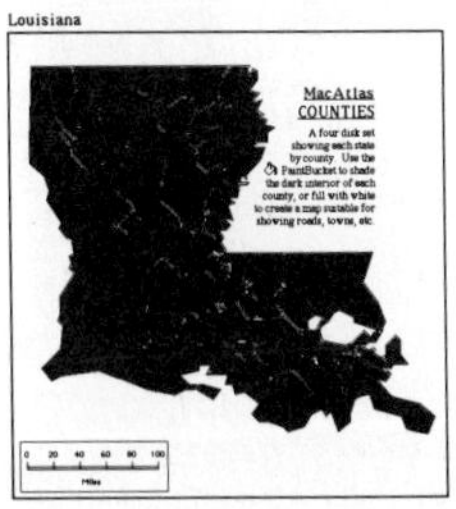

Louisiana Map

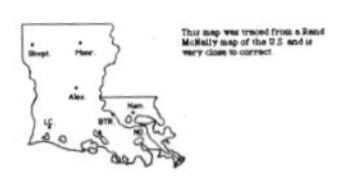

MapGrid

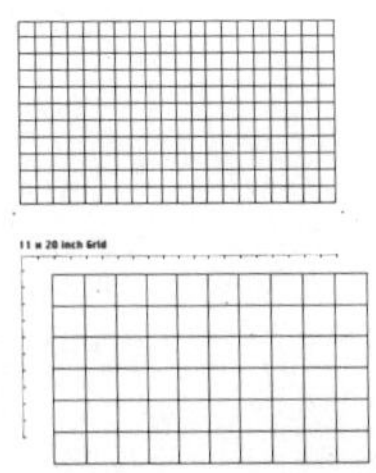

Pictures U1

Continued

MaptoBMUG

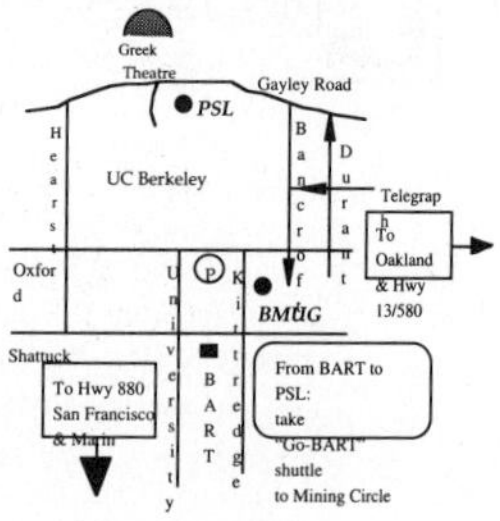

Massachusetts

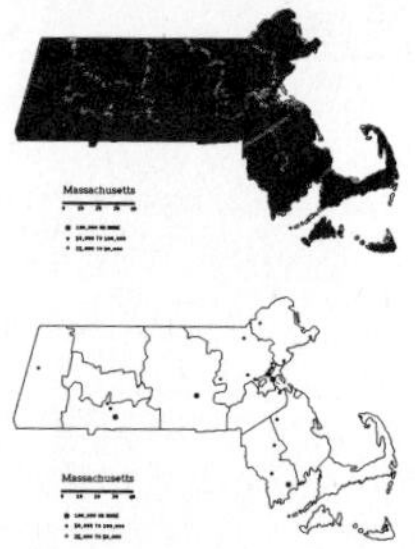

Michigan

Michigan][

New Hampshire

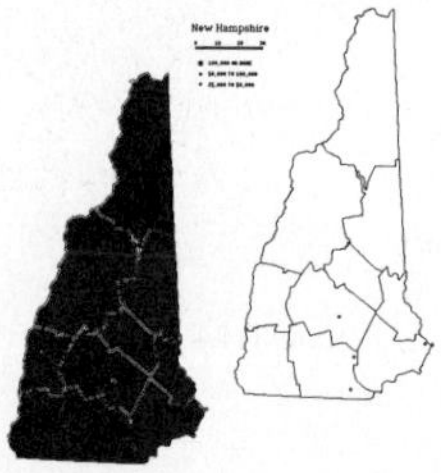

North America

South America

Texas

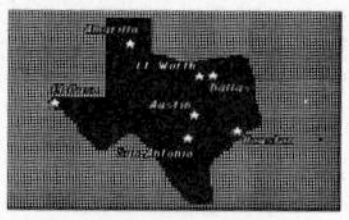

Texas2

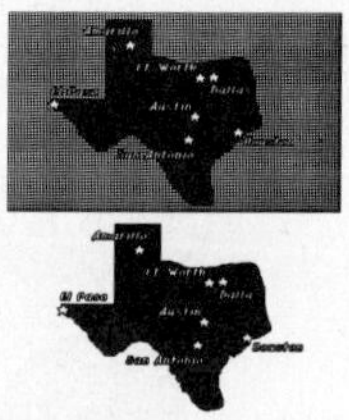

U.S. MAP

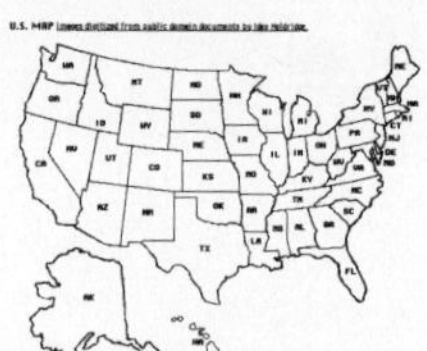

U. S. maps

US Map

Map Pictures

USA info

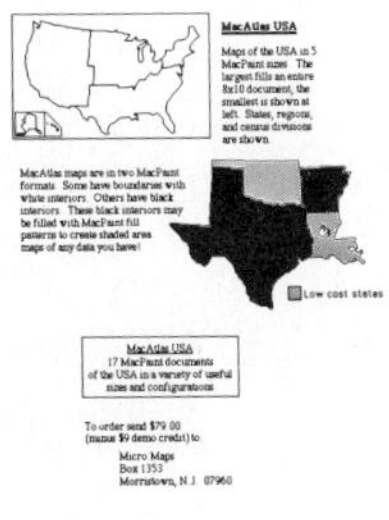

USA Paint Sample

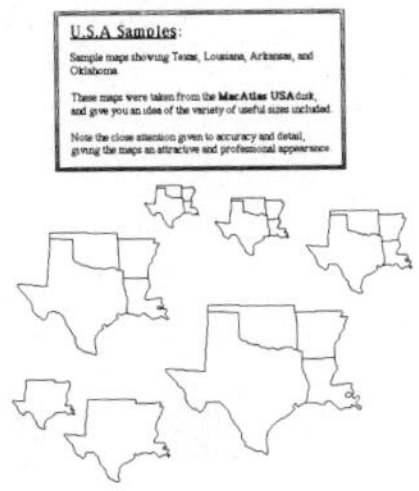

USMapSample

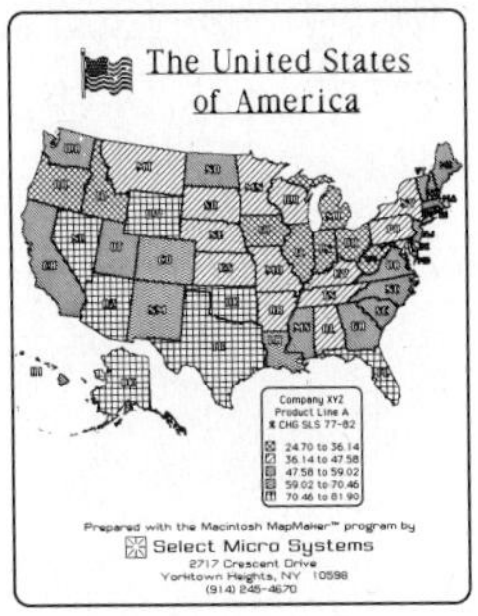

WORLD info

World Map

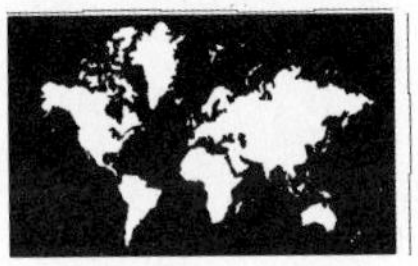

World Map2

WTS

Pictures V1

Computer Pictures

Apple Components

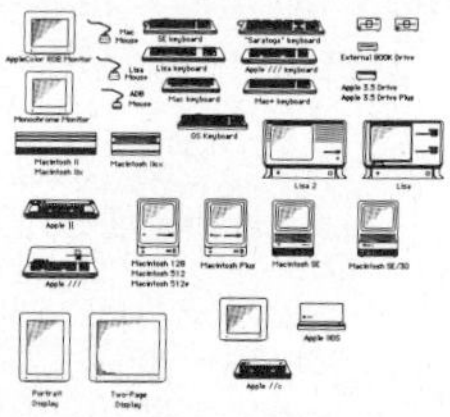

DataComm III

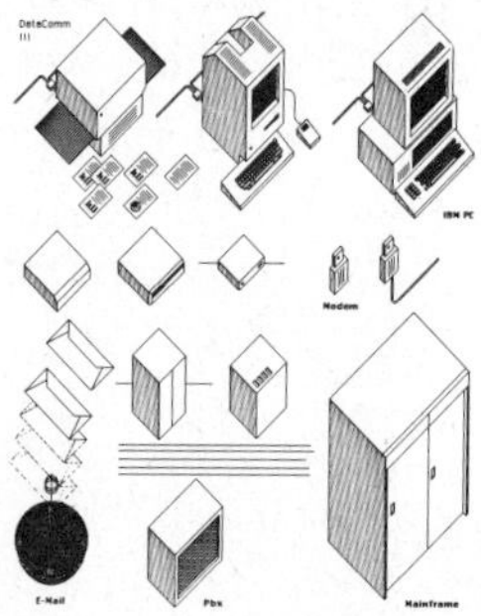

Desk Mac

Happy Mac Friends

Happy Mac work

Mac Portrait

Mac Reflection

Mac SE.SuprPnt

Mainframe

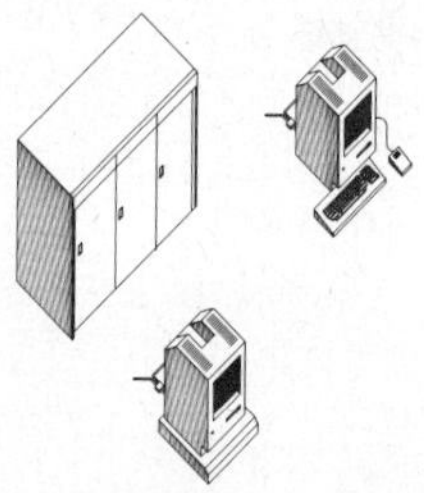

MiniMac

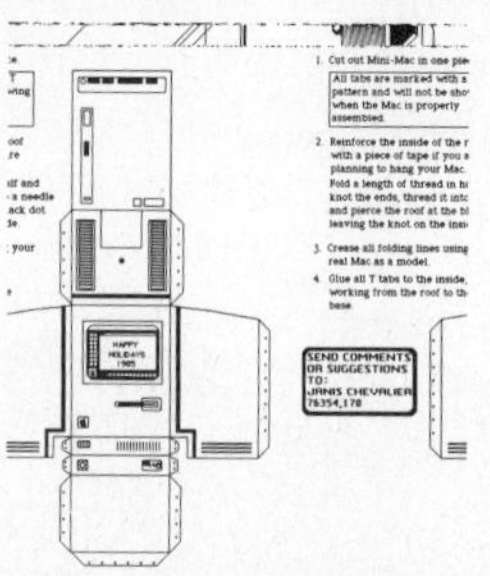

More Macs

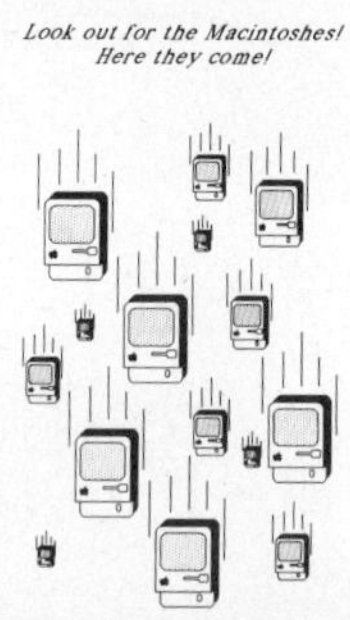

Test Drive

Programming

Tools for programmers of all levels.

Programming A1

Debugging Tools

MacBrowse™ v2.0b1

Description	Author	Info
Macintosh source code browser for developing object-oriented solutions. Parses Object Pascal, C++, or Object Modula-2 codes.	Mary Boetcher Apple Computer, Inc.	**Application** **Freeware** **Size: 461k**

MacsBug v6.2.1

Description	Author	Info
Debugging tool for programmers. Can be useful for nonprogrammers as well for getting out of crashes. Includes brief introductory instruction files.	Apple Computer, Inc.	**Debugger** **Freeware** **Size: 108k**

APL Interpreter

APL 90 v1.05

A demo version of APL90 interpreter.

J.J. Girardot
SYNC
12 Place Hôtel de Ville
42000 Saint-Etienne
FRANCE

Application
Shareware $40.00
Size: 330k

IAPL v1.1B

A free I-APL interpreter for the Macintosh. A manual in Microsoft Word format is included.

Ian A. Clark
Computer Ease-of-Use
9, Hill End, Frosterley,
BISHOP AUCKLAND,
Co.Durham, DL13 2SX
England, UK

Application
Freeware
Size: 253k

Programming C1

Lisp & Gambit Tools

ADX.LSP

A medical application package using XLisp. Lets you start with symptoms and arrive at diagnoses.

Silvio Marugg
CIS: 72037,606

Text Document
Freeware
Size: 150k

Gambit Compiler v1.51

The Gambit Compiler is used to compile a Scheme source program into a binary 'object file' that can either be loaded by the Gambit Interpreter or turned into a full fledged Macintosh application with the Gambit Linker.

Marc Feeley
feeley@cs.brandeis.edu

Application
Freeware
Size: 758k

Gambit Interpreter v1.51

The Gambit Interpreter is a Scheme interpreter that can be used to develop and debug Gambit Scheme programs. It conforms to the IEEE-Scheme standard as well as the R3.99RS report.

Marc Feeley
feeley@cs.brandeis.edu

Application
Freeware
Size: 229k

Gambit Linker v1.51

The Gambit Linker is used to build a Macintosh application program from a runtime library and an arbitrary number of object files produced by the Gambit compiler.

Marc Feeley
feeley@cs.brandeis.edu

Application
Freeware
Size: 5k

XLisp v2.0

XLISP is an experimental programming language combining some of the features of Common Lisp with an object-oriented extension capability.

David Betz
127 Taylor Road
Petersborough, NH 03458

Application
Freeware
Size: 117k

XLisp Tools

Some useful tools for use with XLisp.

Larry Mulcahy

Text Document
Freeware
Size: 119k

Harvest C v1.0

Shareware C compiler for the Macintosh. An integrated development environment, Harvest C is intended to be compatible with the MPW C compiler.

Eric W. Sink
1014 Pomona Drive
Champaign, Illinois 61821
Internet: e-sink@uiuc.edu

Application
Shareware $25.00
Size: 259k

Programming F1

Oberon

MacOberon v2.0

A complete Apple Macintosh II implementation of the new Oberon language and operating system, developed by Niklaus Wirth and Jürg Gutknecht. A large monitor is recommended. Two-disk set.

Michael S. Franz

Application
Freeware
Size: 263k

Programming G1

Forth

Alpha v4.01

A versatile text editor. many features including grep search and ACMDs. Designed for programmers.

Peter Keleher
P.O. Box 1892
Dept. of Computer Science
Rice University
Houston, TX 77251-1892

Application
Shareware $25.00
Size: 278k

Pocket Fourth v0.5

A small compiling interpreter for Forth language. Comes in Application and DA versions. Assembly source code is included.

Chris Heilman
Bitnet: heilman@pc
CIS: 70566-1474

Application
Freeware
Size: 15k

Programming H1

Simple Languages

CAfterDark

A Think C base class for writing graphics modules for Berkeley Systems' After Dark in terms of an object-based abstraction.

Jeff Francis
CS Student, University of Iowa
jfrancis@umaxc.weeg.uiowa.edu
(319) 354-0765

Text Document
Public Domain
Size: 2k

MacABC v1.02.01

ABC is an imperative language originally designed as a replacement for BASIC: interactive, very easy to learn, but structured, high-level, and easy to use. Not a system programming language.

Frank van Dijk, et al.
ABC Distribution
CWI/AA
Postbox 4079, 1009 AB
Amsterdam, The Netherlands
Internet: abc@cwi.nl

Application
Freeware
Size: 273k

MacLessonsInBasic v1.0

Illustrates the use of Microsoft QuickBasic language to draw geometrical figures on the screen.

Carl & Tina Sanders
400 S. Woods Ave.
Los Angeles, CA 90022
213-263-7617

Application
Freeware
Size: 146k

Yerk v3.6.1

A release of Yerk, an object-oriented language originally known as Neon, based on a Forth Kernel with some major modifications. The original Neon was developed by Kriya Systems. Two-disk set.

Bob Loewenstein
Dept. of Astronomy
University of Chicago
Yerkes Observatory
Williams Bay, Wisconsin
53191

Freeware
Size: 20k

Programming K1

Process Monitors

Corner v1.3

This system extension (INIT) gives you the exact cursor position in terms of horizontal and vertical coordinates.

Günther Blaschek
Petzoldstr. 31
A–4020 Linz
Austria / Europe
Bitnet: K331671@ALIJKU11

System Startup Extension
Freeware
Size: 3k

Monitor Process v2.0

This program keeps track of the processes (applications) that are currently running on your Macintosh under System 7. There are a few features to let you play with the processes. Source code included.

Matthew B. Evans
AOL: Spaceship

Application
Freeware
Size: 64k

String Magic v1.1

An application for creating and maintaining string resources. To take advantage of the symbolic names created by String Magic you must develop code using a C or C++ compiler, as the header files generated are in C preprocessor format.

Curt Sellmer
11028 Jollyville Road #342
Austin, TX 78759

Application
Freeware
Size: 76k

Swatch v1.2.2

Lets you view the heap usage using color coded bar graphs, and helps you track down heap bugs. Comes with an INIT that's needed only when running under pre-7 systems.

Joe Holt
Internet: jholt@adobe.com
America Online: Jholt
AppleLink: ADOBE.APDENG
(attn: joe)
(415) 962-2097

Application
Freeware
Size: 28k

TextTranslator v1.2

TextTranslator translates text files from Mac to DOS format and vice versa. Convenient in conjunction with utilities like Dana's DOS Mounter.

Tim Herzog
Produced by Two Bits Worth
198 Western Ave. N. Suite 301
Saint Paul, MN 55102
AOL: Hertim

Desk Accessory
Shareware $10.00
Size: 25k

Window Elephant v1.0d5

To be used with Think C 4.0 Debugger, it remembers where you have placed the source and data windows and restores their positions everytime the Debugger is launched.

dEVoN Hubbard
Reata Software, Inc.
AOL: REATA
AppleLink: REATA.SOFT

System Startup Extension
Freeware
Size: 12k

Sounds

BMUG's sounds library is divided into two parts—sound utilities and the sounds themselves.

Sound-Type Icons

Sound

SoundEdit

Sound

Studio Session

Unknown

Sounds A1

Sound Utilities

Chime v4.0.1

Plays a chime sound on the hour. Sound is stored as an 'snd ' resource, so you can set it to any available sound.

Robert Flickinger

System Startup Extension
Shareware $10.00
Size: 2k

Dawn™ v2.0.2

An INIT and cdev combination that lets you attach a sound to your startup screen(s).

Frank Price
AOC Software
612 Doheny Rd.
Beverly Hills, CA 90210

Control Panel Extension
Shareware $20.00
Size: 47k

Finder Sounds v1.3

A cdev that lets you tag sounds onto actions that you do in the Finder, including moving the mouse or copying files. It's completely configurable. Requires System 6.0.4 or above.

Greg Smith
Bucknell Computer Services
Bucknell University
Lewisburg, PA 17837

System Startup Extension
Freeware
Size: 7k

Format 1 vs Format 2 snds...

A text document explaining the difference between Mac II and HyperCard format sounds.

unknown

TeachText Document
Public Domain
Size: 2k

IBeep2 v2.31

For System 4.1 through 6.0.3 users. Pick sounds to be played at Eject Disk, Shut Down, or Restart.

Riccardo Ettore
67 rue de la limite
1970 W-Oppem
BELGIUM
(32 2) 7679217

Control Panel Extension
Shareware ?
Size: 11k

SndControl v1.1.1

Allows you to link sounds to Finder actions.

Riccardo Ettore
67 rue de la limite
1970 W-Oppem
BELGIUM
(32 2) 7679217

Control Panel Extension
Shareware $25.00
Size: 37k

Sound Mover v1.71

Copies sounds from one file to another, with an interface similar to that of the old Font/DA Mover. Translates many sound formats. Contains documentation within the program. Another must-have for the sound enthusiast.

Riccardo Ettore
67 rue de la limite
1970 W-Oppem
BELGIUM
(32 2) 7679217

Application
Shareware $25.00
Size: 27k

SoundMaster v1.7.2

Sets the sound played by your Mac at 11 different occasions: startup, shutdown, beep, disk insert, etc. Includes docs within the program. A must-have for all sound enthusiasts. Sounds for SoundMaster are on other disks in this section.

Bruce Tomlin
15801 Chase Hill Blvd. #109
San Antonio, TX 78256

Control Panel Extension
Shareware $15.00
Size: 27k

SuperPlay v4.0

Plays SoundCap sounds and turns them into sound resources. Lets you determine the shareware fee—whatever you think the program is worth. Has docs in a separate file. Works with System 7.

John Raymonds
21738 Barbara Street
Torrance, CA 90503

Application
Shareware $?
Size: 16k

Sounds A2

Sound Utilities

Eliza v1.3

Carries on a simple conversation in English between a psychiatrist (the Mac) and a patient (you). Requires MacinTalk. It's based on the classic program by Joseph Weizenbaum.

Charles Hayden
438 River Road
Fair Haven, NJ 07701

Application
Public Domain
Size: 21k

Fonts(Toys1/Toys2)

Fonts for use with TalkingKeys DA, also on this disk.

unknown

Fond/DA Mover
Suitcase
Freeware

MacinTalk v1.31

Speech synthesis driver developed by Apple but no longer officially supported. Utility programs and sample source code are included. Required for most applications that use computer-generated speech.

Apple Computer, Inc.

System File
Freeware
Size: 28k

MacinTalk v2.0

Newer version of the classic text vocalization program, can handle the new SoundManager (System 6.0.7+). Some older programs that need MacinTalk don't work with this; for those use the older version (above).

Apple Computer, Inc.

System File
Freeware
Size: 35k

Moose Frazer v1.0b1

Creates a library of phrases for use with the Talking Moose desk accessory.

Jan Eugenides
PO Box 151
Maynard, MA 01754

Application
Public Domain
Size: 9k

Phonetic Chart

Chart of phonetics for the MacinTalk speech synthesis resource.

unknown

MacWrite Document
Public Domain
Size: 10k

SpeechLab v3.0

Library for MS BASIC programs to allow access to the speech synthesis capabilities of MacinTalk. Docs and assembly language code included.

Kevin J. Willey
4453 Stonecastle Dr. #1102
Dayton, OH 45440
(513) 426-2329

Application
Freeware
Size: 12k

Talking Moose v2.0

A small moose periodically pops up on your desktop and speaks a phrase. Use the Moose Frazer to make a library of phrases. The Meese file is the icon shown in this listing.

Steve Hall
11135 - 50th Ave.
Edmonton, Alberta
T6H 0J1 CANADA

Control Panel Extension
Public Domain
Size: 72k

TalkingKeys v1.1

Speaks each letter as it is typed. Can also speak entire words. Docs in a separate file. Doesn't work with Talking Moose.

Brady Graham
8609 Ingalls Circle
Arvada, CO 80003
CIS: 72376,3327

Desk Accessory
Shareware $15.00
Size: 10k
12" 6 7 32

Sounds A3

Sound Utilities

A.B. Speaks v1.1

Displays the alphabet and speaks the letter clicked on. Also can verbally prompt you to click on a particular letter. Good for small children.

Ed Neu
6761 Deerwood Lane North
Maple Grove, MN 55369

Application
Shareware $5.00
Size: 20k

AppleTones v2.0

Lets user compose music using 12 pre-made building block sounds. Includes docs within the program. Good for learning about repetition, silence, volume, and timbre changes in musical composition.

John R. Meier &
Jon Appleton
Music Department
Dartmouth College
Hanover, NH 03755

Application
Freeware
Size: 71k

CheapBeep v1.0a

Changes the beep sound on your Mac.

Mark P. Bennett

Control Panel
Extension
Freeware
Size: 9k

IgniSound v1.2

Plays a sound when you turn on your Mac.

Steve Bollinger
4297 Sulgrave Drive
Swartz Creek, MI 48473
CIS: 71620,740

Control Panel
Extension
Shareware $10.00
Size: 6k

MacII Beep

Allows you to change the beep sound on a Mac II.

unknown

System Startup
Extension
Public Domain
Size: 2k

Max Yes Master

Plays sound of Max Headroom saying 'Yes, Master.'

Leo Laporte

Application
Public Domain
Size: 18k

Mr. Ed

Plays sound of Mr. Ed, the talking horse, saying 'Hello, I'm Mr. Ed.'

Leo Laporte

Application
Public Domain
Size: 40k

Play Sound v1.0

Plays sounds at 4 different sampling rates. Lets you adjust volume from within the DA.

Claude Johnson
249 Springhill
Rosemère, Québec
J7A 3G2 CANADA

Desk Accessory
Shareware $5.00
Size: 7k

Sounder v1.0

Plays a classic sound at bootup when placed in System Folder. Use ResEdit to change the sound.

Kevin Parichan

System Startup Extension
Freeware
Size: 9k

SpeakIt

Speaks phrases typed into a dialog box. Also reads phrases from a text file.

unknown

Application
Public Domain
Size: 30k

Zippy v1.0

Zippy hangs out in the background and enlightens you with his random words of wisdom. Designed to run as a background application under MultiFinder. MacinTalk is required.

Chuck Shotton
c/o BIAP Systems
PO Box 580622
Houston, TX 77258-0622

Application
Freeware
Size: 24k

Sounds A4

Sound Utilities

BeepINIT

INIT 31

Changes the beep sound on your Mac. Comes with 3 beeps.

Bill Steinberg
John Hardis

System Startup Extension
Public Domain
Size: 4k

ByebyeINIT

Plays a sound when you shut down your Mac. Shareware fee is a donation to your favorite local BBS.

Jim Nitchals
CIS: 71001,2232

System Startup Extension
Shareware $?
Size: 14k

MacTalker

Speaks phrases typed into a dialog box. Also reads phrases from a text file. Includes docs within the program. Needs MacinTalk in the System Folder to work. Comes with several phrases and sounds.

James Joaquin
Viking Technologies, Inc.
PO Box 299
Newport, RI 02840

Desk Accessory
Freeware
Size: 20k

SoundInit

INIT 31

Plays a sound when you start up your Mac. Comes with two sounds.

Bill Steinberg
John Hardis

System Startup Extension
Public Domain
Size: 4k

Utilities
Sounds

Sound Input Device

SID is the complete schematic and source code for building a sound input device for recording sounds and manipulating them on your Mac. Includes testing software. Requires about $60 worth of hardware.	Eric Gould Jeffrey Siegel	**Various File Types** **Freeware** **Size: 183k** 12" 6 7 32

Stand-Alone Grouch v2.5B2

This version of The Grouch is childproof. It does not modify the Finder and draws the animation in a window instead of on the desktop. It does not require the The Grouch extension to be present.	Eric Shapiro Rock Ridge Enterprises 620 Hidden Valley #102 Ann Arbor, MI 48104	**Application** **Freeware** **Size: 313k** 12" 6 7 32

The Grouch v2.5B1

'Oscar The Grouch' is a little guy who lives in your trash can and comes out to visit whenever you empty your trash. From the Sesame Street character.	Eric Shapiro Rock Ridge Enterprises 620 Hidden Valley #102 Ann Arbor, MI 48104	**System Startup Extension** **Freeware** **Size: 314k** 12" 6 7 32

Sounds S1

Sounds

A Little Button

Size: 35k

It's Easy for you...

Size: 36k

Like, wow, man...

Size: 22k

Look, up in the Sky

Size: 101k

Thunder

Size: 277k

Twilight Zone

Size: 266k

Sounds S2

Sounds

Boom
Size: 7k

Dragnet
Size: 169k

Echoes
Size: 64k

F Troop
Size: 56k

Floyd Bells
Size: 91k

Gong
Size: 45k

I Know his Name !
Size: 17k

Number 9
Size: 61k

Screams
Size: 86k

Trying to Think
Size: 32k

Woob Woob
Size: 21k

Yabba Dabba Doo
Size: 66k

Sounds S3

Sounds

Back Off!!

Size: 81k

Dr. Who Theme

Size: 142k

Feed Me All Night Long

Size: 70k

Here's looking at you, kid

Size: 48k

Horse Race

Size: 41k

Knock

Size: 20k

Rooster sound

Size: 38k

That's the machine

Size: 95k

Wecome

Size: 206k

AM/FM Beep
Size: 12k

Arcade Beep
Size: 6k

Ayaaaah!
Size: 13k

Baby sound
Size: 12k

Bassoon & 'Bone Beep
Size: 23k

Beep1
Size: 3k

Boo
Size: 6k

Boom! Ooooh...
Size: 13k

Casio Beep(try me)
Size: 6k

Chimes
Size: 18k

Chimes#2
Size: 19k

Comedy Horn Beep
Size: 8k

Computers
Size: 17k

Danger, Danger
Size: 11k

Door
Size: 8k

Double Sine Beep
Size: 6k

Drop of Water Beep
Size: 3k

Drums
Size: 34k

Extra Special
Size: 44k

FM Beep
Size: 12k

Game over, Man
Size: 13k

Harp-Arppegio
Size: 8k

Hey
Size: 7k

Hey#2
Size: 5k

Sounds S4

Continued

Hey#3
Size: 15k

Horn
Size: 15k

Horn#2
Size: 12k

Jazz Piano Beep
Size: 13k

Kind Warning Beep
Size: 15k

Laughing Warning Beep
Size: 62k

Metal Beep
Size: 9k

Monkey
Size: 3k

Multi-Beep
Size: 11k

No, Will Robinson!
Size: 11k

Oh Bother
Size: 33k

Organ Minor Chord
Size: 9k

Pipe Organ
Size: 15k

Pure Saw Beep
Size: 4k

Robotic Beep
Size: 8k

Shot
Size: 11k

Space Code Beep
Size: 9k

Space Cookies 11k
Size: 14k

Spring Beep
Size: 23k

Square Mod Beep
Size: 8k

Steel-Drum
Size: 4k

Strings
Size: 21k

Strings#2
Size: 7k

Vulcan Mind
Size: 17k

Wail-Guitar

Size: 9k

Wow

Size: 9k

Was It. . ?

Size: 64k

Sounds S5

Sounds

Buse

Size: 67k

Chaocard à tête Jaune

Size: 69k

Choucas

Size: 68k

Grand Corbeau

Size: 193k

MartinetAlpin

Size: 118k

Tétras Lyre

Size: 78k

Ding (old version)

Size: 60k

Ship Horns

Size: 189k

Tic Tac

Size: 44k

Wild Wild West(11hz)

Size: 39k

Jets

Size: 122k

Taxi Horns

Size: 173k

Vacuum Cleaner

Size: 101k

Sounds S7

Sounds

Any Body say Bang

Size: 186k

Cuckoo Clock

Size: 76k

Han han han

Size: 32k

Mah Na Mah Na

Size: 19k

slice of Mah Na Mah Na

Size: 33k

Cuckoo

Size: 6k

Flash 1

Size: 30k

Looney Toon

Size: 119k

Mood Music

Size: 174k

Tu tu tu

Size: 55k

Sounds

Ah.Sound
Size: 6k

Bad disk
Size: 24k

Bark.Sound
Size: 2k

Be back.Sound
Size: 12k

Beep
Size: 8k

Beep sound
Size: 31k

Bells of Eternity
Size: 6k

Bomb
Size: 26k

Disk eject
Size: 6k

Disk Ejection
Size: 32k

Disk Insert
Size: 41k

Disk insert.2
Size: 12k

Disk request
Size: 16k

DragnetBeep
Size: 27k

E.T. Phone Home!
Size: 30k

Eject
Size: 9k

Eject disk
Size: 16k

Game over.Sound
Size: 13k

Insert disk
Size: 17k

Keaggy beep
Size: 20k

Key click
Size: 2k

Oops.Sound
Size: 6k

phoneRing
Size: 24k

PWscream.Sound
Size: 6k

Sounds S8

Continued

Reboot

Size: 17k

Request

Size: 16k

Restart

Size: 28k

Shut down

Size: 8k

Shutdown

Size: 22k

ShutDown sound

Size: 19k

Startup

Size: 62k

Startup sound

Size: 36k

Trying to think.Sound

Size: 32k

Turn Me On...

Size: 21k

Tympani Beep

Size: 20k

Type Key

Size: 3k

Type Return

Size: 5k

Type Space

Size: 4k

TypeKey.Sound

Size: 2k

TypeReturn.Sound

Size: 7k

TypeSpace.Sound

Size: 2k

Welcome.2

Size: 19k

Ac Guitar Hi
Size: 9k

Ac Guitar Lo
Size: 9k

Ac Guitar Maj
Size: 10k

Ac Guitar Min
Size: 9k

Are you sure...
Size: 45k

Bass Guitar Long
Size: 13k

Bass Hi
Size: 10k

Bass Lo
Size: 10k

Crash Cymbal
Size: 12k

E Bass
Size: 8k

Electric Piano 13
Size: 14k

Electric Piano Lo
Size: 7k

Electric Piano Min3
Size: 11k

Fiddle Hi
Size: 16k

Fiddle Short(D4)
Size: 3k

Fiddle Short(G2)
Size: 4k

Fiddle Short(G3)
Size: 4k

Fiddle Short(G4)
Size: 5k

Flute Hi
Size: 19k

Flute Lo
Size: 11k

Flute Mid
Size: 14k

Fuzz Bass
Size: 10k

Greensleeves
Size: 2k

Guitar
Size: 14k

Sounds S9

Continued

Guitar 7
Size: 19k

Guitar(D Maj.)
Size: 9k

Guitar(E min.)
Size: 12k

Guitar(G Maj.)
Size: 11k

HiHatClosed
Size: 2k

HiHatOpen
Size: 8k

Jaw Harp
Size: 9k

Jazz Snare
Size: 2k

Kick+Hat
Size: 9k

Liverpool
Size: 2k

MChop (Lo 5th)
Size: 4k

MDouble bend
Size: 23k

Mguitar Bent 3rd
Size: 14k

Mguitar G3
Size: 16k

Mguitar Hi 4th
Size: 23k

Mguitar Hi Sustain
Size: 16k

MHi-hat
Size: 4k

MKick+Hat
Size: 9k

New Snare
Size: 10k

Orbit
Size: 24k

Rock Snare
Size: 4k

Rooster
Size: 17k

Slide(Pick)
Size: 13k

Snare Normal
Size: 7k

Solo Guitar
Size: 2k

Steel Short
Size: 4k

Synth Shot
Size: 9k

Tenor Hi
Size: 12k

Tombone Lo
Size: 6k

Tombone Mid 2
Size: 5k

Whirl
Size: 16k

Sound of Music
Size: 85k

Synth Bass
Size: 8k

Synth Spring
Size: 12k

Tombone Hi
Size: 3k

Tombone Mid
Size: 4k

Turkey
Size: 7k

Whoosh
Size: 18k

Sounds S11

Sounds

10,000 Marbles
Size: 23k

20 Seconds
Size: 27k

Are you sure...
Size: 45k

Blistered Fingers
Size: 29k

Error, Error
Size: 80k

Expresso...
Size: 87k

Gas Music
Size: 31k

Hallucinating
Size: 34k

Only Knowledge Erased
Size: 86k

The real story
Size: 59k

Turn Me On...
Size: 21k

You Know What ...
Size: 133k

Zzt.snd
Size: 59k

Sounds S12

Sounds

Aliens have landed

Size: 65k

Beware!

Size: 64k

Energy Field

Size: 117k

Everything you know...

Size: 98k

Gollee/eddie 11K

Size: 10k

Hello Seekers...

Size: 134k

No SEX!

Size: 78k

Ranyanaaannnee

Size: 84k

Stranger/Breakfast

Size: 39k

Tennis!?

Size: 15k

Sounds S13

Sounds

20thCenturyFox

Size: 329k

Inquisition

Size: 193k

To the Batmobile

Size: 196k

A Bomb!

Size: 284k

Bomb! Expecting One?

Size: 67k

GhostBuster Rap

Size: 48k

Nuts!

Size: 51k

Better Boing

Size: 8k

Bomb intended for me!

Size: 90k

Hi There/Bundle of kicks

Size: 101k

Special Delivery - a bomb!

Size: 53k

Sounds S15

Sounds

Bring out your dead
Size: 111k

Bumpy Night
Size: 51k

Can'touch this
Size: 88k

Come out to the coast
Size: 36k

EatMyShorts
Size: 11k

Fanfare #1
Size: 74k

Fanfare #2
Size: 104k

Holy Zarquon's Singing Fish!
Size: 33k

I am livin' on Channel Z 11k
Size: 41k

Ordering Pizza?
Size: 17k

Seen Temptation Comin'
Size: 38k

Strange Things...
Size: 34k

Take the bones out
Size: 48k

Telecom

Tools for connecting your Mac to the outside world with a modem.

Telecom A1

ZTerm, etc.

Alice v1.0E

This software is a message reader. To use it, you log on to your favorite BBS (which must support XRS packet format), then download the latest messages in compressed XRS form.

Michael Keller
Mine Design
Voglersheck 15, W-6349
Greifenstein 5
GERMANY

Application
Shareware $10.00
Size: 211k

Batch Binary v0.90

Converts MacBinary files placed in a folder into Mac-formatted files.

Eric Larson
2902 Falls Road
Marcellus, NY 13108
Fidonet: 260/330.0

Application
Shareware $25.00
Size: 25k

CommCloser

CommCloser is a program to close comm ports left open by crashed applications. To use, just run it and pick the appropriate port. It's fairly obvious what to do. One thing to remember: Never close a comm port that's being used.

Russ Nelson
2108 SW Laurel Street
Portland, OR 97201
nelson@catlin.bitnet

Application
Freeware
Size: 11k

Compact Pro v1.32

Compresses and decompresses faster than any other Mac archiver; files' sizes often smaller than StuffIt. Make sure to get SitToCPT if you need to convert StuffIt archives to Compact Pro archives.

Bill Goodman
109 Davis Avenue
Brookline, MA 02146
CIS: 71101,204

Application
Shareware $25.00
Size: 101k

IIfx Serial Switch v1.0

IIfx Serial Switch modifies the serial ports on the Mac IIfx so that they work like the standard Mac serial ports.

Apple Computer, Inc.

Control Panel
Extension
Freeware
Size: 3k

Mac to MacBinary v1.0

A fast and easy way to convert large numbers of Mac-formatted files to MacBinary format. It's a translator for Apple's Macintosh File Translator.

Richard L. Trethewey
PEEK[65]
PO Box 586
Pacifica, CA 94044

AFEdocument
Shareware $5.00
Size: 17k

MacBinary v1.0.1

Converter for files downloaded from computers that do not properly translate MacBinary format files into a standard Mac file. Docs in a separate file.

Gregory J. Smith

Application
Freeware
Size: 17k

MacBinary to Mac v1.0

A fast and easy way to convert MacBinary-formatted files to Mac format. It's a translator for Apple's Macintosh File Translator.

Richard L. Trethewey
PEEK[65]
PO Box 586
Pacifica, CA 94044

AFEdocument
Shareware $5.00
Size: 17k

MacWoof v1.2

MacWoof™ is software that lets you read and send EchoMail and NetMail messages from your Mac. You can set MacWoof to dial and request messages automatically, then read and reply to them at your leisure off-line, thus saving phone bills, etc.

Craig Vaughan
PO Box 2932
Merrifield, VA 22116

Application
Shareware $25.00
Size: 200k
12" 6 7 32

MCS v1.1

A Multichannel Communications System that allows file transfers over noisy phone lines using a proprietary protocol that permits simultaneous download, upload, and chat using different channels. MacBinary II format is used for file transfers.

Yves Lempereur
5311-B Derry Avenue
Agoura Hills, CA 91301

Application
Shareware $15.00
Size: 12k
12" 6 7 32

MultiXfer v0.60

A program designed to transfer files in a queue from one Mac to another. A bit clunky but it works.

Martin Dubuc
U. de Montréal
Montréal, Québec
H3C 3J7 CANADA

Application
Freeware
Size: 47k
12" 6 7 32

spconfig_reset

Resets your serial port on your Mac.

unknown

Application
Freeware
Size: 2k
12" 6 7 32

UnZip v1.10

Docs say it can decompress PKZIP archives versions 1.10, 1.02, 1.01, and 0.92.

Mike O'Connor, et al.
CIS: 76004,1447

Application
Freeware
Size: 50k
12" 6 7 32

zapParam™ 1.0a1 v1.0a1

zapParam wipes out parameter RAM settings stored in your Mac. These settings include mouse speed, double-click speed, menu flash, startup drive, and other settings such as serial port protocols.

Devon Hubbard
Reach Software Corp.

Control Panel
Extension
Freeware
Size: 27k

ZTerm v0.9

Telecom program that features ZModem, YModem, and XModem file transfers; VT100 terminal emulation; ANSI screen control; and a scrollback buffer. This version also does scripting. Comprehensive docs in a separate file.

David P. Alverson
5635 Cross Creek Court
Mason, OH 45040

Application
Shareware $30.00
Size: 197k
12" 6 7 32

Freddie v1.1

An off-line message reader for BBSes.To use this program, the host BBS system must support QWK format packets.

Kem Tekinay
c/o Mondore
75-05 64th Place
Glendale, NY 11385

Application
Shareware $15.00
Size: 824k

OneNet User v1.6

Front-end software for a very promising BBS system called First Class. If you've ever logged on to an MS-DOS-based BBS, you will appreciate the entirely Mac-like interface of this.

SoftArc, Inc.
805 Middlefield Rd., Suite 102
Scarborough, Ontario
MIV 2T9 CANADA

Application
Freeware
Size: 303k

ArcMac v1.2a

An archiving program for transferring files between the Mac and IBM machines. Comes with XARCMAC.EXE and ArcPop.Arc, a Mac archiving program.

D. G. Gilbert
dogStar Software
PO Box 302
Bloomington, IN 47402

Application
Shareware $25.00
Size: 94k

DDExpand™ v3.7

The expand-only version of Disk Doubler, a commercial compression/archiving program.

Salient Software, Inc.
3101 Avalon Court
Palo Alto, CA 94306-3018
(415) 852-9567

Application
Freeware
Size: 134k

EXTRACT.EXE

ExtractorPC: MS DOS utility for unarchiving Macintosh Compact Pro files.

Bill Goodman
109 Davis Avenue
Brookline, MA 02146

MS Works 2.0
Text Document
Freeware
Size: 0k

Extractor v1.20

This program decompresses Compact Pro archives. Can also convert StuffIt 1.5.1 archives.

Bill Goodman
109 Davis Avenue
Brookline, MA 02146
CIS: 71101,204

Application
Freeware
Size: 41k

Fernmail v1.0

An application for reading and sending E-mail via UUCP. 'It is intended to be compatible with UUCP 2.1 (and its pcmail reader/sender application) and Mac/gnuucp (and its MailReader stack).'

Dave Platt
Snulbug Software
1095 Burboyne Street
Mountain View, CA 94043
dplatt@snulbug.mtview.ca.us

Application
Shareware $20.00
Size: 128k

Mac/gnuucp v4.3

A communications program for talking with gnuucp 2.1 sites. Assumes that you have a full 8-bit connection to the remote site. MailReader, on this disk, is the communications front end for this program.

Fort Pond Research
15 Fort Pond Road
Acton, MA 01720
(508) 263-9692

Application
Shareware $20.00
Size: 63k

MacBooz v2.1

Utility to decompress Zoo format archives. (Zoo format is normally used on platforms other than Macintosh.) Also converts text files from UNIX/VMS to Mac format.

Michael Niehaus
Rural Route 1
Box 369
Ferdinand, IN 47532

Application
Freeware
Size: 24k

MacLHa v2.00

LHarc for the Mac. Handles both normal and MacBinary archives.

Kazuaki Ishizaki
CIS: 74340,13
ishiz@muraok.waseda.ac.jp

Application
Freeware
Size: 63k

Telecom B1

Continued

MailReader v4.3

A HyperCard stack front end for Mac/gnuucp (also on this disk). With this stack you can communicate with multiple users on a gnuucp cpu, users on a local area network, etc. (Part of the Mac/gnuucp package.)

Fort Pond Research
15 Fort Pond Road
Acton, MA 01720
(508) 263-9692

HyperCard Stack
Shareware $20.00
Size: 94k

SitToCpt

SitToCpt is a utility for converting archives created by StuffIt into Compactor archives.

Bill Goodman
109 Davis Avenue
Brookline, MA 02146
CIS: 71101,204

Application
Freeware
Size: 28k

UnArjMac v2.21

A simple port of unarj.c to the Mac. Makes minimal use of Mac features.

Robert K. Jung
Village Road West
Norwood, MA 02062
CIS: 72077,445

Application
Freeware
Size: 34k

UNPACKIT.EXE

MS-DOS utility for unarchiving Macintosh PackIt files.

R. (Scott) McGinnis
Merchandise Mart
PO Box 3607
Chicago, IL 60654-0607

MS Works 2.0
Text Document
Shareware $10.00
Size: 10k

UNSIT.EXE v2.3

MS-DOS utility for unarchiving Macintosh StuffIt files.

Brian K. Uechi
GEnie: B.UECHI
CIS: 72330,155

MS Works 2.0
Text Document
Freeware
Size: 21k

USENET Info

Information on USENET, including a list of conference areas, a list of public access UNIX sites, USENET etiquette, and a Q & A file.

unknown

MS Works 2.0
Text Document
Freeware
Size: 262k

btoa/atob Translator v1.0

btoa and atob are UNIX filters that convert 8-bit binary data to 7-bit ASCII data for transmission across channels which only support 7-bit ASCII data. This file is an external module for StuffIt Deluxe.

Raymond Lau

StuffIt Deluxe
Document
Freeware
Size: 9k
12" 6 7 32

MacBinary Translator

This file is an external module for StuffIt Deluxe for encoding and decoding MacBinary-format files.

unknown

StuffIt Deluxe
Document
Freeware
Size: 7k
12" 6 7 32

StuffIt Classic™ v1.6

File compression program that has become the standard on most bulletin boards. A must-have program. Excellent docs in a separate file.

Raymond Lau

Application
Shareware $20.00
Size: 370k
12" 6 7 32

UnStuffIt Deluxe v2.0

UnStuffIt Deluxe uncompresses all StuffIt archives from StuffIt 1.5.1 through StuffIt Deluxe v.2.0.x.

D. Lovato and R. Lau

Application
Freeware
Size: 125k
12" 6 7 32

Telecom D1

UNIX Utilities

BinHex v4.0

Converts files back and forth between binary format and ASCII text format. Useful for transferring files via computers such as mainframes, which do not understand the Macintosh file format.

Yves Lemperuer
28611B Canwood Street
Agoura Hills, CA 91301
(818) 991-6540

Application
Shareware $10.00
Size: 8k

BinHqx v1.02

This program will decode .HQX files.

Rainbow Software
1233-A 7th Avenue
Honolulu, HI 96816

Desk Accessory
Shareware $5.00
Size: 23k

IconUX v1.0

Icon-based front end for UNIX host connections.

Lee Atchison
947 Willowleaf Drive #1302
San Jose, CA 95128
CIS: 73627,2512

Application
Shareware $45.00
Size: 93k

Kermit v0.9(40)

Terminal emulation program (VT100, VT102) that supports the Kermit file transfer protocol developed at Columbia University.

Bill Catchings, et al.
Columbia University
New York, NY

Application
Freeware
Size: 126k

MacCompress v3.2

A compression program that can work on Unix 'compress' format files. Ideal for transferring files between the Mac and UNIX.

Lloyd L. Chambers
PO Box 3442
Stanford, CA 94309

Application
Freeware
Size: 56k

MacLayers v1.0

Provides multiple windows for a Mac connected to a UNIX host.

David W. Trissel

Application
Freeware
Size: 125k

suntar v1.1

suntar is the cheapest way to transfer data between a Macintosh and a UNIX workstation, if a few hardware requirements are met. Use to transfer data from SPARCstations to SuperDrives, tape, etc.

Sauro and Gabriele Speranza
via Cappuccini 18
40026 Imola
ITALY

Application
Freeware
Size: 67k

tar v2.0

Reads and writes tar format archives. Supports different volumes, printing of archive contents, better screen output (for archive contents), and an improved directory selection dialog. Many other features.

Craig Ruff and John Gilmore

Application
Public Domain
Size: 34k

UULite v1.2

A uudecoder. It features multipart file handling and automatic header removal.

Jeff Strobel
260 Greenbrook Drive
Stoughton, MA 02072

Application
Shareware $29.00
Size: 108k

UUTool v2.0.3

An implementation of the 'uuencode' and 'uudecode' binary to text file utilities for the Mac, written by Bernie Wieser. Use to translate binary files into text; compatible with many UNIX implementations.

Octavian Micro Development
10516 Bradbury Drive SW
Calgary, Alberta
T2W 1A6 CANADA

Application
Freeware
Size: 18k
12" 6 7 32

UUTool v2.0.3ç

French version of UUTool 2.0.3, also on this disk.

Octavian Micro Development
10516 Bradbury Drive SW
Calgary, Alberta
T2W 1A6 CANADA

Application
Freeware
Size: 18k
12" 6 7 32

Telecom E1

Text and Graphics Import and Export

FileTyper v1.0.1

Drag a file onto this little gem, and you can edit its file attributes! Neat idea.

Daniel Azuma
21370 Homestead Road
Cupertino, CA 95014-0292

Application
Freeware
Size: 12k

FixSigs

This program changes the file signature of a collection of files dropped on it. One of the Imagery Utilities Package programs.

Jeff Lewis
CIS: 76217,2241
AOL: T Werewolf

Application
Freeware
Size: 6k

GIFConverter v2.2d1

Converts PICT and GIF files to many other formats.

Kevin A. Mitchell
PO Box 803066
Chicago, IL 60680-3066

Application
Shareware $40.00
Size: 284k

Giffer v1.12

Views color pictures. Supports GIF (CompuServe's Graphic Interchange Format) and Mac PICT formats.

Steve Blackstock
40 Bartlett Avenue
Lexington, MA 02173
CIS: 73270,1150

Application
Shareware $20.00
Size: 121k

HeidiTools

A collection of file format conversion utilities for Mac users who exchange data with users of MS-DOS and UNIX-based computers. Provides a convenient front end for those tools, and on-line help to explain the basics.

Biscuit City Software
38 Chamber Street
Newark, DE 19711
(302) 368-1949

HyperCard Stack
Freeware
Size: 216k

HexDump

This program simply dumps any file into a file containing the file's hexadecimal and ASCII representations with the offset from the start of the file (zero) in hexadecimal. One of the Imagery Utilities Package programs.

Jeff Lewis
CIS: 76217,2241
AOL: T Werewolf

Application
Freeware
Size: 27k

Imagery v1.5

A utility that converts a range of graphics files from the IBM PC, Atari ST, UNIX and Amiga computers. The program generates standard TIFF files in TIFF 4.0/5.0 format compatible with many drawing and editing programs.

Jeff Lewis
CIS: 76217,2241
AOL: T Werewolf

Application
Freeware
Size: 103k

JPEG v0.5

A stand-alone JPEG-to-GIF and GIF- to-JPEG converter, meant as an intermediate utility until JPEG support can be added to Imagery. 'There are a number of known and serious problems with this program…use at your own risk.'

Jeff Lewis
CIS: 76217,2241
AOL: T Werewolf

Application
Freeware
Size: 82k

JustPrint

Comes with GIFConverter. Prints out any GLUE format documents.

Kevin A. Mitchell
PO Box 803066
Chicago, IL 60680-3066

Application
Freeware
Size: 4k

Macify v2.8

Transforms text files into a Mac-like form. Can change standard quotes into curly quotes, remove carriage returns, convert spaces runs to tabs, and more. Docs within the program. Very nice. Also comes with Help stack.

Eric Celeste
358 North Parkview
Columbus, OH 43209

Application
Shareware $10.00
Size: 41k

McSink v7.0A

The shareware version of the Vantage DA. Great little editing program; became commercial because it was so well liked. Even comes with 'VCMD' files that behave like macros.

Preferred Software
5100 Poplar Avenue #617
Memphis, TN 38171
(800) 46-6393

Desk Accessory
Shareware $45.00
Size: 93k

TIFF-Fix

This program corrects some peculiarities of the TIFF files generated by Teletypesetting's T-Script v2x PostScript interpreter. One of the Imagery Utilities Package programs.

Jeff Lewis
CIS: 76217,2241
AOL: T Werewolf

Application
Freeware
Size: 31k

TIFFScan

It creates a listing of various information about any given TIFF file. One of the Imagery Utilities Packageprograms.

Jeff Lewis
CIS: 76217,2241
AOL: T Werewolf

Application
Freeware
Size: 37k

Telecom F1

Internet Information

Internet Info

Description	Source	Details
A collection of information files about the Internet.	unknown	**Text Documents** **Freeware** **Size: 323k**

Internet resources guide

Description	Source	Details
Description of the major computers connected to the Internet.	AF Supercomputer Center User Services Group General Atomics Kirtland AFB, NM 87117	**Text Document** **Freeware** **Size: 364k**

Internet Tour v1.3

Description	Source	Details
A HyperCard stack describing the Internet. Interface is first class! You can add information if you wish. Talks about the Internet's history, network, and etiquette.	NSF Network Service Center BBN 10 Moulton Street Cambridge, MA 02138	**HyperCard Stack** **Freeware** **Size: 765k** 12" 6 7 32

Fetch v2.0.6

A program for transferring files. It uses the File Transfer Protocol (FTP) and therefore allows a networked Mac to transfer files with any connected machine that supports FTP. Fetch requires either KSP 1.03 or MacTCP.

Jim Matthews
fetch@dartmouth.edu

Application
Freeware
Size: 138k

HyperFTP v1.3

An interesting front end for FTPing things. You must have MacTCP installed in your System Folder to use HyperFTP.

Douglas Hornig
DUG@CornellC.CIT.Cornell.edu

HyperCard Stack
Freeware
Size: 95k

LeeMail v1.1

Lets you receive and send mail directly to and from your Mac to other machines on the net. It uses the Simple Mail Transfer Protocol (SMTP) to communicate with mailers on other machines. MacTCP (available from Apple) must be installed.

Lee Fyock
520 Boston Road
Billerica, MA 01821
laf@mitre.org

Application
Shareware $10.00
Size: 126k

NetFeed v1.01

A UseNet reader/posting program. Allows you to write scripts to use when you're on-line.

Bill Burns and Brad Boyer

Application
Freeware
Size: 76k

PSIWP v1.6

A front end to an X.500-based White Pages system; supports two paradigms for using the WhitePages: searching and browsing.

PSIWP Shareware Program
Box 3850
Reston, VA 22091

Application
Shareware $35.00
Size: 71k

TheNews v2.02

TheNews gives you a link to net news (also known as USENET), a large semi-structured set of messages written by folks from around the world.

Bill Cramer
504 Winter Wood Drive
Grapevine, TX 76051
uunet!iex!cramer

Application
Shareware $25.00
Size: 198k

Telecom

Text

Programs for processing and massaging text files.

Text A1

Editors and Viewers

Edit II v1.2

A text editor useful in importing database files. Supports stripping or adding of control character and text editing.

Kenneth Seah
ESCware Associates
PO Box 8565
Austin, TX 78713-8565

Application
Shareware $15.00
Size: 55k

File v1.Utah

A simple text editor written in early 1984 when the Mac first came out. Supports only New York, Monaco, and Geneva fonts in 9 or 12 point. A bare-bones editor.

Cary Clark

Application
Public Domain
Size: 19k

FlashWrite v1.1

A control panel that allows you to pop up a text editor by holding down the Command-Shift-Delete keys. Editor supports word wrap.

Andrew Welch
Mark 3 Software
29 Grey Rocks Road
Wilton, CT 06897

Control Panel Extension
Shareware $10.00
Size: 39k

Idealiner v3.4

Outliner program that renumbers properly when items are moved. Each topic has its own text window. User interface OK. Complete documentation. Also imports ThinkTank and Acta.

Clifford Story
Attic Software
PO Box 59229
Schaumburg, IL 60159

Application
Freeware
Size: 133k

MEdit v1.5

Text editor with extensive macro capabilities. Includes a macro compiler; extensive docs in a separate file.

Matthias Aebi
Hirschgartnerweg 25
CH-8057 Zürich
SWITZERLAND

Application
Shareware $25.00
Size: 40k

miniWRITER v1.7

A nice little desk accessory editor that supports word wrap, smart quotes, hyphenation, and more. Use the Font/DA Mover to install in System 6.0.x.

David Dunham
Maitreya Design
PO Box 12085
Eugene, OR 97440

Desk Accessory
Shareware $12.00
Size: 38k

U-Tile+ v1.2

A nice text editor with a friendly interface. Newer than most of the editors around. Disk includes French version too.

David Rand
Université de Montréal
CP 6128, Succursale A
Montréal, Québec
H3C 3J7 CANADA

Application
Shareware $25.00
Size: 123k

Editors and Viewers

Alpha v3.01

An editor for programmers. Includes on-line help (with some C commands) and macro capabilities. Seems fairly sophisticated.

Pete Keleher
PO Box 1892
Rice University
Houston, TX 77251-1892

Application
Shareware $25.00
Size: 236k

Display DA v2.0

A desk accessory that lets you display text. Using ResEdit, you can insert your own text for use as on-line help or an info DA. This DA was used to display the System Errors info in a DA of the same name.

Bill Steinberg
CIS: 76703,1027
AppleLink: X0542
GEnie, MacNet, Delphi: BillS

Desk Accessory
Freeware
Size: 13k

DOCMaker vv3.55

A program for making text documents that can open themselves. Great for making letters or documents for tranfer to other people's machines when you don't know what word processor they have. Formerly known as DOCter.

Mark S. Wall
Green Mountain Software
9404 Valley Lane
Huntsville, AL 35803

Application
Shareware $20.00
Size: 106k

Document Builder v1.0

Creates stand-alone applications from a document, which can contain both text and graphics. Good for distributing documention so the user does not have to use a word processor. Docs in a separate file.

Andrew Welch
Mark 3 Software
29 Grey Rocks Road
Wilton, CT 06897

Application
Shareware $20.00
Size: 48k

ReadMacWrite v85.12.20.spg

Displays MacWrite files on the screen as a teletype and can save as them as ordinary text files.

S. Gillespie
Metaresearch, Inc.
1100 SE Woodward
Portland, OR 97202

Application
Public Domain
Size: 23k

ReadWrite© v1.2

Reads MacWrite, text, and AppleWorks files. Can save a copy of the text as a text file or an AppleWorks file.

PEEK[65]
PO Box 586
Pacifica, CA 94044

Application
Shareware $5.00
Size: 12k

TeachTextMaker v1.1

Create TeachText 1.1 files with this program. It can import, append, and/or edit text documents for inclusion in ReadMe docs.

Karl Pottie
Orkaanstraat 21
B-8800 Rumbeke-Roeselare
BELGIUM

Application
Shareware $15.00
Size: 38k

Viewer v1.05

Displays Glue format files. Glue is a commercial program that allows documents to be 'printed' to a file rather than to a printer.

Solutions, Inc.

Application
Freeware
Size: 45k

Text B1

File Conversion Utilities

Add/Strip v2.89

Expands tabs, converts from WordStar to Mac text file format, curls quotes and apostrophes. Recommended for text file processing.

Jon Wind
2374 Hillwood Drive
Maplewood, MN 55119
CIS: 50167,3444

Application
Shareware $25.00
Size: 91k

AppleWorks-MS Works Translator

Converts AppleWorks files from Apple II ProDOS format to Microsoft Works 1.x file in Mac format. Use in conjunction with Apple File Exchange, which comes with Apple system software.

Productivity Software, Inc.

AFE Document
Freeware
Size: 9k

AppleWorks-MS Works Trans v2.0

Converts AppleWorks files from Apple II ProDOS format to Microsoft Works 2.0 file in Mac format. Use in conjunction with Apple File Exchange, which comes with Apple system software.

Productivity Software, Inc.

AFE Document
Freeware
Size: 12k

Cleanup v1.0

A simple search-and-replace utility that substitutes one character string for another in a text file. Docs within the program.

Michael Sackett
CIS: 76515,160

Application
Freeware
Size: 15k

Conversion v3.0

Converts IBM WordPerfect 4.1/4.2 format files to RTF format, also MS-DOS to Mac text files. The demo version only converts files under 2k in size. Darn!

Martin Simonean
200, De Beaujeu
St Hyacinthe, Québec
QC J2S 7P6 CANADA

Application
Demoware
Size: 41k

Converter v1.5

Removes or modifies characters or strings in a text file. Characters must be specified by their hexadecimal ASCII codes.

Alexander Falk
Leonfeldnerstr. 150/5/13
A4040 Linz
AUSTRIA
(0732) 23-03-27

Application
Shareware $75.00
Size: 35k

EndLine v2.0

Adds carriage returns at the end of lines in text files. Bad user interface: no choice of output file, no access to the Apple menu and desk accessories.

Jeff Fischer

Application
Freeware
Size: 5k

Evolutions v1.01

Converts space runs into tabs, removes control characters, and add/deletes linefeeds. Converts text files to Excel format. Includes documentation within the program.

Kevin M. Hoctor
Emerald Computing Services
2704 N. Loop West, Suite 490
Houston, TX 77008

Application
Shareware $10.00
Size: 21k

File Conversion v1.0

Modifies the file creator for any text file so that double-clicking on the file launches your favorite word processor. Doesn't work with MS Word.

Galen Babcock
MacNews
324 W. Lockford, Suite 3
Lodi, CA 95240

Application
Freeware
Size: 10k

File Converter v1

Converts any character or string to any other that you can type. Has codes for carriage return, linefeed, and tab. Does not allow access to DAs.

Tom Phillips
Phillips Software
1633 Commonwealth Ave.
West Newton, MA 02165

Application
Shareware $5.00
Size: 5k

File Diddler

Lets you strip line feeds and other control characters. Bad user interface, and provides no access to the Apple menu.

R. L. Miller

Application
Public Domain
Size: 17k

Imposters

A set of 4 applications that can be altered with ResEdit to direct your favorite word processor to open an old MacWrite, MPS, MS Word, or QED1 file. System 7 has this capability in the fmap resource.

Al Heynneman
CIS: 70110,611

Application
Public Domain
Size: 10k

Macify v2.8

Lets you transform text files into a Mac-like form: change standard quotes into curly quotes, remove carriage returns, convert space runs to tabs, and more. Docs within the program. Very nice.

Eric Celeste
358 North Parkview
Columbus, OH 43209

Application
Shareware $10.00
Size: 41k

MacWrite Recover v1.0

Converts MacWrite 4.5 documents into standard text files.

Kent Flowers
University of Michigan
MicroGroup

Application
Freeware
Size: 12k

MW -> Text

Converts MacWrite documents into standard text files.

unknown

Desk Accessory
Public Domain
Size: 6k

Quote Converter v.1b

A program for converting dBASE III, Lotus 1-2-3, or Symphony files imported from IBM-compatible machines. Program is from 1988.

Carl Powell III
PCC Software
918 Florence Blvd.
Florence, AL

Application
Shareware $5.00
Size: 38k

Text B1

Continued

Tab Expander v1.11a

Converts tabs to spaces and vice versa. Also replaces the end-of-line character with the appropriate one for Mac, IBM, and UNIX files. Includes a desk accessory version as well.

Ronald G. Parsons
SysCon Consulting
9001 Laurel Grove Drive
Austin, TX 98758

Application
Shareware $5.00
Size: 10k

TabConvertAO

A utility to translate embedded tabs to a user-specified number of spaces. Works on text documents only.

Rico Vaccaro
14 Abilene Lane
Manalapan, NJ 07726

Application
Shareware $5.00
Size: 22k

TabUtil v1.1

Removes and adds tabs; deletes trailing spaces and control characters. Quick and dirty. Creates MDS Edit files.

Chet J. Graham
CIS: 75056,1224

Application
Freeware
Size: 26k

TEXT Ranger

Changes the creator and/or deletes the resource fork of all text files on a disk. Good for transforming generic text files so they open up your favorite word processor when double-clicked.

Darin Adler

Application
Freeware
Size: 10k

Text to Word v1.0

Convert text files to Word files by using this DA. Author found it a minor timesaver.

Carl W. Haynes III
PO Box 2715
W. Lafayette, IN 47903
AOL: CWH3

Desk Accessory
Public Domain
Size: 4k

TextMaster™ v1.4

TextMaster coverts Mac and UNIX text files for porting between the two systems.

Donald Burr
CIS: 72540,3071
AOL: DonaldBurr
dburr@ocf.berkeley.edu

Application
Freeware
Size: 33k

UUTool v2.0.3

A program for encoding and decoding uuencode format files.

Bernie Weiser
Octavian Micro Development
10516 Bradbury Drive SW
Calgary, Alberta
T2W1A6 CANADA

Application
Freeware
Size: 18k

Extractor v1.0

A program for extracting text from resource forks. Extractor can extract text from STR, STR#, TEXT, INTL, intl, MENU, and DITL resources. You can save the extracted text.

Proper Software
CIS: 71545,346
phoffman@well.sf.ca.us

Application
Earthware
Size: 20k

Fix It All

Explains how a sophisticated Mac user can use several file editors and copy programs to recover files from crashed floppies. Written in 1986, most of the information is out of date.

Joseph F. Buchanan
University of Utah

MacWrite
Document
Public Domain
Size: 11k

Laser Quotes

Automatically transforms ordinary quote marks into curly quote marks as you type. Includes docs in a separate file.

Deneba Systems, Inc.
7855 N.W. 12th Street
Suite 202
Miami, FL 33126

System Startup
Extension
Freeware
Size: 2k

LaserLAB v1.0

Fiddles with bitmap images such as those created with MacPaint or other painting programs. Adjusts these images so they look better on a LaserWriter; creates high-resolution effects.

Wayne Moore and Dave Ewing
In Focus Technologies
PO Box 185
Niwot, CO 80544

Application
Freeware
Size: 46k

Loodle v5.2

Loodle is a utility for printing labels for 3.5-inch floppy disks on a LaserWriter. It automatically catalogs disks and can print either 6 or 9 labels per page.

Josh & Nick Franco
TruValue Software
1117 Kagawa Street
Pacific Palisades, CA 90272
CIS: 72571,1010
GEnie: G.FRANCO

Application
Shareware $10.00
Size: 111k

PopChar v1.7

PopChar is a cdev that enables you to generate every possible character that is available in the current font without having to remember keyboard combinations.

Ünther Bláschek
Petzoldstr. 31
A–4020 Linz
AUSTRIA

Control Panel
Extension
Postcardware
Size: 10k

PrettyPrint v2.00

Prints C and Pascal source code that is stored in text files. Makes things look pretty by indenting, boldfacing keywords and Toolbox calls, and italicizing comments. Includes docs in a separate file.

HyperSoft
2124 Kittredge Street #174
Berkeley, CA 94704

Application
Shareware
Size: 32k

Quote INIT v2.0

Automatically changes normal quote marks into the Mac curly quote marks, keeping track of the open and close quotes. Also handles diphthongs and double dashes.

Lincoln D. Stein
44 Boynton Street, #3
Boston, MA 02130

Control Panel
Extension
Shareware $15.00
Size: 9k

Text C1

Continued

Sav-O-Matic v1.51

A contol panel for saving documents in the background at regular intervals. Great if you can't always remember to save your documents while you're working on them. Compatibility with System 7 is unknown.

Bruce Partridge
1209 S. 25th St.
Lincoln, NE 68502

Control Panel
Extension
Shareware $20.00
Size: 12k

Sort v1.11b

Sorts files in alphabetic or numeric order, ascending or descending. Comes with a desk accessory version.

Ronald G. Parsons
SysCon Consulting
9001 Laurel Grove Drive
Austin, TX 98758

Application
Shareware $5.00
Size: 11k

SureSaver™ v1.0

SureSaver automatically saves the file you are working on in most applications at a user-specified time. You can change your preferences by opening up the control panel under the Apple menu and selecting SureSaver.

Kent R. Glenn
Computer Trend, Inc.
4545 N. 36th Street #111
Phoenix, AZ 85018

Control Panel
Extension
Shareware $10.00
Size: 15k

Temperament 2 v2.0 Oz.

Erases MS Word Temp files from your System Folder, preventing the filling up of your System Folder with these files. Supports removal of other types of temporary files.

John Rotenstein
PO Box 165
Double Bay, NSW 2028
AUSTRALIA

Control Panel
Extension
Freeware
Size: 30k

The Cassette Labeler v1.0b1

Creates files for storing information about cassette tapes. A dialog box allows you to record the tape length, type, brand, name, musical artist, and list of songs.

unknown

Application
Public Domain
Size: 57k

Demo ABBRE-V-8™ v1.3

ABBRE-V-8 is a computer shorthand (CAT) that consists of about 180 abbreviations of common words. The demo permits the use of 8 user-defined abbreviations. This ABBRE-V-8ed version shuts itself off after 30 minutes.

L. J. Salmon
PO Box 176
Comptche, CA 95427

Control Panel Extension
Demoware
Size: 102k

Diff v3.14

An application that you can use to compare Macintosh text files, and show what makes them different. Differences are identified and displayed on screen. You may create an optional output file that shows the differences.

Stephan B. Wessels
231 West Fourth Street
#318A
Cincinnati, OH 45202

Application
Public Domain
Size: 41k

DocDoctor Demo

Performs operations on text and MacWrite files, such as counting words and substituting laser fonts for screen fonts. However, the text itself is not displayed on the screen.

David Hawking
Australian National University
GPO Box 4
Canberra ACT 2600
AUSTRALIA

Application
Demoware
Size: 16k

Document Mangle v1.0 Beta

Performs selective global changes to MacWrite files, such as changing all occurrences of one font to another font or adjusting the margins in all rulers of a particular type. Contains docs in a separate file.

Tom Dowdy
Computing Center
Notre Dame, IN 46556
(219) 239-5600

Application
Freeware
Size: 37k

FaceLift v1.02

Reformats fonts, point sizes, and type style information of MacWrite 2.2 and MacWrite 4.5 documents. Useful if you want to print the same file on both an ImageWriter and a LaserWriter.

Paul DuBois/Flat Egg Software
WI Regional Primate Res. Ctr.
1220 Capital Court
Madison, WI 53715-1299

Application
Public Domain
Size: 37k

File Splitter

Splits files into smaller chunks. Lets you split files by using a given chunk size or by specifying that all splits occur at a certain marker character. Comes with a DA for changing the options.

Andrew E. Page
3 Bushnell Drive
Lexington, MA 02173-4901
CIS: 75206,2025

Application
Shareware $3.00
Size: 7k

File Tricks v1.1b

Extracts text from possibly damaged MacWrite files and can substitute laser fonts for screen fonts in MacWrite files.

Ken Flowers

Application
Freeware
Size: 26k

FileSplit v1.1

FileSplit is designed to split large text files into smaller parts. Written with BinHex files in mind, FileSplit breaks large files into 30k sections, small enough to be easily uploaded and mail through most networks.

Richard M. Segal
1060 Morewood Ave.
PO Box 1059
Pittsburgh, PA 15213

Application
Shareware $10.00
Size: 9k

Index v4.5

Produces indexes for MacWrite 4.5 files. Reads one page at a time and allows you to specify words to be added to the index for that page. Documentation is included in a separate file.

Scott Gillespie
Reed College
Portland, OR 97202

Application
Public Domain
Size: 34k

MW II Command Keys

On-line help for MacWrite II.

John Albert

Desk Accessory
Public Domain
Size: 9k

RecoverWordDoc v1.2

Recover text from corrupted MS Word files. Text recovered is in ASCII format and you can save it, import it back into Word, and reformat it. Great for that last attempt before starting from scratch again.

SK Hushing III
PO Box 9745
San Diego, CA 92109

Application
Shareware $5.00
Size: 11k

Rescue v.99

File recovery program for damaged MacWrite 4.5 files. May not work for files created using other versions of MacWrite.

Don Johnson
Rice University

Application
Public Domain
Size: 9k

TextDiff v0.9

Similar to the diff utility on UNIX. Compares two text files and saves differences in a new file. Has documentation, but the result file retains the spirit of UNIX by being difficult to understand.

SignalVideo, Inc.
ICONtact User Group on Delphi (800) 544-4005
(617) 991-3393

Application
Freeware
Size: 18k

Unity v3.1.1

Unity reads text files you select and puts them all into a single file.

Michael O'Rourke
Micro F/X
PO Box 7467
Clemson, SC 29632

Application
Shareware $5.00
Size: 16k

Word Minder v1.0b1

Word Minder is an INIT that deletes the leftover Microsoft Word files you sometimes find in your System Folder. You know the kind: Word Temp 1, Word Temp 2, etc.

AOL: L Products
GEnie: R.Mathews4

System Startup Extension
Freeware
Size: 17k

WordCount v3.01

Counts the number of words in a Microsoft Word 3.x document. MS Word 4.x incorporates this feature so you don't need this unless you have the older version.

Brad Ferguson
CIS: 76354,2733

Application
Freeware
Size: 44k

GoldVarb v1.5

A program for Variable Rule Analysis using tokens, conditions, and cells. Documentation within the program.

David Sankoff, et al.
Université de Montréal
CANADA
(514) 343-7574

Application
Freeware
Size: 172k

INFOMaker v2.6

Converts database files from other computers, such as PCs and mainframes, into formats that can be used by Mac database or spreadsheet programs.

Mark S. Wall
Green Mountain Software
9404 Valley Lane
Huntsville, AL 35803

Application
Shareware $25.00
Size: 109k

NotePad++ v1.2

NotePad utility with a lot of features. Multiple notepads with up to 8 pages per notepad, multiple fonts, styles, and colors within a page, rulers, printing, justification. Has an on-line help screen.

Alexander S. Colwell

Desk Accessory
Freeware
Size: 136k

PasteIt Notes v1.0.1

PasteIt Notes is used to replace those sticky yellow PostIt™ notes that many people have stuck all over the place. Just create a PasteIt Note and stick it on your screen wherever you like. It stays until you move or delete it or you quit PasteIt Notes.

Bruce Beare
3262 Desertwood Lane
San Jose, CA 95132

Application
Shareware $15.00
Size: 84k

Text

Utilities

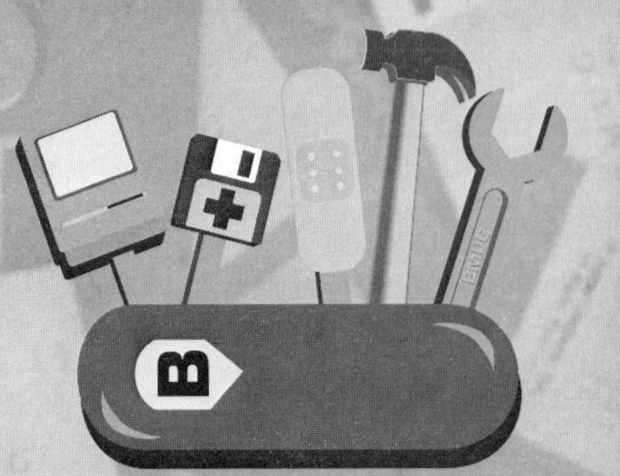

Software for inspecting and modifying files and disks, diagnosing and removing viruses, recovering data, and editing resources.

Utilities A1

System 7 Utilities

AKA

AKA allows you to create aliases in the Finder more easily. When you Option-drag an icon in the Finder, it makes a copy of the item instead of moving it; with AKA, when you Control-drag an item in the Finder, it creates an alias.

Fred Monroe
fredm@apple.com (summer)
rico@caen.engin.umich.edu (fall)
AppleLink: fredom

System Startup Extension
Freeware
Size: 8k

Anchor v1.0

Anchor mounts your network or secondary hard disk. Copy it onto the volume or network you want to mount, make an alias of it, and copy the alias back onto your primary hard disk. Double-click the alias on your primary hard disk.

James Burghardt

Application
Freeware
Size: 4k

AppDisk v1.2

AppDisk is an application that lets you use part of your RAM as a fast disk drive, without restarting your Mac as most INIT/cdev based RAM disks do. It can also save its contents to provide some protection against data loss.

Mark Adams
11215 Research Blvd. #2036
Austin, TX 78759

Application
Shareware $15.00
Size: 20k

Applicon v2.0

Applicon places a tile on your desktop for each running application. Each tile displays the icon and name of the application it corresponds to. Clicking a tile brings the application to the front.

Rick Holzgrafe
rmh@apple.com

Application
Freeware
Size: 48k

basura

When you Command-Delete with basura loaded, the selected items in the front window of the Finder are thrown in the Trash. Option-Command-Delete throws items in the Trash and then empties it.

Fred Monroe
fredm@apple.com (summer)
rico@caen.engin.umich.edu
AppleLink: fredom

System Startup Extension
Freeware
Size: 7k

CClock v2.2.0

CClock is a nifty little program that displays a clock in a window on the Mac. It can be resized and repositioned anywhere on the desktop, and it remembers where you last put it every time it is run.

Stephen W. Martin
2655 S. Peoria
Aurora, CO 80014
CIS: 75126,51

Application
Shareware $15.00
Size: 36k

Customizing Finder 7 Menus

This document describes how to use ResEdit to change Command-key shortcuts in the System 7 Finder.

Alex Narvey
PO Box 332
905 Corydon Ave.
Winnipeg, Manitoba
R3M 3V3 CANADA

Text
Freeware
Size: 19k

dropple menu

When you drag an item from the Finder and drop it on an item in the Apple menu, this hack makes the Finder act as if you had actually dropped it on the file that the Apple menu item represents.

Fred Monroe
fredm@apple.com (summer)
rico@caen.engin.umich.edu
AppleLink: fredom

System Startup Extension
Freeware
Size: 9k

DropSave v.99

With DropSave installed, Shift-clicking on the title bar of a document in an application that has a 'Save As...' menu item creates a document-like icon that can be dropped on a Finder window to save the document in that window.

Dean Yu
nerm@apple.com

System Startup Extension
Freeware
Size: 3k

DTPrinter v1.01MH

DTPrinter allows you to have an icon on your desktop that represents a particular printer. When you drag a document onto the printer icon, it will print to that printer. Useful if you have multiple laser printers, modems, etc.

Leonard Rosenthol
leonardr@sv.portal.com
GEnie, AOL, AppleLink: MACgician

Application
Freeware
Size: 26k

Extensions Manager v1.6

Extensions Manager allows you turn off or on the code that executes at startup in certain system extensions. (Contol Panel, Chooser, and System Startup documents are extensions.)

Ricardo Batista
Apple Computer, Inc.

Control Panel Extension
Freeware
Size: 20k

Finder 7 Menus!

Lets you change the Command-key combinations in the menus of the System 7 Finder. Intended for novice Macintosh users, not just ResEdit freaks!

Adam Stein
Insanely Great Software
126 Calvert Ave. E.
Edison, NJ 08820

Application
Shareware $10.00
Size: 9k

FinderToFront v1.0

FinderToFront is a simple application that makes the Finder the frontmost application at startup. Gets around the problem of having the last application run at startup being left in front when you want the Finder to be in front.

Michael Peirce
Peirce Software
719 Hibiscus Place
San Jose CA 95117

Application
Public Domain
Size: 28k

Helium v2.0

Helium allows you to choose a key combination that inflates System 7's Help Balloons instantly (well, close enough). When you let go of the keys, the Balloons disappear. It also lets you select the font and size of the text that appears in the Balloons.

Robert L. Mathews
PO Box 21271
Oakland, CA 94610-1271

Control Panel Extension
Shareware $5.00
Size: 46k

INITLoader v1.0a7

INITLoader can load extensions from many folders and supports aliases to extensions.

Ian Hendry

Control Panel Extension
Freeware
Size: 35k

Jump In v0.2d1

Part of the Jump Open... package. This INIT allows the Jump Out control panel to remain in resident memory.

Robert W. Thornton
Jump Development Group
1228 Malvern Avenue
Pittsburgh, PA 15217
AppleLink: RThornton

System Startup Extension
Shareware $?
Size: 9k

Utilities A1

Continued

Jump Open... v0.2d1

Allows you to quickly traverse your files at the Finder level to select and open one without leaving a trail of open folder windows. Selecting 'Jump Open...' from the Finder's File menu displays the standard file dialog box.

Robert W. Thornton
Jump Development Group
1228 Malvern Avenue
Pittsburgh, PA 15217
AppleLink: RThornton

Application
Shareware $10.00
Size: 13k

Just Click v1.00

Lets you just click the icon at the far right of the menu bar in System 7 to switch from application to application, just as you could in System 6 MultiFinder, instead of having to pull down the menu and select an application.

Luis A. Bardi

System Startup Extension
Freeware
Size: 9k

Keyboard Menu v1.0

Alters your Keyboard menu to do something. Watch out, this comes from a Hacker's Conference contest!

James W. Walker

System Startup Extension
Freeware
Size: 3k

Kilroy v2.0b1

Brings up a message saying 'Kilroy was here!' at random intervals.

Dave Koziol
PO Box 7794
Ann Arbor, MI 48107

Control Panel Extension
Postcardware
Size: 12k

MountAlias v1.0a3

MountAlias is a control panel that automatically creates aliases to AppleShare volumes every time an AppleShare volume is mounted. These aliases are named and put into a folder according to your specifications.

Jeff Miller
20525 Mariani Avenue
MS: 81EQ
Cupertino, CA 95014
AppleLink: JEFFM

Control Panel Extension
Freeware
Size: 11k

ResEdit 2.1 TMPLs for 7.0

This file contains a number of templates specifically for editing System and Finder 7.0 with ResEdit 2.1. Includes the fmnu TMPL, which enables you to change the new Finder menus.

Fred Hucht
Institute of Theoretical Physics
University of Duisburg
GERMANY

ResEdit Templates
Freeware
Size: 4k

SCSI Accel 7.0 'The Original'

This text file tells how to obtain a version of SCSI Accel that works with System 7.0. SCSI Accel is a software SCSI accelerator that usually speeds up hard drive access for the Mac Plus.

Dave Denowh
2404 26th Street
Rockford, Illinois 61108
(815) 229-5023

Text
Shareware $5.00
Size: 4k

sndConverter v1.2.1

In System 7, the sounds have to be of a special type to use these benefits. sndConverter converts your existing sounds to be System 7.0-compliant.

Joe Zobkiw
AOL: AFL Zobkiw

Application
Freeware
Size: 29k

Switcher v1.1

Switcher allows you to switch between System 6.0.x and System 7. To avoid problems, read the documentation before you use this utility.

Keisuke Hara

Application
Freeware
Size: 43k
12" 6 7 32

System 7 from john

These files, How to Install System 7 and How to Use System 7, will help you get started with System 7. The first document explains how to install System 7 safely; the second discusses many of the new features of System 7.

John Norstad
Academic Computing and Networking
Northwestern University
j-norstad@nwu.edu

Text
Freeware
Size: 104k
12" 6 7 32

System Picker v1.0b10

System Picker is a utility application that allows you to choose the folder that will be the active System Folder upon restart. It can be used to switch between System 6.0.x and System 7, or between customized System Folders.

Kevin Aitken
20990 Valley Green Dr. #635
Cupertino, CA 95014
(408) 974-5899
AppleLink: AITKEN.K

Application
Freeware
Size: 30k
12" 6 7 32

Too Many Lawyers... v1.0

Put this in your System Folder, and it will enforce one of Apple Legal's requirements, and maintain this important existing direction for Apple. Go for it, type the Apple symbol in the Chicago font (Option-Shift-k) and see what happens.

Dave Koziol
PO Box 7794
Ann Arbor, MI 48107

System Startup Extension
Freeware
12" 6 7 32

Trash Chute v2.0

Trash Chute empties the Trash can when you restart or power up your Macintosh. (System 7 doesn't empty the trash automatically as did System 6!) It also deletes items immediately when you drop them on the Trash Chute icon.

Melissa Rogers

Application
Freeware
Size: 6k
12" 6 7 32

Understudy v1.0d3

Understudy provides a means to customize the way the System 7.0 Finder opens documents. This is handy if you want your favorite programs to open text, PICT, PNTG, or other documents that can be opened by more than one application.

Larry Rosenstein
Apple Computer, Inc.
182 Muir Ave
Santa Clara, CA 95051

System Startup Extension
Freeware
Size: 3k
12" 6 7 32

VM-Eject v2.0

VM-Eject modifies your 7.0 Memory cdev (control panel) to allow you to use virtual memory on removable hard disks. This is somewhat risky, so read the documentation before you play with this program.

PB Computing

Application
Freeware
Size: 6k
12" 6 7 32

zapParam™ vv1.0a1

zapParam wipes out parameter RAM settings stored in your Mac. These settings include mouse speed, double-click speed, menu flash, startup drive, and other settings like serial port protocols.

Devon Hubbard
Reach Software Corp.

Control Panel Extension
Freeware
Size: 28k
12" 6 7 32

Color Icon Utilities

Icon Gallery v1.2.2

Icon Gallery is a set of great 256-color icons stored in a format to be installed by SunDesk Strip and used by SunDesk.

Tom Poston
Immedium Design
2114 Lockhart Drive
Charlotte, NC 28203-6040
AOL: TPoston
AppleLink: D4906

Document
Shareware $15.00
Size: 666k
12" 6 7 32

Icon Lab v1.1b

Icon Editor is a MacPaint-like editor to create icl8 color icon resources. The palette used to build an icl8 is the 8-bit system default.

Tom Wasko
4832 - 49th Avenue NW
Calgary, Alberta
T3A 0R9 CANADA

Application
Public Domain
Size: 43k
12" 6 7 32

Bone Factory 7.0 Folders!!

A collection of color icons (icl8s) including a gray-scale icon of Einstein, some folders with eerie faces on them, and other bright color icons and folder icons.

BONE FACTORY

Icon Resouces
Freeware
Size: 13k

Brad & John's Sys. 7 Folder Icons

Cool color icons (icl8s) for folders on the System 7 desktop. Includes folders with landscapes, flags from around the world, animals (including a giraffe), and more!

Brad Sanders & John Calhoun
1134 Ohio, Apt. #1
Lawrence, KS 66044

Scrapbook
Freeware
Size: 330k

Folder Icons

A collection of more than 50 color folder icons (icl8s) for all sorts of stuff ranging from a drop folder to a folder with a water drop on it, and including folder icons for specific programs.

unknown

Icon Resources
Freeware
Size: 55k
12" 6 7 32

Icon Vaults I and II

Under System 7, Icon Vault files provide an easy way to add color icons to programs that do not have them. Just place the Icon Vault file on your hard disk, and you will see color icons for the program that each Icon Vault file supports.

Paul Schliesser
CIS: 71610,3370

Icon Vault Documents
Freeware
Size: 208k
12" 6 7 32

Icons by Immedium Design

This collection of icon families (cicns, icl4s, icl8s, ICN#s, ics#s, ics4s, and ics8s) is a preview of Immedium Design's System 7.0 icons. Includes icons for specific applications as well as icons for the System 7 desktop.

Tom Poston
Immedium Design
2114 Lockhart Drive
Charlotte NC 28203-6040
AOL: TPoston
AppleLink: D4906

Icon Resources
Shareware $20.00
Size: 0k
12" 6 7 32

Other Color Icons

This is a collection of color icons (icl8s) collected from a variety of unknown and unnamed sources. For the most part, they are icons for specific applications including ResEdit, MicroPhone II, and After Dark.

Authors include Shekar M. Krishnan from GooseBump Graphics™ Macintosh User Group
AOL: Shekar 5

Icon Resources
Freeware
Size: 0k
12" 6 7 32

System 7 Color Icons

This collection of color icons (icl8s) has icons for folders, hard drives, applications, documents, and more. Especially awesome are the icons with Macs showing cool displays on their screens.

Young Kim and Andres Kim
6631 Delco Avenue
Canoga Park, CA 91306
AOL: Willfull2
Delphi: YKim

Scrapbook File
Freeware
Size: 0k
12" 6 7 32

System 7.0 icl8s

This is a collection of nifty color icons (icl8s) for the System 7 desktop. Included are icons for the different Macs and standard Mac files, as well as some cool folder icons.

unknown

Icon Resources
Freeware
Size: 0k
12" 6 7 32

Utilities C1

Catalogers

Cat•Mac™

Disk and file cataloging program. Maintains and organizes a library of up to 1000 files. It is a little buggy and should be run in black and white.

Andrew Worth, Paul Bailey, John Moreno
Phoenix Specialties, Inc.
2981 Corvin Drive
Santa Clara, CA 95051

Application
Shareware $10.00
Size: 123k

Catalog+ v2.0 by Charl

Catalog+ is a utility for viewing, printing, or saving information about files. It utilizes regular expressions that allow the user to develop complex statements for matching patterns.

Charles E. Bess
587 N. 480 West
Kokomo, IN 46901

Application
Shareware $5.00
Size: 57k

CatMaker v1987 by NOLA

Disk cataloging program. Creates lists of file names and associated file information. Users can create layouts specifying what information is recorded and can configure the column headings.

Wayne Nolan
Nolan Computer Systems
PO Box 1832
Spring Valley, CA 92077

Application
Shareware $15.00
Size: 29k

Curious Cat v1.0

File cataloger that also records fonts and DAs stored within the System or Font/DA Mover files. May not allow you to catalog on-line volumes.

Robert Boylan
54 Howe Road
Coram, NY 11727

Application
Freeware
Size: 69k

Disk Librarian v1.82a

Creates a consolidated catalog of disks as they are inserted. Catalogs all on-line volumes automatically when it is launched. Offers several sorting and printing options. Has problems with large volumes under MultiFinder.

Little Bit
469 Edgewood Avenue
New Haven, CT 06511

Application
Shareware $20.00
Size: 75k

Disk List/DR vParty Time!

Creates a text file of disk directories. This file is suitable for import into the MD Disk Library HyperCard stack.

Paul Ho
1020 Adams Avenue
Saint Charles, IL 60174
(Modified by Don Rose
PO Box 333
Crystal Lake, IL 60014)

Application
Shareware $10.00
Size: 6k

Index Maker v3.0b1

Index Maker creates an index of files on any or all mounted volumes. You have the option of including the file size and the date and/or time of last modification in the index.

Lon Mc Quillin
PO Box 1676
San Mateo, CA 94401
CompuServe: 75146,3420

Application
Shareware $15.00
Size: 90k

Phantom Catalog

A floppy disk cataloging program. It gives you an icon-based report on the screen that you can save to a text file. It is somewhat buggy under newer systems and has some memory problems under MultiFinder.

Bill Sammons
9313 Vandike St.
Philadelphia, PA 19114

Application
Shareware $?
Size: 62k

QCat v1.4.3

QCat is a utility for cataloging disks. It gives you the option to log only certain types of files and can create log files (text files) using the delimiters of your choice.

Richard De Luca
501 Chemin Witty
Ste-Christine, Québec
J0H 1H0 CANADA
CIS: 72567,3634
GEnie: M.BUSSIERES

Application
Shareware $15.00
Size: 45k
12" 6 7 32

Utilities C2

Catalogers

Dir-Acta-ry

Creates Acta outlines for file directories of disks or folders. Maintains the folder hierarchy by making each folder a topic heading, and each folder and file it contains a sub-topic heading.

David Dunham
James Owen

Application
Freeware
Size: 18k
12" 6 7 32

FileList+ v1.0b19

FileList+ is an extremely fast disk cataloger with powerful search and sort capabilities. It can read and write FileList 1.4 (by Erny Tontlinger) files, for which it is an official update. Supports tab-delimited export of lists!

Bill Patterson
805 Division St.
Greenville, TX 75401
AOL: BillPatt

Application
Freeware
Size: 78k
12" 6 7 32

MacLibrarian v1.0

A file management program. Use it to find duplicate files on your disks. It searches and sorts by any of 10 attributes. It also recognizes StuffIt files and can expand their contents.

Behrouz Poustchi
Epsilon Systems
66 Pellan Way
Kanata, Ontario
K2K 1J8 CANADA
CIS: 70274,3171

Application
Shareware $25.00
Size: 158k
12" 6 7 32

OffLine™ Demo

A disk cataloging program designed to keep track of unmounted volumes.

SNA, Inc.
PO Box 3662
Princeton, NJ 08543
(609) 799-9605

Application
Demoware
Size: 117k
12" 6 7 32

BAD v1.1

Bad 1.1 allows you to format a floppy disk that has bad sectors. It does this by mapping them out when it formats the disk. It automatically prompts you when the Finder cannot verify a disk that you attempted to initialize.

Giuseppe Carnevale
Niutta 36
80128 Napoli
ITALY

System Startup Extension
Shareware $20.00
Size: 11k

Disk Test

Tests 400k or 800k floppies for defects. Does not alter disks in any way. Works fine in MultiFinder, but is modal.

Henry Lowe

Application
Shareware $?
Size: 9k

Disk Timer III

Test the performance of any disk drive by measuring the access time, read/write transfer rates, and overall performance. More sophisticated than DiskTimer II, with a better interface.

Nuvo Labs
245A Tank Fram Road
San Luis Obispo, CA 93401
(805) 544-5766

Application
Public Domain
Size: 33k

DiskBasher v1.1

MacUser's mass storage benchmark that measures hard disk performance by executing a number of writes, seeks, and reads on a temporary file.

Stephan Somogyi
MacUser Labs
950 Tower Lane, 18th Floor
Foster City, CA 94404
CompuServe: 72511,40
AOL: MacUserNWS

Application
Freeware
Size: 24k

Diskette Verify v1.1

Checks single- or double-sided disks by verifying the readability of every block on the disk. The tests it performs are nondestructive.

Harry Starr
90 Haverhill St.
Methuen, MA 01844

Application
Shareware $5.00
Size: 7k

DiskTimer II v1.0...

Runs some simple tests on several aspects of the speed of disk hardware and associated software. The test is run automatically on the volume from which the program is launched; takes several minutes.

unknown

Application
Freeware
Size: 18k

Fast Formatter™ v2.4

Quick disk formatting program handy for initializing a batch of floppies. It also allows you to format a diskette that has bad sectors. Warning: A 'Bad sectors' error message can mean that the disk has faulty media, not just bad sectors!

Beyond Inc.
PO Box 31990
Tucson, AZ 85751
(602) 290-9790

Application
Freeware
Size: 19k

File Scan v3V

Scans all files on a floppy or hard disk checking for errors. It checks both the data and resource forks of files and documents, not the disk media.

Ken Bates
USENET:
decwrl!ssdevo.com!bates

Application
Freeware
Size: 22k

Continued

Flash Formatter Installer

Allows you to install an FKEY that quickly reformats disks. It can erase disks in less than 3 seconds, much faster than the Finder's Erase Disk command. Warning: Erased disks cannot be recovered!

Andrew Welch
Mark 3 Software
29 Grey Rocks Road
Wilton, CT 06897

Application
Shareware $8.00
Size: 43k

Floppy Fixer v1.0

Floppy Fixer is a utility for recovering files from damaged Macintosh diskettes. In addition, it provides easy-to-use tools for identifying and correcting errors in file tags that would cause other file recovery utilities to fail.

Frank Beatrous
309 Barnes Street
Pittsburgh, PA 15221
beatrous@pittvms.bitnet

Application
Shareware $20.00
Size: 94k

Formatter Deluxe v3V

Initializes floppy disks. Good for initializing a large number of disks at once. Has problems redrawing the screen.

Jan Eugenides
MicroSPARC, Inc.
Concord, MA 01742
(617) 371-1660

Application
Freeware
Size: 12k

InUse v2.0

Displays an identifier in the menu bar signaling when a particular SCSI device is accessed.

Sam Barone

Control Panel
Extension
Freeware
Size: 14k

Mount any Hard Disk

Attempts to mount any hard disk connected via a SCSI port.

unknown

Application
Public Domain
Size: 4k

MountEm v1.7

Mounts SCSI drives. Designed for users with removable media drives that require some sort of command to mount new disks when one is ejected and another is inserted.

Bill Steinberg
CIS: 76703,1027
GEnie: BillS

FKEY
Freeware
Size: 6k

QuickFormat! v7.0g

Initializes disks in half the time it takes the Mac in the Finder. Especially helpful for initializing many floppies at one time. Allows you to select how disks are initialized. Very good interface.

Michael J. Conrad
955 Escalon Avenue, #505
Sunnyvale, CA 94086

Application
Shareware $15.00
Size: 100k

SCSI Evaluator v1.07

Evaluates features of your Mac's SCSI bus and devices, such as hard drives. Uses include measuring data transfer rates and checking for bad blocks. Pretty good interface and documentation within the program.

William A. Long
Digital Microwave
PO Box 3527
Mission Viejo, CA 92690

Application
Shareware $20.00
Size: 103k

SCSI Saver v1.1

After your hard drive has been idle for a definable period of time, SCSI Saver attempts to park the heads of the drive to save wear and tear.

Darrell Pfeifer

Control Panel
Extension
Shareware $?
Size: 5k

SCSI Tools

Great utility for checking the status of your SCSI bus and mounting SCSI devices, such as hard disks. Requests that the $5.00 shareware fee be sent to UNICEF.

Paul Mercer
Apple Computer, Inc.
PO Box 160165
Cupertino, CA 95016-0165

Control Panel
Extension
Charityware
Size: 22k

SCSI-Identifier v1.4

SCSI-Identifier is a simple program that tells what SCSI devices are connected to your Mac. It also lets you know if these devices are compatible with Restrospect, a commercial backup utility.

Laurie Gill
Dantz Development Corp.
1510 Walnut Street
Berkeley, CA 94709
(415) 849-0293

Application
Freeware
Size: 36k

SCSIAccel v2.10

Speeds up SCSI drives on the MacPlus by enhancing the throughput of I/O operations for so-called blind read and write operations. Nothing else is affected by it. Disk includes several versions of the extension. Works only on a Mac Plus!

Dolf Starreveld
Dept. of Math and C.S.
University of Amsterdam
Kruislaan 409
1098 SJ Amsterdam
NETHERLANDS

System Startup
Extension
Freeware
Size: 2k

SCSIInfo v1.1

Provides a comprehensive table of information about each SCSI device attached to your computer. In addition to the Reset, Scan, and Mount functions, SCSIInfo can be used to diagnose various problems you may be having with your disk.

Bob Easterday
522 Loumena Lane
San Jose, CA 95111

Control Panel
Extension
Shareware $?
Size: 68k

SCSIOdometer v1.0

SCSIOdometer keeps a running total of the read and write calls and the bites transferred on your hard drive from the time you install the program.

Ray Martin
Optima Technology

Control Panel
Extension
Freeware
Size: 13k

SCSIProbe v3.2

SCSIProbe displays a list of the SCSI devices connected to your Mac. For each device it, lists the SCSI ID, type of device, manufacturer, product number, and version of the driver. It also mounts unmounted devices.

Robert Polic

Control Panel
Extension
Freeware
Size: 20k

Disk Utilities

BackIt v3.03

A file backup utility that lets you specify filename patterns using wildcard characters rather than having to explicitly name each file.

Lars Sundström
Seagull Engineering
Box 909
S-220 09 Lund
SWEDEN
Phone: +46 46 12 54 64

Application
Shareware $12.00
Size: 37k

Comment Editor v1.01

Edits the signature resource of applications. The signature resource holds the version information displayed when you Get Info for the file in the Finder. Use with caution.

Scott Armitage
3048 Lee Avenue N.
Golden Valley, MN 55422

Application
Shareware $10.00
Size: 10k

CompareForks™

Compares the contents of both the data and resource forks of two files. Also has an analysis option providing more details on any differences. Stores results in a text file. Sometimes runs out of memory in MultiFinder.

T. R. Shaw & B. E. Jarrell
OITC
PO Box 73
Melbourne Beach, FL 32951
(305) 983-3714

Application
Shareware $15.75
Size: 57k

Disk Image Filer v1.0

Loads the entire contents of a 400k or 800k floppy into memory and lets you copy it to another floppy or save it in a compressed format. Does not work under MultiFinder.

John Raymonds
CIS: 76174,205

Application
Public Domain
Size: 27k

DiskDup+ v1.2 - Floppy

Disk duplication program. Reads entire contents of a master disk into memory, then writes copies. Doesn't work under MultiFinder.

Roger Bates
Route 1, Box 865
Hillsboro, OR 97124

Application
Shareware $10.00
Size: 9k

DiskNum v0.99

Lets you append a serial number to the name of a floppy disk. Specify a starting value and an increment, then insert a disk. After you rename the disk, the program ejects it and waits for the next disk.

Mark Adams

Application
Freeware
Size: 14k

FileType Lister

Creates a text file listing all the files in a given folder (including sub-folders) having file types that are included in a list of types specified by the user.

Louis King
495 Union Avenue
Memphis, TN 38103
CIS: 71041,171

Application
Shareware $10.00
Size: 13k

Insure vV 1.0

Reminds you of the last time that you backed up your files when you start up your Mac. Also gives you the opportunity to launch your favorite backup program.

Paul Mandel
CIS: 75226,1716
GEnie: P.Mandel

System Startup Extension
Freeware
Size: 16k

InvisiFile v1.0.1

Makes files visible or invisible. Invisible files are not displayed in the Finder (but still appear in Open File dialog boxes in applications). Be careful when using this program!

Robert S. T. Gibson
RR#1 Carrying Place
Ontario
KØK 1LØ CANADA

Application
Shareware $5.00
Size: 14k

MacSnoop™ Demo v1.5.5

A sophisticated file and volume editor that displays hexadecimal and ASCII dumps of files and volumes. Demo version stops working after a certain amount of time.

Art A. Schumer
Evergreen Software, Inc.
15600 NE 8th Street,
Suite A3126
Bellevue, WA 98008
(206) 883-0346

Application
Shareware $25.00
Size: 64k

My Back Up v0.1

Hard disk backup program that supports incremental backups and maintains a journal of all backup activity. You can create small backup sets for saving a few important files at one time.

Rick Giles
Box 207, Acadia University
Wolfville, Nova Scotia
BOP IXO CANADA
(902) 542-7339

Application
Shareware $10.00
Size: 32k

New Creator

New Creator changes the creator of some files. The advantage of using New Creator to do this is that you can do your entire hard disk once and for all. It can search an entire hard disk or just a specific folder for files to change.

Dominic Mazzoni
18518 61st Place West
Lynnwood, WA 98037-7202
(206) 778-5119

Application
Shareware $10.00
Size: 22k

Newer v1.0b1

Full featured backup program. Newer preserves the folder structure on the backup disk. Also, if a copy of a file already exists, it is replaced only if the file being copied is newer than the copy to be overwritten.

George Touchstone
73 Frost St.
Cambridge, MA 02140

Application
Shareware $25.00
Size: 55k

Peeker v1.0

Displays the file type, creator, and signature resource (if present) of a selected file.

Ian McLellan
PO Box 581
Waterloo, Ontario
N2J 4B8 CANADA

Application
Shareware $5.00
Size: 11k

Resource Counter

Counts the number of resource types and number of individual resources in a selected file.

Loftus E. Becker, Jr.

Application
Freeware
Size: 3k

Resource Lister v1.1

Displays a list of resources with the owner type, owner ID, number, resource type, resource ID, resource attributes, size of resource, checksum of resource, and resource name. Can be used to get an overview of all the resources in a file, or to compare the resources in several files.

unknown

Application
Freeware
Size: 12k

Utilities D2

Continued

Serializer

Renames disks with a prefix and a sequential serial number. After specifying the prefix and starting serial number, insert a disk. The program renames and ejects the disk, then waits for the next disk.

Gene Coldwell
Custom Software Products
6300 Innesbrooke
Arlington, TX 76017
GEnie: G.COLDWELL

Application
Freeware
Size: 15k

Version v1.1

Version is a utility for determining the version numbers for each application you own. It scans a disk looking for applications, and when an application is found, it looks at the application's vers resource for the version.

Dana Basken
Rockland Software Company
PO Box 338
Stoneham, MA 02180
AOL: DanaB1

Application
Shareware $5.00
Size: 24k

Version Sleuth v1.0 by Craig

Displays the information stored in the signature resource of an application (NOT the vers resource). Usually it's some text that identifies the version number of the program.

Craig Schmidt
509 Harper Lane
Midland, MI 48640
CIS: 71450,1343

Application
Shareware $?
Size: 19k

Xerisk v0.7

Disk duplication program used by AMUG (Arizona Macintosh User's Group). Can copy two 400k floppies onto one 800k floppy, translating the pseudo-hierarchy of MFS into true HFS folders. Does not work under MultiFinder.

Grand Canyon Code Factory

Application
Freeware
Size: 32k

File Organization Utilities

DesktopFolder v1.0

DesktopFolder brings a feature of System 7 to System 6: the Desktop Folder. Any file saved or moved into the Desktop Folder automatically appears on your desktop, as if the desktop were a folder all to itself.

Pete Gontier
gurgle@well.sf.ca.us
AOL: Zow

System Startup Extension
Freeware
Size: 4k

DisKeeper v1.2.2

DisKeeper is a disk cataloging program. It gives you complete information on your files and folders. Handy for finding invisible files and folders.

J 'Knife-the-Mac' Geagan
pad-parrot productions
7H Laurel Hill Road
Greenbelt, MD 20770
CIS: 71311,301

Application
Shareware $10.00
Size: 158k

FreshStart v1.6

FreshStart lets you get rid of all the random files that clutter up your system. You can also train applications to look in other folders for the files they need with this INIT.

Bob Hablutzel
Wildwood Software
1940 Sherman #316
Evanston, IL 60201

System Startup Extension
Shareware $25.00
Size: 32k

Ghost App v1.0

Creates ghost copies of applications. Good for lazy people who like to keep copies of programs in many folders so they don't have to look around for their favorite applications.

David Camp, Jr.
10751 Fury Lane
El Paso, TX 79935
GEnie: DCAMP

Application
Shareware $10.00
Size: 10k

ListApps v1.0

ListApps quickly produces a list of all applications, INITs, and cdevs on a disk. Use it to rapidly browse a volume for lost or hidden programs.

SK Hushing III
PO Box 9745
San Diego, CA 92169
CIS: 76645,3277
GEnie: SHUSHING

Application
Shareware $5.00
Size: 12k

NamedFolder v1.0

NamedFolder prompts you to enter a folder name each time you create a new folder.

David P. Sumner

System Startup Extension
Freeware
Size: 3k

Set Paths v1.0b2

This cdev allows applications that need Pref files to find them no matter where they are. And even more, if you've moved the Prefs Folder somewhere else, Set File searches until it finds it. Doesn't work with some programs

Bruce Tomlin
15801 Chase Hill Blvd. #109
San Antonio, TX 78256-1037
GEnie: BTOMLIN

Control Panel Extension
Freeware
Size: 18k

Tidy It Up ! v1.0

Tidy It Up! organizes your System Folder and rearranges files and folders by definable categories. Changes are purely cosmetic. Handy if you want a quick iconic reorganization of your System Folder.

Guy Fiems

Application
Shareware $15.00
Size: 84k

Utilities F1

Finder Enhancements

Aesthete v1.0

Lets you specify a SICN (small icon) to be used by MultiFinder when displaying the icon of an application on the right edge of the menu bar. Normally, MultiFinder scales the full-size icon, which is frequently aesthetically unappealing.

David Dunham

System Startup Extension
Freeware
Size: 5k

AltCDEF v1.2

AltCDEF changes the way scroll bars work in standard Mac applications.

Alex Colwell
(213) 607-3550
CIS: 73227,1267

Control Panel Extension
Freeware
Size: 39k

AltWDEF(cdev) v1.4

Adds a Shrink button next to the Zoom button in the title bar of a window. Has plenty of known bugs, but it works fine otherwise. Probably not System 7-compatible.

Alexander S. Colwell
(213) 607-3550
CIS: 73227,1267

Control Panel Extension
Freeware
Size: 31k

AutoMenus v5.01

AutoMenus makes menus stay selected after you release the mouse button. You select menu items by clicking on them; click outside the menu to close it. Supports submenus, and has special features (including Balloon Help) for System 7.0 users.

Michael J. Conrad
955 Escalon Ave., #505
Sunnyvale, CA 94086
CIS: 73457,426

Control Panel Extension
Shareware $10.00
Size: 39k

BarTender v1.0

BarTender enhances the scroll bars on the Macintosh. Has a few tracking problems, but it does make life a little better.

Thomas Chin
804 N. Dubuque St. #4
Iowa City, IA 52245

System Startup Extension
Shareware $7.00
Size: 4k

Big Menu™ v1.0

Adjusts the font size used for the menu bar. Lets you choose either 14- or 16-point; normally, 12-point is used. Good for the vision-impaired or those with high-resolution, large-screen monitors.

Andrew Welch
Mark 3
29 Grey Rocks Road
Wilton, CT 06897

Application
Shareware $8.00
Size: 36k

Big Pat

Awesome!!! Allows you to install large-size patterns (tiles) as desktop patterns on a Mac II.

Charles Dunn
Physics Department
Cornell University
Ithica, NY 14853

Control Panel Extension
Freeware
Size: 9k

Desk Pattern v1.0.1

A cdev for choosing desktop patterns (comes with 200 patterns) especially designed to handle direct color patterns. Aside from how nice they look, they can be set to dither, and they look nice with any number of available colors in different pattern tile sizes.

Brian Lowry
30 Renwick Heights Road
Ithaca, NY 14850
(607) 277-0948

Control Panel Extension
Freeware
Size: 73k

Earth v1.0

Replaces the Apple icon in the menu bar with a rotating image of the earth. Amaze your friends with this great new addition to your Mac desktop. Truly a neat little INIT.

Stefan Bilaniuk
Dept. of Math. & C.S.
Dartmouth College
Hanover, NH 03755

System Startup Extension
Freeware
Size: 3k

Enchanted Menus 88

Causes your menus to pop up at random places on the screen. Great for practical jokes.

IMI Software

System Startup Extension
Freeware
Size: 2k

Following v1.0

Following lets you to change the way your windows and scroll bars look and behave. It has some problems with machines that have Color QuickDraw installed.

Michael, Mark, & Thierry
BP 4125
34091 Montpellier Cedex 02
FRANCE

Control Panel Extension
Public Domain
Size: 48k

Fruits of Passion v2.4

Fruits of Passion enables you to change the Apple icon in the menu bar to another icon in either b&w or color.

Christophe Andres
2 rue de Fréland
67100 Strasbourg
FRANCE

Control Panel Extension
Freeware
Size: 26k

Grouper INIT v1.0

Allows you to select a group of windows, then drag them simultaneously.

Josh Pritikin
6500stom@ucsbuxa.ucsb.edu
GEnie: J.Pritikin

System Startup Extension
Freeware
Size: 6k

HigherMenus v2.0

Claims to let you place a hierarchical menu in the menu bar for quicker access. On the whole, this was totally unreliable. If it did work, it would be very cool. Docs in a separate file.

Dean Yu
20 Krebs Rd.
Plainsboro, NJ 08536

Control Panel Extension
Shareware $5.00
Size: 8k

InvisWin FKey v1.1

This FKEY makes the contents of the front window invisible.

Neal Trautman &
Josh Pritikin
1701 S.W. 42nd Street
Fargo, ND 58103

FKEY Resource
Shareware $3.00
Size: 1k

MenuEdit v1.1

Modifies menus in existing applications or resource files. Alters the text of menu items, Command-key equivalents, associated icons, and hierarchical submenus.

Oliver Steele
1209 Mason Farm Road
Chapel Hill, NC 27514

Application
Freeware
Size: 31k

Continued

MenuTuner v1.0.1

MenuTuner lets you customize the way hierarchical menus work on your Mac by controlling the display timing for these menus.

Carlos A. Weber, M.D.
1407 Aalapapa Drive
Kailua, HI 96734
CIS: 70277,726

Control Panel
Extension
Freeware
Size: 17k

Mover v3.0.4

Allows you to set keys to do various window manipulations when you hold them down.

Robert Polic

Control Panel
Extension
Freeware
Size: 12k

Scroll Limit v1.0

Controls the rate of continuous scrolling. Useful for slowing down scrolling on fast machines where clicking on the up or down arrow scrolls things faster than you like.

Ken McLeod
Blue Cloud Software

Control Panel
Extension
Freeware
Size: 14k

Scroll2 vv2.1b5

Dump this cdev in your System Folder and you can change the scroll arrows on your windows to something more attractive.

Mayson G. Lancaster
1492 W. Colorado Blvd.
Pasadena, CA 91105-1414
CIS: 70441,3263

Control Panel
Extension
Shareware $10.00
Size: 23k

WindChooser v1.01

WindChooser installs a new WDEF and affects all the windows in your System. A WDEF is a window definition, a little piece of code that is responsible for drawing and redrawing and dragging and all sorts of gobbledygook.

Pete Gontier
187 S. Patterson #E
Santa Barbara, CA 93111
CIS: 72261,1754

Control Panel
Extension
Freeware
Size: 12k

Window Cleaner v1.31

Window Cleaner adds a new menu item that aligns all open windows.

Satoshi Nishi
4-17-13 Shimizu
Minami-ku 201
Fukuoka 815
JAPAN

Control Panel
Extension
Freeware
Size: 30k

Windows v1.0b4

Adds a Windows menu that lists the names of all open windows. Selecting a window name from the menu brings that window to the front. Works in the Finder and in most applications.

J. Lindenberg
University of Karlsruhe
Postfach 6980
7500 Karlsruhe 1
GERMANY

Control Panel
Extension
Freeware
Size: 13k

WindowShade v1.1

WindowShade allows you to hide and show windows using a click and Command-key combination.

Robert Johnston
Interactive Technologies, Inc.

Control Panel
Extension
Freeware
Size: 9k

WorkingWind v1.0

A collection of window-handling tools. Send the front window to the bottom, bring the bottom window to the front, select the previous window, close the front window, and select and assign the working window (the main window in use).

Thomas Chin
804 N. Dubuque St. #4
Iowa City, IA 52245
ttchin@icaen.uiowa.edu

System Startup Extension
Shareware $7.00
Size: 6k

ZoomBar v1.7

Lets you shrink a window down to its title bar. This is handy if you often have lots of windows open. Be sure to unshrink title bars before quitting an application where you have used ZoomBar.

Brian Westley
1026 Blair Ave.
St. Paul, MN 55104

Control Panel Extension
Shareware $5.00
Size: 71k

Utilities F2

Finder Enhancements

acur Player

acur Player lets you play animated cursors from inside their resource files.

Jon WInd

Desk Accessory
Freeware
Size: 7k

Black Hole

Instead of trashing your unwanted files in an earthbound receptacle, you can now feed them to the universe's ultimate trash compactor, a black hole. Empty your files past the event horizon. For System 6 only.

Herb Goodman
GEnie: H.M.GOODMAN
CIS: 73300,3273

ResEdit Resource File
Freeware
Size: 8k

BlackHole II

Instead of trashing your unwanted files in an earthbound receptacle, you can now feed them to the universe's ultimate trash compactor, a black hole. Empty your files past the event horizon! System 7-compatible.

Richard Johnson
c/o Space Society
Box 4088
Boulder, CO 80306

ResEdit Resource File
Public Domain
Size: 10k

CatCurs

CatCurs can be used to change the standard watch cursor to a nice moving cat. You need ResEdit to install it into your System file.

Noel Gouveia

ResEdit Resource File
Freeware
Size: 1k

Cursor Edit v1986

Cursor Edit lets you create and edit cursors. The interface is somewhat rough, but some of the editing tools are neat.

Zeba Kimmel
970 SW Mark St.
Newport, OR 97365

Application
Public Domain
Size: 31k

Cursor Wrap

Causes the mouse cursor to wrap around to the other side when it hits the edge of the screen. For example, move the mouse past the left edge of the screen and it reappears on the right edge.

unknown

System Startup Extension
Public Domain
Size: 1k

CursorAnimator v1.0

Cursor Animator replaces the standard Mac cursors (the arrow, watch, plus, crosshair, and I-beam cursors) with the animated or static cursors of your choice. It comes with a number of cursors including a dogcow, a spinning world, and a moon.

Wilhelm M. Plotz
Siedlungsstr. 21
A-4222 St. Georgen/Gusen
AUSTRIA

Control Panel Extension
Freeware
Size: 22k

Cursors! v2.0

A lot of cursor resources. Use ResEdit to install them.

unknown

Resource File
Freeware
Size: 2k

DeskImation™ v2.0

Modifies your Finder so that folder icons look like open folders when you drag a file into a folder or otherwise highlight a folder. Provides a nice touch for those concerned with aesthetics. Has some problems with MultiFinder. Not System 7-compatible.

Andrew Welch
Mark 3 Software
29 Grey Rocks Road
Wilton, CT 06897

Application
Shareware $5.00
Size: 36k

Dragger v1.4

A Control Panel document that lets you drag images such as windows as solids or transparent. The Finder already does this with an outline. Does not work in color and probably not under System 7.

Oliver Steele
University Of North Carolina
Chapel Hill, NC

Control Panel Extension
Freeware
Size: 18k

Layout v1.9

Allows you to change the size and font of text, and the spacing and placement of icons on the desktop. Also lets you configure several other Finder properties.

Michael C. Connor
CIS: 76004,1447

Application
Freeware
Size: 41k

Lefty

Lefty is an INIT that points the Mac's arrow cursor in the other direction. This is especially useful for left-handed people.

Mike Stith
531 Sims Ave.
Columbia, SC 29205
CIS: 76174,1020

System Startup Extension
Freeware
Size: 2k

LunarCrack v1.2

Causes cracks to appear on the screen whenever your Mac beeps. Random jagged lines emanate from the current mouse location, but disappear after the beep. Docs in a separate file.

LunarWare
342 W. Madison
Kirkwood MO 63122

System Startup Extension
Freeware
Size: 3k

MeltCursorINIT v1.2

Causes the cursor to melt away while you are typing. Author admits to some known bugs, but it's cute for kicks.

Gavriel State
21 Sioux Cr.
Ottawa, Ontario
K2H 7E4 CANADA

System Startup Extension
Public Domain
Size: 8k

Shredder Stuff

Set of resources for changing your trash can icon into a shredder. Also adjusts the Finder's menus and dialogs to use the word Shredder instead of Trash.

Brad Ferguson
CIS: 76354,2733

Resource File
Freeware
Size: 8k

Stand-Alone Grouch v2.5B2

This version of The Grouch is childproof. It does not modify the Finder and draws the animation in a window instead of on the desktop. It does not require the The Grouch Extension to be present. See The Grouch description on this disk for more info.

Eric Shapiro
Rock Ridge Enterprises
620 Hidden Valley #102
Ann Arbor, MI 48104

Application
Freeware
Size: 313k

Utilities F2

Continued

The Grouch v2.5B1

Oscar the Grouch is a little guy who lives in your trash can and comes out to visit whenever you empty your trash. From the Sesame Street character.

Eric Shapiro
Rock Ridge Enterprises
620 Hidden Valley #102
Ann Arbor, MI 48104

System Startup Extension
Freeware
Size: 314k

Toilet v6.0.2

Toilet changes the Trash icon into a toilet. Changes all references to the trash and throwing away. Under the Special menu, you 'Flush the Toilet' for that final push into effluvial oblivion.

R. Sefcik

ResEdit Resource File
Freeware
Size: 8k

UFO Cursor

UFO Cursor is a replacement for the Mac's standard watch cursor. It can be installed using ResEdit.

Herb Goodman
CIS: 73300,3273
GEnie: H.M.GOODMAN

ResEdit Resource File
Freeware
Size: 1k

watchCursorINIT v2.0

INIT

watchCursorINIT changes the Mac watch cursor to a clock face (dial) cursor.

Gray Whale Software

System Startup Extension
Freeware
Size: 2k

BundAid v1.2

Scans all files on a disk, checking whether each file whose bundle bit is set does indeed have a BNDL resource. Normally, only executable programs, not data files, have the bundle bit set.

Jim Hamilton
2904 Jubilee Trl.
Austin, TX 78748
CIS: 71640,235

Application
Freeware
Size: 23k

CacheControl v1.3.1

Lets you turn off/on the instruction cache on a 68020 machine (Mac II), and both the instruction and data cache on a 68030 machine (SE/30, IIcx). Some older programs have problems if these caches are on.

Jim Hamilton
2914 Aftonshire Way #13102
Austin, TX 78748

Control Panel
Extension
Shareware $10.00
Size: 6k

CrashGuard v1.0

Attempts to ease the pain of system crashes by not displaying the bomb box. It tries to dump you back into the Finder instead.

Raymond Lau
100-04 - 73rd Avenue
Forest Hills, NY 11375

System Startup
Extension
Shareware $3.00
Size: 1k

CrashSaver Init v1.0

Attempts to gracefully exit back to the Finder when you hit the interrupt switch on the Programmer's Key after a system crash. This program is an INIT; there is also an FKEY version on this disk.

Jack Mello
DailSoft
PO Box 2861
Newport News, VA 23602

System Startup
Extension
Freeware
Size: 1k

CrashSaver Key

Attempts to gracefully exit back to the Finder when you hit an appropriate key combination.

Macazine
DailSoft
PO Box 2861
Newport News, VA 23602

FKEY Resource
Freeware
Size: 1k

Daylight! v2.01

Daylight! makes the Daylight Savings Time changes for you. It can be altered for new daylight savings rules.

Mark D. Malson
3473 Cabbage Palm Ave.
Melbourne, FL 32901
CIS: 71561,1313

Control Panel
Extension
Shareware $5.00
Size: 36k

DeBNDLer v1.1

Solves a problem caused by Adobe PostScript™ font icons when rebuilding the desktop. Speeds up rebuild of desktop by removing bundle information from files for these fonts and makes them DeBDNLer documents (with appropriate icons).

Stephan Somogyi
CIS: 72511,40
MacUserLabs@cup.portal.com
AOL: NETWORKSHOP

Application
Freeware
Size: 33k

General Utilities

DemoQuicKeys v1.0

Demonstration version of a great keyboard macro program. Perform sequences of menu selections, mouse clicks, and keystrokes with the touch of a key. Docs in a separate file. Only for System 6.

Don Brown
CE Software
PO Box 65580
West Des Moines, IA 50265

Control Panel
Extension
Demoware
Size: 67k

Utilities G1

Continued

Desktop Secretary v1.0

Desktop Secretary is an INIT that can perform some of the functions of the Desktop Manager (but doesn't get paid as much). It is designed to substitute for Desktop Manager on locked volumes that have numerous files.

Tom Lippincott
2117 Haste St., Apt. 310
Berkeley, CA 94704
lippin@math.berkeley.edu.

System Startup
Extension
Freeware
Size: 13k

FFP_Control v110 résidenc

Helps speed up Mac's floating-point math. It gives you several options with differing degrees of accuracy.

SGIL
110 Residence Elysees II
78170 La Celle Saint Cloud
FRANCE

Control Panel
Extension
Shareware $30.00
Size: 35k

FinderClick v1.1b

Fixes the problem caused by some poorly written programs where double-clicks are no longer recognized by the Finder. If this happens, select this application and choose Open from the Finder.

Robert S. T. Gibson

Application
Public Domain
Size: 2k

Fix Desktop v2.0

This program is designed to correct inaccuracies in the invisible desktop file that the Finder uses for your disk information (such as icons). Over time, the desktop file can become cluttered with old information, taking up space on your disks.

Anton Rang
215 S. Green Ave.
New Richmond, WI 54017

Application
Freeware
Size: 10k

HellFolderFix

A folder from hell is a folder that is empty but cannot be trashed. This program repairs some 'hellfolders' so that you can throw them out.

John Jeppson
CIS: 76174,2007

Application
Freeware
Size: 13k

immortality v0.94

Automatically opens up a selected desk accessory every time a new application is launched. There's no need for this program under MultiFinder. Contains docs in a separate file.

Ron Risley
1955 Edgemont Street
San Diego, CA 92102
CIS: 73547,240

System Startup
Extension
Freeware
Size: 3k

JumpStart v1.4

Program tries to supercharge an application by rearranging its resources so they load faster. Could be dangerous. Use only on a copy of your applications.

Karl B. Young

Control Panel
Extension
Public Domain
Size: 21k

keyAhead v0.1

Prevents many applications from flushing keystrokes when they start up, allowing you to type ahead as a program is loading. Includes docs in a separate file.

Ron Risley
CIS: 73546,240
GEnie: R-Squared
AppleLink: D0485

System Startup
Extension
Freeware
Size: 2k

MacInTalk v2.0

A newer version of the classic text vocalization program. This version can handle the new Sound Manager implemented in System 6.0.7. Some older programs that need MacInTalk don't work with this, some do.

Apple Computer, Inc.

System File
Freeware
Size: 35k

SetVolume v1.0

An FKEY for changing the volume of your Mac. Can cause problems with the Apple menu.

Dennis W. Manasco, Jr.
4921 East 15th Street
Tulsa, OK 74112
CIS: 74216,366

FKEY
Freeware
Size: 5k

SoftDisk 1.0 S

A hard disk partitioning program that allows you to create files that can be accessed just like a floppy disk. You can 'insert' and 'eject' them, store files and folders on them, etc. Comes with a companion INIT. Docs in a separate file.

Matthias Urlichs
Rainwiesenweg 9
8501 Schwaig 2
GERMANY

Desk Accessory
Shareware $45.00
Size: 16k

SoftwareFPU v2.1

This cdev can be used to fool your IIsi or LC into thinking it has an FPU. Some programs won't run on these machines (they give a 'Coprocessor not installed' error) because they look for an FPU on machines with newer processors. Works in most cases.

Jon Neil & Associates
PO Box 160699
Cupertino, CA 95016

Control Panel
Extension
Shareware $10.00
Size: 43k

SpeedChopper v1.0

SpeedChopper can be configured to consume more or less processor time to control the speed of your Macintosh. Activating and deactivating SpeedChopper is done by typing a user-defined key combination.

Lars Sundström
Seagull Engineering
Box 909
S-220 09 Lund
SWEDEN

Control Panel
Extension
Freeware
Size: 32k

TypeIt4Me v3.0

Gives you the ability to paste text in cases where you are usually not able to. An example is the Open and Save dialog boxes.

Riccardo Ettore
TypeIt4Me
67 rue de la limite
1970 W-Oppem
BELGIUM

System Startup
Extension
Shareware $30.00
Size: 39k

UnBundle v1.0

UnBundle searches the Desktop file for a certain application's icons. The icons are drawn and their resource IDs are listed, along with the type of file each icon is associated with and the FREF ID for the application.

Jack A. Littleton
PO Box 5301
Chico, CA 95927

Application
Shareware $10.00
Size: 17k

Volume Timer v1.0

Volume Timer is a cdev that lets you set 2 different beep volumes for your Mac to automatically switch between at times you set.

Don Sample
20 Deerfield Drive, Apt 1105
Nepean, Ontario
K2G 4L2 CANADA

Control Panel
Extension
Request Ware
Size: 9k

Utilities G2

General Utilities

Big Cheese Key v1.0

This little gem allows you to pop a saved screen shot onto your screen by using a keyboard command. Make your desktop appear to have some impressive work going on when the big cheese drops by!

Andrew Welch
Mark 3 Software
29 Grey Rocks Road
Wilton, CT 06897

Control Panel Extension
Shareware $5.00
Size: 17k

Biorhythm II v4.5

Computes biorhythms of your physical, mental, and emotional health. Produces a plot for any month based on your birthday.

David A. Bailey
7030 Enright Drive
Citrus Heights, CA 95621

Application
Shareware $15.00
Size: 64k

Hours of Daylight

Displays the declination of the sun and the hours of daylight on the current date at a specified latitude.

unknown

Application
Public Domain
Size: 4k

MacAuto! v0.85

A spreadsheet-like application for entering gasoline consumption, gasoline costs, and mileage traveled. Calculates and plots miles/gallon and $/mile.

Scott Silverman
Cra Z Software
PO Box 87
Spotswood, NJ 08884

Application
Freeware
Size: 69k

Morse CDEV v1.0

Generates Morse code signals. Enter text in a dialog box, click on the man's face, and the program emits the Morse code for the text using the Mac's speaker. Includes an INIT and XCMD for HyperCard.

unknown
CIS: 73720,2200

Control Panel Extension
Freeware
Size: 6k

Pict-All v1.0a

Creates an ASCII graphics image of a picture that has been copied to the clipboard. Represents picture by an array of ASCII characters rather than pixels. Very slow.

John Ray
RD #1 13225 Green Road
Wakeman, OH 44889

Application
Shareware $10.00
Size: 47k

Rooter6

Rooter is a program for finding the roots of polynomials of order 10 or less. It uses the QR algorithm to find the roots.

Doug Havenhill
Dynamics and Control

Desk Accessories
Shareware $5.00
Size: 19k

The Hitcher v1.0

Sort of a computer chain letter. The author asks that you enter your name and location in the application and give it to a friend. A scrolling box shows all the people who have passed along the program.

André Airy
3, chemin du coteau
54500 Vandœuvre
FRANCE

Application
Public Domain
Size: 12k

Today v2.01

Today looks at the system date, or a date you supply, then gives a list of interesting things that happened on that date.

Steve C. Johnson
Mitsubishi Electronics
1501 Luna Rd.
Carrollton, TX 75006

Application
Freeware
Size: 27k
12" 6 7 32

Typing Helper v1.0

Typing tutor that displays words one at a time for you to type. Screen has a picture of a keyboard whose letters are highlighted when you type them. Displays speed and accuracy statistics.

Richard Harvey
104 Fieldlard Lane
Sanger, TX 76266

Application
Freeware
Size: 33k
12" 6 7 32

Zoomation! v1.5

Zooms geometric shapes around the screen. Gives you a choice of 8 shapes. Has some problems redrawing the screen.

Andrew Welch
Mark 3
29 Grey Rocks Road
Wilton, CT 06897

Application
Freeware
Size: 14k

Utilities G3

General Utilities

A-Trap Demo v1.0.4

A program for looking at system calls. Works in conjuction with MacsBug. Also known as Simple Sample (Traffic Light).

Apple Computer, Inc.

Application
Freeware
Size: 5k

AATrix Revolver v1

Two applications: Loader and Shooter. Lets you set a different startup application for each day of the week or each day of the month. Neat idea! Docs in a separate file.

A. D. Jensen
AATrix Software
405 Bruce Avenue
Grand Forks, ND 58201

Application
Freeware
Size: 20k

ClockAdjust

ClockAdjust is a combination control panel and INIT that keeps your Mac clock accurate by adjusting its value every week.

James Nitchals
CIS: 71001,2232

Control Panel
Extension
Freeware
Size: 3k

init cdev v3.0

A program that lets you turn cdevs and INITs on and off without removing them from your System Folder. System 6 only. Send the author a postcard if you like his program.

John Rotenstein
PO Box 165
Double Bay, NSW 2028
AUSTRALIA

Control Panel
Extension
Freeware
Size: 26k

Init Manager v1.0b1

Lets you enable/disable individual INITs (startup documents) without having to add/remove them from your System Folder.

Steve Bryan
529 S. 7th Street #625
Minneapolis, MN 55415

Control Panel
Extension
Freeware
Size: 8k

INIT Manager Demo v1.0.0

Organizes startup programs (INITs) by allowing you to keep them in multiple folders. Only INITs in specified folders (and the System Folder) are executed. Demo version does not actually work.

Bob Hablutzel
1940 Sherman #316
Evanston, IL 60201

Control Panel
Extension
Demoware
Size: 5k

Init Mounter v1.0a

This application allows you to run cdevs and INITs after your Mac has started up. Not compatible with MultiFinder or System 7.

Chris Faigle

Application
Freeware
Size: 2k

INIT Tracker v1.0

INIT Tracker gives a detailed report on the INITs and cdevs that are in your System Folder.

Andrew Welch
29 Grey Rocks Road
Wilton CT 06897

System Startup
Extension
Shareware $10.00
Size: 43k

INIT-Scope v1.5

INIT scope gives detailed information regarding what INITs and cdevs are in your System Folder as they load in.

David P. Sumner

1009 Walters Lane
Columbia, SC 29208
(803) 783-2980

Control Panel
Extension
Freeware
Size: 40k
12" 6 7 32

'It's Just a Clock' v1.0a27

A program that displays a clock on the screen. The clock can be analog or digital, and its size is configurable.

Pete Helme
Apple Computer, Inc.
Mac Developer Tech Support
AppleLink: eelpout

Application
Freeware
Size: 24k
12" 6 7 32

Launch v1.3

Rotates startup screens and sounds. User must create a list of specially named startup files, and this program selects the next file in the list on subsequent startups.

Mike Kazmierczak
X Systems
32-F Stratford Hills
Chapel Hill, NC 27514-3239

Application
Shareware $5.00
Size: 37k
12" 6 7 32

MacAClock v1.0.1

Another clock display program that displays an analog face. Colors can be assigned to the clock hands.

Zikif Hamdy
PO Box 782
Corvallis, OR 97339-0782

Application
Freeware
Size: 27k
12" 6 7 32

Menu Clock v3.0

Installs a small digital clock displaying the hour and minutes on the right side of your menu bar. Leaves room for the application icon if running under MultiFinder.

David Phillip Oster

System Startup
Extension
Freeware
Size: 2k
12" 6 7 32

Persistence/DeskClock

DeskClock places a clock on your desktop that looks like raised pieces of the gray desktop.

Darin Adler

System Startup
Extension
Freeware
Size: 7k
12" 6 7 32

Programmer's Key v1.1

Great utility for programmers that uses the reset key on the keyboard to perform the same functions as the Programmer's Key. No more reaching around the side of your Mac to pop into the debugger.

Paul Mercer
PO Box 160165
Cupertino, CA 96016-0165
AppleLink: MERCER1

System Startup
Extension
Freeware
Size: 2k
12" 6 7 32

ShowPict/HidePict

A pair of INITs for displaying a color picture at startup. Uses the picture's own color table instead of the system color table. Color pictures look funny if a color table other than their own is used.

Bill Band

System Startup
Extension
Freeware
Size: 1k
12" 6 7 32

SSSwitcher© v10-20-87

A Screens and Sounds Switcher that randomly selects startup screens, backdrop screens, startup sounds, beep sounds, and shutdown sounds. Picks one of each from all those stored in special folders.

Bob Andris
12155 Terrence AV
Saratoga, CA 95070
(408) 252-5469

Application
Freeware
Size: 41k

SuperClock! v3.9.1

A very nice program that installs a clock in your menu bar. Leaves room for the MultiFinder application icon, hides when a screen saver activates, can toggle between time and date, and has 12- or 24-hour mode.

Steve Christensen
CIS: 76174,1712

Control Panel
Extension
Freeware
Size: 5k

TestDcmd v1.1

Comes with MacsBug. Use it to test dcmd routines.

Michael Tibbit
Apple Computer, Inc.

Application
Freeware
Size: 13k

512KE XPRAM INIT v1.0

Allows owners of Mac 512KEs to use the Sound control panel device (cdev) that comes with System 6.0 and later. Lets you select which sound to use when the Mac beeps.

Scott Armitage

System Startup Extension
Freeware
Size: 2k

Analog board

This MacDraw document is for repairing a bad analog board on a Mac Plus (also 128 and 512K Macs).

D. Heady, MPC
650 S. Park Ave.
Crown Point, IN 46307
(219) 662-0052

MacDraw II Document
Freeware
Size: 22k

DeskZap v2.0b11

Renames, deletes, and copies files. Displays and modifies Finder information. Strips line feeds, control characters, and trailing blanks from text files.

Bruce Tomlin
15801 Chase Hill Blvd. #109
San Antonio, TX 78256

Desk Accessory
Shareware $15.00
Size: 56k

DOS Mounter Demo v0.9

DOS Mounter demo allows you to mount and use MS DOS disks. Of course, you must have a Mac that has one of those 1.4-meg drives. Can only be used with 3.5-inch DOS disks that have been named DEMO* by an MS-DOS machine.

Dayna
50 South Main Street, 5th Floor
Salt Lake City, UT 84144
(801) 531-0203

System Startup Extension
Demoware
Size: 50k

FinderSubstitute

Lets you load up to 35 desk accessories within this program. Allows access to DAs without installing them in your System file. Useful for System 6 only.

Jim Moore

Application
Freeware
Size: 4k

HD Runner v1.1

A Finder replacement that launches applications and opens documents. Docs in a separate file. A clunky little program that doesn't work under MultiFinder or System7.

Dewi Williams
170 Forsythe Road
Magnolia Star Route
Nederland, CO 80466

Application
Public Domain
Size: 19k

IIfx Serial Switch v1.0

IIfx Serial Switch modifies the serial ports on the Mac IIfx so that they work like the standard Mac serial ports.

Apple Computer, Inc.

Control Panel Extension
Freeware
Size: 3k

microLaunch v1.0

A simple Finder replacement that launches other applications and supports desk accessories. Run applications by selecting them using a standard Open File dialog box.

John Doherty
1028 E. Hedrick
Tucson, AZ 85719
GEnie: J.L.Doherty

Application
Shareware $10.00
Size: 8k

MidiBox Paint

Diagram of a universal MIDI/RS-232 (or RS-422) Interface Circuit. For hardware hackers who want to build their own MIDI interface. Parts cost about $25.

R. Guttery
Common Cents Computers

MacPaint
Freeware
Size: 17k

Oasis v2.02

A complete Finder replacement that launches applications, opens documents, creates folders, and manipulates files. Extensive docs within the program.

Jan Eugenides
RR 1 Box 9463
Waterbury Center, VT 05677

Application
Shareware $15.00
Size: 68k

RS-232 description notes

Tables of the serial connectors for the DB-9 and DIN-8 connectors for the Mac. Also shows the pin in/outs for the Mac 25-pin serial, output to the ImageWriter I, ADC 1200 Baud Phone Modem, and Applied Reader Technologies Eprom Programmer.

Thomas Walsh
AOL: ThomasW4

TeachText
Document
Freeware
Size: 10k

SCSI Tester

SCSI Tester traces the different phases of the SCSI protocol.

Roger Feyereisen
46, Rue Pierre Wiser
L-9092 Ettelbruck
LUXEMBOURG

Application
Freeware
Size: 16k

SCSIStart v1.3

Most disks can be jumpered to automatically start the drive spindle when the device powers up, but some cannot. SCSIStart allows you to use these devices by issuing a Start command to a SCSI device. Comes with an INIT too.

Phil Hunt

Application
Freeware
Size: 3k

SE/30 to WP-2 Cable

Shows the pin schematics for the serial ports and cable for connecting the SE/30 to a Tandy WP-2 word processor for transfer of files.

unknown

TeachText
Document
Public Domain
Size: 3k

Servant v0.953

An alternate shell for the Mac that incorporates aspects of the Finder, Switcher, and ResEdit. A truly innovative program that is much better than the Finder in many respects. Definitely not for System 7.

Andy Hertzfeld

Application
Freeware
Size: 128k

SF&I v0.92

A SCSI formatter and installer for techies who want to create their own SCSI driver. Comes with documentation and resources files. Requires ResEdit for adjusting parameters.

Ephraim Vishniac
PO Box 1357
East Arlington, MA 02174

Application
Shareware $10.00
Size: 7k

SID Assembly Help

Instructions for assembling a Cedar Technologies SID Kit. Comes with a diagram showing a correction to their instructions.

Thomas Walsh
AOL: ThomasW4

TeachText Document
Public Domain
Size: 65k

Tiny Finder

Allows you to navigate to a file by using a mechanism similar to the standard Open File dialog box and then launch it.

Kent Kersten
Harrison Systems
437 Atlas Drive
Nashville, TN 37211

Application
Public Domain
Size: 6k

Xpressway Fkey

Puts up a window with the icons of specified applications. Double-clicking on an icon runs the associated program. Not stable under MultiFinder. Comes with a file with the icon shown.

Andrew Welch
Mark 3 Software
29 Grey Rocks Road
Wilton, CT 06897

FKEY
Shareware $10.00
Size: 12k

General Utilities

Eyeballs v1.0

Places a set of eyes in your menu bar that watch you as your work (when they can stay awake...they love to nap).

Ben Haller
Stick Software

System Startup Extension
Freeware
Size: 6k

Fortune II

Displays a random fortune (as in a fortune cookie) once per day or every time you restart your Mac. Similar to the fortune program on UNIX machines. There are both normal and obscene (which may be toggled off) messages.

Arthur Britto II
1850 Arch Street #3
Berkeley, CA 94709
(415) 841-7216

Control Panel Extension
Freeware
Size: 624k

Mac EyeCon v1.0

Mac EyeCon displays a pair of eyes that watch you work. Eyes can be placed anywhere on the desktop, and extra pairs of eyes can be added. This program is designed for use under MultiFinder. Really cool!

Michael C. Koss

Application
Freeware
Size: 9k

Obnoxious

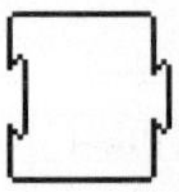

This INIT makes your Mac scream out when you boot up. Also screams at random times. It's...obnoxious! Great for practical jokes.

unknown

System Startup Extension
Public Domain
Size: 23k

Oracle v1.0

Oracle presents you with a random thoughtful quotation each time you start up your computer or once a day, whichever you specify. Oracle has a library of over 1,000 profound readings.

Andrew Welch
Mark 3 Software
29 Grey Rocks Road
Wilton, CT 06897

Control Panel Extension
Shareware $5.00
Size: 300k

AffiniFile MENU

Modified version of the menu for the desk accessory AffiniFile. This version appears as a submenu when using hierDA, a freeware utility available on another BMUG disk.

Dean Wette
CIS: 72317,2034

ResEdit Resource File
Public Domain
Size: 1k

CheckList v1.0

CheckList lets you peek inside PageMaker 4.0 publication files and get information that's difficult to get any other way.

ElseWare Corporation
713 Northeast Northlake Way
Seattle, WA 98105-6429
(206) 547-9623

Application
Shareware $45.00
Size: 178k

DeskWriter (AppleTalk) v2.1

A newer version of the HP DeskWriter printer driver. The older versions have problems with memory management. The AppleTalk version is the least buggy. Comes with normal driver also.

Hewlett-Packard

Chooser Extension
Freeware
Size: 188k

MountImage v1.2ß1

A cdev for mounting Disk Dup+ disk image files as RAM disks. Great for those who want to manipulate the files inside of disk images without having to dup the disk. You can change images while they are mounted!

Steve Christensen

Control Panel Extension
Freeware
Size: 12k

RepairReminders v1.0b4

Repairs Smart Alarms™ reminder files that are damaged during system crashes. May not work on the newer versions of SmartAlarms.

Ngai Tseung Cheung
JAM Software
PO Box 1345
Point Reyes Station, CA 94956

Application
Freeware
Size: 14k

Suitcase II Updater v1.2.11

Suitcase II Updater updates Suitcase II versions 1.2 through 1.2.10 to version 1.2.11. This version is needed for use with System 7.0, but also fixes some problems with earlier system versions.

Software Supply

Application
Freeware
Size: 54k

Utilities J1

Memory Utilities

ApplicationMenu v3.5

Provides a menu of all applications currently running under MultiFinder. This menu drops down when you click on the far right side of the menu bar. For System 6. Comes with an INIT of the same name.

Larry Rosenstein
182 Muir Ave.
Santa Clara, CA 95051
AppleLink: Rosenstein1

Control Panel Extension
Freeware
Size: 11k

Battery Zap

Zaps the parameter RAM by changing the settings back to the factory defaults.

unknown

Application
Public Domain
Size: 1k

CClock v1.4

CClock is a nifty little program that displays a digital clock in a window on the Mac. It is MultiFinder-compatible.

Stephen Martin
13132B E. Kansas Dr. #113
Aurora, CO 80012
CIS: 75126,51

Application
Shareware $5.00
Size: 17k

DA Handler Resizer v1.0

DA Handler Resizer allows you to change the memory request default (16) for the system. This for System 6 only.

Loftus E. Becker, Jr.
CIS: 76703,4054

Application
Freeware
Size: 7k

Earth Idle v1.0

Displays a spinning Earth in a small window. Runs as a background task under MultiFinder to monitor CPU usage. The Earth spins faster when it gets more CPU time.

The Black Swamp Software Co.
1680 Braddock Court
San Jose, CA 95125

Application
Public Domain
Size: 24k

GLA v1.5

GLA stands for Graphic Load Average. It graphically displays the amount of CPU time background tasks are receiving when running under MultiFinder. Docs are in a separate file.

Peter Korn

Application
Freeware
Size: 7k

HeapSpy v1.0

Allows you to graphically look at memory addresses to see if they are purgeable, relocatable, etc. Works with System 7.

Jeff Bock
6418 Chippendale Dr.
Baton Rouge, LA 70817
CIS: 73260,1174

Desk Accessory
Freeware
Size: 9k

HeapTool v1.4

HeapTool is designed to give the Mac enough system heap to operate properly. It gives the Mac a specific amount of system heap after all other INITs have loaded. System 6 only.

Kerry Clendinning
PO Box 26061
Austin, TX 78755
CIS: 76424,2214

Control Panel Extension
Shareware $13.50
Size: 14k

_Launch v3.0

Launch is a small, MultiFinder-compatible program that allows users to start applications and/or switch to other running applications, like the Apple menu in MultiFinder.

Michael Libes
1071 Morewood Ave.
Pittsburgh, PA 15213

Application
Shareware $10.00
Size: 34k

M/F Rating v1.1

Measures the MultiFinder-compatibility of an application by monitoring the amount of CPU time it receives. Friendly applications let others have as much CPU time as possible.

Jim Leitch
Toronto
CANADA

Application
Freeware
Size: 11k

Memdoggie

Displays a memory map of the Mac's RAM when running under MultiFinder. Bombs if run without MultiFinder.

Jeff Hokit
Apple Computer, Inc.

Application
Freeware
Size: 34k

MemINIT cdev v1.0

MemINIT displays the amount of memory you have available, either with a bar on top of the menu bar or by replacing the apple in the Apple menu with a pie chart. Neat cdev.

Seth LaForge
658 Wildcat Canyon
Berkeley, CA 94708
AOL: SethLF

Control Panel Extension
Freeware
Size: 8k

MFMenu v1.1

MFMenu attaches a copy of the MultiFinder Application Switching menu to the MultiFinder icon in the menu bar. The menu pops up when the mouse is pressed in the menu bar between the MultiFinder icon and the right edge of the screen.

Fred D. Reed
IMI SoftWare
121 14th Street
Seal Beach, CA 90740
CIS: 76357,2530

System Startup Extension
Freeware
Size: 3k

Monitor v1.0B1

Monitors the amount of CPU time allocated to background tasks running under MultiFinder.

Ken Bates
decwrl!ssdevo.dec.com!bates

Application
Freeware
Size: 8k

MultiClock v1.2

Now you can have a calendar and analog clock run in the background when you are using MultiFinder.

Martin Simoneau

Application
Freeware
Size: 5k

MultiLaunch v1.0

Lets you use MultiFinder without the memory requirements of the Finder. This saves about 130k of RAM. Launch other applications from within this program instead of the Finder.

Jan Eugenides
RR 1, Box 9463
Waterbury Center, VT 05677

Application
Shareware $10.00
Size: 5k

MultiSet v1.0

Creates sets of applications and/or documents that can be launched all at once when running under MultiFinder. Includes docs in a separate file. Has problems opening documents.

Donald Neff
Neff Systems Group
3286 Knightswood Way
San Jose, CA 95148

Application
Shareware $15.00
Size: 18k

NavCom v1.1

NavCom is a simple MultiFinder background application intended to provide interesting ambience to a Mac screen by giving the illusion that a lot of things are going on. NavCom creates up to 30 small 32 x 32 pixel windows.

Harry R. Chesley

Application
Freeware
Size: 14k

RAM Check v2.0

A nifty program for testing the RAM memory of your Mac. The about box is empty, but everything else checks out fine. May not work on the newest Macs.

Tim Capps and Mike Friese
15180 Transistor Lane
Huntington Beach, CA 92649
(714) 892-8199

Application
Public Domain
Size: 7k

RamDisk+ v2.21

Excellent cdev allows you to set aside some of your Mac's RAM for storing files. Files on a RAM disk are accessed quickly but disappear when you turn off your Mac.

Roger D. Bates
Route 1, Box 865
Hillsboro, OR 97124
(503) 645-3930

Control Panel Extension
Shareware $20.00
Size: 49k

SE/30 SIMM Installation

Describes how to install SIMMs into the SE/30.

John Albert
GEnie: JOHN.ALBERT

Text
Public Domain
Size: 14k

SwapParamRAM

Swaps the values in your parameter RAM with values stored within the program. You can set up the program so that the stored values are a copy of your current parameter RAM values.

Glenn L. Austin

Application
Public Domain
Size: 4k

Take Off v3.0.2

Take Off allows you decide whether the Mac boots under the Finder or Multifinder when you start up. Also allows the direct launching of an application, then returns to either the Finder or MultiFinder when closed. Also has a password feature.

Jim Richardson
10623 Canyoncrest Lane
Houston, TX 77086
CIS: 73307,1131

Application
Shareware $5.00
Size: 23k

Tears v1.0

Displays a window with tears dripping down. Can run as a background task under MultiFinder.

Steve Morein
44 Kinnan Way
Basking Ridge, NJ 07920
CIS: 76545,2472

Application
Freeware
Size: 8k

Tears(MAC II)

Displays a window with tears dripping down. Can run as a background task under MultiFinder. This is a color version of Tears, which is also on this disk.

Steve Morein
44 Kinnan Way
Basking Ridge, NJ 07920
CIS: 76545,2472

Application
Freeware
Size: 9k

TN176 Installing SIMMs

Comes with 5 MacDraw files showing how to install RAM into the IIcx, IIci, 1989 Portable, Plus, SE (with and without jumper), SE/30, II, and IIx.

Apple Computer, Inc.

MacWrite 4.5 Document
Freeware
Size: 220k

ToMultiFinder v4.0

Displays a dialog box at startup time that gives you the choice of running MultiFinder or the regular Finder.

Rich Siegel
11 Hammond Street #9
Waltham, MA 02154
(617) 647-4825

Application
Shareware $15.00
Size: 9k

Waiting

Displays a very small window with an indicator that shows how long applications are waiting for CPU time under MultiFinder.

Erik Kilk

Application
Freeware
Size: 16k

zapPRAM

Resets the parameter RAM on your Mac to the factory default settings.

unknown

Application
Public Domain
Size: 1k

Zippy v2.0

Zippy hangs out in the background and enlightens you with his random words of wisdom. Designed to run as a background application under MultiFinder. MacinTalk is required.

Chuck Shotton
c/o BIAP Systems
PO Box 580622
Houston, TX 77258-0622

Application
Freeware
Size: 45k

Utilities K1

Keyboard Utilities

ADBProbe v1.0.3

Shows the devices connected to the ADB ports on your Mac; lists the address for each. Also lets you reset the ADB bus. Another neat little utility from the author of SCSIProbe.

Robert Polic

Control Panel Extension
Freeware
Size: 5k

ANSI Dvorak v1.0

A Dvorak keyboard for your Mac. System 7 installs by dragging to the System Folder. Use ResEdit to install in System 6.

James W. Walker

Keyboard Resource File
Public Domain
Size: 2k

Clavier Français

A French KeyEd keyboard for the Mac. KeyEd is on this disk.

unknown

KeyEd Keyboard File
Public Domain
Size: 2k

Diacritics

A KeyEd keyboard for the Mac. KeyEd is on this disk.

unknown

KeyEd Keyboard File
Public Domain
Size: 2k

Electric Dvorak Installer

Installer program for changing your keyboard to the Dvorak layout. You can switch back and forth between QWERTY and Dvorak by using the control panel device included in this package.

Tom Phoenix
Box 265-ed
Portland, OR 97207-0265

Application
Freeware
Size: 12k

F1F4 v1.0

Appears to be an early version of the other F1F4 INIT on this same disk; read that one's description and take your pick.

Erny Tontlinger
CIS: 73720,2200

System Startup Extension
Freeware
Size: 1k

F1F4 v1.3

F1F4 is a INIT that translates the function keys F1, F2, F3, and F4 on an Apple extended keyboard to command-Z (undo), Command-X (cut), Command-C (copy) and Command-V (paste). There is a different INIT of the same name on this disk.

David Hirsh
9100 9th Street N., #1004
St. Petersburg, FL 33702

System Startup Extension
Shareware $1.00
Size: 2k

Key Lights v1.0d8

Key Lights is a cdev that makes the Num Lock, Caps Lock, and Scroll Lock lights on an Apple Extended Keyboard sequence in a back and forth motion.

Rick Kaseguma
474 Memorial Drive
Cambridge, MA 02139

Control Panel Extension
HappiWare
Size: 10k

Keyboard Shortcuts v1.3b

Allows Electric Dvorak users to have Dvorak-arranged Command-key shortcuts. It does not affect QWERTY users. Useful with the Electric Dvorak package, version 1.0.

Tom Phoenix
Box 265-ed
Portland, OR 97207-0265

System Startup Extension
Freeware
Size: 2k

KeyEd v0.6.2US

Assigns any ASCII character to any key on the keyboard. Keyboard configurations may be saved and installed in the System file. Useful for working with foreign language character sets.

Samuel Fabien
2, Rue Nollet
75017 - Paris
FRANCE

Application
Shareware $15.00
Size: 54k

KeytransPatch

Modifies the behavior of double-strike keys (used to generate accents and diacritical marks) in System versions 4.0 or later to be the same as in older versions of the System.

Samuel Fabien
2, Rue Nollet
75017 - Paris
FRANCE

System Startup Extension
Freeware
Size: 1k

LaserLister v4.1E

Lists all available LaserWriters. Has options for choosing certain paging and format settings, but there's no documentation that explains the choices.

Patrick W. Dirks
Alan Oppenheimer

Application
Freeware
Size: 14k

Mouse Odometer v1.0

Mouse Odometer watches your cursor and records, in miles, how far it travels on the screen. Adjust its measurements based on your screen resolution. Comes with an INIT.

Sean P. Nolan
Dartmouth HB 2658
Hanover, NH 03755

Application
Shareware $5.00
Size: 37k

Mouse2 v1.4a

Mouse2 doubles the speed of your ADB mouse. It has no effect on the Mac Plus or any other non-ADB mouse.

Ryoji Watanabe
PO Box 160191
Cupertino, CA 95016-0191

Control Panel Extension
Shareware $5.00
Size: 5k

Pointing Device v1.2

This looks an awful lot like the ProPoint INIT. It's basically the same (by the same guy and all). This is a little more recent.

Robert J. Rajewski
Embedded MicroSystems, Inc.

Control Panel Extension
Freeware
Size: 12k

Port~Master™ v1.0

Adjusts the settings for the serial ports (printer and modem ports) that are stored in the parameter RAM of your Mac. Comes with a HyperCard stack that serves as documentation and an installer program.

S. Korean
COM~LINK
485 Brown Briar Circle
Horsham, PA 19044

HyperCard Stack
Freeware
Size: 50k

Utilities K1

Continued

@PortDev/@ResetPorts v2.1.0

@PortDev cdev lets you adjust the PRAM settings for the modem port, as well as the printer port. The @ResetPorts application resets these settings to the factory defaults. Change the memory size of @ResetPorts so it can run in MultiFinder.

Mathew Alan Milroy
C. P. 1375, Station 'H'
Montréal, Québec
H3G 2N3 CANADA

Control Panel
Extension
Freeware
Size: 154k

PrintAid v1.1b1

PrintAid lets you switch the printing application into the background or run something else in its background.

James W. Walker
3200 Heyward Street
Columbia, SC 29205
CIS: 76367,2271

Control Panel
Extension
Freeware
Size: 35k

SafeKeys Init v0.3

Displays a dialog box at startup time that lets you choose which keyboard configuration to use. It changes the keyboard at startup, but the change seems to take two startups to work. If you choose immediate activation, you get a bus error.

Samuel Fabien
2, Rue Nollet
75017 - Paris
FRANCE

System Startup
Extension
Freeware
Size: 6k

SaveATree v1.5

Neat! SaveATree permits the printing of more than one page of text on a single page. Save a tree! Source code is available for $20.

Michael S. Engber
1585 Ridge Avenue
Evanston, IL, 60201
CIS: 70007,3505

Application
Freeware
Size: 67k

SerialPrint II v1.0.1

A DA for printing text on a printer with built-in fonts. Supports ImageWriter, Epson FX, and HP DeskJet printers. Documentation says you must load it using Suitcase II or Master Juggler, not the Font/DA Mover.

Barry Wolman
159 Oxbow Road
Needham, MA 02192
CIS: 71021

Desk Accessory
Freeware
Size: 50k

SmartKeys v2.0

SmartKeys assists Macintosh typists by allowing them to type on the Macintosh as if it were a typewriter. It prevents typing more than one space, converts two consecutively typed hyphens into a dash, and more!

Maurice Volaski
173 Princeton Ave., Apt. #2
Amherst, NY 14226-5006
volaski@contra.med.buffalo.edu

Control Panel
Extension
Freeware
Size: 42k

Standard US KeyBoard

A KeyEd keyboard for the Mac. KeyEd is on this disk.

unknown

KeyEd Keyboard File
Public Domain
Size: 2k

The Namer v2.1

Presents a list of all available LaserWriters and gives you the option of changing their names.

Apple Computer, Inc.

Application
Freeware
Size: 12k

Bomb & Crash Encyclpd. v1.0

A HyperCard stack designed to give you information about system error codes and what to do about them. Nice layout.

Eric C. Thauvin
MacSpect Incorporated
2269 Chestnut St. #338
San Francisco, CA 94123

HyperCard Stack
Shareware $15.00
Size: 301k

Fedit tricks

Tips on how to use Fedit, a former shareware program that is now a commercial product. Fedit is a low-level file editor that lets you inspect and modify the raw data of a file.

Tom Zusag

TeachText Document
Public Domain
Size: 9k

Fix It All

Explains how a sophisticated Mac user can use several file editors and copy programs to recover files from crashed floppies. Written in 1986, most of the information is out of date unless you have an older System (pre-System 6).

Joseph F. Buchanan
University of Utah

MacWrite 4.5 Document
Public Domain
Size: 9k

Fix MacWrite

Explains how to recover a damaged MacWrite file. Much of the information is now out of date.

Joseph F. Buchanan
University of Utah

MacWrite 4.5 Document
Public Domain
Size: 8k

Hard Disk Copy Delays

Compilation of several messages on CompuServe discussing the use of Desktop Manager, which creates a more efficient Desktop file. This topic will interest those with large hard disks.

various

MacWrite 4.5 Document
Public Domain
Size: 28k

Hard drive specs

A list of most of the hard disks manufactured up to mid-1989. Also has the phone numbers of manufacturers if you need more info.

unknown

MacWrite 4.5 Document
Public Domain
Size: 96k

IntroToMacsBug.Write

This document covers the basic MacsBug commands. Intended for testers who have a fairly good understanding of the Macintosh but are not necessarily programmers. For older versions of MacsBug.

Carol Crews

MacWrite 4.5 Document
Public Domain
Size: 38k

MacsBug-MW

This document describes the theory and operation of MacsBug. It also describes the syntax of commands accepted by MacsBug. It is specific to MacsBug 5.1, but can be useful in understanding newer versions.

unknown

MacWrite 4.5 Document
Public Domain
Size: 58k

Resistors

Template for determining the resistance of a resistor based on the color of the bands found on it. Also gives you the color bands if you input a resistance.

Mr. Lynn Wilborn
6677 W. Colfax #367
Lakewood, CO 80214
GEnie: LWILBORN

Excel
Shareware $5.00
Size: 6k
12 6 7 32

+ROM differences

Discusses the differences between the 3 ROM versions for the Mac Plus. These subtle variations do not affect the vast majority of Plus owners.

James MacPhail
CIS: 72027,2155

MacWrite 4.5
Document
Public Domain
Size: 7k
12 6 7 32

Sad Mac Codes

A chart explaining the meaning of those Sad Mac error codes that appear when your Mac fails at powerup. They often indicate a serious hardware error. Hope that you never see one of these!

unknown

Text File
Public Domain
Size: 2k
12 6 7 32

Sad Macs

These documents explain some of the causes of the Mac's Sad Mac error codes.

unknown

TeachText
Document
Freeware
Size: 2k
12 6 7 32

SCSI details

Gives technical details of the SCSI bus and termination. Just right for the wirehead in all of us.

Engineering Department
MicroNet Technology, Inc.

TeachText
Document
?
Size: 14k
12 6 7 32

System Errors Table v3.1

Displays a list of system error numbers and a short description of the error. Explains that little ID number that shows up in the System Bomb dialog box.

Bill Steinberg

Desk Accessory
Freeware
Size: 47k
12 6 7 32

Alchemist

See Clipboard Magician; this DA does most of the dirty work for Clipboard Magician.

unknown

Desk Accessory
Freeware
Size: 18k

Amigator INIT v1.0

Amigator is a utility for faster and easier navigation with any of the standard file dialogs. It pops up an extra menu in all the standard file dialogs (those that allow you to open or save files).

Lluís Bibiloni
c/ Romans 3, 2º 3ª
(08025) Barcelona
SPAIN

System Startup Extension
Shareware $10.00
Size: 39k

Anonymity v1.0

Removes the personalizing information from some applications--in case you misspell your name or move to a different company.

unknown

Application
Public Domain
Size: 3k

ApFont v3.2

A cdev to change the default font used by applications. The default font is the one used by most applications in untitled windows.

Jim Hamilton
2914 Aftonshire Way #13102
Austin, TX 78748

Control Panel Extension
Shareware $5.00
Size: 20k

ChooseCDEV™ v1.0

Sets the icon that appears first in the scrolling list on the left side of the Control Panel desk accessory. Lets you quickly access your most frequently used control panel device.

CE Software
PO Box 65580
West Des Moines, IA 50265
(515) 224-1995

Control Panel Extension
Freeware
Size: 22k

Clipboard Magician v0.65

A software package consisting of two FKEYs, an installer application and a DA. Basically, the DA lets you convert PICTs to ICONs or SICNs, CURS and ICONs to PICTs, and MWRT to TEXT, perform data massaging, etc.

Ed Lai
lai@apple.com
AppleLink: Lai1

various
Freeware
Size: 224k

FetchIt v1.2

FetchIt adds several useful functions to the standard Open and Save dialog box. It pops up a menu when the volume name is clicked on. From there, you can get info on files or find all files that can be opened by the current application.

Scott D. Silverman
PO Box 6379
Haverhill, MA 01831
(508) 373-0977
CIS: 74007,2303

System Startup Extension
Shareware $5.00
Size: 13k

Front & Center™ v.92

Automatically centers any dialog box around the current cursor location. Good for those with large screens who hate guessing where a program will put up its dialog boxes.

Pete Helme
eelpout software
1939 Marshall Ave. #25
St. Paul, MN 55104

Control Panel Extension
Shareware $10.00
Size: 8k

Utilities M1

Continued

GooPanel v1.0a1

GooPanel allows you to open cdevs in their own custom-size windows without having to go through the Control Panel. System 7 now allows you to do this.

Steve Bollinger
Cyberite Systems
909 Church St #C
Ann Arbor, MI 48104-3463

Application
Freeware
Size: 43k

HD Mini-Icon v2.0

Changes the little icon of the hard disk that you see in standard Open File dialog boxes. Works with icons for DataFrame, MagNet, Paradise, Photon, AST, HyperDrive, and SE internal hard drives. Doesn't work with System 7 drivers.

Scott Silverman
Cra Z Software
PO Box 87
Spotswood, NJ 08884

Application
Freeware
Size: 62k

Open-wide v2.4

Open-wide widens the standard file dialog boxes so that you can see long file names. It can also increase the vertical size of the file list. Also re-centers all standard file dialogs according to Apple guidelines.

James W. Walker
3200 Heyward Street
Columbia, SC 29205
CIS: 76367,2271

Control Panel
Extension
Postcardware
Size: 44k

Rebound v0.95

Rebound is an enhancement to the Open and Save dialogs. With Rebound installed, the file list scrolls to and highlights the last opened file or folder for each directory.

Fred D. Reed
IMI SoftWare

System Startup
Extension
Freeware
Size: 4k

Scribe™ v1.0

Lets you sets the default font for applications. Many applications use this font when you create a new document. The normal default font is Geneva.

Andrew Welch
Mark 3
29 Grey Rocks Road
Wilton, CT 06897

Application
Shareware $8.00
Size: 32k

Set BackPat v1.0

Lets you sets the background pattern for a selected application. Stable, but doesn't do much, not many applications use their own background pattern resources.

James Moore

Application
Freeware
Size: 4k

UnScrolly v1.0

UnScrolly allows you to choose to view items in the scrolling icon bar of the Control Panel either by icons or by names. For System 6 only. This is a great little Control Panel for people with lots of Control Panel extensions.

Frédéric Miserey
nOne corp

Control Panel
Extension
Freeware
Size: 4k

Viewer v1.05

Displays Glue format files. Glue is a commercial program that allows documents to be 'printed' to a file rather than to a printer.

Solutions, Inc.

Application
Freeware
Size: 45k

A-Talk

Displays the names, socket numbers, and node numbers of all units connected on an AppleTalk network.

unknown

Desk Accessory
Public Domain
Size: 2k

NetLook™ v1.3-US

NetLook is a small desk accessory that lets you look at all AppleTalk resources on your local network.

Direct Software, Inc.
(415) 347-1590
Fax: (415) 347-7991
AppleLink: D6619

Desk Accessory
Freeware
Size: 1k

NodeCheck v3.0B1

Shows all devices connected on an AppleTalk network, listing the device number, name, and current activity. Appears to be an update to the NetCheck program, also on this disk.

Randy Carr & Mark Davis
Apple Computer, Inc.

Application
Freeware
Size: 42k

SetNode

Sets the ID for AppleTalk nodes.

Jim Hamilton
2914 Aftonshire Way #13102
Austin, TX 78748

Control Panel
Extension
Freeware
Size: 4k

SingleShare v0.9b11

SingleShare is an AppleShare server that does almost as well as AppleShare and in many ways is better than TOPS. It's certainly faster than TOPS in most situations.

Matthias Urlichs
Rainwiesenweg 9
8501 Schwaig 2
GERMANY

Application
Shareware $65.00
Size: 78k

Watch v1.4.3

A program designed to measure packet transfer accuracy over a network. Supports various types of packet protocols and can also remove junk packets during normal traffic. Still has a few bugs.

Brad Parker
brad@cayman.com

Application
Freeware
Size: 87k

Utilities N2

Network Utilities

Apple-Jam

An AppleTalk conference host. Allows up to 20 users to simultaneously chat in conference over an AppleTalk network! What can we say? This is a must-have if you don't want to buy commercial conferencing software for your network.

B. Sutter & H. Wiguna
HealthCare Comm., Inc.
245 S. 84th Street # 300
Lincoln, NE 68510

Application
Freeware
Size: 73k

AppleTalk Alternatives(Text)

AppleTalk Alternatives describes how to build your own connectors for AppleTalk at a fraction of the cost of authentic AppleTalk connectors. It also gives some background information and recommentations for AppleTalk.

Infotek Inc.
56 Cammile
East Patchougue, NY 11772

TeachText
Document
Freeware
Size: 9k

AppleTalk Connector Schematic

AppleTalk Connector Schematic is the technical specifications for an AppleTalk Connector. The drawing is briefly explained in some text included in the file.

Frederick E. Davis

MacPaint
Document
Freeware
Size: 15k

BroadCast v0.5b3

Neat utility for sending message to other machines connected via an AppleTalk network. Displays a message box on the receiving machine containing an icon and text. Has docs in a separate file.

J. Lindenberg
University of Karlsruhe
Postfach 6980
7500 Karlsruhe 1
GERMANY

Chooser
Extension
Freeware
Size: 13k

ClockSynch

Synchronizes the clocks of Macs connected on an AppleTalk network. What a neat idea! You can make the clock time the same for all Macs on a network.

Dave Winer
CIS: 76244,120

Application
Freeware
Size: 20k

Flash Demo v1.1

Great demo that gives you a chance to see a file server network. Comes with DA and HyperCard stack manual.

Beagle Bros., Inc.
6215 Ferris Square, Suite 100
San Diego, CA 92121
(619) 452-5500

System Startup
Extension
Demoware
Size: 65k

FolderShare™ v1.0

Allows AppleShare network users to set the access privileges for newly created folders. By default, only the creator of a new folder has access to it. Has docs in a separate file.

CE Software
PO Box 65580
West Des Moines, IA 50265
(515) 224-1995

Control Panel
Extension
Freeware
Size: 25k

MacInTalk v1.31

Speech synthesis driver developed by Apple but no longer officially supported. Comes with utility programs and sample source code. Required for most applications that use computer-generated speech.

Apple Computer, Inc.

System File
Freeware
Size: 28k

NetBunny v2.5

Run this from your server machine to cause pink Energizer bunnies to run across the entire network's screens! The server has to have 32-bit Color QuickDraw and at least 8 megs of RAM to pull this off. Have fun! Comes with StartWabbit program.

Dean Yu
Cyberite Systems

System Startup
Extension
Freeware
Size: 27k
12" 6 7 32

Public Folder v1.0

Public Folder is a network file transfer and file sharing system. It allows anyone to make files and folders of files available to other users attached to an AppleTalk network.

M. R. Peirce
Claris Corp.
5201 Patrick Henry Dr. MS-C4
Box 58168
Santa Clara, CA 95051-8168

Chooser
Extension
Freeware
Size: 40k
12" 6 7 32

Quick Mount v1.0d7

Mounts file server volumes without going to the Chooser.

B. Gaya & L. Dyer
Apple Computer, Inc.

Application
Freeware
Size: 21k
12" 6 7 32

Utilities P1

Information Utilities

Boot Logger

Creates a text file in your System Folder called Boot Log File. Appends the current date and time to this file each time you restart your Mac. Has docs in a separate file.

Eric D. Boegel

System Startup Extension
Public Domain
Size: 3k

BootMan v1.1

BootMan is designed to display and edit the values of 3 different Macintosh system parameters: system heap size, maximum number of open files, and maximum number of operating system events.

Bill Steinberg
CIS: 76703,1027
AppleLink: X0542
AOL: BillS NYC

Application
Freeware
Size: 27k

Compare-a-Mac v1.0

Shows the number of ticks (1/60ths of a second) it takes your Mac to do drawing, calculating, and fractional multiplication functions. Has a comparative speed list of all Macs from the Plus to the IIfx. Allows you to save results.

Gloria Jacobs
88R Clarendon Avenue
Somerville, MA 02144

Application
Freeware
Size: 25k

DiskStatus v1.0.0

DiskStatus displays the available (or, alternatively, the used) space on all mounted volumes.

Eric Bloodworth
Morpheus Systems
PO Box 10991
Blacksburg, VA 24062

Application
Freeware
Size: 25k

Elapse v2.0.1

Displays the current time, the time when you started up your Mac, and the elapsed time since startup.

Jim Hamilton
2904 Jubilee Trail
Austin, TX 78748
CIS: 71640,235

Application
Shareware $1.00
Size: 6k

Felix v0.4

Displays a dialog box at startup time that lists information about your Mac, such as the name of the boot volume, machine type, memory, CPU type, keyboard type, System version, etc.

Chris Knepper
1839 Alice Street
Santa Cruz, CA 95062

System Startup Extension
Shareware $5.00
Size: 8k

last_boot v1.0d2

On startup, last_boot displays the time your computer was booted and when it was powered down. On shutdown, it displays the total length of time the computer was on.

John Martyniak
CIS: 75176,1760
Delphi & BIX: JMARTYNIAK
GEnie: J.Martyniak

System Startup Extension
Freeware
Size: 4k

LaunchInit v2.0s

An INIT program that records usage statistics when applications are launched. It can record how long the application was in use and which Mac opened it up.

Theodore Wu
85 Easton Ave., Apt. 4E
New Brunswick, NJ 08901

System Startup Extension
Shareware $10.00
Size: 23k

Logger v2.0

Makes entries in a log file (text format) when any of the following events occur: files are created, deleted, or renamed; files or drivers are opened or closed; applications are launched; resource files are opened; the Mac is shut down.

Ricardo Batista
3440 Lebon Drive #4307
San Diego, CA 92122
(619) 587-0623

Control Panel
Extension
Shareware $10.00
Size: 5k

MacEKG™ Demo v1.00

MacEKG is a diagnostic initialization program (INIT) for the Apple Macintosh computer that administers a regimen of logic-intensive diagnostic performance tests each time users boot their machine. This is a demo version.

MicroMat Computer Systems
7075 Redwood Blvd.
Novato, CA 94947
(415) 898-6227

Control Panel
Extension
Demoware
Size: 197k

MacEnvy v2.1

Displays information about your Mac's hardware and system software: machine type, amount of memory, keyboard type, monitor size and resolution, System/Finder versions, etc.

Ken McLeod et al.
Blue Cloud Software Ventures
thecloud@dhw68k.cts.com

Control Panel
Extension
Freeware
Size: 36k

Mug Shot Lite v1.3

Mug Shot II creates a document that lists vital information about your Mac. In this demo, documents cannot be saved and only the first page can be printed.

James K. Miles
Mi Concepts
PO Box 8822
Kentwood, MI 49508
AppleLink, AOL: Mi.Concepts
GEnie: jmiles

Application
Demoware
Size: 45k

ShowSizes v1.0

Shows the sizes of all folders on a disk. Displays the percentage of total disk space occupied by each folder or the percentage of a folder taken up by each of its subfolders. Slick and useful.

John Pugh
PO Box 5509 L-561
Livermore, CA 94550
(415) 423-4239

Application
Freeware
Size: 35k

SysEnvirons

Displays the results of the SysEnvirons Toolbox call, which returns status information about your Mac, such as the machine type, System version, processor type, keyboard type, etc.

Loftus E. Becker, Jr.

Application
Freeware
Size: 4k

System Environment Record

Prints the contents of the SysEnvirons record, which contains status information about your Mac. Fields include the machine type, System version, CPU type, keyboard type, etc.

unknown

Application
Public Domain
Size: 8k

TAA v0.2

TAA (or Technical Assistance Assistance) gives information about your system environment, system files, INITs, DAs, Parameter RAM, device drivers, and printer drivers.

Van Kichline
14454 119th Place N.E.
Kirkland, WA 98034
(206) 820-2680

Application
Freeware
Size: 18k

Utilities P1

Continued

Tattle Tale v1.0.1

Creates a text file that summarizes the name, memory usage, size, and time consumed for all startup documents (INITs). Reports only on INITs that run after Tattle Tale is executed. Comes with companion desk accessory.

Bob Hablutzel
1940 Sherman #316
Evanston, IL 60201
CIS: 76474,154

System Startup Extension
Shareware $5.00
Size: 3k

TattleTale v1.2

One of the more complete system diagnostic and statistics programs available. Gives you a text report on your Mac and SCSI peripherals. Older INIT version is on this disk also. Supports export of information in tab-delimited format.

John Mancino
Decision Maker's Software, Inc.
1910 Joslyn Place
Boulder, CO 80304

Desk Accessory
Earthware
Size: 172k

what v1.0d17

what is a full featured system interrogator. It gives information about your machine, System software, memory, INITs, and more!

John Martyniak
CompuServe: 75176,1760
Delphi & BIX: JMARTYNIAK
GEnie: J.Martyniak

Application
Freeware
Size: 43k

Who's Who v1.0

Displays status information about your Mac, such as the System and Finder version numbers, processor type, keyboard type, etc. Works OK, but it doesn't recognize 68030s and some newer items.

Paolo F. Reda
ZRSoft
ITALY
CIS: 76357,1640

Control Panel Extension
Freeware
Size: 25k

HMG™ ResEdit Primer v6.0

If you want to know some of the nifty things you can do with ResEdit (v2.1+), then this is the program for you. It is a lesson plan for ResEdit.

Herb Goodman
Green Mountain Software
GEnie: H.M.GOODMAN
CIS: 73300,3273
AOL: HMG

Application
Freeware
Size: 608k

ResEdit v2.1.1

ResEdit manipulates resources such as icons, menus, windows, buttons, etc. A required tool for all those who like to tinker with their Mac. New version can do color! BMUG sells a great book on how to use this incredible program.

Apple Computer, Inc.

Application
Freeware
Size: 622k

ResEdit Helper v2.0

Tips and tricks for making effective use of ResEdit, that wonderful resource editor distributed by Apple. About 11 pages. There's a MacWrite version of this file as well. This is for older versions of ResEdit.

Sam Kass
Info-Center BBS
(914) 565-6696

MacWrite 4.5
Document
Freeware
Size: 23k

ResEdit Utilities

'acur' Picker v1.0

'acur' Picker changes the way acur resources are viewed in ResEdit, making it easier to see which cursors a given acur resource refers to.

Chris Reed
3409 Clearview Drive
San Angelo TX 76904
(915) 949-9486

ResEdit Resource Template
Freeware
Size: 2k

DR MAC Utilities

Set of notes about various features of the System, Finder layouts, icons, and fonts. Since it was written in early 1986, much of the information is of historical interest only. Comes with several resources.

Don Rose
DR MAC'S NOTES
PO Box 333
Crystal Lake, IL 60014

Text+Rsc.
Freeware
Size: 45k

FontFkeyDaInitPictSnd

Amazing program for running/displaying fonts, FKEYs, DAs, paintings, and sounds without installing them. Shareware fee is a CD (Compact Disc, Certificate of Deposit, Charitable Donation, or Carol Doda).

Dave Kalin
637 Westholme Ave.
Los Angeles, CA 90024

Application
Shareware $?
Size: 16k

How To Make Icons

A BBS conversation on how to make icons.

From a BBS conversation between Brian Ebarb and David Phillips

Application
Freeware
Size: 18k

IconFill.txt

Discusses how to use ResEdit to modify the Finder 'LAYO' resource to change how color icons are displayed. Icons can have color outlines or be filled with color. For older versions of ResEdit.

Andy Burns
CIS: 76354,2316

Text
Public Domain
Size: 3k

Ogram's DSAT TMPLs

Templates for 'DSAT' resources for use with ResEdit. 'DSAT' resources are used for the system startup alert table, which contains the messages displayed while your Mac is booting up.

Margo Burns
23 Bowen Road
Kittery, ME 03904

ResEdit Resource Template
Public Domain
Size: 9k

resBulker v1991

Designed to let you set resource attributes for specified resource types en masse. ResBulker is not a utility you are likely to use frequently. However, it does fill a void left by other resource utilities such as ResEdit and REdit.

Ken Knight
AOL: KenKnight
Twilight Clone BBS:
(301) 946-8677

Application
Freeware
Size: 29k

ResPeek v2.03

A resource decompiler. Displays the resources contained in a selected file and decompiles resources into a text representation. The release version is available for $25.

Pierre Omidyar
Dark Designs
PO Box 58
Medford, MA 02153

Desk Accessory
Demoware
Size: 21k

ResEdit Utilities

ResTools v2.01

A resource compiler/decompiler that translates between a resource and a text representation of a resource. Similar to Rez/DeRez, which comes with MPW. Docs within the program.

Alan Dahlbom
GEnie: A. DAHLBOM

Application
Freeware
Size: 72k

ResViewer DA

A DA for looking at a few different resource types and modifying them. Can open resource forks of files. Does not work well with other DAs that use HFS calls.

Jim Moore
SoftDisk™, Inc

Desk Accessory
Freeware
Size: 27k

Screen Edit v1.0

Programming utility for setting up window, menu, dialog, alert, and icon resources and creating Lisa Workshop or RMaker source files. Created in early 1985, probably as an alternative (or precursor) to ResEdit.

George Cossey
Dave Holzer

Application
Freeware
Size: 83k

SIZE Editor v1.0

SIZE Editor is a SIZE resource editor to replace the template included with ResEdit (2.1 or higher). It simplifies editing of SIZE resources.

Chris Reed
3409 Clearview Drive
San Angelo, TX 76904
GEnie: J.REED9

ResEdit Resource Template
Freeware
Size: 5k

snd Editor 2.0a4

A 'snd ' resource editor for ResEdit. There is no way of displaying or editing a sound resource with what normally comes with ResEdit; obviously an improvement.

Chris Reed
3409 Clearview Drive
San Angelo TX 76904
(915) 949-9486

ResEdit Resource Template
Freeware
Size: 40k

Sound/PICT Thief v3.0

Copies PICT, snd, ICON, and ICN# resources from a chosen directory into a file in the System Folder called Purloined ResFile. Also scans for the nVIR virus while doing so. Displays window with the PICT and snd resources in the Purloined ResFile.

Jim Moore
GE: J.H.Moore

Application
Freeware
Size: 32k

Utilities S1

Security Utilities

AutoDelete

Deletes a specified set of files. Useful if you use a RAM disk program that automatically loads system files at startup. The copies of any INIT programs you can delete to save space.

John Lim
18 Nottingwood Street
Doncaster East
Victoria, 3109
AUSTRALIA

Application
Freeware
Size: 4k

ChooserUser v1.0b5

ChooserUser lets you control who can change the user name in the Chooser desk accessory. It also allows the user name to be changed at startup, either manually or automatically.

Maurice Volaski
173 Princeton Ave., Apt #2
Amherst, NY 14226-5006
(716) 838-6663

Control Panel
Extension
Freeware
Size: 16k

Complete Delete

Completely erases files by placing zeros in both the data and resource forks. A normal delete removes a file's directory entry but leaves the actual data lying around on the disk. Warning: No recovery of data is possible for files erased with this!

Joel McNamara

Application
Freeware
Size: 4k

DES v2.0

An older implementation of the U.S. National Bureau of Standards data encryption algorithm.

John P. Powers
2406 Richwood Drive
Garland, TX 75042
CIS: 75776,3247

Application
Shareware $15.00
Size: 16k

Enigma v1.1

Encrypts and decrypts files based on a password. Prevents access by unauthorized users. Lets you encrypt any file. Has docs within the program.

Mike Pflueger
19413 N. 75th Drive
Glendale, AZ 85306

Application
Shareware $10.00
Size: 19k

Eraser v1.0B1

Erases floppy disks by overwriting existing contents. Has no menus and no instructions. Hit Command-Q to quit program. Warning: Data on floppies processed by this program are not recoverable!

Darin Adler
Fernando Alves

Application
Public Domain
Size: 33k

Fence v1.0

Fence is a simple and safe password protection program for your disks. Use Fence as the startup application. The window covers the entire screen hiding your desktop. Several neat features found in commercial packages without all the danger.

Jim Walker
Flight Engineering
PO Box 661133
Miami Springs, FL 33266

Application
Shareware $10.00
Size: 40k

FileZero v1.0

Completely erases a file by overwriting its entire contents with zeroes. Merely throwing a file in the trash does not actually erase it; only the directory entry for the file is removed. Warning: Files so erased are not recoverable!

T. R. Shaw and B. E. Jarrell
OITC, Inc.
PO Box 73
Melbourne Beach, FL 32951

Application
Shareware $15.00
Size: 34k

LaserwriterLockout v1.0b5

This lets you control which LaserWriters appear in the Chooser desk accessory. Particularly useful to network environments where access to a particular LaserWriter should be available to only certain nodes on that network.

Maurice Volaski
173 Princeton Ave., Apt #2
Amherst, NY 14226-5006
(716) 838-6663

Control Panel Extension
Freeware
Size: 16k

LockDisk v1.0

A cdev that changes your System disk (the one from which your Mac boots) to read-only status. Dangerous! Use at your own risk!

Brian Bechtel
blob@apple.com
AppleLink: BECHTEL1

Control Panel Extension
Freeware
Size: 28k

LockHD

If made the startup application, this program requests a password before allowing access to the hard disk. Novices may not figure out that this security can be bypassed by booting from a floppy.

Neil Swartz
2740 N. Pine Grove
Chicago, IL 60614
(312) 477-2334

Application
Shareware $5.00
Size: 20k

!MacPassword™ v3.8.8

Provides simple password protection for specified files and folders. At startup, the user must supply the correct password to access these files. Reasonably effective against novices.

Art A. Schumer
Evergreen Software, Inc.
15600 NE 8th St #A3126
Bellevue, WA 98008

Control Panel Extension
Shareware $35.00
Size: 93k

NoControlPanel INIT v1.0b1

NoControlPanel INIT allows system administrators to prevent users from accessing the Control Panel desk accessory from the Apple menu. This program will be particularly useful to Macintosh labs in a university.

Maurice Volaski
173 Princeton Ave., Apt #2
Amherst, NY 14226-5006
(716) 838-6663

System Startup Extension
Freeware
Size: 3k

Passport Demo v2.0

Passport allows you to place a password on your startup disk to control access to your Mac. Somewhat crippled demo in that the password cannot be changed.

Praxitel Inc.
PO Box 15521
Ann Arbor, MI 48106
(313) 485-6278

Control Panel Extension
Demoware
Size: 19k

Password v2.1

Requests a password before allowing access to the hard disk. Must be made the startup application. Novices may not figure out that this security is bypassed by booting from a floppy. It's ugly, but it works OK. Not for MultiFinder or System 7.

Tony Suria
Univ. of Wisconsin - Madison
GEnie: T.Suria

Application
Freeware
Size: 14k

Pickproof v1.2

Simple password protection for hard disks. Make this program your startup application and it prompts for a password. Docs in a separate file. ResEdit can be used to modify the password in the STR# resource.

Dana Basken
GEnie: BASKEN

Application
Freeware
Size: 11k

SecureInit v1.7.2

Lets you set the configuration of your Mac when it starts up. You can have all windows closed, make the System Folder invisible, delete undeclared files, and lock selected files. Could be dangerous.

Dancom Inc.
PO Box 277
CH-1110 Morges
SWITZERLAND

Application
Shareware $30.00
Size: 188k

DarkSide v2.3

DarkSide is a screen saver application for Macintosh computers that run MultiFinder. It runs in the background and has an expandable set of blackouts or faders you can select from.

Tom Dowdy
1180 Lochinvar, #20
Sunnyvale, CA 94087
AppleLink: DOWDY1

Application
Freeware
Size: 15k

Flash-It v2.0.4

Flash-It is a screen dump utility for the Mac. It can capture a screen image, paste it to a document, save it to a separate disk file, and print it very quickly. Has some minor printing problems.

Nobu Toge
PO Box 7114
Menlo Park, CA 94026
CIS: 76334,650

Control Panel
Extension
Shareware $15.00
Size: 39k

MenuPicture v1.01

MenuPicture allows FKEYs to be executed while the mouse is down. This lets the Command-Shift-3 FKEY in the system make screen pictures while you have a menu pulled down.

Douglas S. Wyatt
Opcode Systems
1024 Hamilton Ct.
Menlo Park, CA 94025

System Startup
Extension
Freeware
Size: 2k

MiniScreen v1.0

MiniScreen changes your color monitor's desktop size to that of a dinky, 9-inch monitor. It also gives you the option of choosing the size of your desktop.

Morgan Davis
Beagle Bros, Inc.
6215 Ferris Square #100
San Diego, CA 92121

System Startup
Extension
Public Domain
Size: 3k

ReverseScreen v1.0/1.0b1

Reverses black and white pixels on the screen. Characters become white letters on a black background rather than the usual black letters on a white background. May help the visually impaired. There are two versions of this on disk.

Darin Adler
Apple Computer, Inc.

System Startup
Extension
Freeware
Size: 2k

Screen Maker v1.0.1

Screen Maker converts documents from MacPaint, SuperPaint and FullPaint to StartUpScreens that can be displayed during startup.

B. Atkinson & A. J. Oresteen
452 Orion Rd
Batavia, IL 60510
(708) 879-5678

Application
Public Domain
Size: 7k

ScreenSnap™ v2.2

ScreenSnap allows you to take a snapshot of any rectangular portion. Once created, the snapshot can be inverted, moved, saved as a PICT file, copied to the Clipboard, printed, or just left hanging around on-screen for reference.

M. Hewett & V. Johnson
Knowledge Source, Inc.
814 Fremont St.
Menlo Park, CA 94025-5016

Application
Shareware $11.00
Size: 164k

Utilities T2

Screen Utilities

After Dark Modules

Many of the famous PD modules for the After Dark screen saver. Some work with version 2.0v, the latest stable version of After Dark. BMUG also sells an After Dark Module disk pack. Call for more info.

various

After Dark Modules
various
Size: 1503k

BigZoomIdle

A screen saver of a zooming rectangle. Start it by using the DA.

unknown

Desk Accessory
Public Domain
Size: 3k

Blackout v1.21

Screen saver that blackens your screen after a specified period of inactivity.

Andrew Welch
Mark 3 Software
29 Grey Rocks Road
Wilton, CT 06897

Control Panel Extension
Shareware $5.00
Size: 12k

Eyelixir™ v1.0

Eyelixir is a nifty screen saver. It makes your Mac look like a TV screen blocked out by a lot of interference.

D. Levine & T. Rundgren
Utopia Grokware, Inc.
Sausalito, CA
(415) 331-0714

System Startup Extension
Freeware
Size: 25k

Fuzzy Balls FKEY v1.0

The poor man's screen saver. It displays shaded balls. Every 15 seconds the screen is cleared to black and another set of fuzzy balls is drawn. Ball shading can be reversed.

Jon Wind

ResEdit Resource File
Freeware
Size: 3k

Møire v3.22

A very nice screen saver. After a specified period of inactivity, the screen darkens and a moving moiré pattern is displayed. In color on a Mac II. Docs in a separate file.

John Lim
18 Nottingwood Street
Doncaster East 3109
Victoria
AUSTRALIA

Control Panel Extension
Shareware $10.00
Size: 13k

Stars v1.8

A screen saver. A few minutes of inactivity causes the screen to fade to black, and star patterns zoom by until you resume using your Mac.

unknown

Desk Accessory
Public Domain
Size: 6k

Disinfectant v2.8

THE best virus detection and eradication utility (commercial software included). Works against all known viruses. Excellent on-line help. Installs an INIT that protects you from infection. Works over a network also!

John Norstad
Northwestern University
2129 Sheridan Road
Evanston, IL 60208

Application
Freeware
Size: 320k
12" 6 7 32

Intro to Viruses v2.3

Explains what computer viruses are, how they affect the user, how they spread, how they can be stopped, and more! An attempt to cool virus fever by providing information for the ordinary Macintosh user.

Robert I. Wright
Wright Brothers
1609 Rockglen Ave.
Glendale, CA 91205

HyperCard Stack
Freeware
Size: 108k
12" 6 7 32

Rival Vaccines

Includes the ANTI, CDEF, Frankie, INIT29, MDEF, nVIR, Scores, Trojan Horse, WDEF, and Zuc virus protection files for Rival™, a commercial anti-virus package. The earliest version you need to use all of them is v1.1.4.

Microseeds Publishing, Inc.

Rival Vaccine Resource Files
Freeware
Size: 45k
12" 6 7 32

Virus Encyclopedia

A little behind the times, but still useful information on viruses.

Henry C. Schmitt
The NorthWest of Us
6613 Scott Lane, #17
Hanover Park, IL 60103-3849

HyperCard Stack
Freeware
Size: 93k
12" 6 7 32

VirusDetective v4.03

DA that looks through all files for a specified resource type. Useful in detecting the nVIR virus, which installs a resource of that name in infected files. Docs within the program.

Jeffrey s. Shulman
PO Box 1218
Morgantown, WV 26507-1218
(304) 598-2090

Desk Accessory
Shareware $40.00
Size: 70k
12" 6 7 32

Boaster INIT v1.0

Boaster INIT is for all of you who want to impress co-workers or friends with lots of icons showing at startup. Boaster INIT does nothing useful except for displaying all icons it finds inside Boaster INIT.

unknown

System Startup Extension
Freeware
Size: 45k

Cicn Create.MWrite

Tells you how to create cicn resources.

Paul Smallwood
AOL: AFC Paul

MacWrite 4.5 Document
Public Domain
Size: 21k

Easy Icon v1.1

Easy Icon is a program that lets the unexperienced user easily edit and add icons to HyperCard stacks.

Rolf Rando
13838 Templeton Place
Los Altos Hills, CA 94022
CIS: 72317,603

Application
Freeware
Size: 14k

Explode Cicn v2.0.1

A program for converting cicn icons to an entire icon family. Converts the cicn icon to icl8, ics8, icl4, ics4, ICN#, and ics# resources. Can also be used to convert from icl to cicn format. Comes with source code.

Scott E. Lasley
2404 Cool Spring Road
Hyattsville, MD 20783-2253
CIS: 76324,107

Application
?
Size: 122k

Façade v1.0.1

Neat little utility that lets you change the icons for floppy and hard disks. With ResEdit, you associate a disk name with an icon that is used whenever a disk with that name is mounted.

Greg Marriott
Apple Computer, MS-46Z
20525 Mariani Ave
Cupertino, CA

System Startup Extension
Freeware
Size: 3k

ICN#->ICON

Nice program to convert ICN# to ICON resources.

Jim Hamilton
2914 Aftonshire Way #13102
Austin, TX 78748
CIS: 71640,235

Application
Shareware $5.00
Size: 14k

Icon Extractor v1.1

Takes all icons from ICN# resources in a specified file, transforms them into separate ICON resources, and stores them in a new file. Has docs in a separate file.

John L. Paul
Paul Software Engineering
513 West A Street
Tehachapi, CA 93561

Application
Shareware $1.00
Size: 7k

Icon Hacker v0.9

Provides several editing modes to let you customize icons and ICN#s. Lets you create ICN#s whose selected state looks totally different from their unselected state, and more.

Joe Mastroianni
Killer Owl Productions
43 Woodbrook Dr.
Edison, NJ 08820

Application
Shareware $10.00
Size: 44k

IconMaker v85.12.20.spg.

Icon editor for changing the icons of existing applications. Docs in a separate file.

J. Doenias & S. Gillespie
1100 SE Woodward
Portland, OR 97202
(503) 232-1712

Application
Public Domain
Size: 30k

ICONstructor v1.0

Program for creating icons using a FatBits editor. An icon can be saved as an ICON or ICN# resource.

Lawrence W. Walker
349 Cassidy Ave.
Lexington, KY 40502

Application
Shareware?
Size: 17k

IconWrap v1.2

Icons displayed at startup time can fill up the bottom row of your screen. This INIT causes icons to wrap around to another row rather than just falling off the right edge of the screen.

Ken McLeod
Blue Cloud Software

System Startup Extension
Freeware
Size: 3k

ShowCInit v1.0b1

ShowCInit displays color or b&w icons on the desktop at startup; facilitates the drawing of multiple or animated icons; wraps icons when they reach the end of the screen; provides an option to play a sound at startup.

J. Sternlicht & A. Diaz
3630 Misty Oak Drive, #1607
Melbourne, FL 32901
(407) 727-7737

System Startup Extension
Shareware $1.00
Size: 9k

SicnEdit vJan86

Editor for small icons (SICN resources), which are 16 x 16 bitmap images. Has a FatBits editor with functions for shifting, rotating, and folding images. Very nice interface.

Paul DuBois
1220 Capitol Court
Madison, WI 53706

Application
Freeware
Size: 38k

Utilities X1

Font Utilities

Font Names & Numbers

Describes how to rename and renumber your fonts to avoid font conflicts. This includes how to create NFNT resources using Font/DA Mover 3.8.

Unknown

MacWrite Document
Freeware
Size: 16k

FontDisplay™ Ltd. v5.4.4.A

Displays the entire character set of any Macintosh™ font in an uninstalled suitcase. Multi-bit/color fonts are supported on the Mac II.

Jeffrey S. Shulman
P.O. Box 521
Ridgefield, Connecticut
06877-0521

Application
Shareware $50.00
Size: 87k

Font Lister

Prints out samples of fonts in the system in various type styles.

James G. Eaklor
Wizdom
7862 Allott Avenue
Van Nuys, CA 91402

Text Document
Freeware
Size: 22k

FontMaster '88

Lets you edit existing bitmap fonts to create various styled fonts. Not meant to create fonts from scratch.

T Tauri SoftSystems,
366 Glen Manor Drive,
Toronto, Ontario, Canada
M4E 2X8

Application
Freeware
Size: 59k

Fontsie v3.06

Allows you to have access to fonts stored not in the System file, but in font files on disk. Before you use it, you should configure it with the Configuration program provided.

Loftus E. Becker, Jr.
41 Whitney Street
Hartford, CT 06105

System Startup Extension
Shareware $10.00
Size: 2k

NoFontScaling

Changes the default of font scaling status to 'Disabled'. The +/-FontScaling FKEY still works when this INIT is installed.

Fred D. Reed
IMI SoftWare
121 14th Street
Seal Beach, CA 90740
CIS 76357,2530
GEnie: F.D.REED

System Startup Extension
Freeware
Size: 2k

The Styler v1.0

Prints samples of installed fonts in various styles and sizes.

Peter S. Bryant
P.O. Box 946
Zephyr Cove, Nevada 89448-0946

Application
Shareware $10.00
Size: 31k

Varityper Toolkit v1.0

An extremely useful font utility. Shows character charts for installed fonts, prints font samples, gives info to help avoid font ID conflicts, and searches PostScript files to list the fonts used. Can handle the new TrueType format.

Ken Winograd et al.

Application
Freeware
Size: 128k

Disable page

A short PostScript program for disabling the test page when starting up a LaserWriter. Download it with programs like SendPS. You don't need this if you have LaserWriter Font Utility program that comes with System 7.

John Monaco
CIS: 73317,3677
GEnie: J Monaco

Text Document
Freeware
Size: 1k

Enable page

A short PostScript program for (re)enabling the test page when starting up a LaserWriter. Download it with programs like SendPS. You don't need this if you have LaserWriter Font Utility program that comes with System 7.

John Monaco
CIS: 73317,3677
GEnie: J Monaco

Text Document
Freeware
Size: 1k

FontIconHolder

Keep a copy of this file on your disk to prevent older (non-Adobe) PostScript font files from appearing with a generic document icon when using LaserWriter driver version 5.2 or later.

B. Poulson

Dummy PostScript Font File
Freeware
Size: 1k

FontList.ps

Print out the list of all fonts resident in a PostScript printer. Need a program like SendPS to download this PostScript file to the printer.

Unknown

Text Document
Freeware
Size: 1k

Halftone

Makes clean halftones from grayscale image files.

Chris Capener
P.O. Box
Cupertino, CA 95015-0994

Application
Freeware
Size: 22k

Manual Feed Patch

This PostScript program seems intended to patch the problem of a LaserWriter ignoring the manual feed request. I do not know which version of LaserWriter driver it's meant to be used with.

Unknown

Text Document
Freeware
Size: 1k

N-Font™ v1.0

This allows users to convert the older FONT screen fonts to the newer NFNT screen fonts.

OLDUVAI Corporation

Application
Freeware
Size: 33k

PostScript Files

A collection of PostScript code examples. Includes some utility code, which may not be useful with the latest system software, but may still be of interest if you are studying PostScript programming. One of the files (Mailing Labels.ps) is shareware ($5) by Ray Sanders.

Various authors

Text Files
Freeware
Size: 86k

PostScript® Samples

Examples of PostScript codes. If you are studying PostScript programming, these examples may prove very useful.	Adobe Systems et al.	**Text Documents** **Freeware** **Size: 127k**

PostScript Spooler DA

Sends PostScript program files to a PostScript printer for execution. The DA's name appears as Laser Print under the Apple menu.	MacTutor magazine Sam Roberts	**Desk Accessory** **Freeware** **Size: 4k**

PS Alphabet Samples

26 PostScript files taken from the Colophon 3 Showpage section. These programs demonstrate different techniques and ideas for manipulating PostScript fonts.	Adobe Systems, Inc.	**Text Files** **Freeware** **Size: 72k**

Reset.ps

This tiny PostScript program completely resets LaserWriter, flushing all downloaded fonts.	Unknown	**Text Document** **Freeware** **Size: 1k**

SendPS v2.0

A utility to download a PostScript program or list a straight text file onto a PostScript printer.	Glenn Reid Adobe Systems, Inc.	**Application** **Freeware** **Size: 32k**

ASCII Chart v4.2

A nice utility for displaying all characters in any installed font. Shows key combinations and the character codes in decimal, octal, and hexadecimal numbers. Also font samples in several different formats can be printed or saved to a file.

Jon Wind
CIS: 70167,3444
GEnie: JPWIND
MCI MAIL: J.WIND
AOL: JWIND

Desk Accessory
Shareware $10.00
Size: 60k

BitFont v1.01

Creates a bitmap font from any font which can be drawn on your Macintosh. If you use TrueType or PostScript type 1 fonts with Adobe Type Manager, you can create smooth bitmap fonts of any size.

Peter DiCamillo
Brown University Computing and Information Services
Internet:
Peter_DiCamillo@brown.edu

Application
Freeware
Size: 36k

Font/DA Mover v4.1

Apple's Font/DA Mover. This version (which comes with the TrueType package for System 6) can handle TrueType. Comes with the C source code.

Apple Computer, Inc.

Application
Public Domain
Size: 42k

FreeGeneva

Enables you to remove the three reserved bitmap fonts (Geneva 9, Geneva 12, Monaco 9) from the System file under System 7.

Bryan K. Ressler
AppleLink: BEAKER

Application
Freeware
Size: 9k

SetOutlinePreferred.FKEY

Change a system default behavior so the Font Manager will prefer either TrueType or bitmapped fonts for screen display or printing. Only for System 7 or 6.0.7 with TrueType.

David L. Fowler

FKEY
Freeware
Size: 4k

theTypeBook v2.37

A nice utility that aids in the creation and maintenence of a typeface reference book. It helps people (both clients and employees) select typefaces by demonstrating the various artistic attributes of each face on a printed page.

James Lewis
Golden State Graphics
2137 Candis Av.
Santa Ana, CA 92706

Application
Freeware
Size: 159k

TTConverter v1.0.1

Converts Macintosh TrueType fonts to Windows 3.1 TrueType, and vice versa.

Chris Reed
3409 Clearview Drive
San Angelo, TX 76904-8108

Application
Shareware $10.00
Size: 18k

TrueType™ v1.0

Apple's TrueType INIT (extension). Lets you use TrueType with System 6.0.7.

Apple Computer, Inc.

Extension
Freeware
Size: 104k

Utilities Z1

FKEYs

AntiFreeze

Tries to unfreeze the cursor after a crash that immobilizes it. This doesn't work for all crashes. If it does work, it's best to save whatever you can, then reboot your Mac.

unknown

FKEY File
Public Domain
Size: 1k

BigCursor

Doubles the size of the mouse cursor. Invoking the FKEY again restores the cursor to its original size. Mouse speed slows when the cursor is enlarged.

unknown

FKEY File
Public Domain
Size: 2k

Bomb Alert! FKEY

Displays a list of the 28 system error codes, the ID numbers that show up when your Mac crashes and you get the Bomb alert box.

Andrew Welch
29 Grey Rocks Road
Wilton, CT 06897

FKEY File
Shareware $5.00
Size: 9k

BragKEY

Plays that little tune you hear at baseball games.

unknown

FKEY File
Public Domain
Size: 2k

CacheToggle

Turns the RAM cache on/off. Easier than having to do it manually by going to the Control Panel. Unfortunately, you still need to reboot for the new cache to be implemented. Darn!

David Fry
329A Broadway Street
Cambridge, MA 02139
GEnie: D.FRY

FKEY File
Public Domain
Size: 1k

ClockKey v1.0

Puts up a window displaying the current date and time.

Raymond Lau

FKEY File
Freeware
Size: 1k

Datamagik™'s HomeCursor

Moves the mouse to the home position or top left corner of the screen.

unknown

FKEY File
Public Domain
Size: 1k

Datamagik's ShrinkWindow v0.1

Shrinks the frontmost window so that only the title bar is visible. This leaves the window about 1/4 inch high and 4 inches wide.

unknown

FKEY File
Public Domain
Size: 1k

Date Key v2.05

Types the current time or date at the current insertion point in whatever program happens to be running. Provides several choices for the format of the time and date. Has docs in a separate file. Caution: Modifies the System file!

Loftus E. Becker, Jr.
41 Whitney Street
Hartford, CT 06105
CIS: 70206,67

FKEY File
Shareware $5.00
Size: 3k

DirCreator v1.0

Allows you to create a folder from within an application.

Raymond Lau

FKEY File
Freeware
Size: 2k

DirDelete v1.0

Allows you to delete a folder from within an application.

Raymond Lau

FKEY File
Freeware
Size: 2k

EscapeKey v1.1

Brings up a dialog box that gives you the option of canceling, exiting to the Finder, or shutting down (rebooting).

Paul Nevai
Department of Mathematics
The Ohio State University
Columbus, OH 43210

FKEY File
Freeware
Size: 9k

ExitToShell

Aborts the current application. Handy for running MultiFinder with 1 meg of RAM. Start all your applications, then invoke this FKEY while in the Finder. The Finder quits, freeing up 160K of RAM.

unknown

FKEY File
Public Domain
Size: 1k

FadeKey

Causes the screen to slowly dissolve to black. Clicking the mouse restores the screen. A good, no-frills screen saver, but it's not automatic.

unknown

FKEY File
Public Domain
Size: 2k

Findswell™ Demo v1.0

Puts an extra button in a standard Open File dialog box that brings up a window in which you can install frequently used documents. Easier than trying to remember where you put your documents.

David Dunham
Working Software, Inc.
321 Alvorado St, Suite H
Monterey, CA 93940

System Startup Extension
Demoware
Size: 26k

Fit To Mac

Installer program for an FKEY that places the top left corner of the front window at the top left of the screen and the bottom right corner at the current mouse location.

George Deriso
Leo Laporte

Application
Freeware
Size: 6k

FKey Manager v3.0

A great utility for organizing your FKEYs. Keeps FKEYs in separate files, avoids the 10-FKEY limit, and creates a pop-up menu of FKEYs. Includes a complete manual in a separate file.

Carlos Weber, MD
250 Douglass Street #12
San Francisco, CA 94114
CIS: 70277,726

Application
Freeware
Size: 50k

FKEY-Close Window v1.0

Produces the same effect as clicking in the close box of the front window. Good for those who prefer using the keyboard over the mouse.

Michael Long
729C Nicklaus Drive
Greenwood, IN 46142

FKEY File
Freeware
Size: 1k

Fkey-DA Sampler v3.1

Allows you to run desk accessories and function key programs that are not installed in your System file. Good way to quickly try out DAs and FKEYs.

John Holder
P.O. Box 975
Blue Lake, CA 95525

FKEY File
Shareware $10.00
Size: 5k

Send Window To Rear v1.0

Sends the frontmost window behind all other windows.

Michael Long
729C Nicklaus Drive
Greenwood, IN 46142

FKEY File
Freeware
Size: 1k

Toggle Window Size v1.0

Produces the same effect as clicking in the zoom box of the front window.

Michael Long
729C Nicklaus Drive
Greenwood, IN 46142

FKEY File
Freeware
Size: 1k

FkeyView v2.5

Displays a list of all installed FKEYs showing the name (if present) and the corresponding Command-key number.

John Holder
PO Box 975
Blue Lake, CA 95525

FKEY File
Freeware
Size: 2k

Flush

Flushes the event queue. Useful when you type commands faster than a program can execute them, then change your mind.

unknown

FKEY File
Public Domain
Size: 2k

+/-FontScaling

Toggles the System's scaling of bitmap fonts on and off and reduces the jaggies. Only installed font sizes are shown on-screen when scaling is off. Scaling off also means that your docs may not be WYSIWYG.

IMI Software
121 14th Street
Seal Beach, CA 90740
CIS: 76357,2530

FKEY File
Freeware
Size: 3k

Fontsie v3.06

Allows you to use fonts not installed in the System file. Stores fonts in multiple Font/DA Mover files. Not compatible with SuitCase™. Has docs in a separate file.

Loftus E. Becker, Jr.
41 Whitney Street
Hartford, CT 06105

System Startup Extension
Shareware $10.00
Size: 2k

Formfeed FKEY 1

Performs a form feed on an ImageWriter.

unknown

FKEY File
Public Domain
Size: 1k

KeyPad v1.1

Turns the digit keys on the number keypad into function keys (FKEYs). Just hit a number on the keypad to invoke an FKEY instead of having to hit Shift-Command and the number.

Rick Flott
CIS: 72167,3717

Startup Document
Freeware
Size: 1k

LaserKeyInstaller

Installs an FKEY that prints screen dumps to both the ImageWriter and the LaserWriter. Has options for image smoothing and multiple copies when dumping to a LaserWriter. Includes docs in a separate file.

Lew Rollings
Human-Systems Interface Group
PO Box 1210
Vashon, WA 98070

Application
Shareware $15.00
Size: 7k

LaunchMaker v1.0

Creates and installs a new FKEY to launch any application you select. Has a few bugs. Includes docs in a separate file.

IMI Software
121 14th Street
Seal Beach, CA 90740

FKEY File
Shareware $5.00
Size: 4k

Locate v1.8d1

Searches for lost files. Searches all selected disks for all files that match a filename or portion of a filename that you enter. Has docs in a separate file.

Raymond Lau
100-04 70 Avenue
Forest Hills, NY 11375
CIS: 76174,2617

FKEY File
Shareware $10.00
Size: 12k

MemKey

Compacts memory, then reports how many free bytes are available.

Andrew Welch
29 Grey Rocks Road
Wilton, CT 06897

FKEY File
Shareware $5.00
Size: 2k

MenuSelect v3.1

Takes snapshots of the screen while a menu is open. The built-in Command-Shift-3 FKEY does not do this. Has docs within the program.

John Holder
PO Box 975
Blue Lake, CA 95525

FKEY File
Freeware
Size: 2k

MoveOver INIT

Fixes a problem with System 4.1/Finder 5.5 where the mouse cursor could move one pixel off the right edge of the screen. Not needed for newer Systems. Has docs and source code in a separate file.	Diamond Engineered Software 8890 Robinhood Lane La Jolla, CA 92037 (619) 455-5576	**System Startup Extension** **Freeware** **Size: 1k**

Moving Lines

Blacks out the screen and displays a rapidly moving line-art pattern. Lets you click the mouse or hit a key to exit.	unknown	**FKEY File** **Public Domain** **Size: 2k**

NoFontScaling

Turns off font scaling, which in on by default. Fonts are scaled when there is no built-in font for a specified font size. Comes with an FKEY program that toggles font scaling on/off.	Fred D. Reed IMI Software 121 14th Street Seal Beach, CA 90740	**System Startup Extension** **Freeware** **Size: 2k**

OpenDAs v2.0

Opens up 1 to 10 of the desk accessories installed in your System file. Use the companion application to configure the FKEY. Easier than going to the Apple menu to open commonly used DAs.	John Holder 7365 El Tomaso Way Buena Park, CA 90620	**FKEY File** **Shareware $5.00** **Size: 1k**

Orator™ InstallerFkey v1.1

Installs an FKEY that speaks the time and date when invoked. Installer program does not work under MultiFinder, but the FKEY does.	Mike Whittingham Mark 3 215 Thayer Pond Road Wilton, CT 06897	**Application** **Shareware $5.00** **Size: 49k**

PanicKey v1.16

Displays a picture of a Mac ripped open by an exploding bomb and a man saying 'Arrggh!!' Also plays a short musical tune. Has a cool cursor.	Michael L. Johnson 614 Westview Avenue Trenton, OH 45067	**FKEY File** **Shareware $2.00** **Size: 10k**

Pop-Keys v3.0

A great INIT for popping up the FKEYs installed in your system on a menu! Useful if you can't always remember the proper Command-Shift-# key combinations to use.	Carlos Weber, MD 250 Douglass Street #12 San Francisco, CA 94114 CIS: 70277,726	**System Startup Extension** **Freeware** **Size: 6k**

Printer Burp

Advances a page on the printer.	unknown	**FKEY File** **Public Domain** **Size: 1k**

PrintKey

Ejects a page on an ImageWriter I/II. Sometimes it's more convenient to eject a page from the keyboard rather than fiddling with the buttons on the ImageWriter.

Andrew Welch
29 Grey Rocks Road
Wilton, CT 06897

FKEY File
Shareware $5.00
Size: 2k

Quote INIT v2.0

Automatically changes normal quote marks into the Mac curly quote marks, keeping track of the open and close quotes. Can also handle diphthongs and double dashes.

Lincoln D. Stein
44 Boylton Street, #3
Boston, MA 02130

Control Panel Extension
Shareware $15.00
Size: 9k

Resource Viewer v4.7

Shows all resource types in open files. Displays a list of all the individual resources of a particular type when you click on that type. Lists the ID number, name, and attributes of each resource.

John Holder
P.O. Box 975
Blue Lake, CA 95525

FKEY File
Shareware $5.00
Size: 4k

Restart.FKEY

Performs the same function as selecting Restart from the Special menu in the Finder. Requires System 4.1 or later. Does not save desktop configuration at time of shutdown.

David Gelphman
Bin #88 SLAC
Stanford, CA 94205
(415) 854-3300 x2583

FKEY File
Public Domain
Size: 1k

Reverse Form Feed

Performs a reverse form feed on an ImageWriter.

unknown

FKEY File
Public Domain
Size: 1k

Screen to Clip FKEY

Changes cursor to a right-angle bracket designating the top left corner of a selection box. When you click and drag down and to the right, the contents of the selected area are copied to the Clipboard. Warning: Dragging up to the left crashes your Mac!

unknown

FKEY File
Public Domain
Size: 1k

SFScrollInit v1.0

Great little utility that remembers where you scrolled the last time you opened a file using the standard Open File dialog box. Prevents having to rescroll the next time you go to that folder.

Andy Hertzfeld

System Startup Extension
Freeware
Size: 2k

Shutdown.FKEY

Performs the same function as selecting Shut Down from the Special menu in the Finder. Requires System 4.1 or later. Does not save desktop configuration at time of shutdown.

David Gelphman
Bin #88 SLAC
Stanford, CA 94205
(415) 854-3300 x2583

FKEY File
Public Domain
Size: 1k

Sleep

Screen saver that blacks out the screen and displays the Apple icon at random positions. Restores the screen when you click the mouse.	unknown	**FKEY File** **Public Domain** **Size: 1k**

Space Warp

Screen saver that blackens the screen and displays stars whizzing by. Clicking the mouse or hitting a key restores the screen.	unknown	**FKEY File** **Public Domain** **Size: 2k**

SpecialKey

Places in the Clipboard 4 special characters (Command key, check mark, diamond, and Apple icon) that are sometimes impossible to enter from the keyboard, then pastes them into your file.	Andrew Welch 29 Grey Rocks Road Wilton, CT 06897	**FKEY File** **Shareware $5.00** **Size: 2k**

!THE!Clock

Momentarily displays a small window showing the current time and date.	unknown	**FKEY File** **Public Domain** **Size: 1k**

UnPack FKey v2.0

Unpacks files compressed with PackIt.	Donald Brown CE Software	**FKEY File** **Freeware** **Size: 4k**

Version Reader v5.1

Displays the text of the signature resource and the icons for both the program and the data file of a selected application. Author requests that you send him a postcard if you like the program.	John Holder PO Box 975 Blue Lake, CA 95525	**FKEY File** **Freeware** **Size: 2k**

Window FKEY

Sends the frontmost window to the back, moving all other windows forward one level. Repeated use allows you to riffle through all open windows. Has docs in a separate file.	Charlie Bounds 1235 Kern Ct. Mountain View, CA 94040 CIS: 76515,2154	**FKEY File** **Freeware** **Size: 1k**

Wrap

Causes the mouse cursor to wrap around the edges of the screen. Moving the mouse past the right edge of the screen causes it to reappear on the left side. Works similarly for the other edges.	unknown	**System Startup Extension** **Public Domain** **Size: 1k**

Index

Index

Symbols

A

B

Index

C

Index

Index

Index

K

L

M

Index

N

Index